NAFTA AND SUSTAINABLE DEVELOPMENT

History, Experience, and Prospects for Reform

The North American Free Trade Agreement (NAFTA) and its companion agreement, the North American Agreement on Environmental Cooperation (NAAEC), provide important and often underappreciated protection for the environmental laws of the Party states: Canada, Mexico, and the United States. On the twentieth anniversary of NAFTA's ratification, this book assesses the current state of environmental protection under those agreements. Bringing together scholars, practitioners, and regulators from all three Party states, it outlines the scope and process of NAFTA and NAAEC, their impact on specific environmental issues, and paths to reform. It includes analyses of the impact of the agreements on such matters as bioengineered crops in Mexico, assessment of marine environmental effects, potential lessons for China, climate change, and indigenous rights.

Together, the chapters of this book represent an important contribution to the global conversation concerning international trade agreements and sustainable development.

Hoi L. Kong is an associate professor and Associate Dean Academic at McGill University's Faculty of Law. He has been a visiting professor at universities in the United States, Australia, Hong Kong, and Switzerland. From 2002 to 2003, he was law clerk to Justices Marie Deschamps and Claire L'Heureux Dubé at the Supreme Court of Canada.

L. Kinvin Wroth is a professor of law and former president and dean of Vermont Law School. He has taught land use law, marine law, procedure, legal history, and professional conduct. His coedited work, *Legal Papers of John Adams*, was awarded the American Historical Association's Littleton-Griswold prize. He received his LL.B. from Harvard University.

TREATY IMPLEMENTATION FOR SUSTAINABLE DEVELOPMENT

Over the past three decades, a series of international treaties has entered into force to address pressing global concerns – social and economic development and environmental protection. On climate change, biodiversity and biosafety, desertification, agriculture and seeds, trade, and investment liberalization, new regimes have been established to implement global commitments related to sustainable development, many with nearly universal membership.

Successful domestic implementation of these international treaty regimes is one of the most significant challenges facing international law today. While much has been written on the content and form of treaty law, there is relatively little that examines the transition from international legal theory and treaty texts to domestic regulation and practice.

This new series of books addresses this need and provides a serious contribution to ongoing global debates by conducting a detailed analysis of how myriad new treaty regimes that cover the future's most pressing concerns can be made to work in practice. It is dedicated to our mentor and first Chairman of '' ._ Board of Governors of the Centre for International Sustainable Development Law, The Honourable Mr. Justice Charles Doherty, Puisne judge on the Supreme Court of Canada from February 1, 1989, to August 1, 2003.

Series Editors:

Marie-Claire Cordonier Segger
Markus Wilheim Gehring

NAFTA and Sustainable Development

HISTORY, EXPERIENCE, AND PROSPECTS FOR REFORM

Edited by

HOI L. KONG

McGill University

L. KINVIN WROTH

Vermont Law School

CAMBRIDGE
UNIVERSITY PRESS

University Printing House, Cambridge CB2 8BS, United Kingdom

One Liberty Plaza, 20th Floor, New York, NY 10006, USA

477 Williamstown Road, Port Melbourne, VIC 3207, Australia

314-321, 3rd Floor, Plot 3, Splendor Forum, Jasola District Centre, New Delhi - 110025, India

79 Anson Road, #06-04/06, Singapore 079906

Cambridge University Press is part of the University of Cambridge.

It furthers the University's mission by disseminating knowledge in the pursuit of education, learning and research at the highest international levels of excellence.

www.cambridge.org
Information on this title: www.cambridge.org/9781107482432

© Cambridge University Press 2015

First published 2015
First paperback edition 2018

A catalogue record for this publication is available from the British Library

Library of Congress Cataloging in Publication data
Kong, Hoi L., author.
NAFTA and sustainable development : history, experience, and prospects for reform / Hoi L. Kong, McGill University; L. Kinvin Wroth, University of Vermont School of Law.
   pages   cm
Includes bibliographical references and index.
1. North American Free Trade Agreement (December 1992, 17)   2. Free trade – North America.
3. Sustainable development – Law and legislation – North America.   4. Environmental law – North America.   I. Wroth, L. Kinvin, author.   II. Title.
KDZ944.K66   2015
382´.971073–dc23   2015021270

ISBN 978-1-107-09722-3 Hardback
ISBN 978-1-107-48243-2 Paperback

Contents

List of Editors and Contributors

Betsy Baker, Associate Professor and Senior Fellow for Oceans and Energy, Institute for Energy and the Environment at Vermont Law School, is on leave for 2014–2016 in Anchorage, Alaska, with the University of Washington School of Law, where she is Visiting Professor and Counsel to the Dean for Alaska Programs.

Laurie J. Beyranevand is Associate Professor of Law and Associate Director of the Center for Agriculture and Food Systems at Vermont Law School.

Giselle Davidian, B.C.L., LL.B (McGill), M.Env.Sc. and H.B.Sc. (University of Toronto), is a recent call to the bar of Ontario and recently completed her articles at Willms & Shier Environmental Lawyers LLP in Toronto, where she will return as an associate lawyer in September 2015.

Geoffrey Garver, formerly a member of the Joint Public Advisory Committee of the Commission for Environmental Cooperation and a former director of the CEC's citizen submissions process, is currently Program Coordinator of the project Economics for the Anthropocene, based at McGill. He holds a J.D. from Michigan and an LL.M. from McGill and is a Ph.D. candidate at the McGill School of Environment.

Sébastien Jodoin is an Assistant Professor in the McGill University Faculty of Law and a Faculty Associate of the Governance, Environment & Markets Initiative at Yale.

Avidan Kent holds a Ph.D. from Cambridge University and is Lecturer in Commercial/Trade Law at the University of East Anglia Law School, Norwich, U.K., and an Associate Fellow of the Centre for International Sustainable Development Law, Montreal.

Hoi L. Kong is Associate Professor and Hydro Québec Scholar of Sustainable Development Law and Associate Dean Academic at the McGill University Faculty of Law.

Danni Liang, a visiting scholar at Vermont Law School in 2008–2009, is Associate Professor of Law, Sun Yat-sen University School of Law, Guangzhou, China.

Jingjing Liu, formerly Assistant Professor of Law and Associate Director of Vermont Law School's US-China Partnership for Environmental Law, is a J.S.D. candidate and the Joseph V. Heffernan Fellow at Columbia Law School.

Katia Opalka, B.A., B.C.L., LL.B., McGill, and formerly a legal officer at the Commission for Environmental Cooperation, is an environmental lawyer in private practice in Montreal and an Adjunct Professor at the McGill University School of Environment.

Raul Pacheco-Vega, Ph.D., is Assistant Professor, Public Administration Division, Centro de Investigacion y Docencia Economicas, Campus Región Centro, Aguascalientes, Mexico, and affiliated faculty in the Department of Political Science and the Latin American Studies Program at the University of British Columbia.

Freedom-Kai Phillips is a principal consultant at Bionomos, Ltd., and a Research Fellow with the Biodiversity and Biosafety Law Research Program, Centre for International Sustainable Development Law, Montreal. He holds an LL.B. from Dalhousie and an M.A. from Seton Hall University.

Montserrat Rovalo is a 2013 graduate of the Universidad Autonoma Nacional de Mexico Facultad de Derecho, specializing in international and environmental law. She was an intern with the Commission for Environmental Cooperation, Montreal, and is currently pursuing a Master's degree in international law at the Graduate Institute of International and Development Studies in Geneva, Switzerland.

Nicole Schabus is a Law Professor at the Thompson Rivers University Faculty of Law, Kamloops, B.C., Canada, who has represented a number of First Nations bands in provincial, federal, and international forums.

Paolo Solano is Legal Officer for the Submissions on Enforcement Matters Unit of the Commission for Environmental Cooperation, Montreal, and previously practiced environmental law. He has a law degree from the Universidad Autonoma Nacional de Mexico and has studied at the Georgetown University Law Center.

Pamela Vesilind is a Fellow with the Vermont Law School Center for Agricultural and Food Systems and an Adjunct Instructor in the University of Arkansas School of Law LL.M. Program in Agricultural and Food Law.

Leslie Welts is Staff Attorney for the Vermont Department of Environmental Conservation. She holds a J.D. from Vermont Law School and an LL.M. from the McGill Faculty of Law and has been a consultant and extern at the Commission for Environmental Cooperation.

L. Kinvin Wroth is Professor of Law and former Dean and President at Vermont Law School.

Acknowledgments

The editors, on behalf of all the authors, would like to express their gratitude and thanks to the following organizations and individuals without whose assistance and support this work would not have come into existence:

- The North American Commission on Environmental Cooperation – especially Irasema Coronado, Executive Director, and Paolo Solano, Legal Officer – for providing facilities and other support for the workshop at which most of the chapters in the present work were presented, and the North American Consortium on Legal Education, Vermont Law School, and the Faculty of Law of McGill University for also sponsoring and supporting the workshop.
- The Canadian Embassy's Canadian Studies Grant Program and the Social Sciences and Humanities Research Council of Canada for funding that supported various aspects of the program.
- Marie-Claire Cordonier Segger and Markus W. Gehring, editors of the Cambridge University Press series "Treaty Implementation for Sustainable Development," in which this volume is published, for their continuing support of the project, and our anonymous peer reviewers for their very helpful comments.
- The following student research assistants, whose editorial assistance was essential: John Hutchings, Nicola Langille, Carolyn Poutiainen, Mark Phillips, and Olga Redko of the McGill University Faculty of Law and Katherine Hambley and Elizabeth Tisher of Vermont Law School.
- Ginny Burnham of Vermont Law School for her extensive and patient labor in putting together the final manuscript in proper form for submission to the publisher.

Acknowledgments

The editors, on behalf of all the authors, would like to express their gratitude and thanks to the following organizations and individuals without whose assistance and support this work would not have come into existence:

- The North American Commission on Environmental Cooperation – especially Irasema Coronado, Executive Director, and Paolo Solano, Legal Officer – for providing facilities and other support for the workshop at which most of the chapters in the present work were presented, and the North American Consortium on Legal Education, Vermont Law School, and the Faculty of Law of McGill University for also sponsoring and supporting the workshop.
- The Canadian Embassy's Canadian Studies Grant Program and the Social Sciences and Humanities Research Council of Canada for funding that supported various aspects of the program.
- Marie-Claire Cordonier Segger and Markus W. Gehring, editors of the Cambridge University Press series "Treaty Implementation for Sustainable Development," in which this volume is published, for their continuing support of the project, and our anonymous peer reviewers for their very helpful comments.
- The following student research assistants, whose editorial assistance was essential: John Hutchings, Nicola Langille, Carolyn Poutiainen, Mark Phillips, and Olga Redko of the McGill University Faculty of Law and Katherine Hambley and Elizabeth Tisher of Vermont Law School.
- Ginny Burnham of Vermont Law School for her extensive and patient labor in putting together the final manuscript in proper form for submission to the publisher.

Introduction

NAFTA and Sustainable Development

L. Kinvin Wroth and Hoi L. Kong

Our numbers-obsessed culture reckons progress by the passage of the decades. In January 2014, we recognized the twentieth anniversary of the North American Free Trade Agreement (NAFTA), which took effect on January 1, 1994, after ratification by the United States.[1] Accordingly, this is an appropriate time for decennial stocktaking.

The impact of NAFTA on the environment became a critical issue when it was proposed for ratification in the United States. Fears were expressed that NAFTA would lead the participating governments to weaken environmental policy and regulation in order to encourage trade, in effect engaging in a "race to the bottom" that would result in significant environmental degradation in North America. NAFTA was ratified by the United States only after adoption and acceptance of a side agreement, the North American Agreement on Environmental Cooperation (NAAEC), by NAFTA's other Parties, Canada and Mexico.[2] NAAEC established the North American Commission for Environmental Cooperation (CEC), providing for environmental cooperation and protection in the implementation of NAFTA.

NAFTA and NAAEC were adopted at a time when the principle of sustainability – that development to meet the needs of the present should not compromise the environmental quality necessary to enable future generations to meet their needs – had attained international acceptance and was reflected in recent legislation of the United States and other developed countries designed to regulate development and growth to protect the natural environment.[3] NAFTA and NAAEC reflect the

---

[1] North American Free Trade Agreement, U.S.-Can.-Mex., Dec. 17, 1992, 32 I.L.M. 289 (1993), 32 I.L.M. 605 (1993) (NAFTA).

[2] North American Agreement on Environmental Cooperation, U.S.-Can.-Mex., Sept. 14, 1993, 32 I.L.M. 1480 (1993) (NAAEC). For the political background, see Geoffrey Garver, "Forgotten Promises: The Neglected Environmental Provisions of the NAFTA and the North American Agreement on Environmental Cooperation," Chapter 1 of this volume, at notes 1–3; Katia Opalka, "Sustainable Development, NAFTA, and Water," Chapter 9 of this volume, at notes 3–4.

[3] See World Commission on Environment and Development, Report: Our Common Future, ch. 2, "Toward Sustainable Development," [June 1987], UN Doc. A/42/427 (August 4, 1987), in *UN*

continuing tension between that evolving régime of sustainability and the purpose of free trade to encourage economic development on a global basis.

1. NAFTA AND NAAEC IN A NUTSHELL

The basic structure and provisions of NAFTA and NAAEC form the essential context of the chapters in this volume.

1.1. NAFTA

The Preamble to NAFTA, having set forth ten primarily trade-oriented goals, concludes with additional goals to undertake those purposes "in a manner consistent with environmental protection and conservation; . . . [to] promote sustainable development; [and to] strengthen the development and enforcement of environmental laws and regulations."[4] The objectives of NAFTA, set forth in Article 102, are entirely trade-related, however, and the basic provisions of the Agreement regulate trade in goods, services, cross-border investment, and intellectual property and provide elaborate dispute resolution processes. No single chapter of NAFTA is comprehensively devoted to the environment. Article 104 and Annex 104.1, however, provide that five existing international environmental agreements prevail over NAFTA in the event of inconsistency. Article 2101 provides that environmental and conservation measures of the Party states that are nondiscriminatory and otherwise not inconsistent with NAFTA are not barred by the basic trade provisions of the Agreement. As noted in section 2.1, Chapter 11, concerning cross-border investment, provides some recognition of states' environmental protection interests. NAFTA is overseen by the Free Trade Commission, established by Article 2001, which is composed of cabinet-level representatives of the Parties and is responsible for resolution of disputes about interpretation or application of the agreement as well as for general administration, which it exercises through its Secretariat established by Article 2002.

1.2. NAAEC

The preamble of NAAEC recognizes the importance of cooperative environmental protection in "achieving sustainable development for the well-being of present and future generations."[5] The objectives, set forth in Part One, Article 1, elaborate on

---

Documents: Gathering a Body of Global Agreements, http://www.un-documents.net/ocf-02.htm; Bryan Norton, *Sustainability: A Philosophy of Adaptive Ecosystem Management* (University of Chicago Press, 2005) (examining the theory of sustainability); C.S. Hollings, "Theories for Sustainable Futures," 4(2) *Conservation Ecology* 7 (2000) (examining different perspectives on sustainability); Sustainable Fisheries Act, Pub.L. 104–297, 110 Stat. 3565 (1996), amending 16 U.S.C. §§ 1851–1861.

[4] NAFTA, Preamble.
[5] NAAEC, Preamble.

that point and emphasize cooperation and transparency in serving NAFTA's environmental goals and securing compliance with and enforcement of environmental laws and regulations. In Part Two, the Parties undertake significant commitments to reporting, providing high levels of environmental protection, and establishing effective public and private remedies for violation of environmental laws and regulations. Part Three establishes and describes the functions of the CEC, a tripartite structure consisting of the Council, composed of cabinet-level representatives of the Parties; the Secretariat, consisting of an executive director and staff; and the Joint Public Advisory Committee. Other sections provide for dispute resolution procedures, information sharing, and administration.[6]

2. DISPUTE RESOLUTION PROVISIONS OF NAFTA AND NAAEC

The dispute resolution mechanisms of NAFTA and NAAEC provide the framework in which the provisions of the two agreements are applied in particular circumstances.

2.1. *NAFTA: Chapters 11, 19, and 20*

NAFTA provides three principal dispute resolution mechanisms.[7] The most basic is the intergovernmental dispute resolution process established in Chapter 20, which applies to all disputes between the Parties concerning interpretation or application of the Agreement or Party actions inconsistent with or nullifying it for which the Agreement does not make other specific provision (Article 2004). Article 2005 provides that the responding Party in an environmental dispute that could be resolved under either World Trade Organization (WTO) or NAFTA procedures may require the dispute to be brought in a NAFTA forum. The Chapter 20 process consists of successive steps from consultation between the Parties through conciliation or mediation by the Free Trade Commission to proceedings before an arbitral panel. The Parties to an arbitration are expected to conform to the recommendations provided in the final report of the panel.[8] If a Party fails to comply, the other Party may suspend certain benefits to the noncompliant party through a procedure provided in Article 2019. Very few Chapter 20 proceedings have been completed since 1995.[9]

---

[6] NAAEC, Part Four (Cooperation and Provision of Information), Part Five (Consultation and Resolution of Disputes), Part Six (General Provisions), Part Seven (Final Provisions).

[7] See, generally, David A. Gantz, *Regional Trade Agreements: Law, Policy, and Practice*, pp. 121–27, 133–144 (Durham, N.C.: Carolina Academic Press, 2008); Donald McRae and John Siwiec, "NAFTA Dispute Settlement Process: Success or Failure?," *Biblioteca Virtual del Instituto de Investigaciones Jurídicas de la UNAM* (Mexico City, UNAM, 2010), pp. 363–87.

[8] NAFTA, Arts. 2006 (consultation), 2007 (good offices, conciliation, mediation), 2008–2018 (arbitration).

[9] Gantz, *Regional Trade Agreement*, pp. 142–143 (three proceedings between 1995 and 1998 in which panels were assembled; at least ten consultations).

Chapter 19 provides a separate procedure for disputes concerning the antidumping or countervailing duty laws of a Party.[10] Under Article 1904, the parties agree to forego judicial review of final antidumping or countervailing duty determinations in favor of review of such determinations by bi-national panels established by the Parties from NAFTA rosters and subject to review by Extraordinary Challenge Committees similarly established under Annex 1904.13 by the Parties. Chapter 19 proceedings have seen significantly greater use; as of 2010, 137 proceedings had been filed – 97 against the United States, 22 against Canada, and 18 against Mexico.[11]

Chapter 19 and 20 proceedings are between the Parties, though the governments involved may in fact represent the interests of their subnational units or individual citizens. Chapter 11, governing cross-border investment, provides a unique procedure under which an individual investor may obtain arbitration of a claim against the government of one of the Parties and receive damages for violation of Chapter 11 obligations by federal or state or provincial action. The arbitration is conducted before a three-member panel chosen by the complaining investor and the state, using one of three sets of international arbitration rules. Grounds of challenge under Chapter 11 include violations of the provisions of Articles 1102–1105 concerning standards of treatment for foreign investors and that the state action is an expropriation or taking of the investor's property. The arbitrators' award is binding but may be enforced or revised or annulled in a court of the state where the panel sat. If enforcement proceedings fail, the government of the prevailing investor may bring Chapter 20 dispute resolution proceedings against the other government. Article 1114 allows state measures otherwise consistent with Chapter 11 that ensure that investment activities are "sensitive to environmental concerns and prohibits relaxation of environmental measures by a Party to encourage investment."[12]

Chapter 11 proceedings have been the subject of continuing controversy throughout NAFTA's history. Objections to the process include that the proceedings are commonly used to challenge state environmental, land use, or other important regulatory measures; that they occur largely outside traditional court systems and are not subject to a system of precedent; that they undermine federalism because states or provinces whose laws are challenged do not have standing in the proceedings; and that they have imposed significant costs on taxpayers.[13] That said, it should be noted that between 1995 and 2014, only eighty-four Chapter 11 proceedings have been instituted – twenty-one against the United States, thirty-five against Canada, and twenty-eight against Mexico. There have been eleven awards – six against Canada

---

[10] NAFTA, Arts. 1901–1911 and Annexes 1901.2–1911.
[11] McRae and Siwiec, "NAFTA Dispute Settlement Process," p. 374.
[12] NAFTA, Article 1114(1).
[13] Gantz, *Regional Trade Agreements*, pp. 122–24. See, e.g., Public Citizen, *Table of Foreign Investor-State Cases and Claims under NAFTA and other U.S. "Trade" Deals* (August 2014), p. 1, available at http://www.citizen.org/documents/investor-state-chart.pdf.

(including three settlements) and five against Mexico. Twenty-one claims were dismissed by the panel, twenty-seven never began arbitration or were withdrawn, nine were concluded on other grounds, and sixteen are pending.[14]

2.2. *NAAEC: Article 14 and 15; Part 5*

NAAEC contains a multistage dispute resolution procedure aimed at reviewing and addressing the effectiveness of a Party's enforcement of its environmental law. Article 14 provides for Submissions on Enforcement Matters (SEM) to the CEC Secretariat by any individual or NGO residing in a Party state claiming ineffective enforcement by a Party. The Secretariat is to consider the submission if it meets certain formal requirements, is not aimed at harassing industry, and has been communicated in writing to the Party. The Secretariat may then request a response from the Party if it determines that pursuing the matter, among other things, would advance the goals of the Agreement and private remedies have been unavailing. If the Party's response states that the matter is subject of a judicial or administrative proceeding, the Secretariat is to go no farther. Otherwise, under Article 15, the Secretariat is to advise the Council if preparation of a factual record is warranted and is to prepare it if the Council so directs by a two-thirds vote. In preparing the factual record, the Secretariat may consider information from a variety of sources. Parties may comment on the draft factual record. By a two-thirds vote, the Council may make the final factual record available to the public. Through 2013, 84 SEMs had been pursued – 31 involving Canada, 41 involving Mexico, and 12 involving the United States. Factual records have been prepared in 22 SEMs; five SEMs are currently pending.[15]

Part Five of NAAEC provides a Party-initiated consultation and resolution procedure based on "a persistent pattern of failure" by another Party to enforce its environmental law.[16] If consultation between the parties fails to resolve the matter, a Party may request the Council to undertake conciliation, mediation, or other means to do so. If those efforts fail, the Council, on the request of a party, by a two-thirds vote, may convene an arbitral panel to make findings and conclusions if the initial failure of enforcement involves goods or services traded between Parties or competing with those of another Party. No arbitration proceedings have been undertaken under this provision.[17] If a panel were convened and were to find a persistent pattern of nonenforcement, and the Parties could not agree on a plan to remedy it, the panel could be reconvened on the request of a Party and could

---

[14] These figures are based on a consolidation of the compilations of proceedings on the web page "Foreign Affairs, Trade, and Development Canada," http://www.international.gc.ca/trade-agreements-accords-commerciaux/topics-domaines/disp-diff/nafta.aspx?lang=eng, and Public Citizen, *Table of Foreign Investor-State Cases*, pp. 2–31.

[15] http://www.cec.org/Page.asp?PageID=1226&SiteNodeID=542&BL_ExpandID=502.

[16] NAAEC, Art. 27(1).

[17] See Garver, "Forgotten Promises," Chapter 1 of this volume, at notes 61–86.

ultimately impose a monetary enforcement assessment or a suspension of benefits in the event of nonpayment.[18]

3. THE CONTENTS OF THIS VOLUME

NAFTA has been the subject of much academic commentary, with the trade elements of NAFTA dominating the discussion.[19] As discussed earlier, NAFTA contains a commitment to sustainable development, and scattered provisions of it partially reflect that commitment, but the adoption of NAAEC was politically necessary to its successful ratification. The objectives of NAAEC echo the aspiration, inherent in the concept of sustainability, to balance the economic, environmental, and human costs of development. The process established by NAAEC aims to protect the Parties' environmental laws from the effects of NAFTA by ensuring that different environmental standards adopted by the Parties do not lead to distortions that cause increased trade to result in increased environmental degradation.

This volume seeks to address this underappreciated and underdeveloped aspect of NAFTA. Its chapters were initially presented as papers at a preliminary workshop held on June 14, 2013, at the Montreal facilities of the Secretariat of the CEC. The workshop, coordinated by this volume's editors, was jointly sponsored by the McGill University Faculty of Law, Vermont Law School, and the CEC. It was the product of a longstanding relationship between Vermont Law School and McGill intended to take advantage of Vermont's leadership in environmental law and McGill's leadership in international and comparative law and sustainable development.[20] Sixteen individuals affiliated with McGill, Vermont Law School, the CEC, and other academic and governmental or other institutions in the United States, Canada, and Mexico, and representing a variety of perspectives, made presentations at the workshop. The present volume contains 16 chapters, 15 presented as papers at the workshop and one prepared for the workshop that could not be offered there.

The chapters are grouped in three parts focused on three general themes.

---

[18] NAAEC, Arts. 39–41.

[19] See Sébastien Jodoin, "Pathways of Influence in the NAFTA Regime and Their Implications for Domestic Environmental Policy-Making in North America," Chapter 14 of this volume, at notes 1–4; Gantz, *Regional Trade Agreements*, pp. 122–24.

[20] Following a successful series of conferences and exchanges that began in the 1990s, the two faculties in August 2006 formally established the "Vermont-McGill Initiative on Cross-Border Sustainability." For publications resulting from these joint efforts, see Symposium, "Law and Civil Society," 15 *Ariz. J. Int'l & Comp. L.* 1–317 (1998); Symposium, "Quebec, Canada and First Nations: The Problem of Secession," 23 *Vt. L. Rev.* 699–859 (1999); Symposium, "Mountain Resorts: Ecology and the Law," 26 *Vt. L. Rev.* 509–751 (2002); Symposium, "Accommodating Differences: The Present and Future of the Law of Diversity," 30 *Vt. L. Rev.* 431–937 (2006); "Joint McGill-Vermont Law School Workshop on Water," 34 *Vt. L. Rev.* 855–973 (2010); "Joint Cross-Border Conference on Sustainability," 13 *Vt. J. Envtl. L.* 417–573 (2012). These activities have enjoyed significant support from Canadian Studies Program Enhancement and Conference grants awarded by the Government of Canada through the Canadian Embassy in Washington.

3.1. *Part I: Process: NAFTA and NAAEC*

Part I examines the procedures with which compliance by NAFTA Parties with its sustainability goals can be assessed.

Geoffrey Garver provides an overview of the development of NAFTA and NAAEC and a general evaluation of their implementation.[21] He then explores three provisions intended to support environmental goals, which have been largely neglected: NAFTA Article 1114(2) and other provisions that sought to discourage the Parties from weakening existing environmental protections; the provisions of NAAEC Part V providing Party-to-Party dispute resolution in cases of persistent failure to enforce environmental laws; and NAAEC Article 10(7) obligating the CEC to develop a process for transboundary environmental impact assessment. He concludes that these failures illustrate the more general proposition that the environmental protection features of NAFTA are overmatched by the international trade purposes of the Agreement.

Giselle Davidian addresses the purposes and functions of NAAEC's Submissions on Enforcement Matters (SEM) and the effectiveness of the process.[22] Asserting that a duty of public accountability, including procedural justice, is a developing principle of international law, she examines the SEM process to determine the degree to which it applies that principle. She concludes that the success of SEM in countering the "race to the bottom" effect is offset by failures of process, including lack of access, politicized use of the process by the CEC, lack of clear procedural provisions governing Council proceedings, lack of independence for the CEC Secretariat, and lack of oversight and enforcement provisions for its conclusions. After reviewing other examples, she offers recommendations designed to increase the independence of the process, increase public participation, and depoliticize it. She concludes that failure to make such changes will leave the process so weak that it would be preferable to develop an adversarial process for addressing noncompliance with NAAEC.

Paolo Solano explores the meaning and scope of the concept of "environmental law," an essential element of a complaint to be submitted in the SEM process.[23] Parties responding to complaints have consistently argued for a narrow definition of "environmental law," and the CEC Council has also taken a narrow view. In an extensive body of decisions on submissions, however, the Secretariat has developed a detailed and nuanced broad view. The chapter details those decisions in nine procedural and substantive areas of domestic law. Mr. Solano concludes that the broad view is necessary and appropriate under the international law principle of

---

[21] Geoffrey Garver, "Forgotten Promises: The Neglected Environmental Provisions of the NAFTA and the NAAEC," Chapter 1 of this volume.

[22] Giselle Davidian, "Should Citizens Expect Procedural Justice in Nonadversarial Processes? Spotlighting the Regression of the Citizen Submission Process from NAAEC to CAFTA-DR," Chapter 2 of this volume.

[23] Paolo Solano, "Choosing the Right Whistle: The Development of the Concept of Environmental Law under the Citizen Submissions Process," Chapter 3 of this volume.

effectiveness to carry out the purposes of NAAEC and to sustain public respect for the process.

Montserrat Rovalo analyzes the status of the NAAEC provision that upon notice of pending judicial or administrative proceedings, the Secretariat should not proceed with a SEM complaint.[24] New SEM guidelines have eliminated the requirement that the Secretariat provide reasons for its decision not to proceed. She analyzes the scope and meaning of the NAAEC provision and describes the Secretariat's interpretation of the provision in specific cases under the former guidelines as well as the positions of the Parties and Council on the question. Noting that providing reasons is essential to the integrity of the SEM process, she assesses the impact of the New Guidelines on the process and advances some proposals to mitigate their possible negative implications.

Leslie Welts identifies procedural barriers caused by increasingly formal interpretations in the implementation of NAAEC's procedural requirements for submissions in the SEM process.[25] The procedural burden has risen for submissions, decreasing the public's access to information and limiting the ability of the public to hold the Parties accountable for enforcing their environmental laws. This shift has the effect of stifling submissions and hindering the NAAEC's prime tool for achieving its sustainable development goals. Ms. Welts analyzes the Secretariat's interpretation of NAAEC's procedural requirements over time and assesses how the increasingly heavy burden impacts the CEC's success in implementing NAAEC's sustainable development goals. She concludes that this interference demonstrates a need to revisit the procedural requirements to encourage increased public participation via citizen submission in order to improve prospects of achieving those goals.

3.2. *Part II: Specific Environmental Issues under NAFTA and NAAEC*

Part II addresses the application of various NAFTA, NAAEC, and related measures to specific problems and in specific settings.

Pamela Vesilind considers the effect of NAFTA and NAAEC on sustainability issues in Mexican farmed animal agriculture.[26] She notes that the ten-year assessment of these issues did not consider the effect on hog farming and the environment of intensive livestock operations (ILO) undertaken by U.S. interests in Mexico with impetus provided by NAFTA. Two efforts by indigenous agricultural and environmental interests use the CEC SEM process to address this issue. Ms. Vesilind suggests that the process was ineffective because of the narrow scope of NAAEC,

---

[24] Montserrat Rovalo, "Pending Proceedings in the New Guidelines for Submissions on Enforcement Matters: An Improved Regression?," Chapter 4 of this volume.
[25] Leslie Welts, "Form Over Substance: Procedural Hurdles to the NAAEC Citizen Submission Process," Chapter 5 of this volume.
[26] Pamela Vesilind, "Downward Harmonization: Mexico's Industrial Livestock Revolution," Chapter 6 of this volume.

the inadequate nature of Mexican environmental regulation, the fundamental disconnect between the engine of free trade and traditional agriculture, and finally that NAFTA was basically designed to advantage U.S. and Canadian industrial agriculture at Mexico's expense.

Laurie Beyranevand analyzes the impact of NAFTA on U.S. and Canadian agricultural biotechnology policies' influence over Mexico's environment and agriculture.[27] NAFTA lifted the barriers that had prevented bioengineered crops from entering Mexico. Though the CEC agreed in a report that bioengineered corn from the U.S. and Canada represented a threat to Mexico's traditional maize crop, many other crops remained at risk of bioengineered imports from the U.S. and Canada, which had allowed their production under regulations developed on a cost-benefit basis. Neither country addressed the risk to Mexican agriculture, however. Professor Beyranevand recommends a variety of solutions suggested by the CEC and a joint U.S.-Canadian effort to assess the risks for Mexican agriculture and develop a tripartite regime to address them.

Betsy Baker considers the methods used to assess NAFTA's effect on the marine environment and possible lessons for the CEC from the experience of other ocean assessment measures.[28] She notes the amount of NAFTA's ocean area and describes assessment processes generally and the World Ocean Assessment (WOA) to be completed in 2014. Describing the tools available to and used by the CEC to address marine environmental issues, including reports, ecological scorecards, and works such as its 2012 *North American Environmental Atlas*, she proposes methods by which the CEC can participate in ongoing ocean assessment activities.

Katia Opalka draws on her experience as a legal officer at the CEC to provide a personal reflection on NAFTA's impact on sustainable development in water policy.[29] After a discussion of the development of NAFTA and NAAEC, in which she had a role, Ms. Opalka describes the current state of the CEC's role with water issues, with examples of a number of activities and SEM proceedings. She concludes that water issues have not been a major part of the CEC's agenda because national sovereignty concerns have deterred the Parties and their leaders from making a sustained commitment to a CEC role.

Nicole Schabus considers the effect of NAFTA and NAAEC on indigenous people's rights.[30] She argues that indigenous peoples in North America have managed their resources and territories sustainably and maintained sustainable economies as, for example, with the salmon fisheries of the Pacific Northwest. Though colonization

---

[27] Laurie Beyranevand, "Agricultural Biotechnology and NAFTA: Analyzing the Impacts of U.S. and Canadian Policies on Mexico's Environment and Agriculture," Chapter 7 of this volume.

[28] Betsy Baker, "Assessing Assessments of NAFTA's Marine Environment: The Commission for Environmental Cooperation Meets the World Ocean Assessment," Chapter 8 of this volume.

[29] Katia Opalka, "Sustainable Development, NAFTA, and Water," Chapter 9 of this volume.

[30] Nicole Schabus, "Indigenous Peoples in North America: Bridging the Trade and Environment Gap to Ensure Sustainability under NAFTA and NAAEC," Chapter 10 of this volume.

has marginalized indigenous peoples, indigenous rights are today recognized in many international instruments, and NAFTA also should recognize and implement them. She examines Canada's regulation and deregulation of collective lands and describes the proceedings brought by indigenous peoples of British Columbia before WTO and NAFTA tribunals claiming Canadian intrusions on their lands. She also sets out the role indigenous peoples can play in ensuring environmental, cultural, and economic sustainability through their knowledge of traditional environmental concerns.

Freedom-Kai Phillips discusses the effect of regional approaches to renewable energy regulation and emissions reduction on global competitiveness.[31] He notes that climate change has emerged as an increasingly prevalent threat globally. Although NAFTA Parties are employing individual policy measures domestically, the NAAEC has the additional potential to assist Parties in combating climate change together in a comprehensive and efficient manner. Capitalizing on the experience of the European Union, NAFTA Parties have an opportunity to integrate their individual climate change strategies. By leveraging lessons learned, Parties can collectively increase policy effectiveness and decrease costs of implementation.

Avidan Kent considers the effect of the sustainable development principle on public participation in arbitration proceedings under NAFTA Chapter 11 governing foreign investment.[32] After reviewing the general principle of public participation and access, as well as its role in international law and, specifically, NAFTA and NAAEC, the chapter describes the challenges to providing for participation in Chapter 11 disputes and its "creeping acceptance in those proceedings." After reviewing the current practice in a number of specific cases, Dr. Kent notes the example of the EU and UNCITRAL as models for future development under Chapter 11 and makes recommendations based on those sources.

Danni Liang and Jingjing Liu in their joint paper discuss lessons that China can learn from the NAFTA experience in addressing impacts of free trade on the environment, in particular the concerns over the potential for a "race to the bottom" in light of lax environmental regulations and weak enforcement in China at a time of rapid economic engagement.[33] They describe cases under NAFTA Chapter 11 and the risks of sacrificing environmental concerns to investor interests that they reflect, then argue for an evolution of process that will resolve that conflict. After a review of China's current challenges and well-developed environmental laws but weak enforcement structure, the authors recommend that China incorporate

[31] Freedom-Kai Phillips, "Climate Change, Sustainable Development, and NAFTA: Regional Policy Harmonization as a Basis for Sustainable Development," Chapter 11 of this volume.

[32] Avidan Kent, "The Principle of Public Participation in NAFTA Chapter 11 Disputes," Chapter 12 of this volume.

[33] Danni Liang and Jingjing Liu, "Preventing Environmental Deterioration from International Trade and Investment: How China Can Learn from NAFTA's Experience to Strengthen Domestic Environmental Governance and Ensure Sustainable Development," Chapter 13 of this volume.

provisions related to environmental protection and sustainable development into all international trade and investment agreements and that it be prepared for potential investor–state arbitration claims.

3.3. *Part III: Proposals for Reform and Lessons Going Forward*

Part III looks at the operation of NAFTA and NAAEC from broader jurisprudential and methodological perspectives.

Sébastien Jodoin provides "a theoretical account" of the ways in which the NAFTA regime may influence domestic environmental policy in the Party states.[34] After a review of the compartmentalized approach of present scholarship on this question, Professor Jodoin analyses four pathways of influence – international rules, international norms, markets, and direct access to policy-making – and how they affect policy development. His purpose is to demonstrate the roles of the pathways, rather than to provide a comprehensive treatment of environmental policy-making. After analyzing the operation and effect of each pathway, he concludes that NAFTA does not appear to have actually exerted pervasive, sustained, or significant positive or negative influence on environmental policy-making but calls for further research to dig deeper into that conclusion.

Hoi Kong examines the NAAEC SEM process to demonstrate how deliberative democracy offers a theoretical framework justifying the process, explains why and how the process falls short of fully realizing its deliberative democratic potential, and proposes reforms to the process consistent with NAAEC's limits.[35] His analysis begins with an account of deliberative democracy and its relation to the ideas of Lon Fuller and attempts to demonstrate why and how it can be extended to the transnational context. He then examines in detail the structure and processes of NAAEC and shows how the SEM process was founded on ideas that resonate with the aspirations of deliberative democratic theory, yet has been widely understood to have been a disappointment. In the final section, he proposes reforms that acknowledge the limits of the NAAEC, while seeking to vindicate deliberative democratic aspirations.

Raul Pacheco-Vega proposes a methodology for evaluating the way in which environmental NGOs can affect policy under NAFTA.[36] Noting that the evidence concerning the causal mechanisms and exact effects that increased transnational commercial activity has on specific ecosystems has been inconclusive, Professor Pacheco-Vega states that, nevertheless, there are significant collateral or indirect environmental consequences of NAFTA, such as innovative citizen participation

---

[34] Sébastien Jodoin, "Pathways of Influence in the NAFTA Regime and Their Implications for Domestic Environmental Policy-Making in North America," Chapter 14 of this volume.

[35] Hoi L. Kong, "The Citizen Submissions Process in the NAAEC: Theory and Practice in Deliberative Democratic Institutional Design for Transnational Institutions," Chapter 15 of this volume.

[36] Raul Pacheco-Vega, "Assessing ENGO Influence in North American Environmental Politics: The Double Grid Framework," Chapter 16 of this volume.

mechanisms and strong cross-border mobilization of environmental activists. He summarizes the results of empirical investigations that he has conducted over the past fifteen years on the coalition-building mechanisms deployed by environmental nongovernmental organizations (ENGOs) involved in the development and use of information dissemination such as the pollutant release and transfer registries (PRTRs). He also outlines a proposed methodology that can be used to assess degrees of influence of ENGO coalitions on domestic policy-making and makes a case for its use within North American environmental politics.

4. CONCLUSION

This collection of essays aims at two goals. It at the same time aspires to be a fitting testament to the twentieth anniversary of NAFTA's entering into force and a significant contribution to this book series' aspiration to assess the implementation of sustainable development treaties. The two aspirations are related. The collection examines from a rich diversity of perspectives one of the least-studied aspects of the NAFTA regime, namely the provisions, most notably in the NAAEC, that govern sustainable development in the trade region. As the editors of this collection and the organizers of the conference from which it emerged, we have brought together researchers from all three member countries of NAFTA. Some of the contributors to this volume are senior academics, while others are researchers on the cusp of their academic careers. Some contributors bring us an insider's perspective of the CEC, while others offer a viewpoint from private practice. We believe that this rich kaleidoscope of perspectives sheds new light on the various ways in which the member countries of NAFTA have succeeded or failed to make effective the regime's sustainable development aspirations. And we hope that the collection contributes thereby to the global conversation that this collection seeks to initiate into the ways in which sustainable development treaties in different regions around the world have been implemented.

PART I

Process: NAFTA and NAAEC

1

Forgotten Promises

Neglected Environmental Provisions of the NAFTA and the NAAEC

Geoffrey Garver

1. INTRODUCTION

One of the political hot potatoes that President George H. W. Bush passed off to President Bill Clinton in 1993 was getting the United States Congress to adopt legislation implementing the North American Free Trade Agreement (NAFTA),[1] which was signed late in President Bush's term. To help get the NAFTA through Congress, and to meet his campaign promises to bolster the quite modest environmental and labor provisions in the text of the NAFTA, President Clinton hastily negotiated side agreements with Canada and Mexico on labor and on the environment in the first year of his presidency. The environmental side agreement, the North American Agreement on Environmental Cooperation (NAAEC),[2] was intended to address concerns that liberalized trade among Canada, Mexico, and the United States would increase environmental harms due to the increased scale of economic activity; create havens for polluting industries, for example, along the United States–Mexico border; and trigger a "race to the bottom" in which the governments would weaken environmental regulations or enforcement in order to attract economic benefits of trade.[3] The NAAEC came into effect on January 1, 1994. It created the trinational Commission for Environmental Cooperation (CEC), headed by a council made up of the top environmental official of each country, and imposed on the government Parties various obligations designed to minimize environmental concerns related to the NAFTA.

---

[1] North American Free Trade Agreement between the Government the United States of America, the Government of Canada and the Government of the United Mexican States, San Antonio, December 17, 1992, in force January 1, 1994, (1993) 32 ILM 296; Can. TS 1994 No. 2, 32.
[2] September 14, 1993, in force January 1, 1994, (1993) 32 ILM 1480; Can. TS 1994 No. 3.
[3] See Pierre Marc Johnson and André Beaulieu, *The Environment and NAFTA: Understanding and Implementing the New Continental Law* (Washington, DC: Island Press, 1996), pp. 23–4, 36–7, 40–7, 245–6; Joseph A. McKinney, *Created from NAFTA: The Structure, Function, and Significance of the Treaty's Related Institutions* (Armonk, NY: M. E. Sharpe, 2000), pp. 90–1.

Together the NAFTA and the NAAEC contain various provisions to address these concerns. The NAFTA, described further in Section 2, discourages weakening of environmental measures, encourages the upward harmonization of environmental laws and regulations, gives certain multilateral environmental agreements qualified precedence over the NAFTA, and constrains assertions that a country's environmental protection measures constitute a nontariff trade barrier. The NAAEC, also described further in Section 2, imposes soft obligations on Canada, Mexico, and the United States to maintain high levels of environmental protection, to effectively enforce their environmental laws, and to ensure due process in the treatment of environmental claims in domestic proceedings. It also gives the CEC Council the authority to engage the governments in a broad program of environmental cooperation and requires the council to consider the environmental impacts of the NAFTA on an ongoing basis and to work toward an agreement on transboundary environmental impact assessment. To ensure the governments fulfil their obligation to effectively enforce their environmental laws, the NAAEC establishes two measures: a citizen-driven accountability mechanism able to yield detailed investigative reports, called factual records, on allegations that a Party has failed to effectively enforce its environmental law and a Party-to-Party dispute resolution process that can lead to monetary sanctions or to the loss of NAFTA benefits.

In its first twenty years, the CEC has produced a sustained cooperative program that has yielded some important results,[4] especially in early years when, for example, the CEC assisted Mexico in phasing out DDT[5] and began issuing its annual *Taking Stock* report, which combines pollutant, release, and transfer information from the three countries.[6] As of May 2013, the citizen-driven submissions on enforcement matters (SEM) mechanism had received eighty-one submissions and generated seventeen factual records – although the impact of factual records generally has been quite limited.[7] Overall, measured against its potential to foster aggressive policies on pressing regional and global environmental challenges, particularly related to energy and climate change, the CEC has fallen short.[8] Further, several important environmental provisions of the NAFTA and the NAAEC have been either neglected or abandoned, casting doubt on the environmental promise and legacy of the agreements.

---

[4] See Scott Vaughan, "Thinking North American Environmental Management," in Thomas J. Courchene, Donald J. Savoie, and Daniel Schwanen (eds.), *The Art of the State II: Thinking North America* (Montreal: Institute for Research on Public Policy, 2004), folio 5, pp. 20–1.

[5] See Commission for Environmental Cooperation, "DDT no longer used in North America" (2003), http://cec.org/Storage/50/4285_DDT_en.pdf.

[6] See Commission for Environmental Cooperation, "Taking stock," http://cec.org/Page.asp? PageID=924&SiteNodeID=483.

[7] See Pierre Marc Johnson et al., "Ten Years of North American Environmental Cooperation: Report of the Ten-year Review and Assessment Committee to the Council of the Commission for Environmental Cooperation," June 15, 2004, p. 46, http://cec.org/Storage/79/7287_TRAC-Report2004_en.pdf.

[8] See Vaughan, "Thinking North American Environmental Management," pp. 23–5.

Yet some of these neglected provisions have become boilerplate elements in the environmental frameworks negotiated in post-NAFTA trade deals to which Canada, Mexico, or the United States have signed on, raising the concern that they provide "green" cover for trade deals that do little in practice to confront the global ecological challenges that have been increasing – while also becoming ever more apparent – as regional and global trade has expanded.[9]

This chapter focuses on three of the most prominent neglected environmental instruments of the NAFTA and the NAAEC: one that aimed to address fears of a potential "race to the bottom" in levels of environmental protection, another that responded to concerns about weak environmental enforcement, and a third that created an expanded opportunity to examine the environmental effects of North American economic activity.

The results, in short, have been disappointing. As for the first instrument, the three governments have evidently completely ignored the mild mandate to prevent weakening of environmental protections in the NAFTA countries that the states were given most explicitly in the NAFTA's Article 1114(2). The second, the Party-to-Party dispute resolution process set out in Part V of the NAAEC, which aims to provide a remedy for persistent patterns of weak enforcement of environmental laws, has never come to life. Finally, Canada, Mexico, and the United States have failed to conclude the agreement on transboundary environmental impact assessment (TEIA) that is called for in the NAAEC's Article 10(7).

Section 2 places these provisions in the context of the entire framework for trade and the environment that the NAFTA and the NAAEC establish. Section 3 describes the provisions that relate to nonregression of environmental protections and discusses the Parties' failure to implement them despite the weakening of several environmental laws in Canada, Mexico, and the United States since the NAFTA and the NAAEC came into effect. Section 4 presents an analysis of the failure to implement the Party-to-Party dispute resolution in Part V of the NAAEC. Section 5 presents and analyzes the governments' unsuccessful attempts to reach an agreement on TEIA. The conclusion summarizes the implications of the failure to make use of these neglected provisions, especially in light of the adoption of the first two by numerous subsequent agreements,[10] and suggests that the NAFTA and the NAAEC have established "tragic institutions"[11] because they resist change and occupy policy space that better alternatives should fill.

---

[9] On increasing ecological concerns associated with trade, see, e.g., Duncan Pollard et al. (eds.), *Living Planet Report 2010: Biodiversity, Biocapacity and Development* (Gland, Switzerland: WWF International, 2010), pp. 78–9; Chris Hails et al. (eds.), *The Living Planet Report* (Gland, Switzerland: WWF International, 2008), pp. 28–9.
[10] See infra notes 107 and 108 and accompanying text.
[11] Brigham Daniels, "Emerging commons and tragic institutions" (2007) 37:3 *Envtl. L.* 515 at 520–1, 539–41.

2. SUMMARY OF THE NAFTA AND THE NAAEC ENVIRONMENTAL PROVISIONS

At the time of its adoption, promoters of the NAFTA called it the most environmental trade agreement to date.[12] Yet its environmental provisions were insufficient to allay environmental concerns regarding expanded trade in North America. The NAAEC addressed at least some of those concerns, and together the NAFTA and the NAAEC established the basic approach to trade and environment that the North American countries have followed, with various permutations, in their subsequent trade deals. This section presents an overview of the key environmental provisions of the NAFTA and the NAAEC and places the neglected provisions noted in Section 1 in the context of this framework.

2.1. *Environmental Provisions of the NAFTA*

The preamble to the NAFTA states the resolve of the NAFTA governments to "UNDERTAKE [their NAFTA obligations] in a manner consistent with environmental protection and conservation; . . . [to] STRENGTHEN the development and enforcement of environmental laws and regulations; and [to] PROMOTE sustainable development."[13] The text then expands on these objectives. It provides at least some protection to the Parties' existing environmental commitments against potential accusations that they amount to trade barriers and to the Parties' ability to adopt and maintain environmental standards, and it promotes harmonization of the Parties' standards while encouraging higher levels of environmental protection and discouraging backsliding.

In the event of an inconsistency with the NAFTA, Article 104 of the NAFTA gives qualified precedence to several international environmental agreements: the Convention on International Trade in Endangered Species of Wild Flora and Fauna (CITES), the Montreal Protocol on Substances that Deplete the Ozone Layer, the Basel Convention on the Control of Transboundary Movements of Hazardous Wastes and their Disposal, and bilateral agreements between the United States and Canada on the movement of hazardous wastes and between the United States and Mexico on environmental protection in the United States–Mexico border area. The NAFTA also affirms the Parties' right to adopt environmental standards according to their desired levels of environmental protection, and to impose those standards on other Parties' goods and services, so long as doing so advances a "legitimate objective" and is nondiscriminatory.[14] Further, the NAFTA requires the Parties to

---

[12] See Johnson and Beaulieu, *The Environment and NAFTA*, p. 66; Greg Block, "Trade and environment in the western hemisphere: Expanding the North American Agreement on Environmental Cooperation into the Americas" (2003) 33:3 *Envtl. L.* 501 at 503.
[13] NAFTA, Preamble.
[14] Ibid., Article 904.

"work jointly to enhance the level of safety and of protection of human, animal and plant life and health, the environment and consumers"[15] and to work toward making their environmental standards compatible without weakening them.[16] The dispute resolution process in Article 20 of the NAFTA applies to Party-to-Party disputes regarding the standard-setting provisions and consistency with multilateral environmental agreements, but to date no such disputes have been initiated.[17]

The most explicit provision in either the NAFTA or the NAAEC that prohibits backsliding, or regression, in levels of environmental protection – albeit softly – is the NAFTA's Article 1114(2). It states:

> The Parties recognize that it is inappropriate to encourage investment by relaxing domestic health, safety or environmental measures. Accordingly, a Party should not waive or otherwise derogate from, or offer to waive or otherwise derogate from, such measures as an encouragement for the establishment, acquisition, expansion or retention in its territory of an investment of an investor. If a Party considers that another Party has offered such an encouragement, it may request consultations with the other Party and the two Parties shall consult with a view to avoiding any such encouragement.[18]

This, along with other provisions in the NAFTA and the NAAEC that reinforce the nonregression obligation, is the first of the neglected provisions; it will be examined in more detail in Section 3.

2.2. *Key Provisions of the NAAEC*

The NAAEC, adopted in light of criticism that the NAFTA did not sufficiently allay environmental concerns, expanded on the NAFTA's environmental provisions. It also institutionalized a cooperative program for environmental protection and conservation in North America in the CEC and created new mechanisms to enhance public participation in the achievement of North American environmental objectives. Two key measures included in the NAAEC to promote public participation in the work of the CEC are the provision for a process to receive citizen submissions on enforcement matters in Articles 14 and 15, and the creation of the Joint Public Advisory Committee (JPAC),[19] which engages the North American public in

---

[15] Ibid., Article 906(1).

[16] Ibid., Article 906(2).

[17] Indeed, the NAFTA Secretariat reports that only three disputes have been filed under the Article 20 dispute resolutions proceedings, none directly involving an environmental issue. See NAFTA Secretariat, "Dispute settlement, decisions and reports," http://www.nafta-sec-alena.org/Default.aspx?tabid=95&language=en-US.

[18] NAFTA, Article 1114(2).

[19] See NAAEC, Article 16. The JPAC is a 15-member committee made up of five citizens from each country, whose mandate is to provide advice to the CEC Council on any matter covered by NAAEC.

order to fulfill its mandate to advise the CEC council on the implementation of the NAAEC.

In regard to enhancing levels of environmental protection without regression, the preamble of the NAAEC reaffirms "the importance of the environmental goals and objectives of the NAFTA, including *enhanced* levels of environmental protection."[20] This principle reappears among the objectives of the agreement set out in Article 1, the first of which is to "foster the protection and improvement of the environment in the territories of the Parties for the well-being of present and future generations."[21] By stating a goal of enhancing or improving the environment and environmental protection, these provisions evidence an intention to establish a policy against regression of environmental protections. This implied principle of nonregression is carried forward in the obligations of the NAAEC Parties in Article 3, which states:

> Recognizing the right of each Party to establish its own levels of domestic environmental protection and environmental development policies and priorities, and to adopt or modify accordingly its environmental laws and regulations, each Party shall ensure that its laws and regulations provide for high levels of environmental protection and shall strive to continue to improve those laws and regulations.[22]

Clearly, however, the obligation to "strive to continue to improve" environmental laws and regulations is only an implied obligation not to weaken them, and even so, the obligation would be stronger if it were simply "to improve" them. Yet Article 3 is the clearest expression in the NAAEC of a nonregression principle that reinforces the NAFTA's Article 1114(2).

Other provisions of the NAAEC provide additional reinforcement of the weak nonregression obligation in the NAFTA and the NAAEC. Article 10(3)(*b*) states that

> [t]he Council shall strengthen cooperation on the development and continuing improvement of environmental laws and regulations, including by . . . *without reducing levels of environmental protection*, establishing a process for developing recommendations on greater compatibility of environmental technical regulations, standards and conformity assessment procedures in a manner consistent with the NAFTA.[23]

Article 10(6)(*b*) gives the CEC Council a direct role in the implementation of NAFTA Article 1114(2), requiring it to

> provid[e] assistance in consultations under Article 1114 of the NAFTA where a Party considers that another Party is waiving or derogating from, or offering to waive or otherwise derogate from, an environmental measure as an encouragement to

---

[20] Ibid., Preamble [emphasis added].
[21] Ibid., Article 1(*a*).
[22] Ibid., Article 3.
[23] Ibid., Article 10(3)(*b*) [emphasis added].

establish, acquire, expand or retain an investment of an investor, with a view to avoiding such encouragement.

To allay concerns that Canada, Mexico, or the United States would use weak environmental enforcement to gain economic advantages, Article 5 of the NAAEC requires "each Party [to] effectively enforce its environmental laws and regulations" "with the aim of achieving high levels of environmental protection and compliance with its environmental laws and regulations."[24] Article 5 also includes a list of potentially appropriate governmental action in fulfilling that obligation. The wording of Article 5 pairing effective environmental enforcement with high levels of environmental protection suggests, again by implication, that weakening enforcement would be a form of environmental regression that would run counter to the NAAEC.

Articles 6 and 7 enhance the requirements of Articles 3 and 5 by requiring the Parties to ensure access to private remedies for environmental harms and to ensure that the Parties' administrative, quasijudicial, and judicial proceedings allow remedies for environmental harms and accord procedural guarantees. The SEM mechanism in Articles 14 and 15 and the Party-to-Party dispute resolution process in Part V subject the Party's enforcement obligation in Article 5 to independent review. Part V, the second neglected provision examined in this Chapter, is discussed in detail in Section 4.

The NAAEC also put into effect provisions regarding environmental impact assessment, an important tool for considering holistically the environmental implications of economic development, including cumulative effects and other impacts that can contribute to providing an overview of the scale effects of economic activities (that is, more trade-stimulated economic activity means more impact). Article 2(1)(e) obligates each Party to "assess, as appropriate, environmental impacts."[25] Article 10(6)(g) requires the CEC Council to "consider[] on an ongoing basis the environmental effects of the NAFTA." Article 10(7) states:

> Recognizing the significant bilateral nature of many transboundary environmental issues, the Council shall, with a view to agreement between the Parties pursuant to this Article within three years on obligations, consider and develop recommendations with respect to:
>
> a. assessing the environmental impact of proposed projects subject to decisions by a competent government authority and likely to cause significant adverse transboundary effects, including a full evaluation of comments provided by other Parties and persons of other Parties;
> b. notification, provision of relevant information and consultation between Parties with respect to such projects; and
> c. mitigation of the potential adverse effects of such projects.

---

[24] Ibid., Article 5(1).
[25] Ibid., Article 2(1)(e).

The unsuccessful implementation of Article 10(7), the third neglected provision examined in this chapter, is discussed in detail in Section 5.

3. NAFTA ARTICLE 1114(2): AN IMPOTENT SHIELD AGAINST ENVIRONMENTAL BACKSLIDING

A policy and at least a soft obligation not to weaken environmental protections is established both by explicit provisions like the NAFTA's Article 1114(2) and by other provisions discussed in Section 1.2, which strongly imply that environmental backsliding runs counter to the spirit and letter of both the NAFTA and the NAAEC. Investigations to determine whether a race to the bottom in environmental protection has resulted from the NAFTA have not revealed any clear economic shifts as a result of differences in levels of environmental protection in the three countries.[26] Examples of environmental backsliding do appear to exist, however, and illustrate the weakness of the nonregression provisions in the NAFTA and the NAAEC.[27] The failure of the NAFTA governments to formally raise concerns regarding such cases has left the potential of NAFTA Article 1114(2) untapped and undeveloped.

3.1. *Examples of Post-NAFTA Environmental Backsliding*

In Canada, the most prominent recent examples of the weakening of environmental protection were adopted as part of the federal budget implementation acts of 2009, 2010, and 2012, in which significant rollbacks of environmental law were effected under the guise of budgetary and fiscal measures, and were thus subjected to little public scrutiny or debate. The most severe of these, the Jobs, Growth and Long-term Prosperity Act, 2012,[28] and the Jobs and Growth Act, 2010, which together implemented the 2012 federal budget, plainly weaken Canadian environmental protections in several ways. Most notably, these Acts (1) amended the federal Species at Risk Act (SARA)[29] by eliminating the five-year term limit on permits to engage in activities that affect species protected by SARA or their critical habitat, and exempted certain pipeline projects from the requirement to respect reasonable measures to protect critical habitat of species protected under SARA;[30] (2) replaced the Canadian Environmental Assessment Act, 1992, with the Canadian Environmental Assessment Act, 2012, which greatly reduced the number of projects subject to federal

---

[26] See Chris Wold, "Taking stock: Trade's environmental scorecard after twenty years of 'trade and environment'" (2010) 45:2 *Wake Forest L. Rev.* 319 at 334. C.f. Block, "Trade and Environment," p. 503.

[27] See Ignacia S. Moreno et al., "Free trade and the environment: The NAFTA, the NAAEC, and implications for the future" (1999) 12:2 *Tulane Envtl. L. J.* 405 at 433.

[28] SC 2012, c. 19.

[29] SC 2002, c. 29.

[30] Jobs, Growth and Long-term Prosperity Act, ss. 163, 165.

environmental assessment, reduced the number of factors to be considered in conducting assessments, shortened the time for completing environmental screenings and full environmental assessments, and limited opportunities for public participation by tightening the criteria for members of the public wishing to participate in a federal environmental assessment;[31] and (3) weakened the federal Fisheries Act by increasing the level of harm to fish or fish habitat that would need to be shown in order to prove a violation of the Act, reducing the kinds of fisheries subject to the Act, and expanding the ability of the federal government to exempt activities or undertakings from the Act even if they cause harm to fish or fish habitat.[32]

The Jobs and Economic Growth Act,[33] which implemented the 2010 budget, weakened several provisions of the Canadian Environmental Assessment Act, 1992,[34] for example, by giving the federal government increased discretion to limit or eliminate the application of environmental impact assessment requirements for certain projects and activities.[35] The Budget Implementation Act, 2009,[36] weakened the scope of the Navigable Waters Protection Act by limiting the types of activities and projects that require environmental impact assessment and other review.[37]

Canada's abandonment in 2011 of its obligations to reduce emissions of greenhouse gases under the Kyoto Protocol on climate change[38] and its related repeal in 2012 of the Kyoto Protocol Implementation Act[39] are further examples of backward movement on environmental protection.[40] Likewise, Canada's apparent reduction of its federal environmental spending by roughly forty percent in the period 1993 to 1997 could itself be seen as a form of regression.[41]

In Mexico, one example of regression in environmental protection since 1994 was the dilution in 2004 of a regulation on the protection of wetlands and mangroves.[42] Noting that environmental improvements in Mexico that some expected NAFTA

---

[31] Ibid., s. 52.

[32] Ibid., ss. 132–56.

[33] RSC 2010, c. 12.

[34] See ibid., ss. 2153–71.

[35] Ibid., s. 2155. See letter from Richard D. Lindgren, Counsel, Canadian Environmental Law Association, to James Rajotte, Chair, Standing Committee on Finance, House of Commons (May 13, 2010), http://cela.ca/publications/re-bill-c-9-proposed-changes-canadian-environmental-assessment-act.

[36] RSC 2009, c. 2.

[37] Ibid., ss. 317–40.

[38] Environment Canada, *Canada's Withdrawal from the Kyoto Protocol* (May 28, 2012), http://ec.gc.ca/Publications/default.asp?xml=EE4F06AE-13EF-453B-B633-FCB3BAECEB4F.

[39] Jobs, Growth and Long-term Prosperity Act, s. 699.

[40] See Government of Canada, "Canada lists emissions target under the Copenhagen accord" (2010), http://ec.gc.ca/default.asp?lang=En&news=EAF552A3-D287-4AC0-ACB8-A6FEA697ACD6 (setting emissions reduction targets for 2020 that are significantly higher than Canada's obligations under the Kyoto Protocol for 2012).

[41] See Vaughan, "Thinking North American Environmental Management," p. 12. See also Moreno et al., "Free trade and the environment," p. 437; Block, "Trade and Environment," p. 517.

[42] See Francisco Flores-Verdugo et al., "La topografía y el hidroperíodo: dos factores que condicionan la restauración de los humedales costeros" (2007) Sup. 80 *Boletín de la Sociedad Botánica de México* 33

to produce have not occurred, one set of commentators contended that "Mexico's poor environmental record is mostly due to a weakening of the commitment to environmental protection in the post-NAFTA period. Indeed, real spending and inspection levels in manufacturing have declined since NAFTA, and the environmental impacts have been well documented."[43]

Prominent backsliding examples from the United States date back to at least 1995, with the passage of the Emergency Supplemental Appropriations for Additional Disaster Assistance, for Antiterrorism Initiatives, for Assistance in the Recovery from the Tragedy that Occurred at Oklahoma City, and Rescissions Act, 1995.[44] That law created a salvage timber harvest program that reduced or eliminated the application of the National Environmental Policy Act[45] and other environmental laws to the logging of certain salvage timber sales and some specific controversial timber sales in the Northwestern United States.[46] More recent examples[47] include the repeal in 2003 of a rule[48] that had defined total maximum daily loads of water pollution under the Clean Water Act,[49] the weakening in 2003 of the regulations on the types of modifications of major air pollution sources that would require more stringent pollution controls under the Clean Air Act's[50] "New Source Review" provisions,[51] and the rollback in 2008 of the Stream Buffer Zone rule that prohibited surface mining activities within 100 feet of streams.[52]

---

at 35 (discussing a 2004 amendment to the Ministry of the Environment and Natural Resources' regulation NOM-022-SEMARNAT-2003 that allowed mangroves to be destroyed as long as the destruction was compensated).

[43] Eduardo Zepeda, Timothy A. Wise, and Kevin P. Gallagher, "Rethinking trade policy for development: Lessons from Mexico under NAFTA," *Carnegie Endowment for International Peace* December 7, 2009, p. 16, http://carnegieendowment.org/publications/index.cfm?fa=view&id=24271.

[44] Pub. L. 104–19, 109 Stat. 104.

[45] 42 USC §§ 4321ff (1969).

[46] 1995 Rescissions Act, subss. 2001(b)–(d), (k). See Moreno et al., "Free trade and the environment," pp. 440–1 (discussing this law and another budgetary measure in 1995 that reduced funding of certain environmental activities of the EPA and the U.S. Fish and Wildlife Service).

[47] For a more comprehensive set of examples of alleged rollbacks in U.S. environmental laws under the administration of President George W. Bush, see Charles Pope, "Bush uses rule book to roll back protections," *Seattle Post-Intelligencer*, March 15, 2005, http://www.seattlepi.com/national/216007_regs15 .html; Emily Cousins, Robert Perks, and Wesley Warren, *Rewriting the Rules: The Bush Administration's First-Term Environmental Record* (New York: Natural Resources Defense Council, 2005).

[48] U.S. Environmental Protection Agency, Withdrawal of Revisions to the Water Quality Planning and Management Regulation and Revisions to the National Pollutant Discharge Elimination System Program in Support of Revisions to the Water Quality Planning and Management Regulation, 68 Fed. Reg. 13608 (2003).

[49] 33 USC §§ 1251ff (1972).

[50] 42 USC §§ 7401ff (1955).

[51] U.S. Environmental Protection Agency, Prevention of Significant Deterioration (PSD) and Non-Attainment New Source Review (NSR): Equipment Replacement Provision of the Routine Maintenance, Repair and Replacement Exclusion, 68 Fed. Reg. 61248 (2003).

[52] US Department of the Interior, Final Rule on Excess Spoil, Coal Mine Waste, and Buffers for Perennial and Intermittent Streams, 73 Fed. Reg. 75814 (2008). See also Natural Resources Defense Council, "EPA allows mining companies to destroy America's streams," December 2, 2008, http://nrdc.org/media/2008/081202.asp.

A final example of post-NAFTA weakening of environmental law in the United States underscores one of the key false promises of NAFTA: that it would open a new era of North American integration in which new opportunities in Mexico would reduce the incentive to migrate north. The Illegal Immigration Reform and Immigrant Responsibility Act of 1996[53] authorizes the Secretary of the Department of Homeland Security to forego all legal requirements that apply to the construction of physical barriers (namely, a fence) and roads in the border zone between the United States and Mexico. Between 2005 and 2008, the secretary exercised this power five times[54] in order to bypass important environmental requirements that otherwise applied[55] to the construction of fences in California and Texas along a significant portion of the United States–Mexico border.

3.2. *The Failure to Implement NAFTA Article 1114(2) and Related Non-Regression Provisions*

The actual experience and practice of the Parties in the seventeen years since the NAFTA and the NAAEC took effect confirm the weakness of the agreements' nonregression provisions. Neither the Parties nor commentators appear to view non-regression of environmental protections as a strict mandate. As the earlier examples show, the Parties have on occasion weakened environmental protections with no consequences pursuant to the NAFTA or the NAAEC. Neither the NAFTA nor the NAAEC contains a reliable means of enforcing the nonregression provisions; Party-to-Party consultations are the sole remedy.

Pierre-Marc Johnson and André Beaulieu aptly describe the nonregression provision in Article 3 and most of the other Party obligations in the NAAEC as "akin to unilateral declarations of intention since they are not enforceable under the NAAEC."[56] Noting that the NAAEC contains fact-finding and reporting provisions that may help bring to light the Parties' conformity with these obligations, they claim "[i]t will necessarily fall to NGOs and, to a lesser extent, to the Secretariat to monitor the implementation of these obligations and publicize governmental lapses."[57] As for the nonregression language in the NAFTA itself, commentators have

---

[53] Pub. L. 104–208, Div. C, 110 Stat. 3009–546, as amended by the REAL ID Act of 2005, Pub. L. 109–13, Div. B, 119 Stat. 302, as amended by the Secure Fence Act of 2006, Pub. L. 109–367, 120 Stat. 2638, as amended by the Department of Homeland Security Appropriations Act, 2008, Public Law 110–61, Div. E, Title V, s. 564, 121 Stat. 2090 (2007).

[54] See 70 Fed. Reg. 55622 (September 22, 2005), 72 Fed. Reg. 2535 (January 19, 2007), 72 Fed. Reg. 60870 (October 26, 2007), 73 Fed. Reg. 19077 (April 8, 2008), 73 Fed. Reg. 19078 (April 8, 2008).

[55] The exempted laws include the National Environmental Policy Act; the Endangered Species Act; the Clean Water Act; the Clean Air Act; the Safe Drinking Water Act; the Resource Conservation and Recovery Act; the Comprehensive Environmental Response, Compensation and Liability Act; and the Migratory Bird Treaty Act.

[56] Johnson and Beaulieu, *The Environment and NAFTA*, p. 146.

[57] Ibid., p. 149.

characterized NAFTA Article 1114(2) as a statement of "common policy" that "is not mandatory."[58]

The practice of the Parties supports these views. First, despite instances of environmental backsliding, no Party has initiated consultations regarding regression of environmental protections as provided for in NAFTA Article 1114(2), and the rollback of environmental laws and regulations has never been on the agenda of the CEC Council, despite the mandate they are conferred in NAAEC Article 10(6)(*b*). Second, the NAFTA Parties have established neither criteria indicating what qualifies as regression of environmental protections or procedures nor guidelines for consultations or other means of enforcing the nonregression provisions. Simply put, formal or informal enforcement of those provisions has never been part of the CEC's agenda, and it is difficult to imagine the Parties departing from their record of inaction. The Parties' triple roles as members of the CEC Council, which oversees the NAAEC; as governments subject to the NAAEC's provisions; and as partners in the CEC's cooperative programs create inherent conflicts and disincentives in the enforcement of Article 3 and other NAAEC obligations that make progress on meaningful implementation of the nonregression provisions a formidable challenge.[59]

Whether the examples of environmental backsliding mentioned in the previous section are treaty violations undoubtedly raises issues of interpretation under NAFTA Article 1114(2) or the various provisions of the NAAEC that reinforce the nonregression obligation. In Article 1114(2), what kinds of environmental measures are considered relevant, what is the meaning of the terms "waive" and "otherwise derogate from," and what kind of "encouragement for the establishment, acquisition, expansion or retention in its territory of an investment of an investor" must be shown? Given the very soft nature of the sole remedy of consultation, one would expect these terms to be given a broad and liberal meaning.[60] However, the

---

[58] Sanford E. Gaines, "Protecting investors, protecting the environment: The unexpected story of NAFTA chapter 11," in David L. Markell and John H. Knox (eds.), *Greening NAFTA: The North American Commission for Environmental Cooperation*(Stanford, CA: Stanford University Press, 2003), p. 173, p. 195, note 44. See also Vaughan, "Thinking North American Environmental Management," p. 8.

[59] This inherent conflict of interest has received considerable attention in the context of Articles 14 and 15, but the Council has taken virtually no action to alleviate those concerns. See JPAC, "Advice to Council 03–05" (2003), http://cec.org/Page.asp?PageID=122&ContentID=1274 (noting "an emerging perception of Council being in conflict of interest" and recounting public testimony at a JPAC meeting that "Council is having a hard time differentiating their role-when they are acting as a Council and when they are acting individually as Parties"); Geoff Garver, "Tooth decay" (2008) 25:3 *The Environmental Forum* 34 at 38 ("[p]roviding the CEC secretariat with greater discretion to define the scope of factual record investigations would address a fundamental concern about the process: the inherent conflict of interest that the NAFTA governments face in being both council members who vote on factual records and also, since the council is composed of the three countries' environmental ministers, targets of individual submissions"); David Markell, "The role of spotlighting procedures in promoting citizen participation, transparency and accountability" (2010) 45:2 *Wake Forest L. Rev.* 425 at 440.

[60] Certainly, the Canadian prime minister's statements to Latin American investors in April 2012 that touted recent changes to Canadian environmental law as a reason to invest in resource development

government Parties – both individually and together as the CEC Council – have done nothing to provide clarity on these questions.

4. PART V OF THE NAAEC: A PANDORA'S BOX THAT WILL NEVER BE OPENED

Part V of the NAAEC (Articles 22 to 36) explicitly targets widespread or systemic failures to effectively enforce environmental laws in the NAFTA countries and establishes Party-to-Party dispute resolution with potential sanctions as the remedy. Article 22 provides that "[a]ny Party may request in writing consultations with any other Party regarding whether there has been a persistent pattern of failure by that other Party to effectively enforce its environmental law."[61] If consultations fail to resolve the matter, the council can appoint an arbitral panel to prepare a report and, if necessary, assess a "monetary enforcement assessment."[62] Article 36 provides that failure to pay a monetary enforcement assessment can lead to suspension of benefits under the NAFTA. When the NAAEC was negotiated, Part V was seen as the teeth sought by environmentalists to hold the governments to account in the event of weak environmental enforcement.[63]

None of the NAAEC Parties has ever put Part V to the test by initiating a dispute with another Party. In fact, twenty years after the NAAEC took effect the Parties have not adopted rules of procedure for Part V, as required under Article 28, and they have not developed a roster of arbitrators, as called for under Article 25.

As time progresses, Part V looks more and more like a set of "false teeth" included in the NAAEC in order to ensure the NAFTA's approval by the United States Congress.[64] There are good reasons to believe that the NAAEC governments will never put Part V to use because of political dynamics built into the structure of Part V and because of past recommendations that a moratorium be placed on its implementation.

The structural obstacles to implementation and use of Part V are significant.[65] NAAEC defines a "persistent pattern" for the purposes of Article 22 as "a sustained or recurring course of action or inaction beginning after the date of entry into force of this Agreement."[66] The agreement also provides that A Party has not failed to

---

in Canada would seem to qualify squarely as the kind of encouragement that Article 1114(2) was intended to dissuade. See John Vizcaino, "Stephen Harper sells resource-friendly economy to Latin American execs," *Toronto Star*, April 12, 2012, http://thestar.com/business/2012/04/14/stephen_harper_sells_resourcefriendly_economy_to_latin_american_execs.html.

[61] NAAEC, Article 22(1).
[62] See ibid., Articles 23, 24, 31–4.
[63] See Vaughan, "Thinking North American Environmental Management," p. 9.
[64] See ibid., pp. 7–9.
[65] See ibid., pp. 9–13.
[66] NAAEC, Article 45(1).

"**effectively enforce its environmental law**" . . . where the action or inaction in question by agencies or officials of that Party:

(a) reflects a reasonable exercise of their discretion in respect of investigatory, prosecutorial, regulatory or compliance matters; or
(b) results from *bona fide* decisions to allocate resources to enforcement in respect of other environmental matters determined to have higher priorities.[67]

To succeed in a Part V dispute, a Party would have to overcome these vague definitions in establishing its case and fending off potential defenses and would also have to show that the alleged failure to effectively enforce environmental law

relates to a situation involving workplaces, firms, companies, or sectors that produce goods or provide services:

(a) traded between the territories of the Parties; or
(b) that compete, in the territory of the Party complained against, with goods or services produced or provided by persons of another Party.[68]

Consequently,

the outcome will be much less certain than in a typical trade dispute, with completely different stakes and a greater potential for backfiring. [Further,] every plaintiff in these dispute resolution processes is also a potential defendant in a future case, and therefore has a reduced incentive to develop the strongest possible arguments favoring the plaintiff position. It is hard to imagine a government arguing for an expansive definition of what qualifies as a failure to effectively enforce, or for a limited interpretation of defenses that apply to the reasonable exercise of enforcement discretion and bona fide allocation of resources to higher priorities.[69]

For all these reasons, dispute resolution under Part V of the NAAEC "is a Pandora's box no government is likely to open."[70]

The second principal reason that Part V is not likely to be implemented is fears that even the potential for Part V dispute proceedings renders the SEM mechanism under the NAAEC's Articles 14 and 15 less effective.[71] Article 14 allows any person residing or nongovernmental organization established in North America to file a submission with the secretariat of the CEC asserting that one of the NAAEC Parties is failing to effectively enforce its environmental laws. The secretariat can "request[] a response

[67] Ibid.
[68] Ibid., Article 24.
[69] Garver, "Tooth decay," p. 39. See also Vaughan, "Thinking North American Environmental Management," pp. 9–10.
[70] Garver, p. 39.
[71] See Vaughan, "Thinking North American Environmental Management," pp. 11–12; Johnson et al., "Ten Years of North American Environmental Cooperation," p. 38.

from the Party"[72] and then recommend the development of a factual record to the council.[73] With a two-thirds majority vote of the council,[74] the secretariat conducts a detailed investigation into the allegations and produces a factual record,[75] which requires a two-thirds majority vote of the council for publication.[76] A factual record provides information that allows members of the public to decide for themselves if the Party has failed to effectively enforce its laws, but it may not provide a conclusion of its own, make recommendations, or require a remedy.

The SEM process has a long history of controversy, linked mostly to the fact that the NAAEC Parties have dual roles both as members of the council voting on the preparation and publication of factual records and overseeing the process, and as individual Parties that are targeted by the process. Perhaps as a consequence, contrary to the apparent purpose of the process, the council has severely restricted the ability of submitters to raise widespread, systemic cases of weak enforcement that are the types of assertions most likely to reveal a weak regime of environmental protection.[77] In recommending the production of a factual record in response to the Migratory Birds submission, the secretariat noted that submissions raising widespread or systemic allegations of ineffective enforcement are especially suited to the process:

> [A]ssertions that the failure to enforce extends beyond a single facility or project portend, at least potentially, a more extensive or broad-based issue concerning the effectiveness of a Party's efforts to enforce its environmental laws and regulations. In other words, the larger the scale of the asserted failure, the more likely it may be to warrant developing a factual record, other things being equal. If the citizen submission process were construed to bar consideration of alleged widespread enforcement failures, the failures that potentially pose the greatest threats to accomplishment of the Agreement's objectives, and the most serious and far-reaching threats of harm to the environment, would be beyond the scope of that process.[78]

Nonetheless, in voting to authorize factual records, the council has on several occasions either limited the scope of the factual records to isolated incidents that were not the main focus of the submissions, or required submitters to provide specific evidence for all cases involved in a widespread or systemic pattern of weak enforcement.[79]

---

[72] NAAEC, Article 14(2).
[73] Ibid., Article 15(1).
[74] Ibid., Article 15(2).
[75] Ibid., Article 15(2)–(6).
[76] Ibid., Article 15(7).
[77] See John H. Knox and David L. Markell, "Evaluating citizen petition procedures: Lessons from an analysis of the NAFTA Environmental Commission" (2012) 47:3 *Texas Intl. L. J.* 505 at 525–6.
[78] SEM-99-002 (*Migratory Birds*), Recommendation pursuant to Article 15(1) (December 15, 2000), p. 10.
[79] See especially SEM-97-006 (*Oldman River II*), Council Resolution 01–08 pursuant to Article 15(2) (November 16, 2001); SEM-99-002 (*Migratory Birds*), Council Resolution 01–10 pursuant to

As a result of the limitations imposed by the council on the scope of factual records and other aspects of the process, the SEM mechanism has not lived up to its potential.[80] Moreover, the governments' mostly tepid responses to factual records to date suggest this is not a particularly promising means to hold the Parties to account for weak enforcement. The NAAEC does not require a government that is the subject of a factual record to take any action or to respond in any other way following its publication. Despite calls to make some kind of commitment to follow up on factual records, the council has stated firmly in the past that the follow-up to factual records is a matter of domestic policy of the individual governments.[81] More recently, the council adopted measures that "call for Parties to follow up on concluded submissions with information on any new developments and actions taken regarding matters raised in such submissions."[82] Nonetheless, the impact of the submissions process and factual records has been modest to date, with some positive effects in specific cases.[83] In cases such as the Migratory Bird and Pulp and Paper factual records, the process had no discernible impact on the enforcement practices of the government concerned.

One reason suggested to explain the council's action to limit claims of widespread failures to enforce environmental law under Articles 14 and 15 is that these cases might establish the "pattern" required to succeed in a dispute proceeding under Part V.[84] Perhaps it is an awareness that Part V is likely to remain dormant, given its Byzantine procedures and the daunting challenge in raising a successful case, that has prompted calls for a moratorium on Part V consultations, in order to encourage the SEM process, which has been active, to produce more effective results.[85]

In the governance proposal that accompanies the CEC strategic plan for 2010 to 2015,[86] the Council indicated that it could direct officials representing the three governments to resume negotiation of model rules for the NAAEC Part V dispute resolution process, which the Parties had undertaken from 1997 to 2000. However, the Parties have not resumed negotiations as of February 2014.

Article 15(2) (November 16, 2001); SEM-98–004 (*BC Mining*), Council Resolution 01–11 pursuant to Article 15(2) (November 16, 2001); SEM-00–004 (*BC Logging*), Council Resolution 01–12 pursuant to Article 15(2) (November 16, 2001); SEM-02–001 (*Ontario Logging*), Council Resolution 03–05 pursuant to Article 15(2) (April 22, 2003); SEM-02–003 (*Pulp and Paper*), Council Resolution pursuant to 03–16 (December 11, 2003). See also Block, "Trade and Environment," p. 541; Garver, "Tooth decay," pp. 36–7.

[80] For a summary of other limitations the Council has imposed, see Garver, "Tooth decay."

[81] See letter from Alternative Representative for Canada Norine Smith to 2002 JPAC Chair Jonathan Plaut (June 14, 2002), http://cec.org/Storage/25/1591_Council-Lessons-learned-04.pdf.

[82] Commission for Environmental Cooperation, "CEC Ministerial Statement, 2012," http://cec.org/Page.asp?PageID=122&ContentID=25241.

[83] See Johnson et al., "Ten Years of North American Environmental Cooperation," p. 46.

[84] Vaughan, "Thinking North American Environmental Management," pp. 11–12.

[85] Johnson et al., "Ten Years of North American Environmental Cooperation," p. 55.

[86] Commission for Environmental Cooperation, "Governance proposal," p. 7, http://cec.org/Storage/101/10004_Governance_Proposal_May_2010_final2e.pdf.

5. NAAEC ARTICLE 10(7): A LOST OPPORTUNITY TO EXPAND ENVIRONMENTAL IMPACT ASSESSMENT

Article 10(7) of the NAAEC derives from the notion in Principle 2 of the 1992 Rio Declaration on Environment and Development – building on Principle 21 of the 1972 Stockholm Declaration on the Human Environment – that "States have . . . the responsibility to ensure that activities within their jurisdiction or control do not cause damage to the environment of other States or of areas beyond the limits of national jurisdiction."[87] The preamble to the NAAEC explicitly reaffirms this principle. Article 10(7) obligates the CEC Council to develop recommendations on various aspects of TEIA within three years of the effective date of the treaty's entry into force with a view to an agreement. Almost twenty years on, despite considerable effort by the Parties, a North American TEIA agreement has not been finalized.[88]

The 1991 Convention on Environmental Impact Assessment in a Transboundary Context, or Espoo Convention, to which Canada is a Party, provides a prototype for assessing transboundary environmental impacts through an international agreement. In addition, Canada, Mexico, and the United States all have federal and subnational laws and regulations on environmental impact assessment that, despite differences, could form the building blocks for a North American TEIA agreement. The challenge under the NAAEC has been to create reciprocal TEIA obligations using existing domestic requirements on environmental impact assessments.

Negotiation of a TEIA draft text began after the CEC Council instructed negotiators in 1995 to be guided by overarching principles for TEIA that emphasized the transboundary nature of pollution, good neighborliness, respect for existing national and subnational processes, cost effectiveness and efficiency, complementarity, and public participation.[89] These overarching principles formed the basis of the Parties' efforts from 1996 to 1999 to negotiate the recommended draft text of a TEIA agreement. The CEC Secretariat facilitated the negotiations by providing background analysis and by hosting, at its Montreal headquarters office, meetings of a trinational working group of Party delegates. Consistent with the text of Article 10(7), the negotiations focused on Party-to-Party notification of projects and provision of relevant information, the actual assessment of transboundary environmental impacts, consultations between Parties regarding any conflicts in regard to transboundary impacts, and mitigation of adverse impacts.[90]

---

[87] Rio Declaration on Environment and Development, UNEP, 1992, UN Doc. A/Conf.151/Rev. 1, 31 ILM 874, Principle 2.

[88] Much of the chronology of the TEIA negotiations is drawn from Geoffrey Garver and Aranka Podhora, "Transboundary environmental impact assessment as part of the North American Agreement on Environmental Cooperation" (2008) 26:4 *Impact Assessment and Project Appraisal* 253.

[89] Commission for Environmental Cooperation, "Council resolution 95–07" (October 13, 1995).

[90] The author was a member of the U.S. delegation at those negotiations.

In June 1999, despite the completion of a nearly complete draft text,[91] the negotiations broke down because of difficulty establishing reciprocity on the treatment of projects subject to approval only by subnational (as opposed to federal) governments.[92] In a June 1999 communiqué, the CEC Council seemed to indicate a shift to "'good neighbor' agreements based on reciprocity" between subnational governments, such as individual states or provinces.[93]

Since 1999, despite pressure from the JPAC,[94] progress toward resuming negotiation of a TEIA agreement has been slow, and the role of the CEC has diminished. In its communiqué following the annual council session in 2001, the council stated simply that "[w]ith respect to transboundary environmental impact assessment, an informal, productive process is continuing."[95] In a March 2003 letter to the JPAC that makes the lack of movement clear, the council stated:

> Although substantial progress has been made in the development of the TEIA agreement, the Parties have had difficulty in agreeing on the manner in which the Agreement would address projects subject to approval at the sub-Federal level, due to differences in the Federal systems of each country. Government to government contacts are continuing to explore potential solutions to this problem.[96]

In 2004, funding for support of implementation of Article 10(7) was eliminated entirely from the CEC budget.[97]

The three governments subsequently announced that under the Security and Prosperity Partnership (SPP), which Canada, Mexico, and the United States undertook in 2005, they would "[s]eek to conclude a transboundary environmental impact

[91] Commission for Environmental Cooperation, Draft North American Agreement on Transboundary Environmental Impact Assessment (October 1997), http://cec.org/Storage/92/8900_Draft-TEIA_Agreement-Oct97_en.doc.

[92] The CEC Council stated in 1999 that "Council members agreed to work with their respective negotiators and individual border states and provinces to build 'good neighbor' agreements based on reciprocity." Commission for Environmental Cooperation, "Council communiqué – 1999," http://cec.org/Page.asp?PageID=122&ContentID=1292.

[93] Ibid.

[94] Commission for Environmental Cooperation, "JPAC advice to Council 02–12," December 10, 2002, http://cec.org/Page.asp?PageID=122&ContentID=992.

[95] Commission for Environmental Cooperation, "CEC Council communiqué – 2001," http://cec.org/Page.asp?PageID=122&ContentID=1290.

[96] Letter from Judith Ayres, Assistant Administrator, Office of International Affairs, United States Environmental Protection Agency, to JPAC Chair Gustavo Alanis-Ortega (March 24, 2003), http://cec.org/Storage/24/1583_Counci-Response-02-12_en.pdf.

[97] Commission for Environmental Cooperation, *Operational Plan: 2004–2006* (2004), p. 48, http://cec.org/Storage/27/1791_2004-OperationalPlan_en.pdf. The government of Canada has said the Council met its obligations under Article 10(7) in 1997, before the draft TEIA agreement was even completed. See "Joint response from the Departments of Environment, Foreign Affairs and International Trade, and Transport [to the] petition submitted by [the] Sierra Legal Defence Fund concerning the implementation of the North American Agreement on Environmental Cooperation," August 9, 2006, http://oag-bvg.gc.ca/internet/English/pet_166_e_28901.html.

assessment cooperation agreement for proposed projects by June 2007."[98] The SPP
set out a policy framework for North American security and prosperity but had no
formal connection to the NAFTA, the NAAEC, or the CEC. TEIA negotiations
made little progress through the SPP.[99]

In 2011, following a public meeting that included a discussion of the NAAEC's
Article 10(7) and the negotiation of a TEIA agreement, the JPAC advised the council
as follows:

> Noting that efforts to pursue a North American TEIA agreement through the Secu-
> rity and Prosperity Partnership have ceased, JPAC supports the renewal of efforts
> to finalize a North American TEIA agreement, consistent with Article 10(7) of the
> NAAEC.... JPAC [recommends] that the Council approve a review of case studies
> of projects or activities in North America with transboundary impacts, develop pilot
> projects for implementing TEIA mechanisms with respect to specific projects, and
> direct the Secretariat to commission a short and focused review of lessons learned
> in the implementation in Europe of the Convention on Environmental Impact
> Assessment in a Transboundary Context.[100]

In response,[101] the council referred to the governance proposal that accompanies
the CEC strategic plan for 2010 to 2015,[102] which notes that the council could direct
its officials to resume discussions pursuant to NAAEC Article 10(7). The council
also said it would "consider opportunities that demonstrate the most efficient and
effective means to implement [TEIA] mechanisms" and that it remains open to
relevant reviews by the secretariat.[103] Neither the council nor the secretariat has
proceeded with any activities related to TEIA since that time.

6. CONCLUSION

Global and regional ecological challenges related to climate change, biodiversity
loss, excessive human introduction of nitrogen and phosphorous, overfishing, and the
use of land and fresh water have steadily grown more pressing in the past twenty years

[98] Security and Prosperity Partnership, "Report to leaders, June 2005," http://spp-psp.gc.ca/eic/site/spp-psp.nsf/eng/00098.html.
[99] See Security and Prosperity Partnership of North American, "Prosperity priorities," http://spp-psp.gc.ca/eic/site/spp-psp.nsf/eng/00052.html.
[100] JPAC, "Advice to Council no: 11–01," http://cec.org/Page.asp?PageID=122&ContentID=17599.
[101] Letter from Dan McDougall to Irasema Coronado, June 17, 2011, CEC Council response to JPAC Advice 11–01, http://cec.org/Storage/127/15201_Letter_from_Council_-_JPAC_Advice_11-01.pdf.
[102] Commission for Environmental Cooperation, "Proposal to examine the governance of the CEC and the implementation of the NAAEC," http://cec.org/Storage/101/10004_Governance_Proposal_May_2010_finalze.pdf.
[103] Letter from Dan McDougall to Irasema Coronado, June 17, 2011, CEC Council response to JPAC Advice 11–01, http://cec.org/Storage/127/15201_Letter_from_Council_-_JPAC_Advice_11-01.pdf.

along with awareness of them.[104] International trade is increasingly a driver of these challenges.[105] These trends make clear the urgency of developing strong measures to prevent backsliding in environmental protection, to ensure effective enforcement, and – most critically[106] – to counter the ecologically negative scale effects of expanded economic activity. The ongoing risk of economic crises such as the global recession of 2008 and 2009, which can tempt governments to roll back environmental regulation or enforcement and to expediently promote environmentally damaging development in order to stimulate economic growth and job creation, underscores the need for such protections.

Are the NAFTA and the NAAEC suitable occupants of their policy space, and are they allowing governments the potential to use all of the tools at their disposal to drive a transition to an economy that lives within ecological limits? The evidence is scant that they are. The three provisions discussed in this chapter were adopted to provide key guarantees that liberalized trade would promote stronger environmental protection and enforcement and improved analysis of environmental impacts to address scale effects. Not only have these been ignored in the context of the NAFTA and the NAAEC, but versions of the NAFTA's Article 1114(2) have also come to appear in virtually every subsequent trade deal that the United States and Canada have entered into,[107] and versions of Part V of the NAAEC appear in most subsequent United States trade agreements.[108] These empty provisions take up policy space that

---

[104] See Johan Rockström et al., "Planetary boundaries: Exploring the safe operating space for humanity" (2009) 14:2 *Ecology and Society* 32, http://ecologyandsociety.org/vol14/iss2/art32/; James Gustave Speth, *The Bridge at the Edge of the World: Capitalism, the Environment and Crossing from Crisis to Sustainability* (New Haven, CT: Yale University Press, 2008), pp. 1–5.

[105] See Hails et al., *The Living Planet Report*, pp. 28–9.

[106] See generally Vaughan, "Thinking North American Environmental Management."

[107] See, e.g., Free Trade Agreement between Canada and the Republic of Colombia, Lima, November 21, 2008, in force August 15, 2011, Can. TS 2011 No. 11, Article 815; Free Trade Agreement between Canada and the Republic of Panama, Ottawa, May 14, 2010, in force April 1, 2013, Can. TS 2013 No. 9, Article 9.16; Free Trade Agreement between Canada and the Republic of Peru, Lima, May 29, 2008, in force August 1, 2009, Can. TS 2009 No. 15, Article 809; Free Trade Agreement between the Government of Canada and the Government of the Republic of Chile, Santiago, December 5, 1996, in force July 5, 1997, Can. TS 1997 No. 50, Article G-14; Dominican Republic–Central America–United States Free Trade Agreement, May 28, 2004, (2004) 43 ILM 514, Article 17.2(2); United States–Colombia Free Trade Agreement, November 22, 2006, in force May 15, 2012, Article 18.3(2), http://ustr.gov/trade-agreements/free-trade-agreements/colombia-fta/final-text; United States–Peru Trade Promotion Agreement, April 12, 2006, in force February 1, 2009, Article 18.3(2), http://ustr .gov/trade-agreements/free-trade-agreements/peru-tpa/final-text; United States–Panama Trade Pro-motion Agreement, June 28, 2007, not yet in force, Article 17.3(2), http://ustr.gov/trade-agreements/ free-trade-agreements/panama-tpa/final-text; United States–Chile Free Trade Agreement, June 6, 2003, in force January 1, 2004, (2003) 42 ILM 1026, Article 19.2(2); United States–Australia Free Trade Agreement, May 18, 2004, in force January 1, 2005, (2004) 43 ILM 1248, Article 19.2(2).

[108] See, e.g., US–Colombia FTA, Articles 18.3(1), 18.12; CAFTA, Articles 17.2(1), 17.10; US–Peru TPA, Articles 18.3(1),18.12; US–Panama TPA, Articles 17.3(1), 17.11; US–Chile FTA, Articles 19.2(1), 19.6; US–Australia FTA, Articles 19.2(1), 19.7.

might otherwise be occupied by effective innovations able to address the aggregate ecological effects of an increasingly globalized economy.

The NAFTA governments know how to adopt more rigorous tools if they want to. They did so in the NAFTA's Chapter 11 by waiving their sovereign immunity so as to allow private investors to seek monetary awards for breach of the NAFTA's investor protections through binding arbitration.[109] The dispute settlement mechanism in Part V of the NAAEC, submissions on enforcement matters under the NAAEC's Articles 14 and 15, and the environmental consultations otherwise allowed under the NAAEC or the NAFTA are at best weak cousins to the investor dispute mechanism in the NAFTA.[110] In light of the contribution of regional and global trade to looming ecological challenges like climate change, this differentiation in the governmentally granted power to access publicly financed remedies reflects a troublesome imbalance. Without a meaningful attempt to hold each other to account in regard to environmental backsliding or other environmental shortcomings, or to give critical issues such as climate change paramount importance in regional decision making, the perception that the NAFTA and the NAAEC are mere paper tigers against North American ecological challenges is likely to continue and to solidify.

Overcoming the stagnancy of trade policy in North America will be difficult in part because of the general difficulty in transforming institutions that have achieved stability – in this case, an entire series of trade agreements built around an outdated and unambitious approach in regard to trade and environment – even where the conditions and assumptions under which those institutions were established have changed significantly or have been shown to be faulty.[111] This phenomenon of maintaining "tragic institutions"[112] – that is, institutions created to address an aspect of the tragedy of the commons that have become ineffective but difficult to change – is likely exacerbated where pressures in addition to the bureaucratic tendency to maintain budgets and programs are considerable. In the case of the North American approach to trade and the environment, a key factor is the expediency of reproducing a model when doing so does not appear to come with any significant political cost.

The approach of the North American partners to international trade and the environment is a reflection in large measure of the global approach – with the possible exception of Europe, where for more than sixty years the European Union member countries have accepted supranational authority in the environment and other domains beyond trade and finance. The key features of the global trade and

---

[109] NAFTA, Articles 1115–38.

[110] C.f. discussion of the asymmetry in how the investor dispute provisions of Chapter 11 of the NAFTA affects national sovereignty as compared to Articles 14 and 15 of the NAAEC, in Chris Tollefson, "Games without frontiers: Investor claims and citizen submissions under the NAFTA regime" (2002) 27:1 *Yale J. Int'l. L.* 141 at 145–7.

[111] See Daniels, "Emerging commons and tragic institutions," pp. 520–1, 539–41.

[112] Ibid.

finance system are its increasingly doubtful assumption that mobile capital and limited market regulation lead to long-term social and environmental well being; its consistent undervaluation of environmental values, biodiversity, and ecological integrity; its enduring assumption that measures to protect the environment, public health, or other public goods or commons are disguised barriers to trade; its near blindness to overconsumption and aggregate ecological impacts of economic activity; and its apparent assumption that comparative advantage – a bedrock justification for international trade – remains an important factor in a world with few meaningful restrictions on the movement of capital.[113] In light of the momentum this set of features encourages along a path to ecological catastrophe, the assumption that they will ensure that boundaries between ecological security and catastrophe will be respected must be severely questioned. Each of the elements of the institutional infrastructure that supports the current regime of international trade and finance, such as those included in the NAFTA and the NAAEC, should face serious scrutiny as to their ability to respect those boundaries.

Stable institutions can help solve the tragedy of the commons, but "with a change of circumstances and values sensible institutions can morph into tragic institutions."[114] In the context of trade and environment in North America, a key change in circumstances since 1994 is the significant new information regarding the accelerating regional and global ecological crisis, especially climate change. According to Daniels, institutions are much more likely to be adaptive and to respond to environmental challenges that public participation, transparency, and impact analysis can reveal if they have the capacity to (1) prepare those who control commons resources to be flexible and adaptive, (2) be "continually expos[ed] to competing values" so as to foster integrated management of multiple values rather than single uses of commons resources, (3) "[w]ithin sensible bounds, allow trading among users," (4) "[b]uild mechanisms to internalize externalities," (5) "[p]rovide incentives for users to conserve the commons," (6) give legal rights to those affected by the use of commons to challenge decisions regarding management of the commons, and (7) "[i]f necessary, buy out interests of entrenched users."[115] With these criteria in mind, it becomes clear that a more fundamental reform of North America's trade and environment model is needed – one that reckons with the aggregate scale effects of the regional and global trade and finance regime in radical new ways.

[113] See generally William E. Rees, "Globalization and sustainability: conflict or convergence?" (2002) 22:4 *Bull. of Sci., Tech. & Soc.* 249; Nathan Pelletier, "Of laws and limits: An ecological economic perspective on redressing the failure of contemporary global environmental governance" (2010) 20:2 *Global Environmental Change* 220.
[114] Daniels, "Emerging commons and tragic institutions," p. 565.
[115] Ibid., 566–8.

2

Should Citizens Expect Procedural Justice in Nonadversarial Processes? Spotlighting the Regression of the Citizen Submissions Process from NAAEC to CAFTA–DR

Giselle Davidian

1. INTRODUCTION

Since the proliferation of international free trade agreements (FTAs) toward the end of the twentieth century and the corresponding neglect for environmental consequences, the mission of environmental activists and nongovernmental organizations (NGOs) has been to hold states accountable for implementing their environmental laws and policies. Public participation has many advantages: it strengthens the relationship between government and civil society, it enhances comprehensive decision making, and it encourages sustainable business practices.[1] Where a public complaint process exists, citizens are an important source of information concerning potential environmental violations.

The North American Agreement on Environmental Cooperation (NAAEC or the "Agreement")[2] is significant for establishing a citizen participation process for the Commission for Environmental Cooperation's (CEC) Secretariat to consider Submissions on Enforcement Matters (SEM), and consequently opening up the realm of international law to the influences of nonstate actors. By presenting a submission, citizens and NGOs are able to direct a spotlight on any of the three North American Free Trade Agreement (NAFTA)[3] signatories to address their failure to enforce domestic environmental law. As the first model of its kind, however, it has been described as a dead-end process that subjects submitters to a serious

---

[1] Susan Casey-Lefkowitz et al., "The Evolving Role of Citizens in Environmental Enforcement," paper delivered at the Fourth International Conference on Environmental Compliance and Enforcement, Chiang Mai, Thailand (April 22, 1996) at 2.

[2] North American Agreement on Environmental Cooperation, September 14, 1993, in force January 1, 1994, (1993) 32 ILM 1480; Can TS 1994 No 3.

[3] North American Free Trade Agreement between the Government of the United States of America, the Government of Canada and the Government of the United Mexican States, San Antonio, December 17, 1992, in force January 1, 1994, (1993) 32 ILM 296; Can TS 1994 No 2.

accountability gap and a lack of procedural justice.[4] As a result, the CEC has struggled to adequately fulfill its duties as "regional facilitator, convener, statistician and watchdog."[5]

This paper will examine the substantive and procedural features of the CEC SEM process and consider whether it offers the public due process in enforcing domestic environmental protection laws. First, it will investigate the need for procedural justice in the so-called "spotlighting mechanism"[6] by asking: does the state owe individuals a duty to be the object of review? It will consider the strengths and weaknesses of other international fact-finding and compliance models, namely the World Bank Inspection Panel, the European Union Citizen Complaint Process, and the International Civil Aviation Organization's Universal Safety Oversight Audit Program. Next, it will examine Articles 14 and 15 of the NAAEC SEM process and consider their successes and failures in achieving NAAEC objectives. Finally, it will compare the SEM processes of the NAAEC and those of the Dominican Republic–Central America–United States Free Trade Agreement (CAFTA–DR).[7] The paper will conclude with recommendations and speculate on the viability of the nonadversarial spotlighting trend, a task of particular importance considering that many subsequent FTAs have been modeled after the NAAEC. This paper contends that procedural justice cannot result from nonadversarial fact-finding processes in which Member States engage in face-saving practices that politicize the process and reject global administrative principles, most notably transparency and accountability.[8] If structural problems cannot be resolved and governments cannot agree to engage collaboratively, future citizen submission processes should move to an adversarial method, one with effective sanctions for noncomplying Member States.

2. APPLYING GLOBAL ADMINISTRATIVE PRINCIPLES TO FACT-FINDING

The perceived legitimacy of international agreements has been sought to be increased, in response to a demanding public, by moving toward achieving the

---

4   David Markell, "The Role of Spotlighting Procedures in Promoting Citizen Participation, Transparency, and Accountability" (2010) 45 *Wake Forest Law Review* 425 at 452. See also Geoff Garver, "Tooth Decay: Examining NAFTA's 'Environmental Teeth'" (2008) 25 *The Environmental Forum* 34.

5   Chris Wold, "Evaluating NAFTA and the Commission for Environmental Cooperation: Lessons for Integrating Trade and Environment in Free Trade Agreements" (2008) 28 *Saint Louis University Public Law Review* 201 at 222.

6   Spotlighting mechanisms allow citizens the opportunity to direct a spotlight onto government enforcement practices that they feel are inadequate.

7   Dominican Republic–Central America–United States Free Trade Agreement, May 28, 2004, (2004) 43 ILM 514, Chapter 17 [CAFTA–DR].

8   For a definition of global administrative principles, see Carol Harlow, "Global Administrative Law: The Quest for Principles and Values" (2006) 17 *European Journal of International Law* 187 at 195 (in which she defines global administrative law principles as comprising: "accountability, transparency and access to information, participation, the right of access to an independent court, due process rights, including the right to be heard and the right to reasoned decisions and reasonableness").

global administrative ideals of accountability, transparency, public participation, and due process.[9] Complaint and grievance mechanisms have been particularly effective in incorporating the views and interests of citizens while striving for exemplary global governance.[10] Yet to some, soft law complaint mechanisms are regarded as a deceptive means of concealing the reluctance of states to set up an international legal framework with binding targets and clear enforcement devices.[11]

Complaints and grievances mechanisms have the capacity to provide a useful and accessible avenue by which affected parties can pursue breaching parties. They strive to engage communities beyond their borders and incorporate previously marginalized views and the interests of civil society.[12] In an environmental context, for instance, communities are able to express concerns regarding the preservation of ecosystems, species, and climate systems – issues that transcend regional boundaries. An example is the Office of the Compliance Advisor/Ombudsman (CAO), an independent post that reports to the President of the World Bank Group.[13] The CAO responds to complaints through mediated settlements headed by the CAO Ombudsman, or through compliance audits that ensure adherence to relevant policies.[14]

2.1. *Duty of States to Be the Object of Review*

Does a state owe its citizens a duty to be the object of review? A growing number of civil society members would answer this question in the affirmative. The alleged duty arises especially in light of an increasing demand for public accountability

---

[9]   Harlow, "Global Administrative Law," p. 195.

[10]   Duncan French and Richard Kirkham, "Complaint and Grievance Mechanisms in International Dispute Settlement," in Duncan French, Matthew Saul, and Nigel D. White (eds.), *International Law and Dispute Settlement: New Problems and Techniques* (Oxford: Hart Publishing, 2010), p. 57. Meanwhile, critics of the soft law approach contend that processes may lack the legitimacy, surveillance, and enforcement mechanisms offered by hard law. Joseph F. DiMento and Pamela M. Doughman, "Soft Teeth in the Back of the Mouth: the NAFTA Environmental Side Agreement Implemented" (1998) 10 *Geo Int'l Envtl L Rev* p. 736.

[11]   John J. Kirton and Michael J. Trebilcock, "Introduction: Hard Choices and Soft Law in Sustainable Global Governance," in John K. Kirton and Michael J. Trebilcock (eds.), *Hard Choices, Soft Law: Voluntary Standards in Global Trade, Environment and Social Governance* (Aldershot, UK: Ashgate Publishing, 2004), pp. 3, 6. The authors define "soft law" as follows: "Soft law . . . refers to regimes that rely primarily on the participation and resources of nongovernmental actors in the construction, operation, and implementation of a governance arrangement" (p. 9).

[12]   French and Kirkham, "Complaint and Grievance Mechanisms," pp. 61–62.

[13]   The CAO reviews complaints from communities affected by development projects undertaken by the private sector lending and insurance members of the World Bank Group, the International Finance Corporation ("IFC"), and the Multilateral Investment Guarantee Agency (MIGA).

[14]   Online: http://www.cao-ombudsman.org. Based on the results of the ombudsman assessment, CAO specialists either work with the stakeholders to develop a jointly agreed process of assisted negotiation or determine that a collaborative solution is not possible and transfer the case to CAO Compliance for appraisal. If an audit is merited, the CAO typically employs an independent panel of experts to conduct the investigation. The audit is based on a review of documents, interviews, and observation of project activities and outcomes.

in response to the perceived weakening of governmental authority as a result of globalization, which has entailed the greater control of transnational corporations and the ease of cross-border public sharing of news and ideas though social media. At the same time, the shift toward a rights-based development approach has encouraged citizens to act as legitimizers and watchdogs of state policies.[15] Citizens are aware of the dire repercussions that would arise if the actions of states, nonstate actors, and individuals were not at the very least confined by domestic laws, especially in the environmental and sustainable development context.

Former Secretary-General of the United Nations, Kofi Annan, for instance, has acknowledged the critical roles that civil society groups play "as partners, advocates and watchdogs" in attaining sustainable development.[16] Yet, to outsiders, international and intergovernmental organizations can have the appearance of private, exclusive clubs. Increasing the perceived legitimacy of international governance is therefore an important objective, and one that requires states to allow public scrutiny of such organizations.

Maintaining public administrative accountability is crucial to the concept of the rule of law as developed in Canada, the United States, and Mexico.[17] Yet despite each individual nation's commitment to the ideal that no person (natural and moral) or government is above the law, the rule of law within an international setting is still emerging. As former Canadian Minister of Foreign Affairs, Bill Graham, has stated:

> Our societies are based upon the rule of law, and the sustainable, shared global future that we seek must have the same basis, however difficult it may be to obtain universal acceptance of the rules and establish effective means of enforcement. Examples close to home illustrate the point: we do not dispense with domestic law

---

[15] Mark R. Goldschmidt, "The Role of Transparency and Public Participation in International Environmental Agreements: The North American Agreement on Environmental Cooperation" (2001–2002) 29 *Environmental Affairs L Rev* p. 351. See also Emanuele Rebasti, "Beyond consultative status: which legal framework for enhanced interaction between NGOs and intergovernmental organizations?" in Pierre-Marie Dupuy and Luisa Vierucci (eds.), *NGOs in International Law: Efficiency in Flexibility?* (Cheltenham, UK: Edward Elgar, 2008), p. 21, pp. 52ff.

[16] Secretary-General Kofi Annan, "Address to the World Summit on Sustainable Development," (address delivered at the World Summit on Sustainable Development, Johannesburg, September 2, 2002) [unpublished], http://www.un.org/events/wssd/statements/sgE.htm.

[17] Mary Liston, "Governments in Miniature: The Rule of Law in the Administrative State" in Colleen Flood and Lorne Sossin (eds.), *Administrative Law in Context: A New Casebook* (Emond-Montgomery Publishing, 2008), pp. 77–114. In Canada, the Rule of Law is the principle that no one is above the law. Law is based upon fundamental principles that can be discovered, but that cannot be created through an act of will. In the United States, the underlying assumption about the Rule of Law is that limits must be placed on government, since the tendency of government is to grow. Instead, individual, inalienable rights are officially recognized as being fundamental to the United States' form of government and are enumerated in the U.S. Bill of Rights. In Mexico, the Rule of Law refers to the capacity of the judiciary to uphold, interpret, and enforce the principles and laws that assure the constitutionally prescribed functioning of government and protect individual rights and property in a predictable yet equitable way.

because we know some will defy the law; nor do homeowners consider stronger locks an adequate substitute for the law.[18]

Even so, other uniform standards may be applied. To take one example, due to the international nature of the NAAEC, the Agreement is applied in accordance with the rules of interpretation set out in Articles 31 and 32 of the Vienna Convention on the Law of Treaties.[19] Therefore, while universally applicable ideas of the rule of law may be elusive, other internationally accepted standards may be of help.

Global treaties publicly embody a set of universally applicable expectations, including prohibited and required practices and policies. In addition, they establish a measure of predictability and accountability. Treaties contribute to the development of international goals as well as approaches toward attaining those goals; they also present references to guide states' activities and domestic legislation, providing a focal point for discussion and negotiations on agreements. By requiring each state to implement its own laws with respect to the environment, it becomes critical to the principle of responsible government that NAAEC signatories allow the public to assess government compliance.

2.2. *Considering Other Fact-Finding Processes*

This section surveys other international fact-finding and compliance models: the World Bank Inspection Panel, the European Union Citizen Complaint Process, and the International Civil Aviation Organization (ICAO) Safety Oversight and Audit Process. The purpose is to consider the ways in which global administrative principles are applied and to consider the factors that can operate in the SEM process.

2.2.1. World Bank Inspection Panel

The World Bank Inspection Panel is a quasiindependent body created to hold the World Bank (WB) accountable for failures to follow its own internal policies and procedures. The three-member Panel investigates claims brought by citizens who are likely to be affected by an action or omission of the WB resulting from such a failure.[20]

---

[18] United Nations Conference on Disarmament, 2002, 898th Mtg, UN Doc CD/PV.898.
[19] *Vienna Convention on the Law of Treaties*, May 23, 1969, 1155 UNTS 331; Can TS 1980 No 37 (entered into force January 27, 1980), Articles 31 and 32. Canada and Mexico are parties to the Convention. The United States is not a party to the Convention, but it has accepted that the application of rules on interpretation apply as customary international law to treaties.
[20] Note that the failure must have had, or threatens to have, a material adverse effect. A request can be filed by any two or more adversely affected people living in the project area. In special cases, an executive director of the World Bank may file the request. See World Bank, Inspection Panel, August 19, 1994. Operating Procedures, http://www.worldbank.org/inspectionpanel. Members are appointed by the Board for nonrenewable periods of five years. They are "selected on the basis of their ability to

The policies and procedures are designed to ensure that WB operations provide social and environmental benefits, avoid harm to people and the environment, and provide greater transparency of investments.

The Panel is independent of the WB's management; it reports directly to the Board of Executive Directors and is provided with separate resources to discharge its functions. This independence ensures the Panel's impartiality. Upon receiving a complaint, the Panel conducts an initial review and subsequently informs the Board of Executive Directors whether, in its recommendation, a full investigation is warranted.[21] If the Board authorizes the investigation, the Panel may assess allegations and has access to all resources – including WB staff, pertinent records, and internal accountability and evaluation teams – to do so. It reports its findings and recommendations to the WB management and Board of Executive Directors.[22] Management has six weeks to prepare a report for the Board indicating its recommendations for responding to the Panel's findings. It is then up to the Board to announce what remedial measures, if any, the WB will undertake.

The WB process is similar to that of SEM, since in each case an independent body (Panel or Secretariat, respectively) is responsible for investigating and reporting on noncompliance. Both are nonbinding and nonjudicial processes that are intended to be a forum of last resort. Submitters must first exhaust other available remedies prior to filing a claim. Investigations in each model are triggered by the "fire alarm" of citizen complaints that point a spotlight at the actions of WB. However, the spotlight on compliance with duties in each model can be especially hindered when parties are unwilling to be the target of investigation. Internal investigations remain voluntary and self-imposed.

The transparency of the WB process is further weakened by the Panel's inability to oversee the implementation of remedial measures and assess whether proposed measures would satisfy the concerns of the claimants in compliance with WB policies.[23] The process has been criticized for having the effect of shielding the WB from accountability by encouraging staff to panel-proof their activities and weaken their policies.[24] Such practices lead to a "race to the bottom" for FTAs, discussed in Section 3 of this chapter. Avoiding such detrimental consequences is the ultimate

deal thoroughly and fairly with requests brought to them, their integrity and their independence from Bank Management, and their exposure to developmental issues and to living conditions in developing countries:" International Bank for Reconstruction and Development, Resolution No. IDA 96–6, *The Inspection Panel* (September 22, 1993).

21 International Bank for Reconstruction and Development, Resolution No. IDA 96–6.
22 Ibid.
23 Dana L. Clark, "The World Bank and Human Rights: The Need for Greater Accountability" (2002) 15 *Harvard Law School Human Rights Journal* 206 at 218: the author contends that "[a]lthough people affected by World Bank projects have rights under the policy framework and an adequate forum for raising concerns about violations, they are frequently denied an effective remedy."
24 See Natalie Laura Bridgeman, "World Bank Reform in the 'Post-Policy' Era" (2001) 13 *The Georgetown International Environmental Law Review* 1013.

objective of the SEM process. Therefore, successes and lessons learned from the WB Inspection Panel experience are directly informative to the CEC Secretariat in administering the SEM process.

2.2.2. European Union Complaint Process

European Union (EU) law obliges each Member State to properly implement and enforce EU legislation domestically.[25] Citizens have a right to lodge a complaint to the Commission against a Member State for purported infringements of EU law. The burden imposed on complainants is low because citizens do not have to demonstrate a formal interest in bringing proceedings, nor do they have to demonstrate that they were principally and directly affected by the Member State's infringement.[26] Pursuant to Article 226 of the Treaty Establishing the European Community, the Commission maintains discretionary powers to launch the complaint process or to refer the case to the Court of Justice of the European Communities.[27]

The Commission must ensure complainants are informed of each decision made and steps taken following the lodging of a complaint.[28] The aim is to complete an investigation (that is, by issuing a formal notice or closing the case) within a year from the date of initial registration of the complaint, and the complainant must be informed in case of delay. To ensure transparency, Commission decisions on infringement cases are published online within a week of their adoption. Complainants have the additional recourse of referring the matter to the European Ombudsman if they feel that they were subject to maladministration by the Commission.[29]

The process aims to follow the principles of good administration as defined by Article 41 of the Charter of Fundamental Rights of the European Union.[30] In 2001, the European Code of Good Administrative Behaviour (the Code) was adopted to

---

[25] If a member state fails to comply with Community law, it is subject to the infringement procedure set out in Article 226 of the Treaty Establishing the European Community: Consolidated Version of the Treaty Establishing the European Community, November 10, 1997, [1997] OJ C 340/3; 37 ILM 79.

[26] EC, Commission communication to the European Parliament and the European Ombudsman on relations with the complainant in respect of infringements of Community law, [2002] OJ, C 244/5 at 6.

[27] EC, Commission communication [2002] at 5.

[28] EC, Commission communication [2002] at 7–8. Decisions include: formal notice, reasoned opinion, referral to the Court or closure of the case.

[29] Under Articles 21 and 195 of the Treaty Establishing the European Community, as well as the European Code of Good Administrative Behaviour (EC, *Sitting of Thursday, September 6, 2001*, [2001] Annex 5–2045/2002).

[30] Article 41 of the Charter of Fundamental Rights of the European Union (EC, Charter of Fundamental Rights of the European Union, [2000] OJC 364/1) enumerates the following rights and duties as part of the right to good administration: the right to have one's affairs "handled impartially, fairly and within a reasonable time" (Article 41(1)), the right to be heard, the right to access one's file, and the duty of the administration to give reasons for its decisions (Article 41(2)) and language rights (Article 41(4)).

provide guidelines for Commission staff to follow in their relations with the public. It also establishes a mechanism through which members of the public may submit complaints with the Secretariat-General of the Commission concerning an alleged failure to abide by the principles set out in the Code.[31] The Code sets out general principles with respect to its relations with the public. These principles include procedural rights and duties (the right to fair and impartial treatment, the right to be heard and the duty to state reasons), substantive rights (data protection), general principles of European administrative law (proportionality), and rules of ethical behavior and good administrative service (courtesy).

The EU complaint mechanism produces a concrete outcome by either issuing a formal notice for opening proceedings against the Member State in question, or closing the case indefinitely.[32] In the EU model, the decision maker (that is, the Commission) is also the primary investigator of the facts, unless the Ombudsman is requested to further investigate. Sources of EU administrative law are found primarily in the Lisbon Treaty, Community legislation and case law of Community courts, and decisions made by the European Ombudsman.[33] The EU ensures that citizens are provided good administration by empowering an Ombudsman to investigate grievances.[34]

Despite the noted differences, the two systems are similar in that they both assess the noncompliance of states with the law. Just as the SEM Secretariat passes on the results of the investigation to the Council once complete, the EU Commission passes on results of the fact-finding investigation to a separate body if proceedings are warranted.

While accountability under EU law represents a model of good governance and serves a symbolic function of administrative reform, it has been criticized for adopting a value that is too broad and ill-defined.[35] At the very least, the EU method provides a strong aspirational model for a legally binding complaint mechanism that places

---

[31] European Code of Good Administrative Behaviour. As seen earlier, complaints may also be lodged with the European Ombudsman: http://www.euro-ombudsman.eu.int.

[32] EC, Commission communication [2002] at 7.

[33] Paul P. Craig, "EU Administrative Law" (New York: Oxford University Press, 2006) at 280. Article 41 of the Charter enumerates the following rights and duties as part of the right to good administration: the right to have one's affairs handled impartially, fairly and within a reasonable time (paragraph 1), the right to be heard, to access one's file and the duty of administration to give reasons for its decisions (paragraph 2), as well as noncontractual liability of the EU (paragraph 3) and language rights (paragraph 4).

[34] The Ombudsman has advocated for a general code of good administration arguing that the existing Code, which elaborates on the meaning of the right to good administration in Article 41, should be transformed into formal law. Paul P. Craig, "EU Administrative Law" (New York: Oxford University Press, 2006) at 280.

[35] Dorte Sindbjerg Martinsen and Torben Beck Jørgensen, "Accountability as a Differentiated Value in Supranational Governance" (2010) 40 *The American Review of Public Administration* 742 at 747 (the idea that accountability must be supported by its co-values: "responsibility, responsiveness, transparency, integrity, controllability, and rule of law").

high value in good administration. The SEM process can adopt from the EU system the objective of attaining concrete outcomes. The EU system might also inspire possible models for investigating grievances and providing good governance.

2.2.3. ICAO Safety Audits

The International Civil Aviation Organization (ICAO), a specialized United Nations agency established by the Chicago Convention,[36] provides a final example of international regulation that investigates noncompliance. The role of the ICAO is to provide safety and security standardization and technical guidance on the proper functioning of international civil aviation, which it does through the development and issuance of Standards and Recommended Practices (SARPs), the production of detailed guidance material, a safety and security audit process, and international conferences and workshops.

Based on the principles of equality, state responsibility for the common good, and accountability, the Chicago Convention requires Contracting States to implement SARPs adopted by the Council.[37] ICAO members cooperate to secure the highest attainable degree of uniformity with respect to standards and must only notify the organization if they find it "impracticable" to comply in all respects with standards and procedures.[38] In practice, members have not regarded compliance with the Council's standards as compulsory. As a result, the ICAO Secretariat does not presume compliance from a lack of disclosure.

In an effort to add sharper teeth to its functioning, the ICAO developed the Universal Safety Oversight Audit Program (USOAP) to conduct regular, mandatory, and harmonized safety audits for each contracting country. The audits assess the effective execution of safety oversight systems and evaluate the implementation of safety SARPs. There are three audit phases: (1) the preaudit phase entails establishing the safety oversight system in place and identifying any discrepancies with SARP practices; (2) the on-site phase verifies the information provided and establishes recommendations; and (3) the postaudit phase includes the submission of a report and the publication of the Final Safety Oversight Audit Report on the ICAO website to ensure transparency and inform all countries of each other's strengths and weaknesses.[39] A Corrective Action Plan is developed where there are instances of noncompliance, complete with findings, recommendations, and action deadlines.

[36] Convention on International Civil Aviation, December 7, 1944, 15 UNTS 295; Can TS 1944 No 36.
[37] ICAO can set rules for its own enforcement unless a majority of the member states object to the proposed rules within three months: Articles 54(*l*) and 90 of the Convention on International Civil Aviation.
[38] Convention on International Civil Aviation, Articles 37 and 38. Revisions to the Convention are available online: http://www.icao.int/publications/pages/doc7300.aspx.
[39] See ICAO Council, 174th Sess., Procedure of Transparency and Disclosure, ICAO Doc C-WP/12497 (2005).

If the state fails to provide corrective action to resolve the safety concern, it will be contacted to determine why action was not taken.[40] Member states are notified of unresolved safety concerns. The ICAO has developed initiatives to improve the implementation of SARPs in regions with a lack of technical, financial, or human resources, making the process less adversarial and more cooperative.[41]

Both SEM and USOAP are based on voluntary compliance. USOAP's mandate to increase transparency and disclosure has been effective because of the normative implications inherent in noncompliance (that is, states naturally want to protect their aviation industries, airspaces, passengers, and goods from safety risks introduced by noncompliant states). The SEM process is similar because developing factual records of noncompliance may motivate states to limit or impose conditions on trade for a particular practice and location of a documented breach.

Whereas the ICAO establishes uniform standards, SEM adheres to the enforcement of individual domestic law only. Critics of the USOAP claim that the development of states accepting standardized rules and regulations as binding may significantly relax the tradition of state sovereignty entrenched in the positivist approach.[42] However, flexible and modern SARPs of the ICAO have proven to be a more effective approach to regulating aviation.[43]

2.3. *Procedural Justice to Enable Public Participation*

If the SEM process is to achieve and maintain legitimacy under international law, then submissions must be addressed under established global administrative principles, including procedural justice. Procedural justice can be regarded as "the extent to which citizens value a process because of its procedural features."[44] In the context

---

[40] ICAO Council, 179th Sess., Review of the Memorandum of Understanding (MOU) relating to the conduct of safety oversight audits under the comprehensive systems approach, ICAO Doc C-MIN 179/12 (2006) §49.

[41] Initiatives include: ICAO Technical Co-operation Bureau; the Implementation Support and Development Branch; the International Financial Facility for Aviation Safety; and a partnership system to analyze causes and develop solutions: see Jimena Blumenkron, "Implications of Transparency in the International Civil Aviation Organization's Universal Safety Audit Program," http://www.iilj.org/GAL/documents/V5.Blumenkron at 9.

[42] Conway W. Henderson, *Understanding International Law* (Chichester, UK: Wiley-Blackwell, 2010), p. 89.

[43] Thomas Buergenthal, *Law-Making in the International Civil Aviation Organization* (Syracuse, NY: Syracuse University Press, 1969), pp. 101ff. See also "Worldwide and Regional Trends in Aviation Safety" (presented at the Directors General of Civil Aviation Conference on a Global Strategy for Aviation Safety, March 20–22, 2006), ICAO Doc DGCA/06-WP/2 § A-3: rate of safety-related accidents involving passenger fatalities in scheduled air transport operations worldwide for the period 1994–1999 was 1.3 and for the period 2000–2004 declined to 0.8.

[44] David L. Markell and Tom R. Tyler, "Using Empirical Research to Design Government Citizen Participation Processes: A Case Study of Citizens' Roles in Environmental Compliance and Enforcement" (2008) 57 *Kansas Law Review* 1 at 4.

of the CEC, procedural justice should, through the notion of separation of powers, prevent a party under investigation from undermining the independence of the fact finder of the investigation. Without the actual and perceived legitimacy of the SEM process by the public, submissions will cease and the process will collapse.

Eleven years after the NAAEC came into effect, the Almaty Guidelines on Promoting the Application of the Principles of the Aarhus Convention in International Forums were created.[45] They represent the first official, accomplished attempt to deal comprehensively with public participation at the international level. The Almaty Guidelines were established "to provide general guidance to Parties on promoting the application of the principles of the [Aarhus] Convention in international forums in matters relating to the environment."[46] The Guidelines recognize the importance of public participation in international environmental matters by emphasizing the close relation between public participation and the principle of sustainable development. This association is a requisite for good governance and a tool for enhancing the quality of international implementation processes.[47] Transparency of public participation policies, including rules for access to information and mechanisms for application review, is emphasized primarily to prevent abusive processes that lead to undesirable outcomes. Procedural requirements include reasonable time frames for different stages, opportunities to participate in decision-making processes, and transparent and clearly stated standards.[48]

It is questionable whether the soft character of the Guidelines' contents "will bear significantly on the conduct of . . . state members" in international forums.[49] While successful in significantly furthering participatory opportunities of NGOs in international forums when dealing with environmental issues, the language of the Guidelines reflects their nonbinding nature and the desire of states to retain a large margin of discretion in their application. This problem is shared with SEM, as public participation processes inherently threaten to embarrass governments by exposing their noncompliance. Institutional support is therefore critical to their success.[50] As the next section will describe, such support includes an independent Secretariat and a committee of experts to serve as watchdogs over the process.

---

[45] Promoting the Application of the Principles of the Aarhus Convention in International Forums, ESC Dec II/4, UNESCOR, 2005, ECE/MP.PP/2005/2/Add.5 [Almaty Guidelines].

[46] Article 1 of Almaty Guidelines.

[47] Articles 11 and 12 of Almaty Guidelines. Article 11 states: "Access to information, public participation and access to justice in environmental matters are fundamental elements of good governance at all levels and essential for sustainability."

[48] Articles 35 and 36 of Almaty Guidelines.

[49] Attila Tanzi, "Controversial developments in the field of public participation in the international environmental law process" in Dupuy and Vierucci (eds.), *NGOs in International Law*, pp. 135, 148.

[50] John H. Knox, "Separated at Birth: The North American Agreements on Labor and the Environment" (2004) 26 *Loyola of Los Angeles International and Comparative Law Review* 359 at 386.

3. EFFECTIVENESS OF NAAEC CITIZEN SUBMISSION PROCESS

The negotiation of the NAFTA side agreement on the environment was essentially an afterthought prompted by then-presidential candidate Bill Clinton, who declared that he could not support NAFTA unless it was accompanied by supplemental agreements on environmental protection and labor issues.[51] While the United States, Mexico, and Canada (the Parties) did not reopen NAFTA to revise substantive rules about trade liberalization and the environment, the Parties successfully negotiated an environmental side agreement known as the North American Agreement on Environmental Cooperation.

The primary goal of the environmental side agreement is to maintain the integrity of domestic environmental law enforcement. Article 3 establishes levels of protection. While recognizing each country's right to create its own laws, Article 3 stipulates that each Party "shall ensure that its laws and regulations provide for high levels of environmental protection and shall strive to continue to improve those laws and regulations."[52] Thus, each Party is at liberty to make sovereign decisions about the nature and content of its environmental laws, but is restricted from reducing their efficacy. The issue of enforcement, as opposed to the adequacy of the environmental legislation, was the main concern in formulating the NAAEC.

There are two possible avenues to address noncompliance. First, governments may seek an assessment of a Party engaged in a persistent pattern of failure to enforce applicable environmental laws, which may lead to monetary enforcement sanctions. The second is a citizen submission process that allows groups or individuals to allege a Party's breach of environmental laws. This paper considers the effectiveness of the latter avenue, the Submission on Enforcement Matters process.

3.1. *Outlining the SEM and Factual Record Preparation Processes*

The guiding body of the CEC is the Council, made up of the U.S. EPA Administrator, the Mexican Secretary of the Environment, and the Canadian Environment Minister. The Council hires the Executive Director, who in turn hires Secretariat staff from the three countries. Aside from helping Parties to implement a cooperative environmental work program, the Secretariat has a duty to investigate citizen SEMs. The third body of the CEC is the Joint Public Advisory Committee (JPAC), composed of fifteen citizens (five from each of the three countries). Its role is to advise the Council on matters of public concern within the scope of the Agreement.

---

[51] Presidential Candidate Governor Bill Clinton, "Address" (delivered at University of North Carolina, October 4, 1992), cited in Gary C. Hufbauer, Jeffrey J. Schott, et al., *NAFTA Revisited: Achievements and Challenges* 154, note 1 (2005). See Charles F. Doran and Alvin Paul Drischler, *A New North America Cooperation and Enhanced Independence* 129, note 26 (1996).

[52] Article 3 of NAAEC.

The Agreement includes an obligation for the Parties to maintain high standards of environmental protection and to effectively enforce environmental laws.

3.1.1. Article 14: The Citizen Submission on Enforcement Matters Process

A significant CEC responsibility is the implementation of the SEM process, through which citizens may file submissions alleging that any of the three signatory countries "is failing to effectively enforce its environmental law."[53] The Secretariat reviews submissions based on criteria specified in Article 14(1) and in the Guidelines to the SEM.[54] Where these criteria are met, the Secretariat may determine whether the submission merits requesting a response from the concerned Party. The Secretariat considers whether the submission alleges harm to the submitter, whether the submission raises a matter whose further study would advance the goals of the NAAEC, "whether private remedies available under the Party's law have been pursued," and whether "the submission is drawn exclusively from mass media reports."[55] The Party must advise the Secretariat within thirty (or, exceptionally, sixty) days following the request if the matter is the subject of a pending judicial or administrative proceeding, if the matter was previously subject to a judicial or administrative proceeding, or if private remedies are available (and whether they have been pursued).[56] A submission is barred from proceeding if the matter is currently the subject of a pending judicial or administrative proceeding.

3.1.2. Article 15: Factual Record Preparation

Aided by the Party's response, the Secretariat considers whether a factual record should be developed. If it determines that such action is appropriate, the Secretariat may inform the Council of its decision and corresponding reasons.[57] If, on the other

---

[53] Article 14 of NAAEC.
[54] Article 14(1) of NAAEC. The submission must: be written in Spanish, French, or English; clearly identify the person(s) or organization(s) making the submission; provide "sufficient information to be reviewed by the Secretariat, including any documentary evidence on which the submission may be based"; appear to be "aimed at promoting enforcement rather than at harassing industry"; indicate that "the matter has been communicated in writing to the relevant authorities"; include copies of relevant correspondence between the submitter and the authorities concerning the matters at issue in the submission; and be "filed by a person or an organization residing or established in the territory of a Party." Commission for Environmental Cooperation, Guidelines for Submissions on Enforcement Matters under Articles 14 and 15 of the North American Agreement on Environmental Cooperation (Montreal: Commission for Environmental Cooperation, 2013). Especially Articles 3 to 5 of the Guidelines: The submission must not exceed 15 pages of typed, letter-sized paper, excluding supporting documents, and must clearly identify the environmental law(s) at issue.
[55] Article 14(2) of NAAEC.
[56] Article 14(3) of NAAEC.
[57] Article 15(1) of NAAEC.

hand, it finds that a factual record is not warranted, the Secretariat must unilaterally dismiss the submission, providing a reasoned basis for its decision to do so.

By a two-thirds vote, the Council may instruct the Secretariat to prepare a factual record.[58] In conducting the investigation necessary to develop the factual record, the Secretariat may consider information that is: publicly available, submitted by interested NGOs or private persons, submitted by JPAC, developed by the Secretariat, or collected by independent experts.[59] Upon completion of the factual record, the parties have forty-five days to comment on its accuracy.[60] After the incorporation of "appropriate" comments, the final factual record is resubmitted to the Council.[61] By another two-thirds vote, the Council may make the final factual record publicly available within sixty days of its submission.[62]

3.2. *Successes: The First of its Kind*

3.2.1. Offsetting the "Race to Bottom" Effect

Free trade agreements have been criticized for bringing about a "race to the bottom" (or competitiveness) effect by decreasing environmental standards. Since free trade makes it easier for industries to relocate to countries with laxer regulatory standards, the resulting environmental damage is greater than it would have been had there not been free trade.[63] The SEM process, despite its avoidance of harmonized standards, has been successful in substantially offsetting the race to the bottom effect.[64]

There are other environmental impacts that come into play with trade liberalization, namely scale and technique effects.[65] While the scale effect describes the negative environmental consequences of scalar increases in economic activity, the technique effect accounts for the "positive environmental consequences of increases in income that call for cleaner production methods."[66] Scale effects occur because lowering trade barriers causes an expansion of economic activity. If the nature of the activity is unchanged while the scale continues to grow, a corresponding increase

[58] Article 15(2) of NAAEC.
[59] Article 15(4) of NAAEC.
[60] Article 15(5) of NAAEC.
[61] Article 15(6) of NAAEC.
[62] Article 15(7) of NAAEC.
[63] For further discussion of this argument, see for example Durwood Zaelke, Paul Orbuch, and Robert F. Housman (eds.), *Trade and the Environment: Law, Economics, and Policy* (Washington, DC: Island Press, 1993) at Part III: Trade and Environmental Conflicts at 147.
[64] Bradley N. Lewis, "Biting Without Teeth: The Citizen Submission Process and Environmental Protection" (2007) 155 *University of Pennsylvania Law Review* 1229 at 1231.
[65] Gene M. Grossman and Alan B. Krueger, "Environmental Impacts of a North American Free Trade Agreement" in Peter M. Garber (ed.), *The Mexico-US Free Trade Agreement* (Cambridge, MA: MIT Press, 1993), p. 13, pp. 14–15.
[66] Werner Antweiler, Brian R. Copeland, and M. Scott Taylor, "Is Free Trade Good for the Environment" (2001) 91 *American Economic Review* 877 at 878.

of exploitation of natural resources occurs. Although little attention has been given to the scale effects of the NAAEC, they are considered to be much more serious than competitiveness effects.[67] A focus on scale and capacity building is most effective if it is considered before an FTA has come into force. Technique effects, on the other hand, can potentially lead to a decline in adverse environmental effects. This is because free trade may encourage multinational corporations to transfer cleaner technologies to developing countries. Furthermore, if economic liberalization increases income levels, community dynamics of the wealthier area may change, resulting in citizen demands for a cleaner environment.

3.2.2. Nonadversarial in Nature

The fact that the NAAEC does not impose uniform environmental standards, combined with its broader goal of fostering the improvement of the North American environment, makes SEM a cooperative process, at least in theory. The soft-law approach is meant "to enhance government accountability and transparency" by expanding opportunities for public involvement in governance.[68]

The publication of a factual record officially validates community or individual concerns and spotlights nonenforcement issues. As a report of the independent review committee stated, SEM makes it possible for "some 350 million pairs of eyes to alert the Council of any 'race to the bottom' through lax environmental enforcement."[69] With greater public awareness, public pressure may even shame government officials into acting promptly to rectify concerns.

3.2.3. Secretariat Granted a Degree of Independence

The Secretariat's responsibilities include providing technical, administrative, and operational support, along with any other assistance needed by the Council. It has been praised for the rigorous manner in which it reviews submissions and maintains the integrity of the SEM process.[70] In order for the process to work efficiently, however, the Secretariat must have sufficient autonomy to select submissions, investigate allegations, and prepare factual records. As noted in considering other fact-finding models described in Section 2 of this chapter, independence is essential to enabling impartiality.

At the outset, Article 11(4) grants the Secretariat a degree of independence. The Secretariat is managed by the Executive Director and has an international character,

---

[67] Wold, "Evaluating NAFTA" at 204–05.
[68] Markell, "Spotlighting Procedures" at 426.
[69] Independent Review Committee of the NAAEC, "Four-Year Review of the North American Agreement on Environmental Cooperation: Report of the independent review Committee" (June 1998), http://www.cec.org/Storage/60/5224_NAAEC-4-year-review_en.pdf at 5.
[70] Wold, "Evaluating NAFTA" at 228.

which implies independence and neutrality. The autonomy of the Secretariat –
clearly set out in the Agreement – is essential to the functioning of the SEM process.
In practice, however, the autonomy granted to the Secretariat is often overshadowed
by Council's actions. This will be discussed under the disadvantages described in
the following section.

3.2.4. Citizen Advisory Body: JPAC

The inclusion of a Joint Public Advisory Committee to provide the Council with
advice on matters within the scope of the Agreement is unprecedented among
intergovernmental organizations. As yet another avenue for involving public participation, JPAC is composed of fifteen independent citizens (five appointed from each
country) working on a voluntary basis.[71] JPAC has been instrumental in advocating
for the effectiveness and scope of the citizen submission process. As of May 2013, in
more than forty instances JPAC has provided letters, advice, and commentaries to
the Council, of which at least eight are on matters related to SEM.[72] JPAC has raised
concerns about the Council limiting the independence of the Secretariat; neglect-
ing timeliness and transparency in deciding whether to develop a factual record;
giving overbroad, unsubstantiated claims of confidentiality; limiting the scope of
review for factual records; creating a conflict of interest through its decision-making
role; and failing to follow up factual records.

The effectiveness of JPAC is uncertain, given that its numerous complaint submissions have been ignored or pushed aside. JPAC has been adamant about addressing
the Council's lack of timeliness in responding to JPAC advice despite the fact that
methods for improving the Council's responsiveness have been established. In a 2008
letter to JPAC, the CEC Council dismissed the idea of incorporating JPAC's plan to
follow up on resolutions of issues raised in published factual records, claiming that
the review would go beyond the scope of the NAAEC. The Council's consistent and
uncooperative behavior suggests it is opposed to integrating an auditing function to
assess the nature of its actions.

3.3. *Failures of SEM*

The CEC Council's continual practice of sabotaging the SEM process and preventing an independent and meaningful investigation has diminished its accountability
and transparency, as well as meaningful public participation and due process. As a

---

[71] For selection criteria, see Article 16 of NAAEC.
[72] For example: JPAC Advice 08–01, "Submissions on Enforcement Matters: From Lessons Learned
      to Following Up Factual Records" (February 27, 2008); JPAC Advice 03–05: "Limiting the scope of
      factual records and review of the operation of CEC Council Resolution 00–09 related to Articles 14
      and 15 of the North American Agreement on Environmental Cooperation" (December 17, 2003).

result, the CEC has struggled to meet expectations and balance its roles as "regional facilitator, convener, statistician and watchdog."[73]

Citizens have filed a total of eighty-four submissions to date.[74] While the distribution of submissions per year has remained relatively stable, with an average of just under five submissions per year, the fact that there were only two submissions filed in 2012 raises concerns about the viability of the SEM process. There is an apparent lack of public confidence emerging.[75]

Of the eighty-four submissions to the CEC, there have been a disproportionate number of Mexican and Canadian submissions.[76] Only twelve of eighty-four submissions have been from the United States and only one of these resulted in the production of a factual record.[77] The disproportionately small number of U.S. submissions compared to its neighbors has raised further doubts concerning the viability of the SEM process.[78] It is plausible that U.S. citizens may prefer to go through its citizen suit process rather than attempt to surmount the hurdles presented by the CEC. The following points will address SEM failures that may explain its diminishing credibility.

3.3.1. Accessibility: Too Many Hurdles to Pass through the Gate

The SEM process places an unduly cumbersome burden on the submitter to provide sufficient information. The criteria outlined in Article 14(1) for allowing a submission to be considered in the first place are adhered to pedantically by gatekeepers (that is, the Secretariat, and in some instances the Council).[79] If documentary evidence is missing from a submission that can be easily accessed, the Secretariat will not assume responsibility for collecting it. Instead, it will reject the application, dampening interest in the process, frustrating the group or individual, and wasting time and resources.

---

[73] Wold, "Evaluating NAFTA" at 222.
[74] See CEC, Registry of Citizen Submissions: http://www.cec.org/Page.asp?PageID=751&SiteNodeID=250.
[75] See letter from Devon Page, Executive Director of EcoJustice, to Evan Lloyd, Executive Director of the Commission for Environmental Cooperation (January 17, 2011), http://www.ecojustice.ca/media-centre/media-release-files/cec-withdrawal-letter.
[76] According to the CEC Registry, 41 of 84 submissions were from Mexico and 31 of 84 submissions from Canada.
[77] Note that one other U.S. factual record is in the process of being developed (SEM-04–005 (*Coal-fired Power Plants*)).
[78] John H. Knox, "A New Approach to Compliance with International Environmental Law: The Submissions Procedure of the NAFTA Environmental Commission" (2001) 28 *Ecology Law Quarterly* 1 at 105–106.
[79] For example, see: *Ontario Logging* submission (SEM-02–001 (*Ontario Logging*), Submission pursuant to Article 14 (February 4, 2002)); *Alberta Tailings Ponds* determination (SEM-10–002 (*Alberta Tailing Ponds*), Determination pursuant to Article 14(1) (September 3, 2010)).

In the *Ontario Logging* submission, the Council challenged the Secretariat's discretion to determine whether a submission had sufficient information.[80] The submitters claimed that clear-cutting activity destroyed over 85,000 migratory bird nests in central and northern Ontario through the use of a statistical model. Council rejected the estimated value and instead demanded that submitters provide evidence of the number of nests actually destroyed.[81] Essentially, Council was requiring submitters to prepare their own factual record in support of the allegations, even though the Canadian government could have easily found the information itself.[82]

While other fact-finding examples, such as the EU complaint process, assist citizens in making submissions, the SEM process leaves submitters to their own devices. This hands-off approach goes against the very objectives of the NAAEC, particularly to "increase cooperation between the Parties to better conserve, protect, and enhance the environment."[83] Instead, the submitter is expected to conduct research, collect evidence, and submit all relevant documentation. This process is confusing to newcomers and demanding on time, money, and resources.[84] Furthermore, it is difficult for submitters to subscribe to the process if the chance of their submissions being denied at the entry point is high. The presumption should not be that the submitter has the resources for further study; rather, the onus should be on the Secretariat.[85] Considering the high evidentiary burden imposed on the submitter, there is a severe disproportion between controls set at the entry levels and the possible end outcome. The citizen suit process available in the United States is arguably a better option for U.S. complainants when considering that it places a similar burden on the citizen but offers a more enticing outcome than SEM.[86] This may explain why there has only been one factual record prepared for the United States to date.[87]

3.3.2. Council Members Are Not Required to Justify Votes

The Council is not required to justify outcomes of either vote. By failing to provide reasons for deciding whether it approves the development of the factual record and

[80] *Ontario Logging* submission. For Council Resolution, see: SEM 02–001 (*Ontario Logging*), Council Resolution 03–05 pursuant to Article 15 (April 22, 2003).
[81] Wold, "Evaluating NAFTA" at 229. Council noted that the submission was "based in large part on an estimation derived from the application of a descriptive model, and does not provide facts related to cases of asserted failures to enforce environmental law": *Ontario Logging* Council Resolution 03–05.
[82] Garver, "Tooth Decay" at 37.
[83] Article 1(c) of NAAEC.
[84] JPAC Advice 08–01, "Submissions on Enforcement Matters." See also Jane Gardner, "Analysis Articles 14 and 15 of the NAAEC Council's 'Emerging Conflict of Interest'" (April 28, 2004), http://www.cec.org/Storage/56/4831_Discussion-paper-28%20Apr_en.pdf at 6, relaying comments made at a 2003 public meeting: "[I]t should be up to the Secretariat to determine the sufficiency of information; all evidence does not have to be submitted at the start of the process."
[85] Jane Gardner, "Analysis Articles 14 and 15" at 6.
[86] See text at notes 107–118 of this chapter.
[87] SEM-99–002 (*Migratory Birds*), Submission pursuant to Article 14 (November 17, 1999). As noted earlier, one other U.S. factual record is in the process of being developed (*Coal-fired Power Plants*).

whether it chooses to make a document publicly available, the Council undermines transparency and due process.

3.3.3. Council Can Restrict the Scope of the Factual Record

The Council has restricted the scope of factual records on several occasions, impeding the Secretariat's fact-finding role. A 2003 report by the Environmental Law Institute (ELI) discussed four instances in which the Council significantly limited the scope of the factual records. In each case (*BC Mining, BC Logging, Migratory Birds,* and *Oldman River II*), the Secretariat had requested a broad-scoped investigation to consider widespread and systematic breaches by the Party.[88] In significantly narrowing the scope of each investigation, the Council "dramatically changed" the nature of the factual record, effectively excluding important issues from the Secretariat's consideration.[89] In doing so, the Council patently obstructed the public participation and accountability objectives of SEM.

Another example of the Council limiting the scope of an investigation is the *Species at Risk* submission, in which EcoJustice, on behalf of fourteen Canadian and U.S. environmental organizations, made a submission asserting that the Canadian federal government was failing to enforce the Species at Risk Act (SARA)[90] with respect to at least 197 species identified as being at risk in Canada.[91] More than three years after the Secretariat made a recommendation for further investigation, the CEC Council passed a resolution instructing the Secretariat to prepare a factual record for only two of the allegations, and drastically limited the scope to eleven species. The submitters alleged that the species were "cherry picked" to show Canada in its best light. EcoJustice subsequently withdrew its submission on the basis that the Council had: (1) materially delayed resolving whether to produce the factual record; (2) incorrectly limited the scope of the factual record, inconsistent with the NAAEC spirit; and (3) "arbitrarily limited the scope of the factual record in a

---

[88] David L. Markell, "Governance of International Institutions: A Review of the North American Commission for Environmental Cooperation's Citizen Submissions Process" (2005) 30 *North Carolina Journal of International Law and Commercial Regulation* 759 at 774. Examples include: *BC Mining* (SEM-09–004 (*BC Mining*), Council Resolution 01–11 pursuant to Article 15(2) (November 16, 2001)): Council instructed the Secretariat to develop a factual record with regard to only one of the three mines highlighted as examples in the submission; *BC Logging* (SEM-00–004 (*BC Logging*), Council Resolution 01–12 pursuant to Article 15(2) (November 16, 2001)): Council limited factual record to two alleged violations in the Sooke watershed (rather than public/private lands throughout BC); *Migratory Birds* (SEM-99–002 (*Migratory Birds*), Council Resolution 01–10 pursuant to Article 15(2) (November 16, 2001)): Council limited scope of factual record to two specific cases identified as examples in the submission; *Oldman River II* (SEM-97–006 (*Oldman River II*), Council Resolution 01–08 pursuant to Article 15(2) (November 16, 2001)): Council limited scope to Sunpine Forest Products Access Road (rather than broader area).

[89] Markell, "Governance of International Institutions," at 775.

[90] *Species at Risk Act,* SC 2002, c 29.

[91] SEM-06–055 (*Species at Risk*), Submission pursuant to Article 14 (October 6, 2006).

manner designed to frustrate objective evaluation of Canada's failure to enforce the SARA."[92] Since the controversy, EcoJustice, formerly a main submitter, has refused to engage in the SEM process.

3.3.4. Council Has Delayed Voting

The Council has been notorious for delaying votes on factual record recommendations and the publication of factual records. The recent 2012 Guidelines,[93] which resulted from the SEM Modernization Taskforce, have set a sixty-day time frame for voting on the preparation of factual records and a sixty-day time frame for voting on their publication.[94]

Prior to the implementation of the recent Guidelines, the JPAC Lessons Learned report urged the CEC to reduce total wait time to a two-year maximum for reviewing submissions, preparing factual records, and authorizing their release.[95] The recommendation was of no avail: the average length of time it has taken the CEC to release factual records is approximately five tears and five months (see Table 2.1 note), a time period that effectively makes any anticipated record "stale and irrelevant."[96] Such delays have inhibited public enthusiasm for participating in the enforcement of domestic environmental laws.[97] As the legal maxim goes: justice delayed is justice denied. Recent agreements on public participation in international forums, such as the Almaty Guidelines, have emphasized the importance of reasonable time frames for ensuring due process.[98] Following the New Guidelines, the critical next step is to observe subsequent determinations, responses, and votes to determine whether the revised deadlines will result in changed and improved behavior.

3.3.5. Citizen Has No Role after Initial Submission

Although SEM empowers citizens to challenge failures in enforcing environmental laws, once the assertions are submitted, the citizen has no role in the investigation. As discussed, citizens are a valuable resource to the CEC and can provide much

[92] Letter from Devon Page.
[93] Commission for Environmental Cooperation, Guidelines for Submissions on Enforcement Matters under Articles 14 and 15 of the North American Agreement on Environmental Cooperation (Montreal: Commission for Environmental Cooperation, 2013).
[94] Articles 15(2) and 15(7) of NAAEC.
[95] Joint Public Advisory Committee, "Lessons Learned: Citizen Submissions under Articles 14 and 15 of the North American Agreement on Environmental Cooperation: Final Report to the Council of the Commission for Environmental Cooperation" (June 6, 2001), http://www.cec.org/Storage/40/3253-rep11-e-final_EN.PDF.
[96] Letter from Devon Page. The letter continued: "The Submitters consider the Council's delay particularly egregious given that the submission contemplates Canada's failure to enforce a protective law for endangered species defined as 'facing imminent extirpation or extinction.'"
[97] Letter from Devon Page.
[98] Article 35 of Almaty Guidelines.

TABLE 2.1. *Duration to Produce SEM Factual Records*

Factual Record	Country	Date Submission Received by CEC*	Date Factual Record Released*	Duration: Submission to Factual Record
ALCA-Iztapalapa II				
SEM-03–004	Mexico	17 June 2003	2 June 2008	5 years
Aquanova				
SEM-98–006	Mexico	20 October 1998	23 June 2003	4 years, 7 months
BC Hydro				
SEM-97–001	Canada	2 April 1997	12 June 2000	3 years, 2 months
BC Logging				
SEM-00–004	Canada	15 March 2000	11 August 2003	3 years, 5 months
BC Mining				
SEM-98–004	Canada	29 June 1998	12 August 2003	5 years, 2 months
Cozumel				
SEM-96–001	Mexico	17 January 1996	25 October 1997	1 year, 9 months
Lake Chapala II				
SEM-03–003	Mexico	23 May 2003	23 January 2013	9 years, 8 months
Metales y Derivados				
SEM-98–007	Mexico	23 October 1998	11 February 2002	3 years, 4 months
Migratory Birds				
SEM-99–002	United States	19 November 1999	24 April 2003	3 years, 5 months
Molymex II				
SEM-00–005	Mexico	6 April 2000	8 October 2004	4 years, 6 months
Montreal Technoparc				
SEM-03–005	Canada	14 August 2003	24 June 2008	4 years, 10 months
Oldman River II				
SEM-97–006	Canada	4 October 1997	11 August 2003	5 years, 10 months
Ontario Logging				
SEM-02–001	Canada	6 February 2002	5 February 2007	5 years
Ontario Logging II				
SEM-04–006	Canada	12 October 2004	5 February 2007	2 years, 4 months
Pulp and Paper				
SEM-02–003	Canada	8 May 2002	5 February 2007	4 years, 9 months
Quebec Automobiles				
SEM-04–007	Canada	3 November 2004	6 December 2012	8 years, 1 month
Río Magdalena				
SEM-97–002	Mexico	15 March 1997	11 December 2003	6 years, 9 months
Tarahumara				
SEM-00–006	Mexico	9 June 2000	9 January 2006	5 years, 7 months
			Average	4 years, 10 months*

* The average increased to 5 years and 5 months as a result of release of four factual records after compilation of Table 2.1. See SEM-04-005, SEM-05-003, SEM-06-003, SEM-006-004. Dates were compiled from factual records found at http://www.cec.org/Page.asp?PageID=924&SiteNodeID=543.

information during the course of an investigation. As a cooperative process, SEM should increase meaningful public participation in the exchange of documents.[99] In the EU complaint process, for example, the Commission keeps complainants abreast of decisions made at each step of the process through written correspondence. Complainants have a chance to clarify the grounds for their complaints at any point during the procedure. Upon closure of the case, the Commission describes the reasons for which the case is being closed, but invites the complainant to submit comments within a four-week period.[100] The EU practice validates its higher regard for the citizen's role in aiding enforcement.

3.3.6. The Secretariat Is Not Actually Independent

The relationship between the Secretariat and the Council is not defined in detail in the Agreement. While the Executive Director appoints and supervises the Secretariat, the Council has a general responsibility "to oversee the Secretariat."[101] Furthermore, the Council may "reject any appointment that does not meet the general standards."[102]

There is an inherent conflict of interest in the organizational structure of the CEC bodies, whereby the Council can ultimately undermine the Secretariat's discretion and reject a submission, narrow the scope, delay voting, or decide not to require a factual record to be prepared – all without justification. Even when it acts within its role, however, the Council's discretion to determine essentially whether a Party should be investigated for not enforcing its laws creates a conflict and diminishes procedural justice. The Council is unable to differentiate when it is acting as the Council and when members are acting individually as Parties.[103] An excerpt from a letter by the Canadian National Advisory Committee to the Canadian government further expands on this issue:

> The Article 14 and 15 process puts the members of the Council in a difficult position. . . . They must vote on whether to support an investigation into the actions of their own country or a fellow Council member's country. This creates the potential for an apparent conflict of interest. It was the reason the Honourable Sergio Marchi, Canada's former Minister of the Environment, recommended at the 1996 Council meeting in a public statement that he wanted to make a practice

---

[99] David L. Markell, "Understanding Citizen Perspectives on Government Decision Making Processes as a Way to Improve the Administrative State" (2006) 36 *Environmental Law* 651 at 683.

[100] EC, Commission communication [2002] at 8.

[101] Article 10.1(c) of NAAEC.

[102] Article 11.3 of NAAEC.

[103] Gardner, "Analysis Articles 14 and 15" at 6. See also Katia Opalka, "Inside the NAFTA Environmental Commission" (2010) White Paper [unpublished]. The author, a former CEC legal officer, offers a counterargument: "we all wear different hats, and if someone can be trusted to be an environment minister, then surely that person can do a good job at leading the implementation of the NAFTA environmental agreement."

of unanimously accepting recommendations by the Secretariat for factual records because to do so otherwise could create the appearance of a conflict of interest, or create animosity among parties.[104]

The Council's lack of respect for the limits on its authority has weakened the intended credibility of the process.[105] To reestablish SEM's integrity, the Council must adhere to the self-imposed limits of the NAAEC and respect the roles of the Secretariat and citizens. Thus, the Secretariat must be sufficiently independent from the CEC Council and its findings should be strictly impartial.

3.3.7. No Standard Establishing the Grounds for Voting Against Publishing Factual Record

As mentioned while discussing SEM successes, the official validation of community concerns by a published factual record presents the opportunity for prompt government officials to take appropriate substantive remedial steps. However, with no standard establishing the grounds upon which the Council can vote against publishing a factual record, the advantage that may justify the time and effort by submitters to initiate the investigation dissipates. It is inappropriate to have the Council, composed of the actual Parties who are the subjects of the factual records, decide whether or not to publish a document that may discredit the Parties' effectiveness in enforcing domestic laws.

In the *Metales y Derivados* submission, the Mexican government from the outset insisted that its response to the submission be kept confidential.[106] That designation prevented the public release of the response in its entirety, holding it under a veil of secrecy. In the end, the Council unanimously approved the public release of the final factual record, but did not draw conclusions as to whether Mexico had failed to enforce its laws.

3.3.8. Dead End Outcome

The final outcome of SEM offers only a factual record – the NAAEC does not require governments to address issues raised in the record or to take preventative action. The SEM process offers neither remedies nor sanctions. An accurate factual record would ideally expose a Party's mistakes and prompt it to reexamine and adjust regulatory and enforcement policies to prevent future occurrences. The SEM process may also

[104] Letter from Canadian NAC on the NAAEC to the Canadian government (March 13, 2003), cited in Gardner, "Analysis Articles 14 and 15."
[105] Markell, "Governance of International Institutions" at 762. See also Chris Tollefson, "Games Without Frontiers: Investor Claims and Citizen Submissions Under the NAFTA Regime" (2002) 27 *Yale Journal of International Law* 141 at 180–182.
[106] SEM-98–007 (*Metales y Derivados*), Submission pursuant to Article 14 (October 23, 1998).

create a subsidiary bilateral effect among NAAEC parties seeking compliance to use diplomatic or other intergovernmental channels to induce behavioral changes.[107] Thus, the process is meant not only to facilitate self-corrective action, but also to encourage compliance by external pressures. However, the publication of factual records has the potential to serve as a trigger for the bilateral dispute settlement process outlined in Part V of the NAAEC.

The value of a spotlight function is questionable given the way the Council has eroded the credibility of the process.[108] This may be partially due to the refusal of member governments to treat citizen submissions as a cooperative process. Governments are reluctant to discredit themselves. As a result, the SEM process fails to accomplish the underlying triple goal of being an effective tool that facilitates public participation, supports government transparency, and promotes the effective enforcement of environmental law in North America.[109] In some cases (for example, *Metales y Derivados* and *Montreal Technoparc*) the government has been willfully negligent in preparing a meaningful response to the occurrences. The examples highlight the futility of effecting any substantive change to the underlying regulatory enforcement policies.

The *Metales y Derivados* case concerns a former battery and lead waste recycling facility located in Mexico that was shut down and subsequently abandoned by its U.S. owner. Complaints by neighboring community members about Metales' pervasive environmental violations were ignored for years. By the time Mexican environmental officials finally instituted criminal enforcement proceedings, the owner had fled across the border to the United States, leaving behind thousands of tons of waste and contaminated soil containing lead and other heavy metals. The CEC factual record, released in 2002, concluded that the site created a "grave risk to human health."[110] The factual record declined to make conclusions as to whether Mexico had failed to effectively enforce its environmental law. Despite the recognized health risks, on-site toxic waste remained uncontrolled until 2008.[111] While the *Metales* case promoted transparency in the SEM process, "it failed to bring about substantive environmental improvements, enhance enforcement activities, and improve public participation in environmental governance."[112]

Montreal Technoparc involves a former historic industrial and municipal landfill owned by the city of Montreal.[113] The submitters presented water quality results

[107] Tseming Yang, "The Effectiveness of the NAFTA Environmental Side Agreement's Citizen Submission Process: A Case Study of Metales y Derivados" (2005) 76 *University of Colorado Law Review* 443 at 457.
[108] Wold, "Evaluating NAFTA" at 232.
[109] Commission for Environmental Cooperation, *Guidelines for Submissions* (2013).
[110] SEM-98-007 (*Metales y Derivados*), Factual Record pursuant to Article 15 (February 7, 2002).
[111] Community signed a landmark cleanup agreement in 2004 with the Mexican government. The cleanup was completed in 2008 with independent community monitoring.
[112] Yang, "Effectiveness" at 445.
[113] SEM-03-005 (*Montreal Technoparc*), Submission pursuant to Article 14 (August 18, 2003).

showing levels of toxic pollutants discharged from the site to be excessively above Canadian Water Quality Guidelines (for example, polychlorinated biphenyl [PCB] levels in the discharges were about 8.5 million times the guideline value of 0.001 μg/L for PCBs).[114] The submitters asserted that the Technoparc discharges were an offense under section 36(3) of the federal Fisheries Act,[115] which Canada had failed to enforce.[116] The factual record was released after almost five years, revealing that the site had over 4 million liters of diesel fuel mixed in the water and that water toxicity levels exceeded the lethal limits for fish. Despite the presence of exceedingly high levels of contaminants, uncertainties surrounding ownership made it difficult to trace the source and impose corrective measures. The *Montreal Technoparc* factual record resulted in no changes to Canada's enforcement of the Fisheries Act and the Water Quality Guidelines. The city of Montreal has since created a project to impose monitoring and remediation of the site.[117]

Factual records highlight the failure to enforce environmental laws against polluters and to take citizen complaints seriously. If the official response to proven violations is as minimal as it has been in *Metales* and *Montreal Technoparc*, the CEC submission process cannot be expected to produce substantive changes to the underlying regulatory enforcement policies. The process lacks a follow-through capacity to monitor a NAFTA Party's compliance with its environmental laws following the publication of a factual record concluding that there has been clear noncompliance.[118] In following its mandate, the CEC must consider ways to facilitate public awareness of postrecord actions by the relevant Party.

4. BEYOND NAAEC: APPLYING THE PROCESS TO CAFTA–DR

The CAFTA–DR agreement, signed in 2004, includes an environmental chapter that established the Central American Commission for Environment and Development (CCAD).[119] Similar to the CEC, the CCAD includes an Environmental Affairs Council (EAC or the "Council") and Secretariat. The goal of the environmental program is to identify specific areas of environmental concern and develop work programs that are not necessarily linked to trade liberalization. Project funding is available through the joint U.S. Enviromental Protection Agency (EPA)–United

---

[114] Montreal Technoparc Submission.

[115] *Fisheries Act*, RSC 1985, c F-14.

[116] Section 36(3) of the *Fisheries Act* prohibits the deposit of a deleterious substance into water frequented by fish or in any place under any conditions where the substance may enter such water.

[117] See the project online: http://ville.montreal.qc.ca/portal/page?_pageid=7237,74839583&_dad=portal &_schema=PORTAL.

[118] David L. Markell, "The Commission for Environmental Cooperation's Citizen Submission Process" (2000) 12 *Georgetown International Environmental Law Review* 545 at 571. See also JPAC Advice 08–01, "Submissions on Enforcement Matters."

[119] Chapter 17 of CAFTA–DR. Note that some authors have pointed to this as an important change, but it is of more symbolic importance as there is no legal difference.

States Agency for International Development (USAID) program on environmental capacity building.[120]

There are some proactive tools that have been implemented. For example, Chapter 17 requires Parties to create rosters of environmental experts to serve when disputes arise. In addition, U.S. agencies give technical assistance and training to officials in the region acting in the roles of environmental law enforcement and implementation. These aids are perhaps warranted given the greater disparity in economic resources among member states of CAFTA–DR, which likely translates to a lack of uniformity in environmental regulations.[121] Still, CAFTA–DR's initiatives have been regarded as insufficient in dealing with scale issues of trade.[122] The CAFTA–DR SEM process allows even less independence for the Secretariat and eliminates the role of the JPAC.[123] The changes reflect an effort by the United States to eliminate independent assessment of trade-environmental issues.[124]

4.1. *Changes Made to SEM: Examining Chapter 17*

The CAFTA–DR Submission on Environmental Law Enforcement Matters is modeled after NAAEC's SEM process.[125] The entities involved in CAFTA–DR's citizen submission process are the Secretariat for Enforcement Matters, the Environmental Cooperation Commission, and the EAC. The Secretariat is a public entity that receives and considers public submissions, and is responsible for preparing factual records regarding such submissions. The Council is composed of cabinet-level officials who meet annually to oversee the implementation of Chapter 17.

Submission requirements are almost identical to those of the NAAEC SEM, with the only major difference being that the submission for CAFTA–DR is not limited to persons or organizations residing or established in the territory of a Party.[126]

---

[120] Capacity building for CAFTA–DR includes: strengthening institutional and legal frameworks, increasing compliance and implementation of Multilateral Environmental Agreements, creating an air pollution monitoring network, improving wastewater regulations, improving solid waste management, establishing safe chemical management, and implementing pollution release and transfer registries.

[121] Nathaniel Hemmerick Hunt, "One Step Forward, Two Steps Back: The Central American Free Trade Agreement and the Environment" (2007) 35 *Georgia Journal of International and Comparative Law* 545 at 550 (see also Hunt's discussion about Central American countries not having appropriate regulations, making enforcement impossible).

[122] Wold, "Evaluating NAFTA" at 243.

[123] Article 17.7 of CAFTA–DR.

[124] Wold, "Evaluating NAFTA" at 206.

[125] As in NAAEC's SEM, the main objective of Chapter 17 is the promotion of environmental protection through the effective implementation of each Party's domestic laws; each Party retains the ability to establish its own level of domestic environmental protection. Article 17.13 defines environmental law as "any statute or regulation of a Party, or provision thereof, the primary purpose of which is the protection of the environment, or the prevention of a danger to human, animal, or plant life or health" through control of pollutants and toxic chemicals and conservation of wild flora and fauna.

[126] The CAFTA–DR process requires that every submission meet six criteria listed in Chapter 17.7.2 of CAFTA–DR: it must (a) be in writing in English or Spanish; (b) identify the person or entity

U.S. submitters are excluded from the process because of their access to the NAAEC SEM; however, a person of a Party other than the United States may file a submission alleging that the United States is failing to effectively enforce its environmental laws.[127]

The Secretariat uses a similar set of guidelines in determining whether a submission merits requesting a response from the Party, but does so "taking into account guidance regarding those goals provided by the Council and the Environmental Cooperation Commission established under the ECA [Environmental Cooperation Agreement]."[128] This suggests an attempt by the Secretariat to reduce the accessibility issues discussed in Part Three. The Secretariat has published a document with further clarifications as to submission requirements;[129] however, it is unclear if other steps have been taken to assist submitters.

If the Secretariat decides that a factual record is warranted, it notifies the Council in writing. A vote by one member of Council is all that is required to create a factual record; if Council takes no action, the submission will be dismissed.[130] The Secretariat can use all submitted information along with external sources to prepare the factual record. Once submitted, the Council has sixty days to vote on publishing the final factual record. One vote is sufficient for publication. If there are no votes within sixty days, the Secretariat will notify the Council and submitter and the factual record will not be published.

4.1.1. No Advisory Committee

The CAFTA–DR SEM excludes the role of an advisory committee such as the NAAEC JPAC as a means for citizens to advise the Council on a voluntary basis. JPAC been persistent in voicing concerns about substantive and procedural action by the NAAEC Council and, at the very least, has facilitated debate by scrutinizing decisions and advocating for the public.[131] Removing that role suggests member states' reluctance to hear public inquiry and advice.

---

making the submission; (c) provide sufficient evidence on which the submission may be based; (d) promote enforcement of the law rather than harassing industry; (e) show that the matter has been communicated to the Party and any responses from the Party; and (f) filed by a person of a Party.
[127] Chapter 17.7.3 of CAFTA–DR.
[128] Chapter 17.7.4(b) of CAFTA–DR.
[129] Environmental Affairs Council, Working Procedures for Submissions on Environmental Law Enforcement Matters under Chapter 17 of the Dominican Republic-Central America-United States Free Trade Agreement. See online: http://www.saa-sem.org/index.php?option=com_content&view=Article&id=52&Itemid=208&lang=us.
[130] Chapter 17.8.2 of CAFTA–DR.
[131] Ten-Year Review and Assessment Committee, "Ten Years of North American Environmental Cooperation: Report of the Ten-Year Review and Assessment Committee to the Council of the Commission for Environmental Cooperation" (June 15, 2004), http://www.cec.org/Storage/79/7287_TRAC-Report2004_en.pdf at 35 (the report considers JPAC's dual role as watchdog to the Parties and a strategic partner to the Council as creating both "philosophical and operational challenges").

4.1.2. Curtailed Independence of Secretariat

The Secretariat is a much smaller entity under CAFTA–DR, consisting of a General Coordinator and a Technical Assistant, both appointed by the Council for a two-year term. The Secretariat is "under the sole direction and supervision of the Council" and its mandate is limited to reviewing citizen submissions alleging failures to enforce environmental law effectively and in the preparation of factual records.[132] The Secretariat cannot prepare reports without first obtaining government approval, and the Council maintains authority to decide whether and in what way to create factual records, changing the scope, making final edits, and deciding to publish results. The decision to curtail the independence of the Secretariat may be due to the United States' skepticism of the discretion given to the CEC Secretariat.[133]

4.1.3. Establishment of Environment Affairs Council

CAFTA–DR's Council has developed an Environmental Cooperation Agreement (ECA) to elaborate on the role of environmental matters and to create processes for Parties to establish joint work programs to address conservation and other matters.[134] The work plans specifically allocate resources to harmonizing environmental regulations, implementing and enforcing environmental law, and strengthening environmental impact assessments. The ECA budget is about U.S. $19 million, but fluctuates according to availability of resources.[135] Regardless, it is much higher than the CEC's budget of $3 million ($9 million on a triennial basis), which has remained constant since the inception of NAAEC despite market fluctuations.[136]

4.1.4. No Supermajority Requirement

Although the CAFTA–DR Council retains authority for deciding whether the Secretariat should prepare a factual record and whether the factual record should be made public, there is no longer a requirement of a supermajority of votes. Instead, a single Party's vote can instruct the Secretariat to proceed on either action.

---

[132] Agreement Establishing a Secretariat for Environmental Matters under the Dominican Republic–Central America–United States Free Trade Agreement (July 27, 2006), http://www.oas.org/dsd/Tool-kit/Documentos/MOduleII/CAFTA%20-%20Agreement%20to%20Establish%20Secretariat.pdf, Article 3.

[133] Wold, "Evaluating NAFTA" at 239.

[134] Chapter 17.5.2 of CAFTA–DR.

[135] Agreement among the Governments of Costa Rica, the Dominican Republic, El Salvador, Guatemala, Honduras, Nicaragua, and the United States of America on Environmental Cooperation (February 18, 2005), http://www.oas.org/dsd/Tool-kit/Documentos/MOduleII/CAFTA%20Environmental%20Cooperation%20Agreement.pdf, Article VIII.1: "All cooperative activities under the Agreement shall be subject to the availability of funds and of human and other resources, and to the applicable laws and regulations of the appropriate Parties."

[136] Opalka, "NAFTA Environmental Commission."

4.1.5. Recommendations by Council

The Council must consider the final factual record and provide recommendations "as appropriate" to the ECA "including recommendations related to the further development of the Party's mechanisms for monitoring its environmental enforcement."[137] Providing advice for improving enforcement gives the process more value and a greater chance of attaining Chapter 17's objectives. Nevertheless, the words "as appropriate" suggest a voluntary basis.

4.1.6. Deadlines for Preparation of Factual Record

The working plan establishes a deadline of 180 days for the Secretariat to complete a factual record, though this deadline may be extended for another 180 days.[138] The 2012 NAAEC Guidelines also establish a 180-day deadline for the Secretariat to complete a factual record, but without the option of extension. The implementation of the deadlines has been effective for CAFTA–DR, but is yet to be proven effective for NAAEC since the Guidelines were only published in July 2012.[139]

4.1.7. Failure to Fix Flaws of NAAEC

By allowing the Council even greater authority and diminishing the independence of the Secretariat, the CAFTA–DR SEM process fails to resolve some of the NAAEC's oajor institutional flaws. There are no checks on Council's power to override decisions of the Secretariat. As in the NAAEC process, there are no provisions preventing Council from deciding that submissions do not meet requirements or for narrowing the scope of investigation. Furthermore, there are no deadlines imposed on Council to act on recommendations of the Secretariat.

4.1.8. CAFTA–DR SEM in Practice

Since 2007, thirty-two submissions have been filed: one or two filed per year between 2007 and 2009, ten filed in 2010, eight filed in 2011, two in 2012, five in 2013, two in 2014, and one in 2015. Many of the submissions in 2010–2011 were suspended and resubmitted, inflating the apparent number of submissions. The process has resulted in the publication of only three factual records: *Marine Turtles Dominican Republic* (CAALA/o7/oo1), *Residencial Villa Veranda El Salvador* (CAALA/10/oo1), and

---

[137] Chapter 17.8.8 of CAFTA–DR.
[138] Environmental Affairs Council, Working Procedures for Submissions on Environmental Law Enforcement Matters under Chapter 17 of the Dominican Republic-Central America-United States Free Trade Agreement, at 16.1. See http://www.saa-sem.org/images/stories/pdf/base_legal/ Procedimientos%20de%20Trabajo%20SECRETAR%C3%8DA%20DE%20ASUNTOS%20AMBIEN TALES%20CAFTA-DR%20Versi%C3%B3n%20Bilingue.pdf.
[139] See Commission for Environmental Cooperation, *Guidelines for Submissions* (2013).

West Bay Roatan Honduras (CAALA/11/004).[140] In *Laguna del Tigre Fonpetrol Guatemala* (CAALA/10/006), the Secretariat suspended the preparation of a factual record after it received additional information from the Party.[141] In an even stranger scenario, the Secretariat recommended the preparation of a factual record in *Omoa Honduras* (CAALA/10/007), and shortly after issued a correction, annulling its recommendation to prepare a factual record.[142] It is unclear whether the political context of repressive regimes and lower environmental standards among CAFTA–DR member states has suppressed the use of the citizen submission process.[143]

5. RECOMMENDATIONS

As previously stated, in response to the concerns raised that the SEM process takes too long, is scope-limiting, and leads to a dead-end result, an SEM modernization taskforce was created in 2011 that implemented time goals and New Guidelines in July 2012. While it is too soon to judge the effectiveness of the implemented changes, the JPAC has remained skeptical that the New Guidelines will continue to raise or reinforce barriers. Under the 2012 Guidelines, the SEM process should now take approximately two years from start to end, and the Secretariat must explain any delays.[144] While there is an exhaustion requirement of private remedies for petitioners,[145] the JPAC has expressed concern that the CEC does not do enough to help the public "understand how the SEM process or other avenues of relief may help them to resolve environmental issues."[146] Finally, the 2012 Guidelines establish a more nuanced approach to dealing with pending judicial or administrative proceedings, precluding the Council from stopping the process in its tracks once it

---

[140] CAALA/07/001 (*Marine Turtles Dominican Republic*), Factual Record (January 2011). See online: http://www.saa-sem.org/expedientes/factual_record_caala_07_001.pdf.CAALA/10/001. (*Residencial Villa Veranda El Salvador*), Factual Record (August 2012). See online: http://www.saa-sem .org/expedientes/factual_record_caala_10_001_english.pdf.CAALA/11/004. (*West Bay Roatan*), Factual Record (October 2013). See online: http://www.saa-sem.org/expedientes/factural_record_caala_11_004_ west_bay_roatan.pdf. See also CAALA/13/004 (*Cuyamel II Honduras* (preparation of factual record recommended, 4/16/15).

[141] CAALA/10/006 (*Laguna del Tigre Fonpetrol Guatemala*), Informe al Consejo de Asuntos Ambientales CAFTA-DR (June 2012). See online: http://www.saa-sem.org/docs/suspension_10_006.pdf.

[142] CAALA/10/007 (*Omoa Honduras*), Errata (March 2011). See online: http://www.saa-sem.org/index .php?option=com_content&view=article&id=88%3Acaala10007-omoa-n&catid=40%3A2010&Item id=198&lang=us.

[143] Wold, "Evaluating NAFTA" at 237 (the author suggests that the history of violence and repressive regimes in the context of CAFTA–DR "is likely to stifle the use of the citizen submission process," making it adversarial rather than cooperative).

[144] In addition, electronic submissions are not accepted. See Commission for Environmental Cooperation, *Guidelines for Submissions* (2012).

[145] Commission for Environmental Cooperation, *Guidelines for Submissions* (2013) at 5.6, 7.3, 7.5.

[146] CEC, Joint Pub. Advisory Comm., Advice to Council No: 12–01: Re: SEM Task Force Proposals for Changes to the Guidelines for Submissions on Enforcement Matters (SEM) (May 23, 2012). http://www.cec.org/Storage/137/16238_JPAC_Advice_12–01-Final-en.pdf.

has begun.[147] While the revisions address many concerns, such as temporal delays, they leave some problems unresolved, such as scoping, and present new exhaustive requirements for petitioners.[148] The critical next step is to observe whether the revisions will result in effective changes and improved behavior. What follows are further recommendations for improvement.

5.1. *Eliminate Government Role in Factual Record Determination*

Government actors, regardless of whether they are acting for the Council or the Party, should not be granted the power to determine whether a factual record is warranted for the conflict of interest reasons already noted. A focus on enforcement failures has unfortunately put governments on the defensive, making them more inclined to undermine the process in order to avoid embarrassment. Instead, a separate and independent group should make an impartial decision based on the preliminary information presented. The WB Inspection Panel provides a good model for a process that sets up an independent fact finder dependent on the Board of Executive Directors to determine whether an investigation is warranted. The subject of the investigation (WB management) can comment on the proceedings but cannot vote. This type of organizational structure would increase both actual legitimacy and the public's perception of procedural justice.

5.2. *Role of Secretariat as Fact Finder and Issue Resolver*

In order for the Secretariat to be given the requisite autonomy to perform its functions freely, the Council must renounce its control and ability to manipulate the SEM process. In addition, the Secretariat should be given a greater role to be able to help resolve the issues discovered during the fact-finding process. The focus should be on resolving environmental enforcement problems, rather than assigning blame. The Secretariat's role should mirror that of the Commission in the EU Complaint Process, working in partnership with the complainant to find solutions. The CEC Secretariat should also adopt the practice of helping the complainant gather documentation for the submission.

---

[147] Commission for Environmental Cooperation, *Guidelines for Submissions* (2013) at 9.6.

[148] For example, Guideline 5.6(c) states that the Secretariat is guided by whether or not "the Submitter" pursued private remedies. This addition makes the process even more burdensome on the Submitter. As it stands, if documentary evidence is missing from a submission that can be easily accessed, the Secretariat will not assume responsibility in collecting it. Instead, it will reject the application, dampening interest in the process, frustrating the group or individual, and wasting time and resources. The presumption should not be that the Submitter has sufficient resources for further study or to pursue private remedies. It will be difficult for complainants to subscribe to the process if the chance of their submissions being denied at entry point is high.

5.3. *Increase Participation of Public throughout Process*

SEM should be regarded as a collaborative process among the submitters and the CEC units. Citizens have much to offer the SEM process as advocates for environmental protection with a wealth of knowledge. CEC should make use of this untapped resource by involving citizens throughout the investigation. As in the EU complaint process, submitters should be notified at each stage and allowed to comment and provide supplemental information to help the fact finder. At the end of the investigation, the submitter should be involved in creating and implementing recommendations with the objective of preventing future recurrences of nonenforcement.

5.4. *Official Recommendations Based on Factual Record*

Recognizing that environmental harm is usually irreversible, preventing future damage requires not only that past enforcement failures are documented in factual records, but that steps for action are developed and implemented as well. The ICAO safety audit provides a good example of proactive reporting complete with recommendations and action deadlines. NAAEC member states should also be subject to such obligations and unresolved concerns should be immediately revealed to other Parties and to the public through the website. If noncompliance with recommendations is due to a lack of resources (whether technical, financial, or human), the Secretariat, Council, and public participants should mimic the ICAO's practice of developing initiatives to assist the member states with their compliance, making the process more cooperative rather than adversarial. Initiatives may include training enforcers, allocating funds, and introducing new technologies to track progress of an issue and communicate it to the public.

By adding official recommendations and including a follow-up of enforcement, the SEM process is likely to make citizens more confident about the effectiveness of the process and accordingly more willing to use it. Follow-up instruments can include auditing, such as on-site assessments and monitoring reports. These mechanisms will help add value to the SEM process and reach the objectives of the NAAEC.

5.5. *Increase Funding*

The suggestions made up until this point cannot be fulfilled without sufficient funding. The contrast of trade-induced growth of NAFTA and the environmental focus introduced by the NAAEC should have translated into a more substantial environmental budget to compensate for the degradation brought on by industrialization. A U.S. $9 million budget for an intergovernmental body is clearly insufficient. CAFTA–DR's much larger budget has allowed it to create rosters of environmental experts, provide technical assistance and training, and create work programs focusing on specific areas of environmental concern.[149] Furthermore, realistic funding will secure more efficient resources and reduce lengthy delays in the preparation of factual records. Ensuring adequate funding will make it less possible for financial pressure to detract support from the CEC's commitment to strengthening and expanding participation of the North American public in the protection of its shared environment.

5.6. *Depoliticize the Process*

Countless academic articles have been written on improving NAAEC's SEM process. JPAC has not been silent about its recommendations either. Accordingly, one can confidently assume that the CEC knows what steps to take if it wants to restore public confidence in the process and ensure that NAAEC objectives are met. Nevertheless, the Council continues to overstep its role, delay the process, and obstruct citizen complaints from being investigated.

The greatest threat to the effective use of SEM is the politicization of the process. The signatory governments have treated SEM as adversarial rather than cooperative, sabotaging the process at every opportunity.[150]

There is also the issue of disproportionality of submissions. Mexico, the main original target of the Agreement, has as expected had the most submissions. Canada had apparently not anticipated placing a close second on the noncompliance leaderboard and having its environmental practices scrutinized. It has consequently acted defensively by refusing to provide information, placing temporal limitations on allegations, and delaying the SEM process.[151] The disproportionately small number of U.S. submissions compared to those of its neighbors likely also has mounted tensions and made the process more adversarial.[152]

The SEM process must be rethought to deflect government hostility and should instead be recognized as a collaborative process for enhancing government outcomes. There is much to be learned from the EU and ICAO processes, but without the political will to act cooperatively, fixing structural flaws will be futile.

It is disconcerting that the SEM process has been duplicated almost verbatim to form the environmental chapters of other FTAs, as seen with CAFTA–DR, given its ineffectiveness in reaching its objectives. Such practice suggests that the United States is not actually interested in maintaining environmental protection laws, but rather that the inclusion of an environmental chapter provides an appearance of legitimacy. The fact that a broken process with inherent structural flaws and lack

---

[149] See CAFTA-DR web site for current programs in place, http://www.caftadr-environment.org.
[150] Wold, "Evaluating NAFTA" at 205.
[151] SEM-02–003 (Pulp and Paper), Submission pursuant to Article 14 (May 6, 2002).
[152] Knox, "A New Approach" at 105–106.

of political will is essentially being copied and pasted into other FTAs diminishes credibility of the more recent FTAs, the accountability of the relevant governments, and the public's right to be heard. Unless major changes are made immediately, the history of the structural eroding of the process "indicates that it may not be the most appropriate model for future FTAs."[153]

If FTA signatories cannot commit to upholding environmental values and subscribing to implement both their cooperative and enforcement mandates, an adversarial approach should be taken instead. Proponents of hard law argue that it offers greater potential for results, since it is more durable, more predictable, and usually more transparent.[154] At the very least, implementing an adversarial process with harmonized standards and sanctions for noncompliance would increase the accountability of member states and prevent them from shying away from enforcing laws.

6. CONCLUSION

The NAAEC SEM process, later implemented in CAFTA–DR and other FTAs, stands out as an innovative tool for both affected stakeholders and member states. The mechanism seeks to engage a range of communities and incorporate the previously marginalized concerns of civil society.[155] It furthermore has the potential to remove geopolitical borders, and instead view North America as a series of interconnected terrestrial and marine ecosystems.[156] Unfortunately, the process has yet to live up to its expectations in practice due to a combination of structural flaws and a lack of political will.

The principles of global administrative law imply that NAFTA's signatory governments should be accountable for providing citizens with a duty to be the object of review and allow citizens a proper forum in which to voice their concerns about environmental noncompliance. Despite well-documented breaches, SEM submitters have become increasingly frustrated with the procedural flaws and numerous obstacles presented by the process. The submission on Montreal's Technoparc is a case in point: the factual record confirms the breach, yet the situation persists eight years later.

Among the Council, there is widespread resistance to facilitating the SEM process as a cooperative and collaborative exercise between citizens and the CEC. Members of government have resented the limitations imposed by SEM on trade, and have been embarrassed by findings of policy violations and nonenforcement.

---

[153] Wold, "Evaluating NAFTA" at 232.
[154] Kirton and Trebilcock, *Hard Choices, Soft Law*, p. 350.
[155] French and Kirkham, "Complaint and Grievance Mechanisms," pp. 61–62.
[156] Opalka, "NAFTA Environmental Commission."

There is ample room to develop further accountability mechanisms to ensure fundamental principles of procedural due process are satisfied. An impartial, independent party should properly investigate legitimate concerns of citizens, and environmental protection laws should be enforced accordingly. An independent submission review process, timely factual records that conclude by describing action to be taken (with timelines), and subsequent monitoring and follow-up reporting by the CEC can help rectify some of the issues. If the NAAEC fails to implement effective changes such as those outlined in this paper, this important experiment in reconciling free trade and environmental protection will be viewed as a politically convenient way to avoid actually accounting for environmental noncompliance. Unless the Council is able to depoliticize its involvement and rethink the preferred approach, SEM should be regarded as an inadequate tool for future FTAs.

REFERENCES

International Agreements

Almaty Guidelines on Promoting the Application of the Principles of the Aarhus Convention in International Forums, May 27, 2005, Decision II/4 of MOP, doc. ECE/MP.PP/2005/2/Add.5

Central America-Dominican Republic-United States Free Trade Agreement, August 5, 2004, ch. 17.

Commission of the European Communities, "Commission Communication to the European Parliament and the European Ombudsman on Relations with the Complainant in Respect of Infringements of Community Law," Brussels, March 20, 2002, 141 at 4.

Convention on International Civil Aviation, December 7, 1944, 15 UNTS 295. 2000 revision is available online: <www.icao.int/icaonet/dcs/1300.html>.

EC Treaty (Treaty of Rome), European (Economic) Community, March 25, 1957. (Entered into force January 1, 1958.)

European Code of Good Administrative Behaviour, European Communities, September 6, 2001.

International Bank for Reconstruction and Development, IBRD 93–10, Resolution No. IDA 96–6, "The Inspection Panel," September 22, 1993, online: <www.inspectionpanel.org>.

North American Agreement on Environmental Cooperation, September 14, 1993, 32 I.L.M. 1480. (Entered into force January 1, 1994.)

Session of the ICAO Council. Review of the Memorandum of Understanding (MOU) relating to the conduct of safety oversight audits under the comprehensive systems approach, 179th Sess., 12th Mtg., Subject No. 14.5: Safety Oversight, ICAO Doc. C-MIN 179/12 (2006) §49.

Vienna Convention on the Law of Treaties, May 22, 1969, 155 U.N.T.S. 331.

World Bank Inspection Panel, *Operating Procedures* (1994). *Online:* WB <http://www.worldbank.org/inspectionpanel>.

Secondary Material: Monographs

Buergenthal, Thomas. *Law-Making in the International Civil Aviation Organization.* Syracuse, NY: Syracuse University Press. 1969.

Craig, Paul P. *EU Administrative Law.* New York: Oxford University Press. 2006.

Dupuy, Pierre-Marie and Luisa Vierucci. *NGO's in International Law, Efficiency in Flexibility?* Cheltenham, UK: Edward Elgar Publishing Limited. 2008.

French, Duncan and Matthew Saul. *International Law and Dispute Settlement*. Portland, OR: Hart Publishing. 2010.

Grossman, Gene, and Alan Krueger. "Environmental Impacts of a North American Free Trade Agreement," in *The US – Mexico Free Trade Agreement*. Ed. Peter Garber. Cambridge, MA: MIT Press. 1993.

Henderson, Conway W. *Understanding International Law*. West Sussex, UK: Wiley-Blackwell Publication. 2010.

Kirton, John J. and Michael J. Trebilcock. *Hard Choices, Soft Law: Voluntary Standards in Global Trade, Environment and Social Governance*. Aldershot, England: Ashgate Publishing. 2004.

Flood, Colleen and Lorne Sossin. *Administrative Law in Context: A New Casebook*. Emond-Montgomery Publishing. 2008.

Secondary Material: Articles

Antweiler, Werner, et al. "Is Free Trade Good for the Environment." (2001) 91 4 *The American Economic Review* 877.

Bridgeman, Natalie. "World Bank Reform in the 'Post-Policy' Era." (2001) 13 *Geo Int'l Envtl L Rev* 1013.

Casey-Lefkowitz, Susan, William J. Futrell, Jay Austin, and Susan Bass. "The Evolving Role of Citizens in Environmental Enforcement." Paper delivered at the Fourth International Conference on Environmental Compliance and Enforcement in Chiang Mai, Thailand, April 22, 1996, unpublished.

Currie, Duncan. "United States Unilateralism and the Kyoto Protocol, CTBT and ABM Treaties: The Implications Under International Law." Greenpeace publication (*R. v Bush*), June 9, 2001. <http://archive.greenpeace.org/climate/climatecountdown/legalsum.htm>.

Clark, Dana L. "The World Bank and Human Rights: The Need for Greater Accountability." (2002) 15 *Harv Hum Rts J* 218.

DiMento, Joseph F. & Pamela M. Doughman. "Soft Teeth in the Back of the Mouth: the NAFTA Environmental Side Agreement Implemented." (1998) 10 *Geo Int'l Envtl L Rev* 651, 658–81.

Garver, Geoff. "Tooth Decay: Examining NAFTA's 'Environmental Teeth.'" (2008) 25(3) *The Environmental Forum* 34–39.

Goldschmidt, Mark R. "The Role of Transparency and Public Participation in International Environmental Agreements: The North American Agreement on Environmental Cooperation." (2001–2002) 29 *Environmental Affairs L Rev* 343–398.

Harlow, Carol. "Global Administrative Law: The Quest for Principles and Values." (2006) 17(1) *Eur J Int Law* 187–214.

Knox, John H. "A New Approach to Compliance with International Environmental Law: The Submissions Procedure of the NAFTA Environmental Commission." (2001) 28 *Ecology LQ*.

Knox, John H. "Separated at Birth: The North American Agreements on Labor and the Environment." (2004) 26 *Loy LA Int'l & Comp LJ* at 359–387.

Lewis, Bradley N. "Biting Without Teeth: The Citizen Submission Process and Environmental Protection." (2007) 155 *U Penn LR* 1229–1268.

Markell, David L. "Governance of International Institutions: A Review of North American Commission for Environmental Cooperation's Citizen Submissions Process." (2005) 30 *NCJ Int'l L & Com Reg* at 759–794.

Markell, David L. "The Role of Spotlighting Procedures in Promoting Citizen Participation, Transparency, and Accountability." (2010) 45 *Wake Forest L Rev* 425–467.

Markell, David L. and Tom R. Tyler. "Using Empirical Research to Design Government Citizen Participation Process: A Case Study of Citizens' Roles in Environmental Compliance and Enforcement." (2008) 57 *Kan L Rev* 1.

Markell, David L. "The Commission for Environmental Cooperation's Citizen Submission Process." (1999) 12 *Geo Int'l Envtl L Rev* at 545–574.

Markell, David L. "Understanding Citizen Perspectives on Government Decision Makin Processes as a Way to Improve the Administrative State." (2006) 36 *Environmental Law* 683.

Martinsen, Dorte Sindbjerg and Torben Beck Jørgensen. "Accountability as a Differentiated Value in Supranational Governance." (2010) 40(6) *The American Review of Public Administration* 742–760.

Wold, Chris. "Evaluating NAFTA and the Commission for Environmental Cooperation: Lessons for Integrating Trade and Environment in Free Trade Agreements." (2008) 28 *St Louis U Pub L Rev* 201–252.

Yang, Tseming. "The Effectiveness of the NAFTA Environmental Side Agreement's Citizen Submission Process: A Cast Study of Metales y Derivados." (2005) 76(2) *U Colo L Rev* 443–502.

Speeches

Annan, S-G Kofi. "Address to the World Summit on Sustainable Development." Secretary-General address delivered at the World Summit on Sustainable Development, Johannesburg, September 2, 2002, unpublished, <http://www.un.org/events/wssd/statements/sgE.htm>.

Clinton, Presidential Candidate Gov. Bill "Address." Address delivered at University of North Carolina, October 4, 1992, unpublished.

Graham, Hon. Bill. "Notes For An Address by the Honourable Bill Graham, Minister of Foreign Affairs." Address delivered at the United Nations Conference on Disarmament, Geneva, March 19, 2002, unpublished, <http://webapps.dfait-maeci.gc.ca/minpub/Publication.asp?publication_id=380961>.

Other

CEC, Joint Pub. Advisory Comm., Advice to Council No: 08–01: Submissions on Enforcement Matters: From Lessons Learned to Following Up Factual Records (Feb. 27, 2008). Available at: http://www.cec.org/files/pdf/ABOUTUS/JPACAdvice-0801_SEM_en.pdf.

CEC, Joint Pub. Advisory Comm., Advice to Council No: 12–01: Re: SEM Task Force Proposals for Changes to the Guidelines for Submissions on Enforcement Matters (SEM) (May 23, 2012). *Available at:* http://www.cec.org/Storage/137/16238_JPAC_Advice_12–01-Final-en.pdf.

Four-Year review of the North American Agreement on Environmental Cooperation: Report of the independent Review Committee (June 1998), p. 5.

Gardner, Jane. "Emerging Conflict of Interest" JPAC Discussion Paper: Analysis Articles 14 and 15 of the NAAEC Council's (April 28, 2004), unpublished.

Opalka, Katia. "Inside the NAFTA Environmental Commission." (2010) White Paper, unpublished.

Commission for Environmental Cooperation. *Guidelines for Submissions on Enforcement Matters under Articles 14 and 15 of the North American Agreement on Environmental Cooperation*. Montreal: Commission for Environmental Cooperation. 2013. http://www.cec.org/Storage/152/17779_SEM_booklet_PDF_en_final.pdf.

Environmental Affairs Council. *Working Procedures for Submissions on Environmental Law Enforcement Matters under Chapter 17 of the Dominican Republic-Central America-United States Free Trade Agreement*. Environmental Affairs Council, 2010. http://www.saa-sem .org/index.php?option=com_content&view=article&id=52&Itemid=208&lang=us.

3

Choosing the Right Whistle

The Development of the Concept of Environmental Law under the Citizen Submissions Process

Paolo Solano[1]

1. INTRODUCTION

This chapter discusses the development of the concept of environmental law under the Submissions on Enforcement Matters (SEM) process of the North American Agreement on Environmental Cooperation (NAAEC). After almost twenty years in force, the fairness of the SEM process is still criticized by a variety of authors and its effectiveness remains the consistent subject of debate. This once-novel mechanism, however, has now gained the maturity to merit a review of its history. Such a review, I suggest, reveals that SEM may require a tune-up to bring it in line with current approaches to public participation.

The need for reevaluation was recently underscored by an attempted modernization process undertaken by the Parties to the NAAEC. After over a year of discussions that did ultimately result in changes to the administration of the SEM process, the only substantial progress was the establishment of timelines for every step of the complaint process. This chapter assesses a key aspect when considering a submission, namely whether the provisions invoked by the submitter constitute "environmental law" as it appears in Article 45(2) of the NAAEC. This is a pivotal concept that has been interpreted expansively by the Secretariat of the Commission for Environmental Cooperation (CEC) in numerous determinations. However, some of the responses filed by the NAAEC Parties have contended that it should instead be interpreted narrowly and allow few laws and regulations to proceed for further consideration following the initial screening process.

[1] The author is a legal officer at the Secretariat of the Commission for Environmental Cooperation CEC. Information in this paper is in the public domain; it does not necessarily reflect the opinion of the Parties to the North American Agreement on Environmental Cooperation or the CEC Secretariat and may not be construed as the policy of the CEC Secretariat with respect to any particular submission. I wish to thank the student editor, Mark Phillips, whose incisive comments have greatly improved the quality of this paper. I remain responsible for any errors or omissions. The views expressed in this chapter are mine alone.

For the purposes of determining whether a legal provision is admissible for analysis under the SEM process, the term "environmental law" is defined in Article 45(2) of the NAAEC.[2] One of the first tasks of the Secretariat of the CEC on receiving a submission is to determine whether the laws cited therein fit in the category of "environmental law," which the NAAEC explicitly creates.

This category encompasses statutes or regulations applicable to Canada, the United States, or Mexico that, in their entirety or according to their specific provisions, have as their primary purpose the protection of the environment or the prevention of a danger to human life or health.

Over the course of the Secretariat's past 160 determinations made under Articles 14 and 15,[3] it has often addressed the question of whether a provision qualifies as "environmental law" and thus merits further review under the submissions process. The definition of environmental law has been explored in detail by the Secretariat and its interpretation has been disputed on multiple occasions by the Party responding to a submission. The meaning of "environmental law" has also been disputed by the CEC Council[4] – which is also charged with overseeing the Secretariat – through Council resolutions, a practice that has drawn criticism for encroaching on the Secretariat's authority. Indeed, the role of the Secretariat is to process citizen submissions "as well as the parameters of that authority are set out in the Agreement" and "[i]n no instance is the exercise of this authority stated to be subject to the approval of the Council."[5] The extensive practice of interfering with the functions specifically assigned to the CEC Secretariat's processing of submissions has thus "undermined the legitimacy of its results."[6] Without addressing the extent to which such behavior conforms to international law, this paper aims to contrast divergent positions on the circumstances that allow a provision of a statute or regulation to qualify under NAAEC's Article 45(2).

After twenty years of the NAAEC's existence, a review and reexamination of significant moments in the implementation of this treaty – the most important

---

[2] North American Agreement on Environmental Cooperation, September 14, 1993, in force January 1, 1994, (1993) 32 ILM 1480; Can. TS 1994 No. 3.

[3] Figure according to author's database, last updated September 15, 2013, based on information available in the registry of the CEC.

[4] The CEC Council is composed of the Canadian, Mexican, and U.S. ministers of the environment or their equivalent.

[5] Donald M. McRae, "Inclusion in a factual record of information developed by independent experts and the autonomy of the secretariat of the CEC in the Article 14 and 15 process" (2008) 26 *North American Environmental Law and Policy* 1 at 22, http://permanent.access.gpo.gov/lps117824/CCE_26_english.pdf.

[6] Lucas Gifuni, "The CEC Council's discretionary decision making under Article 15 of the NAAEC and its legality at international law," June 14, 2011, paper submitted to the Meeting of the North American Consortium on Legal Education (NACLE) Comparative Environmental Law Research Project, p. 9, http://nacle.org/sites/default/files/Washington%20Workshop%20-%20Lucas%20Gifuni%20Paper%20-%20NAAEC%20art%2014-15%20-%202011-10%5B1%5D.pdf.

regional agreement toward protection of shared environments in North America – is now due. These years have seen the accumulation of a body of precedent and of doctrine addressing the concept of environmental law, which may further inform and guide the administration of citizen submissions. My intent is to contribute an insider's perspective to the ongoing debate on possible future revision by the NAAEC Parties.

The Secretariat's attempts to further develop the scope of qualifying provisions under NAAEC Article 45(2) are in constant conflict with the Council's views on the proper meaning of environmental law. Recently a Council resolution prevented the Secretariat from considering standards issued by the Ministry of Health aimed at protecting human health through the control of air emissions.[7] Responses from Mexico, the concerned Party responding to submissions, have maintained that environmental crimes under the Federal Criminal Code of Mexico do not meet the definition of environmental law;[8] that provisions of the Mexican Biosafety Law on Genetically Modified Organisms are not admissible;[9] that water law and more precisely water rights allocation laws cannot be considered for a factual investigation;[10] and that only laws enforced by environmental authorities may be considered environmental law.[11]

There follows an account of a practice undertaken by the Council and the NAAEC Parties that may lead to practical interference with key, independent functions specifically designated to be carried out by the CEC Secretariat. While this is an overview from the perspective of an active CEC staff member, this chapter focuses its analysis on submissions related to alleged failures to effectively enforce environmental law on the part of the government of Mexico. However, one should keep in mind that even if the Secretariat is not bound by the principle of stare decisis,[12] it does interpret NAAEC in accordance with Article 31(1) of the 1969 Vienna Convention on the Law of Treaties,[13] and as "suggested by general canons of statutory

---

[7] SEM-05–003 (*Environmental Pollution in Hermosillo II*), Council resolution 12–04 pursuant to Article 15(1) (June 15, 2012).

[8] EM-06–003 (*Ex Hacienda El Hospital II*) and SEM-06–004 (*Ex Hacienda El Hospital III*), Response pursuant to Article 14(3) (January 10, 2007), unofficial translation, p. 58.

[9] SEM-09–001 (*Transgenic Maize in Chihuahua*), Response pursuant to Article 14(3), (May 3, 2010), unofficial translation, p. 25.

[10] SEM-03–003 (*Lake Chapala II*), Council resolution 08–01 pursuant to Article 15(1) (May 30, 2008).

[11] Supra note 9.

[12] SEM-97–001 (*BC Hydro*), Notification pursuant to Article 15(1) (April 27, 1998), p. 8.

[13] Vienna Convention on the Law of Treaties, May 23, 1969, in force January 27, 1980, (1969) 8 ILM 679; 1155 UNTS 331. The convention is in force in Canada and Mexico, but although the United States signed it on April 24, 1970, it has not ratified it. U.S. Courts have considered the Vienna Convention as a general codification of customary international law. See e.g. *Fujitsu Ltd.* v. *Federal Express Co.*, 247 F 3d 423 (2nd Cir. 2001): "[W]e rely upon the Vienna Convention here 'as an authoritative guide to the customary international law of treaties.' Because the United States 'recognizes the Vienna Convention as a codification of customary international law,' it 'considers the Vienna Convention in dealing with day-to-day treaty problems'" [citations omitted].

interpretation."[14] For that reason, even if a determination refers to a specific Party, the outcome affects the others in future situations.

2. INTERPRETATION OF NAAEC

That the CEC Secretariat is part of an international organization and that it is competent to interpret NAAEC was established in *Drilling Waste in Cunduacán*.[15] The Council and the Parties to NAAEC do not play a direct role in determining whether a submission is admissible under Article 14(1) of NAAEC.[16] However, in response to a Joint Public Advisory Committee review of NAAEC, the Council stated that "countries that are parties to international agreements are solely competent to interpret such instruments."[17] More recently, the Council underscored its "capacity as governing body" in the new Guidelines for Submissions on Enforcement Matters under Articles 14 and 15 of the North American Agreement on Environmental Cooperation (Guidelines).[18] Clearly departing from Council Resolution 00–09, which stated the Parties were the "sole" entities authorized to interpret NAAEC, the Secretariat argued that it is "neither a court nor a dispute resolution body" but that in order to carry out its functions under Articles 14 and 15 "it must necessarily be able to interpret" NAAEC provisions applicable to the SEM process[19] and based this conclusion on the doctrine of effectiveness.[20] Even though the Secretariat has systematically interpreted NAAEC Articles 14 and 15 (and related provisions), a question that has not been fully resolved is the extent to which the Secretariat may interpret domestic laws when considering whether a provision meets the NAAEC definition. Although the Parties have never specifically raised an objection, the Secretariat often refers to national jurisprudence in its determination process in order to avoid arriving at undesirable results. For example, the Secretariat has had to verify whether a zoning program was considered a "law" by domestic courts[21] and

[14] SEM-97–001 (April 27, 1998) Notification, p. 8, n. 9.
[15] SEM-07–005 (*Drilling Waste in Cunduacán*), Determination pursuant to Article 14(3) (April 8, 2009), p. 7.
[16] NAAEC, Article 10(1)(c), (d).
[17] Council resolution 00–09 Matters related to Articles 14 and 15 of the Agreement (June 13, 2000), http://cec.org/Page.asp?PageID=122&ContentID=1143.
[18] Commission for Environmental Cooperation, Guidelines for Submissions on Enforcement Matters under Articles 14 and 15 of the North American Agreement on Environmental Cooperation, February 2013, p. 5, http://cec.org/Storage.asp?StorageID=10838.
[19] SEM-07–005 (*Drilling Waste in Cunduacán*), Determination pursuant to Article 14(3) (April 8, 2009), p. 7.
[20] See "Eritrea-Ethiopia boundary commission: Statement by the commission," November 27, 2006, in UNSC, 2006, UN Doc. S/2006/992, pp. 9–34, p. 14.
[21] The Secretariat determination that a zoning program is not law according to Mexican courts can be consulted at: SEM-09–001 (*Wetlands in Manzanillo*), Determination pursuant to Article 14(1) (October 9, 2009), p. 9. On this submission, the Secretariat confirmed that it must consider domestic courts in considering this question in SEM-09–001 (*Wetlands in Manzanillo*), Notification pursuant to Article 15(1) (August 19, 2013), p. 18.

the extent to which constitutional provisions may be considered environmental law from an enforcement perspective.

The Secretariat has also stated that the SEM process is not intended to serve as a standard setting review mechanism,[22] nor to open a legislative forum.[23] It has clarified that Articles 14 and 15 do not create a judicial review process and that in practice it is incapable of causing interference or creating duplication of efforts because it is not a court or tribunal, and so parallel and conflicting outcomes (*lis pendens*) cannot arise.[24]

In light of this conceptual understanding one must ask whether the Secretariat should then consider domestic legal interpretation when considering whether legislation, or a provision thereof, qualifies for SEM review. On this point, the Inter-American Court of Human Rights prefers to consider "domestic legal regimes," as the concept of "laws" must not be "divorced from the context of the legal system which gives meaning to the term 'laws' and affects its application."[25] A similar approach has been adopted by the European Court of Human Rights, which concluded that "the word 'law' in the expression 'prescribed by law' covers not only statute but also unwritten law."[26] Thus, the Secretariat clearly must interpret both NAAEC and domestic law to fulfil its function in processing citizen submissions, which requires the consideration of environmental laws within their greater context.

3. EXPANDING AND RESTRICTING THE NAAEC'S CONCEPT OF ENVIRONMENTAL LAW

NAAEC Article 45(2) provides a detailed definition of the meaning of environmental law. The definition includes the words "statute or regulation, or provision thereof," meaning that in theory a submission may assert failure to effectively enforce a whole law and not only a single provision, as in the *Magdalena River* and *Polar Bears*

---

[22] "[T]he submission focuses on the enactment of a law . . . [y]et the enactment of a law does not . . . provide facts upon which to charge a failure to enforce" SEM-95-002 (*Logging Rider*), Determination pursuant to Article 14(1) (December 8, 1995), p 4. The "standard setting" notion was later developed in SEM-98-003 (*Great Lakes*), Determination pursuant to Article 14(1) (December 14, 1998), p. 5.

[23] "Article 14 was not intended to create an alternate forum for legislative debate." SEM-95-001 (*Spotted Owl*), Determination pursuant to Article 14(1) (September 21, 1995), p. 5. The notion that the CEC Secretariat is not a court was further elaborated in *Minera San Xavier*.

[24] "[T]he Secretariat . . . does not issue any judgments or take any actions which have legal effect. [Thus] Secretariat Determinations are not binding on the Parties or submitters, and Factual Records are not rulings or judicial opinions on an asserted failure of effective enforcement of environmental law" (SEM-07-001 (*Minera San Xavier*) Determination pursuant to Article 15(1) (July 15, 2009), p. 13).

[25] The Word "Laws" in Article 30 of the American Convention on Human Rights (Uruguay) (1986), Advisory Opinion OC-6/86, Inter.-Am. Ct HR (Ser. A) No. 6, para. 20.

[26] *The Sunday Times v. United Kingdom* [1979] ECHR 1; (1980) 2 EHRR 245, para. 47.

submissions.[27] Most importantly, it embraces the concept of "primary purpose" that includes the protection of the environment and human life or health. NAAEC Article 45(2) lists three practices that constitute environmental law:

(i) the prevention, abatement or control of the release, discharge, or emission of pollutants or environmental contaminants,
(ii) the control of environmentally hazardous or toxic chemicals, substances, materials and wastes . . . or
(iii) the protection of wild flora or fauna, including endangered species, their habitat, and specially protected natural areas.

From these three categories the NAAEC excludes "worker safety or health" and "exploitation . . . of natural resources" (including "subsistence or aboriginal harvesting"). Finally, NAAEC includes an important interpretation guideline, which holds that "the primary purpose of a particular statutory or regulatory provision . . . shall be determined by reference to [the] primary purpose [of the provision in question], rather than to the primary purpose of the statute or regulation of which it is part."[28]

The first time the Secretariat addressed how the term "environmental law" should be interpreted was in *Biodiversity*.[29] In this matter, the Secretariat laid an important building block for future submissions in considering "that the term 'environmental law' should be interpreted expansively,"[30] and that a restrictive view would not be consistent with NAAEC objectives. Subsequent determinations adopted this expansive approach.[31]

In contrast, the Parties to NAAEC have consistently argued for a more limited understanding of the meaning of environmental law. In *Transgenic Maize in Chihuahua*, for example, Mexico alleged that consideration of the provisions under Article 45(2) must be under restrictive criteria.[32] This position has been repeatedly adopted in other responses to citizen submissions, notably in *Wetlands in*

[27] SEM-97–002 (*Magdalena River*), Notification pursuant to Article 15(1) (February 5, 2002), p. 9; SEM-11–003 (*Protection of Polar Bears*), Submission pursuant to Article 14(1) (November 30, 2011).
[28] SEM-95–002 (December 8, 1995) Determination, p. 3.
[29] See SEM-97–005 (*Biodiversity*), Submission pursuant to Article 14(1) (December 16, 1997).
[30] SEM-97–005 (*Biodiversity*), Determination pursuant to Article 14(1) (May 26, 1998), pp. 2–3. This does not mean, however, that adopting such a view released the Secretariat from the obligation to provide reasons when considering future submissions.
[31] While it is desirable that administrative decision making is conducted in a fair and efficient manner and that reasons be provided during the submissions process, it is also evident that "the universal requirement of reasons may also strengthen an unwelcome trend towards the excessive legalization of much of the administrative process. For instance, writing formal reasons for a decision, especially with an eye to the construction of a body of precedent, often elevates to the level of 'agency law' a question that is essentially factual or judgmental, and particular to the case being decided. The proliferation of agency law . . . may . . . divert the agency's focus from substantive issues to the interpretation of earlier decisions." J. M. Evans, H. N. Janisch, and David J. Mullan, *Administrative Law*, 4th edition (Toronto: Emond Montgomery, 1995), p. 482.
[32] SEM-09–001 (*Transgenic Maize in Chihuahua*), Response pursuant to Article 14(3) (May 3, 2010), unofficial translation, pp. 2–3.

Manzanillo[33] and *Los Remedios National Park II*, where Mexico underscored that assessment of provisions should follow a narrow approach.[34]

In the following I give an account of the Secretariat's practice in considering the concept of environmental law. This account includes consideration of a broad spectrum of legal instruments, including treaties, constitutional provisions, criminal law, water law, and biodiversity law. This chapter concludes by suggesting guiding parameters grounded in the principle of effectiveness and by considering whether returning to the doctrine of implied powers may further improve the work of the Secretariat.

3.1. *Consideration of the Term "Laws or Regulations"*

The Secretariat has already addressed whether the definition in question extends to treaties entered into by independent states under international law and whether their provisions may be considered under the process in Articles 14 and 15. In *Biodiversity*, the submitters asserted that Canada was failing to effectively enforce the Convention on Biological Diversity and alleged that the ratification instrument was a legally binding "regulation."[35] In its determination, the Secretariat affirmed "a critical distinction between 'international' and 'domestic' legal obligations."[36] The issue came back before the CEC almost ten years later when a group of NGOs filed the *Devil's Lake* submission[37] and the Secretariat was asked to consider whether provisions of the Treaty Relating to Boundary Waters between the United States and Canada (Boundary Waters Treaty) met the definition of environmental law.[38] In doing so, the Secretariat partially grounded its reasoning on a WTO appellate panel opinion that considered that 'laws or regulations'... refer to... the domestic legal system of a WTO Member."[39]

The Secretariat accepted that matters falling under Articles 14 and 15 may be also fall under other international agreements, insofar as the treaty in question is incorporated into the domestic legal system. Compared to other determinations, *Devil's Lake* addressed this question in detail and concluded that in Canada and

---

[33] "[T]he determination of which provisions constitute environmental law pursuant to the Agreement must be done with special care and with adherence to strict criteria" SEM-09–002 (*Wetlands in Manzanillo*), Government of Mexico response pursuant to Article 14(3), unofficial translation, (October 11, 2010), pp. 3–4.

[34] "In Mexico's perspective, analysis of provisions constituting environmental law as per defined in the Agreement, must be conducted with special care and adopting a restrictive criteria," my own translation of SEM-09–003 (*Los Remedios National Park II*), Government of Mexico response pursuant to Article 14(3) (December 20, 2010), p. 3.

[35] SEM-97–005 (*Biodiversity*), Submission pursuant to Article 14(1) (December 16, 1997), p. 1.

[36] SEM-97–005 (*Biodiversity*), Determination pursuant to Article 14(1) (May 26, 1998), p. 4.

[37] SEM-06–002 (*Devil's Lake*), Submission pursuant to Article 14(1) (March 24, 2006).

[38] Ibid., pp. 7–8.

[39] WTO, Mexico: Tax Measures on Soft Drinks and Other Beverages: Report of the Appellate Body, WTO Doc. WT/DS308/AB/R (2006), p. 28.

the United States, self-executing treaties or those implemented through legislation may be considered under Articles 14 and 15. The Secretariat then reached the conclusion that the Boundary Waters Treaty is not a "law or regulation" because the United States has not adopted legislation implementing any of its provisions. It also found that when it had been considered by courts, they found that it is self-executing neither through directly enforceable provisions nor by a federal action for noncompliance.[40] All that being said, there is evidence that even if the United States has the ability to choose the means by which to implement its international obligations – in this case, a court judgment – it is expected to do so within reasonable time.[41] This particular question has not reached the CEC, but it would not be surprising were the Secretariat to choose to maintain consistency with these prior determinations.

The Secretariat addressed a similar question when processing a submission asserting failure to effectively enforce an international treaty adopted by Mexico, and thus considered whether a treaty incorporated into the Mexican law becomes domestic as well as the functioning of the incorporation system. The Mexican courts have found that, pursuant to Article 133 of the Mexican Constitution,[42] international treaties are the supreme law of the land[43] and are incorporated into the domestic legal regime through this Mexican constitutional mechanism.[44] Based on the method by which international treaties are adopted within the Mexican legal system, the Secretariat reached the conclusion that an international treaty incorporated into domestic law

[40] The determination quotes the following comment by John Knox: "I think most observers would say that is going to be a long shot for Manitoba to convince a Federal Court that the 1909 Treaty obligation [under Article IV] is self-executing, and get an injunction against North Dakota. . . . There have been relatively few efforts to argue that the 1909 Treaty is self-executing in U.S. law, and they have failed when brought by a private individual" (SEM-06–002, p. 5, n. 20). See also John Knox, "Environment: Garrison dam, Columbia river, the IJC, NGOS" (2004) 30 Can.–USLJ 129 at 136–7.

[41] Request for Interpretation of the Judgment of March 31, 2004 in the Case Concerning Avena and Other Mexican Nationals (*Mexico v. United States of America*), [2009] ICJ Rep. 3, p. 18.

[42] "This Constitution, the laws issued by the Congress of the Union and all the Treaties issued in conformity, celebrated and that are celebrated by the President of the Republic, will be the Law Supreme of the Union. Judges from each State will adhere to this Constitution, laws and treaties, notwithstanding the provisions in their contradiction that may exist in the Constitutions and State laws." Article 133 of the Mexican Constitution, as translated in SEM-09-002 (*Wetlands in Manzanillo*), Determination pursuant to Article 14(1) (October 9, 2009), p. 6, n. 29.

[43] See "Tratados internacionales. Son parte integrante de la ley suprema de la unión y se ubican jerárquicamente por encima de las leyes generales, federales y locales. Interpretación del artículo 133 constitucional" ["International Treaties. Integral part of the supreme law of the land and hierarchically above general, federal and local laws. Interpretation of Constitutional Article 133"], in Suprema Corte de Justicia de la Nación, *Semanario Judicial de la Federación y su Gaceta*, vol. XXV, April 2007, pp. 6ff.

[44] See "Tratados internacionales. Incorporados al derecho nacional. Su análisis de inconstitucionalidad comprende el de la norma interna" ["International Treaties. Incorporated to the national law. Its analysis of inconstitutionality also includes the domestic law"], in Suprema Corte de Justicia de la Nación, *Semanario Judicial de la Federación y su Gaceta*, vol. XXVI, July 2007, pp. 2725–2727.

may in effect be considered. Thus in *Wetlands in Manzanillo* the Secretariat concluded that provisions of the Ramsar Convention[45] qualified as environmental law and could be considered by the Secretariat. In its response pursuant to Article 14(3), Mexico expressly conceded that the Ramsar Convention is environmental law, but contended that the convention did not apply to the alleged enforcement matters because the area in question was not designated by Mexico as a Ramsar site under Article 2(1) of the Ramsar Convention.[46] The Secretariat recommended the production of a factual record that ultimately did not include the Ramsar Convention. However, the same treaty was again raised by a submission in *Tourism Development in the Gulf of California* and further consideration is still being given to a revised submission by the Secretariat.[47]

Another relevant case is *Transgenic Maize in Chihuahua*, in which the submitters asserted that Mexico was failing to effectively enforce provisions intended to control, inspect, investigate, and assess risks associated with transgenic maize in Chihuahua, Mexico. Provisions of the Cartagena Protocol[48] were cited by the submitters[49] that require Mexico to provide adequate protection to ensure the safe transfer, handling, and use of living modified organisms in a manner that prevents or reduces the related risks to biological diversity.[50] The Secretariat concluded that the Cartagena Protocol was incorporated into the domestic legal system of Mexico and that it may be considered for further analysis under NAAEC.[51]

Another issue addressed by the Secretariat is whether other instruments whose effects are similar to those of laws can qualify as "environmental law." In one case, citing a Mexican court ruling, the Secretariat determined that a zoning program does not qualify as "law" under NAAEC. While a zoning program is an administrative act that citizens must observe, the Secretariat did not consider such as environmental law. Mexican courts have ruled on the scope of zoning plans, finding that although they provide rules, they do not constitute law in a material sense nor do they exist at

---

[45] Convention on Wetlands of International Importance Especially as Waterfowl Habitat, Ramsar, Iran, February 2, 1971, in force December 21, 1975, 996 UNTS 245 (No. 14583), as modified by the Paris Protocol, December 3, 1982, and the Regina Amendments, April 28, 1987.

[46] Ibid., Article 2(1) establishes that "Each Contracting Party shall designate suitable wetlands within its territory for inclusion in a List of Wetlands. . . . The boundaries of each wetland shall be precisely described and also delimited."

[47] SEM-13–001 (*Tourism Development in the Gulf of California*), Determination pursuant to Article 14(1) (May 24, 2013), p. 10.

[48] Cartagena Protocol on Biosafety to the Convention on Biological Diversity, Montreal, May 15, 2000, in force September 11, 2003, (2000) 39 ILM 1027; 2226 UNTS 208.

[49] The submitters referred to over 90 provisions in six different laws and regulations, while the provisions cited from the Cartagena Protocol included Articles 1, 2, 8, 9, 10, 15, and 16. See SEM-09–001 (*Transgenic Maize in Chihuahua*), Submission pursuant to Article 14(1) (January 26, 2009).

[50] C.f. Cartagena Protocol, Articles 1, 2(2).

[51] SEM-09–001 (*Transgenic Maize in Chihuahua*), Determination pursuant to Article 14(1)(2) (March 3, 2010), p. 8.

the same level of normative hierarchy as law, and rather their existence, application, and enforceability derive entirely from the laws from which they originate.[52]

However, a provision that does not qualify as "law or regulation" may nonetheless be an implementation device. In other words, a product of policymaking that serves as an enforcement tool, when poorly implemented, may lead to a factual investigation under Article 15(1). For example, without specifically addressing the question of whether Total Maximum Daily Loads (TMDLs) qualified as "environmental law," the Secretariat determined that failure to adopt TMDLs could be subject for further review in a factual investigation[53] which upon implementation, "become part of the federal law of water pollution control."[54] TMDLs are essentially a calculation of the maximum amount of a pollutant a water body can receive,[55] and "[a]lthough a TMDL itself imposes no enforceable requirements; it can serve as an assessment and planning tool that local, state, and federal authorities can use to impose controls or pollution reduction targets for the purpose of achieving the applicable water quality standards."[56] More recently, in *Wetlands in Manzanillo*, the Secretariat reached the conclusion that although an agreement between state and federal governments did not qualify as law, it served as an implementation device of state laws, enforcement of which may be addressed in a factual record.[57] In a similar way, the Secretariat concluded in a case related to Alberta oil sands that an agreement between the federal government and the province of Alberta to enforce the Canadian Fisheries Act[58] does not constitute environmental law,[59] but rather a mechanism "intended to help coordinate and streamline both Canada's and Alberta's regulatory activities relating to the protection of the environment."[60]

---

[52] "Programas de desarrollo urbano emitidos conforme a la Ley de Desarrollo Urbano del Estado de Puebla, son normas de character general supeditadas a la ley que les da origen (legislación vigente en 2001)" ["Urban development programs issued under the *Puebla* State Urban Development Act are general rules subordinated to the law from which they originate"], in Suprema Corte de Justicia de la Nación, *Semanario Judicial de la Federación y su Gaceta*, vol. XXI, May 2005, p. 1511 (Administrative Collegiate Court for the Sixth Circuit).

[53] "Because TMDLs addressing air sources of mercury have been developed for numerous waterways in several states despite the complexities involved in doing so, and because EPA has not exercised its statutory authority to establish TMDLs for mercury in any of the ten states of concern, the Secretariat concludes that the response leaves open central questions that the submission raises regarding development of mercury TMDLs in the states for which no judicial proceeding relating to development of mercury TMDLs is pending." SEM-04–005 (*Coal-fired Power Plants*), Notification pursuant to Article 15(1) (December 5, 2005), p. 26 [footnotes omitted].

[54] Ibid., p. 22 quoting Arkansas, 503 U.S. at 110 n. 13.

[55] U.S. Environmental Protection Agency, *Developing Effective Nonpoint Source TMDLs: An Evaluation of the TMDL Development Process* (2007), p. ES-1, http://epa.gov/evaluate/tmdfinal.pdf.

[56] SEM-98–003 (*Great Lakes*), United States of America response pursuant to Article 14(3) (December 3, 1999), p. 48.

[57] SEM-09–001 (August 13, 2010) Notification, p. 11.

[58] RSC 1985, c. F-14.

[59] SEM-10–002 (*Alberta Tailings* Ponds), Determination pursuant to Article 14(1)(2) (December 11, 2013), p. 9.

[60] Ibid.

Thus one must be careful when considering "laws or regulations" because these vary depending on the legal system to which they belong: they may comprise any law-like element at any of a number of levels in the hierarchy – from constitutions to standards – and take on a different meaning when considered as implementation devices rather than laws.

3.2. *Who Shall Be the Authority to Enforce the Law?*

The submissions process has led to unusual responses from the Party in question in attempts to impose additional requirements restricting the way a particular provision must be interpreted and whether it meets the NAAEC definition. In Mexico's response to the Secretariat in *Transgenic Maize in Chihuahua*, for example, it argued that according to the domestic legal system, enforcement of the Biosafety Law's provisions[61] falls to agencies with a different scope of authority than the central environmental ministry.[62] The Secretariat was to proceed to review Mexican provisions requiring inspection of genetically modified maize, for example, whose enforcement fell under the purview of customs authorities, and thus Mexico maintained that these did not qualify as environmental law.[63]

Similarly, in *Sumidero Canyon II* Mexico maintained that provisions allocating authority to enforce Article 170 of the Ley General del Equilbrio Ecologico y la Proteccion al Ambiente (LGEEPA) fall within the category of Article 45(1), thus automatically excluding them from consideration in the SEM process. Mexico maintained that a list of possible emergency measures that can be carried out in the face of high-risk or environmentally damaging activities does not properly fall within the SEM's jurisdiction and must be automatically excluded. From Mexico's perspective, this means that when a provision allows for discretionary enforcement, although this may constitute environmental law, it cannot be brought before the SEM. Thus, implementing a provision that gives an authority powers to, say, temporarily shut down a facility, always confers a certain degree of discretion. However, what will remain unclear is whether a given instance in which the measure was carried out was effective or not, and it is at that point that the exercise of discretion should be scrutinized. At the time this paper was drafted, the Secretariat was still developing its conclusions on how it will consider the issue of discretion in *Sumidero Canyon II* and whether to recommend a factual record.[64]

---

[61] Ley de Bioseguridad de Organismos Genéticamente Modificados [Genetically Modified Organisms Act], DOF March 18, 2005.

[62] SEM-09–001 (May 3, 2010) Government of Mexico Response, Unofficial translation, p. 25.

[63] See Ley de Bioseguridad de Organismos Genéticamente Modificados, Article 18, paras. I, II, IV, V, provisions which are enforced by the Mexican customs authority (*Secretaría de Hacienda y Crédito Público*) because they prevent imports of genetically modified seeds.

[64] For updates related to the *Sumidero Canyon II* submission, see http://cec.org/Page.asp?PageID=2001&ContentID=25135.

3.3. *Constitutional Laws*

The Secretariat does not uniformly maintain its expansive view of what is included in environmental law. One counterexample has been its consideration of guiding principles such as those commonly found in constitutional law, an approach that can be tracked back to 2005[65] when the Secretariat first adopted a positivist approach and argued that the right to a healthy environment affirmed in Article 6 of the Mexican Constitution might be quite challenging to enforce or even to analyze in terms of effective enforcement because it includes no specific provisions that translate its general principles into concrete action.[66] Written constitutions may incorporate the right to a healthy environment through constitutional reform; for example, Mexico enlarged the scope of the constitutional protection of the environment to include access to water and sanitation.[67]

Without secondary laws that address these constitutional rights, it may be quite difficult to realize them effectively. The Secretariat has seen submissions addressing environmental law enforcement through statutory provisions, in some cases also backed by the constitution. This approach is consistent with a decision of the Mexican Judiciary holding that environmental rights are to be protected by secondary laws implementing constitutional rights.[68]

On August 30, 2005, the submission *Environmental Pollution in Hermosillo II* was filed before the CEC Secretariat asserting that Mexico was "failing to effectively enforce Article 4 of the [Mexican] Constitution," along with several secondary provisions.[69] When considering the admissibility of Article 4, the Secretariat concluded – partially based on a domestic judicial decision – that the provision could not be considered under the submissions process since it did not specify how governments are to implement its protections.[70] A detailed review of the decision in

---

[65] SEM-05–003 (*Environmental Pollution in Hermosillo II*), Determination pursuant to Article 14(1)(2) (November 9, 2005), p. 7.

[66] There is evidence that countries where the right to a healthy environment is recognized under constitutional laws face practical obstacles to its effective implementation. See generally David R. Boyd, *The Environmental Rights Revolution: A Global Study of Constitutions, Human Rights and the Environment* (Toronto: UBC Press, 2012).

[67] "Whatever may be the advantages of a so-called 'unwritten' constitution, its existence imposes special difficulties on teachers bound to expound its provisions." A. V. Dicey, *Introduction to the Study of the Law of the Constitution*, 10th ed. (London: MacMillan & Co, 1965), p. 4.

[68] A circuit court has stated in this respect that "precisamente la definición de su contenido debe hacerse con base en una interpretación sistemática, coordinada y complementaria" ["specifically, its content must be defined on the basis of a systematic, coordinated, and complementary interpretation"]. "Medio ambiente adecuado para el desarrollo y bienestar. Concepto, regulación y concreción de esa garantía" ["Adequate environment for environment and well-being: concept, regulation and realization of that guarantee"], in Suprema Corte de Justicia de la Nación, *Semanario Judicial de la Federación y su Gaceta*, vol. XXI, January 2005, pp. 1799–1800.

[69] SEM-04–002 (*Environmental Pollution in Hermosillo II*), Submission pursuant to Article 14(1) (August 30, 2005), p. 13.

[70] "Si bien la redacción del artículo 4° constitucional mexicano garantiza el derecho que toda persona tiene a tener un medio ambiente adecuado, este artículo no define por sí mismo de manera concreta

question[71] revealed that the Mexican Circuit Court had actually rejected traditional positivism and had instead adopted a purposive approach that is more consistent with contemporary legal thought.[72] The court argued against a literal interpretation of the constitutional right to a healthy environment, and held that courts must undertake a teleological interpretation guided by the Magna Carta and the domestic statutory context.[73]

The Secretariat has now also rejected the positivist view through the combined effect of several of its determinations: it first held that constitutional provisions may further guide the analysis of effective enforcement,[74] then stated that Article 4 may "only [be] considered where there is a necessary element in effective enforcement of the environmental law at issue,"[75] and finally considered that this constitutional provision "may be included in [the] analysis provided that it is complemented by the analysis of [other] environmental laws in question."[76] Although Mexico initially challenged the Secretariat's position,[77] it eventually accepted it in its subsequent responses to submissions.[78]

Until now, the CEC Secretariat has admitted constitutional provisions for further consideration only when submitted alongside provisions from other statutes and regulations: it has never considered fundamental norms on their own in a citizen submission. It remains an open question whether there are circumstances in which a submission based on a constitutional norm in isolation can be considered by the Secretariat.

3.4. *Criminal Law*

Due to the importance of the legal protection of the environment, even criminal prosecution can be deployed to deter acts that cause harm to the environment as a

---

y específica de que forma debe darse esta obligación por parte del gobierno" [Transl. by author: "Although Article 4 of the Mexican Constitution ensures the right to an adequate environment, it does not define by itself, in a specific and concrete form, how this government obligation is to be implemented"], in SEM-04–002 (*Environmental Pollution in Hermosillo II*), Determination pursuant to Article 14(1)(2) (November 9, 2005), p. 7.

71 "Medio ambiente adecuado."

72 Carlos M. Baquedano Gorocica, Análisis del criterio sostenido por el Cuarto Tribunal Colegiado en Materia Administrativa del Primer Circuito dentro del Amparo en revisión 28/2004 (2011), p. 4, http://carlosbaquedano.com/wp-content/uploads/2011/02/An%C3%A1lisis-del-criterio-sostenido-por-el-Cuarto-Tribunal.final_.pdf.

73 "Medio ambiente adecuado," p. 1799.

74 SEM-06–006 (*Los Remedios National Park*), Determination pursuant to Article 14(1) (January 19, 2007), pp. 4–5.

75 SEM-09–001 (*Transgenic Maize in Chihuahua*), Determination pursuant to Article 14(1) (January 6, 2010), p. 5.

76 SEM-09–002 (October 9, 2009), Determination, p. 6.

77 SEM-06–006 (July 16, 2007), Response, pp. 48–49.

78 "Esta Parte coincide con la interpretación del Secretariado . . ." ["This Party agrees with the Secretariat's interpretation . . ."] SEM-09–002 (*Wetlands in Manzanillo*), Response pursuant to Article 14(3) (October 11, 2010), p. 73.

last resort. The criminal sanction is restrained by *favor libertatis* so that only once preventive measures have been exhausted may it be set in motion.[79]

One of the earliest examples of criminal penalties in international environmental law was adopted in the 1992 Basel Convention, which provides "that illegal traffic in hazardous wastes . . . is criminal,"[80] and requires the introduction of domestic enforcement instruments in Article 9(5).[81] In Mexico, environmental offences were first included in the LGEEPA in 1992 and in the Federal Criminal Code in 1996.[82]

At the CEC, a submission filed in 1998 was the first to assert a failure to enforce the criminal law, specifically with respect to gasoline leaks that led to catastrophic explosions in Guadalajara, Mexico.[83] As a result of the release of hydrocarbons and other explosive substances into the underground sewer of the Reforma sector in Guadalajara, a series of explosions killed 204 people, injured 1,460, and led to 1,148 cases of destroyed or damaged buildings and other property.[84] Because the submitters failed to connect applicable provisions to any practical enforcement issue, the Secretariat did not request a response from the government of Mexico.[85] However, the Secretariat determined that "provisions specifying environmental crimes are, by virtue of their primary purpose, 'environmental law' under the definition in . . . the NAAEC,"[86] an important precedent.

A group of submitters later filed a complaint before the Secretariat asserting that the Mexican government was failing to effectively enforce its environmental laws with respect to an abandoned lead smelter that posed a health risk to neighboring communities. It was not until this submission, *Metales y Derivados*, that Article 415 of the Federal Criminal Code was held to qualify as environmental law, as it "establishes criminal penalties for environmental offences, directed to protecting human health and the environment."[87] The Secretariat considered Article 415 of the Federal

---

[79] María Calvo Charro, *Sanciones medioambientales* (Madrid: Marcial Pons Ediciones Jurídicas y Sociales, 1999), p. 11.

[80] Basel Convention on the Control of Transboundary Movements of Hazardous Wastes and their Disposal, March 22, 1989, in force May 5, 1992, (1989) 28 ILM 657; (1999) 1673 UNTS 125, Article 4(3).

[81] "Each Party shall introduce appropriate national/domestic legislation to prevent and punish illegal traffic. The Parties shall co-operate with a view to achieving the objects of this Article."

[82] Código Penal Federal [Mexican Federal Criminal Code], Articles 414–23.

[83] SEM-98–001 (*Guadalajara*), Submission pursuant to Article 14(1) (January 9, 1998), Unofficial translation, p. 5.

[84] Ibid.

[85] SEM-98–001 (*Guadalajara*), Determination pursuant to Article 14(1) (September 13, 1999), p. 4. It should be noted that even in the case a Party is requested to file a response to a submission, pursuant to Guideline 10.1 the Secretariat may proceed to consider "in light of any response provided by the Party." Although there is no specific obligation to file a response, NAAEC Parties have never failed to do so.

[86] Ibid.

[87] Although the factual record did not investigate enforcement of the Código Penal Federal [Mexican Federal Criminal Code]. See SEM-98–007 (*Metales y Derivados*), Recommendation pursuant to Article 15(1) (March 6, 2000), pp. 6, 10.

Criminal Code as aiming to protect the human health and the environment[88] by imposing fines and prison sentences for carrying out activities involving hazardous waste without authorization[89] and recommended preparation of a factual record. Provisions of the Federal Criminal Code were also at issue in the *ALCA-Iztapalapa II* factual record, which included information on administrative[90] and criminal prosecution actions[91] instituted by Mexico related to management of hazardous materials.

At the time this chapter was written, a factual record on enforcement of the criminal law was under development pursuant to a submission filed in 2006. In *Ex Hacienda El Hospital II*, a group of residents in the vicinity of Cuautla, Morelos – about 150 kilometers from Mexico City – filed a submission with the CEC Secretariat asserting that Mexico was failing to effectively enforce the provisions of its Federal Criminal Code with respect to the closure, dismantling, and decommissioning of a paint pigment facility formerly operated by BASF Mexicana. The submitters maintained that Mexico did not enforce Federal Criminal Code provisions with respect to alleged illegal disposal of hazardous waste inside the facility and in the neighboring community of El Hospital. In its response, Mexico argued that the Criminal Code provisions do not "formally" qualify as environmental law because they form part of a "criminal conduct catalogue" and, relying on the definition of crime,[92] concluded that "strictly speaking the provisions of the Federal Penal Code" fall outside of the NAAEC Article 45(2) definition.[93]

Despite factual records and numerous determinations that have provided adequate reason to consider provisions of the Federal Penal Code of Mexico as environmental law, there has been a sustained resistance by Mexico in allowing a public investigation of the effectiveness of enforcement of environmental laws. To date, I have encountered no compelling reason effective enforcement actions should not be within the scope of factual investigations.

3.5. *Water Allocation and Water Quality Laws*

Council Resolution 08–01 authorized the Secretariat to develop a factual record pursuant to the *Lake Chapala II* submission and included several limitations on the scope of the investigation, including some based on the definition of environmental

---

[88] SEM-98–007 (*Metales y Derivados*), Notification pursuant to Article 15(1) (March 6, 2000), p. 6.
[89] Código Penal Federal [Mexican Federal Criminal Code], Article 415 ss. I, in force in 1999. See the Secretariat translation at SEM-98–007 (*Metales y Derivados*), Recommendation pursuant to Article 15(1) (March 6, 2000), p. 6, n. 6.
[90] SEM-03–004 (*ALCA-Iztapalapa II*), Factual record pursuant to Article 15(2) (June 2, 2008), pp. 56–58.
[91] Ibid., pp. 59–66.
[92] "Delito es el acto u omisión que sancionan las leyes penales" ["A crime is an act or omission punished by criminal laws"], Código Penal Federal, Article 7, first paragraph.
[93] SEM-06–003 (*Ex Hacienda El Hospital II*) and SEM-06–004 (*Ex Hacienda El Hospital III*), Response pursuant to Article 14(3) (January 10, 2007), unofficial translation, p. 58.

law.[94] In particular, the Council excluded "legislation, or provisions thereof, primarily addressing issues of water distribution." The Council sought to exclude laws that relate to natural resources distribution, which fall outside the NAAEC definition. Indeed, the agreement explicitly states that "exploitation . . . of natural resources"[95] is not considered environmental law and the Council interpreted this – perhaps with good reason – to include provisions related to water rights allocation. Mexico, however, considered that the limitation encompassed the entire National Waters Act (*Ley de Aguas Nacionales*, LAN),[96] which includes important water quality provisions. But a finding that the cited LAN provisions are environmental law in the sense of NAAEC Article 45(2) is clearly supported by previous determinations in which the Secretariat found that legal provisions governing water pollution control and water quality are environmental law, not only in Mexico[97] but also in the United States[98] and Canada.[99] Moreover, the Council has unanimously authorized the preparation of factual records with respect to water quality–related law, with Mexico voting affirmatively in every case,[100] and in *Aquanova* the Secretariat prepared a factual record on Mexico's alleged failure to effectively enforce provisions of its National Waters Act and its regulations.[101] Likewise, the Secretariat has previously found that the primary purpose of water pollution control–related law "is environmental protection or the prevention of a hazard to human health, principally through the prevention and control of pollutant releases."[102]

Several LAN provisions quoted in the *Lake Chapala II* submission later formed part of the factual record made public on January 22, 2013, which includes

[94] SEM-03–003 (*Lake Chapala II*), Council resolution 08–01 pursuant to Article 15(1) (May 30, 2008).
[95] NAAEC Article 45(2)(*b*).
[96] Ley de Aguas Nacionales (LAN) [National Waters Act], DOF December 1, 1992.
[97] See SEM-98–006 (*Aquanova*), Notification pursuant to Article 15(1) (August 4, 2000), pp. 5–6; SEM-97–002 (February 5, 2002), Notification, p. 6; SEM-06–003 (*Ex Hacienda El Hospital II*), Determination pursuant to Article 14(1) and (2) (August 30, 2006), p. 9.
[98] SEM-04–005 (*Coal-fired Power Plants*), Determination pursuant to Article 14(1) and (2) (February 24, 2005), p. 8, in relation to the Clean Water Act.
[99] See SEM-97–003 (*Quebec Hog Farms*), Notification pursuant to Article 15(1) (October 29, 1999), p. 7 (in relation to the regulation respecting the prevention of water pollution in livestock operations); SEM-98–004 (*BC Mining*), Notification pursuant to Article 15(1) (May 11, 2001), p. 11 (in relation to s. 36(3) of the Canadian Fisheries Act); SEM-03–005 (*Montreal Technoparc*), Notification pursuant to Article 14(1) and (2) (September 15, 2003), p. 3 (also in relation to Fisheries Act, s. 36(3)).
[100] SEM-98–006 (*Aquanova*), Council resolution 01–09 pursuant to Article 15(1) (November 16, 2001); SEM-97–002 (*Magdalena River*), Council resolution 02–02 pursuant to Article 15(1) (March 7, 2002); SEM-04–005 (*Coal-fired Power Plants*), Council resolution 08–03 pursuant to Article 15(1) (June 23, 2008); SEM-98–004 (*BC Mining*), Council resolution 01–11 pursuant to Article 15(1) (November 16, 2001).
[101] SEM-98–006 (*Aquanova*), Factual record pursuant to Article 15 (June 23, 2003) addresses the effective enforcement of LAN Articles 86 paragraph III; 88; 119 paragraphs I, II and VIII; 4; 9; and 92, as well as Reglamento de la Ley de Aguas Nacionales [Regulations to the National Water Law, RLAN] Articles 134, 135, 137, and 153.
[102] SEM-97–002 (February 5, 2002), Notification, p. 6.

considerable information on water quality in the Santiago and Verde Rivers as well as Lake Chapala in central Mexico.[103]

3.6. *Biodiversity Laws*

Construction of a body of exceptions to what constitutes environmental law is well demonstrated in *Transgenic Maize*, when Mexico argued in a contentious response that provisions of its Biosafety Law[104] did not meet NAAEC Article 45(2)'s high bar. Although environmental protection was *one* of the purposes of the law in question, Mexico maintained that the act itself could not be considered environmental law, that the Biosafety Law can only be addressed under a restrictive criteria,[105] and that in any event only provisions enforced by environmental authorities can be considered under the SEM process. Mexico thus argued, for instance, that provisions establishing the procedures to safely release genetically modified organisms including the requirement to obtain a permit to introduce GMOs into the environment cannot be considered by the SEM process, and that its "institutional capacities do not constitute matters within the scope of NAAEC since: i) they . . . do not refer to the effective enforcement of environmental law . . . , and ii) they relate to assessment of the effectiveness of the Parties' policies, laws, and institutions."[106] The Secretariat, however, found that because the provisions in question had instrumental value in that they contribute to environmental protection, they do in fact qualify as environmental law despite Mexico's position.

3.7. *Health Laws*

In Resolution 12–04 the Council authorized the development of a factual record with respect to atmospheric pollution levels in the city of Hermosillo, Sonora. The submission was filed on August 30, 2005, and a factual record was recommended in April 2007. It was not until June 2012 – five years later – that the Council finally voted in favor of instructing the Secretariat to develop the factual record. The Council's resolution included a paradox, however: the Secretariat was directed to develop a factual record on air pollution in Hermosillo, but prohibited from discussing enforcement actions related to criteria air pollutants. Issued by the Ministry of Health, standards for the so-called "criteria air pollutants"[107] are aimed at protecting human health

---

[103] SEM-03-003 (*Lake Chapala II*), Factual record pursuant to Article 15 (October 9, 2012), http://cec.org/lakechapala.

[104] Ley de Bioseguridad de Organismos Genéticamente Modificados.

[105] SEM-09-001 (May 3, 2010) Response, pp. 24, 27.

[106] Ibid., p. 7.

[107] Instituto Nacional de Ecología y Cambio Climático, *Contaminantes criterio*, http://www.inecc.gob.mx/calaire-indicadores/523-calaire-cont-criterio. For "criteria air pollutants," see, for example, the EPA's website referring to a set of National Ambient Air Quality Standards for six principal pollutants, which are called "criteria" pollutants: http://www.epa.gov/air/criteria.html.

yet did not meet the high bar to be considered environmental law according to the Council's narrow conception. The Council's reasons for its unanimous vote were never made public and the resolution simply states that the provisions' "primary purpose is *not* to protect the environment or prevent danger to human life or health through the prevention, abatement or control of the release, discharge or emission of pollutants or environmental contaminants."[108]

Since no advice to the Council from Mexico regarding the criteria air standards was ever made public, we can only speculate on the reasoning underlying Council Resolution 12–04. The standards in question establish reference levels for criteria air pollutants to protect human health, so the most plausible explanation is that a narrow view of Article 45(2)'s definition excludes the provisions because they do not directly *control* the release of pollutants. Council Resolution 12–04 will have a long-term effect on any future submissions that assert a failure to effectively enforce criteria air quality standards, as the Council considers the standards themselves to be inadmissible. The *Environmental Pollution in Hermosillo II* factual record is yet another casualty of strict scoping limits imposed by the Council given its interpretation of NAAEC.

These decisions run counter to *Metales y Derivados*, in which the Secretariat's main purpose in considering the development of a factual record was "to understand Mexico's enforcement efforts to prevent an imminent risk to the environment and dangerous repercussions to public health,"[109] and the decision to investigate was backed by a unanimous vote of Council.[110] *Metales y Derivados* is one of the few CEC submissions that led to tangible results. In particular, the submitter recognized the visibility that the process had brought to the issue[111] and, perhaps as a result, on January 28, 2009 the Environmental Protection Agency and Semarnat, Mexico's environmental ministry, jointly announced completion of the clean up of the *Metales y Derivados* lead smelter site.[112]

3.8. *Zoning Laws*

City planning, zoning bylaws, urban development programs, and environmental planning have also been subject to admissibility challenges imposed by the Secretariat and by Mexico. As discussed earlier, the Secretariat has determined that

---

[108] SEM-05–003 Council Resolution 12–04 [emphasis added].

[109] SEM-98–007 (March 6, 2000), Recommendation, p. 2.

[110] SEM-98–007 (*Metales y Derivados*), Council resolution pursuant to Article 15(2) (May 16, 2000).

[111] Letter from from César Luna, Environmental Health Coalition, to the Joint Public Advisory Committee (January 31, 2001).

[112] U.S. Environmental Protection Agency, "U.S. EPA, Mexican environmental agencies celebrate cleanup of former abandoned lead smelter / Over 42,000 tons of dangerous lead contained," January 28, 2009, http://yosemite.epa.gov/opa/admpress.nsf/o/F2FBFB057587A0418525754C00763C42.

zoning plans do not meet the definition of *law* and thus a submission based solely on violation of an urban development program cannot be reviewed.[113] The situation is otherwise when a submission cites a specific law in connection with an urban development program. For instance, the Secretariat may recommend the production of a factual record when an environmental permit was issued which conflicts with zoning plans, especially in areas designated for conservation and low-impact activities.[114] The Secretariat may also inquire into environmental obligations when a Party implements a zoning program based on, for instance, human settlements or even environmental impact laws.

Mexico has argued, however, that zoning laws and their environmental planning implementation instruments should not be considered within the process in two responses to citizen submissions. In its response to *Los Remedios National Park*, Mexico argued that urban development matters do not constitute environmental law.[115] Mexico's response did not identify the circumstances that require the Secretariat to refrain from considering urban development laws; the Secretariat discounted the Party's reasoning on this point, as most of the issues to be decided related to protection and management of national parks laws.[116]

In *Wetlands in Manzanillo*, Mexico reiterated its argument that provisions whose purpose is to "establish the content of the municipal urban development plans" should be excluded from the SEM process.[117] The Secretariat was not persuaded and held instead that environmental land use planning could be analyzed so long as only the environmental features of land use were considered, including restoration of ecological stability and protection of the environment.[118]

3.9. Procedural Laws

The Secretariat has also considered the circumstances under which which laws establishing procedural norms should be admissible. The Secretariat has generally excluded provisions related to due process of law, as it did in *Guadalajara* with regards to certain criminal procedure provisions.[119] The Secretariat's exclusion of

---

[113] SEM-09-002 (October 9, 2013), Determination, p. 9, pursuant to Article 15(1) (August 19, 2013), p. 50.

[114] See SEM-09-002 (*Wetlands in Manzanillo*), Notification of Mexico response pursuant to Article 14(3) (July 15, 2007), Article 14(3) (December 2), SEM-09-003 (*Los Remedios National Park II*), Government of Mexico response pursuant to Article 14(3) (December 2), p. 10.

[115] See SEM-06-006 (*Los Remedios National Park*), Determination pursuant to Article 14(1) and (2) (November 11, 2010), pp. 4–5.

[116] SEM-09-003 (*Los Remedios National Park*), Response ("... it should be noted that [the provision in question] does not meet the requirements of NAAEC, since its primary purpose is ... the establishment of the content of municipal urban development programs"), p. 18.

[117] SEM-09-006 (*Guadalajara*), August 19, 2013, Determination, pursuant to Article 14(1) (September 13, 1999).

such provisions has decreased in recent years when considering laws that create a comprehensive administrative framework to support the enforcement of a particular law.

The Secretariat, when considering a genetically modified organisms law in *Transgenic Maize*, concluded that "the establishment of a comprehensive administrative regime, comprising a legal-judicial framework on the one hand and a framework of sanctions for violations on the other, does not appear to be conceived . . . as an end itself."[120] The Secretariat recalled[121] that "to assume a conception of punitive power as a metajuridical 'good' . . . is to justify maximalist models of criminal law with few or no limits on punishment."[122] Indeed, when the law or a penalty comes to constitute an end in itself, we should question whether the legal regime can still be considered part of a democratic order. Given this awareness, procedural law protections within the environmental law regime may come to be more easily admitted in CEC proceedings.

4. CONCLUSION: LESSONS DRAWN FROM THE PRINCIPLE OF EFFECTIVENESS

Article 45(2) is the linchpin of the Article 14(1) machinery. A narrow interpretation of the definition of environmental law restricts potential investigation of enforcement practices that the Council – and often the Party in question – have deemed to be external to the Submissions process. This questionable practice should in the future be tempered by the principle of effectiveness and the doctrine of implied powers.

In international law, the principle of effectiveness requires that a treaty must be interpreted in a manner that makes its guaranteed rights "practical and effective," not "theoretical and illusory."[123] Likewise, the Secretariat should be expected to interpret NAAEC as a purposive whole to promote internal consistency between its various provisions.[124] The Secretariat must be able to interpret Articles 14 and 15 in harmony with NAAEC Article 45(2) and especially Article 1, reading the agreement as a complete entity. The Secretariat implicitly relied on the principle of effectiveness until it explicitly justified the approach in *Drilling Waste in Cunduacán*.[125] Indeed, the Secretariat has explicit authority to determine whether a provision qualifies as

---

[120] SEM-09-001 (*Transgenic Maize in Chihuahua*), Notification pursuant to Article 15(1) (December 20, 2010), pp. 17–18.

[121] Ibid., p. 18, n. 143.

[122] Luigi Ferrajoli, *Derecho y razón: Teoria del garantismo penal* (Madrid: Trotta, 2001), p. ___, as translated in SEM-09-001, Notification (December 20, 2010), p. ___.

[123] *Artico v. Italy* [1980] ECHR 4 at para. 33.

[124] See *Stec and Others v. the United Kingdom* (dec.) [GC], nos. 65731/01, 65900/01, §§ 47–8, ECHR 2005-X; *Demir and Baykara v. Turkey*, application no. 34503/97, ___ of November 12, §§ 65–8, http://hudoc.echr.coe.int/sites/eng/pages/search.aspx?i=001-81___

[125] SEM-07-005 (*Drilling Waste in Cunduacán*), Determination pursuant ___ (April 8 ___) p. 7.

environmental law and is entitled to consider a law's domestic interpretation in order to avoid a "divorce" between the legal concept as analyzed by an international body and the context of domestic legal systems.[126]

On the other hand, the doctrine of implied powers could instead be invoked to procedurally support the Secretariat's practice of expanding the scope and meaning of NAAEC. However, because the Secretariat has the express authority to determine whether a provision qualifies as "environmental law," there is likely no specific need to rely on implied authority. Thus in my opinion the Secretariat does not need to rely on any subsidiary power when considering whether a provision qualifies under Article 45(2), because it enjoys the authority to do so conferred directly by Article 14(1) of the agreement, and perhaps confirmed by Guideline 5.1.

As pointed out by McRae, the issue becomes complex when the Council exercises its control over the Secretariat when conducting business as the CEC governing body.[127] Council actions may suggest that, when it acts as the governing body, under the doctrine of implied powers it is further considering legal provisions for investigation or revising the scope of enforcement to be undertaken in a factual record. However, an administrative body should be careful to only exercise its implied powers for the purpose of achieving objectives emanating from its authorizing instrument, in this case the NAAEC. Thus, the Council's exercise of authority as the governing body of the CEC may, for instance, expand the scope of a factual investigation. McRae suggests as an example that the Council may agree to include a recommendation and a "determination of whether a Party has failed to effectively enforce its environmental law."[128] Similarly, the Council may also exercise its implied authority as the governing body to further enhance compliance and enforcement of environmental laws under Article 1 of the agreement by allowing inclusion of comments, opinions, recommendations, or even conclusions related to findings.[129]

In closing, I must acknowledge that there are positive recent signs pointing toward an improvement in Secretariat and Council dynamics. The inclusion of time limits in Guideline 19 is having important effects in terms of ensuring the delivery of long-awaited determinations and factual records by the end of 2013. The promptness of the SEM process is a key necessity for the long-term success of the CEC, but it must be balanced with procedural thoroughness to ensure the credibility of the mechanism. Promptly issuing determinations at the early stages of the procedure will improve the process, but at the point of developing a factual record, it will become more difficult to meet the target deadlines set by the Guidelines. The main reason for this is that development of a factual record is particularly time-intensive and requires developing questionnaires, conducting interviews, and following up with

[126] The Word "Laws" in Article 30 of the American Convention on Human Rights, para. 20.
[127] McRae, 23.
[128] Ibid., 15.
[129] NAAEC, Article 1(g)–(h).

cross-interviews. The recent changes to the SEM process may still prove it unable to deliver concrete results and further, substantial changes may still be necessary.

Legal technocrats must by now be aware that the static and lackluster implementation of Article 45(2) is only further alienating the North American public, and ignores that environmental issues are constantly evolving; a pure vision of law is appealing in theory, but has limited effects on the matters brought before the CEC. Interpreting each word in isolation from the greater context of NAAEC's objectives may lead, for example, to treat criteria air standards, criminal provisions against the environment, water quantity laws, biodiversity laws, zoning laws, and even constitutional norms as outside of the scope of Articles 14 and 15 process.[130] An interpretation of Article 45(2)'s provisions as part of a whole may be required to achieve an effective NAAEC implementation. Guided by the principle of effectiveness, the Secretariat must affirm its authority to independently assess a law to determine if it qualifies under NAAEC Article 45(2). In turn, the Council should use its implied powers to pursue objectives under Article 1 of the agreement by expanding the meaning, object, and purpose of factual records and not to limit or narrow the environmental laws in question. If we fail to do so, our generation may never witness renewed vitality within the SEM process.

---

[130] "In considering the question before the Court upon the language of the Treaty, it is obvious that the Treaty must be read as a whole, and that its meaning is not to be determined merely upon particular phrases." *Competence of the International Labour Organization in Regard to Internal Regulation of the Conditions of Labour of Persons Employed in Agriculture* (1922), Advisory Opinion, PCIJ (Ser. B) No. 2 at para. 24.

4

Pending Proceedings in the New Guidelines for Submissions on Enforcement Matters

An Improved Regression?

Montserrat Rovalo

1. INTRODUCTION

Article 14(3)(a) of the North American Agreement on Environmental Cooperation (NAAEC) establishes that when a Party notifies the Secretariat that a "judicial or administrative proceeding" is pending, the Secretariat shall not proceed with the submission. Departing from past practice and procedure, New Guideline 9.6 provides that no reasoning by the Secretariat for such termination is required. Moreover, such notification may be delivered "at any other point in the submission process." These changes to the guidelines are fundamental to the integrity and fairness of the SEM Process.

This chapter includes an analysis of the scope and meaning of NAAEC Article 45(3) and an overview of the Secretariat's interpretation before the guidelines' reform in July 2012. This chapter also overviews the Parties' and Council's positions. It then assesses the impact of the New Guidelines on the SEM Process and advances some proposals to mitigate their possible negative implications.

One of the most important features incorporated into the North American Agreement on Environmental Cooperation (NAAEC, or the Agreement) is the Submissions on Enforcement Matters (SEM) process under Articles 14 and 15. Since 1995, when the Secretariat received its first submission,[1] the mechanism has been widely used by U.S., Canadian, and Mexican citizens to assert that their governments are not effectively enforcing their environmental law. Although a higher number of Canadian submissions were initially received by the Secretariat, overall it has been Mexican citizens who have submitted the most.[2]

---

[1] SEM-95–001 (*Spotted Owl*), Submission pursuant to Article 14 (June 30, 1995).
[2] See Raúl Pacheco-Vega, "Las denuncias ciudadanas sobre cumplimiento ambiental en América del Norte (1996–2012): perspectivas sobre la sociedad civil ambientalista norteamericana" (2013) 8 NORTEAMÉRICA, 77–108.

With the intention of providing some guidance to the Secretariat, the Council of the Commission for Environmental Cooperation – constituted of the ministers of the environment of the United States, Canada, and Mexico – developed in 2000 the Guidelines for Submissions on Enforcement Matters under Articles 14 and 15 of the NAAEC (Former Guidelines).[3] These guidelines were revised and amended in July 2012 (becoming the New Guidelines).[4] Although the modifications introduced by the New Guidelines were not numerous, they focused on fundamental aspects of the SEM process, which could radically change the Secretariat's practice.

One of these aspects relates to the concept of "pending proceedings." When a Party notifies the Secretariat that the matter of a submission is the subject of a pending administrative or judicial proceeding, the Secretariat shall proceed no further according to NAAEC Article 14(3). Under the Former Guidelines, the Secretariat was required to explain its reasons for terminating the submission process in each case, and thus was able to explore the concept and elements of a pending proceeding through its determinations. According to the New Guidelines, the Secretariat's reasoning is no longer required.

2. THE SEM PROCESS

2.1. *A Brief Summary*

NAAEC Articles 14 and 15 establish a process that allows any nongovernmental organization or person residing or established in the territory of one of the Parties to present a submission to the Secretariat of the CEC asserting that a Party is failing to effectively enforce its environmental law. The Secretariat initially evaluates the admissibility of the submission on the basis of six criteria listed in Article 14(1). If the Secretariat determines that all criteria are met, it then, guided by the provisions of Article 14(2), analyzes whether the submission merits requesting a response from the Party. Finally, if the Secretariat considers that the submission, in light of the Party's response, warrants the development of a factual record – and in the absence of procedural obstacles – it shall so inform the Council and provide its reasons in accordance with Article 15(1).

A factual record is a research-based document that provides "an objective presentation of the facts relevant to the matter(s) raised in a submission."[5] The Secretariat shall prepare a factual record if the Council instructs it to do so by a two-thirds vote.

[3] Commission for Environmental Cooperation, *Bringing the Facts to Light: A Guide to Articles 14 and 15 of the North American Agreement on Environmental Cooperation* (Montreal: Commission for Environmental Cooperation, 2000).
[4] Commission for Environmental Cooperation, *Guidelines for Submissions on Enforcement Matters under Articles 14 and 15 of the North American Agreement on Environmental Cooperation* (Montreal: Commission for Environmental Cooperation, 2013).
[5] Ibid., 12.2.

Once prepared, the Secretariat presents a draft factual record to the Council, and the Parties may provide comments on its accuracy. These comments shall later be incorporated by the Secretariat as appropriate. Finally, the Secretariat submits the final factual record to the Council, which decides – by a two-thirds vote again – whether to make it publicly available.

The SEM Process operates as a "soft law" "spotlighting" instrument aimed to improve government accountability and transparency and citizen access to information.[6] It materializes some of NAAEC's objectives – which include, inter alia, enhancing compliance with, and enforcement of, environmental laws and regulations, and promoting transparency and public participation in their development.[7] Even though a factual record is the most illustrative way to "bring the facts to light," not every submission warrants the development of a factual record, as sometimes Parties' responses to submitters' assertions may also meet NAAEC's objectives.

2.2. *Procedural Obstacles for the Preparation of a Factual Record*

Regardless of the Secretariat's assessment of the submitters' assertions and the Parties' responses, the NAAEC envisages some procedural obstacles that prevent further analysis on whether to recommend preparation of a factual record.

The admissibility requirements established under NAEEC Article 14(1) constitute the first obstacle for the development of a factual record. If they are not fulfilled, the submitters are given sixty workings days under the New Guidelines to file a revised submission, after which time the process is terminated if no submission is delivered or if the Secretariat determines again that the revised submission is inadmissible. Among the admissibility requirements is the criterion that a submission must assert that a Party is failing to effectively enforce its *environmental law*, which is defined in NAAEC Article 45(2). Consequently, the Secretariat cannot further proceed with a submission invoking law outside of this realm.[8]

Once the Secretariat determines that the submission meets the Article 14(1) criteria, other procedural obstacles might exist when the Secretariat determines whether the submission merits requesting a response from the Party. In so doing, the Secretariat shall consider whether: the submission alleges harm to the submitters; it raises matters of which further study would advance NAAEC's goals; it is drawn exclusively from mass media reports; and, most importantly, private remedies available under the Party's law have been pursued.[9]

---

[6] David Markell, "The Role of Spotlighting Procedures in Promoting Citizen Participation, Transparency, and Accountability" (2010) 45 *Wake Forest Law Review*, 425–67 at 426.

[7] North American Agreement on Environmental Cooperation, September 14, 1993, in force January 1, 1994, (1993) 32 ILM 1480; Can TS 1994 No 3. Articles 1(g) and 1(h).

[8] See Chapter 3 of this volume, Paolo Solano, "Choosing the Right Whistle: The Development of the 'Environmental Law' Concept under the Citizen Submissions Process."

[9] NAAEC, Article 14(2).

Additionally, the Council has the power to stop the process and instruct the Secretariat not to prepare a factual record, despite the reasons given by the latter in its recommendation of whether a factual record is warranted.[10]

Perhaps one of the strictest procedural obstacles – giving absolutely no margin of discretion to the Secretariat – is concerned with the existence of pending judicial or administrative proceedings related to the subject matter of submissions. The purpose of the present chapter is to analyze this particular feature in light of the text of NAAEC and the Former Guidelines, to identify the main patterns of the Secretariat's previous practice when applying and interpreting NAAEC Article 14(3)(a), and then to provide an a priori assessment of the changes introduced by the New Guidelines on this matter.

3. PENDING ADMINISTRATIVE OR JUDICIAL PROCEEDINGS

Legally speaking, a "pending" proceeding generally refers to that which is begun but not yet completed, which is in process of settlement or adjustment.[11] However, NAAEC provides a definition of a "pending administrative or judicial proceeding" for the purposes of Articles 14 and 15. According to Articles 31 and 32 of the Vienna Convention on the Law of Treaties, which establish the customary rule on treaties interpretation,[12] a treaty "shall be interpreted in good faith in accordance with the ordinary meaning to be given to the terms of the treaty in their context and in light of its object and purpose" and "[a] special meaning shall be given to a term if it is established that the parties so intended."[13] Given that the NAAEC is an international treaty, it is only necessary to interpret the concept contained in Article 45(3) in accordance with this general rule of interpretation. On several occasions, the Secretariat has intended to apply the referred articles of the Vienna Convention in its analysis of Articles 14 and 15.

Article 14(3) establishes that the Party shall advise the Secretariat within thirty days or, in exceptional circumstances, within sixty days of delivery of the request of a response by the latter:

---

[10] NAEC, Article 15(2).

[11] Black's Law Dictionary Free Online Legal Dictionary, 2nd ed., "pending."

[12] The general rule of interpretation contained in Articles 31 and 32 has been recognized as customary international law by the International Court of Justice (*Case concerning the Territorial Dispute (Libyan Arab Jamahiriya v Chad)*, [1994] ICJ Rep 6 at 41; *Case concerning Kasikili/Sedudu Island (Botswana v Namibia)* [1999] ICJ Rep 1045 at 18). This recognition has also been reflected in the International Tribunal for the Law of the Sea (*Responsibilities and Obligations of States Sponsoring Persons and Entities with respect to Activities in the Area*, Advisory Opinion (February 1, 2011) at 57). See Anthony Aust, *Modern Treaty Law and Practice*, 2nd ed. (Cambridge: Cambridge University Press, 2007), pp. 11–14.

[13] Vienna Convention on the Law of Treaties, Vienna, May 23, 1969, in force January 27, 1980, 1155 UNTS 331; (1969) 8 ILM 679.

(a) Whether the matter is the subject of a pending judicial or administrative proceeding, in which case the Secretariat shall proceed no further, and
(b) Of any other information that the Party wishes to submit, such as
   (i) Whether the matter was previously the subject of a judicial or administrative proceeding, and;
   (ii) Whether private remedies in connection with the matter are available to the person or organization making the submission and whether they have been pursued.

3.1. *Concept*

3.1.1. Article 45(3)

NAAEC Article 45(3) establishes the definition of "judicial or administrative proceedings," for the purposes of Article 14(3), in the following terms:

(a) A domestic judicial, quasi-judicial or administrative action pursued by the Party in a timely fashion and in accordance with its law. Such actions comprise: mediation; arbitration; the process of issuing a license, permit, or authorization; seeking an assurance of voluntary compliance or a compliance agreement; seeking sanctions or remedies in an administrative or judicial forum; and the process of issuing an administrative order; and
(b) An international dispute resolution proceeding to which the Party is party.

3.1.2. Secretariat's Interpretation

In its first determinations, the Secretariat began analyzing the scope of Articles 14(3)(a) and 45(3). The Parties frequently notified the Secretariat of alleged pending proceedings and requested – in some cases even demanded – that the Secretariat terminate the process of the submissions. The Secretariat considered these articles for the first time in the Oldman River I submission in 1997.[14] Since then, the Secretariat has applied and interpreted them in more than twenty submissions. Probably without the intention of departing from the text of NAAEC, the Secretariat has developed important criteria through its reasoning in different submissions.

The Secretariat has referred several times to Articles 31 and 32 of the Vienna Convention.[15] In so doing, it has interpreted the terms of NAAEC's provisions, particularly those relating to administrative and judicial proceedings, according to

---

[14] SEM-96–003 (*Oldman River I*), Determination pursuant to Article 15(1) (April 2, 1997), pp. 3–5.
[15] The Vienna Convention has been in force in both Canada and Mexico since January 27, 1980. The United States signed the Vienna Convention, but has not ratified it. Nonetheless, the general rule of interpretation contained in Articles 31 and 32 is binding on the United States as customary international law.

a plain reading of its terms. When the literal interpretation has not been enough, it has looked for other possible interpretations of terms within the broader context of other NAAEC provisions. Moreover, it has sometimes referred to previous decisions of the Secretariat.[16] In the interpretation of Article 45(3), the Secretariat has analyzed its various elements independently in different determinations.

3.1.2.1. "JUDICIAL, QUASI-JUDICIAL OR ADMINISTRATIVE ACTION". The Secretariat has established that the concept of "judicial, quasi-judicial or administrative action" should be defined narrowly to fulfill and promote the objectives and rationale of the NAAEC and also to give meaning to the SEM process.[17]

3.1.2.2. "PURSUED BY THE PARTIES". In *Oldman River I*, the Secretariat considered that the term "Party" is employed consistently throughout NAAEC to refer to a government signatory to the Agreement – that is, to the governments of Canada, the United States, or Mexico. Hence, the drafters of Article 45(3) limited its scope to the actions pursued by governments to secure compliance with environmental law. In the Secretariat's words, it applies "where a government is actively engaged in pursuing enforcement-related measures against one or more actors implicated in an Article 14 submission."[18]

The Secretariat has referred to the examples listed in Article 45(3) to support its interpretation, since those kinds of actions "are taken almost exclusively by the official government bodies charged with enforcing or implementing the law."[19]

When a pending proceeding has been initiated and pursued by a private entity, the practice of the Secretariat has been not to include it within the scope of Article 45(3).[20] For example, in *El Boludo Project* submission, the Secretariat established that a citizen complaint procedure (*denuncia popular* in Mexican law) cannot be considered a pending proceeding in terms of NAAEC as it is not initiated by a Party, although it may lead to inspection and surveillance proceedings under certain circumstances that could meet the Article 45(3)(a) definition.[21] The same

[16] Although not obliged by the principle of stare decisis, "the Secretariat must attempt to ensure a modicum of predictability and thus fairness in its practice with regard to Articles 14 and 15, for example, by taking into account lessons learned from previous Determinations and Factual Records." (SEM-07-001 (*Minera San Xavier*), Determination pursuant to Article 15(1) (July 15, 2009), paras. 32–3. See SEM-97-001 (*B.C. Hydro*), Recommendation pursuant to Article 15(1) (April 27, 1998), p. 8.)

[17] *B.C. Hydro* Recommendation, p. 9; SEM-00-004 (*BC Logging*), Notification pursuant to Article 15(1) (July 27, 2001), p. 16.

[18] *Oldman River I* Determination, p. 3.

[19] Ibid. See, e.g., SEM-06-003 and SEM-06-004 (*Ex Hacienda El Hospital II* and *Ex Hacienda El Hospital III*), Notification pursuant to Article 15(1) (May 12, 2008), p. 11.

[20] *Oldman River I* Determination, p. 4; SEM-98-005 (*Cytrar I*), Determination pursuant to Article 15(1) (October 26, 2000), p. 11; SEM-04-005 (*Coal-fired Power Plants*), Notification pursuant to Article 15(1) (December 5, 2005), p. 14.

[21] SEM-02-004 (*El Boludo Project*), Notification pursuant to Article 15(1) (May 17, 2004), p. 5.

has been said in relation to civil lawsuits and complaints before a human rights ombudsman.[22]

3.1.2.3. "IN A TIMELY FASHION". In general terms, the Secretariat has interpreted the requirement of a proceeding to be made "in a timely fashion" to mean that the action must have been pursued in a "vigorous manner," in accordance with time limits established by law and without undue delay.[23] When analyzing the lapsing of administrative procedures – particularly in relation to Mexican law – due to the expiration of the period established for the authority to render a decision, the Secretariat has considered the procedure to be no longer pending and therefore not pursued "in a timely fashion" under Article 45(3).[24]

In its response to the *Coronado Islands* submission, Mexico emphasized its disagreement with the Secretariat's interpretation on this matter. According to Mexico, the appeals for review (*recursos de revisión*) do not cease to be pending simply because the Secretariat considers that the final resolution was not issued in a timely fashion. On the basis of a literal interpretation, Mexico claimed that the term "pending" means that its resolution or termination is awaiting and does not imply any period of time.[25]

In the *Coronado Islands* Article 15(1) notification, the Secretariat confirmed its previous interpretations and stated that:

> [In Mexican law] administrative orders must be issued within three months following the filing of an appeal. Where the authority fails to act, the law fills the legal void by establishing that the appeal is deemed to be denied. For the purposes of the NAAEC, upon expiry of the period ... any subsequent action taken by the Party ... is not considered timely.[26]

3.1.2.4. "IN ACCORDANCE WITH THE PARTY'S LAW". In relation to the last requirement in the definition of Article 45(3)(a), the Secretariat has established that the proceeding must be grounded in the statutory or common law of the Party in question,[27] which means that the alleged "pending proceeding" should not be *ultra vires*.

3.1.2.5. "AN INTERNATIONAL DISPUTE RESOLUTION PROCEEDING TO WHICH THE PARTY IS PARTY". The definition of "pending proceeding" established in Article

[22] SEM-03–003 (*Lake Chapala II*), Notification pursuant to Article 15(1) (May 18, 2005), pp. 16–18.

[23] *B.C. Hydro* Recommendation, p. 9.

[24] See *El Boludo Project* Notification, pp. 6–8; SEM-05–001 (*Crushed Gravel in Puerto Peñasco*), Determination pursuant to Article 15(1) (October 24, 2005), pp. 10–11; SEM-05–002 (*Coronado Islands*), Notification pursuant to Article 15(1) (January 18, 2007), pp. 12–14.

[25] SEM-05–002 (*Coronado Islands*), Government of the United Mexican States Response pursuant to Article 14(3) (January 10, 2006), pp. 10–11.

[26] *Coronado Islands* Notification, pp. 13–14.

[27] *B.C. Hydro* Recommendation, p. 9.

45(3)(b) has been invoked in two instances to request the Secretariat to proceed no further with a submission. This has been done by the United States and Mexico in the *Methanex* and *Cytrar II* submissions, which referred to proceedings before arbitral tribunals in which the respective governments were parties.[28]

In contrast with the concept envisaged in Article 45(3)(a), for an international dispute resolution proceeding to be considered a "pending proceeding," it is not necessary for the Party to have initiated it; the Party only needs to be a party of it. In this regard, the Secretariat has recognized that the mechanism created by Chapter 11 of NAFTA for the settlement of investment disputes,[29] and the mechanism administered by the International Center for the Settlement of Investment Disputes (ICSID),[30] qualify as international dispute resolution proceedings usually initiated by private entities.

In the *Methanex* submission, the Secretariat decided to proceed no further, as there existed a pending international proceeding before an arbitral tribunal established under NAFTA Chapter 11. In this proceeding, both the submitter and the United States were parties, and the proceeding referred to the same matter as that of the submission. This was not the case in the *Cytrar II* submission, where the submitters were different subjects from the private enterprise that initiated an arbitral proceeding against Mexico. The Secretariat continued with the submission on the basis that in order to terminate the SEM process, "there must be a reasonable expectation that the 'pending judicial or administrative proceeding' invoked by the Party will address and potentially resolve the matters raised in the submission."[31]

3.2. *Article 14(3)(a) of NAAEC*

3.2.1. Importance of Article 14(3)(a) for the SEM Process

Article 14(3)(a) is one of the few provisions in NAAEC with the ultimate effect of terminating a submission process and therefore limiting citizens' access to information. According to the Secretariat, it is an exceptional way to terminate submissions[32] and the Secretariat has described it as a "peremptory clause."[33]

The Secretariat has established that it is neither a court nor tribunal; the SEM process is not adversarial; its determinations are not binding; and factual records are

---

[28] SEM-99–001 and SEM 00–002 (*Methanex*), Government of the United States Response pursuant to Article 14(3) (May 30, 2000); SEM-01–001 (*Cytrar II*), Government of the United Mexican States Response pursuant to Article 14(3) (June 1, 2001); SEM-01–001 (*Cytrar II*), Government of the United Mexican States Response pursuant to Article 14(3) (July 19, 2001).

[29] *Methanex* Determination pursuant to Article 14(3) (June 30, 2000), p. 4.

[30] *Cytrar II* Determination pursuant to Article 14(3) (June 13, 2001), p. 4.

[31] *Cytrar II* Notification pursuant to Article 15(1) (July 29, 2002), pp. 5–6.

[32] SEM-06–006 (*Los Remedios National Park*) Determination pursuant to Article 15(1) (March 20, 2008), p. 8; SEM-07–005 (*Drilling Waste in Cunduacán*), Determination pursuant to Article 14(3) (April 8, 2009), para. 30.

[33] *B.C. Hydro* Recommendation, p. 10.

not rulings or judicial opinions.[34] In this sense, the Secretariat has considered that *lis pendens* cannot occur.[35]

Nonetheless, the Secretariat has avoided interfering nonjudicially with ongoing proceedings of the Parties when issuing its determinations, particularly when recommending a factual record. The Secretariat has interpreted the inclusion of Article 14(3)(a) in NAAEC as the intention of the Parties to exclude a review of enforcement matters being actively pursued by any of them.[36]

3.2.2. Former SEM Guidelines

According to Former Guideline 9.4, if a Party informed the Secretariat that the matter raised in a submission was the subject of a pending judicial or administrative proceeding, as defined in NAAEC Article 45(3), the Secretariat was supposed to proceed no further with the submission, and to notify the submitter and the Council of its reasons for terminating the submission process.

As the Secretariat has interpreted the restriction envisaged in Article 14(3)(a) as an exception, and as it was required by the Former Guidelines to explain its reasoning for terminating a submission process, the Secretariat has been able to develop the limits and conditions of this article.[37]

3.2.3. Secretariat's Practice and Interpretation through its Determinations under Articles 14(3) and 15(1) of NAAEC

When the Parties have mentioned the existence of pending proceedings in their responses under Article 14(3)(a) of NAAEC and have therefore requested the Secretariat to proceed no further with the submission process, the latter has consistently interpreted that provision in a restrictive manner. This restrictive interpretation reflects the Secretariat's intention of promoting NAAEC's objectives of transparency and public participation, and of giving meaning to the SEM process designed "to scrutinize the Parties' commitments to effectively enforce their environmental laws."[38]

In this regard, the Secretariat has established that "[o]nly those proceedings *notified* [by a Party] *pursuant to Article 14(3)* and *categorized in Article 45(3)(a)* may preclude the Secretariat from proceeding further" [emphasis added].[39] Consequently,

---

[34] *Minera San Xavier* Determination, paras. 32 and 44; SEM-08–001 (*La Ciudadela Project*), Determination pursuant to Article 15(1) (August 12, 2010), para. 46.

[35] Ibid., para. 44. See SEM-09–001 (*Transgenic Maize in Chihuahua*), Determination pursuant to Article 15(1) (December 20, 2010), para. 75.

[36] *B.C. Hydro* Recommendation, p. 7.

[37] The text of Article 14(3) does not explicitly indicate any role for the Secretariat other than to proceed no further. The Council likely simply gave effectiveness to this article through the Former Guidelines.

[38] *B.C. Hydro* Recommendation, p. 9.

[39] *Minera San Xavier* Determination, para. 35.

when a Party has referred to a pending judicial or administrative proceeding in its response to a submission, but has not requested the Secretariat to proceed no further in accordance with Article 14(3)(a), the Secretariat has omitted dismissing *motu pro-prio* the submission and has examined the pending proceeding directly under Article 15(1). For example, in the *Cytrar I* submission, the Secretariat determined, among other reasons, that Article 14(3)(a) was not applicable because Mexico's response did not request the Secretariat to stop proceedings in accordance with that article.[40]

When the Party has adequately notified the Secretariat of the existence of a pending proceeding, but has provided little or no information – as has occurred with Mexico's responses on several occasions under the plea of confidentiality – the Secretariat has sometimes requested more information from the Party.[41] Without that information, "the possibility exist[ed] that a submission could be terminated without presenting the required *reasons* why such decision was made."[42] As the Secretariat could not apply Article 14(3)(a) "on the mere assertion of a Party to that effect,"[43] in cases in which it has lacked the necessary information, it has simply proceeded to the analysis of Article 15(1).[44]

The Secretariat in its practice has intended to strictly examine the fulfillment of all requirements established in the definition of "pending administrative or judicial proceedings" under Article 45(3). It has on some occasions dismissed the applicability of Article 14(3)(a) when the action had not been pursued by the Party,[45] or when it had not been pursued in a timely fashion.[46] The Secretariat has construed the legal standard established under Article 14(3)(a) as requiring two facts: (1) the existence of a pending judicial or administrative proceeding under Article 45(3); and (2) the pending proceeding and the allegations raised in the submission to have the same subject matter.[47] Moreover, the onus of proving the same subject matter lies on the Party invoking it.[48]

---

[40] *Cytrar I* Determination, p. 10. See also SEM-98–006 (*Aquanova*), Notification pursuant to Article 15(1) (August 4, 2000), p. 26; SEM-02–003 (*Pulp and Paper*), Notification pursuant to Article 15(1) (October 8, 2003), p. 17; *Minera San Xavier* Determination, para. 36.

[41] The Secretariat has requested additional information when the Party delivered its response in the thirty-day limit established under Article 14(3) and not under the exceptional sixty-day limit (see *Cytrar II* Determination; SEM-06–006 (*Los Remedios National Park*), Secretariat Information Request pursuant to Article 21(1)(b) (November 27, 2007); SEM-07–001 (*Minera San Xavier*), Secretariat Information Request pursuant to Article 21(1)(b) (March 7, 2008)).

[42] Transgenic Maize in Chihuahua Determination, para. 76.

[43] *Cytrar II* Determination, p. 5.

[44] See, e.g., SEM-00–006 (*Tarahumara*), Notification pursuant to Article 15(1) (August 29, 2002), p. 17; *La Ciudadela Project* Determination, para. 61; *Transgenic Maize in Chihuahua* Determination, para. 76.

[45] See *Oldman River I* Determination; *El Boludo Project* Notification; *Lake Chapala II* Notification; *Coal-fired Power Plants* Notification; *Minera San Xavier* Determination.

[46] See *El Boludo Project* Notification, pp. 7–8; *Coronado Islands* Notification, pp. 12–14.

[47] *B.C. Hydro* Recommendation, p. 2; SEM-98–004 (*BC Mining*), Notification pursuant to Article 15(1) (May 11, 2001), p. 15; *Aquanova* Notification, p. 26; *Methanex* Determination, p. 4; *Cytrar II* Determination, p. 4; *El Boludo Project* Notification, p. 4; *Lake Chapala II* Notification, p. 17.

[48] *Cytrar II* Notification, p. 7.

The Secretariat has determined that only those proceedings intended to conclude within a definable period and that have a definable goal fall within the scope of Article 14(3)(a). To the contrary, activities that are "solely consultative, information-gathering or research-based" do not fall within the scope of that article.[49] The fear behind the Secretariat's analysis has been that Parties "could effectively shield non-enforcement of [their] environmental laws from scrutiny simply by commissioning studies or holding consultations."[50] For example, in the *BC Mining* submission, the Secretariat considered that inspections and testing do not fall within Article 45(3) because they are "information-gathering steps that might, but do not necessarily, lead to further enforcement action."[51] A similar rationale applied to warning letters – which the Secretariat determined are not administrative orders[52] – and criminal investigations.[53]

By interpreting Article 14(3)(a) in accordance with Article 31 of the Vienna Convention, the Secretariat has concluded that the exclusion from the SEM process – particularly from the development of a factual record – of matters that are currently the subject of judicial or administrative proceedings is required by "the two-pronged criteria applied by the Secretariat":[54] (1) the need to refrain from interfering with pending litigation, and (2) the need to avoid a duplication of effort.[55]

Regarding the first aspect, as has already been mentioned, the Secretariat does not consider itself a court of law, and its determinations do not have legal effect. The Secretariat cannot interfere with ongoing domestic proceedings in the same way that domestic court judgments can. Nonetheless, it has undertaken to avoid actions that could cause unintended nonjudicial interference.[56]

Regarding the second aspect, the Secretariat has considered that a duplication of enforcement effort could arise if a Party would seek enforcement through one or some of the measures mentioned in Article 45(3)(a) and the Secretariat, in developing a factual record, would require the Parties to embark on additional actions regarding the same matters. In such a case, the Secretariat's factual record could lead to a "commitment of additional resources or diversion of existing resources."[57]

---

[49] *B.C. Hydro* Recommendation, p. 9.
[50] Ibid.
[51] *BC Mining* Notification, p. 17.
[52] "Administrative orders" within the meaning of Article 45(3) must contain, at least, "a directive with immediate legal effect that compels or enjoins an activity so as to promote compliance with the law" (Ibid.).
[53] According to the Secretariat, criminal investigations are not of same nature as those actions explicitly mentioned in Article 45(3)(a), and they do not always have a clear beginning and endpoint; nonetheless, they might lead to a judicial or administrative proceeding falling within that article (*BC Logging* Notification, p. 17). See *Aquanova* Notification, p. 26; *Pulp and Paper* Notification, p. 17; *Los Remedios National Park* Determination, pp. 9–10.
[54] *B.C. Hydro* Recommendation, p. 11.
[55] Ibid., p. 10. The Secretariat has applied consistently the same criteria in subsequent determinations or notifications (e.g., *Coal-fired Power Plants* Notification, p. 14; *BC Logging* Notification, p. 17).
[56] *Minera San Xavier* Determination, paras. 44–5. See *Lake Chapala II* Notification, p. 18.
[57] Ibid., para. 46.

3.2.4. The Recourse to Article 15(1)

A common practice of the Secretariat regarding this stage of the SEM process has been to interpret Article 14(3)(a) restrictively. As a consequence, the Secretariat has terminated submissions in accordance with this article in only a few cases,[58] and has examined those "pending proceedings" that fall outside the scope of Article 45(3)(a) in the Article 15(1) recommendations.

In contrast to Article 14(3)(a), by which the Secretariat "shall" proceed no further, the text of Article 15(1) provides the Secretariat with a wide margin of discretion: "If the Secretariat *considers* that the submission, in the light of any response provided by the Party, warrants developing a factual record, the Secretariat shall so inform the Council and provide its reasons" [emphasis added].

The NAAEC in this provision explicitly instructs the Secretariat to provide its reasons to recommend the development of a factual record, which depends on the Secretariat's discretion in evaluating the Parties' responses.

The language of Article 14(3)(a) clearly requires the Secretariat to dismiss a submission when a pending administrative or judicial proceeding exists. The text of Article 15(1), on the other hand, does not indicate the factors that the Secretariat should consider in its decision making.[59] When the Secretariat has determined that an alleged pending proceeding does not fit within the definition envisaged in Article 45(3)(a), e.g., because the action was initiated by a private party, such as the submitter, it has nonetheless evaluated the pending proceeding in many submissions so as to determine whether to recommend, or not, the development of a factual record.[60]

In this regard, the Secretariat has considered two factors to be relevant to its determinations: (1) the similarity between the subject matter of the submissions and that of the pending proceedings and (2) the impact that the remedy sought may have on the submissions' enforcement matters. These two issues have been considered with the aim of avoiding the "two-pronged" risks of duplicating efforts and interfering with pending processes.[61] These two issues were also in line with Former Guideline 7.5, which was concerned with the risks posed when private remedies were pursued by the submitters.[62]

For example, when finding that a criminal investigation cannot constitute a pending proceeding under Article 14(3)(a) of NAAEC, the Secretariat has nonetheless found that a factual record is not warranted as long as the criminal investigation remains active and ongoing. Due to the "degree of secrecy and sensitivity"[63]

---

[58] See *Methanex* Determination; *Drilling Waste in Cunduacán* Determination.
[59] *Methanex* Determination, p. 3.
[60] See, e.g., *Oldman River I* Determination; *B.C. Hydro* Recommendation; *Cytrar I* Determination; *Cytrar II* Notification; *Lake Chapala II* Notification; *Minera San Xavier* Determination.
[61] See *Oldman River I* Determination, p. 4; *B.C. Hydro* Recommendation, p. 10.
[62] See *Minera San Xavier* Determination, paras. 36 and 45.
[63] *BC Logging* Notification, p. 17.

of criminal investigations, factual records could present a risk of interfering and disclosing information, investigative techniques, or the identities of relevant people.[64]

It should also be mentioned that the Secretariat has, on some occasions, determined the partial applicability either of Article 14(3)(a) or Article 15(1). When it has found the existence of a pending proceeding in light of the Parties' responses falling within the purview of Article 45(3)(a), it has decided to proceed no further in relation to those proceedings, but not in relation to all the allegations of the submissions.[65] In some of its Article 15(1) Notifications to the Council, the Secretariat has excluded pending proceedings – which fall outside the scope of Article 45(3)(a) – from the scope of the recommendation to prepare a factual record.[66]

3.2.5. Parties' Positions and Perspectives

It is possible to infer the Parties' opinions toward Article 14(3)(a) from their responses to submissions. It is also possible to infer the Council's position from its resolutions instructing the Secretariat whether it should prepare a factual record in accordance with NAAEC Article 15(2).

From all the submissions for which the Secretariat has requested a response from the Parties, on twenty-one occasions they have argued the existence of a pending proceeding and have requested the Secretariat to proceed no further. Canada has argued pending proceedings on five occasions, Mexico on fourteen, and the United States only on two.[67] Despite the Parties' assertions as to the importance of the SEM Process, mentioning the existence of pending proceeding to stop the process could be considered a frequent practice.

In this regard, Canada has affirmed that it considers Articles 14 and 15 to be "among the most important provisions" of the NAAEC.[68] However, Canada has also asserted that factual records must not be prepared with respect to issues that are the subject of contemporaneous domestic proceedings,[69] and therefore has "respectfully" requested the Secretariat to proceed no further.[70] Canada has argued that, *inter alia*,

---

[64] Ibid.

[65] See *BC Mining* Notification; *Ex Hacienda El Hospital II* and *Ex Hacienda El Hospital III* Notification; *Los Remedios National Park* Determination; *Transgenic Maize* Determination; SEM-09-003 (*Los Remedios National Park II*), Determination pursuant to Article 15(1) (July 27, 2011); SEM-09-002 (*Wetlands in Manzanillo*), Notification pursuant to Article 15(1) (August 19, 2013).

[66] See *BC Logging* Notification; *Pulp and Paper* Notification; *Coal-fired Power Plants* Notification.

[67] See Annex I.

[68] SEM-97-001 (*B.C. Hydro*), Government of Canada Response pursuant to Article 14(3) (July 21, 1997), p. 1.

[69] SEM-98-004 (*BC Mining*), Government of Canada Response pursuant to Article 14(3) (September 8, 1999), p. 5.

[70] *BC Mining* Response, p. 4; SEM-06-005 (*Species at Risk*), Government of Canada Response pursuant to Article 14(3) (February 8, 2007), p. 3.

criminal proceedings, warning letters, and appeals procedures constitute "pending proceedings" in terms of Article 45(3)(a).

The United States has stated that it "believes that the Articles 14 and 15 process is a critical component of the cooperative efforts for environmental protection among the Parties to the NAAEC."[71] The United States has also declared itself to be "a strong supporter" of the SEM process.[72] The United States even asserted that Article 14(3) was partially intended to prevent litigants from using the SEM process as "an alternative mechanism for obtaining information that would be useful in certain types of other proceedings."[73] Pursuant to Article 14(3)(a) the United States has proclaimed that the Secretariat is barred from further considering submissions.[74]

Mexico's position has been somewhat more controversial. In its response to the *Coronado Islands* submission, Mexico argued that NAAEC only requires the Party to notify the Secretariat if the subject of the submission is that of a pending proceeding, and that the interpretation of the Agreement is a power conferred only to the Parties and not to the Secretariat. Moreover, the Mexican government highlighted that only a Party's judiciary may interpret a Party's law, rather than the Secretariat.[75]

It seems that Mexico moderated its radical position in its subsequent responses to other submissions in which it notified the Secretariat of the existence of pending administrative and judicial proceedings.[76] For instance, in its response to the *Los Remedios National Park II* submission, Mexico stated that "[t]he Mexican government clearly understands the proceeding envisaged by NAAEC and the inclusion of this section [in relation to Articles 14(1), (2), and (3)] in the Response does not have as its object to formulate a rejoinder not contemplated in the mentioned Agreement, but only to promote a more careful review by the Secretariat of those assumptions that should govern its performance in the admission and processing of citizen

---

[71] SEM-99–001 and SEM 00–002 (*Methanex*), Government of the United States of America Response pursuant to Article 14(3) (May 30, 2000), p. 1.

[72] Ibid.

[73] Ibid., p. 9.

[74] SEM-04–005 (*Coal-fired Power Plants*), Government of the United States of America Supplemental Response pursuant to Article 14(3) (September 29, 2005), p. 3.

[75] *Coronado Islands* Response, pp. 10–11.

[76] See SEM-06–006 (*Los Remedios National Park*), Government of the United States of Mexico Supplemental Response pursuant to Article 21(1)(b) (February 26, 2008); SEM-07–001 (*Minera San Xavier*), Government of the United States of Mexico Supplemental Response pursuant to Article 21(1)(b) (June 5, 2008); SEM-07–005 (*Drilling Waste in Cunduacán*), Government of the United States of Mexico Supplemental Response pursuant to Article 21(1)(b) (May 15, 2008); SEM-08–001 (*La Ciudadela Project*), Government of the United States of Mexico Supplemental Response pursuant to Article 21(1)(b) (May 26, 2010); SEM-09–001 (*Transgenic Maize in Chihuahua*), Government of the United States of Mexico Response pursuant to Article 14(3) (May 3, 2010); SEM-09–003 (*Los Remedios National Park II*), Government of the United States of Mexico Response pursuant to Article 14(3) (December 20, 2010).

submissions, on an analysis framework that respects the scope of cooperation among the Parties"[77] [unofficial translation].

3.2.6. The Inferred Council's Position

Besides the individual attitudes of the Parties toward the "pending proceedings" reflected in their responses to submissions, it is interesting to examine the Council's attitude as well. The Council instructs the Secretariat, by a two-thirds vote, to prepare a factual record.[78] The Council may provide comments on the accuracy of the draft factual record submitted by the Secretariat,[79] and also decides by a two-thirds vote whether to make the final factual record publicly available.[80] According to the NAAEC, the Council only has the power to intervene in the SEM process when the Secretariat submits to it a recommendation to prepare a factual record; before this particular moment, the process relies on the Secretariat's analysis and decisions, and the Council is only informed by the Secretariat.[81]

In relation to the existence of a pending proceeding, the Council's attitude toward the Secretariat's analysis can be inferred from its resolutions instructing the preparation of factual records. As neither the NAAEC nor the Former Guidelines required the Council – in contrast to the Secretariat[82] – to explain the reasons for its decisions,[83] one can only speculate about its motives and intentions. The text of the Council's resolutions is nonetheless revealing.

To start with, in seven submissions in which the Secretariat has considered the alleged pending proceedings not to fall within the scope of Article 14(3)(a) and has recommended to the Council the preparation of a factual record, the Council

---

[77] Los Remedios National Park II Response, p. 2.
[78] NAAEC, Article 15(2).
[79] Ibid., Article 15(5).
[80] Ibid., Article 15(7).
[81] See Former Guidelines, 3.8, 7.1, 7.2, 9.4, 9.5, 9.6, 10.1, and 14.1.
[82] Former Guideline 10.1 established, "If the Secretariat considers that the submission, in light of any response provided by the Party or after the response period has expired, warrants developing a factual record, the Secretariat will so inform the Council . . . the Secretariat will provide sufficient explanation of its reasoning to allow the Council to make an informed decision. . . . The Council may request further explanation of the Secretariat's reasons."
[83] Former Guideline 10.4 established, "The Secretariat will prepare a factual record if the Council, by a two-thirds vote, instructs it to do so. If the Council votes to instruct the Secretariat not to prepare a factual record, the Secretariat will so inform the Submitter and will inform the Submitter that the submission process is terminated." Fortunately, with the New Guidelines, the Council must provide its reasons when instructing the Secretariat to prepare a factual record. However, it remains unclear whether the Council is required to do so when instructing the Secretariat not to prepare it. The relevant New Guideline 10.4 now establishes, "If the Council, by at least a two-thirds vote, instructs it to do so, the Secretariat will prepare a factual record in accordance with those instructions. The Council will provide its reason(s) for the instructions in writing and they will be posted on the public registry."

has either partially concurred in or totally diverged from the Secretariat's opinion. The Council has considered the Parties' responses in many cases, and practically ignored the Secretariat's analysis.[84]

For instance, in the *BC Mining* submission, Canada claimed that actions it had taken in relation to three mines – the Britannia, Tulsequah Chief, and Mt. Washington mines – constituted pending judicial or administrative proceedings within the meaning of Articles 14(3)(a) and 45(3)(a) and requested the Secretariat to proceed no further. The Secretariat considered that none of the actions taken by Canada in relation to the three mines fell within the definition of those provisions, as provincial permits were no longer the subject of pending proceedings and inspections, testing, and warning letters do not fall within the scope of those provisions.[85] However, the Council stated that it had been informed by Canada that "at this time there are no pending judicial or administrative proceedings regarding the Britannia Mine and that proceedings relating to the Tulsequah Chief and Mt. Washington Mines are still pending."[86] Consequently, the Council instructed the Secretariat to prepare a factual record with respect to the Britannia Mine and to terminate the submission process with respect to the assertions concerning the other two.[87] The Council did not specify to which proceedings Canada was referring, and did not mention its considerations of the Secretariat's analysis on this issue.

In the *Tarahumara* submission, the Secretariat found that the information provided by Mexico in its response was insufficient to terminate the submission in accordance with Article 14(3)(a), and recommended the preparation of a factual record.[88] However, the Council, "[having been informed] by Mexico that the administrative proceedings related to the citizen complaints referenced under headings H and M of the submissions [were] no longer pending,"[89] instructed the Secretariat to prepare a factual record. Even though the Council followed the Secretariat's recommendation in this regard, in relation to the pending proceedings it was the Mexican notification that was considered relevant and not the Secretariat's analysis.

[84] See SEM-97–001 (*B.C. Hydro*), Council Resolution 98–07 pursuant to Article 15(2) (June 24, 1998); SEM-98–004 (*BC Mining*), Council Resolution 01–11 pursuant to Article 15(2) (November 16, 2001); SEM-00–006 (*Tarahumara*), Council Resolution 03–04 pursuant to Article 15(2) (April 22, 2003); SEM-01–001 (*Cytrar II*), Council Resolution 02–13 pursuant to Article 15(2) (December 10, 2002); SEM-02–003 (*Pulp and Paper*), Council Resolution 03–16 pursuant to Article 15(2) (December 11, 2003); SEM-03–003 (*Lake Chapala II*), Council Resolution 08–01 pursuant to Article 15(2) (May 30, 2008); SEM-06–005 (*Species at Risk*), Council Resolution 10–05 pursuant to Article 15(2) (December 20, 2010).
[85] *BC Mining* Notification, p. 17.
[86] *BC Mining* Council Resolution 01–11, pp. 1–2.
[87] Ibid.
[88] *Tarahumara* Notification, pp. 17, 18, and 20.
[89] *Tarahumara* Council Resolution 03–04, p. 1.

Moreover, in the *Cytrar II* submission, Mexico asserted that the matter of the submission was also the subject of an arbitration proceeding to settle an international investment dispute between Técnicas Medioambientales Tecmed, S.A. (a partner of Cytrar S.A. de C.V.) and Mexico. The Secretariat was unable to determine that both processes – the submission and the arbitration proceeding – shared the same subject matter, since Mexico failed to provide sufficient information. The Secretariat was unable to ascertain the subject of the arbitration proceeding, and could not derive this information from the relationship of the companies in question.[90] After requesting additional information from Mexico, the Secretariat recommended a factual record.[91] Once again, the Council considered that Mexico, in its response, "informed the Secretariat, pursuant to Article 14(3)(a) of the NAAEC, that the matter at issue in the submission is the subject of a pending international dispute resolution proceeding before the International Centre for Settlement of Investment Disputes."[92] Without further explanation or reference to the Secretariat's recommendation, the Council instructed it not to prepare a factual record.[93]

With these examples at hand, the opinion of those who believe that the actions and decisions of the Council "have eroded public confidence in the process," and who have expressed concern about its neutrality,[94] seems to be justified.

4. NEW SEM GUIDELINES

4.1. *Comparison with Former SEM Guidelines*

The NAAEC explicitly requires the Secretariat to provide reasons for its decision-making in only one provision – in Article 15(1) concerning the recommendation of a factual record – and implicitly in Articles 14(1) and 14(2) concerning the admissibility of the submissions and the request of a response, respectively. However, the Parties have extended this requirement to particular steps of the SEM process through the New Guidelines.[95]

---

[90] *Cytrar II* Determination, pp. 4–5.
[91] *Cytrar II* Notification.
[92] *Cytrar II* Council Resolution 02–13.
[93] Ibid.
[94] Markell, "Role of Spotlighting Procedures," 440.
[95] Although the guidelines do not constitute as such an amendment to the NAAEC, they could be considered to represent a "subsequent agreement between the parties regarding the interpretation of the treaty or the application of its provisions" under Article 31(3)(a) of the Vienna Convention. Furthermore, Former Guideline 18.1 established that the guidelines do not intend to modify the Agreement and that in case of conflict among their provisions, those of the Agreement prevail to the extent of the inconsistency; New Guideline 18.1 expresses a similar point.

Under the Former Guidelines, the Secretariat was supposed to provide its reasons in four circumstances: (1) when determining whether a submission met the criteria set out in Article 14(1);[96] (2) when assessing whether a submission merited requesting a response from the Party concerned;[97] (3) when notifying the Council and the submitter of the existence of a pending proceeding and the consequent termination of the submission process;[98] and when recommending the development of a factual record.[99] In this regard, the New Guidelines remain the same or were slightly modified, with the exception of one: that concerning the notification of the existence of pending proceeding under Article 14(3)(a).[100]

Former Guideline 9.4 established that:

> If the Party informs the Secretariat that the matter raised in the submission is the subject of a pending judicial or administrative proceeding, as defined in Article 45(3) of the Agreement, the Secretariat will proceed no further with the submission, *and will notify the Submitter and the Council of its reason(s)* and that the submission process is terminated [emphasis added].

The corresponding New Guideline 9.6 establishes that:

> If, in its response under Article 14(3), the Party informs the Secretariat and explains in writing that the matter raised in the submission is the subject of a pending judicial or administrative proceeding, as defined in Article 45(3) of the Agreement, the Secretariat *will proceed no further* with the submission and *will promptly notify* the Submitter and the Council, in writing, that the submission process is terminated without prejudice to the Submitter's ability to file a new submission. If the Party informs and provides the written explanation *at any other point* in the submission process prior to a Council instruction that a factual record be prepared, the Secretariat *should consider* terminating the process to avoid the potential for duplication or interference. If the Party informs and provides the written explanation after the Secretariat has been instructed by the Council to prepare a factual record, the Secretariat *is to proceed* with the factual record unless Council directs otherwise [emphasis added].

According to the New Guideline, if a Party notifies the Secretariat of the existence of a pending proceeding regarding the matter raised in a submission, the Secretariat

---

[96] Former Guidelines, 6.1, 6.3 and 7.2.

[97] Ibid., 7.2.

[98] Ibid., 9.4.

[99] Ibid., 9.6 and 10.1.

[100] See New Guidelines, 6.1, 6.3, 7.2, 9.8, and 10.1 (for examples of similarities to Former Guidelines). In accordance with New Guideline 8.1, when the Secretariat determines that the submission does not merit a response from the Party, the process is terminated and the Secretariat is supposed to notify the Council and the submitter in accordance with New Guideline 7.2. In addition, when the Secretariat, the Council, or a Party does not meet an applicable deadline, it should provide a written explanation in accordance with New Guideline 15.1(k).

will proceed no further and will notify the submitter and the Council that the submission process is terminated without further reasoning or explanation.

This assumption is based on a literal interpretation of the New Guideline. First of all, a removal of the words "of its reasons" from the Former Guideline and the introduction of "promptly" in the new one can be appreciated. In the new text, the Party must not only inform the Secretariat of the existence of a pending proceeding, but also must explain its reasons in a written form. This obligation is reinforced by the addition of New Guideline 15.1(g), which establishes that the Registry will include "the Party's written explanation that the matter(s) raised in the submission is the subject of a pending judicial or administrative proceeding, if applicable." Moreover, the use of different words in the second and third part of the New Guideline 9.6 leads to the same conclusion: the Secretariat "should consider" terminating the process when the notification is presented at any other point of the process before the Council instructs the preparation of a factual record, as opposed to "is to proceed" when the Council has instructed preparation of a factual record.[101] The terms "should consider" seem to enable the Secretariat to explain the reasons of its determination if it decides to proceed no further; the absence of these terms seems to indicate that the Secretariat is not allowed to give its reasons in the other two cases described in New Guideline 9.6. If the Parties had intended to consider the Secretariat's reasoning, they would not have altered the drafting of the Former Guideline or would have introduced different terms.

Consequently, the Party's own explanation – concerning how the matter raised in the submission is the subject of a pending judicial or administrative proceeding in terms of Article 45(3) of NAEEC – will probably constitute the last word on the matter. Apparently, the New Guidelines shift the power of making a determination of a pending proceeding to the Party in question. Additionally, the time at which a response is submitted under Article 14(3) is not the only procedural opportunity for the Parties to notify the Secretariat of the existence of a pending proceeding. Parties are now allowed to give such notification at any other point afterwards, either before or after the Council's instruction to prepare a factual record.

4.2. *Implications for the SEM Process*

When read and analyzed carefully, the subtle changes to Former Guideline 9.4 may have important implications in the Secretariat's interpretation and application of Article 14(3)(a). What are the reasons for this reform? The New Guidelines could be a response to the Secretariat's practice of restrictively interpreting Article 14(3)(a) and using its discretionary powers under Article 15(1), a practice the Parties may

---

[101] New Guidelines, 9.6.

116 *Montserrat Rovalo*

consider inconvenient. In addition, perhaps the Parties disliked how the Secretariat contradicted their views on what constitutes pending proceedings in their respective legal systems. However, these mere speculations can hardly be proven.

Nonetheless, it is logical to posit that the New Guidelines legitimize and legalize a previous practice in which the Council ignored the Secretariat's reasoning and considered only the Parties' assertions. As has elsewhere been mentioned, "while [the Parties] publicly embrace the values that underlie the process – transparency, accountability, stronger environmental protection – they have in practice sought to circumscribe it."[102]

Considering that the Council already has a veto power regarding the development of factual records,[103] the implicit danger in New Guideline 9.6 is that it creates a new type of veto, which is directly and individually vested in the Parties. This danger is underlined by the fact that the Parties have shown in the past a tendency to assert the existence of pending administrative or judicial proceedings. If the dismissal of submissions on this ground becomes a common practice in the future, citizens' trust in the SEM process may be reduced, and they may present fewer submissions.

As to the transparency of the process, theoretically transparency will be assured by the Parties' duty to provide a written explanation and publish it in the Registry. Considering that the Parties, particularly Mexico, used to notify the Secretariat of the existence of pending proceedings but failed to clarify these assertions under a confidentiality argument, the mentioned duty seems to constitute an improvement. However, it is unclear from the text of the New Guidelines what would happen if the Parties' explanations were incomplete or insufficiently clear, or if they were to argue the existence of a pending proceeding that does not conform to the definition contained in Article 45(3) based on the criteria already developed by the Secretariat. Under these scenarios, perhaps, the Secretariat may be able to find an opportunity to analyze the alleged existence of pending proceedings.

One of the main critiques of the SEM process since its creation has been the inherent procedural injustice in its design and implementation, as the Parties play a double role: that of being the "targets"[104] of the submissions and that of having decisional power in the process.[105] Unfortunately, New Guideline 9.6 seems to further tilt the SEM process in favor of the Parties.

[102] Ten-year Review and Assessment Committee, "Ten Years of North American Environmental Cooperation," *Report of the Ten-year Review and Assessment Committee to the Council of the Commission for Environmental Cooperation* (June 15, 2004).
[103] Markell, "Role of Spotlighting Procedures," 456.
[104] David Markell, "The North American Commission for Environmental Cooperation After Ten Years: Lessons About Institutional Structure and Public Participation in Governance" (2004) 26 *Loyola of Los Angeles International & Comparative Law Review*, 341–57 at 347.
[105] Pacheco-Vega, "Las denuncias ciudadanas," 97.

5. NECESSARY REFORM OF THE NEW GUIDELINES?

Considering this analysis of the New Guidelines, the inferences from its interpretation, and the possible consequences that may arise from its application, venturing to suggest some new reforms could be useful. It must be clarified, however, that these proposals lack an empirical basis, as Article 14(3)(a) has not yet been interpreted in light of the New Guidelines. The following constitute a priori suggestions that aim to improve the goals of transparency, justice, and impartiality in the SEM Process.

5.1. *Mandatory Reasoning from Council, Parties, and Secretariat*

Positive aspects of the New Guidelines include the introduction of time limits for the different steps of the citizen submission process, and the duty for Council, Parties, and the Secretariat to provide a written explanation in case of delay.

In accordance with NAEEC and the New Guidelines, the Secretariat must explain its reasons when writing Article 14(1) determinations,[106] requesting a response from the Parties,[107] and deciding whether the submission warrants the development of a factual record.[108] Equally, in their responses to submissions, the Parties must explain how they are enforcing their environmental law or how the matter of a submission is the subject of a pending proceeding.[109] Moreover, the Council is now supposed to provide its reasons when instructing the Secretariat to prepare a factual record.[110] Consequently, all of these documents shall be published in the Registry of the CEC.[111]

Notwithstanding these positive features, the New Guidelines do not specify whether the Council should also explain its reasons when instructing the Secretariat not to develop a factual record. This reasoning is undoubtedly of interest to submitters and citizens. The Council's motives are also not required with respect to its decisions concerning the publication of factual records. With the aim of achieving a higher degree of transparency and access to information, the publication of the Council's, Secretariat's, and Parties' reasoning in every decision, determination, notification, or response should be the general rule.

5.2. *Secretariat: Final Word on the Applicability of Article 14(3)(a)*

Bearing in mind that the existence of a pending proceeding under Article 14(3)(a) constitutes an ipso facto ground for the termination of a submission process, the

---

[106] New Guidelines, 6.1 and 7.2.
[107] Ibid., 7.2.
[108] NAAEC, Article 15(1); New Guidelines, 9.8 and 10.1.
[109] Ibid., 9.4 and 9.6.
[110] Ibid., 10.4.
[111] Ibid., 10.2 and 15.1(f), (g), (h)(i), (h)(ii), (h)(iv), (h)(vi).

applicability of that article should be restrained. Termination of the submission process should be exceptional. With the aim of achieving fairness and impartiality, it is preferable (from a citizen's perspective) to give the Secretariat the last word on the applicability of the article – rather than to leave the decision to the Parties, which have an accused-judge personality in the process.

In this regard, it could be argued that the drafting of the New Guideline 9.6 goes against the object and purpose of NAAEC. However, this hypothesis will be mainly confirmed by future practice of the Parties and the Secretariat. Furthermore, the Secretariat has developed a full set of criteria regarding pending administrative and judicial proceedings. Although the Secretariat is not obliged to follow these criteria, it has tried to apply them coherently and consistently. Without diminishing the importance of the Parties' reasoning when arguing the applicability of Article 14(3)(a), leaving the final decision to the Secretariat would reduce the risk of using fragmented, inconsistent criteria for the article's application.

6. CONCLUSIONS

The language of Article 14(3)(a) is quite straightforward and does not give any discretion to the Secretariat to evaluate whether to terminate the submission process, since it obliges the Secretariat to stop the process when a pending proceeding exists. The Former Guidelines allowed the Secretariat to reason and determine whether a pending proceeding existed in terms of Article 45(3)(a). In addition, by restrictively interpreting Article 14(3)(a) with the aim of promoting NAAEC's objectives, the Secretariat still evaluated pending proceedings falling outside the scope of Article 45(3)(a) in its Article 15(1) recommendations.

It is clear from the New Guidelines that the Parties will now decide whether a pending proceeding exists and whether the Secretariat should proceed no further, unless the latter finds an alternative provision or interpretation in NAAEC to continue assessing the Parties' responses in this regard. The Secretariat will find itself in a very difficult position if it acknowledges that there is no pending proceeding under NAAEC Article 45(3)(a) and, yet, has to terminate a submission.

Perhaps the Council did not envisage the possible negative consequences of the guideline reform on this matter, although this potential explanation seems somewhat naive. Unfortunately, the Parties' intention to have more control over the process seems more likely.

As the Secretariat has already established, the SEM process is designed to scrutinize the Parties' commitments to effectively enforce their environmental laws. Thus, having an independent and impartial arbitrator defining the existence of pending proceedings and the applicability of Article 14(3)(a) is preferable. For this main reason, reform to the New Guidelines has been suggested so as to restore the final word on this matter to the Secretariat. This proposal is unlikely to be received favorably by the Parties in light of their past positions, and any such reform will probably not occur without at least having tested the New Guidelines for a few years.

Pending Administrative or Judicial Proceedings*

Number	Party	Submission	Party Argues Pending Proceedings	14(3)(a) Determination	15(1) Determination or Notification	Secretariat Recommends Factual Record	Council Instructs Factual Record
1	Canada	SEM-96-003 (Oldman River I)	Yes		x	No	
2	Canada	SEM-97-001 (B.C. Hydro)	Yes		x	Yes	Yes
3	Canada	SEM-98-004 (BC Mining)	Yes		x	Yes	Yes
4	Mexico	SEM-98-005 (Cytrar I)	No		x	No	
5	Mexico	SEM-98-006 (Aquanova)	No		x	Yes	Yes
6	USA	SEM-99-001 and SEM-00-002 (Methanex)	Yes	x			
7	Canada	SEM-00-004 (BC Logging)	Yes		x	Yes	Yes
8	Mexico	SEM-00-006 (Tarahumara)	Yes		x	Yes	Yes
9	Mexico	SEM-01-001 (Cytrar II)	Yes	x		Yes	No
10	Canada	SEM-02-003 (Pulp and Paper)	No		x	Yes	Yes
11	Mexico	SEM-02-004 (El Boludo Project)	Yes		x	Yes	Withdrawal of Submission
12	Mexico	SEM-03-003 (Lake Chapala II)	Yes		x	Yes	Yes
13	USA	SEM-04-005 (Coal-fired PowerPlants)	Yes		x	Yes	Yes
14	Mexico	SEM-05-001 (Crushed Gravel in Puerto Peñasco)	No		x	No	
15	Mexico	SEM-05-002 (Coronado Islands)	Yes		x	Yes	Withdrawal of Submission
16	Mexico	SEM-06-003 and SEM-06-004 consolidated (Ex Hacienda El Hospital II and III)	Yes		x	Yes	Yes
17	Canada	SEM-06-005 (Species at Risk)	Yes		x	Yes	Yes
18	Mexico	SEM-06-006 (Los Remedios National Park)	Yes		x	No	
19	Mexico	SEM-07-001 (Minera San Xavier)	Yes		x	No	
20	Mexico	SEM-07-005 (Drilling Waste in Cunduacán)	Yes	x			
21	Mexico	SEM-08-001 (La Ciudadela Project)	Yes		x	No	
22	Mexico	SEM-09-001 (Transgenic Maize in Chihuahua)	Yes		x	No	
23	Mexico	SEM-09-003 (Los Remedios National Park II)	Yes		x	No	
24	Mexico	SEM-09-002 (Wetlands in Manzanillo)	Yes		x	Yes	Pending

* Based on information available in the Registry of the CEC at www.cec.org.

LIST OF REFERENCES

International Materials

Case concerning *Kasikili/Sedudu Island (Botswana v Namibia)* [1999] ICJ Rep 1045.
Case concerning the *Territorial Dispute (Libyan Arab Jamahiriya v Chad)*, [1994] ICJ Rep 6.
North American Agreement on Environmental Cooperation, September 14, 1993, in force January 1, 1994, (1993) 32 ILM 1480; Can TS 1994 No 3.
Responsibilities and Obligations of States Sponsoring Persons and Entities with respect to Activities in the Area, Advisory Opinion (February 1, 2011).
Vienna Convention on the Law of Treaties, Vienna, May 23, 1969, in force January 27, 1980, 1155 UNTS 331; (1969) 8 ILM 679.

CEC Documents

Commission for Environmental Cooperation, *Bringing the Facts to Light: A Guide to Articles 14 and 15 of the North American Agreement on Environmental Cooperation* (Montreal: Commission for Environmental Cooperation, 2000).
Commission for Environmental Cooperation, *Guidelines for Submissions on Enforcement Matters under Articles 14 and 15 of the North American Agreement on Environmental Cooperation* (Montreal: Commission for Environmental Cooperation, 2013).
SEM-00–004 (*BC Logging*), Recommendation pursuant to Article 15(1) (July 27, 2001).
SEM-00–006 (*Tarahumara*), Council Resolution 03–04 pursuant to Article 15(2) (April 22, 2003).
SEM-00–006 (*Tarahumara*), Recommendation pursuant to Article 15(1) (August 29, 2002).
SEM-01–001 (*Cytrar II*), Council Resolution 02–13 pursuant to Article 15(2) (December 10, 2002).
SEM-01–001 (*Cytrar II*), Determination pursuant to Article 14(3) (June 13, 2001).
SEM-01–001 (*Cytrar II*), Recommendation pursuant to Article 15(1) (July 29, 2002).
SEM-02–003 (*Pulp and Paper*), Council Resolution 03–16 pursuant to Article 15(2) (December 11, 2003).
SEM-02–003 (*Pulp and Paper*), Recommendation pursuant to Article 15(1) (October 8, 2003).
SEM-02–004 (*El Boludo Project*), Recommendation pursuant to Article 15(1) (May 17, 2004).
SEM-03–003 (*Lake Chapala II*), Council Resolution 08–01 pursuant to Article 15(2) (May 30, 2008).
SEM-03–003 (*Lake Chapala II*), Recommendation pursuant to Article 15(1) (May 18, 2005).
SEM-04–005 (*Coal-fired Power Plants*), Government of the United States of America Supplemental Response pursuant to Article 14(3) (September 29, 2005).
SEM-04–005 (*Coal-fired Power Plants*), Recommendation pursuant to Article 15(1) (December 5, 2005).
SEM-05–001 (*Crushed Gravel in Puerto Peñasco*), Recommendation pursuant to Article 15(1) (October 24, 2005).
SEM-05–002 (*Coronado Islands*), Government of the United Mexican States Response pursuant to Article 14(3) (January 10, 2006).
SEM-05–002 (*Coronado Islands*), Recommendation pursuant to Article 15(1) (January 18, 2007).
SEM-06–003 and SEM-06–004 (*Ex Hacienda El Hospital II and Ex Hacienda El Hospital III*), Recommendation pursuant to Article 15(1) (May 12, 2008).
SEM-06–005 (*Species at Risk*), Council Resolution 10–05 pursuant to Article 15(2) (December 20, 2010).

SEM-06–005 (*Species at Risk*), Government of Canada Response pursuant to Article 14(3) (February 8, 2007).

SEM-06–006 (*Los Remedios National Park*), Government of the United Mexican States Supplemental Response pursuant to Article 21(1)(b) (February 26, 2008).

SEM-06–006 (*Los Remedios National Park*), Recommendation pursuant to Article 15(1) (March 20, 2008).

SEM-06–006 (*Los Remedios National Park*), Secretariat Information Request pursuant to Article 21(1)(b) (November 27, 2007).

SEM-07–001 (*Minera San Xavier*), Government of the United Mexican States Supplemental Response pursuant to Article 21(1)(b) (June 5, 2008).

SEM-07–001 (*Minera San Xavier*), Recommendation pursuant to Article 15(1) (July 15, 2009).

SEM-07–001 (*Minera San Xavier*), Secretariat Information Request pursuant to Article 21(1)(b) (March 7, 2008).

SEM-07–005 (*Drilling Waste in Cunduacán*), Determination pursuant to Article 14(3) (April 8, 2009).

SEM-07–005 (*Drilling Waste in Cunduacán*), Government of the United Mexican States Supplemental Response pursuant to Article 21(1)(b) (May 15, 2008).

SEM-08–001 (*La Ciudadela Project*), Government of the United Mexican States Supplemental Response pursuant to Article 21(1)(b) (May 26, 2010).

SEM-08–001 (*La Ciudadela Project*), Recommendation pursuant to Article 15(1) (August 12, 2010).

SEM-09–001 (*Transgenic Maize in Chihuahua*), Government of the United Mexican States Response pursuant to Article 14(3) (May 3, 2010).

SEM-09–001 (*Transgenic Maize in Chihuahua*), Recommendation pursuant to Article 15(1) (December 20, 2010).

SEM-09–002 (*Wetlands in Manzanillo*), Notification pursuant to Article 15(1) (August 19, 2013).

SEM-09–003 (*Los Remedios National Park II*), Government of the United Mexican States Response pursuant to Article 14(3) (December 20, 2010).

SEM-09–003 (*Los Remedios National Park II*), Recommendation pursuant to Article 15(1) (July 27, 2011).

SEM-95–001 (*Spotted Owl*), Submission pursuant to Article 14 (June 30, 1995).

SEM-96–003 (*Oldman River I*), Recommendation pursuant to Article 15(1) (April 2, 1997).

SEM-97–001 (*B.C. Hydro*), Council Resolution 98–07 pursuant to Article 15(2) (June 24, 1998).

SEM-97–001 (*B.C. Hydro*), Government of Canada Response pursuant to Article 14(3) (July 21, 1997).

SEM-97–001 (*B.C. Hydro*), Recommendation pursuant to Article 15(1) (April 27, 1998).

SEM-98–004 (*BC Mining*), Council Resolution 01–11 pursuant to Article 15(2) (November 16, 2001).

SEM-98–004 (*BC Mining*), Government of Canada Response pursuant to Article 14(3) (September 8, 1999).

SEM-98–004 (*BC Mining*), Recommendation pursuant to Article 15(1) (June 29, 1998).

SEM-98–005 (*Aquanova*), Recommendation pursuant to Article 15(1) (August 4, 2000).

SEM-98–005 (*Cytrar I*), Recommendation pursuant to Article 15(1) (October 26, 2000).

SEM-99–001 and SEM 00–002 (*Methanex*), Determination pursuant to Article 14(3) (June 30, 2000).

SEM-99–001 and SEM 00–002 (*Methanex*), Government of the United States of America Response pursuant to Article 14(3) (May 30, 2000).

Additional Secondary Sources

Aust, Anthony. *Modern Treaty Law and Practice*, 2nd ed. Cambridge: Cambridge University Press, 2007.

Black's Law Dictionary Free Online Legal Dictionary, 2nd ed.

Markell, David. "The North American Commission for Environmental Cooperation After Ten Years: Lessons About Institutional Structure and Public Participation in Governance." (2004) 26 *Loyola of Los Angeles International & Comparative Law Review*, 341–57.

Markell, David. "The Role of Spotlighting Procedures in Promoting Citizen Participation, Transparency, and Accountability." (2010) 45 *Wake Forest Law Review*, 425–67.

Pacheco-Vega, Raúl. "Las denuncias ciudadanas sobre cumplimiento ambiental en América del Norte (1996–2012): perspectivas sobre la sociedad civil ambientalista norteamericana." (2013) 8 *NORTEAMÉRICA*, 77–108.

Solano, Pablo. "Choosing the Right Whistle: The Development of the 'Environmental Law' Concept under the Citizen Submission Process," Chapter 3 of this volume.

Ten-year Review and Assessment Committee. "Ten Years of North American Environmental Cooperation." *Report of the Ten-year Review and Assessment Committee to the Council of the Commission for Environmental Cooperation* (June 15, 2004).

5

Form over Substance

Procedural Hurdles to the NAAEC Citizen Submission Process

Leslie Welts

1. INTRODUCTION

The North American Agreement on Environmental Cooperation's (NAAEC) sustainable development objective is intended to be carried out by the Commission on Environmental's Cooperation (CEC) citizen submission process. However, the CEC Secretariat has interpreted the NAAEC's procedural requirements for citizen submissions in an increasingly formalistic manner. As a result, the procedural burden has risen for NAAEC submissions, decreasing the public's access to information and limiting the ability of the public to hold the Parties accountable for enforcing their environmental laws. Consequently, the procedural burden has the effect of stifling submissions and hindering the NAAEC's prime tool for achieving its sustainable development goals. This chapter analyzes the Secretariat's interpretation of NAAEC's procedural requirements over time and assesses how the increasingly heavy burden impacts the CEC's success in implementing NAAEC's sustainable development goals. This chapter concludes that this interference demonstrates a need to revisit the procedural requirements to encourage increased public participation via citizen submission in order to improve prospects of achieving NAAEC's sustainable development goals.

Canada, the United States of America, and Mexico adopted the NAAEC in 1993 as a side agreement to the North American Free Trade Agreement (NAFTA).[1] The purpose of its adoption was as a safeguard to prevent liberalized trade between Canada, the United States, and Mexico (the Parties) from resulting in harm to the environment.[2] The NAAEC set broad environmental objectives, such as

---

[1] John H. Knox and David L. Markell, "The Innovative North American Commission for Environmental Cooperation," in David L. Markell and John H. Knox (eds.), *Greening NAFTA: The North American Commission for Environmental Cooperation* (Stanford, CA: Stanford University Press, 2003), pp. 8–9.

[2] Knox and Markell, "The Innovative North American Commission," pp. 1, 8.

"conservation, protection and enhancement of the environment"[3] through the Parties' "cooperation in these areas in achieving sustainable development for the well-being of present and future generations."[4]

The NAAEC established the CEC to administer the processes aimed at achieving these goals.[5] The CEC is composed of three bodies: the Council, the Secretariat, and the Joint Public Advisory Committee (JPAC).[6] The JPAC consists of five citizens from each country[7] who advise the Council on matters within the scope of the NAAEC.[8] The Secretariat, which is the administrative body of the CEC, is charged with providing technical, administrative, and operational support to the Council.[9] The Council, which is the governing body of the CEC,[10] is charged with overseeing the Secretariat[11] and with providing a forum for discussions of environmental matters within the scope of the NAAEC.[12]

The NAAEC also established two important processes for achieving its objectives: the Party dispute consultation process[13] and the citizen submission process.[14] Although the Party dispute consultation process has not yet been used, citizens of all three countries have actively used the citizen submission process since its inception.[15] This citizen submission process allows members of the public – either individuals or nongovernmental organizations – to charge a Party with failure to enforce its environmental laws by submitting its assertion to the Secretariat.[16] If a submission meets certain substantive and procedural requirements under the NAAEC, the Secretariat must then conduct an investigation into the matter and, ultimately, develop a factual record regarding the asserted failure of enforcement.[17] This factual record serves as a spotlight in that the Secretariat draws no legal conclusions[18] and issues no punishments.[19] Instead, the factual record is a tool that enables governmental

---

[3] Article 1(c) of the North American Agreement on Environmental Cooperation, Washington, Ottawa, and Mexico City, September 14, 1993, in force January 1, 1994, 32 ILM 1480.
[4] Preamble of the NAAEC.
[5] Article 8(1) of the North American Agreement on Environmental Cooperation (NAAEC).
[6] Article 8(2) of the NAAEC.
[7] Article 16(1) of the NAAEC.
[8] Article 16(4) of the NAAEC.
[9] Article 11(5) of the NAAEC.
[10] Article 10(1) of the NAAEC.
[11] Article 10(1)(c) of the NAAEC.
[12] Article 10(1)(a) of the NAAEC.
[13] Articles 22–36 of the NAAEC.
[14] Articles 14–15 of the NAAEC.
[15] Thomas Hale, "Citizen Submission Process of the North American Commission for Environmental Cooperation" in Thomas Hale and David Hale (eds.), *Handbook of Transnational Governance: Institutions & Innovations* (Cambridge: Polity Press, 2011), p. 120.
[16] Article 14 of the NAAEC.
[17] Article 15 of the NAAEC.
[18] Hale, "Citizen Submission Process," 120.
[19] See Chris Wold, "Evaluating NAFTA and the Commission for Environmental Cooperation: Lessons," (2008) 28 *St. Louis Univ. Public L. Rev.* 201, 231–232.

transparency and accountability. Moreover, the factual record provides the public with an important means for participation.

Criticisms of the citizen submission process have focused on "the ability of governments to delay reports and limit their scope, the lack of authority of the Secretariat to reach legal conclusions, and the absence of any consistent mechanism to follow up on reports."[20] Other critics have focused on the conflicts inherent in the CEC's governing structure: the Council has the final say on whether the Secretariat should develop and release factual records that spotlight its member countries' own alleged failures.[21] Although these are important issues that warrant further exploration, this chapter focuses instead on the procedural aspects of the citizen submission process. This chapter contends that the Secretariat's interpretation of the NAAEC's procedural requirements has become unduly burdensome on submitters and is interfering with the purposes of the process and the sustainable development objective of the NAAEC.

Section 1 presents background information on sustainable development principles as they relate to the NAAEC. Section 2 closely considers the Secretariat's implementation of the NAAEC's procedural requirements and discusses how its interpretation of these requirements has served to limit the scope of acceptable submissions. Section 3 analyzes how these barriers interfere with the NAAEC's sustainable development objective. This chapter concludes that the Secretariat should broaden its view of what satisfies certain procedural requirements and that the structure of the CEC should be reconsidered to reduce conflicts of interest.

2. THE NAAEC AND SUSTAINABLE DEVELOPMENT

Sustainable development principles are deeply ingrained in the function and purpose of the NAAEC and the CEC. Article 1 of the treaty lists "promote sustainable development based on cooperation and mutually supportive environmental and economic policies" as a formal treaty objective.[22] The NAAEC preamble recognizes "the importance of conservation, protection and enhancement of the environment . . . in achieving sustainable development for the well-being of present and future generations."[23] When the Independent Review Committee (IRC), a committee established by the CEC to conduct the objective four-year review required by the terms of the NAAEC,[24] conducted the first official review of the CEC, it

---

[20] John Knox, "Neglected Lessons of the NAFTA Environmental Regime" (2010) 45 *Wake Forest L. Rev* 391, 411.
[21] Chris Wold, et al., "The Inadequacy of the Citizen Submission Process of Articles 14 & 15 of the North American Agreement on Environmental Cooperation" (2004) 26 *Loyola of Los Angeles International and Comparative Law Review* 415, 426.
[22] Article 1(b) of the NAAEC.
[23] Preamble of the NAAEC.
[24] The NAAEC Review Committee of the Commission for Environmental Cooperation Call for Comments, COMMISSION FOR ENVIRONMENTAL COOPERATION (Dec. 2, 1997), http://www.cec.org/Page.asp?PageID=122&ContentID=1804&SiteNodeID=366.

noted that the long-term value of the NAAEC and the CEC would be measured by the contribution the CEC makes to sustainable development in North America.[25] The IRC also explained that the CEC had a unique opportunity to "play an important role in the achievement of sustainable development as the North American economy becomes increasingly linked."[26] In short, the CEC has made sustainable development a key goal of NAAEC enforcement; a goal that extends beyond merely counteracting the environmental effects of liberalized trade.[27]

2.1. *Principles of Sustainable Development*

Before discussing how the CEC integrates sustainable development in its operations, it is necessary to first define the concept. However, the task of defining "sustainable development" is challenging because "international understanding of both sustainability and development has evolved a great deal in recent decades."[28] The NAAEC does not define sustainable development in its provisions and has instead left it to the Parties to interpret.[29] Sustainable development is most commonly defined in international law as development that "meets the needs of the present without compromising the ability of future generations to meet their own needs."[30] This definition was first put forward in a 1987 United Nations report entitled "Our Common Future."[31] Over time and many international debates, policymakers have come to recognize three central "pillars" of sustainable development – environmental protection, economic growth, and social equity – for which states are collectively responsible.[32]

---

[25] Final Report of the Independent Review Committee, "Four-Year Review of the North American Agreement on Environmental Cooperation" (1998) at 5, http://www.cec.org/Storage/60/5224_NAAEC-4-year-review_en.pdf&sa=U&ei=XEymUa6VBbi-4AOfmYC4Dw&ved=0CAkQFjAB&client=internal-uds-cse&usg=AFQjCNFW4ZNeYRh2VTMz77V6kDQgis1lEA ("the long-term value of NAAEC and the Commission will be measured not so much by a technically defined environment and trade 'ruler,' but rather by the contribution the CEC makes to improved environmental conditions for all people in North America, in the context of changing economic patterns – in short, by its contribution to sustainable development in North America").

[26] Final Report of the Independent Review Committee, 9.

[27] David L. Markell, "The Role of Spotlighting Procedures in Promoting Citizen Participation, Transparency, and Accountability" (2010) 45 *Wake Forest Law Review* 425, 465.

[28] Marie-Claire Cordonier Segger, "The Role of International Forums in the Advancement of Sustainable Development" (2009) 10 *Sustainable Dev. L. & Pol'y* 4 at 4.

[29] Article 45 of the NAAEC.

[30] Cordonier Segger, "The Role of International Forums," 5.

[31] Cordonier Segger, "The Role of International Forums," 5 (citing U.N. World Commission on Environment and Development, *Report of the World Commission on Environment and Development: Our Common Future*, U.N. Doc. A/42/427 (Aug. 4, 1987), http://www.un-documents.net/wced-ocf.htm)).

[32] Ibid., 6 (citing the Johannesburg Declaration on Sustainable Development UN Department of Economic and Social Affairs, Johannesburg Declaration on Sustainable Development, U.N. Doc. A/Conf.199/200, http://www.unescap.org/esd/environment/rio20/pages/Download/johannesburgdeclaration.pdf).

Once international policymakers and legal scholars reached consensus as to the pillars of sustainable development, their focus turned to developing legal and policy mechanisms to realize these pillars.[33] Despite reaching some consensus on the pillars, sustainable development remains a concept lacking in clarity that often creates diverse interpretations of how to put it into practice.[34] Several international debates have ensued in an effort to enumerate principles for putting the concept of sustainable development into practice, and the 2002 New Delhi Declaration principles have emerged as the current standard.[35] As a result, international agreements often seek to address specific sustainability challenges related to economic, environmental, and social aspects of development through the adoption of certain operational mechanisms influenced by the New Delhi Declaration principles.[36] The New Delhi Declaration, which was produced as a result of the International Law Association meeting in 2002, offers seven "Principles of International Law Relating to Sustainable Development."[37] These principles were intended to serve as a tool informing policy and legal arrangements.[38] Of the seven principles, two are particularly relevant to the NAAEC: the principle of public participation and access to information and justice (Principle 5) and the principle of good governance (Principle 6).[39]

The principle of public participation and access to information and justice recognizes a "right of access to appropriate, comprehensible and timely information held by governments" related to sustainable development and "access to effective judicial or administrative procedures," including redress and remedy, as essential principles of the international law of sustainable development.[40] The principle of good governance calls on states to adopt "democratic and transparent decision-making procedures and financial accountability," to "combat official or other corruption," and to "respect the principle of due process in their procedures."[41]

In accordance with these New Delhi principles, the NAAEC contemplates that its sustainable development objective, like its other objectives, is to be accomplished by each Party enforcing its environmental laws and regulations, providing citizen

---

[33] Cf. ibid., 10.

[34] Maja Goepel, "Formulating Future Just Policies: Applying the Delhi Sustainable Development Law Principles" (2010) 2 *Sustainability* 1694 at 1694–95; see also David Markell (2010), p. 465 ("We are early on in understanding how best to configure our governance institutions to promote the unwieldy concept of sustainable development").

[35] Cordonier Segger, "The Role of International Forums," 10.

[36] Ibid., 13–14.

[37] International Law Association, "ILA New Delhi Declaration of Principles of International Law Relating to Sustainable Development," April 2, 2002, 2 *Int'l Envtl. Agreements: Politics, Law and Econ.* 209 (2002). U.N. Doc A/CONF.199/8.

[38] Cordonier Segger, "The Role of International Forums," 10.

[39] International Law Association, "ILA New Delhi Declaration of Principles of International Law Relating to Sustainable Development," 215.

[40] Ibid., 213, 215.

[41] Ibid., 215.

access to legal remedies, and assuring procedural due process for administrative and judicial proceedings.[42] The NAAEC supplements these internal enforcement mechanisms by providing two CEC procedural mechanisms for furthering its sustainable development goals: a consultation procedure for resolving Party disputes[43] and a citizen submission process.[44] Both processes emphasize effective enforcement of environmental laws through public participation and good governance principles.

2.2. *Party Dispute Consultation Procedure*

The consultation procedure "allows one country to submit a claim against another for a persistent pattern of failure to effectively enforce its domestic environmental laws in a manner that affects trade between the countries, with ultimate recourse to fines or snap-back tariffs."[45] The process promotes the sustainable development principles of public participation of good governance because the Parties are able to submit claims against one another, giving them each the opportunity to participate in decision-making processes made by the others. In addition, the process promotes good governance because it holds Parties accountable for their enforcement of environmental laws.

The consultation procedure gives the CEC "teeth" to remedy lax enforcement of domestic environmental laws,[46] but, as of May 2013, no Party has used the consultation procedure, and it seems that no party has any intention of doing so.[47] As a result, the citizen submission process has garnered significantly more attention.

2.3. *Citizen Submission Process*

The NAAEC's citizen submission process is a mechanism that enables residents of Canada, the United States, and Mexico to make submissions that "bring the facts to light concerning the enforcement of environmental legislation on the books of any

---

[42] David A. Gantz, "Labor Rights and Environmental Protection Under NAFTA and Other U.S. Free Trade Agreements" (2011) 42 *U. Miami Inter-Am. L. Rev.* 297, 311. See also Articles 5–7 of the NAAEC.
[43] Articles 22–36 of the NAAEC.
[44] Article 14 of the NAAEC.
[45] Linda J. Allen, "The North American Agreement on Environmental Cooperation: Has it Fulfilled its Promises and Potential? An Empirical Study of Policy" (2012) 23 *Colo. J. Int'l Envtl. L. & Pol'y* 121, 144.
[46] Allen, "Promises and Potential," 144.
[47] Geoff Garver, "Tooth Decay: Examining NAFTA's 'Environmental Teeth,'" (2008) 25 *The Environmental Forum* 34, 38 (contending that "the dispute resolution process has been a 'true paper tiger'" because "[n]one of the NAFTA governments has given the slightest indication that it has considered, or ever will consider, using the process to hold one of its trading partners accountable for weak enforcement of environmental laws"). See also Allen, "Promises and Potential," 144.

of the three countries."[48] This process is known as the Submissions on Enforcement Matters or SEM process.[49]

Under NAAEC Article 14, individuals or nongovernmental organizations can submit written assertions that a Party is failing to effectively enforce an environmental law to the CEC Secretariat.[50] If the Secretariat determines that the submission meets the procedural requirements provided in Article 14, the Secretariat will request a response from the Party against whom the assertions are made.[51] The Secretariat will then consider the Party's response and determine whether the submission warrants developing a factual record.[52] The factual record, which is drafted by independent experts coordinated by the Secretariat, draws from a wide range of technical expertise.[53] The factual record is intended to be an objective document that outlines "the history of the issue, the obligations of the Party under the law in question, the actions of the Party in fulfilling those obligations, and the facts relevant to the assertions made in the submission."[54] The Secretariat is not permitted to draw legal conclusions, offer remedies, or impose sanctions in factual records.[55] In other words, the factual record is meant "to create an objective picture of the party's enforcement or lack thereof."[56] Thus, the factual record serves as a "fire alarm" rather than a means for citizens to seek sanctions against their governments.[57]

Like the Party dispute consultation procedure, the citizen submission process promotes the sustainable development principles of public participation of good governance. The process promotes public participation in that it gives individuals and nongovernment actors the opportunity to participate in decision-making processes by giving them access to a fire alarm. The process also promotes public participation by ensuring that the public has access to information on the effective enforcement of environmental laws, as the public release of factual records is the end goal of every submission.[58]

---

[48] Commission for Environmental Cooperation, "Bringing the Facts to Light: A Guide to Articles 14 and 15 of the North American Agreement on Environmental Cooperation" (2007) at 1, http://www.cec.org/Storage/41/3331_Bringing%20the%20Facts_en.pdf.

[49] Commission for Environmental Cooperation, "Submissions on Enforcement Matters," http://www.cec.org/Page.asp?PageID=1212&SiteNodeID=210&BL_ExpandID=156.

[50] CEC, "Bringing the Facts to Light," 1.

[51] CEC, "Bringing the Facts to Light," 1.

[52] Article 15(1) of the NAAEC.

[53] Hale, "Citizen Submission Process," p. 119.

[54] CEC, "Bringing the Facts to Light," 1.

[55] Article 15(3) of the NAAEC; Wold, "Evaluating NAFTA," 231–32.

[56] Hale, "Citizen Submission Process," p. 119.

[57] Kal Raustiala, "Police Patrols and Fire Alarms in the NAAEC" (2004) 26 *Loy. L.A. Int'l & Comp. L. Rev.* 389, 390; Markell, "The Role of Spotlighting," 430. For a seminal work on the "fire alarm" versus "police patrol" models of government oversight, see Matthew D. McCubbins and Thomas Schwartz, "Congressional Oversight Overlooked: Police Patrols Versus Fire Alarms" (1984) 28 *American Journal of Political Science*, 165.

[58] Commission on Environmental Cooperation, "Guidelines on Enforcement Matters" (2012), 1, http://www.cec.org/Storage/152/17779_SEM_booklet_PDF_en_final.pdf. Although the CEC maintains all

The process has also often been cited as a prime model of accountability and good governance.[59] The process was intended to "gently nip" governments that failed to effectively enforce their environmental laws by shining the spotlight on enforcement.[60] Such spotlighting increases the transparency of government decision-making processes and provides individuals and nongovernment actors with the ability to hold the government accountable for these processes.

The citizen submission process was expected to generate a good deal more submissions than the CEC has received to date. According to one study, "Given the importance of lax enforcement during the NAFTA negotiations, some negotiators of the NAAEC anticipated that the CEC would receive hundreds, if not thousands, of citizen submissions annually."[61] Through 2013, the Secretariat had received only eighty-four citizen submissions – fewer than five each year on average – and had prepared twenty-two factual records. The most submissions the Secretariat has received in a single year is seven (1997, 1998, 2004, and 2006). Moreover, the incoming submissions appear to be dwindling in recent years. The Secretariat has received four or fewer submissions per year in the years since 2009, and it received a record low of only two submissions in 2012.[62] One submitter became so frustrated with the lengthy process that it went so far as to withdraw its submission in 2011.[63]

Despite unmet expectations regarding the use of the citizen submissions process, many legal scholars regard it as the "centerpiece"[64] and "most innovative and closely-watched aspect of the [NAAEC]."[65] The process is also cited as a prime example of a process that emphasizes "new governance" principles, such as facilitating public participation and promoting government transparency.[66]

public documents on its website in its Registry of Submissions, Commission on Environmental Cooperation, "Registry of Submissions," http://www.cec.org/Page.asp?PageID=751&SiteNodeID=250, not all factual records are made public. Guideline 13.1. If the Council does make a factual record public, the Secretariat must post it on the online registry. CEC Guideline 15.1(j).

[59] Wold, "The Inadequacy of the Citizen Submission Process," 416 ("Many had regarded the Citizen Submission Process as a potential model for accountability and governance for a new breed of international institutions – a positive response to globalization that gives citizens a voice in the often impenetrable affairs of international organizations").

[60] Garver, "Tooth Decay," 34.

[61] Allen, "Promises and Potential," n. 122.

[62] CEC Registry, http://www.cec.org/Page.asp?PageID=751&SiteNodeID=250.

[63] EcoJustice withdrawal letter, January 17, 2011, by EcoJustice Executive Director Devon Page, http://www.ecojustice.ca/media-centre/media-release-files/cec-withdrawal-letter (accusing Council of material delay in deciding whether to produce a factual record and of incorrectly and arbitrarily limiting the scope of the factual record, frustrating both "letter and spirit of the NAAEC" and enforcement of Canada's Species at Risk Act).

[64] Markell, "The Role of Spotlighting," 430.

[65] Wold, "The Inadequacy of the Citizen Submission Process," 416.

[66] John H. Knox and David L. Markell, "Evaluating Citizen Petition Procedures: Lessons From an Analysis of the NAFTA Environmental Commission," (2012), pp. 506, 507.

3. SECRETARIAT INTERPRETATION OF NAAEC ARTICLE 14(1)

Having discussed the general citizen submission process in its context as intended to further the NAAEC's sustainable development goals, this chapter now turns to how the Secretariat analyzes submissions. In particular, this section focuses on how the Secretariat interprets the NAAEC's procedural requirements set forth in Article 14(1).[67]

Submissions to the Secretariat must meet certain criteria before the Secretariat may proceed with the submission process and request a response from the applicable Party. These procedural requirements are set forth in Article 14(1) and (2) of the NAAEC. Because the Article 14 requirements are fairly general, the CEC published supplemental citizen enforcement guidelines in 1995, revised in 2012,[68] to "describe and clarify the manner in which the public submission process should be implemented."[69]

Article 14(1) provides several mandatory criteria for all submissions, whereas Article 14(2) lists guidance criteria for the Secretariat to consider when deciding whether to request a response from a member state. Submissions that do not meet Article 14(1) requirements are not further considered. If those requirements are met, the Secretariat will determine whether a response is merited under Article 14(2). Although Article 14(2) is an important part of the process, this chapter focuses on the threshold requirements of Article 14(1).

Article 14(1) provides:

> The Secretariat may consider a submission from any non-governmental organization or person asserting that a Party is failing to effectively enforce its environmental law, if the Secretariat finds that the submission:
>
> (a) is in writing in a language designated by that Party in a notification to the Secretariat;
> (b) clearly identifies the person or organization making the submission;
> (c) provides sufficient information to allow the Secretariat to review the submission, including any documentary evidence on which the submission may be based;
> (d) appears to be aimed at promoting enforcement rather than at harassing industry;

---

[67] For a detailed discussion of these issues, see Paolo Solano, "Choosing the Right Whistle: The Development of the concept of Environmental Law under the Citizen Submission Process," Chapter 3 in the present collection.

[68] Paul Stanton Kibel, "Awkward Evolution: Citizen Enforcement at the North American Environmental Commission," (2002) 32 *Envtl. L. Reporter* 10769, 10773.

[69] Guidelines for Submissions on Enforcement Matters under Article 14 and 15 of the North American Agreement on Environmental Cooperation (as amended July 11, 2012), http://www.cec.org/Storage .asp?StorageID=10838. The original 1995 Guidelines were amended in 1995 and again in 2012. Kibel at 10773.

(e) indicates that the matter has been communicated in writing to the relevant authorities of the Party and indicates the Party's response, if any; and

(f) is filed by a person or organization residing or established in the territory of a Party.[70]

The Secretariat typically opens submission determinations with the declaration that Article 14(1) is "not intended to be an insurmountable screening device."[71] The Secretariat first used this language in its Article 14(1) Biodiversity Determination in 1998.[72] The Secretariat explained in that determination that "Article 14(1) should be given a large and liberal interpretation, consistent with the objectives of the NAAEC and the provisions of the Vienna Convention on the Law of Treaties."[73]

However, the Secretariat's explanation of its "insurmountable" language has since evolved; it is now declared to mean "that the Secretariat will interpret every Submission in accordance with the NAAEC and the Guidelines, yet without an unreasonably narrow interpretation and application of those Article 14(1) criteria."[74] The Secretariat's new interpretation – that it should consider submissions "without an unreasonably narrow interpretation" – is a good deal narrower than "a large and liberal interpretation." The modern interpretation implies that the Secretariat has taken an increasingly narrow view of Article 14(1)'s procedural requirements – enough so that it must clarify that its view is not "unreasonably narrow." This trend is of particular concern since this interpretation provides the lens through which the Secretariat examines submissions to determine whether they pass procedural muster. With this

[70] Article 14(1) of the NAAEC.

[71] For example, see SEM-13–002 (*Louisiana Refinery Releases*) Determination in accordance with Article 14(1) of the North American Agreement on Environmental Cooperation (August 12, 2013) at 4, available at http://www.cec.org/storage/151/17765_13–2-DETN_en.pdf; see also SEM-12–002 (*St. Lawrence River Wind Farms*) Determination in accordance with Article 14(1) of the North American Agreement on Environmental Cooperation (April 3, 2013) at 5, available at http://www.cec.org/storage/146?17222_12–2-DETN14; and SEM-11–003 (*Protection of Polar Bears*) Determination in accordance with Article 14(1) of the North American Agreement on Environmental Cooperation (Dec. 5, 2011) at 9, available at http://www.cec.org/storage/142/16760_11–3-DET14(1)(2)_en.pdf.

[72] SEM-97–005 (*Biodiversity*) Determination pursuant to Article 14(1) of the North American Agreement on Environmental Cooperation (May 26, 1998) at 2, http://www.cec.org/Storage/67/6133_97–5-DET-E .pdf. Before 1997, Article 14(1) Determinations were brief notifications to the submitting party that their submission met "initial screening criteria under 14(1)." The Secretariat first issued a lengthy and analytical Article 14(1) determination in August, 1997. See SEM-97–004 (*Biodiversity*) Determination pursuant to Articles 14 and 15 of the NAAEC (August 25, 1997), http://www.cec.org/Storage/67/6133_97–5-DET-E.pdf. In 1998, in response to the Animal Alliance of Canada's *Biodiversity* submission, the Secretariat first used the now-common "insurmountable" language.

[73] SEM-97–005 (*Biodiversity*) Determination pursuant to Article 14(1) of the North American Agreement on Environmental Cooperation (May 26, 1998) at 2, http://wwws.cec.org/Storage/67/6133_97–5-DET-E.pdf.

[74] SEM-11–003 (Protection of Polar Bears) Determination in accordance with Article 14(1) of the North American Agreement on Environmental Cooperation (Dec. 5, 2011) at 9, http://www.cec.org/storage/142/16760_11–3-DET14(1)(2)_en.pdf.

in mind, we now look to the Secretariat's analysis of the Article 14(1) requirements themselves.

3.1. *Article 14(1) Opening Sentence*

The Secretariat has long "recognize[d] that meaning must be given not only to the specific criteria delineated in Article 14(1)(a)–(f), but also to the opening words of the section."[75] This requirement is important to consider because these opening words provide three relatively high hurdles that submitters must overcome. The opening sentence of Article 14(1) provides that "[t]he Secretariat may consider a submission . . . asserting that a Party *is failing* to *effectively enforce its environmental law*."[76] This sentence has the effect of limiting submissions to those that: (1) involve at least one "environmental law"; (2) allege a failure to "effectively enforce" this environmental law; and (3) assert that the failure is one that is ongoing in nature.[77] The Secretariat has developed extensive requirements about what constitutes an environmental law, what qualifies as a failure, and when a failure is considered ongoing. Each of these requirements is addressed in turn.

3.1.1. "Environmental law"

The first source of law for what constitutes an environmental law is the definition in the NAAEC itself.[78] Article 45(2) of the NAAEC defines the term "environmental law," "for the purposes of Article 14(1)," as the legal provisions of a Party "the primary purpose of which is the protection of the environment, or "prevention of a danger" to human life or health."[79] Article 45 not only defines "environmental law," but also clarifies what the term excludes. Article 45(2) explicitly excludes legal provisions "directly related to worker safety or health[80] and those "the primary purpose of which is managing the commercial harvest or exploitation, or subsistence or aboriginal harvesting, of natural resources."[81]

The Secretariat has stated that "the term 'environmental law' should be interpreted expansively" because "[i]t would not be consistent with the purposes of the NAAEC to adopt an unduly restrictive view of what constitutes a statute or regulation which is primarily aimed at protection of the environment or prevention

---

[75] *Biodiversity*-Article 14(1) Determination, A14/SEM/97–005/09/14(1) at 2–3.

[76] Article 14(1) of the NAAEC (emphasis added).

[77] David L. Markell, "The Commission for Environmental Cooperation's Citizen Submission Process" (2000) 12 *Geo. Int'l Envtl. L. Rev.* 545 at 551.

[78] SEM-98–001 (*Guadalajara*) Article 14(1) Determination pursuant to Article 14(1) of the North American Agreement for Environmental Cooperation (September 13, 1999) at 3, http://www.cec.org/Storage/67/6142_98–1-DET-E.pdf.

[79] Article 45(2)(a) of the NAAEC.

[80] Article 45(2)(a)(iii) of the NAAEC.

[81] Article 45(2)(b) of the NAAEC.

of a danger to human life or health."[82] The Secretariat has found that the basic environmental laws of each Party fall within this definition, including Canadian federal and provincial laws,[83] Mexican federal laws,[84] and U.S. federal laws.[85] The Secretariat has also found that legal provisions specifying environmental crimes are considered environmental law for the purposes of the NAAEC where such provisions provide sanctions for violations of mandatory prevention and control measures that may harm human life or health and the environment. In the Guadalajara Determination, the Secretariat noted: "it is clear that provisions specifying environmental crimes are, by virtue of their primary purpose, 'environmental law' under the definition in Article 45(2) of the NAAEC. These provisions sanction violations of mandatory prevention and control measures that may harm human life or health and the environment."[86]

Narrow interpretations of the express exclusions in Article 45(2) have limited the scope of submissions that assert failures to effectively enforce legal provisions directly related to worker safety or health[87] or that have as their primary purpose the exploitation or harvesting of natural resources.[88] Moreover, the Secretariat has also found that the definition of environmental law excludes international legal instruments that have not been incorporated into domestic law, because these international agreements are not laws "of a party."[89] The result of this narrow interpretation of

[82] SEM-97–005 (*Biodiversity*) Determination pursuant to Article 14(1) of the North American Agreement on Environmental Cooperation (May 26, 1998) at 2, http://www.cec.org/Storage/67/6133-97–5-DET-E .pdf.

[83] See, e.g., Canada Fisheries Act (SEM-97–001), Canadian Environmental Assessment Act (SEM-97–006), Quebec Environment Quality Act (SEM-04–07).

[84] See, e.g., General Environmental Protection and Ecological Equilibrium Law (SEM-96–001).

[85] National Environmental Policy Act (SEM-96–004), Clean Air Act (SEM-98–003), Clean Water Act (SEM-04–005).

[86] SEM-98–001 (*Guadalajara*) Article 14(1) Determination (September 13, 1999) at 4, http://www.cec .org/Storage/67/6142-98–1-DET-E.pdf (dismissed on other grounds). See SEM 98–001 (Metales y Derivados), http://www.cec.org/Page.asp?PageID=2001&ContentID=2372&SiteNodeID=250&BL_ ExpandID (final factual record).

[87] NAAEC, Article 45(a). See SEM-05–003 (*Environmental Pollution in Hermosillo II*), Council Resolution 12:04, http://www.cec.org/Storage/139/16377_05–3-RES_en.pdf (direction to develop factual record).

[88] NAAEC, Article 45(b); SEM-00–006 (*Tarahumara*) Determinación conforme a los artículos 14(1) y 14(2) (Nov. 6, 2001) at 11, http://www.cec.org/Storage/70/6427_ACF187.pdf (characterizing a law requiring consultation with indigenous peoples before exploiting state-owned mineral resources as non-environmental because the law's primary purpose was covered under Article 45(b)); but see SEM-09–005 (*Skeena River Fishery*) Determination pursuant to Article 14(1)(2) at 10–11, http://www.cec.org/ Storage/88/8490/_09–5-DET_14_1_2_en.pdf (ultimately characterizing a commercial fishing license law as "environmental" only after rejecting the counterargument that the law's primary purpose was "the commercial harvest or exploitation, or of subsistence fishing, or of aboriginal harvesting of natural resources").

[89] See SEM-98–003 (*Great Lakes*) Determination pursuant to Article 14(1) and Article 14(2) of the North American Agreement on Environmental Cooperation (September 8, 1999) at 4–5, http://www.cec.org/ Storage/69/6310_ACF1786.pdf (finding that neither the Great Lakes Water Quality Agreement nor the 1986 Agreement Between the Government of the United States of America and the Government of Canada Concerning the Transboundary Movement of Hazardous Waste should be considered

"environmental law" is that citizens are precluded from triggering the fire alarm on their country through the submission process if it fails to follow through on an international agreement. Since citizens are already precluded from domestic relief by nature of the international commitments not being incorporated into domestic law, this interpretation effectively bars citizens from holding their country accountable for its international commitments. As a result, this interpretation is contradictory to the CEC objective to enable citizens to shine a spotlight on the country for failing to effectively enforce its environmental laws.

3.1.2. "Assertion" of "failure to effectively enforce"

The Secretariat has established multiple requirements related to a submission's assertion. In its *Biodiversity* determination, The Secretariat explained:

> [T]he language of an "assertion" supports a relatively low threshold under Article 14(1), a certain amount of substantive analysis is nonetheless required at this initial stage. Otherwise, the Secretariat would be forced to consider all submissions that merely "assert" a failure to effective enforce environmental law.[90]

Consequently, the Secretariat has developed certain standards for assertions: (1) the assertion must be made explicitly with a positive statement as to the legal provisions involved, the failure alleged, and properly document the failure;[91] (2) the assertion must not be alleging a deficiency in the law itself;[92] and (3) the assertion must not be a challenge to standard-setting practices reserved to the Parties to establish.[93]

First, the assertion must be explicit, indicative, and properly documented and reasoned.[94] The Secretariat has clarified that the assertion must contain a positive statement that a Party is failing to effectively enforce its environmental law and should also sufficiently document the alleged failures of a Party, including any acts

---

"environmental law" because these agreements "had not been imported into domestic law by way of statute or regulation pursuant to a statute"); SEM-97–005 (*Biodiversity*) Determination pursuant to Article 14(1) of the North American Agreement on Environmental Cooperation (May 26, 1998) at 3–4, http://www.cec.org/Storage/67/6133-97-5-DET-E.pdf (finding that the UN Convention on Biological Diversity did not qualify as "environmental law" because, though Canada ratified the convention, the convention was not Canadian law because it had not been incorporated into domestic law by way of statute or regulation).

[90] SEM-97–005 (*Biodiversity*) Article 14(1) Determination (May 26, 1998) at 4.

[91] *Iona Wastewater Treatment* Determination, at 18–19 citing *Tailings Ponds* Determination at para 28. See also Guidelines 5.1 and 5.3 (2012).

[92] *Coal-fired Power Plant* Determination (December 16, 2004) SEM-04–005 at 4, *Iona Wastewater Treatment* Determination at 20 (and see SEM-98–003 (*Great Lakes*), Articles 14(1) and 14(2) Determination (September 8, 1999) at 7–9, item III.A.3.)

[93] SEM-04–005 (*Coal-fired Power Plants*), Determination (December 16, 2004) at 4; SEM-98–003 (*Great Lakes*), Determination pursuant to Articles 14(1) and 14(2), 5 NAELP 164, 171–73 (September 8, 1999).

[94] *Iona Wastewater Treatment* Determination, at 18–19 citing *Tailings Ponds* Determination at para 28. See also Guidelines 5.1 and 5.3 (2012).

or omissions to enforce its environmental law.[95] Mere citation of legal provisions without a clear connection to an assertion and the alleged acts or omissions of a Party in failing to effectively enforce an environmental law also does not meet the criteria of Article 14(1).[96] This requirement is sensible because submissions need to be articulated clearly enough to allow the Secretariat to properly understand the scope of the request.

Next, the Secretariat has clarified that the submission must allege a failure to effectively enforce the cited provisions of law and not a deficiency in the law itself.[97] Presumably, citizens can put pressure on local legislators to amend legal provisions with deficiencies and therefore it appears appropriate at first glance for the Secretariat to leave such assertions to domestic matters. However, upon closer review, one learns that this is only the case for citizens of the country as to which they are submitting a submission. The NAAEC permits submissions from persons or organizations "residing or established in the territory of a Party" and does not specify that such persons or organizations are limited to submitting assertions regarding the Party in which they reside.[98] Therefore, submitters from one Party's territory can make a submission against another one of the Parties. In such a scenario, the submitter would not have the benefit of being able to lobby their local government for legal reform. As a result, that submitter is precluded from access to the government transparency and accountability the citizen submission process is meant to promote.

Finally, the Secretariat has established that it will not consider assertions that challenge the kind of standard-setting power that the NAAEC Parties have reserved to themselves.[99] The Secretariat clarified in the *Coal-fired Power Plants* determination that specific legal obligations that a Party imposes on itself and fails to effectively enforce are a more appropriate subject of an assertion than standard-setting decisions.[100] This interpretation is troubling because it shields the Parties from being held accountable to the public if they set extremely lax environmental standards. In fact, it effectively cuts the submitter entirely out of the decision-making process because submitters are not entitled to challenge the appropriateness of the standard, but rather only the Party's effective enforcement of the standard. Again, citizens of the Party under question can presumably lobby their local government, but persons residing in the territory of one of the other Parties are left without recourse.

---

[95] *Protection of Polar Bears* Determination at 11; Guideline 5.1 (2012).

[96] *St. Lawrence River Wind Farms* Determination, SEM-12–002 at 8.

[97] *Coal-fired Power Plant* Determination (December 16, 2004) SEM-04–005 at 4, *Iona Wastewater Treatment* Determination at 20; cf. SEM-98–003 (*Great Lakes*), Articles 14(1) and 14(2) Determination (September 8, 1999) at 7–9, item III.A.3.)

[98] See NAAEC art. 14(1)(f).

[99] SEM-04–005 (*Coal-fired Power Plants*), Determination (December 16, 2004) at 4; SEM-98–003 (*Great Lakes*), Determination pursuant to Articles 14(1) and 14(2), 5 NAELP 164, 171–73 (September 8, 1999).

[100] SEM-04–005 (*Coal-fired Power Plants*), Determination (December 16, 2004) at 4.

3.1.3. "Is failing": A Temporal Requirement

The Secretariat has consistently interpreted the phrase "is failing to effectively enforce" to mean that the failure must be ongoing in nature.[101] For example, the Secretariat dismissed the Canadian Environmental Defence Fund's submission because it was filed three years after the program at issue came into effect.[102] Specifically, the submission must demonstrate that the failure is ongoing on the date the Submission is made,[103] and the submitter carries the burden of proof in demonstrating "'how such failure is allegedly occurring' with 'sufficiently documented reasons.'"[104]

The Secretariat's standard for demonstrating the necessary temporal requirement requires the submitter to engage in a delicate balancing act. The submission must allege a failure that is persistent and ongoing in nature, yet must also list concrete examples to sufficiently document this failure. This requirement calls on submitters to be broad in their assertions and specific in their proof – two conflicting standards. Either the submission is properly broad in its assertion that the problem is persistent and ongoing or it must list examples that submitter hopes will not become obsolete before the Secretariat considers the submission. As a result, the temporal requirement has become unduly burdensome.

3.2. *Article 14(1): Six Listed Criteria*

Once a submission clears the hurdles in the opening sentence of Article 14(1), the Secretariat determines whether it meets the requirements set forth under Article 14(1)'s six listed criteria. These six criteria require that a submission alleging a Party's failure to enforce its environmental law:

[101] See, e.g., SEM-99–002 (*Migratory Birds*), Secretariat of the Commission for Environmental Cooperation Determination pursuant to Article 14(1) and (2) of the North American Agreement on Environmental Cooperation (December 23, 1999) at 4, http://www.cec.org/Storage/71/6481_ACF183D .pdf ("The Submission focuses on asserted failures to enforce that are ongoing. It thereby meets the jurisdictional requirement in the first sentence of Article 14(1)."); SEM-09–004 (*Quebec Mining*), Determination in accordance with Article 14(1) of the North American Agreement on Environmental Cooperation (October 20, 2009) at 6, http://www.cec.org/Storage/96/9339_09–4-DETN_14_1__en.pdf.

[102] SEM-97–005 (*Biodiversity*) Determination pursuant to Article 14(1) of the North American Agreement on Environmental Cooperation (May 26, 1998) at 3, http://www.cec.org/Storage/67/6133_97–5-DET-E .pdf.

[103] SEM-11–003 (*Protection of Polar Bears*) Determination in accordance with Article 14(1) of the North American Agreement on Environmental Cooperation (Dec. 5, 2011) at 10, http://www.cec.org/storage/ 142/16760_11–3-DET14(1)(2)_en.pdf.; SEM-10–003 (*Iona Wastewater Treatment*) Secretariat for the Commission for Environmental Cooperation Determination in accordance with Article 14(1) and (2) of the North American Agreement for Environmental Cooperation (December 16, 2011) at 18, http://www.cec.org/Storage/131/15587_10–3-DET_14(1)(2)_en.pdf.

[104] SEM-10–003 (*Iona Wastewater Treatment*) Secretariat for the Commission for Environmental Cooperation Determination in accordance with Article 14(1) and (2) of the North American Agreement for Environmental Cooperation (December 16, 2011) at 19, http://www.cec.org/Storage/131/15587_ 10–3-DET_14(1)(2)_en.pdf. (quoting *Tailings Ponds* Determination at para 28) (citing Guidelines 1.1, 5.1 and 5.3; *Quebec Mining*, at 5, item III).

(a) [I]s in writing in a language designated by that Party; (b) clearly identifies the person or organization making the submission; (c) provides sufficient information to allow the Secretariat to review the submission, including any documentary evidence on which the submission may be based; (d) appears to be aimed at promoting enforcement rather than at harassing industry; (e) indicates that the matter has been communicated in writing to the relevant authorities of the Party and indicates the Party's response, if any; and (f) is filed by a person or organization residing or established in the territory of a Party.[105]

Requirements (a), (b), (e), and (f) are simple checkbox requirements and therefore unnecessary to discuss at length. However, requirements (c) and (d) present bigger challenges to submitters.

3.2.1. Article 14(1)(c)

Under Article 14(1)(c), the submission must provide "sufficient information to allow the Secretariat to review the submission, including any documentary evidence on which the submission may be based."[106] This task can prove quite difficult for complicated submissions, especially given that submissions are limited to fifteen pages in length.[107] The page limit does exclude supporting information, but it does not give submitters much space for making a case. Rather, the page limitation implies that the submission should be brief, to the point, and need not provide the Secretariat with a legal treatise on the matter. Guideline 5.3 supports this interpretation in its clarification that "[s]ubmissions must contain a succinct account of the facts on which such an assertion is based."[108]

Taken together with the observations that the NAAEC uses the term "assert" instead of a more formal term, such as "allege" or "claim," and that the NAAEC leaves the fact-gathering responsibility largely to the Secretariat, the NAAEC may be construed as intending to restrict the burden placed on citizens submitters. In short, the NAAEC's provisions imply that it is the role of the submitter to pull the fire alarm and the role of the Secretariat to investigate whether a fire is burning. Nevertheless, the Secretariat has rejected submissions that failed to provide extensive evidence in support of their assertions on the grounds that the submissions did not comply with the requirements of Article 14(1)(c).

A prime example where the Secretariat pedantically interpreted Article 14(1)(c) occurred when the Secretariat rejected the Alberta Tailings Ponds submission in 2010.[109] In its determination, the Secretariat found that the submitters failed to meet

---

[105] Article 14(a)–(f) of the NAAEC.
[106] Article 14(1)(c) of the NAAEC.
[107] Guideline 3.3.
[108] Guideline 5.3.
[109] See SEM-10-002 (*Alberta Tailings Pond*) Determination in accordance with Article 14(1) of the North American Agreement for Environmental Cooperation (September 3, 2010) at 16–17, http://www.cec.org/Storage/93/9018_10-2-DETN_14_1_en.pdf.

the requirements of Article 14(1)(c), in part because they neglected to attach the relevant documents referenced in the submission.[110] The Secretariat explained:

> Not providing a referenced document or a series of documentation in a Submission does not automatically result in a Submission failing to meet the requirement set out in NAAEC Article 14(1)(c). Yet relevant factual documents that may provide the Secretariat with information to properly assess an assertion, and that are cited in the Submission should generally form part of the Appendices.[111]

This statement built upon the Secretariat's Notification that a Factual Record is Warranted in the *BC Logging* enforcement matter, in which it noted that it was a good practice for submitters to include referenced documents and that, at a minimum, submitters "should make every effort to attach relevant portions of all documentation supporting assertions that are central to a submission, unless that documentation is easily accessible to the public, the Parties and the Secretariat through the internet or other widespread and readily available means."[112] The Secretariat raised the standard in the Alberta Tailings Ponds Determination by taking the *BC Logging* determination's explanation that including referenced documents was a good practice to mean that these documents "should generally form part of the Appendices."[113]

What is more, the Secretariat apparently declined to apply the exception for easily accessible documents in the *Alberta Tailings Ponds* determination: the Secretariat faulted the submitters for not attaching relevant federal case law to their submission,[114] though federal case law is presumably "easily accessible to the public, the Parties and the Secretariat through the internet or other widespread and readily available means." However, the Secretariat's interpretation in the *Alberta Tailings Ponds* determination may have been an anomaly because in 2011, the Secretariat applied the easily accessible exception in its *Protection of Polar Bears* determination.[115] In that determination, the Secretariat noted, "Most of the scientific research and government documents that the Submitter relies upon have been provided in the Exhibits.... In each case where documents have not been provided

---

[110] See SEM-10–002 (*Alberta Tailings Pond*) Determination in Accordance with Article 14(1) of the North American Agreement for Environmental Cooperation (Sept. 3, 2010) at 16–17, http://www.cec.org/Storage/93/9018_10–2-DETN_14_1__en.pdf.

[111] SEM-10–002 at para. 40.

[112] SEM-10–002 (*Alberta Tailings Pond*) Determination in Accordance with Article 14(1) of the North American Agreement for Environmental Cooperation (Sept. 3, 2010) at 16 n. 91, http://www.cec.org/Storage/93/9018_10-2-DETN_14_1__en.pdf, http://www.cec.org/Storage/93/9018_10–2-DETN_14_1__en.pdf (quoting SEM-00–004 (*BC Logging*) Article 15(1) Notification to Council that Development of a Factual Record is Warranted (July 27, 2001) at 4.

[113] SEM-10–002 at 16 para. 40.

[114] SEM-10–002 at 17 para. 40.

[115] SEM-11–003 (*Protection of Polar Bears*) Determination in accordance with Article 14(1) of the North American Agreement on Environmental Cooperation (Dec. 5, 2011) at 13 para. 44, http://www.cec.org/storage/142/16760_11–3-DET14(1)(2)_en.pdf.

by the Submitter, the documents are referenced and readily accessible."[116] Similarly, in the *Tourism Development in the Gulf of California* determination, the Secretariat rejected the submission under Article 14(1)(c), but provided an analysis as to why certain documents that were not included nor readily accessible would assist the Secretariat in determining whether a factual record was warranted.[117]

It remains unclear whether the Secretariat will reject future submissions based on failure to attach all relevant reference documents.[118] Even assuming the Secretariat follows the interpretation employed in the *Polar Bear* determination and accepts submissions that do not attach easily accessible documents in their appendices, the Secretariat has nevertheless made the Article 14(1)(c) standard more stringent. The shift from the *BC Logging* determination's standard (that attaching reference documents is a good practice) to the *Alberta Tailings Ponds* standard (that these documents should generally form part of the appendices) demonstrates the Secretariat's increasingly high standards for submissions.

The Secretariat's increasingly stringent view of what is required under Article 14(1)(c) may be a symptom of the influence the Council has on the Secretariat. For example, in 2002, the Secretariat determined that the *Ontario Logging* submission was specific enough to warrant a factual record and notified the CEC Council of this recommendation.[119] But, despite the Secretariat's recommendation, the Council resolved not to develop a factual record because the submission's assertions were "based in large part on an estimation derived from the application of a descriptive model."[120] By rejecting the submitters' estimations of environmental damage and requiring the submitters to provide data that the environmental damage had actually occurred, the Council resolution effectively raised the standard for meeting Article 14(1)(c), because, without the council's approval, the Secretariat cannot develop a factual record.[121] Critics cite this particular Council action as a blatant demonstration of its attempts to erode the authority and independence of the Secretariat and to block submitters from successfully triggering the fire alarm.[122] The Alberta Tailings Ponds

---

[116] SEM-11–003 (*Protection of Polar Bears*) Determination in accordance with Article 14(1) of the North American Agreement on Environmental Cooperation (Dec. 5, 2011) at 13 para. 44, http://www.cec .org/storage/142/16760_11–3-DET14(1)(2)_en.pdf.

[117] SEM-13–001 (*Tourism Development in the Gulf of California*) Determination in accordance with Article 14(1) of the North American Agreement on Environmental Cooperation (May 24, 2013) at 27 paras. 103–113, http://www.cec.org/Storage/151/17742_13–1-DETN_14(1)_en.pdf.

[118] Through 2013, the Secretariat has not addressed this issue in any determinations since the *Tourism Development in the Gulf of California* Determination. See CEC Registry, http://www.cec.org/Page .asp?PageID=751&SiteNodeID=250.

[119] SEM-02–001 (*Ontario Logging*) Article 15(1) Notification to Council that Development of a Factual Record is Warranted (November 12, 2002) at 16, http://www.cec.org/Storage/72/6598_02-1-ADV2_en .pdf.

[120] Council Resolution 02–05 (April 22, 2003) at 1.

[121] Article 15(2) of the NAAEC. See also Guideline 10.1.

[122] Garver, "Tooth Decay," 37 ("Again, the council rejected an approach that would promote transparency and public access to government-held environmental information, in favor of an approach that

Determination demonstrates that the Secretariat will likely follow the Council's view of the requirements under Article 14(1)(c).

3.2.2. Article 14(1)(d)

Under Article 14(1)(d), submissions must "appear[] to be aimed at promoting enforcement rather than at harassing industry."[123] In making this determination, the Secretariat will consider whether: "(a) the submission is focused on the acts or omissions of a Party rather than on compliance by a particular company or business; especially if the Submitter is a competitor that may stand to benefit economically from the submission; and (b) the submission appears frivolous."[124]

The Secretariat rejected a 2011 submission under Article 14(1)(d), in part because it "*appear[ed] at least feasible*" that the submitter stood to benefit from its submission.[125] This standard makes it difficult for a conscientious company to blow the whistle on a government's failure to enforce environmental laws within its own industry. Under Article 14(1) as interpreted in submissions and Guidelines 5.1 and 5.3, specific facts demonstrating an ongoing failure must be provided. That showing by a conscientious company may well lead the Secretariat to find that the company is targeting a competitor, resulting in rejection of the submission under Article 14(1)(d). The Secretariat may be effectively obstructing the very citizens who are in the best position to observe a fire – those at conscientious or "green" companies – from triggering the fire alarm. Such obstruction frustrates the purpose of the citizen submission process: to enhance public participation and government transparency.

This part has examined the Secretariat's interpretation of Article 14(1) by considering how the Secretariat's treatment of each requirement has evolved since the NAAEC's entry into force. This analysis reveals that each requirement presents certain hurdles for submitters and the height of many of these hurdles has increased over time. It is possible that some of these changes have occurred as result of the Council's influence, as exemplified by the Council's resolution to raise the standard for 14(1)(c) factual support required to warrant a factual record, and the Secretariat's subsequent decision, in the Alberta Tailings Pond case, to heighten the standard for documentary support. It is equally possible that the Secretariat's limited resources have forced it to be more discerning in its recommendations for factual record

---

limits access to the process."); and Chris Wold, "Evaluating NAFTA," 228 ("Further evidence of the Council's effort to undermine the citizen submission process and erode the Secretariat's independence can be found in the Ontario Logging submission").

[123] Article 14(1)(d) of the NAAEC.

[124] Guideline 5.4 (2012).

[125] SEM-11–001 (*PCB Treatment in Grandes-Piles, Quebec*) Determination in accordance with Article 14(1) of the North American Agreement on Environmental Cooperation (April 12, 2012) at 8, http://www.cec.org/Storage/136/16134_11-1-DETN_14_1_en.pdf.

development. Although these speculations may warrant further exploration, this chapter does not purport to determine the cause of the changes, but rather to discuss how their occurrence impacts the CEC's ability to achieve the NAAEC's sustainable development objective.

4. SECRETARIAT INTERPRETATION AND SUSTAINABLE DEVELOPMENT

As discussed in Section 2, the CEC has shown a genuine commitment to the NAAEC's sustainable development principles since its establishment. The NAAEC includes sustainable development objectives, such as to "foster the protection and improvement of the environment . . . for the well-being of present and future generations"[126] and to "increase cooperation between the Parties to better conserve, protect, and enhance the environment."[127] The NAAEC established the CEC and its Secretariat to administer the processes intended to carry out these objectives. Both the party dispute consultation process and the citizen submission process incorporate the important principles of public participation and good governance set forth in the New Delhi Declaration for achieving sustainable development, and the citizen submission process has been lauded as a model for achieving public participation and transparency.[128] But certain blockades are preventing these models from achieving their sustainable development objectives. The Secretariat's increasingly heightened procedural scrutiny of submissions hinders the NAAEC's sustainable development objectives by cutting off an important means for public involvement and government transparency and accountability.

This part recaps the NAAEC's sustainable development objectives, the relevant New Delhi Declaration principles for achieving sustainable development, and how the Secretariat's interpretation of its responsibilities under Article 14 is frustrating its objectives under the Preamble and Article 1.

4.1. *Public Participation*

The New Delhi Declaration's principle of public participation and access to information and justice recognizes "a right of access to appropriate, comprehensible and timely information held by governments" related to sustainable development and of "access to effective judicial or administrative procedures," including redress and remedy, as essential principles of the international law of sustainable development.[129] The various procedural hurdles imposed by the Secretariat collectively interfere with the public participation principle of sustainable development because

---

[126] Article 1(a) of the NAAEC.
[127] Article 1(c) of the NAAEC.
[128] See Section 2.3.
[129] International Law Association, "ILA New Delhi Declaration of Principles of International Law Relating to Sustainable Development."

they limit the public's access to information and the public's ability to participate in decision-making processes. For example, the public's access to information is currently inhibited because few factual records are being developed. Through 2013, only a little more than one-quarter of the submissions filed have made it to the factual record stage.[130] In addition, the Secretariat's procedural hurdles preclude many submitters from engaging in the decision-making processes and from accessing the administrative proceedings offered through the citizen submission process.

The Secretariat is interpreting several specific procedural requirements of the NAAEC in such a way that they interfere with public participation. Most notably, as discussed in Section 3, the Secretariat's interpretation of the terms "environmental law" and "assertion" hinder the public's access to information. By narrowly interpreting express exclusions from the definition of "environmental law" and by excluding international environmental instruments that have been ratified but not yet implemented in a Party's domestic law from the definition, the Secretariat is depriving the public of the benefit of the citizen submission process's fire alarm in regard to these matters. Further, the Secretariat's interpretation that "assertions" excludes challenges to deficiencies in the laws themselves or standing-setting practices obstructs submitters by shielding Parties that purposely set low environmental standards. Such obstruction prevents the public from accessing information about that Party's allegedly lax standards and serves as an incentive for Parties to adopt lax standards in an effort to avoid the scrutiny of a factual record. What is more, this interpretation prevents submitters within the territory of another Party from participating in the decision-making process altogether because they are unable to lobby the government of another Party for legal reform.

The Secretariat's interpretation of Article 14(1)(d) requirements is also interfering with the public participation principles of sustainable development. This interpretation precludes greener companies from blowing the whistle on a Party for failing to effectively enforce an environmental law if it is *at least feasible* that they may stand to benefit economically from the submission. This interpretation also precludes an important stakeholder from participating in the citizen submission process, because, next to the Party itself, regulated industries are in the best position to know if a Party is effectively enforcing its environmental laws. Eliminating these companies' ability to make submissions serves to discourage companies from complying with environmental laws that the Party itself is not interested in enforcing.

Clearly, the Secretariat's procedural hurdles are disqualifying many submissions. In the context of the sustainable development principle of public participation, it is undeniable that several of these interpretations are limiting the public's access to information and ability to participate in the process. Because the citizen submission process's focal point is providing the public with information by "bringing

---

[130] Of 84 submissions, only 22 have been developed, or are currently in development of, a factual record. CEC Registry, http://www.cec.org/Page.asp?PageID=751&SiteNodeID=250.

the facts to light," the fact that the Secretariat's interpretations are creating these
hindrances is at odds with the citizen submission process's intent and purpose and
interferes with the NAAEC's sustainable development objectives. Submitters are
unable to hold the Parties accountable for failing to implement their international
obligations. Similarly, Parties are not held accountable for weak environmental
laws. These interpretations inhibit submitters' ability to seek transparency in such
decisions.

4.2. *Good Governance*

The New Delhi Declaration's principle of good governance promotes transparent decision-making procedures and government accountability.[131] The CEC has
successfully facilitated transparency and accountability in many ways. The citizen
submission process is an innovative tool for enlightening the public on the Parties'
enforcement of environmental laws. The process achieves transparency by making environmental information publicly available. The process also holds Parties
accountable for their actions and omissions, although not by sanctioning them, but
rather through the potential for embarrassment caused by publicly releasing a factual record. It is also important to note that the CEC's webpage serves as a good
model for maintaining transparency. The CEC webpage maintains a registry of
submissions and is updated regularly with correspondence regarding submissions,
Party responses, and Council resolutions.[132]

However, the CEC may not be as successful in promoting its own good governance as it appears at first glance. In particular, the CEC has been criticized
for Council actions that serve to erode the independence of the Secretariat.[133]
Good governance requires clear boundaries of authority and respective roles, yet the
Council has worked over time to subtly alter those boundaries.[134] It seems likely that
these actions may explain some of the Secretariat's increasingly stringent procedural
requirements – requirements that hinder submitters from successfully using the
process to achieve transparency and accountability in Parties' environmental governance.

The Secretariat's interpretations may or may not be a symptom of the Council's
misconduct. In any event, it is clear that these increasingly stringent procedural
barriers are muddling the transparency the citizen submission process is meant to

[131] International Law Association, "ILA New Delhi Declaration of Principles of International Law Relating to Sustainable Development."
[132] CEC Registry of Submissions, http://www.cec.org/Page.asp?PageID=751&SiteNodeID=250.
[133] See David L. Markell, "The CEC Citizen Submission Process: On or Off Course?" in David L. Markell
and John H. Knox (eds.), *Greening NAFTA: The North American Commission for Environmental
Cooperation* (2003); see also Wold, "The Inadequacy of the Citizen Submission Process"; and Garver,
"Tooth Decay."
[134] Markell and Knox, "Greening NAFTA," 284.

achieve. What is more, these barriers are serving to shield the Parties from public scrutiny. Given that the citizen submission process carries no sanctions or legal conclusions, these burdensome procedural requirements are disproportionate.

4.3. *Proposed Solutions*

The Secretariat's view of NAAEC's procedural requirements has drastically narrowed the scope of what constitutes an acceptable submission. The consequence is that fewer submissions make it through the process, which stifles public participation and good governance. Since public participation and good governance are the principles through which the NAAEC's sustainable development objective is to be achieved, their asphyxiation interferes with the CEC's ability to achieve the NAAEC's purpose. Although the Secretariat's narrowing view may be a result of the Council's conflict of interest, the Secretariat should not allow this influence to seep into its administration of the citizen submission process. Two suggestions may aid the Secretariat in resolving these challenges (1) the Secretariat should broaden its view of what satisfies certain procedural requirements and (2) the structure of the CEC should be reconsidered to reduce conflicts of interest. The first suggestion is more modest than the latter. The Secretariat could easily expand its interpretations to encourage more submissions. For instance, the CEC could amend its guidelines to clarify that submitters need not include reference documents in the submission appendices if the documents are easily accessible. Various tweaks in the CEC guidelines could easily accomplish a broadening of Article 14(1)'s procedural requirements.

The second suggestion is much more challenging, but it is also essential, given that the power to authorize development of a factual record ultimately rests with the Council. Currently, the Secretariat is charged with assessing incoming submissions that make assertions against the Parties. Since the Parties are the governing body of the CEC, this puts the Secretariat in an awkward position of shining the proverbial spotlight on its own boss. It is hardly surprising that such a scenario has allowed Party agendas to seep into the citizen submission process. The most effective way to resolve this issue is to ensure the Secretariat is fully independent from the Council, and that the Council – composed of the very Parties against whom assertions are made – no longer has the final word on whether to develop a factual record. One way to do this is to have an independent body vote on whether to develop and release factual records. Although the CEC can amend its guidelines to broaden the scope of acceptable submissions, the conflict of interest problems will likely continue until the Secretariat has greater independence.

5. CONCLUSION

Notwithstanding the CEC's admirable efforts to achieve the NAAEC's sustainable development objectives, the Secretariat's implementation of the citizen submission process has raised several hurdles. In particular, the Secretariat's narrowing interpretations of the process's procedural requirements has served to hinder the very principles the citizen submission process was established to enhance, notably public participation and good governance. If the CEC allows the hurdles to continue to escalate, this action will severely interfere with the CEC's ability to achieve the sustainable development goals of the NAAEC. Should the CEC choose to address this issue, modest solutions are available in the form of amendments to the guidelines. However, these solutions are only temporary. If the CEC wishes to address the fundamental problem, it will need to find a way to eliminate the inherent conflict of interest caused by the Council's oversight of the Secretariat.

PART II

Specific Environmental Issues under NAFTA and NAAEC

6

Downward Harmonization

Mexico's Industrial Livestock Revolution

Pamela Vesilind

1. INTRODUCTION

As the North America Free Trade Agreement (NAFTA)[1] and the North American Agreement on Environmental Cooperation (NAAEC)[2] reach the twenty-year milestone, environmentalists and policymakers from Mexico, the United States, and Canada are gathering to assess the environmental implications of economic integration among dissimilar trading partners. A central question in these discussions: whether NAAEC and the Commission for Environmental Cooperation (CEC) have successfully promoted an "upward harmonization" of environmental protection law among the member nations.

The same question was posed on NAFTA's ten-year anniversary. Numerous CEC representatives and observers agreed then that relaxed trade policies under NAFTA had modernized Mexico's manufacturing and crop agriculture sectors without negatively impacting the environment.[3] However, these assessments did not consider how relaxed trade and foreign investment rules had rapidly transformed the hog and poultry farming sectors to the substantial detriment of Mexico's scarce natural resources. By 2004, many family and commercial farms had already been displaced by high-volume intensive livestock operations (ILOs).[4] As one industry observer described it, the industrial pork sector was "just at the start of the curve[;] . . . poised for massive expansion, integration, and consolidation."[5]

---

[1] North American Free Trade Agreement, U.S.-Can.-Mex., Dec. 17, 1992, 32 I.L.M. 289 (1993), 32 I.L.M. 605 (1993) [hereinafter NAFTA].

[2] North American Agreement on Environmental Cooperation, U.S.-Can.-Mex., Sept. 14, 1993, 32 I.L.M. 1480 (1993) [hereinafter NAAEC].

[3] Greg M. Block, "The North American Commission for Environmental Cooperation and the Environmental Effects of NAFTA: A Decade of Lessons Learned and Where They Leave Us," *Loyola of Los Angeles International & Comparative Law Review* 26 (2004), 459 n. 67.

[4] In the United States, the common term is Concentrated Animal Feeding Operation or CAFO.

[5] Jerry Speir et al., *Comparative Standards for Intensive Livestock Operations in Canada, Mexico, and the United States* (Montreal: Commission for Environmental Cooperation, 2003), p. 2,

The direct and indirect impacts of ILO hog production on the Mexican environment were, and continue to be, devastating. Rivers, streams, and lakes downstream from ILOs are contaminated by untreated waste containing nitrogen, phosphorus, pathogens, antibiotics, and other pharmaceuticals. Groundwater aquifers are being depleted at an alarming rate. Open-air pits of liquid and solid wastes emit ammonia, hydrogen sulfide, and particulate matter (PM) – all associated with respiratory ailments.[6] They also emit greenhouse gases (GHGs) including methane, carbon dioxide, and nitrous oxide.[7]

Yet the CEC appears reluctant to address environmental regulations of the intensive livestock production industry. Twice in the last decade, the CEC sidestepped its obligations under NAAEC to assess the effectiveness of a member nation's enforcement strategies. And although the livestock sector presents the most attainable and cost-effective opportunities for preventing air and water contamination and mitigating GHG emissions,[8] no CEC climate change policy working groups have addressed industrial animal agriculture to date.

Why not? This chapter explores several possible explanations. First, it explains how NAFTA's relaxed trade rules, combined with Mexico's NAFTA-related policies, allowed American producers to rapidly industrialize Mexico's hog farming and pork production sectors. This is followed by an overview of the environmental impacts of industrial pork production. The final section considers several legal, political, and practical aspects that may influence the CEC's authority, political will, and resources for promoting "upward harmonization" of environmental protection regimes in the North American free trade zone.

2. LIBERALIZED TRADE AND THE INDUSTRIALIZATION OF MEXICAN HOG FARMING

In pre-NAFTA Mexico, most domestic pork was produced from hogs raised in smaller- or medium-scale commercial farms and family-run farms. Under NAFTA, domestic production doubled and Mexico developed a thriving pork export business (albeit not to NAFTA member nations), but few traditional farms remain. In the ILO model, hogs are raised in high-density warehouses; the largest facilities house

---

http://www.cec.org/Storage/49/4168_Speir-etal_en.pdf (quoting "Making Moves in Mexico," *Successful Farming Magazine* (Oct. 2001)).

[6] Alexandra G. Ponette-González and Matthew Fry, "Pig Pandemic: Industrial Hog Farming in Eastern Mexico," *Land Use Policy* 27 (2010), 1109, http://www.academia.edu/314615/Pig_Pandemic_Industrial_Hog_Farming_In_Eastern_Mexico (last visited Mar. 14, 2014).

[7] United Nations Conference on Trade and Development, *Wake Up Before it is Too Late: Make Agriculture Truly Sustainable Now for Food Security in a Changing Climate* (Geneva: United Nations Publications, 2013), pp. 2–6, http://unctad.org/en/PublicationsLibrary/ditcted2012d3_en.pdf.

[8] United Nations Food and Agriculture Organization, *Livestock's Long Shadow: Environmental Issues and Options* xxi–xxii (Rome: U.N. Food and Agriculture Organization, 2006), ftp://ftp.fao.org/docrep/fao/010/a0701e/a0701e.pdf [hereinafter Livestock's Long Shadow].

tens of thousands of hogs. Clusters of these warehouses dot the rural landscapes of six states producing half of the nation's pork: Jalisco, Sonora, Guanajuato, Yucatán, Michoacán, and Tamaulipas.

The story of this transformation begins in the United States. By the 1980s, market leaders such as Murphy Family Farms, Carroll's Foods, and Prestage Farms were industrializing animal husbandry and building a production model that would forever alter the American rural landscape and way of life. In the 1950s, three million farmers raised hogs; in 1992, 240,000 hog facilities were in their place.[9] These facilities housed hogs in herds of 5,000 or more, where producers could refine cost-efficient feed conversion technologies, selective breeding methods, and pharmaceutical regimens to ensure predictable and rapid growth.[10] They built broad distribution channels through acquisition, exclusive contracting, and vertically integrated supply chains.[11] Today in the United States, fewer than 70,000 operators produce the pork sold domestically or exported to other nations. Many self-described "hog farmers" are contractors for major producers, temporarily housing and feeding hogs they do not own.[12]

By comparison, Mexico's agricultural policies supported regional pork production and distribution networks operating at low volumes.[13] A few major commercial pork operators expanded herd sizes during the 1980s, but they did not incorporate the confinement techniques or the genetic uniformity and growth enhancement technologies that were widely adopted in the United States and Canada. Mexico's trade barriers mostly protected domestic pig farmers from less-expensive American pork imports, and the government generously subsidized sorghum (feed grain). Under these supports, Mexican pork production tripled between 1972 and 1983.[14]

By the mid-1980s, these farmer-friendly programs and policies had become incompatible with the country's aspirations to join the global marketplace.[15] Presidents

---

[9] Nigel Key and William McBride, *The Changing Economics of U.S. Hog Production* (Washington, D.C.: USDA Economic Research Service, 2007), pp. 5, 15–17, http://www.ers.usda.gov/ersDownload Handler.ashx?file=/media/244843/err52.pdf.

[10] Ibid., pp. 4–5.

[11] Marcy Lowe and Gary Gereffi, *A Value Chain Analysis of the U.S. Pork Industry* (Durham, N.C.: Center on Globalization, Governance & Competitiveness, Duke University, 2008), pp. 9–18, http://www.cggc.duke.edu/environment/valuechainanalysis/CGGC_PorkIndustryReport_10-3-08 .pdf.

[12] Speir et al., above note 5, p. 8.

[13] S. Patricia Batres-Marquez et al., *The Changing Structure of Pork Trade, Production, and Processing in Mexico*, MATRIC Briefing Paper 06-MBP 10 (Mar. 2006), pp. 10–13, http://www.card.iastate.edu/ publications/dbs/pdffiles/06mbp10.pdf; see also Daniel Lederman, et al., *Lessons from NAFTA for Latin America and the Caribbean Countries: A Summary of Research Findings*, 95–109 (Washington, D.C.: World Bank, 2005) (discussing various agriculture-related reform efforts), http://www.econ.umn .edu/~tkehoe/classes/NAFTAWorldBank.pdf.

[14] Leland Southard, "Mexico's Pork Industry Structure Shifting to Large Operations in the 1990's," *Agriculture Outlook* (Sept. 1999), 27.

[15] Mexico signed onto the World Trade Organization General Agreement for Trade and Tariffs (GATT) in 1986, and various regional and bilateral trade agreements with other nations. Kevin P. Gallagher,

Carlos Salinas de Gortari (1988–1994) and Ernesto Zedillo Ponce de León (1994–2000) believed that flexible trade and investment policies with Mexico's North American neighbors were critical for economic development.[16] The Salinas government began divesting itself from agricultural production and introduced variously successful reforms[17] aimed at encouraging farmers to modernize production and raise sanitary standards.[18] Feed subsidies were replaced by price controls, and then by price guarantees tied to international market prices.[19] Livestock producers received funding to develop irrigation canals for managing animal waste and to improve pastureland quality.[20] Nevertheless, hog farmers and pork producers struggled under these policies, and production plummeted.

Perhaps the most transformative policy changes were those allowing foreign direct investments (FDIs) and total foreign ownership of businesses and land.[21] Around the same time, Mexico finally granted full land ownership to the *elijardos*, peasants and farmers who had possessed only limited property interests in their farm land since the Mexican Revolution.[22] Combined, these last two initiatives left rural peasants vulnerable to exploitation by creditors and foreign investors.

When NAFTA took effect in 1994, Mexican pork producers could not meet domestic demand,[23] a disparity that favored U.S. producers. NAFTA's tariff rate

Free Trade and the Environment: Mexico, NAFTA, and Beyond (Stanford, Calif.: Stanford University Press, 2004), pp. 7–8.

[16] M. Angeles Villarreal, *NAFTA and the Mexican Economy* (Washington, D.C.: Congressional Research Service, 2010), p. 1, http://www.fas.org/sgp/crs/row/RL34733.pdf; Gustavo Alanis-Ortega and Ana Karina González-Lutzenkirchen, "No Room for the Environment: The NAFTA Negotiations and the Mexican Perspective on Trade and the Environment," in Carolyn L. Deere and Daniel C. Esty, *Greening the Americas: NAFTA's Lessons for Hemispheric Trade* (Cambridge, Mass.: MIT Press, 2002), pp. 45, 47–48; Marla Dickerson, "NAFTA Has Had its Trade-Offs for the U.S.," *Los Angeles Times* (Mar. 03, 2008), http://articles.latimes.com/2008/mar/03/business/fi-nafta3 (last visited Mar. 14, 2014); Greg Woodhead, *NAFTA's Seven Year Itch: Promised Benefits Not Delivered to Workers*, AFL-CIO Policy Statement (2002), p. 1, http://www.citizenstrade.org/ctc/wp-content/uploads/2011/05/nafta_at_seven.pdf.

[17] Ana de Ita, "Land Concentration in Mexico after PROCEDE," in Peter Rosset et al. (ed.), *Promised Land: Competing Visions of Agrarian Reform* (New York: Food First Books, 2006), pp. 148, 151.

[18] Lederman et al., above note 14, p. 98.

[19] Lederman et al., above note 14, p. 96–98.

[20] Lederman et al., above note 14, p. 98.

[21] Gallagher, above note 16, p. 4 (referring to Mexico's policy and regulatory transformation as a type of "trade package" that includes "the liberalization of both trade and investment, the increase in structural adjustment programs for the least developed countries, and the decreasing role of government in developed and developing countries alike"); Gustavo Alanis-Ortega and Ana Karina González-Lutzenkirchen, above note 17, p. 47. Mexico also lifted its requirement that foreign-owned businesses conduct operations in consideration of local economies. Timothy A. Wise and Betsy Rakocy, *Hogging the Gains from Trade: The Real Winners from U.S. Trade and Agricultural Policies* (Medford, Mass.: Tufts University Global Development & Environment Institute, 2010), p. 3, http://www.ase.tufts.edu/gdae/Pubs/rp/PB10-01HoggingGainsJan10.pdf [hereinafter Hogging the Gains].

[22] De Ita, above note 18, p. 151; Lederman et al., above note 14, p. 99.

[23] L. Martin Cloutier et al., *Local Environmental Protection and Trade: The Cases of Hog Production in Canada and Mexico* (Montreal: Commission for Environmental Cooperation, 2003), p. 15,

quota (TRQ) program, crafted to correct for these imbalances, levied short-term trade restraints on agricultural products designated as particularly sensitive to trade pressures. A country's TRQ product was assigned a tariff fee schedule and trade quota, authorizing the country to assess tariffs for all imports exceeding that year's quota. Year-over-year, the quota limits rose as the corresponding tariff rates decreased. To deter inexpensive imports from the U.S. and Canada, Mexico reserved nine-year TRQs for live hogs and pork products.[24]

However, the TRQs were feeble deterrents. The 1994 peso crisis left many agrarian support programs unfunded, just as transnational corporations Smithfield Foods, Cargill, ConAgra Foods, and Tyson Foods began investing heavily in subsidiary partnerships with Mexico's mid-tier and major pork and poultry producers.[25] Smithfield, the largest investor, established at least nine subsidiaries in Mexico and spent $22 million to obtain half ownership of Agroindustrial del Noroestehich, which had operations in Hermosillo, Mexico City, and Guadalajara. The American corporations also invested in large swatches of agrarian land, especially in Jalisco, Sonora, and Guanajuato. Here, they erected industrial livestock warehouses and dug expansive hollows for animal waste lagoons.[26]

By 1999, Smithfield had established Mexico's first vertically integrated supply chain, in the border state of Sonora. Smithfield's partnership with Agrofarms (the largest hog breeder) and Grupo Alpro (a well-established meat processor and distributor)[27] enabled the corporation to lower production costs enough to develop an export market in Japan.[28] ConAgra USA established a similar venture with Campi, to form Univasa Corporation, a fully-integrated, 30,000-hog facility for breeding, gestating, farrowing, slaughtering, and processing hogs.[29] Another Smithfield investment, in Agroindustrius Unidas de Mexico (AMSA), created the behemoth Granjas

---

fig. 1, http://www3.cec.org/islandora/en/item/1928-local-environmental-protection-and-trade-en.pdf (illustrating decline in pork production).

[24] Gary Clyde Hufbauer and Jeffrey J. Schott, *NAFTA Revisited: Achievements and Challenges* (Washington, D.C.: Institute for International Economics, 2005), pp. 283–85. Additional antidumping protections are provided in the WTO, allowing complaining countries to assess extra import taxes when "imports rise due to low import prices." Lederman et al., above note 14, p. 101.

[25] Speir et al., above note 5, p. x (characterizing foreign investment amounts as "significant" but difficult to verify); Steven Zahniser and Zachary Crago, *NAFTA at 15: Building on Free Trade*, WRS-09–03 (United States Department of Agriculture, Economic Research Service, 2009), pp. 12–13 (discussing growth of Mexican affiliates of U.S. multinational food companies).

[26] Ponette-González and Fry, above note 6, 1107, 1108.

[27] Smithfield Press Release, *Smithfield Foods Announces Completion of Joint Venture in Mexico* (Sept. 20, 1999), http://investors.smithfieldfoods.com/releasedetail.cfm?releaseid=297149 (last visited Mar. 14, 2014).

[28] Speir et al., above note 5, p. xi; S. Patricia Batres-Marquez et al., "Mexico's Changing Pork Industry: The Forces of Domestic and International Demand," *Choices* 22 (2007), 7, 8; U.S. Meat Export Federation, *Mexico Pork*, (Oct. 2008), p. 1, http://www.usmef.info/TradeLibrary/files/MEXICO%20PORK%20SMP%20FY09.pdf (discussing opportunities for market expansion).

[29] Monte W. Fuhrman, DVM, "Hog Heaven: Is it on the Yucatán Peninsula of Mexico?," *Swine Health & Production* 4 (1996), p. 41, http://www.aasv.org/shap/issues/v4n1/v4n1p41.pdf.

Carroll de Mexico (GCM) complex in the Perote Valley of Veracruz. By 2008, GCM's production volume was unmatched in Mexico. It kept 56,000 breeding sows and nearly a million hogs in production for slaughter across the Perote Valley.[30]

Liberalized trade policies under NAFTA also enabled these corporations to cir- cumvent the Mexican feed markets and create implicit subsidy systems for their busi- ness partners.[31] Cargill's Yucatán-based feed mill, for example, became the exclusive supplier for Grupo Porcicola Mexicano (GPM), another of Mexico's largest verti- cally integrated pork producers.[32] Cargill and its competitors imported U.S. feed at prices 15 to 23 percent below production costs[33] and awarded preferential volume discounts to their largest ILO partners in Mexico. These artificially underpriced imports far exceeded TRQ limits, but Mexico chose not to assess tariffs[34] – even as traditional commercial farms and subsistence farmers paid twice as much for domes- tically produced feed. Perhaps emboldened by Mexico's passivity, U.S. producers flooded the Mexican market with live hogs. By minimizing feed, land, and labor costs, Mexican-based (but American-owned) intensive livestock producers and pork processors captured the consumer market with historically low prices.[35]

Small- and medium-sized commercial farms were driven out of business, unable to compete with modern production methods. Even pork imports from the United States were less expensive than pork from backyard *camposino* farms. The Mexican government attempted to correct the trade imbalance by offering favorable credit terms to the largest domestic producers, but these attempts were offset by incre- mentally less restrictive tariff quotas and rising domestic consumption demands.[36] When the TRQs terminated in 2003, it was estimated that another 18,000 Mexican hog farms would go under.[37] After fifteen years of free trade in North America, imports of U.S. pork had risen by 700 percent,[38] making Mexico a top importer of

---

[30] Each of GPM's sixteen facilities had a "unit" devoted to one stage in the farrow-to-finishing (birth-to-fattening) cycle. One "unit" was made up of as many eighteen hog warehouses. Ponette-González and Fry, above note 6, p. 1108.

[31] Hogging the Gains, above note 22, p. 2.

[32] Speir et al., above note 5, p. xi.

[33] Hogging the Gains, above note 21, p. 2 (discussing 1996 Farm Bill deregulation of commodities markets).

[34] Hogging the Gains, above note 22, p. 3; Lederman et al., above note 14, p. 101.

[35] Hufbauer and Schott, above note 25, p. 295 and n. 26; Hogging the Gains, above note 22, p. 1; Batres-Marquez et al., above note 14, pp. 9–13.

[36] Cloutier et al., above note 23, p. 20, fig. 6 (illustrating disparity between pork imports and exports in Mexico); Batres-Marquez et al., above note 14, pp. 2–6 (noting that, in the hog and pork TRQ programs' final year, U.S. pork exports to Mexico rose 67%, while Mexican exports to the U.S. rose very little).

[37] Hufbauer and Schott, above note 25, p. 289 n. 10. Of domestically produced pork, one-third still came from backyard farms, but it was sold fresh, locally. Ponette-González and Fry, above note 6, p. 1107 (reporting that the remaining 28% of domestic pork consumed was produced by backyard farms (10–50 pigs), which sold the fresh meat locally).

[38] United Nations Food and Agriculture Organization, *Livestock Sector Brief: Mexico* (2005), pp. 11– 12, http://www.fao.org/ag/againfo/resources/en/pubs_sap.html (last visited Mar. 14, 2014); Hogging the

hogs, pork, and animal feed.[39] Free trade was a double-edged sword. In the end, the technological advances Mexico sought for its agricultural producers rendered many of them obsolete.

3. THE ENVIRONMENTAL EFFECTS OF INDUSTRIAL LIVESTOCK PRODUCTION

The environmental impacts of industrial hog production methods are well documented. The impacts of Mexico's transformation have been similar to those in rural North Carolina, where hog waste effluents have severely contaminated the Haw River and its tributaries.[40] In the decade or so prior to NAFTA, Mexico's aquatic resources were already strained by governmental support programs that rewarded producers for increasing their herd sizes. The relaxed trade and foreign investment policies that ushered in the intensive breeding and farrowing model only exacerbated these challenges.

Transitions from conventional pig farming to industrial-style production wreak havoc on hydrologic systems because, whereas small farms typically do not generate more manure than they can manage, high-volume facilities do. Manure from most pasture-raised animals can improve the soil's nutrient content. But intensive livestock operations must store and dispose of tons of untreated animal waste.

In all but the most advanced systems, liquid and solid wastes are collected on-site, in outdoor anaerobic pits.[41] As the solid waste sinks to the bottom, the liquid waste putrefies from lack of oxygen, creating conditions favorable to more than 300 volatile organic compounds (VOCs), many of them toxic.[42] Often, the untreated liquid waste is disposed of by spraying it on fields as fertilizer. If the soil is able to absorb the waste, it may filter toxins before they reach groundwater.[43] However, if the soil is

---

Gains, above note 22, p. 3. Western Organization of Resource Councils et al., Press Release, *Livestock Producers from Mexico, Canada and United States Seek New Trade Policy & Market Reforms* (Feb. 13, 2009), https://www.commondreams.org/newswire/2009/02/13-16 (last visited Mar. 14, 2014) (emphasizing the dramatic increase in imports of U.S. pork).

[39] U.S. Meat Export Federation, above note 29, p. 1; "US Loses Near-Monopoly on Mexico Sorghum Imports," *Agrimoney.com* (Mar. 21, 2013), http://www.agrimoney.com/news/us-loses-near-monopoly-on-mexico-sorghum-imports-5647.html.

[40] Speir, et al., above note 5, p. ix; see generally Stuart Allen et al., *North Carolina Hog Farming: From Family Farms to Corporate Factories* (University of North Carolina Kenan-Flagler Business School, MBA White Paper, 2007), https://extranet.kenan-flagler.unc.edu/kicse/ORIG%20Shared%20Documents/North_Carolina_Hog_Farming.pdf.

[41] Pew Commission on Industrial Farm Animal Production, *Putting Meat on the Table: Industrial Farm Animal Production in America* (2008), pp. 33, 77–81 (2008), http://www.ncifap.org/_images/PCIFAPFin.pdf/.

[42] Environmental Protection Agency, *Inventory of U.S. Greenhouse Gas Emissions and Sinks: 1990–2008* (Washington, D.C.: EPA, 2010), § 6.2, http://www.epa.gov/climatechange/Downloads/ghgemissions/508_Complete_GHG_1990_2008.pdf.

[43] However, pastures overloaded with nitrate can compromise the health of grazing cattle. Speir et al., above note 5, p. 3.

frozen or becomes saturated, the excess runoff eventually ends up in storm systems and waterways, where nitrogen and phosphorous in the untreated waste deplete the oxygen. The ability of a moving body of water to recover is compromised by repeated discharges directly into the waterway. This leads to eutrophication, when levels of dissolved oxygen are so low that the water becomes uninhabitable to fish. Water quality is further degraded by fine particulate matter and residual contaminants such as antibiotics and hormones.

In Mexico, waste effluent discharges and runoff from hog ILOs have adulterated surrounding surface waters and their tributaries and groundwater reservoirs.[44] Repeated overapplications of manure in Yucatán, for example, have contaminated numerous underground aquifers. Mexico's soil and water conservation programs, including efforts to reduce the use of nitrogen crop fertilizer and some of the most persistent pesticides, have been undermined by agricultural waste disposal practices. Intensive livestock operations also require disproportionally more water to operate, especially in warmer climates. As a result, underground aquifers nearby ILO clusters have been drained at accelerated rates since the mid-1990s.[45] Finally, anaerobic manure pits emit high levels of ammonia and hydrogen sulfide, air pollutants known to jeopardize human and animal health, and methane and nitrous oxide, two GHGs contributing to climate change.[46]

Experts at the Organisation for Economic Co-Operation and Development (OECD) and the United Nations Food and Agriculture Organization (FAO) are among the many scientists who agree that, although industrialized agriculture is attractive to developing nations in the short term, the model cannot scale to meet global demands for inexpensive animal protein.[47] The only viable methods for delaying or mitigating the environmental effects of intensive livestock production are, according to the OECD, consumer pressure and environmental regulations.[48]

4. THE CEC AND INTENSIVE LIVESTOCK PRODUCTION ISSUES

The CEC has documented the effects of industrial livestock operations in Mexico since the late 1990s, but the Secretariat's first citizen submission involving

---

[44] Organisation for Economic Co-Operation and Development, *Environmental Performance of Agriculture in OECD Countries Since 1990* (Paris: OECD Publications, 2008), p. 395 [hereinafter OECD Country Trends].

[45] Ponette-González and Fry, above note 6, p. 10.

[46] OECD Country Trends, above note 46, p. 396. A significant amount of the methane emissions are from the anaerobic manure pits, not from the animals themselves. EPA, above note 43. OECD estimated that agricultural GHGs made up 8% of the total GHG emissions. The OECD first observed Mexico's steep rise in agricultural GHGs between 1990 and 1996 (up 43%). During this period, pork production rates were stable; only production methods changed. OECD Country Trends, above note 46, p. 396.

[47] Livestock's Long Shadow, above note 8, p. 6 ("Environmental degradation at its current scale and pace is clearly a serious threat for the sustainability of natural resources[,] . . . [and] if left unchecked . . . may threaten not only economic growth and stability but the very survival of humans on the planet").

[48] See generally OECD Country Trends, above note 46.

industrial hog production originated in Canada. In the *Quebec Hog Farms* submission, nearly twenty nongovernmental organizations documented widespread violations of Quebec's Environmental Quality Act (EQA) and its "Regulation respecting the prevention of water pollution in livestock operations."[49] They alleged that hog ILOs in the Quebecois river basins of Chaudiére, Yamaska, and l'Assomption[50] were exceeding herd-size and manure-spreading limits and operating illegally in numerous other ways: violating manure siting and storage specifications; ignoring recordkeeping requirements; refusing to register with the government; and failing to obtain a Certificate of Authorization for establishing, expanding, or modifying large facilities. Moreover, the submission alleged, the provincial government was regularly certifying noncomplying operators and subsidizing them with manure management program funds. Canada refuted these allegations, recounting its efforts to enforce regulations and contain the effects of livestock waste effluents and citing new legislation designed to improve the enforcement process.[51] After considering Canada's response to these allegations, the Secretariat recommended to the Council that it develop a factual record to analyze the effectiveness of these new and existing enforcement methods. Nonetheless, the Council denied the recommendation, and the submission failed.[52]

Six years later, the CEC received a submission challenging Mexico's enforcement of environmental regulations on wastewater. Unlike *Quebec Hog*, which dealt primarily with environmental regulations specifically for livestock producers, the submission for *Lake Chapala II* involved governmental enforcement of general pollution and water quality law in the Lerma-Chapala-Santiago-Pacifico watershed area located in and around the state of Jalisco.[53] The submitters asserted, among other claims, that the federal Ministry of Environment and Natural Resources (SEMARNAT) and various state and regional entities were failing to monitor, report, and apply water quality recovery methods mandated by the Ley General del Equilbrio Ecologico y la Proteccion al Ambiente (LGEEPA). Consequently, residents along the polluted Santiago River, especially those in Juanacatlán, Jalisco, were becoming sick. Among the affected waterways was the Lerma River, which flows into Lake Chapala, the primary source of drinking water for Guadalajara and surrounding areas.[54] The compromised water levels in Mexico's largest lake also severely jeopardized waterbird habitat.

[49] *Quebec Hog Farms*, SEM-97–003, Canadian Response, p. 4 (Sept. 9, 1997) (citing Submission, p. 5 (April 9, 1997)), http://www.cec.org/Storage/67/6094_97-3-RSP-E.pdf.

[50] *Quebec Hog Farms*, Article 15(1) Notification to Council that Development of a Factual Record is Warranted, p. 2 (Oct. 29, 1999), http://www.cec.org/Storage/67/6103_97-3-ADV-E.pdf.

[51] *Quebec Hog Farms*, Canadian Response, above note 51, p. 2.

[52] *Quebec Hog Farms*, Council Resolution, p. 1 (May 16, 2000), http://www.cec.org/Storage/67/6106_97-3-res-e.pdf.

[53] *Lake Chapala II*, SEM-03–003, Submission, pp. 7–10 (May 23, 2003), http://www.cec.org/Storage/143/16933_03-3-SUB_en.pdf. Although the submission covered a larger region, the final factual record was confined to Lake Chapala and parts of the Santiago River and Verde River Basins.

[54] Ibid., pp. 6–8.

Much of the water contamination was attributable to discharges from the thousands of hog ILOs along the Santiago, Verde, Zula, and Lerma Rivers.[55] The discharges from six extremely large facilities were identified as causing the most severe impacts. Testing at one ILO revealed that water discharges had "high, acute toxicity" levels. Another five facilities were discharging untreated hog waste at volumes equivalent to that of 200,000 people, as measured by their impacts on dissolved oxygen levels.[56] A decade after the CEC received the submission, it published a factual record for *Lake Chapala II*. As the next section explains, this record did little to address governmental enforcement failures related to livestock waste disposal.

5. ATTEMPTING TO EXPLAIN THE CEC'S RECORD

5.1. *Possibility 1: NAAEC Terms Limit the CEC's Scope of Review*

Why have the environmental effects of industrial hog production in Mexico received comparatively little attention from the CEC? One possible answer lies in the NAAEC itself. The Preamble hints at NAAEC's internal conflict: on the one hand it seeks to promote sustainable development and the "conservation, protection and enhancement of the environment" in the three Party nations; on the other hand, it affirms the Parties' sovereign rights "to exploit their own resources pursuant to their own environmental and development policies," so long as they limit environmental damage to the confines of their own borders.[57] The CEC's scope of authority to influence environmental policy flows from these diametrically opposed goals.

NAAEC's most limiting mechanism is also its cornerstone. The Article 14 citizen submissions process[58] has been heralded as "an important experiment in 'new governance'" that empowers citizens to promote effective enforcement of environmental laws.[59] Yet it allows the Secretariat to consider only submissions that involve existing environmental regulations, not assertions of regulatory inadequacy or general allegations of poor environmental stewardship. To be reviewable by the Secretariat, a submission must allege that a Party has failed to "effectively enforce"

---

[55] *Lake Chapala II*, SEM-97–003, Factual Record for Submission, pp. 61–71, 72–93 (Jan. 22, 2013), http://www.cec.org/Storage/150/17567_Lake_Chapala_II_Factual_Record_en.pdf (documenting hog farm discharges, as well as those from food and tequila industries and dairy producers).

[56] Ibid., p. 65.

[57] NAAEC, above note 2, Preamble, 32 I.L.M. at 1482.

[58] NAAEC, above note 2, Art. 14, 32 I.L.M. at 1488.

[59] John H. Knox and David L. Markell, "Evaluating the Citizen Petition Procedures: Lessons From an Analysis of the NAFTA Environmental Commission," *Texas International Law Journal* 47 (2012), 505. Knox represented the U.S. in NAAEC negotiations, as an attorney with the U.S. State Department. Markell was the first Director of the Submissions on Enforcement Matters Unit within the Secretariat. Ibid., n. a1.

its regulations and the allegation must be based on publicly available information ("mass media reports").[60] In addition, the submitters must allege actual injury resulting from the Party's failure to effectively enforce its laws.[61]

A submission meeting these criteria and other minor requirements under Article 14(1) authorizes the Secretariat to request a response from the Party. This step provides the Party several opportunities for concluding the Secretariat's inquiry: by demonstrating that the matters asserted by the submitters are the subject of past, current, or pending administrative or judicial proceedings, or that the submitters have neglected to exhaust their private remedies.[62] Article 14(c)'s text does not expressly state that a Party may refute submission assertions enough to satisfy the Secretariat that a factual record is unnecessary, but the CEC has interpreted the process this way.

To illustrate this point: if a Party is able to demonstrate sufficient *attempts* to enforce its environmental regulations, such as by employing several of Article 5's nonexhaustive list of acceptable enforcement strategies, the Secretariat may conclude that the Party is meeting its obligation to "*effectively* enforce its environmental laws and regulations through appropriate governmental action."[63] Put another way, the inquiry process may be terminated if the Party demonstrates attempts to enforce its regulations, irrespective of whether the Party has found the attempts to be "effective."

This interpretation transforms the Party's requirement from one of demonstrating compliance with its official regulatory laws to one of demonstrating compliance with NAAEC Article 5. On its face, this is not an arduous requirement. Only several of Article 5's enforcement instruments, such as penalties or sanctions, are punitive. Most of the acceptable strategies are decidedly more passive, such as voluntary compliance programs, inspections, certification and recordkeeping requirements, and public education campaigns.[64] This inserts unpredictability into the process. Moreover, in accepting a Party's response that it has employed several Article 5 enforcement strategies, the Secretariat – or Council – concludes that the submitters' assertions had been deemed unfounded.

The *Quebec Hog Farms* and *Lake Chapala II* submissions illustrate this problem. In *Quebec Hog Farms*, Canada's Article 14(c) Party response argued that a factual record was inappropriate because, among other reasons, Quebec had implemented Article 5-approved enforcement strategies, including incentive-based, voluntary manure management programs aimed at helping producers upgrade their animal waste storage and disposal processes. Additionally, the Party argued, three months after the submission's filing date Quebec had amended

---

[60] NAAEC, above note 2, Art. 14(1), (2)(d), 32 I.L.M. at 1488.
[61] NAAEC, above note 2, Art. 14(2)(a), 32 I.L.M. at 1488.
[62] NAAEC, above note 2, Art. 14(3)(a), 32 I.L.M. at 1488.
[63] NAAEC, above note 2, Art. 5(1), 32 I.L.M. at 1483 (emphasis added).
[64] NAAEC, above note 2, Art. 5(1), 32 I.L.M. at 1483.

its regulation to approve EQA enforcement efforts in the livestock production sector.[65]

In its recommendation to the Council that it develop a factual record of the submission, the Secretariat observed that Canada's response "le[ft] open several central questions of fact relating to whether the Party is effectively enforcing the environmental laws at issue."[66] Although Quebec's voluntary compliance programs were acceptable Article 5 enforcement strategies, the Secretariat was unconvinced that they amounted to *effective* enforcement of "legally binding, enforceable limits" on herd sizes and the "legally enforceable requirements governing . . . manure-spreading and storage."[67] With respect to Quebec's recently adopted regulations, a factual record would evaluate "the nature of these efforts and their effectiveness."[68] The Secretariat was particularly troubled by the assertion that hog producers were receiving governmental subsidies, while disregarding livestock herd size limits or manure storage and spreading regulations. A record was warranted to expose the breadth of noncompliance in the hog industry.

The Secretariat's doggedness may have been due in part to the submission's persuasive documentation about the industry's flagrant offenses. The submission cited a report by the Quebec Auditor General from 1995 to 1996 as well as a third-party report endorsed by the Canadian Ministry of Agriculture, the Quebec Ministry of Environment of Wildlife (MEF), and members of the industry.[69] The Auditor General Report raised the alarm that Quebec's water quality problems could become far worse, considering the 15 percent increase in pork production between 1992 and 1997, and that "few concrete measures [had] been taken to manage previously existing [manure] surpluses."[70] Runoff from overapplication of manure on land had become the region's greatest cause of nonpoint source pollution.

When the Council voted 2–1 to prevent the Secretariat from pursuing a factual record, it must have been a blow to the Secretariat. The two Council members in the majority issued no details regarding the vote allocation or reasoning. Perhaps this experience shaped the Secretariat's approach in *Lake Chapala II.*

In its response to the *Lake Chapala II* submission, Mexico stipulated that the Santiago and Verde Rivers were contaminated by untreated municipal and industrial waste and that a high percentage of livestock operations were violating discharge standards.[71] Nevertheless, Mexico asserted, a factual record was unnecessary because the appropriate regulatory authorities were addressing these

---

[65] *Quebec Hog Farms*, Canadian Response, above note 51, p. 5.

[66] *Quebec Hog Farms*, Notification to Council, above note 52, p. 2.

[67] *Quebec Hog Farms*, Notification to Council, above note 52, pp. 2–3.

[68] *Quebec Hog Farms*, Notification to Council, above note 52, pp. 2–3.

[69] *Quebec Hog Farms*, Notification to Council, above note 52, p. 11.

[70] *Quebec Hog Farms*, Notification to Council, above note 52, p. 15.

[71] *Lake Chapala II*, SEM-03–003, Article 15(1) Notification to Council that Development of a Factual Record is Warranted, p. 10 (May 18, 2005), http://www.cec.org/Storage/73/6721_03-3-RSP_es.pdf.

problems, and they had initiated sanctions proceedings against some of the ILO violators.

As in *Quebec Hog Farms*, the Secretariat moved to develop a factual record, in part to discover "information allowing for an analysis of whether Mexico is effectively enforcing its environmental law . . . so as to prevent the alleged environmental deterioration and water imbalance of the watershed and of Lake Chapala."[72] Although it sent the recommendation in May 2005, the Council delayed its authorization until January 2008. The authorization was burdened by caveats that confined the record's scope and neutralized its deterrent effect. In addition to limiting the geographic scope of inquiry, it directed the Secretariat to

> describe actions undertaken by Mexico in compliance with the regulations cited in the title of this decision, but to refrain from including any form of assessment of the effectiveness of the Party's policies or legislation.[73]

Moreover, the Council ordered the Secretariat to notify the Parties (not the Council) of "its overall work plan for gathering relevant facts" and provide them "opportunit[ies] to comment on that plan."[74] Party comments during this process are not part of the public record, so it is unclear whether this requirement contributed to the unprecedented length of time it took the CEC to publish the factual record – nearly a decade after the submission had been filed.[75]

In the end, the *Lake Chapala II* factual record was a far cry from the document the Secretariat intended to develop – and what Article 14 authorizes it to develop. The record is a recitation of the decade-long dispute. It repurposes outdated production numbers and scientific data[76] and painstakingly avoids drawing "conclusions regarding the meaning of these facts" or "the effectiveness of any of Mexico's policies or laws."[77] Incredibly, it even presents alternative theories regarding Lake Chapala's condition and whether any decline in its productivity is attributable to naturally occurring conditions, not wastewater effluents.[78]

---

[72] Ibid., p. 19.

[73] *Lake Chapala II*, SEM-03–003, Council Resolution, p. 2 (May 30, 2008), http://www.cec.org/Storage/73/6727_03-3-RES_en.pdf.

[74] Ibid. In addition to decreasing the geographic scope of the factual record, the Council instructed the Secretariat to refrain from addressing any issues related to water supply and distribution, because Mexico argued this issue was not an environmental concern.

[75] In 2009, SEMARNAT increased its number of regional water monitoring stations and raised the quality standards for sections of the Santiago and Verde Rivers closest to municipalities. Mexico cited these efforts as evidence of its compliance with NAAEC. Importantly, the raised standards had no practical effect on the rivers' actual quality, because even under the lower standards, the waters exceeded maximum pollutant discharge levels. See *Lake Chapala II*, Notification to Council, above note 73, pp. 9–10.

[76] Much of the factual record uses data collected by SEMARNAT and Conagua between 2001 and 2006, and from a 2006 CEC report. See generally *Lake Chapala II*, Factual Record, above note 57.

[77] *Lake Chapala II*, Factual Record, above note 57, pp. 16, 41.

[78] *Lake Chapala II*, Factual Record, above note 57, pp. at 32–33.

Quebec Hog Farms and *Lake Chapala II* illustrate how the CEC's organizational structure and allocation of power can inhibit it from fully realizing its mission to promote harmonization of environmental protection laws. Of its three branches – the Council, the Secretariat, and the Joint Public Advisory Committee (JPAC) – the Council is the smallest and most powerful. Its three representatives are hand-selected by their respective Parties. Together, they set the CEC's agenda, allocate the budget, control the publication of information, and retain final veto authority. As in *Quebec Hog Farms*, the submissions process is "structurally biased in favor of [any two] governments"[79] who vote, by secret ballot,[80] to deny or grant authorization for the development of a factual record. A vote to deny, in effect, bars the Secretariat from conducting any further inquiry, even on a general level.[81]

Even without heavy-handed oversight from the Council, the citizen submission process's sunshine effect may not be enough to influence Party behavior.[82] When it strips the Secretariat of its ability to expose a trade partner's failures to effectively enforce its own environmental laws, the Council removes the "citizen" from the citizen process by resurrecting the opaqueness NAAEC was supposed to eliminate. Without the power of transparency, the CEC's value is strictly advisory.

5.2. *Possibility 2: Mexico Lacks Adequate Environmental Regulations*

A second possibility is that Mexico's environmental laws do not go far enough to protect its resources from the by-products of industrial livestock production. As the previous section discusses, the CEC may only assess citizen submissions citing current environmental regulation. Although the CEC may recommend specific standards or regulations to Party nations, these recommendations are not binding.[83] Thus, if Mexico's environmental laws are comparatively substandard, the CEC can only advise the Party about how it might harmonize its regulations with those in the U.S. and Canada. When it comes to regulating the externalities

---

[79] Knox and Markell, above note 61, p. 524. Although consensus is required for many Council decisions, Article 15 is an exception.

[80] NAAEC, above note 2, Art. 13(1), 32 I.L.M. at 1487. See also *Quebec Hog Farms* (SEM-97–003); *Lake Chapala* (SEM-97–007); *Cytar I* (SEM-98–005); *Cytar II* (SEM-01–001); *Cytar III* (SEM-03–006); *Great Lakes* (SEM-98–003); *Mexico City Airport* (SEM-02–002); *Ontario Power Generation* (SEM-03–001). Documents are available at http://www.cec.org/Page.asp?PageID=1226/SiteNodeID=545 (last visited Mar. 14, 2014).

[81] NAAEC, above note 2, Art. 13(1), 32 I.L.M. at 1487–88 (allowing the Secretariat to prepare reports for the Council on "any other environmental matter related to the . . . Agreement[, but that these] . . . environmental matters shall not include issues related to whether a Party has failed to enforce its environmental laws and regulations").

[82] See Knox and Markell, above note 61, p. 521 (observing that the CEC submission records between 1995 and 2011 suggest that few potential submitters in the United States are aware of the NAAEC citizens submission process).

[83] NAAEC, above note 2, Art. 10(6)(d), 32 I.L.M. at 486; but see NAAEC, Art. 10(5)(b), 32 I.L.M. at 486.

of intensive livestock operations, however, no NAFTA member stands out as a leader.

NAFTA and other international trade agreements have influenced Mexico's legislative agenda. In 2007, environmental sustainability became a "key dimension" of the federal agenda.[84] Mexican environmental laws have more in common with U.S. and Canadian laws than not. General authority is distributed across national, state (or provincial), and local governments, and many state-level standards mirror those imposed by federal authorities. The primary Mexican environmental law, established under the Salinas administration, is the LGEEPA.[85] The SEMARNAT, Mexico's equivalent to the U.S. Environmental Protection Agency (EPA), sets national environmental policy goals and standards under LGEEPA and other environmental laws. The National Water Commission (Conagua), a division of SEMARNAT, sets overall policies, standards, and regulations under the National Water Law.

As in the United States, Mexican state-level water commissions are the primary enforcers of wastewater storage and disposal regulations. They review the nutrient or manure management plans submitted by ILOs and are tasked with monitoring and reporting how these waste disposal plans are carried out. In the last decade, more water resource management authority has been delegated to local basin councils (the source of another complaint in the *Lake Chapala II* submission). Regional governmental authorities run general land-use permit programs, and local zoning regulations apply setback restrictions for ILOs near residential zones and waterways.

Across North America, environmental regulations for agricultural production are woefully outdated, drafted in "a world of smaller farms."[86] Exemptions for agricultural production are increasingly anachronistic as applied to intensive livestock and poultry facilities, which are more industrial than agricultural.[87] For example, all three countries prohibit point-source discharges of untreated sewage into waterways,

---

[84] Organisation for Economic Co-Operation and Development, *Environmental Performance Reviews: Mexico 2013 Assessment and Recommendations*, Ch. 2, para. 1, http://www.oecd.org/env/country-reviews/oecdenvironmentalperformancereviewsmexico2013assessmentandrecommendations.htm (last visited Mar. 14, 2014).

[85] Gallagher, above note 16, p. 63.

[86] Speir et al., above note 5, p. 2; see also Livestock's Long Shadow, above note 8, p. 4 ("Public policies, in developed and developing countries alike, barely keep pace with rapid transformations in production technology and structural shifts in the sector"); Darryl Jones et al., Organisation for Economic Co-Operation and Development, *Agriculture, Trade and the Environment: The Pig Sector* (Paris: OECD Publications, 2003), p. 13–14, http://www.oecd-ilibrary.org/content/book/9789264104174-en (last visited Mar. 14, 2014) (discussing the struggle of many countries in dealing with increasing environmental degradation).

[87] See *Quebec Hog Farms*, Canadian Response, above note 51, p. 2 (explaining Quebec's preference for "incentive measures to ensure enforcement and to reach environmental goals" because "[t]he special nature of the agricultural sector and the types of pollution it produces have led to many innovative regulatory enforcement methods").

with exceptions. The Mexican National Water Law features a permitting and licensing system for point source discharges into public waterways, but – like the Clean Water Act in the United States – it does not regulate agricultural nonpoint source effluents.

States and provinces in all three countries have dealt with devastating waste overflow events in areas with heavy concentrations of hog farms. Yet none of the three countries requires that animal waste be treated before being used for fertilizer, nor regulates the residual antibiotics, hormones, and other pharmaceuticals in the waste.[88] Air pollution laws fail to assess or restrict emissions of ammonia, hydrogen sulfide, methane, nitrous oxide, and other pollutants associated with anaerobic waste decomposition. Although ILOs are a significant source of GHGs, climate change legislation has yet to catch up with industrial meat production.

Environmental regulations in Canada, Mexico, and the United States are inadequate, but industrial agriculture is not entirely exempt from permitting programs, waste management requirements, and other attempts to mitigate wastewater contamination. Underenforcement remains a pressing problem. This includes enforcement of the pollution controls on direct discharges into rivers and tributaries in the Lerma-Chapala-Santiago-Pacifico water basin discussed in *Lake Chapala II* and other CEC reports on industrial livestock production. Similarly, effective enforcement of Quebec's livestock and waste management regulations undoubtedly would have alleviated some of the submitters' injuries. Thus, NAAEC's goal, to promote the effective enforcement of *existing* environmental laws, remains relevant.

5.3. *Possibility 3: Liberalized Trade and Agricultural Practices Are Not Linked*

A third possible explanation is that the CEC is skeptical about the existence of a causal relationship between NAFTA-related policies and the environmental impacts of industrial pork production in Mexico. Identifying cause-and-effect relationships between trade liberalization and environmental harms can be relatively simple or enormously complex.[89] The automobile manufacturing sector, for example, has relatively straightforward connections with trade policy and pollution.[90] Greg Block, who served with the Secretariat until 2002,[91] finds the causal connections between NAFTA policies and "the spread of U.S.-style [Concentrated Animal Feeding Operations; CAFOs]" into Mexico, and connections between CAFO practices and their

---

[88] Speir et al., above note 5, pp. 107, 110.
[89] Block, above note 3, pp. 457–58.
[90] Gallagher, above note 16, p. 2 (concluding that this makes the industry a frequent subject of studies).
[91] Block served as Head of the Legal Division from 1994 to 1995 and named Director of Programs in 1995.

"potential environmental considerations" less than straightforward, on the far side of the "causality continuum."[92]

Kevin Gallagher, a member of the NAAEC Advisory Council, has theorized that Mexico's increased pollution problems are not attributable to NAFTA-related trade and investment policies, because no "mass migration of heavily polluting firms" crossed the U.S.-Mexican border after the trade treaty took effect.[93] Gallagher is referring to firms he calls "dirty industries," those that produce iron and steel, chemicals, cement, pulp and paper, beer and malt, automotives, rubber, and aluminum.[94]

It follows, Gallagher continues, that the increase of environmental problems were the result of "market failures" attendant to NAFTA policies, and that Mexico could have prepared for these conditions by preemptively enacting stricter environmental regulations.[95] Block also advances the theory that Mexico failed to anticipate how "the influx of CAFO-produced pork and poultry" would impact the country.[96] Had the government considered these impacts, he argues, it could have erected "environmental and social safety nets and safeguards" before instituting agriculture and land use reforms that – combined with liberalized trade and investment policies – welcomed the CAFO influx.[97] A flaw in this line of reasoning is that any regulations rigorous enough to prevent or vigorously mitigate environmental injuries attendant to the CAFO influx necessarily would be (1) broader and more stringent than the regulations applied to CAFOs in the U.S. and Canada, and (2) challenged by these two countries as barriers to trade.

A corollary theory is that liberalized trade merely accelerated Mexico's preexisting market trends toward agricultural industrialization. Therefore, environmental harms associated with this acceleration cannot be said to have been *caused* by NAFTA policies.[98] This theory is advanced by distinguishing "direct" environmental impacts of liberalized trade in the form of policy shifts from pressures on environmental quality exerted by increases in scale. As CEC's former head of economics Scott Vaughn suggested in 2004, environmental degradation is "rarely, if ever" directly related to changes in scale because trade liberalization also introduces

---

[92] Block, above note 3, pp. 457–59 (describing the spectrum of possible linkages as the "causality continuum" between trade and environmental impact).

[93] Gallagher, above note 16, p. 2.

[94] Gallagher, above note 15, p. 57.

[95] Gallagher, above note 15, pp. 2, 10 (suggesting that without "proper environmental policies in place, economic integration can exacerbate environmental problems"); see Karel Mayrand and Marc Paquin, *The CEC and NAFTA Effects on the Environment: Discussion Paper* (Montreal: Unisfèra International Centre, 2003), p. 4 (noting NAFTA's influence on regional economics).

[96] Block, above note 3, p. 466.

[97] Block, above note 3, pp. 463, 466 ("While trade and investment liberalization measures are not solely responsible for these important changes, they largely set the rules of the game and fix expectations by key market players").

[98] Block, above note 3, p. 459 n. 67 (dismissing arguments to the contrary as "lack[ing] analytical rigor" for this reason).

technological improvements and harmonized standards that compensate for these pressures.[99]

It is apparent that others within the CEC disputed the conclusion that technological advances facilitating increased livestock production offset environmental harms.[100] As early as 1997, the CEC chose western feedlot cattle production as one of three focus areas for designing an analytic model to recognize links between environmental conditions and trade-related economic or institutional development. Between 1999 and 2006, the CEC published multiple studies documenting the increasingly severe environmental and public health effects of industrialization in the livestock sector across North America.[101]

In any respect, it is undisputed that monitoring and regulating industrial livestock production is uniquely difficult. A 2003 CEC assessment of *Quebec Hog Farms* and *Lake Chapala II* concluded that three commonalities made industrial meat production especially challenging to monitor: (1) the difficulties in establishing causation on a case-by-case basis, (2) the heterogeneity and size of CAFOs/ILOs, and (3) the amount of nonpoint source pollution involved.[102]

It is inherently difficult to assess the enforcement and effectiveness of regulations on wastewater contaminants, considering the variable property of water and the complexity of finding the origins of nonpoint source contamination.[103] It is even more difficult when the contamination is downstream from more than one ILO, as is usually the case. Potential litigants injured by wastewater contamination commonly find this causation issue a barrier to common law remedies, a reality acknowledged in *Quebec Hog Farms*.[104]

Moreover, federal and state regulatory agencies in the United States and Mexico struggle to gather data about ILOs and CAFOs and their waste management

---

[99] Scott Vaughn, "The Greenest Trade Agreement Ever?: Measuring the Environmental Impacts of Agricultural Liberalization," in *NAFTA's Promise and Reality: Lessons from Mexico for the Hemisphere* (Washington, D.C.: Carnegie Endowment for International Peace, 2004), p. 61, http://carnegieendowment.org/files/nafta1.pdf.

[100] See, e.g., Commission for Environmental Cooperation, *Ten Years of North American Environmental Cooperation* (Montreal: CEC, 2004), pp. 26–28; Speir et al., above note 5, pp. 16–17, 25–26; Cloutier et al., above note 24, p. 19; Commission for Environmental Cooperation, *Free Trade and the Environment: The Picture Becomes Clearer* (Montreal: CEC, 2002), pp. 16–17, http://www3.cec.org/islandora/en/item/1871-free-trade-and-environment-picture-becomes-clearer-en.pdf; Commission for Environmental Cooperation, *The North American Mosaic: A State of the Environment Report* (Montreal, CEC: 2001), pp. 23, 26, 33, http://www.cec.org/storage/62/5428_mosaic-2008_en.pdf.

[101] See, e.g., Cloutier et al., above note 24; Speir et al., above note 5.

[102] Cloutier et al., above note 24, p. 7; see also Speir et al., above note 5, pp. vi–vii (recognizing that ILOs and CAFOs create "serious public health and environmental issues" that are "unique to this industry").

[103] See OECD Country Trends, above note 46, p. 211 (noting that it is difficult to isolate agriculture's impact to water quality).

[104] *Quebec Hog Farms*, Notification to Council, above note 52, p. 9.

practices.[105] Without adequate data, regulators are unable to discern which facilities are adopting management practices that prevent water contamination. Despite the overwhelming presence of hog ILOs in the *Lake Chapala* area of investigation, the Factual Record sidestepped analysis of hog waste contamination. It explained:

> It is important to emphasize the difficulty in analyzing the waste outputs from livestock-raising operations.... and the fact that, in some cases, there is a lack of wastewater discharge permits issued by [SEMARNAT–Conagua]. It was thus not possible to include an exhaustive analysis of hog farming pollution sources in the area of interest.[106]

With the exception of some high-tech facilities in Sonora, a U.S. border state, most ILOs are technologically inferior and dominate rural, economically disadvantaged areas. The geographic isolation tends to obscure pollution problems, turning them into local issues.[107] Most of the other hog ILOs are found in five states: two on the Gulf of Mexico (Yucatán and Tamulipas), and three in the central Pacific Ocean region (Jalisco, Guanajuato, and Michoacán), which supply domestic consumers, including those in nearby Mexico City.

6. CONCLUSION

A final possible explanation is that the Commission for Environmental Cooperation is only as influential as the Parties intended it to be when NAAEC and NAFTA were drafted.[108] During NAAEC negotiations, optimistic proponents imagined a spirit of cooperation that could power an "upward harmonization" of environmental policies encouraging transparency and inclusion. In the case of Mexico's industrial livestock revolution, NAAEC's "cooperation" does more to preserve the status quo in the United States and Canada.

---

[105] Although the EPA records information about the number of CAFOs with NPDES permits, this is a small minority of the total number of industrial farms. A permit is not required for nonpoint source emissions of untreated animal waste. In 2012, the EPA published a draft rule for collecting this data and making it available to the public. After considerable resistance from the industrial agriculture lobby, the agency withdrew the draft rule. See National Pollutant Discharge Elimination System (NPDES) Concentrated Animal Feeding Operation (CAFO) Reporting Rule, 77 Fed. Reg. 42, 679 (July 20, 2012).

[106] Lake Chapala II, Factual Record, above note 57, pp. 63–64 (referring to a report from the SEMARNAT-Conagua 2007 Compendium that 12% of punishable violations cited by Conagua were "related to discharge of wastewater without permission"). The Secretariat was also hampered by SEMARNAT's overly-broad definition of "wastewater," which did not distinguish between animal waste and other effluent discharges. *Lake Chapala II*, Factual Record, above note 57, pp. 63–64 n.418.

[107] Jones et al., above note 88, p. 13; Cloutier et al., above note 24, p. 8.

[108] Mexico and Canada's resistance to NAAEC is well documented. Mexican negotiators were particularly concerned that the United States would use protectionist barriers erected under the guise of environmental concerns. Alanis-Ortega and González-Lutzenkirchen, above note 17, pp. 42–44, 51.

In the early 1990s, NAFTA's adoption was feverishly opposed by the National Farmers Union and trade organizations for growers of fruit, vegetables, peanuts, wheat, and sugar cane, and numerous other American agricultural organizations. Absent from these protests and lobbying campaigns were their colleagues from the National Pork Producers Council, National Cattlemen's Association, National Milk Producers Council, American Soybean Association, and U.S. Feed Grains Council. As evidenced by the overwhelming success enjoyed by American pork corporations conducting business in Mexico, their pro-NAFTA lobbying efforts were well timed and wisely targeted.

7

Agricultural Biotechnology and NAFTA

Analyzing the Impacts of U.S. and Canadian Policies on Mexico's Environment and Agriculture

Laurie J. Beyranevand

1. INTRODUCTION

Since its inception, agricultural biotechnology has dramatically affected the world's food production methods. Because it has the potential to both increase agricultural productivity as well as provide significant benefits to human and animal health,[1] many commentators and experts tout biotechnology as the sustainable tool to combat the many challenges associated with global warming and changing weather patterns. Moreover, genetically engineered (GE) crops are viewed as the necessary means by which the world can adequately begin to address global food insecurity issues. As of 2011, the United States held the position as the global leader in the production of biotech crops with the largest acreage, at over 170 million acres, while Canada was the fifth highest producer, holding over 25 million acres of genetically engineered crops.[2] Industrialized nations have long been the leaders in the cultivation and development of these crops, yet recent studies show that developing nations are quickly following suit and taking the lead in biotech crop production with 52 percent of the world's current market originating in those countries.[3] Most countries that choose to utilize these technologies have planted only one crop variety, the most popular being corn, cotton, and soybeans, whereas the United States and Canada have adopted several

---

[1] Ernest G. Jaworski, "The Impact of Biotechnology on Food Production," in National Research Council (ed.), *Biotechnology and the Food Supply: Proceedings of a Symposium* (Washington, DC: The National Academies Press, 1988), p. 9, http://www.nap.edu/openbook.php?record_id=1369&page=9.

[2] International Service for the Acquisition of Agri-Biotech Applications, *Global Status of Commercialized Biotech/GM Crops: 2011, Slides and Tables*, ISAAA (2011), http://www.isaaa.org/resources/publications/briefs/43/pptslides/default.asp (last visited Feb. 2, 2014) (The United States plants maize, soybean, cotton, canola, sugarbeet, alfalfa, papaya and squash. Similarly, Canada produces GE canola, maize, soybean, and sugarbeet).

[3] International Service for the Acquisition of Agri-Biotech Applications, Global Biotech/GM Crop Plantings Increase 100-fold from 1996: *Developing Countries, Including New Adopters Sudan and Cuba, Now Dominate Use of the Technology*, ISAAA (Feb. 20, 2013), http://www.isaaa.org/resources/publications/briefs/44/pressrelease/ (last visited Feb. 2, 2014).

different varieties of crops.[4] In contrast, Mexico, while adopting only two different crop varieties, cotton and soybeans, is still considered a "biotech mega country"[5] because these two crops comprise almost 500,000 acres of the country's arable land, which only accounts for 13.1% of the country's total land area.[6] While Mexico commercially produces only two crops, as of 2009, 31 transgenic crop varieties were approved for production, including corn.[7]

It has been suggested that the development and proliferation of these "super crops" directly coincided with the development of free trade agreements.[8] Specifically, the North American Free Trade Agreement (NAFTA) lifted the barriers on trade that originally prevented these plants from entering Mexico, and consequently introduced bioengineered crops into a country that still largely relied on traditional agricultural methods of food production. Concerns about the effects of these introductions led 21 indigenous communities in Mexico, along with Mexican environmental and advocacy groups, to petition the Commission for Environmental Cooperation (CEC), the organization created to implement the goals set forth in the North American Agreement on Environmental Cooperation (NAAEC) in 2002. Specifically, these groups asked the CEC to analyze "the impacts of transgenic introgression into landraces of maize in Mexico."[9] Mexico is a historical center of diversity for maize, which makes it a crop of cultural significance within the country. Consequently, the introduction of genetically engineered corn into Mexico was considered an issue of great environmental import, due to the very real potential for crop contamination from cross-pollination, which would, in turn, threaten the country's crop biodiversity.[10]

While Mexico has taken significant steps to prevent the cross-pollination of transgenic corn varieties with traditional and wild varieties by creating transgenic free zones and isolating production of bioengineered varieties, the fact remains that, as corn is an open pollinator, it has been virtually impossible to eliminate the risk of introgression. The CEC has recognized that bioengineered varieties of corn present threats to the biodiversity of Mexico's crops, create the potential for displacement of traditional farming methods, and introduce serious threats to the environment from increased use of pesticides.[11] However, while corn warrants discussion, because of its historical significance to the country and the recognized instances of transgression,

---

[4] International Service for the Acquisition of Agri-Biotech Applications, above note 3.

[5] Ibid.

[6] Ibid.; The World Bank, *Data: Arable land (% of land area)*, http://data.worldbank.org/indicator/AG .LND.ARBL.ZS/countries (last visited Feb. 2, 2014).

[7] Gerardo Otero and Gabriela Pechlaner, *Is Biotechnology the Answer? The Evidence from NAFTA* (2009), p. 28, http://www.sfu.ca/~otero/docs/NACLA-2009.pdf.

[8] Ibid., p. 27.

[9] Commission for Environmental Cooperation, *Maize and Biodiversity, The Effects of Transgenic Maize in Mexico* (2004), p. 6, http://www.cec.org/Storage/56/4837_Maize-and-Biodiversity_en.pdf.

[10] Ibid.

[11] Ibid., p. 4.

it is not the only product of agricultural biotechnology that presents a threat to Mexico's environment. Each bioengineered crop approved for commercialization presents its own unique set of considerations for the sustainability of Mexico's agricultural system, environment, and economy. Since Mexico must abide by trade agreements with the United States and Canada, both of which take the regulatory position that genetically engineered crops are substantially equivalent to their conventional counterparts, but also the European Union, which takes a more protective and precautionary approach to the products of agricultural biotechnology, the country is in the difficult position of trying to comply with very different sets of standards for its agricultural exports.

Consequently, it is critical for the United States, Canada, and Mexico to develop better assessment methodologies of the risks presented to all three countries, each of which has separate and distinct concerns, before a bioengineered crop is approved and commercialized for sale to each of the member countries. The United States is currently in the process of reconsidering some of its policies regarding the treatment of genetically engineered crops and, in particular, how farmers who use these technologies can coexist with farmers who choose not to, given the issues of cross-pollination.[12] Accordingly, the time may be ripe for the NAFTA signatory countries to reconsider their approaches to regulation and trade of these products in order to more fully meet the objectives stated in the NAAEC to "foster the protection and improvement of the environment in the territories of the Parties for the well-being of present and future generations" and "promote sustainable development based on cooperation and mutually supportive environmental and economic policies."[13] While the current regulatory policies adopted in the United States and Canada to address agricultural biotechnology fail to adequately protect the environment and agriculture of Mexico, there are opportunities for substantial improvements that would allow for better assessment and coordination of research and information among the Parties and work to benefit everyone.

2. AGRICULTURAL BIOTECHNOLOGY

Farmers have used agricultural technology in the form of genetic modification or selective breeding for generations to increase yields, develop crop resistance, and isolate specific desirable traits, among other reasons.[14] Although the terms are often

---

[12] See, e.g., United States Department of Agriculture, Advisory Committee on Biotechnology & 21st Century Agriculture (AC21), *Draft Charge*, http://www.usda.gov/wps/portal/usda/usdahome? contentid=AC21Main.xml&contentidonly=true (last visited Feb. 2, 2014) (USDA Secretary, Tom Vilsack, reconvened the Advisory Committee on Biotechnology and 21st Century Agriculture to address issues of coexistence between GE and non-GE farmers).

[13] North American Agreement on Environmental Cooperation, U.S.-Can.-Mex., Sept. 14, 1993, *International Legal Materials* 32 (entered into force Jan. 1, 1994), 1483.

[14] "Biotechnology is the application of scientific and engineering principles to the processing or production of materials by biological agents to provide goods and services. Agricultural biotechnology

used synonymously, in the United States, the agencies responsible for regulating these products differentiate the practice of genetic modification from genetic engineering in the sense that the former relies on sexual reproduction while the latter most commonly occurs upon the insertion of foreign genetic material.[15] Farmers were experimenting with genetic modification or hybridization prior to any formal understanding of genetics, but the work of Gregor Mendel in this field led to a much greater understanding of selective breeding.

In the simplest of terms, Mendel found that hereditary traits are controlled by genes, which exist in pairs that are equally separated into gametes, or eggs and sperm, meaning that each gamete contains only one part of the gene pair.[16] When gametes are combined from parent cells to form progeny, this happens randomly, and without regard to which member of the gene pair is carried, allowing for the expression of different traits.[17] Mendel's discoveries broadened and refined the field of selective breeding in agriculture, due to this new understanding of inheritance.[18]

Ultimately, however, the process of cross-hybridization is inevitably unpredictable and imprecise because the process is random and relatively uncontrolled – it can take many attempts at a cross before the offspring expresses the desired traits. Consequently, genetic engineering, which typically involves isolating specific genes from one organism and transferring them into another organism, has been heralded as a breakthrough in scientific innovation that increases predictability, but requires much less effort and time. Genetic engineering or recombinant DNA technology,

encompasses a growing list of techniques that range from simple probes to determine whether an individual plant or animal is carrying a specific gene to measurement of the activity of all an organism's genes (its genome) simultaneously. One technique common in agricultural biotechnology is the integration of a gene from one species into the genome of another. This technique is commonly referred to as genetic engineering, and the resulting product is described as transgenic (having a foreign gene)." National Research Council, *Global Challenges and Directions for Agricultural Biotechnology: Workshop Report* (Washington, D.C.: The National Academies Press, 2008), p. 10, http://www.nap.edu/catalog/12216.html.

[15] Genetic engineering is the "[m]anipulation of an organism's genes by introducing, eliminating or rearranging specific genes using the methods of modern molecular biology, particularly those techniques referred to as recombinant DNA techniques." United States Department of Agriculture, *Glossary of Agricultural Biotechnology Terms*, http://www.usda.gov/wps/portal/usda/usdahome?navid=BIOTECH_GLOSS&navtype=RT&parentnav=BIOTECH (last visited Feb. 2, 2014). "Genetic modification," on the other hand, is defined as "[t]he production of heritable improvements in plants or animals for specific uses, via either genetic engineering or other more traditional methods. Some countries other than the United States use this term to refer specifically to genetic engineering." Ibid. The term genetic modification includes "more traditional methods" such as hybridization or cross-breeding.

[16] A. J. F. Griffiths et al., "Mendel's Experiments," in *An Introduction to Genetic Analysis*, 7th ed. (New York: W. H. Freeman, 2000), http://www.ncbi.nlm.nih.gov/books/NBK22098/.

[17] Ibid.

[18] A. M. Wieczorek and M. G. Wright, "History of Agricultural Biotechnology: How Crop Development has Evolved," *Nature Education Knowledge* 3 (2012), 9, http://www.nature.com/scitable/knowledge/library/history-of-agricultural-biotechnology-how-crop-development-25885295.

while capable of producing desirable traits with a degree of precision and uncertainty unmatched by traditional breeding techniques, is, however, not without its critics.

Agricultural biotechnology and genetic engineering were developed, in large part, to respond to the problems associated with the Green Revolution. Specifically, while the Green Revolution resulted in the creation of higher-yielding crops, those crops required more intensive inputs in the form of fertilizers and herbicides, which generated a host of unanticipated environmental issues.[19] Scientists who remain critical of biotechnology argue that insufficient funding was dedicated to research regarding the health and ecological implications of GE organisms during the initial years.[20] Moreover, the industries engaged in research and development focused on an agenda dominated largely by profit and the search for traits, such as herbicide resistance, that could bolster sales of preexisting products such as agri-chemicals and pesticides.[21] Whereas farmers had traditionally identified crop varieties based on a wide array of beneficial traits, the new GE seeds created brand recognition for a specific genetic trait associated with a specific chemical herbicide.[22] To protect their investments, biotech companies developed "technology use agreements," stating that the companies owned the seed and specifying that farmer purchasers were required to use only the company's herbicides on the crop even when other generic versions existed, prohibited from saving seed from one season to the next, and subject to the company's right to inspect the farm for up to three years after the seed's initial planting.[23]

Cited as the means by which many developing countries can survive and perhaps even thrive, despite the effects of global warming, agricultural biotechnology incorporates new varieties of plants that are "able to better withstand abiotic stress like droughts, floods, saline water, heat and cold."[24] However, in most instances, those countries that might stand to gain the most from such technologies are also the least able to afford them.[25] Taking into account the fact that climate change has been tied to the very countries responsible for developing and proliferating biotechnology, the ethical issues become more acute.[26] Many developing countries have yet to adopt the practices of large-scale industrialized agricultural operations and, in turn, have

---

[19] National Research Council, above note 14, p. 9.
[20] Peter Andree, *Genetically Modified Diplomacy: The Global Politics of Agricultural Biotechnology and the Environment* (Vancouver: UBC Press, 2007), p. 41.
[21] Ibid., pp. 41–42.
[22] Ibid., p. 42.
[23] Ibid., p. 43.
[24] C. A. Timmermann, H. van den Belt, and M. J. J. A. Korthals, "Climate-ready GM Crops, Intellectual Property and Global Justice," in Carlos M. Romeo Casabona, Leire Escajedo San Epofanio, and Aitziber Emaldi Cirion (eds.), *Global Food Security: Ethical and Legal Challenges* (The Netherlands: Wageningen Academic Publishers, 2010), p. 153.
[25] Ibid.
[26] Ibid.

been able to preserve their rich biodiversity of plant species.[27] These plants serve as the foundation for innovations and advances in biotechnology, yet the developing countries are often unfairly, or not at all, compensated for the tremendous role they play in preserving agrobiodiversity.[28] Many argue that the biotechnology industry will cease to exist without preserving biodiversity, as the variety in plants and their genetic material either become the basis of or provide information for the products of biotechnology.[29] When considering this issue, it becomes apparent why many developing countries feel they are being slighted when they collaborate with industry to develop solutions to a problem for which they are largely not responsible, and then must pay exorbitant prices for the efforts of their collaboration.[30] Finally, due to the restrictive provisions included in most of the contracts governing the products of biotechnology, many farmers are required to abandon their traditions of seed saving, making the price of innovation even greater. Commentators argue that providing economic value to conservation practices would serve to benefit all parties.[31]

From an environmental perspective, some commentators suggest that introducing transgenic crops, or those created through the process of genetic engineering, presents no additional risks to the environment than introduction of their conventional counterparts.[32] This notion is based on the premise that conventional agriculture is responsible for its own share of environmental risk and damage. However, other commentators suggest that genetically engineered crops present a tremendous amount of environmental harm. The categories of risk most commonly associated with the introduction of GE plants and crops "include those associated with the movement of the transgenes, impacts of the whole plant through escape, and through impacts on agricultural practices, non-target organism effects, and resistance evolution."[33]

Despite the large amounts of agricultural acreage devoted to GE crops, as the global leader in their production, the United States still lacks a system by which it can monitor the impacts of large scale plantings, due to inadequate "baseline ... and comparative data on environmental impacts of previous agricultural practices."[34]

---

[27] Ibid., p. 155.
[28] Ibid.
[29] Ottavio Janni, "Biotechnology and developing Countries: The Struggle Over Intellectual Property Rights and Implications for Biodiversity Conservation," in R. E. Evenson and V. Santaniello (eds.), *The Regulation of Agricultural Biotechnology* (Cambridge, Mass.: CABI Publishing, 2004), p. 120 ("Developing countries hold both the richest areas for biodiversity and the most threatened ones, and as such biodiversity conservation is a particularly pressing issue for them").
[30] Timmermann, above note 24, p. 156.
[31] Janni, above note 29.
[32] See generally National Research Council, *Environmental Effects of Transgenic Plants: The Scope and Adequacy of Regulation* (Washington D.C.: The National Academies Press, 2002), http://www.nap.edu/catalog/10258.html.
[33] Ibid., p. 7.
[34] Ibid., p. 13.

In other words, the United States lacks a system that provides the necessary "environmental monitoring of agricultural and natural ecosystems" that could allow for an analysis of the "status and trends of the nation's biological resources."[35] Biotech crops are developed so rapidly that scientists remain concerned about the potential for "unknown biosafety hazards" and ill effects on the environment.[36] Consequently, despite assurances from the United States' regulatory agencies engaged in monitoring and enforcing the development and planting of GE crops that the process is closely regulated to prevent environmental risks associated therewith, the evidence suggests that perhaps those agencies lack the necessary concrete data to accurately make those determinations.

3. THE U.S. APPROACH TO THE REGULATION OF AGRICULTURAL BIOTECHNOLOGY

The United States is the lead nation in both producing and planting genetically engineered crops, making the approach it has taken toward their regulation both influential and significant. In the United States, three agencies share the responsibility of regulating the products of agricultural biotechnology: the United States Department of Agriculture (USDA), the Food and Drug Administration (FDA), and the Environmental Protection Agency (EPA). While no single federal law addresses biotechnology, the Office of Science and Technology Policy (OSTP) created the Biotechnology Science Coordinating Committee (BSCC)[37] to develop an "interagency coordinating committee," with representatives from each of the involved agencies, "to coordinate science issues related to research and commercial applications of biotechnology."[38] Importantly, the BSCC was charged only with coordinating scientific information between the agencies, and was not intended to address any issues related to the problems surrounding regulatory oversight.

Despite this mandate to coordinate responsibilities among the agencies, the BSCC was criticized for the fact that it became involved in issues of regulatory policy rather than science, conducted much of its business outside of the discerning eyes of the public, and ultimately failed to meet its obligation of developing consistent

---

[35] Ibid., pp. 13–14.

[36] Robert L. Paarlberg, Raymond F. Hopkins, and Lisa Ladewski, "Regulation of GM Crops: Shaping an International Regime," in R. E. Evenson and V. Santaniello (eds.), *The Regulation of Agricultural Biotechnology* (Cambridge, Mass.: CABI Publishing, 2004), pp. 4–5.

[37] Proposal for a Coordinated Framework for Regulation of Biotechnology, 49 Fed. Reg. 50,856, 50,858 (Dec. 31, 1984).

[38] Coordinated Framework for Regulation of Biotechnology; Establishment of the Biotechnology Science Coordinating Committee, 40 Fed. Reg. 47,174, 47,175–76 (Nov. 14, 1985) (The express purposes of the BSCC were to: "Serve as a coordinating forum for addressing scientific problems, sharing information, and developing consensus; [p]romote consistency in the development of Federal agencies' review procedures and assessments; [f]acilitate continuing cooperation among Federal agencies on emerging scientific issues; and[i]dentify gaps in scientific knowledge").

standards to guide agency decision making in this regard.[39] Ultimately, the BSCC sought the assistance of the National Research Council of the National Academies of Science to consider scientific information that was relevant to decisions about the "the introduction of genetically modified organisms and microorganisms and plants into the environment."[40]

In 1986, with the help of the BSCC,[41] the OSTP published its revised Coordinated Framework for the Regulation of Biotechnology.[42] This was the group's second attempt at developing a coordinated agency response to biotechnology and outlined the regulatory framework that remains largely unchanged to date. The Coordinated Framework is premised on the policy that "[r]ecombinant DNA techniques have opened up new and promising possibilities in a wide range of applications and can be expected to bring considerable benefits to mankind."[43] Moreover, the OSTP determined that developing new laws to regulate the products of genetic engineering was unnecessary because the health and safety laws in existence at the time were better able to provide instant regulatory oversight and guidance than would new legislation.[44] Additionally, because of the broad range of products developed through biotechnology, the OSTP could not envision any alternative that would effectively regulate the field.[45] Ultimately, the regulatory focus was, and remains, on the end product of the technology rather than the process.

The Coordinated Framework was drafted in a manner that was intended to provide guidance on the decisions that required regulatory approval and review and those that did not.[46] By way of example, the Framework addressed the fact that, within agriculture, new plants, animals, and microorganisms had long been introduced into the environment without federal regulation, and only some of those that were nonnative or pathogenic would now require federal oversight.[47] However,

---

[39] Al Gore, "Planning a New Biotechnology Policy," *Harvard Journal of Law and Technology* 5 (1991), 23; Linda Maher, "The Environment and the Domestic Regulatory Framework for Biotechnology," *Journal of Environmental Law and Litigation* 8 (1993), 139–40 (citing Bureau of National Affairs, *United States Biotechnology: A Legislative and Regulatory Roadmap*, BNA *Special Report on Biotechnology* #27 (Aug. 1989) (In part, the emphasis on policy may have been due to several Bush appointees to the Committee who were lawyers rather than scientists.).

[40] National Research Council, *Field Testing Genetically Modified Organisms: Framework for Decisions*, (Washington, D.C.: The National Academies Press, 1989), p. 1, http://www.nap.edu/catalog.php?ecord_id=1431.

[41] Maher, above note 39, p. 140 (The original chairman of the BSCC, David Kingsbury, helped draft the Coordinated Framework.).

[42] Coordinated Framework for Regulation of Biotechnology, 51 Fed. Reg. 23,302, 23, 302 (June 26, 1986).

[43] Ibid., p. 23,308.

[44] Ibid., p. 23,303.

[45] Ibid.; Maher, above note 39, p. 138 ("Biotechnology is a multi-discipline science, and at times, its products cross traditional barriers that distinguish foods from pesticides, medicines from poisons, and even tomatoes from fish").

[46] Coordinated Framework for Regulation of Biotechnology, 51 Fed. Reg. at 23,302.

[47] Ibid., p. 23, 303. ("Within agriculture, for example, introductions of new plants, animals and microorganisms have long occurred routinely with only some of those that are not native or are pathogenic requiring regulatory approval. It should be noted that microorganisms play many essential and varied

this oversimplification of the issues ignored the fact that the referenced introductions occurred through conventional breeding techniques, such as cross-breeding and hybridization, rather than by genetic engineering. Consequently, the OSTP explicitly provided that not all experiments involving the environmental release of genetically engineered organisms would be subject to prior approval.[48] This exception was especially true for plant applications, since those were determined to present low risk.[49]

Each of the responsible agencies developed individual statements of policy in response to the Coordinated Framework, and in response, the OSTP suggested that each responsible agency needed to conduct its assessments on a "case by case basis" taking into consideration the safety of the product, but also addressing the usefulness of the product.[50] The OSTP's wording in the Coordinated Framework demonstrated a clear policy decision that the products of genetic engineering were not only identical to their nongenetically engineered counterparts, but also had the potential to be superior.[51] Such flexibility in oversight was considered necessary to facilitate the growth of this sector. However, concerns remain that the safety of these products has become secondary to their utility.

Unfortunately, despite its best efforts, the Coordinated Framework provided little useful guidance to the responsible agencies. The OSTP's disjointed discussion of the existing mechanisms by which federal laws were able to regulate the products of genetic engineering in spite of the fact that these laws had never before considered the issue of biotechnology proved problematic. In other words, the OSTP had left the bulk of regulation in the hands of a group of agencies that were unable to reach consensus regarding how best to regulate these products.

In 1992, the OSTP issued its final statement of policy to provide the responsible agencies with the "proper basis" by which they were to engage in decision making within the bounds of the discretion afforded by the statutory framework.[52] Specifically, the policy included three principles that presently guide federal oversight of introductions of genetically engineered products into the environment. First, agencies should focus their decisions on the product of biotechnology rather than the process by which it has been created.[53] Next, the agencies should base their

---

roles in agriculture and the environment and that for decades agricultural scientists have endeavored to exploit their advantages through routine experimentation and introduction into the environment; and as a rule these agricultural and environmental introductions have taken place without harm to the environment.")

[48] Coordinated Framework for the Regulation of Biotechnology, 51 Fed. Reg. at 23,305.

[49] Ibid.

[50] Proposal for a Coordinated Framework, 49 Fed. Reg. at 50858.

[51] "While the recently developed methods are an extension of traditional manipulations that can produce similar or identical products, they enable more precise genetic modifications, and therefore hold the promise for exciting innovation and new areas of commercial opportunity." Coordinated Framework for the Regulation of Biotechnology, 51 Fed. Reg. at 23,302.

[52] Exercise of Federal Oversight Within Scope of Statutory Authority: Planned Introductions of Biotechnology Products Into the Environment, 57 Fed. Reg. 6,753, 6,753 (Feb. 27, 1992).

[53] Ibid.

decisions on the particular risks posed by the product rather than the fact that it has been developed through biotechnology.[54] Finally, organisms that possess "new phenotypic trait(s)" that have not been found to pose a greater risk than the "parental organisms" should not be subject to a greater level of oversight than the original unaltered organism.[55]

According to the OSTP, the risk-based approach provided for in the final policy achieved the necessary balance between ensuring safety and not unnecessarily hindering innovation and development.[56] This approach reflected the conclusions of the National Research Council, which had determined that genetically engineered organisms do not necessarily pose a greater risk than organisms that have not been subject to the same processes.[57] Consequently, the final policy makes clear that federal oversight may be duplicative of industry research in some instances, and agencies should be conscious of this fact while taking care not to waste resources.[58] The precaution witnessed in the early stages of policy development was replaced by a risk-based approach that essentially employs a cost-benefit analysis.[59] Critics of this approach argue that it has led to the weak exercise of statutory authority on the part of the responsible agencies[60] and has allowed for the "deregulation of

---

[54] Ibid.

[55] Ibid., p. 6, 756.

[56] Ibid.

[57] Ibid., p. 6, 755, citing National Research Council, above note 40. Specifically, the findings of the NRC indicated:

"1. The same physical and biological laws govern the response of organisms modified by modern molecular and cellular methods and those produced by classical methods. (p. 15)

"2. Information about the process used to produce a genetically modified organism is important in understanding the characteristics of the product. However, the nature of the process is not a useful criterion for determining whether the product requires less or more oversight. (pp. 14 and 15)

"3. No conceptual distinction exists between genetic modification of plants and microorganisms by classical methods or by molecular techniques that modify DNA and transfer genes. (p. 14)

"4. Crops modified by molecular and cellular methods should pose risks no different from those modified by classical methods for similar traits. As the molecular methods are more specific, users of these methods will be more certain about the traits they introduce into the plants. (p. 3)

"5. In many respects, molecular methods resemble the classical methods for modifying particular strains of microorganisms, but many of the new methods have two features that make them even more useful than the classical methods."

[58] Ibid., p. 6, 757. Critics suggest that because this policy is based "in large part on a policy determination that agencies and companies should not have to waste resources on unnecessary testing and evaluation ... it [provides] an excuse for regulatory agencies to avoid their responsibilities." Thomas O. McGarity, "Seeds of Distrust: Federal Regulation of Genetically Modified Foods," *University of Michigan Journal of Law Reform* 35 (2002), 431.

[59] Some considered this a watershed moment for both the regulation of biotechnology and of risk assessment generally. Peter Mostow, "Reassessing the Scope of Federal Biotechnology Oversight," *Pace Environmental Law Review* 10 (1992), 232.

[60] Douglas A. Kysar, "Preferences for Processes: The Process/Product Distinction and the Regulation of Consumer Choice," *Harvard Law Review* 118 (2004), 559 (citing Rebecca Bratspies, "The Illusion of Care: Regulation, Uncertainty, and Genetically Modified Food Crops," *New York University Environmental Law Journal* 10 (2002), 297; Gregory N. Mandel, "Gaps, Inexperience, Inconsistencies, and

large-scale environmental releases of transgenic plants," causing profound impacts for the individuals choosing not to invest in these technologies.[61]

4. CANADIAN AND MEXICAN APPROACHES TO THE REGULATION OF BIOTECHNOLOGY

4.1. *The Canadian Approach*

Canada is considered a member of the "biotech bloc" with the United States and devoted 10 percent of its government's research budget to biotechnology in the 1990s.[62] The Canadian approach to regulating the products of genetic engineering is remarkably similar to the regulatory scheme in the United States, as its focus is also on the products generated from biotechnology rather than the processes used in the development. Consequently, the Canadian government developed regulations to address plants with novel traits (PNTs), which are those plants "that do not have a history of production and safe consumption in Canada."[63] PNTs may have been modified using "biotechnology, mutagenesis, or conventional breeding techniques."[64] One notable difference between the Canadian and U.S. regulatory scheme is that not all plants developed through genetic engineering are considered PNTs.[65]

While many jurisdictions in Canada require some level of regulatory oversight for new GE crops, regulatory oversight by the Canadian Food Inspection Agency (CFIA), the agency that, along with Health Canada and Environmental Canada, is responsible for assessing the safety of GE crops, is triggered only when a plant expresses a new trait, meaning some plants created through biotechnology will escape oversight while some conventionally modified crops may fall within the agency's purview.[66] As in the United States, three agencies share the responsibility of regulating products developed through biotechnology: the CFIA, Health Canada, and Environment Canada.[67] Moreover, rather than developing a new set of laws

Overlaps: Crisis in the Regulation of Genetically Modified Plants and Animals," *William and Mary Law Review* 45 (2004), 2167; McGarity, above note 59).

[61] David J. Earp, Ph.D., "The Regulation of Genetically Engineered Plants: Is Peter Rabbit Safe in Mr. McGregor's Transgenic Vegetable Patch?," *Environmental Law* 24 (1994), 1658.

[62] Andree, above note 20, p. 40.

[63] Stuart J. Smyth and Alan McHughen, "Regulation of Genetically Modified Crops in USA and Canada: Canadian Overview," in Chris A. Wozniak and Alan McHughen (eds.), *Regulation of Agricultural Biotechnology: The United States and Canada* (New York: Springer, 2012), p. 16.

[64] Canadian Food Inspection Agency, *Plants with Novel Traits*, http://www.inspection.gc.ca/plants/plants-with-novel-traits/eng/1300137887237/1300137939635 (last visited Feb. 2, 2014).

[65] Smyth and McHughen, above note 63.

[66] Ibid., pp. 15–17.

[67] Canadian Food Inspection Agency, *Regulating Agricultural Biotechnology in Canada: An Overview*, http://www.inspection.gc.ca/plants/plants-with-novel-traits/general-public/overview/eng/1338187581090/1338188593891 (last visited Feb. 2, 2014).

and regulations to address these products, the Canadian government adopted the approach taken by the United States and developed a framework for regulation that "build[s] on existing laws and expertise."[68] In other words, "agricultural products of biotechnology are regulated under the same broad legislation and structures, with the addition of some new regulations and administrative procedures, as agricultural products produced in more traditional ways."[69]

The CFIA is the agency with primary responsibility for regulating the performance and usefulness of the products of biotechnology and ensuring their safety from an environmental perspective.[70] Comparatively speaking, this agency performs many of the same functions as the USDA. Specifically, the agency exercises its authority under the purview of four different statutes, namely, the Seeds Act, the Fertilizers Act, the Feeds Act, and the Health of Animals Act.[71] In addition to its commitment to using existing legislation as a means of regulation rather than develop new laws, the CFIA is committed to focusing on "product characteristics" rather than production methods, "conduct[ing] evaluations for each product on the basis of its unique characteristics and . . . establish[ing] appropriate safety levels based on the best scientific information."[72] When conducting these evaluations, safety is not defined as "the complete absence of risk, but rather as the level of 'acceptable risk.'"[73] Additionally, agency officials do not undertake independent testing of the products but instead generally analyze the data submitted by the applicants performing experiments in limited instances to confirm results.[74]

The CFIA engages in a three-stage assessment process that considers the environmental release of the product, as well as its use as an animal feed.[75] During the first stage, plants must be grown in a confined facility that utilizes growing conditions specified in the biosafety guidelines developed by Health Canada and the Medical Research Council.[76] In stage two, the developer must obtain approval from the CFIA prior to engaging in confined field trials, which are limited in number, size,

---

[68] Ibid.
[69] Ibid.
[70] Ibid.
[71] Ibid.; see also Smyth and McHughen, above note 63, pp. 16–18. (The Seeds Act assesses "genetic uniformity, stability and uniqueness ('uniqueness' here means the new cultivar must be genetically modified or genetically different from all earlier varieties)." Additionally, the Seeds Act develops "thresholds for environmental safety risks such as geneflow, invasiveness, weediness and impact on non-target organisms." The Feeds Act develops the thresholds for "potential risks due to allergenicity, toxicity, digestibility and dietary exposure relating to animal feeding." Finally, the Food and Drugs Act "establishes risk thresholds for allergenicity, toxicity, metabloization, nutrition and dietary exposure relating to human consumption.")
[72] Canadian Food Inspection Agency, above note 67.
[73] Ibid.
[74] Smyth and McHughen, above note 63, p. 17.
[75] Ibid., p. 26.
[76] Ibid.

and distance.[77] These field trials occur over several years in different locations that encompass the places where the crop might be adopted, and the data generated from these trials is used by the CFIA when conducting the safety assessments in the third stage.[78] In the final stage, the developer must submit the scientific data and information collected from the field trials to the CFIA, which reviews the data and forms the basis of its final decision to allow the developer to apply for unconfined commercial production of the crop.[79]

Health Canada derives its authority to address the potential human health impacts of these products from the Food and Drugs Act and sets their safety standards.[80] Before any genetically engineered products can be sold as food or animal feed, they must be approved by the agency after review of detailed scientific data submitted by the manufacturers.[81] Additionally, Health Canada is responsible for assessing the potential risks of "new substances" used in any product regulated by the Food and Drugs Act on human health and the environment.[82] The agency does not review all foods that are new to the market in Canada, excluding those with a prior history of safe use in other countries and those with only "minor processing change[s]."[83] Consequently, only those processes that are unique and present "substantial changes in the composition of the food" will be subject to review.[84] Once the field trial data is submitted to the CFIA, this information is then analyzed by Health Canada to assess the "nutritional, toxicity and allergenicity data."[85] Commentators suggest that the more novel the food product, the less transparent the process is with regard to the submission of scientific data.[86]

Finally, Environment Canada is responsible for determining whether the PNT can be identified as a toxic substance presenting harm to humans and the environment.[87] Of the three agencies, this agency exercises the least regulatory authority over the PNT process.[88] Overall, however, the shared regulatory approach is not only similar to, but consistent with the approach taken by the United States.[89] The two countries have engaged in efforts to ensure such consistency since 1998 and are considered by some to be an "international beacon for science-based regulation."[90]

---

[77] Ibid.
[78] Ibid., pp. 26–27.
[79] Ibid., p. 27.
[80] Ibid., p. 28.
[81] Ibid.
[82] Ibid.
[83] Ibid.
[84] Ibid.
[85] Ibid.
[86] Ibid.
[87] Ibid., pp. 30–31.
[88] Ibid., p. 31.
[89] Ibid.
[90] Ibid.

4.2. *Mexican Approach*

Since 1988, Mexico has allowed the field testing of certain bioengineered crops.[91] However, while one of the first countries to adopt agricultural biotechnology for experimental reasons, Mexico's agricultural sector continues to invest primarily in the production of conventional crops.[92] Some commentators suggest that regulatory policy addressing biotechnology in the country is directly tied to trade agreements and a desire to access global markets.[93] Mexico and Canada are parties to the United Nations' Convention on Biological Diversity[94] while the United States is only a signatory, and of the three, Mexico is the only country that is also a party to the Convention's supplementary Cartagena Protocol on Biosafety (hereinafter Protocol).[95] The Protocol is an international treaty adopted as a supplementary agreement to the Convention that regulates the transboundary movement of living modified organisms (LMOs).[96] From the Canadian perspective, the Protocol lacks "clarity and predictability in terms of its implementation and enforcement."[97] The United States was concerned about "contradictory language" in the Protocol pertaining to protections for intellectual property.[98] Incidentally, none of the countries

[91] Aarti Gupta and Robert Falkner, "The Influence of the Cartagena Protocol on Biosafety: Comparing Mexico, China and South Africa," *Global Environmental Politics* 6 (Nov. 2006), 33, http://www.mitpressjournals.org/doi/pdf/10.1162/glep.2006.6.4.23.

[92] United States Department of Agriculture Foreign Agricultural Service, *Mexican Government Continues to Support Biotech Crops* (July 14, 2000), p. 8, http://gain.fas.usda.gov/Recent%20GAIN%20Publications/Biotechnology%20-%20GE%20Plants%20and%20Animals_Mexico%20City_Mexico_14-07-2010.pdf.

[93] Ibid.

[94] United Nations Conference on Environment and Development: Convention on Biological Diversity, *International Legal Materials* 31 (opened for signature June 5, 1992), 818. The CBD was adopted during the Rio Earth Summit and provides a global legal framework for addressing issues related to biodiversity. Convention on Biological Diversity, *Introduction*, http://www.cbd.int/convention/bodies/intro.shtml (last visited Feb. 2, 2014); see also Convention on Biological Diversity, *List of Parties*, http://www.cbd.int/information/parties.shtml (last visited Feb. 2, 2014).

[95] Cartagena Protocol on Biosafety to the Convention on Biological Diversity, *International Legal Materials* 39 (Jan. 29, 2000), 1027.

[96] Ibid. Under the Protocol, a "living modified organism" "means any living organism that possesses a novel combination of genetic material obtained through the use of modern biotechnology." Ibid. A "living organism" is defined as "any biological entity capable of transferring or replicating genetic material, including sterile organisms, viruses and viroids." Ibid. See generally Convention on Biological Diversity, *About the Protocol*, http://bch.cbd.int/protocol/background/ (last visited Feb. 2, 2014).

[97] Government of Canada, Agriculture and Agri-Food Canada, *The Biosafety Protocol*, http://www.agr.gc.ca/eng/industry-markets-and-trade/agri-food-trade-policy/trade-topics/the-biosafety-protocol/?id=1384287629516 (last visited Feb. 2, 2014).

[98] Thomas P. Redick, "The Cartagena Protocol on Biosafety: Precautionary Priority in Biotech Crop Approvals and Containment of Commodities Shipments," *Colorado Journal of International Environmental Law and Policy* 18 (2007), 59, citing Victor M. Marroquin-Merino, "Wildlife Utilization: A New International Mechanism for the Protection of Biological Diversity," *Law and Policy in International Business* 26 (1995), 317 (noting that while the Convention gave Parties rights to genetic resources, its "controversial provisions on the protection of intellectual property and the transfer of biotechnology" stopped the United States from adopting the Convention). While the Clinton administration signed

that export the products of genetic engineering have ratified the Protocol.[99] Despite the fact that neither the United States nor Canada is a party to the Protocol, both countries have expressed a willingness to work with the parties subject to it to address the concerns raised by LMOs.[100]

The regulatory approach reflected in the Protocol is a precautionary one that requires countries to have adequate information before consenting to the import of the products of biotechnology.[101] This approach emphasizes the potential for risks in stark contrast to the science-based approach requiring proof of harm taken by countries such as the United States and Canada. Mexico's ratification of the Protocol in 2002 helped ensure approval of its own Biosafety Law in 2005, as the Protocol required each party to pass legislation to "harmonize its domestic laws with its international obligations."[102] The Biosafety Law explicitly adopted the precautionary approach, making decision makers subject to its considerations. Yet, there are currently no guidelines within the law addressing how they are to do so.[103] Additionally, while the various recommendations, standards, and instruments addressing biotechnology developed by organizations such as the Organisation for Economic Co-Operation and Development (OECD), the Food and Agriculture Organization of the United Nations (FAO), the World Health Organization (WHO), and the Codex Alimentarius Commission (CAC) are not binding on Mexico, arguably, it should consider their recommendations when regulating in this field as a member country of those organizations.[104]

Prior to the passage of its Biosafety Law in 2005, Mexico's Congress developed the Committees for Science and Technology and Environment, Natural Resources and Fisheries to engage in studies considering how to balance the country's valuable natural resources with its "international obligations to promote free trade."[105] However, many in the country were concerned about the effects of genetically engineered crops on native species of maize and successfully persuaded the government

the treaty, the U.S. Senate has not ratified the Convention. See ibid., pp. 333–34; United States Department of Agriculture, *Forest Service: International Program, Convention on Biological Diversity,* http://www.fs.fed.us/global/aboutus/policy/multi/bind.htm#4 (last visited Feb. 2, 2014).

[99] Gupta and Falkner, above note 91, p. 32.

[100] Commission for Environmental Cooperation, above note 9, p. 13.

[101] Ibid. Some commentators distinguish between the "precautionary principle" adopted by the EU and the "precautionary approach" reflected in the Protocol suggesting the former applies in "situations of high uncertainty with a risk of irreversible harm" whereas the latter applies when "the level of uncertainty and potential costs are merely significant and the harm is less likely to be irreversible." Alicia Gutierrez Gonzalez, *The Protection of Maize Under the Mexican Biosafety Law: Environment and Trade* (2010), p. 99.

[102] United States Department of Agriculture Foreign Agricultural Service, *Mexican Government Continues to Support Biotech Crops* (July 14, 2000), p. 8, http://gain.fas.usda.gov/Recent%20GAIN%20 Publications/Biotechnology%20-%20GE%20Plants%20and%20Animals_Mexico%20City_Mexico_ 14–07–2010.pdf.

[103] Gonzalez, above note 101, p. 99.

[104] Ibid., pp. 112–13.

[105] Ibid., p. 114.

to enact a law criminalizing the storing or release of genetically engineered crops into the environment.[106] The committees, however, recognized that biotechnology had the ability to provide benefits to the country in terms of human, plant, and animal health, as well as economic development.[107] Following these determinations, the Mexican Biosafety Law was written to enable the realization of these benefits, while complying with the provisions of the Cartagena Protocol, and regulates "the contained use, handling, transport, packaging and identification [of GMOs], [the] [i]ntentional release of GMOs into the environment; GMOs for use as food or feed or for processing...; [and] transboundary movements (import/export) and transit."[108]

Under the Mexican Biosafety Law and the rules implementing its provisions, three different agencies share authority to develop the country's policies related to biotechnology,[109] while the Inter-Ministerial Commission on Biosecurity and Genetically Modified Organisms (CIBIOGEM) is responsible for coordinating and creating the procedures that require a reasonable consideration of the potential risks associated with the handling of the products of biotechnology, but lacks an enforcement mechanism.[110] CIBIOGEM is a committee in the executive branch[111] and is comprised of a few different agencies, including the National Council of Science and Technology (CONACYT), and the representatives of the following Secretariats: Agriculture, Environment and Natural Resources, Health, Treasury, Economy, and Education.[112] The Commission also receives counsel and advice from various technical and advisory groups and receives input from different sectors with expertise in the field of biosafety.[113] Finally, four main secretariats fall under the purview of CIBIOGEM, whose function is to regulate the "import, export and release of [genetically engineered organisms] into the environment."[114]

The main function of the Biosafety Law is to "prevent, avoid or reduce" *potential* risks to the human and natural environment, in addition to protecting Mexico's biological diversity.[115] Under the law, risk assessments are performed on a "case-by-case basis" and require the following:

[106] Gupta and Falkner, above note 91, p. 34.
[107] Gonzalez, above note 101, p. 114.
[108] Ibid., pp. 114–15.
[109] United States Department of Agriculture Foreign Agricultural Service, above note 102, p. 2.
[110] Gonzalez, above note 101, pp. 116–17; United States Department of Agriculture Foreign Agricultural Service, above note 102, p. 4.
[111] Gonzalez, above note 101, p. 115.
[112] United States Department of Agriculture Foreign Agricultural Service, above note 102, p. 4.
[113] Gonzalez, above note 101, p. 116 (The members of these sectors are "allowed to participate through opinions, studies and consultations in order to generate knowledge and expertise to support public policies and promote research on biotechnology and biosafety").
[114] Ibid., p. 117.
[115] Ibid., p. 123.

(i) an identification of any novel characteristics associated with the GMO that may [present] possible risks to biological diversity;

(ii) [a]n evaluation of the likelihood of these risks being realized, taking into account the level and kind of exposure of the GMO;

(iii) [a]n evaluation of the consequences should these possible risks be realized; [a]n estimation of the overall risk posed by the GMO based on the evaluation of the likelihood and consequences of the identified possible risks being materialize; [a] recommendation as to whether or not the possible risks are acceptable or manageable, including where necessary, identification of strategies to manage these possible risks.[116]

While the law mandates that the requirements of the risk assessments shall be established by regulations, norma official mexicana (NOMs), these have not yet been completed.[117]

From the perspective of the United States, Mexico's regulatory approach toward biotechnology sends "mixed signals."[118] Specifically, the USDA cites the government of Mexico's decision to authorize the commercial cultivation of 253,000 hectares of genetically engineered soybeans in 2012 as contradictory to its decision to delineate centers of origin and corn genetic diversity in the country in 2011.[119] Because Mexico is a "mega diverse country" and a "cent[er] of origin and genetic diversity,"[120] it forbids the release of genetically engineered organisms in those areas that are considered centers of origin for native species and plants.[121] The government's decision to develop a map with the aforementioned delineations has been controversial among many different interests, including "government, industry, and academic."[122] However, others suggest the Mexican government has not taken sufficient measures to protect its native species, environment, and traditional methods of farming. Critics cite the failure to include a mechanism in the Biosafety Law that comports with the principals in the Protocol and requires advanced informed agreement before the importation of certain products of genetic engineering.[123] The country appears to be conflicted in its attempts to access the international trade markets, while ensuring economic prosperity and preservation of cultural and environmental heritage.

---

[116] Ibid., p. 125.

[117] Ibid., p. 126.

[118] United States Department of Agriculture Foreign Agricultural Service, *Mexico Cautiously Moves Forward with Biotechnology* (Jul. 19, 2012), p. 1, http://gain.fas.usda.gov/Recent%20GAIN%20Publications/Agricultural%20Biotechnology%20Annual_Mexico%20City_Mexico_7-19-2012.pdf.

[119] Ibid.

[120] Gonzalez, above note 101, p. 133.

[121] Ibid., p. 133; United States Department of Agriculture Foreign Agricultural Service, above note 118, p. 6.

[122] United States Department of Agriculture Foreign Agricultural Service, above note 118.

[123] Gupta and Falkner, above note 91, p. 35.

5. IMPACTS ON MEXICO AND RECOMMENDATIONS FOR
A UNIFORM SYSTEM OF REGULATION

5.1. *Impacts*

Some suggest that "[t]he acronym NAFTA can be heard in a Mexican farmer's conversation almost as often as drought."[124] This discontent stems from NAFTA's troubling impacts on the Mexican agricultural sector, which many attribute to the asymmetries among the parties that existed at the time of signing and persist currently.[125] Specifically, the agreement is viewed as having been "poorly negotiated" for Mexico in the sense that its most economically sensitive products were not excluded as they were for Canada, it bears the burden of high import quotas, and the agreement excludes any provisions for the "possibility of review, suspension, moratorium, or the use of other instruments for protecting domestic production."[126] Overall, it is estimated that NAFTA's provisions related to agriculture greatly favor the United States to Mexico's detriment, as exports to the country are high and the United States holds a "major share" of the high-value foods (meat and poultry, dairy, and snack foods) market.[127]

Regarding the import of the products of biotechnology, Mexico has signed a "Trilateral Agreement"[128] with its NAFTA partners, which requires labels on bulk commodity imports that state they may contain genetically engineered organisms.[129] Critics of the Agreement note that it was negotiated by a representative of the Ministry of Agriculture in the absence of adequate discussion with other members of government, and therefore does not have their support.[130] The Agreement is controversial in the sense that the labeling requirement is only necessary when the genetically engineered materials exceed 5 percent,[131] which represents the unintended or adventitious presence percentage used by the United States in stark contrast to the 0.9 percent allowance in the European Union.[132] Arguably, the adoption of this high

---

[124] Richard Manning, *Food's Frontier: The Next Green Revolution* (Berkeley, Calif.: University of California Press, 2000), p. 151.

[125] Manuel Angel Gomez and Rita Schwentesius Rindermann, "NAFTA's Impact on Mexican Agriculture: An Overview," in Juan M. Rivera, Scott Whiteford, and Manuel Chavez (eds.), *NAFTA and the Campesinos: The Impact of NAFTA on Small-Scale Agricultural Producers in Mexico and the Prospects for Change* (Chicago, Ill.: University of Scranton Press, 2009), p. 3.

[126] Ibid.

[127] Bert R. Pena and Amy Henderson, Symposium, "U.S.-Mexico Agricultural Trade and Investment After NAFTA," *United States-Mexico Law Journal* 1 (1993), 275.

[128] Gupta and Falkner, above note 91, p. 36.

[129] Ibid.; United States Department of Agriculture Foreign Agricultural Service, above note 102, p. 8.

[130] Gupta and Falkner, above note 91, p. 36.

[131] Ibid.

[132] National Research Council, *The Impact of Genetically Engineered Crops on Farm Sustainability in the United States* (2010), p. 172, http://www.nap.edu/openbook.php?record_id=12804, citing Matty Demont and Yann Devos, "Regulating Coexistence of GM and Non-GM Crops Without Jeopardizing Economic Incentive," *Trends in Biotechnology* 26 (2008), 353–58; Organic Foods Production Act of

threshold runs "counter to the spirit, if not (yet) the letter of the Cartagena Protocol (given that the debate about thresholds is yet to take place in the global context)."[133]

The issue of the impacts of agricultural biotechnology in Mexico became the focus of international attention in 2001 when *Nature* published a controversial study alleging the cross-pollination of traditional maize landraces with genetically engineered varieties.[134] The following year, "21 indigenous communities of Oaxaca and three Mexican environmental groups, Greenpeace México, the Mexican Center for Environmental Law (*Centro Mexicano de Derecho Ambiental* – Cemda), and the Union of Mexican Environmental Groups" petitioned the CEC, the tri-national organization developed to address environmental concerns arising under NAFTA, to engage in an analysis of "the impacts of transgenic introgression into landraces of maize in Mexico."[135] Pursuant to its authority under Article 13 of the North American Agreement on Environmental Cooperation,[136] the CEC agreed to study the issue and prepare a report for the CEC Council and the environment ministers or their counterparts in each of the NAFTA countries.[137]

As part of its study, the CEC noted that the United States has either approved or granted nonregulated status to twenty varieties of genetically engineered maize while Canada has done the same for approximately ten.[138] In contrast, Mexico has approved six varieties for import as food, for feed, or processing, but not for commercial cultivation.[139] However, based on these discrepancies in regulation, imports to Mexico could contain both approved and unapproved varieties of transgenic maize as the United States and Canada do not require specific labeling.[140]

The CEC's report made several key findings regarding the potential and reality of gene flow between transgenic and native varieties of maize, impacts to biodiversity, concerns about potential health implications, and issues regarding the sociocultural significance of the crop to the Mexican people.[141] Corn is the "basic staple food for human consumption" in the country.[142] Specifically, the report determined

1990, 7 U.S.C. §§ 6501–6522 (1990). ("For example, in the United States, voluntary labeling of food as GE-free is allowed as long as a product contains less than 5-percent adventitious presence of GE material. In contrast, the EU allows up to 0.9-percent adventitious GE material in non-GE food, animal feed, and products labeled as organic if the GE crop has been approved in the EU; otherwise, the threshold is zero.")

[133] Gupta and Falkner, above note 91, p. 36.
[134] David Quist and Ignacio H. Chapela, "Transgenic DNA Introgressed into Traditional Maize Landraces in Oaxaca, Mexico," *Nature* 414 (2001), 541–43.
[135] Commission for Environmental Cooperation, above note 9, p. 6.
[136] North American Agreement on Environmental Cooperation, above note 13, pp. 1487–88.
[137] Commission for Environmental Cooperation, above note 9, p. 6.
[138] Ibid., p. 13.
[139] Ibid.
[140] Ibid.
[141] Ibid., pp. 15–25.
[142] Alejandro Nadal and Timothy A. Wise, *The Environmental Costs of Agricultural Trade Liberalization: Mexico-U.S. Maize Trade Under NAFTA* (June 2004), p. 4, http://ase.tufts.edu/gdae/pubs/rp/DP04NadalWiseJuly04.pdf.

that there is evidence of gene flow from transgenic varieties into the landraces of native maize.[143] The CEC postulates that such gene flow occurs when GE grain is imported into a rural community by way of a government agency and then planted by farmers on an experimental basis.[144] If there are native landraces in the same fields or near vicinity, then cross-pollination can occur.[145] This process of introduction has occurred without any mechanisms requiring consent or approval by the local, impacted communities.[146] Additionally, Mexican farmers have traditionally saved and traded their seeds, and because some of those might be genetically engineered, the gene flow can be perpetuated.[147] Once such gene flow has occurred, removal of "transgenes that have introgressed widely into landraces is likely to be very difficult and may in fact be impossible."[148]

The CEC's findings with respect to impacts on biodiversity were less conclusive and suggested that the impacts of GE corn on plants and animals are "[n]either negative nor positive," while the impacts on native varieties of maize remain unknown.[149] Regarding health implications, the report acknowledges "[t]here is no empirical evidence that the process of producing GM crops is hazardous or beneficial *per se* to animal or human health."[150] However, the products of agricultural biotechnology need further evaluation of their effects.[151] Because Mexicans hold a special reverence for maize, many consider the introgression of GE varieties of corn as an "unacceptable risk" to traditional agricultural practices and regard it as "contamination."[152] Finally, while the United States and Canada evaluate risks for GE crops within their borders, they fail to perform risk assessments of the consequences of such products beyond their borders prior to export.[153] Because Mexico has no process by which GE crops are systematically monitored, the impacts and risks are largely unknown.[154]

5.2. Recommendations

Currently, no framework exists for a universal system of regulation for the products of biotechnology among the United States, Canada, and Mexico that takes into account the special needs of each country. Specifically, because the United States and Canada are developed countries that are both producers and exporters of the

[143] Commission for Environmental Cooperation, above note 9, p. 16.
[144] Ibid.
[145] Ibid.
[146] Ibid., p. 24.
[147] Ibid.
[148] Ibid., p. 17.
[149] Ibid., p. 19.
[150] Ibid., p. 20.
[151] Ibid.
[152] Ibid., p. 23.
[153] Ibid., p. 25.
[154] Ibid.

technologies while Mexico is a developing country that largely imports these products, there is a clear need to develop a system of regulation that adequately serves to protect the interests of each country while safeguarding the resources each has deemed valuable.

Following the passage of NAFTA, advocates and critics expressed deep concern about the financial impacts of the trade agreement on Mexico, given its status relative to the United States and Canada. Many suggest these fears have been realized, as exports of corn from the United States to Mexico have increased significantly since the implementation of NAFTA, and the resulting environmental and social consequences to both countries remain the topic of much debate.[155] The agricultural system in the United States is drastically different from the traditional farming methods used by Mexican farmers and peasants. In attempting to compete with the United States, Mexico's methods of agricultural practices that are less reliant on chemicals and serve to promote and support biodiversity are yielding to the more environmentally destructive practices used by large-scale agricultural operations in the United States.[156]

After engaging in its study in Mexico, the CEC made many recommendations, several of which are useful in considering how the policies regarding the regulation of agricultural biotechnology could be adapted between the three countries. First, the CEC suggested that the responsible agencies in each of the three countries "should develop and implement better methods for detecting and monitoring the spread of specific transgenes, such as unique identifying genetic markers (including the specific transgene locus) and the transgene products (such as specific Bt proteins) that can be recognized easily, reliably, and inexpensively."[157] Moreover, the countries should assess and manage the risks associated with these products in a comprehensive manner by sharing research and identifying the risks posed not just in one of the countries, but all three.[158] In some instances, this may mean that a particular product is not suitable for release in all countries.[159] Given that Mexico is a developing country that primarily imports these technologies, the United States and Canada are in a better position to conduct these assessments. Finally, to provide for better "regulatory oversight, there should be greater information exchange among regulators in the three countries in order that no products are released without the knowledge of all three governments."[160]

Ultimately, the CEC's suggestions are not unique or groundbreaking. In the United States, there has been a strong push for the responsible regulatory agencies to do a better job of assessing the long-term impacts of such technologies. Currently, the

[155] Nadal and Wise, above note 142, p. 2.
[156] Ibid., p. 26.
[157] Commission for Environmental Cooperation, above note 9, p. 27.
[158] Ibid., p. 31.
[159] Ibid.
[160] Ibid.

USDA has no mechanism by which to continue to review a genetically engineered crop once it has been deregulated by the agency. The existing monitoring system focuses on "the simplest ecological scales, even though the history of environmental impacts associated with conventional breeding points to the importance of large-scale effects."[161] Consequently, scientific bodies in the United States have long recommended that regulators begin to consider the effects of transgenes on "regional farming practices [and] systems."[162] This issue has been of significance in the United States and is an issue for any country receiving exported bioengineered products.

Because the United States has conducted more environmental reviews of these products than any other country, it remains in the best position to assess the potential impacts from a regulatory perspective.[163] However, the issues and considerations may not be the same for all importing countries, making the review process deficient in some regards. As discussed, maize producers in Mexico have a different set of concerns than do producers in the United States. It has been recognized that "the global scientific capacity to conduct locally relevant environmental risk analyses is sorely deficient, and this needs immediate attention."[164] Perhaps this attention should come in the form of U.S. and Canadian assessment of the specific risks faced by Mexico as it imports the products of biotechnology from those two countries. Recognition of this factor as part of ongoing discussions about how to properly ensure the achievement of the goals set forth in the NAAEC will be critical. Any system whereby the United States and Canada take into greater consideration the environmental impacts and risks associated with these products can result in substantial protection of Mexico's rich natural resources, which, ultimately, works to the benefit of all three countries.

[161] National Research Council, above note 32, p. 15.
[162] Ibid.
[163] National Research Council, above note 32, p. 247.
[164] Ibid.

8

Assessing Assessments of NAFTA's Marine Environment

The Commission for Environmental Cooperation Meets the World Ocean Assessment

Betsy Baker

1. INTRODUCTION

Imagine, for a moment, the marine area of the North American Free Trade Agreement (NAFTA)[1] as a blue blanket enveloping the North American continent. It cloaks the Canadian Archipelago and fills the Beaufort Sea; it wraps the coasts and continental shelves off of Nunavut, the Inuvialuit Settlement Region, the Northwest Territories, and the state of Alaska. Abutting Russian waters, it cups the Chukchi Sea and funnels through the Bering Strait. It connects the Aleutian and Pribilof islands in the ring of fire, and surrounds Hawaii. It laps the continent's western coast from British Columbia to Chiapas via Washington, Oregon, California, Baja California, Oaxaca, and other states. It warms the Gulf of Mexico from the Yucatan to Florida, channels the Gulf Stream from the mid-Atlantic seaboard, sweeps along the Maritime Provinces, fills the Hudson Bay and contains the icy waters of the Davis Strait.[2] Combined, the Exclusive Economic Zones (EEZs) of Canada, Mexico, and the United States cover over fifteen million square kilometers of ocean, almost two and a half times the size of Australia's EEZ.[3] The NAFTA marine areas, which are

---

[1] North American Free Trade Agreement, U.S.-Can.-Mex., Dec. 17, 1992, 32 I.L.M. 289 (1993), 32 I.L.M. 605 [hereinafter NAFTA].

[2] This litany does not name all areas potentially covered by the NAFTA marine area. In Annex 45 to the North American Agreement for Environmental Cooperation (NAAEC), each state defines its territory to include certain marine areas. For Mexico these include the islands of Guadalupe and Revillagigedo in the Pacific; for the United States they include Puerto Rico. For all three states "territory" includes "any areas beyond the territorial seas . . . within which, in accordance with international law . . . and its domestic law, [the state in question] may exercise rights with respect to the seabed and subsoil and their natural resources." Mexico's definition of territory also references the United Nations Convention on the Law of the Sea (LOS), as it was the only NAFTS state party to the LOS in 1993 when the NAAEC was signed (it entered into force Jan. 1, 1994). Canada joined the LOS Convention in 2003; the United States is still not party.

[3] Total: 15,494,705 km²: Canadian EEZ = 6,006,154 km²; Mexican EEZ = 3,269,386 km²; United States EEZ = 6,219,165 km². Pew Charitable Trusts, Sea Around Us Project: Fisheries, Ecosystems & Biodiversity, http://www.seaaroundus.org#/eez/ (last visited 14 Mar. 2014). For a map of the NAFTA

not necessarily conterminous with the three EEZs, also contain some of the highest net primary productivity rates in the world.[4]

The creation of the EEZ as a new maritime zone by the 1982 UN Convention on the Law of the Sea heralded a new era for coastal states in relation to marine resources.[5] As coastal states were required to take account of other states' interests in this new zone, multilateralism eventually became the operative rule for managing substantial portions of ocean space.[6] The entry into force of NAFTA twelve years later, in 1994, and the simultaneous creation of the Commission for North American Environmental Cooperation (CEC) added a regional component to how Canada, Mexico, and the United States regarded their neighboring marine areas. The CEC, established by Part III of the North American Agreement on Environmental Cooperation (NAAEC),[7] is responsible for annual reports, including regular assessments of the region's environment.[8] These annual CEC reports have not been systematic in their treatment of NAFTA's ocean areas, but individual CEC initiatives on the marine environment have produced such useful tools as the 2009 book *Marine Ecoregions of North America*,[9] *The North American Environmental Atlas*,[10] and ecological "scorecards" for marine protected areas (MPA).[11]

marine regions, see http://www.cec.org/Page.asp?PageID=122&ContentID=1324&SiteNodeID=498& BL_ExpandID= (last visited May 28, 2015).

[4] Michael A. Huston and Steve Wolverton, "The Global Distribution of Net Primary Production: Resolving the Paradox," *Ecological Monographs* 79 (Aug. 2009), 343 ("Net primary production, the rate at which plants convert carbon dioxide and water into energy-rich carbon compounds, is the foundation for all life on Earth. . . . [T]he highest productivity is in the high latitudes, particularly in the northern hemisphere"). See also PEW Charitable Trusts, *Sea Around Us*, to compare productivity for, e.g., the U.S. East Coast (796 mgC·m^{-2}·day^{-1}) and U.S. West Coast (885) with China (755), Chile (771), or Somalia (882); U.S. Department of the Interior, Bureau of Ocean Energy Management, Regulation and Enforcement, Alaska OCS Region, *Chukchi Sea Planning Area, Oil and Gas Lease Sale 193 In the Chukchi Sea, Alaska, Final Supplemental Environmental Impact Statement, Volume I*, OCS EIS/EA BOEMRE 2011–041 (2011), p. ES3, available at http://www.boem.gov/ak193/ (last visited May 26, 2015). ("Primary productivity (pelagic as well as benthic) in the Chukchi Sea shelf region is considered the highest of any shelf region in the world due to the influence of several ocean currents").

[5] Yoshifumi Tanaka, *A Dual Approach to Ocean Governance: The Cases of Zonal and Integrated Management in International Law of the Sea* (Abingdon, U.K.: Ashgate Publishing Group, 2008), pp. 5–6.

[6] Tanaka, *Dual Approach*, p. 5.

[7] North American Agreement on Environmental Cooperation, U.S.-Can.-Mex., Sept. 14, 1993, 32 I.L.M. 1480 (1993) [hereinafter NAAEC].

[8] Under NAAEC Art. 12(3), the annual report of the NAFTA CEC "shall periodically address the state of the environment in the territories of the Parties."

[9] Tara A.C. Wilkinson et al., *Marine Ecoregions of North America* (Montreal: Commission for Environmental Cooperation, 2009), http://www.cec.org/storage/83/7831_marineecoregions-web_en.pdf.

[10] Commission for Environmental Cooperation, *North American Environmental Atlas* (2012), http://www.cec.org/Page.asp?PageID=924&SiteNodeID=495&AA_SiteLanguageID=1 (last visited Mar. 14, 2014) [hereinafter CEC Atlas]. The atlas is an online service that includes comprehensive information about NAFTA's marine regions (last visited May 28, 2015).

[11] Douglas Hyde et al., *A Guide to Ecological Scorecards for Marine Protected Areas in North America* (Montreal: Commission for Environmental Cooperation, 2011), p. 1, http://www3.cec.org/islandora/en/ item/4184-guide-ecological-scorecards-marine-protected-areas-in-north-america-en.pdf [hereinafter CEC Scorecards].

How do these NAFTA initiatives for assessing and better understanding North American marine areas relate to a more recent phenomenon: a profusion of global "assessment platforms" and mechanisms, all of which generate and consume science information[12] and some of which focus on marine areas? These assessments are not environmental impact assessment (EIA) tools but rather comprehensive studies of scientific literature and other information available about the state of the environmental sector in question. An early and influential assessment was the 2004 Arctic Climate Impact Assessment.[13] The most recent, the World Ocean Assessment (WOA), was initiated in 2011 under the auspices of the General Assembly. The WOA will be "the first global integrated assessment of the state of the marine environment, including socio-economic aspects" and was to be completed by 2014.[14]

This chapter examines the relationship between NAFTA marine environment initiatives and the global assessment platforms that have developed in recent years. It begins with a brief history of assessment platforms as consolidators of science information. The chapter then introduces the legal bases for environmental initiatives developed under the NAAEC, describes those initiatives, and examines how they function. It concludes by suggesting ways in which the NAFTA marine initiatives can benefit from and contribute to the growing network of assessment platforms for the marine environment and how they can connect with tools being developed for marine area management elsewhere in the world.[15]

2. INFORMATION ASSESSMENT PLATFORMS

In the first decade of the twenty-first century, information "assessment platforms" have emerged as a means for consolidating and reviewing existing studies on the state of an environmental sector such as climate, oceans, or biodiversity. While these assessments are typically based in some form of agreement or memorandum of

---

[12] For the purposes of this paper, "science information" means existing information that is synthesized or consolidated for policy purposes. This is distinct from the production of new science, which the assessment platforms presented in this paper do not do. I understand "science" as pure and applied science based on method, peer review, and the acceptance of uncertainty as part of the scientific process. See, e.g., Helen Quinn, "What is Science?," *Physics Today* (July 2009), pp. 8–9 ("To oversimplify, scientists think of science both as a process for discovering properties of nature and as the resulting body of knowledge, whereas most people seem to think of science, or perhaps scientists, as an authority that provides some information – just one more story among the many that they use to help make sense of their world"). Quinn's latter definition approximates the term "science information" as used in this paper.

[13] ACIA, *Arctic Climate Impact Assessment* (Cambridge: Cambridge University Press, 2005), http://www.acia.uaf.edu/pages/scientific.html (last visited Mar. 14, 2014).

[14] United Nations, Oceans & Law of the Sea, Background Information on a Regular Process for Global Reporting and Assessment of the State of the Marine Environment including Socio-Economic Aspects (2011), para. 28, http://www.un.org/Depts/los/global_reporting/regular_process_background.pdf (last visited May 28, 2015) [hereinafter RP Background Paper].

[15] This chapter does not discuss transboundary EIAs under NAAEC Art. 10(7), which have generated only modest literature. See, e.g., John H. Knox, "The North American Commission for Environmental Cooperation and Transboundary Pollution," *Environmental Law Reporter* 34 (2004), 10142; Jameson Tweedie, "Transboundary Environmental Impact Assessment Under the North American Free Trade Agreement," *Washington & Lee Law Review* 63 (2006), 849.

Betsy Baker

understanding (MOU), they are (directly) tied neither to formal EIA requirements nor to specific reporting obligations under international agreements. All such assessment platforms aim to provide policy makers with independent, integrated scientific assessments of existing knowledge about a certain environmental sector, such as biodiversity or oceans, but they do not produce new science.[16] They are used to gather, process, consolidate, and assess science information, understood for the purposes of this chapter to mean existing information that is collected or synthesized for policy purposes.

The Millennium Ecosystem Assessment (MA) is the most significant precursor to today's biodiversity assessment platforms.[17] The MA produced five volumes of reports between 2001 and 2005 that were designed to provide reliable scientific data for environmental policy makers through a "comprehensive global evaluation of the condition of the five major ecosystems: forests, freshwater systems, grasslands, coastal areas and agroecosystems."[18] The MA reflected the then-current state of scientific knowledge on biodiversity and ecosystem services and was considered "a paragon of how research can be brought to bear on the issue" of sustainable development.[19]

The latest in this series of assessment initiatives to trace their lineage to the MA is the Intergovernmental Science-Policy Platform on Biodiversity and Ecosystem Services (IPBES).[20] Launched in April 2012, IPBES aims to be to the science of biodiversity and ecosystem services what the Intergovernmental Panel on Climate Change is to climate science.[21] IPBES is an independent intergovernmental body and, in many ways, picks up where the MA left off in 2005, covering both terrestrial and marine biodiversity.

[16] For example, a "key point" about the WOA is that it "will make use of, and be fundamentally built upon, existing assessments: these will include the results of major international marine programmes, such as the assessments of the Intergovernmental Panel on Climate Change, and the Census of Marine Life . . ., the outputs of agencies like the UN Food and Agriculture Organisation . . ., and the assessments produced by regional seas organizations and regional fisheries management bodies." United Nations World Ocean Assessment, *About* (2013), http://www.worldoceanassessment.org/?page_id=6 (last visited Mar. 14, 2014).
[17] Millennium Ecosystem Assessment, *Ecosystems and Human Well-being: Synthesis* (Washington, D.C.: Island Press, 2005), www.unep.org/maweb/documents/document.356.aspx.pdf, http://www3.cec.org/islandora/en/item/4184-guide-ecological-scorecards-marine-protected-areas-in-north-america-en.pdf (last visited May 28, 2015).
[18] Kofi Annan, "Sustaining Our Future," in *We the Peoples: The Role of the United Nations in the 21st Century* (New York: United Nations, 2000), https://www.un.org/en/events/pastevents/pdfs/We_The_Peoples.pdf (last visited May 28, 2015).
[19] "Leadership at Johannesburg," *Nature* 418 (Aug. 22, 2002), 803.
[20] For background on the MA, the WOA, and IPBES, see Betsy Baker, "Marine Biodiversity, Ecosystem Services and Better Use of Science Information," in Harry N. Scheiber et al. (eds.), *Securing the Ocean for the Next Generation*, Papers from the Law of the Sea Institute, UC Berkeley–Korea Institute of Ocean Science and Technology Conference, held in Seoul, Korea, May 2012, http://www.law.berkeley.edu/files/Baker-final.pdf (last visited May 28, 2015).
[21] See, e.g., United Nations Environment Programme, Report of the Second Session of the Plenary Meeting to Determine Modalities and Institutional Arrangements for an Intergovernmental Science-Policy Platform on Biodiversity and Ecosystem services, UNEP/IPBES.MI/2/9 (May 18, 2012), App'x I, para. 1(a), (c), http://www.ipbes.net/component/docman/doc_download/982-ipbes-mi-2-9-report-of-panama-meeting-and-resolution-establishing-ipbes.html?Itemid=58 (last visited May 28, 2015).

Specific to the world's oceans, recent efforts to establish a mechanism for comprehensive assessment of the marine environment and marine biodiversity include the Regular Process, with roots in the 2002 Johannesburg World Summit on Sustainable Development,[22] and two related assessments: the Assessment of Assessments (AoA)[23] and WOA. The WOA will be "the first global integrated assessment of the state of the marine environment, including socio-economic aspects" and is to be completed by 2014.[24] The WOA continues the work of the AoA (the first phase of the Regular Process) by carrying the Johannesburg themes of sustainability for marine areas into the twenty-first century and supporting the Regular Process with a new level of expertise and data management technologies. The WOA engages a 200-plus member Pool of Experts, the coordinators of which are to meet with the Commission on Sustainable Development (CSD) regularly – and for the first time in May 2014 – to brief the CSD on the progress of the WOA.[25]

The science information that feeds into such information assessment platforms can come from many sources, including independent academic studies and from international agreements, such as biodiversity conventions and other multilateral environmental agreements. But it does not appear that data or science information generated from states by complying with monitoring or other environmental reporting or informational requirements under agreements such as NAFTA ever finds its way into the assessment platforms, that is, unless such reporting data is somehow analyzed in literature that, in turn, is incorporated into one of the information assessment platforms.[26]

3. CEC TOOLS FOR THE MARINE ENVIRONMENT AND THEIR LEGAL BASIS IN THE NAAEC

The CEC has developed several tools that are useful for better understanding the North American Marine Environment, including the book on *Marine Ecoregions*

---

[22] Johannesburg Plan of Implementation of the World Summit on Sustainable Development, Sept. 4, 2002, para. 36(b), http://www.un.org/est/sustdev/documents/WSSD_POI_PD/English/WSSD_PlanImpl.pdf (last visited May 28, 2015) [hereinafter JPOI]. The JPOI called for establishing a "Regular Process" for "global reporting and assessment of the state of the marine environment." Ibid. The Regular Process, now formally established as a mechanism reporting to the General Assembly, held its first meeting in 2011 and initiated the first cycle of the WOA. The 2009 AoA Report recommended a mechanism for the Regular Process that builds on existing institutions to process and integrate "all available information" on ocean use. United Nations Environment Programme & International Oceanographic Commission of UNESCO, *An Assessment of Assessments, Findings of the Group of Experts. Start-up Phase of a Regular Process for Global Reporting and Assessment of the State of the Marine Environment including Socio-economic Aspects*, UNEP (DEPI)/RS.12 /4 (2009), p. 12, http://www.unep.org/regionalseas/globalmeetings/12/wp04-assessment-of-assessments.pdf [hereinafter AoA Report] (last visited May 28, 2015).

[23] AoA Report.

[24] RP Background Paper, para. 22.

[25] See United Nations, Oceans & Law of the Sea, *Revised Draft Timetable*, http://www.un.org/depts/los/global_reporting/global_reporting.htm (last visited May 28, 2015).

[26] A search for literature discussing connections between conventional reporting requirements and information assessment platforms yielded limited results.

of North America, the *North American Marine Atlas*, and the ecological scorecards introduced earlier.[27] How do these tools relate to the legal structure underlying the NAAEC, bearing in mind that the majority of CEC environmental cooperation initiatives are voluntary?[28]

NAAEC Article 8 establishes the CEC, or Commission, which comprises a Council, a Secretariat,[29] and a Joint Public Advisory Committee (JPAC); Article 16 establishes the fifteen-member JPAC, which may provide advice to the Council or technical support to the Secretariat on matters arising under the agreement.[30] Of the fifty-one articles that comprise the body of NAAEC, only one makes specific reference to marine or ocean matters: Article 10(2)(g) states that the Council may consider, and develop recommendations regarding, "transboundary and border environmental issues, such as the long-range transport of air and *marine* pollutants."[31] Annex 45 of NAAEC, however, makes clear that the Agreement applies to the marine environment in the same way as to terrestrial components of the North American environment.[32]

The NAAEC provides for two kinds of reporting: mandatory Annual Reports from the CEC, and voluntary independent Secretariat reports.[33] Under NAAEC Article

[27] Wilkinson et al., *Marine Ecoregions of North America*; CEC Atlas; Hyde et al., *Guide to Ecological Scorecards.*

[28] The CEC engages primarily in "voluntary environmental cooperative initiatives." Linda J. Allen, "The North American Agreement on Environmental Cooperation: Has It Fulfilled Its Promises and Potential? An Empirical Study of Policy," *Colorado Journal of International Environmental Law and Policy* 23(2012), 133 (listing the North American Biodiversity Information Network as an example of "initiatives that have been effective at facilitating cooperation between the countries").

[29] For analyses of how these NAAEC bodies function, see, e.g., David L. Markell, "The North American Commission For Environmental Cooperation After Ten Years: Lessons About Institutional Structure and Public Participation in Governance," *Loyola of Los Angeles International & Comparative Law Review* 26 (2004), 341; Chris Wold, "Evaluating NAFTA and the Commission for Environmental Cooperation: Lessons for Integrating Trade and Environment in Free Trade Agreements," *Saint Louis University Public Law Review* 28 (2008), 201; and Paul Stanton Kibel, "The Paper Tiger Awakens: North American Environmental Law After the Cozumel Reef Case," *Columbia Journal of Transnational Law* 39 (2001), 414–18 (providing both an excellent case study and general discussion of the CEC's Secretariat role in North American environmental law through 2000).

[30] Kibel, "The Paper Tiger Awakens," p. 414. ("The CEC has three main institutional components: (1) the Council of Ministers, composed of the senior environmental ministers/officials from Canada, Mexico, and the United States; (2) the Secretariat, the administrative body of the CEC, with an Executive Director appointed directly by the Council of Ministers ('Council'); and (3) JPAC, a fifteen person advisory committee comprised of five non-governmental representatives from each of the signatories. Because the Council meets only once a year, and because JPAC has only advisory responsibilities, most of the substantive work of the CEC, and of implementing the NAAEC, is delegated to the Secretariat." (Citations omitted.))

[31] NAAEC, Art. 10(2)(g) (emphasis added).

[32] See NAAEC, Annex 45, which contains country-specific definitions of "territory." As discussed in note 2, above, all three NAFTA countries include marine areas in their Annex 45 definitions.

[33] Both types of reports are available on the CEC website. Annual Reports from 1995 to 2009 are posted at http://www.cec.org/Page.asp?PageID=30107&SiteNodeID=648 (last visited Mar. 14, 2014), and the Independent Reports, eight over the period 1995–2013, at http://www.cec.org/Page.asp?PageID=924&SiteNodeID=332 (last visited Mar. 14, 2014).

12(3), the annual report of the CEC "shall periodically address the state of the environment in the territories of the Parties."[34] In practice, the Annual Reports do not evidence a consistent method for analyzing the state of the NAFTA environment, terrestrial or marine, but serve largely to apprise the reader of the CEC's overall activities. However, anecdotally and occasionally the Annual Reports do contain notable marine developments. The 2009 Annual Report, for example, highlighted not only the Marine Ecoregions book and the Marine Atlas but also voluntary protective measures for conservation of the leatherback turtle and the humpback whale.[35] In the early years of the NAAEC, the Annual Reports referenced the CEC's role in establishing pilot programs in the Gulf of Maine and the Bight of California under the Global Programme of Action (GPA) for the Protection of the Marine Environment from Land-based Activities in North America.[36]

The independent Secretariat reports are based on Article 13 of NAAEC, which makes it possible for, but does not require, the Secretariat to prepare a report for the Council on any matter within the scope of the annual program established by the Council. Under Article 13(1), the Council must be notified of, and may object to, such a report being undertaken. Allen has observed that the independent Secretariat reports "may have had some impact [but] their effectiveness is limited because their recommendations are not binding on the countries or other affected stakeholders and because the CEC has no well-defined follow-up role once the report is released."[37] To date, the Secretariat has prepared eight Independent Reports from 1995 to 2013, none of which focuses on recognizably marine issues.[38]

---

[34] NAAEC, Art. 12(3).

[35] Commission for Environmental Cooperation, *Annual Report* (2009), p. 7 [hereinafter 2009 Annual Report], http://www.cec.org/Storage/151/17762_CEC_2009_AR-e3-rev.pdf (last visited May 28, 2015). ("As part of the continued implementation of the Marine North American Conservation Action Plans (NACAP), the CEC implemented training programs on conservation of the leatherback turtle. During 2009, it also conducted programs to share scientific data and new estimates of the abundance of humpback whales in the North Pacific. . . . Under NACAP efforts, the CEC continued its program on incidental *vaquita marina* by-catch through a prototype net; the use of the alternative gear for local fishermen in the Sea of Cortes, and the construction and operation of the sea turtle excluder device (TED) affixed to an alternative fishing gear.")

[36] See, e.g., Commission for Environmental Cooperation, *Annual Report* (1999), p. 21, http://www.cec .org/Storage/93/9091_ar98_en.pdf; CEC, *Annual Report* (1998), p. 18, http://www.cec.org/Storage/93/ 9094_ar99_en.pdf (last visited May 28, 2015); Lawrence P. Hildebrand and Aldo Chircop, "A Gulf United: Canada-U.S. Transboundary Marine Ecosystem-Based Governance in the Gulf Of Maine," *Ocean & Coastal Law Journal* 15 (2010), 357 n. 84, in which the authors discuss the Global Programme of Action Coalition for the Gulf of Maine, indicating that "GPAC was formed under the auspices of the North American Free Trade Agreement (NAFTA). NAFTA's Commission for Environmental Cooperation (CEC) selected the Gulf of Maine as the location for a pilot project designed to reduce pollution and protect coastal habitats, an initiative in which the Council has been both interested and involved."

[37] Allen, "The North American Agreement," 132–33 (citations omitted).

[38] CEC Secretariat Independent Report topics include "Electricity and the Environment," "Maize and Biodiversity," and "Sustainable Freight Transportation." All eight reports are available at http://www.cec.org/Page.asp?PageID=924&SiteNodeID=332 (last visited Mar. 14, 2014).

NAAEC's very general provisions regarding environmental reporting and the Agreement's lack of specific references to the marine environment have not prevented the CEC from producing well-regarded practical tools for students, scholars, and managers of the NAFTA marine environment. The voluntary nature of these projects and the CEC's broad remit to promote cooperation on environmental issues[39] renders them possible without a direct mandate in the NAAEC.

The CEC's *Marine Ecoregions of North America*[40] "outlines a system of classification and map that creates consistent, standardized and understandable units out of the vastness of the continent's ocean and coastal waters. This system can be scalable, ecosystem-oriented, and linked to existing maps and classifications."[41] Experts from all three NAFTA countries worked together to "describe and map the North American oceanic and coastal waters, classifying them into twenty-four marine ecoregions according to oceanographic features and geographically distinct assemblages of species."[42] While the NAAEC did not introduce the idea of ecoregions, the book and its precursors are acknowledged as a successful example of implementing the concept.[43] Indeed, the 1997 CEC map of North American ecoregions[44] that preceded the 2009 book is cited as a "notable exception" to the usual practice of visualizing superimposed political divisions, boundaries, and governance structures over features and landscapes that, in the natural world, know no physical boundaries.[45]

Similarly, the *North American Environmental Atlas* identifies itself as "Maps without Borders."[46] The Atlas is the joint product of the mapping agencies of all three NAFTA countries[47] and has proven useful enough that other entities have incorporated Atlas products into such outcomes as mapping the Deepwater Horizon oil spill in relationship to marine protected areas in the Gulf of Mexico.[48]

---

[39] Under NAAEC, Art. 10(1), "[t]he Council shall be the governing body of the Commission and shall: . . . (f) promote and facilitate cooperation between the Parties with respect to environmental matters."

[40] Wilkinson et al., *Marine Ecoregions of North America*.

[41] 2009 Annual Report, p. 7.

[42] 2009 Annual Report, p. 7.

[43] Anastasia Telesetsky, "Ecoscapes: The Future of Place-Based Ecological Restoration Laws," *Vermont Journal of Environmental Law* 14 (2012), 53off (including NAFTA's marine ecoregions in her discussion of how ecoregions evolved as a concept and pointing to its inclusion in work by the World Wildlife Fund).

[44] Commission for Environmental Cooperation, *Ecological Regions of North America: Towards a Common Perspective* (1997), http://www.cec.org/storage/42/3484_eco-eng_en.pdf (last visited May 28, 2015).

[45] Cuauhtémoc León et al., "Challenges for Managing the North American Coastal Zone," *Ocean & Coastal Law Journal* 9 (2004), 282–83 and n. 3.

[46] See CEC Atlas; see also 2009 Annual Report, p. 7.

[47] CEC Atlas.

[48] For example, "[u]sing the CEC's marine protected areas and marine ecoregions maps, GreenInfo Network created this image and Google Earth tour that shows the Deepwater Horizon oil spill in relationship to the Gulf of Mexico's marine ecosystes." CEC Atlas, *Deepwater Horizon Oil Spill*, http://www.cec.org/Page.asp?PageID=122&ContentID=2915&SiteNodeID=631&BL_ExpandID= (last visited 14 Mar. 2014).

Ecological Scorecards for the North American Marine Protected Area Network (NAMPAN) are another voluntary mechanism created by the CEC. The CEC introduced ecological scorecards in 2011 for the limited purposes of assessing the condition of marine protected areas in the NAFTA region and in the hope that the scorecard would eventually "foster systematic environmental monitoring."[49] As seen, the reporting requirements of the NAAEC do not extend to systematic environmental *monitoring* by each state.[50] The CEC makes clear that "The scorecards do not replace well-designed, sustained monitoring programs and reporting used by the MPA agencies themselves that should continue to be relied upon for agency-approved reporting on ecosystem condition and trends. Instead, the scorecards can serve as a tool to identify gaps in knowledge, to bridge gaps between technical/scientific communities and the public-at-large, and to allow comparisons across a broad region."[51]

The preceding language is quoted at length because it does two things. It underlines the importance of the relationship between the ecological scorecards and national reporting authorities that may have specific monitoring requirements. The language also helps relate the ecological scorecards to provisions under the NAAEC that aim to improve comparability of environmental protection standards in each of the three NAFTA member countries. Under Article 10(3),

> The Council shall strengthen cooperation on the development and continuing improvement of [national] environmental laws and regulations, including by:
>
> (a) promoting the exchange of information on criteria and methodologies used in establishing domestic environmental standards; and
> (b) without reducing levels of environmental protection, establishing a process for developing recommendations on greater compatibility of environmental technical regulations, standards and conformity of assessment procedures in a manner consistent with the NAFTA.[52]

Use of the ecological scorecards across North American MPAs has the potential to bring greater uniformity to the types of environmental information gathered by each state and the means by which it is collected.

---

[49] Hyde et al., *Guide to Ecological Scorecards*, p. 1. ("It is hoped that this tool and the process will contribute to the betterment of science- and evidence-based ocean stewardship, increase civic engagement in MPA management, and expand North Americans' understanding of ecosystem health. This in turn should further improve regional- and continental-scale conservation strategies and foster systematic environmental monitoring.")

[50] Monitoring is not mentioned under NAAEC, Art. 2(1), whereby each party makes General Commitments with respect to its territory to "(a) periodically prepare and make publicly available reports on the state of the environment;" and "(e) assess, as appropriate, environmental impacts."

[51] Commission for Environmental Cooperation, North American Marine Protected Areas Network, *Condition Reports*, http://www2.cec.org/nampan/mpas (last visited 14 Mar. 2014) [hereinafter CEC NAMPAN].

[52] NAAEC, Art. 10(3).

The CEC North American Ecological Scorecards, while not mandatory, are a step in the direction of "greater compatibility" if not of environmental technical regulations in each state, of making assessments of marine protected areas more uniform between Canada, Mexico, and the United States. They are designed for use in ten priority areas for marine conservation identified under the Baja to Bering project, by the three national agencies responsible for MPA oversight.[53] Through the scorecards, the agencies seek to "share evidence-based ecological information through scorecards that refine monitoring information into concise, easily understood, ecosystem health assessments."[54]

Ecological scorecards are not unique to NAFTA but are a product of evolving management approaches to MPAs. Like the information assessment platforms discussed earlier, MPAs also relate back to the 2002 Johannesburg World Summit on Sustainable Development (WSSD).[55] In the case of marine protected areas, nations at the WSSD committed to creating "representative networks [of MPAs] by 2012."[56] Other regions with MPAs have adopted ecological scorecards as a management tool. For example, the Contracting Parties to the Oslo-Paris Agreement on Protection of the Marine Environment for the North-East Atlantic (OSPAR) introduced rapid self-assessment checklists[57] and ecological scorecards[58] as some of a variety of guidances and tools used to identify, select, and manage MPAs.[59] Under its Joint Assessment and Monitoring Program (JAMP), the OSPAR Contracting Parties have developed a sophisticated, consistent methodology for environmental assessment monitoring that is common to all fifteen of its member states and extends beyond MPAs.[60] As management of marine areas, protected or otherwise, continues to grow

[53] The Baja to Bering (B2B) project has identified 28 priority marine conservation areas; of these ten were selected for the Ecological Scorecard pilot. See Lance Morgan et al., *Marine Priority Conservation Areas: Baja California to the Bering Sea* (Montreal: Commission for Environmental Cooperation of North America and the Marine Conservation Biology Institute, 2005), pp. 5, 14; Hyde et al., *Guide to Ecological Scorecards*, p. 3.

[54] See CEC NAMPAN.

[55] See JPOI.

[56] JPOI, para. 32(c). ("32. In accordance with chapter 17 of Agenda 21, promote the conservation and management of the oceans through actions at all levels, giving due regard to the relevant international instruments to: . . . (c) Develop and facilitate the use of diverse approaches and tools, including the ecosystem approach, the elimination of destructive fishing practices, the establishment of marine protected areas consistent with international law and based on scientific information, including representative networks by 2012.")

[57] OSPAR Convention for the Protection of the Marine Environment of the North-East Atlantic, *Guidance for the Design of the OSPAR Network of Marine Protected Areas: A Self-assessment Checklist* (Reference number: 2007–6).

[58] OSPAR Convention for the Protection of the Marine Environment of the North-East Atlantic, *Guidance to Assess the Effectiveness of Management of OSPAR MPAs: A Self-assessment Scorecard* (Reference number: 2007–5).

[59] OSPAR Commission, *Network of Marine Protected Areas*, http://www.ospar.org/content/content.asp?menu=00700302210000_000 (last visited 14 Mar. 2014).

[60] See, e.g., OSPAR Commission, Joint Assessment and Monitoring Programme 2010–2014 (OSPAR Agreement 2010–4), http://webcache.googleusercontent.com/search?q=cache:Ln_bLeHZrWwJ:www

in importance in North America, OSPAR's JAMP may have model character for the NAFTA member states in cooperating to develop "conformity of assessment procedures" under NAAEC Article 10(3)(b) discussed earlier.

4. CONCLUDING OBSERVATIONS: CONNECTING THE CEC'S MARINE ENVIRONMENT CONSERVATION INITIATIVES TO THE WORLD OCEAN ASSESSMENT

This chapter has attempted to outline the basic structure and functions of two separate developments under international law, neither of which amounts to a binding legal obligation per se: (1) information assessment platforms such as the World Ocean Assessment, and (2) voluntary tools the CEC has developed under the NAAEC for cooperation to protect the North American marine environment. This study concludes by offering some initial thoughts on how these two different undertakings can complement each other. It does so by identifying pathways (beyond membership in the WOA expert groups) for Canada, Mexico, and the United States to impart to the WOA lessons learned in the NAAEC context about developing tools for marine conservation.

In 2012, the WOA began hosting a series of regional workshops[61] to, among other things:

- Enhance dialogue between marine experts within Governments, international government organizations and regional initiatives
- Develop an inventory of environmental and socioeconomic marine assessments
- Consider the linkages among assessments, including driving factors and the state of the marine environment
- Identify marine assessment capacity-building needs and consider means to address those needs.[62]

A recurring theme of the workshop for the Western Caribbean Region (WCR) – the existence of numerous information gaps – provides a good focal point for linking CEC initiatives to the WOA. The CEC has successfully addressed some gaps for the

---

.ospar.org/html_documents/ospar/html/10-04e_jamp.doc+&cd=1&hl=en&ct=clnk&gl=us (last visited May 28, 2015).

[61] See United Nations World Ocean Assessment, *General Information*, http://www.worldocean assessment.org/?page_id=20 (last visited 14 Mar. 2014).

[62] United Nations General Assembly, *Final Report of the Fourth Workshop Held under the Auspices of the United Nations in Support of the Regular Process for Global Reporting and Assessment of the State of the Marine Environment, Including Socioeconomic Aspects*, Miami, United States of America, November 13–15, 2012, paras. 2–3, Annex to the Note verbale dated January 2, 2013 from the Permanent Mission of the United States of America to the United Nations addressed to the Secretary-General, A/67/687, http://www.worldoceanassessment.org/wp-content/uploads/2013/01/Workshop-Report-w-Annexes.pdf (last visited May 28, 2015).

NAFTA Region, such as the need for a regional Atlas.[63] The CEC North American Marine Atlas could provide model character to the WCR and, indeed, to other regions of the WOA. One must keep in mind that the WOA will not produce new knowledge, but it could assess the need for (or existence of) tools such as the CEC Marine Atlas based in part on how such tools are being used in decision making by responsible authorities.

Other information gaps identified at the WOA-WCR workshop include the need for "[s]tandardized protocols and methods across the region for comparability" and "[r]eliable, consistent monitoring programmes that continue beyond the initial assessments."[64] Again, the CEC has developed tools for the North American marine environment that can be used as benchmarks for assessing comparable issues in other regions of the world. The CEC Ecological Scorecards, while not a substitute for a consistent monitoring program, offer guidance for developing a more sophisticated and regular approach to monitoring across different national systems.

Another conclusion of the WOA-WCR workshop was the need for improved science communication and integration. The workshop Final Report noted that there is no lack of data and information; "however, they are not always readily available or synthesized in a usable form."[65] In the end, the need for information in "usable form" lies behind the perennial calls for science and information to inform decision making. The WOA-WCR workshop, too, identifies the need for "Science-to-policy approaches to ensure that research informs decision-making. Research needs to be planned and designed to meet management needs by engaging decision makers in design as well as implementation."[66]

The CEC has been able to produce such practical and effective tools for conservation of the North American marine environment in part because decision makers have been engaged at some level in designing them. The respective national agencies, though not the only stakeholders responsible for overseeing MPAs, were involved in identifying the ten priority conservation areas under the Bering to Baja initiative; they were also engaged in designing the Ecological Scorecards, again working with other stakeholders and outside experts.[67] A fact that should be emphasized

---

[63] UN, *Final Report of the Fourth Workshop*, para. 10. ("A dynamic, living atlas of the Wider Caribbean region marine environment. . . . The challenge is not the production of individual data products, but the generation of harmonized data sets to maximize the impact and benefit for scientific analyses and syntheses. The Global Ocean Observing System Regional Alliance for the IOCARIBE region (IOCARIBE-GOOS) is a potential mechanism for such an atlas. The Caribbean Marine Atlas project of the Intergovernmental Oceanographic Commission represents a first step in this process.")

[64] UN, *Final Report of the Fourth Workshop*.

[65] UN, *Final Report of the Fourth Workshop*. ("An important amount of information is not published (grey literature) or exists only as internal reports of the public or private sector. Scientific results need to be synthesized and culled to identify key coherent messages relevant to management and policy agendas.")

[66] Ibid.

[67] See Morgan et al. *Marine Priority Conservation Areas*; Hyde et al., *Guide to Ecological Scorecards*; CEC NAMPAN.

in closing is that the structure of the NAAEC itself is what allows for engagement of the appropriate authorities from all three NAFTA member states in the development of such tools, and for the engagement of others with the expertise to promote the conservation of the North American marine environment. The WOA assessment will do well also to assess the strength of the legal structures that are available for regional cooperation around all parts of our blue planet.

9

Sustainable Development, NAFTA, and Water

Katia Opalka[1]

1. INTRODUCTION

The North American Free Trade Agreement (NAFTA)[2] was signed six months after the 1992 Rio Declaration on Environment and Development,[3] which likely explains how the term "sustainable development" ended up in the preamble to NAFTA. That wasn't enough to get NAFTA through Congress, though, so in 1993 U.S. Trade Representative Mickey Kantor announced that there would be environmental and labor side-agreements in exchange for Congress agreeing to drop a clause-by-clause review of the treaty text in favour of a simple, up-down vote.[4] It worked. NAFTA passed. Speaking bluntly, you might say the environment was pork. At the time, during a gap year between undergrad and law school, I was an intern at the Canadian Embassy and I was in the room, taking notes, when Mr. Kantor made his announcement. Little did I imagine that I would one day work on implementing the environmental agreement.

We need to remember what that time was like. I had just completed a degree in history at McGill where during a course titled "History of the Soviet Union

---

[1] This chapter is a personal take on NAFTA and the environment from an environmental law practitioner who spent the better part of seven years investigating domestic environmental law enforcement in North America as a legal officer in the Secretariat of the NAAEC Commission on Environmental Cooperation. Statements made in the text are subjective. The reader is expected to have a general understanding of international trade and environmental law developments in the period 1994–2014. Citation is minimal.

[2] North American Free Trade Agreement, U.S.-Can.-Mex., Dec. 17, 1992, 32 I.L.M. 289 (1993), 32 I.L.M. 605 (1993) [hereinafter NAFTA].

[3] United Nations Conference on Environment and Development, Rio de Janiero, Braz., June 3–14, 1992, *Rio Declaration on Environment and Development*, U.N. Doc. A/CONF.151/26/Rev.1 (Vol. I), Annex I (Aug. 12, 1992).

[4] Testimony of Ambassador Mickey Kantor, United States Trade Representative, Before the Subcommittee on International Trade, Committee on Ways and Means, U.S. House of Representatives, March 11, 1993.

from Stalin to Gorbachev," in the fall of 1989, the professor gave up teaching and chose instead to read to us from the day's newspaper coverage of events in Moscow. In 1992 I spent a semester in Berlin studying philosophy of history at Humboldt University where, to my surprise, there was considerable ambivalence about access to the West. In addition, Neo-Nazi groups were gathering followers and it became commonplace to attend 100,000 person rallies where such groups and their detractors clashed violently.

The North American Agreement on Environmental Cooperation (NAAEC), as the environmental side agreement was entitled,[5] took effect on the same day as NAFTA: January 1, 1994. At the time, the Soviet Union was already in the rearview mirror. The Free Trade Agreement of the Americas (FTAA) was looming on the horizon. Countries were realigning. There was a sense that history was over[6] and an expectation that in the post–Cold War world, free trade plus sustainable development would achieve, for all of us, what regular capitalism and communism hadn't: an improvement in the human condition motored by self-interest and conditioned by ecological constraints. Lest we forget, NAAEC, like NAFTA, was drafted on the premise that a whole other continent (South America) would be joining our free trade area in the not too distant future, creating a sustainable, free-trading hemisphere.

In 1994, the NAAEC-mandated Commission for Environmental Cooperation (CEC or the Commission) had to get up and running. A Secretariat needed to be established. Party meetings convened. It was exciting. The swanky Montreal offices of the new entity, located in the Quebec government-owned Montreal World Trade Center next door to the Secretariat of the United Nations Convention on Biological Diversity, were designated as supranational space, complete with private elevator, flags, and a handful of environmental experts drawn from the three countries. These people had diplomatic status, of a sort, and were meant to be wholly independent from influence by government officials. Pay scales were inspired by the UN. The environment ministers of the three countries, meeting in council at least once a year, were nominally in charge. Independent legal experts were hired to field complaints from civil society about environmental law enforcement and recommend investigations where appropriate. The Council would commission work from the Secretariat and then advise the Parties on what to do in order for sustainable development to occur.

Except that North America is not Europe and a careful reading of the NAAEC makes clear that there was absolutely no intention of creating a new, supranational order of government. There are no EU directives for us. Furthermore, while the NAAEC was a first in putting environment ministers in charge of running an

---

5   North American Agreement on Environmental Cooperation, U.S.-Can.-Mex., Sept. 14, 1993, 32 I.L.M. 1480 (1993) [hereinafter NAAEC].
6   See generally Francis Fukuyama, *The End of History and the Last Man* (New York: Free Press, 1992).

international organization, the State Department, Foreign Affairs, and the *Secretaria de Asuntos Internacionales* – the entities tasked by each of the countries with protecting national sovereignty – made sure no one got carried away. Draft Council resolutions were pored over by legal experts to make sure the CEC did nothing to bind the Parties, whether on purpose or by accident. No commitments, no standards, no policy. There would be no North American anything, except, maybe, maps.

And in the meantime, everything else kept going. The Soviet Bloc faded away. China and India came into their own. The new round of World Trade Organization (WTO) negotiations was a flop and the FTAA was shelved, in its place a growing stack of bilateral trade agreements and foreign investor protection agreements. Ten years into NAFTA, North America was no longer very exciting, except maybe as a post-9/11 security perimeter or a fortress of energy independence. Now it has been twenty years. Climate change makes biodiversity conservation seem like a luxury from a bygone era. We had just begun protecting the environment from people when protecting people from the environment became our number one priority. This is the context for examining the role of NAFTA and its institutions on the question of water.[7]

2. WATER

Before there were borders there were aquifers, lakes, rivers, and oceans. The lines that separate the United States from Canada and Mexico run through water bodies and out into the sea. Along the borders there have been water issues for as long as and even before the countries existed. From an environmental perspective, those issues fall into two broad categories: water sharing and water pollution. Of course, there is now a third category, one that falls under public safety: protecting people and assets from extreme weather. What follows is a brief description of formal and informal responses.

2.1. *Binational Institutions*

For the Canada–U.S. border, the International Joint Commission (IJC), established under the 1909 Boundary Waters Treaty, exists to support and monitor joint efforts to implement commitments under bilateral air and water quality agreements, and to resolve disputes.[8] At the U.S.–Mexico border, the International Boundary and Water Commission performs a role similar to that of the IJC.[9] In addition, the

---

[7] See generally Christine Elwell, *NAFTA Effects on Water: Testing for NAFTA Effects in the Great Lakes Basin* (Sierra Club of Canada, 2001), http://www.sierraclub.ca/national/programs/ sustainable-economy/trade-environment/nafta-great-lakes.pdf.

[8] International Joint Commission, *About the IJC*, IJC (2014), http://www.ijc.org/en_/About_the_IJC (last visited May 28, 2914).

[9] International Boundary & Water Commission, *About Us*, IBWC (2014), http://www.ibwc.state.gov/ home.html (last visited May 28, 2014).

Border Environment Cooperation Commission (BECC), established in 1993 under a side agreement to NAFTA, together with the North American Development Bank (NADBank), supports the design and implementation of environmental infrastructure projects in the border region, with a strong emphasis on those related to water and wastewater.[10]

2.2. *Cross-Border Environmental Assessment*

North America has bilateral water-related institutions, but what about continental issues? For example, could there be one set of rules for dealing with cross-border environmental assessment, regardless of which U.S. border is in play? NAAEC Article 10(7) requires the Council to work on a transboundary environmental impact assessment agreement:

> Recognizing the significant bilateral nature of many transboundary environmental issues, the Council shall, with a view to agreement between the Parties pursuant to this Article within three years on obligations, consider and develop recommendations with respect to:
>
> a) assessing the environmental impact of proposed projects subject to decisions by a competent government authority and likely to cause significant adverse transboundary effects, including a full evaluation of comments provided by other Parties and persons of other Parties;
> b) notification, provision of relevant information and consultation between Parties with respect to such projects; and
> c) mitigation of the potential adverse effects of such projects.

Though a draft of such an agreement has been ready since the late 1990s, there is no indication that the Parties are in any rush to move forward on this front.[11]

There are some core issues standing in the way of supranational environmental assessment in North America. To understand these issues, it is best to be practical. A given project may benefit the economy of one region of one province or state a great deal. The federal government will be careful not to interfere unduly with that jurisdiction's assessment of how the economic and social benefits stack up against the environmental costs. Now imagine the federal government requiring that province or

---

[10] Report of the House Ways and Means Committee, 103rd Cong., An Act to Implement the North American Free Trade Agreement, H.R. 3450, Nov. 15, 1993. As stated in the report, section 542 would authorize the President to accept membership in a North American Development Bank. The bank would be a multilateral bank with stock held by member states. The bill would authorize the United States to subscribe to 150,000 shares of capital stock and the appropriation of $1,500 million to purchase the stock. It would appropriate $56.25 million in 1995 for the first paid-in stock subscription, and would provide an authorization of appropriations for the remaining amount without fiscal year limitation.
[11] See generally Neil Craik, "Transboundary Environmental Assessment in North America: Obstacles and Opportunities," in C.J. Bastmeijer and T. Koivurova (eds.), *Practising International Environmental Impact Assessment* (Martinus Nijhoff, Leiden/Boston, 2008), http://www.aals.org/am2007/thursday/craik.pdf.

state to turn down the project because of a cost-benefit analysis done by a jurisdiction in a neighboring country, or because of objections in a neighboring country to the effect of the project on the global commons. Under the constitution, this may be difficult to do. Politically, it makes no sense.

An alternative to moving forward with a trilateral agreement is a political fix: the leaders of the three countries commit to consulting each other and making cooperation happen. An example would be the 2005 Canada–U.S.–Mexico Security and Prosperity Partnership (SPP),[12] an initiative led by a prime minister and two presidents. For a time, there was a sort of SPP work program, and this program included several items from the CEC's mandate, notably as regards cooperation on pressing energy matters and trade and environment issues. It was exciting at first, but history showed that while high-level engagement certainly attracts a great deal of NGO and media attention, it is not a solution for multifaceted, ongoing challenges such as cross-border environmental impacts. For that, staff, structures, and the like are required. In fact, not long after it got started, the SPP fizzled. The countries had new leaders with new priorities.

In the absence of a continental environmental/energy policy with a supranational board issuing binding rulings in bilateral or trilateral disputes about projects or policies with cross-border impacts, the next best thing is a solid network of relationships among federal, state, and local government employees. As suggested by Professor Neil Craik, any trilateral agreement on transboundary environmental assessment should probably be a framework agreement that builds on existing practice and provides agencies with the flexibility they need to accommodate competing interests on a case-by-case basis.[13]

2.3. *Progress on Three Fronts*

So far, then, we can say that NAFTA itself has given rise to one key water-related institution, the Mexico–U.S. BECC. In addition, though, via the NAAEC, NAFTA has helped the countries move forward on three fronts: creating a shared vision of the North American environment, including as regards water, aligning data-gathering and reporting mechanisms to allow for comparisons across jurisdictions over time and giving the Secretariat and the public standing to draw attention to water-related problems.

NAFTA and its institutions have gone some way toward providing better data for tracking the state of the environment and making environment-related policy decisions in North America. For example, the CEC *Taking Stock* report[14] is quite well known. It is an annual compilation of data from across the continent on pollutant

[12] Security and Prosperity Partnership of North America, *About SPP*, SPP (2009), http://www.spp-psp.gc.ca/eic/site/spp-psp.nsf/eng/h_00003.html (last visited May 28, 2014).
[13] Above note 11, pp. 4–5.
[14] Commission for Environmental Cooperation, *Taking Stock Online*, CEC (2014), http://www.cec.org/Page.asp?PageID=924&SiteNodeID=1097 (last visited May 28, 2014).

releases and transfers to environmental media, including water. However, and more importantly, although the NAAEC states that the Council shall serve as a forum for the discussion of environmental matters falling within its scope, the CEC has been ignored at key moments, in key files. Absent legal and political commitments by the countries, the decision whether to channel a particular environmental matter through the rather public forum of the CEC has been left up to mid-level government employees acting on the basis of national and subnational – or even personal – priorities.[15]

The CEC has helped us begin to see North America in ecological terms. This brings us back to the maps I mentioned earlier. When policymakers are provided with the means to literally see the big picture, problems and potential solutions are easier to spot.

The great map showing wetlands in North America[16] is a CEC accomplishment. The impetus behind conserving and restoring North America's wetlands, however, came from concerns raised and decisions made well before 1994.[17] Furthermore, the North American Waterfowl Management Plan, which seeks to conserve migratory species by conserving and restoring their habitat, is not managed by the CEC, though it did lead to the North American Bird Conservation Initiative,[18] with which the CEC was intimately involved for a time, helping identify important bird areas across the continent.

There is an entity called the Trilateral Committee for Wildlife and Ecosystem Conservation and Management[19] that deals directly with these initiatives. This committee was established in 1995, has its own web site, www.trilat.org, is composed exclusively of staff from governmental environmental agencies, has a detailed program of work and a host of subcommittees, and has held formal annual meetings every year since 1996. It is not part of the CEC.

2.4. *Obstacles to Progress*

Whether a group of countries turns to an international body for advice or delegates management functions to that body depends on a host of factors that, once they

---

[15] *See* Council of the Commission for Environmental Cooperation, *Terms of Operation – Working Groups* (Montreal: CEC, 2012), http://www.cec.org/Storage/143/16910_ToO-Final-6Aug2012docx-clean.pdf.

[16] Commission for Environmental Cooperation, *Wetlands, 2004*, CEC (2014), http://www.cec.org/Page.asp?PageID=122&ContentID=1323&SiteNodeID=498&BL_ExpandID= (last visited May 28, 2014).

[17] *See generally* Minister of Environment, Canadian Wildlife Service, *North American Waterfowl Management Plan: A Strategy for Cooperation* (Ottawa: Canadian Wildlife Service, 1986), http://nawmp.wetlandnetwork.ca/Media/Content/files/NAWMP%20Original.pdf.

[18] North American Bird Conservation Initiative, *Vision*, NABCI (2014), http://www.nabci.net/vision.htm (last visited May 28, 2014).

[19] Trilateral Committee for Wildlife and Ecosystem Conservation and Management, *Background: About the Trilateral Committee*, Trilateral Committee (2012), http://www.trilat.org/about-the-trilateral (last visited May 28, 2014).

are described, make good sense. For example, is there a shared sense, among the countries, that the international body is going to add value in the form of financial or human resources? Can that body do the work better, faster, cheaper than the countries could on their own? Is there a political advantage to one, two, or all three countries in entrusting the matter or commissioning advice or "a list of options" from the international body, knowing that the document and related activities will likely be made public?

The IJC (Canada–U.S.) is a good example of an institution that complains, albeit very politely, about not being listened to. In its reports, the IJC points out that Canada and the United States have made many commitments to each other in bilateral agreements, and that despite data showing worrying trends on the ground, the countries are relatively unresponsive to the IJC's suggestions.[20] IJC reports land on very cluttered desks in Washington, D.C., and Ottawa. The countries will not delegate decision-making authority to the IJC (i.e., "you deal with it"), but neither will they use the IJC's priorities – notably, the environment comes first – when making decisions at the national level. Likewise, the CEC Secretariat prepared a "North American Boundary and Transboundary Inland Water Management Report" in 2001,[21] and it was duly shelved.

2.5. The CEC: Failures and Successes

Canada and the United States have an agreement that contains a formula for sharing the power of the Columbia River to generate electricity.[22] For years, NGOs and aboriginal groups have complained that the agreement ignores the needs of nature and the rights of First Nations. It has proven very difficult for both countries to accept the concept of working toward an arrangement that would meet peak energy demand and also avoid or minimize disruption or destruction of habitat upon which wildlife and people rely. This file – the Columbia River Treaty – has not been discussed in the NAFTA/NAAEC context.

Related to this topic, early in the life of the CEC, the Secretariat received a citizen complaint about a utility in Canada operating hydro dams without due regard to effects on fish and fish habitat. The complaint resulted in the publication of a report (the *BC Hydro* factual record) detailing provincial efforts to ramp up water use planning.[23] Almost twenty years later, the province faces the vexing issue

---

[20] International Joint Commission, *Reports and Publications*, IJC (2014), http://www.ijc.org/en_/Reports_and_Publications (last visited May 28, 2014).

[21] Commission for Environmental Cooperation, *North American Boundary and Transboundary Inland Water Management Report* (Montreal: CEC, 2001), http://www3.cec.org/islandora/en/item/1803-north-american-environmental-law-and-policy-volume-7-en.pdf.

[22] Columbia River Treaty, U.S.-Can., Sept. 16, 1964.

[23] BC Hydro, SEM-97–001, Final Factual Record (April 2, 1997), http://www.cec.org/Storage/68/6220_BC-Hydr-Fact-record_en.pdf.

of how to reconcile the "green energy" benefits of run of the river hydro dams and their inevitable impacts on aquatic ecosystems. The whole file – hydroelectric power dams – could have been referred to the CEC for development of a North American approach or plan, but it was not. The closest thing that happened was a 2002 independent Secretariat report on the environmental impacts of deregulation in the electricity sector.[24] That report did not mention *BC Hydro* or fish habitat, focusing instead on air quality impacts from coal-fired power generation.

Another long-standing transboundary water issue concerns sediment contamination in the bed of Lake Roosevelt, in Washington State. Lake Roosevelt is actually a man-made reservoir created to power the Grand Coulee Dam. The incredibly powerful current of the Columbia River comes to a near standstill in the reservoir. This is where objects carried along by the current over great distances finally come to rest. That includes slag from a smelter in Trail, British Columbia, that has been in operation for over a century. Slag used to be discharged into the river and then carried off by the current. It traveled across the border and down into Lake Roosevelt. U.S. courts held that the smelter used Lake Roosevelt to dispose of its waste, even if those who operated the smelter did not know where the slag was ending up.[25]

Canada would have liked to handle this situation through diplomatic means, or if not, then at least through a joint referral to the IJC. Instead, the U.S. allowed a citizen-driven suit to follow its course through the courts under U.S. domestic environmental law. Under that process, judges would decide whether a company operating in Canada could be liable for environmental damage caused in the United States. The matter has never made it to the CEC.

There have been water-related citizen complaints about environmental law enforcement that raise Canada–U.S. border environmental issues. An example is *Devils Lake*, in which submitters claimed that polluted water from the United States would make its way into Canada through a new outfall and eventually reach Lake Winnipeg, with potentially devastating consequences.[26] There was also *St. Clair River*, where submitters claimed that industrial pollution entering the river in Sarnia, Ontario, was causing harm in the United States.[27] Both were dismissed

24 Secretariat of the Commission for Environmental Cooperation, *Environmental Challenges and Opportunities of the Evolving North American Electricity Market* (Montreal: CEC, 2002), http://www3.cec.org/islandora/en/item/959-environmental-challenges-and-opportunities-evolving-north-american-electricity-en.pdf.

25 *See* Pakootas v. Teck Cominco Metals, Ltd., 452 F.3d 1066, 1080 (9th Cir. 2006) (CERCLA. applies as a matter of domestic law where "release" of pollutant was leaching of slag, which occurred in U.S.); 2012 WL 6546088 (E.D. Wash. 2012), appeal dismissed, 9th Cir. 13–35024 (4/26/13) (defendant liable for future response costs); 563 Fed. Appx. 526 (2/26/14) (award of attorneys' fees to plaintiffs vacated).

26 Devils Lake, SEM-06-002, Submission (Mar. 30, 2006), http://www.cec.org/Storage/83/7867_06-2-SUB_en.pdf.

27 St. Clair River, SEM-07–004, Submission (July 25, 2007), http://www.cec.org/Storage/83/7900_07–4-SUB_en.pdf.

because the submitters based their claims on treaty provisions instead of domestic environmental law.

A good example of a file that could – probably should – have had some CEC input and in the end was not even resolved by the IJC is ballast water regulations published by the State of New York. The regulations were meant to address the growing threat that invasive species found in ballast water pose to native species in the Great Lakes.[28] The regulations were to be very strict. Quebec and Ontario complained loudly, as did the lobby group representing the shipping industry in Canada. Washington stepped in and overrode New York, setting lower federal standards.[29] Then Canada followed suit.[30] No one talked to the CEC.

In the lead-up to the ratification of NAFTA, several states and California in particular worried that NAFTA would affect their ability to set environmental standards that are more exigent than those of the U.S. Environmental Protection Agency (EPA). I know because I attended congressional committee hearings on the topic. The case of the New York State ballast water regulations is a good example of those fears coming true, but not because of NAFTA.

Earlier I mentioned the North American Waterfowl Management Plan and the North American Bird Conservation Initiative. Both of those initiatives are closely related to citizens' ability to imagine the continent not as a place for people but as home to species that are genetically configured to know where they are, where they need to go, and where to stop along the way. They use the continent fully, moving around with the seasons, choosing the best places to live out key periods of their life cycles.

Hunters, farmers, and politicians in North America have long known that actions in a neighboring country can have a devastating effect on populations of migratory species. Early in the life of the CEC, the Parties to the NAAEC accepted a public request that the CEC Secretariat, pursuant to NAAEC Article 13 and with the instruction of Council, look into what may have caused the deaths of thousands of migratory birds in the Silva Reservoir in Mexico.[31] The answer, avian botulism, left open many questions. Yes, the proximate cause was botulism, a disease linked to naturally occurring bacteria found in mud at the bottom of lakes. But what was the ultimate cause? Why so many birds in one place at one time? Also worth noting: the Silva Reservoir report was the first and the last time an Article 13 investigation began with a request from the public.

---

[28] "Editorial: Another tough ballast rule dumped overboard," *Detroit Free Press* (Mar. 14, 2012), http://www.freep.com/article/20120310/OPINION01/203100316/Editorial:%20Another%20tough%20ballast%20rule%20dumped%20overboard (last visited May 28, 2014).

[29] See Tim Anderson, "Sinking States' Role in Ballast Water Rules," *Stateline Midwest* (December 2011), http://www.csgmidwest.org/policyresearch/documents/ballast.pdf.

[30] *See* Regulations Amending the Vessel Pollution and Dangerous Chemical Regulations, http://canadagazette.gc.ca/rp-pr/p2/2013/2013-05-08/html/sor-dors68-eng.html.

[31] Commission for Environmental Cooperation, *CEC Secretariat Report on the Death of Migratory Birds at the Silva Reservoir* (Montreal: CEC, 1995).

Mysterious mass deaths caused by avian botulism have occurred at various locations throughout North America. When the CEC released the Secretariat's very first Article 13 report, the botulism question could have earned a spot on the long-term CEC agenda. The question is, what would the long-term connection be? As hands-on as commissioning research? Engaging with the scientific community to coordinate efforts? Publishing periodic reports? That question of what, exactly, the Secretariat's role on environmental issues should be has not been answered yet, or rather, there is a different answer every few years. The Parties – that is to say, the three countries – do not want the CEC to be a catalyst for joint action on environmental problems. And yet the CEC is also not allowed to do the seemingly less controversial but much more resource-intensive job of comprehensive reporting on the state of the North American environment.

Another example involving birds and water is the *Coronado Islands* citizen submission, alleging a failure by Mexico to effectively enforce its environmental assessment rules in connection with the review and authorization of a liquefied natural gas (LNG) terminal that would have been located offshore, twelve miles from Tijuana.[32] The terminal was designed to use the Coronado Islands as a breakwater. The Coronado Islands are home to a rare species of migratory bird. When the project was authorized, the U.S. Fish and Wildlife Service changed the listing priority number for this bird, the Xanthus's Murrelet, from a five to a two.[33] The Secretariat recommended a factual record investigation into how the project was assessed and authorized. Before the Council could vote on the recommendation, Chevron canceled the project. Mexico asked the Secretariat to withdraw its recommendation. The Secretariat did.

The submitters in *Coronado Islands* were very concerned about the risk of a catastrophic explosion. Though it was highly unlikely to occur, if it did happen, the main island would be blown to pieces. But the submitters also fretted about the best-case scenario. Even if the terminal operated without incident, the submitters alleged, ship traffic and its attendant noise and risk of collisions would interfere with marine mammals that travel up and down the West Coast. The area around the terminal would cease to provide quality habitat for fish and other organisms that birds feed on. Habitat quality would be impaired by water pollution, changes in water temperature from the discharge of cooling water, and destruction of the sea floor ecosystem. This would be in addition to bird fatalities (fatal light attraction) or decline in nesting success caused by the presence of floodlights that must stay on at night to maintain navigation safety.

---

[32] *Coronado Islands*, SEM-05–002, Submission (May 3, 2005), http://www.cec.org/Storage/83/7861_05–2–SUB_en.pdf.

[33] Endangered and Threatened Wildlife and Plants; Review of Native Species That Are Candidates or Proposed for Listing as Endangered or Threatened; Annual Notice of Findings on Resubmitted Petitions; Annual Description of Progress on Listing Actions, 70 Fed. Reg. 24,870, 24876–77 (May 11, 2005).

The *Coronado Islands* submission, like the much earlier *Cozumel* submission[34] (wharf building for cruise ships ignoring impacts on coral reefs), raised questions that would fit nicely on a North American environmental agenda: how to align research, policy, legislation, and enforcement in the three countries to improve knowledge of interconnected marine ecosystems and reduce impacts from passenger and industrial ships and port/docking facilities. For a time, the Secretariat looked into air pollution associated with tanker traffic, but that item did not stay on the agenda for long.[35]

The CEC's biodiversity program, which no longer exists or is now called something else, did some very interesting work related to ocean use. Everyone who worked at the CEC in the 2000s has at least heard of B2B. In other circles, B2B means business to business, but at the CEC it refers to Baja-to-Bering. Hearing that term often enough helps erase the mental image of North America as three pieces. Instead of borders, the CEC helped with the process of identifying and mapping "priority conservation areas" (aspirational language; not marine protected areas) along the Pacific Coast. CEC involvement went as far as supporting the preparation of a North American Conservation Action Plan for the humpback whale.[36] This was good work.

One file that could have been a catalyst for cooperative action is the *Lake Chapala* submission.[37] The submitters claimed that while the public had been consulted on formulation of federal water policy in Mexico, the public was shut out when the policy was put into action. They claimed that the policy requirement to put environmental protection first was not being honored in water allocation deals being struck behind closed doors by state governors and water license holders from the Lake Chapala watershed. The CEC was allowed to investigate, but its mandate was restricted to water pollution; there would be no questions asked about water allocation. Furthermore, the Council resolution instructing the Secretariat to prepare a factual record narrowed the scope of the investigation to one dam project (since canceled) on one river in the watershed.

No one can blame the parties for wanting to keep the CEC out of domestic water disputes. It is hard for policymakers to see how domestic debates over water protection and conservation are anyone else's business. In fact, people sometimes hold the mistaken belief that the NAAEC citizen submission process requires complainants to find a link to trade in order for their submission to be admissible. Industry representatives have grumbled that submitters – particularly in Canada – have used

34 Cozumel, SEM-96–001, Submission (Jan. 17, 1996), http://www.cec.org/Storage/83/7862_ACF96B .pdf.
35 See Ron Orol, "Air Pollution from Ships a Growing Concern," *CEC Newsletter* (Summer 2005), http://www.cec.org/Page.asp?PageID=122&ContentID=2544&SiteNodeID=451 (last visited May 28, 2014).
36 Commission for Environmental Cooperation, *North American Conservation Action Plan for the Humpack Whale* (Montreal: CEC, 2005), http://www.cec.org/Storage/59/5158_NACAP-Humpback-Whale_en.pdf.
37 Lake Chapala, SEM-97–007, Submission (Oct. 10, 1997), http://www.cec.org/Storage/69/6259_ACFA1B.pdf.

the process for purposes far removed from the concerns that prompted the inclusion of Articles 14 and 15 in the NAAEC.[38] For example, they point to the large number of submissions invoking the federal Fisheries Act habitat protection and pollution prevention provisions and claim that NGOs are trying to use the NAAEC to upset Canada's constitutional division of powers.[39]

The citizen submissions process has allowed submitters to draw international attention to water-related environmental law enforcement issues that confront all jurisdictions to varying degrees.

In *Rio Magdalena*, for example, it turned out that while the federal government had financed the construction of municipal wastewater treatment plants, there was no budget to operate the plants and municipal wastewater was simply flowing through the plants on its way to the river.[40] *Iona Wastewater Treatment* is a file in which the government response has been to draw a distinction between toxic releases that result from operational errors and those that follow from shortcomings in the treatment method or plant size.[41] In *Montreal Technoparc*, where a former landfill was leaking diesel laced with polychlorinated biphenyls (PCBs) into the Saint Lawrence River, the question was whether there was any point in channeling groundwater from the site to the municipal sewer, since the municipal wastewater treatment plant could not remove the PCBs and they would therefore end up in the river anyway.[42] These files have not given rise to a trilateral initiative on municipal wastewater treatment.

In *Coal-Fired Power Plants*, environmental organizations from the United States and Canada argued that the United States failed to take into account mercury entering U.S. waterways from coal-fired power plants (through deposition from smokestack emissions or in wastewater from the plants) when it calculated the contaminant load for those waterways.[43] The interesting issue there is that removing mercury from smokestack emissions by trapping it in water has resulted in there being a lot of mercury-laden wastewater that needs to be disposed of. *Ontario Power Generation* alleged that emissions from Ontario's coal-fired power plants were causing Fisheries Act violations in the form of unauthorized aerial deposits of mercury into fish-bearing waters.[44]

[38] Personal conversation with Cam Avery, Joint Public Advisory Member, November 2001.
[39] Ibid.
[40] Rio Magdalena, SEM-97–002, Submission (Mar. 15, 1997), http://www.cec.org/Storage/88/8481_97-2-SUB-S.pdf.
[41] *Iona Wastewater Treatment*, SEM-10–003, Submission (May 7, 2010), http://www.cec.org/Storage/87/8394_10-3-SUB_en.pdf.
[42] *Montreal Technoparc*, SEM-03–005, Submission (Aug. 14, 2003), http://www.cec.org/Storage/83/7890_03-5-SUB_en.pdf.
[43] *Coal-fired Power Plants*, SEM-04–005, Submission (Sept. 20, 2004), http://www.cec.org/Storage/83/7860_04-5-SUB_en.pdf.
[44] *Ontario Power Generation*, SEM-03–001, Submission (May 1, 2003), http://www.cec.org/Storage/84/7963_01-SUB-CECf.pdf.

BC Mining, in turn, raised the question of what the federal government of Canada is doing about orphaned/abandoned mines that leak acidic water into the environment, killing aquatic ecosystems.[45] The Council refused to let the Secretariat investigate another question raised in the submission, about how mining project proponents calculate acid-generating potential and what the government is doing to enforce the Fisheries Act pollution prevention provisions against operating mines that produce acid mine drainage. *Pulp and Paper* performed a similar exercise with respect to effluent from pulp and plants that is acutely lethal to fish and with respect to which there are no prosecutions.[46]

Aquanova addressed the illegal destruction of mangroves,[47] *BC Logging* dealt with logging to the edge of small streams,[48] and *Oldman River II* examined a road that was built across the headwaters of rivers and streams considered by provincial fisheries biologists to be prime fish habitat in Alberta.[49] In all three of those files, the issue was the effect of industrial development on surface waters that serve critical ecosystem functions.

2.6. The Proper Role of the CEC?

Each of the submissions mentioned here raises issues that are common to the three countries. However, there is nothing in the NAAEC that requires the Council to do anything after an investigation is completed into a matter raised by a submitter. I maintain that this does not mean that nothing happens. It only means that whatever notice is taken, in government, of the work of the CEC Secretariat is kept under wraps. There may be bilateral or even trilateral discussions regarding some of these matters, but they are not public and not known to Secretariat personnel.

There is a question, which is valid, regarding the difference between a supranational organization (which is what I understand by "international organization") and an intergovernmental organization. Early in the life of the CEC, there was a lot of sensitivity amongst Secretariat personnel regarding the independence of the staff from government. In other words, whether someone was a U.S. or Mexican national was not supposed to matter once that person took up a job at the CEC because that person was now working for the CEC and not for a country. To underscore: Secretariat staff did not represent a country or its interests. What followed from this

[45] *BC Mining*, SEM-98–004, Submission (June 29, 1998), http://www.cec.org/Storage/84/7960_98–4-SUB-E.pdf.
[46] *Pulp and Paper*, SEM-02–003, Submission (May 8, 2002), http://www.cec.org/Storage/83/7896_01-SUB.pdf.
[47] *Aquanova*, SEM-98–006, Submission (Oct. 20, 1998), http://www.cec.org/Storage/83/7857_98–6-SUB-OS.pdf.
[48] *BC Logging*, SEM-00–004, Submission (March 15, 2000), http://www.cec.org/Storage/84/7959_00–4-SUB-E.pdf.
[49] *Oldman River II*, SEM-97–006, Submission (Oct. 4, 1997), http://www.cec.org/Storage/68/6226_97–6-SUB-E.pdf.

understanding was that the NAAEC itself was supreme, and the Council's decisions, taken under the aegis of the NAAEC, laid out a cooperative program of work that was truly "supranational."

To make sure that the program of work was translated into reality, the NAAEC allowed the Council to create working groups and define their role. Those working groups, and their relationship with Secretariat staff, play a central role in determining whether the CEC is a supranational or an intergovernmental organization. When Secretariat experts are at the wheel, directing the working groups to produce deliverables as mandated by Council resolutions, then the CEC is a supranational organization. When Secretariat staff is reduced to carrying out solely secretarial tasks, such as making photocopies and booking hotels and airline tickets for working group members, then the CEC is an intergovernmental organization, since anyone who matters (working group members) works for, is paid by, and is beholden to, one of the three countries.

3. CONCLUSION

To summarize and conclude then, it can be said that water, as part of the pollution prevention or biodiversity conservation equation, has landed on the CEC agenda now and again since 1994, either as a piece of the cooperative work program or as the focus of an independent Secretariat report or citizen submission. However, except for a brief period in the 2000s, when there was a short-lived focus on freshwater,[50] water in and of itself has not held the CEC's attention. I submit that this is because the protection of national sovereignty has prevented the CEC as an institution from capturing the imaginations of and securing a sustained commitment from the countries and their leaders.

---

[50] See generally Commission for Environmental Cooperation, *Draft Options for a CEC Role in the Sustainable Use and Conservation of Freshwater in North America* (Montreal: CEC, 2002), http://www3 .cec.org/islandora/en/item/1906-draft-options-cec-role-in-sustainable-use-and-conservation-freshwater- in-en.pdf.

10

Indigenous Peoples in North America

Bridging the Trade and Environment Gap to Ensure Sustainability under NAFTA and NAAEC

Nicole Schabus

1. INTRODUCTION

Indigenous peoples in North America over thousands of years managed their resources and territories sustainably and maintained sustainable economies. Colonization, associated exploitation of indigenous lands, and international trade have marginalized indigenous peoples economically. Government regulation has been used to undermine these indigenous economies to secure access for nonindigenous actors.

Today, indigenous rights are recognized in international instruments that provide remedies against colonization. International trade agreements, such as the North American Free Trade Agreement (NAFTA), should also recognize and implement indigenous rights.

Focusing on Canada, this chapter demonstrates how failing to recognize indigenous rights in the implementation of NAFTA can lead to economic uncertainty for investors, and how taking indigenous rights and knowledge into account can ensure more environmentally, culturally, socially, and economically sustainable development. In the twenty years since NAFTA's entry into force, indigenous peoples have secured further international recognition of their rights. Multilateral environmental agreements increasingly recognize indigenous control over lands and resources and the role that indigenous peoples and their knowledge play in ensuring sustainable development. Indigenous peoples have standing in international law, and their rights must be taken into account when accessing lands and resources. Indigenous peoples can be the bridge between economics and trade on one side and environment and culture on the other. Indigenous peoples bridge the existing gap because their rights range from economic to cultural and include jurisdictional elements that relate to protecting the environment and accessing lands and resources.

2. SUSTAINABLE INDIGENOUS ECONOMIES IN NORTH AMERICA AND THE IMPACT OF COLONIZATION AND GOVERNMENT REGULATION

2.1. *Indigenous Economies*

Indigenous peoples in North America interacted with the diverse environments and ecosystems of the continent for thousands of years prior to the arrival of Europeans. It is well documented that indigenous peoples' cultures, societies, and economies have been shaped by their respective environments. Similarly, indigenous peoples in North America have modified their environments.[1] It is suggested that one of the motivations was "to increase the overall abundance and accessibility of wild species of plants and animals . . . [which] often involved substantial and ongoing investments of labour – sometimes communal, sometimes at smaller kin unit levels – on particular, well-recognized, and sometimes specifically demarcated parcels of land (or water)."[2]

In many regions this intensive interaction between indigenous peoples and the natural environment resulted in highly complex societies and wealth-creation economies.

In the Pacific Northwest, indigenous economies have been centered around the sustainable management and use of salmon. Archaeological evidence documents the resilience of Pacific Northwest salmon populations and the associated socioeco- logical system over the last 7,500 years. The evidence shows that indigenous peoples sustainably used, rather than overfished, the resource despite the facts that the region supported extremely high human population densities and that these communities had the technology to greatly reduce salmon populations.[3] The evidence further shows that this resilience is best explained by generalized resource use and social institutions regulating fishing. Furthermore,

> [a]s historic and contemporary records illustrate, Indigenous peoples of the Pacific Northwest engaged in complex rituals that reflected and contributed to core beliefs related to native animals and plants, and the landscape in which people lived. Traditions and institutions of First Nations peoples and Native Americans incorpo- rated explicit monitoring of resource use and proprietorship, which helped convert open-access resources into common-pool ones.[4]

---

[1] For detailed descriptions of different indigenous societies and their interaction with the environment, see Bruce D. Smith, ed., *The Subsistence Economies of Indigenous North American Societies: A Handbook* (Washington, D.C.: Smithsonian Institution Scholarly Press, 2011).

[2] Bruce D. Smith, "Shaping the Natural World: Patterns of Human Niche Construction by Small-Scale Societies in North America," in Smith, *The Subsistence Economies*, pp. 604–05.

[3] Sarah K. Campbell and Virginia L. Butler, "Archaeological Evidence for Resilience of Pacific North- west Salmon Populations and the Socioecological System over the Last ~7,500 Years," *Ecology and Society* 15 (2010), 2.

[4] Campbell and Butler, "Archeological Evidence," p. 16.

Salmon is considered a cultural "keystone species" for indigenous peoples in the Pacific Northwest. Ecologists refer to keystone species to indicate that some species play an integral role in the overall structure and function of ecosystems.[5] Ethnobotanist Dr. Nancy Turner further developed the term "cultural keystone species" to describe species that are the underpinning of a culture.[6] Cultural keystone species play a fundamental role in the diet and ceremonies of the indigenous peoples, and without these species the societies they support would be fundamentally different.[7] This makes the conversation about salmon all the more important and means that indigenous peoples must be involved in ensuring salmon's sustainable management and use, as much today as in the past.

2.2. *Colonization and Regulation*

It is well-documented that the impact of colonization was devastating to indigenous peoples and their cultures and economies.[8] The main driver of colonization was economic: to gain access to lands and resources under the control of indigenous peoples. Over time, government regulations increasingly were used to limit indigenous peoples' access to their lands and resources and to marginalize indigenous economies.

   This can be explained by returning to the example of salmon, which formed the basis of indigenous wealth-creation economies and its fishery was controlled by indigenous peoples, even in early colonial times. Historical records document that indigenous peoples played a key role in the trade for salmon. Salmon was one of the principal exports for the Hudson Bay Company (HBC) from the Pacific Northwest. Professor Douglas Harris, who has researched Aboriginal fisheries extensively, explains that the HBC only briefly tried to deploy its own workers on the Lower Fraser in the 1840s and instead decided to purchase fish from Aboriginal fishers,[9] as previously. James Douglas, the first governor of the province of British Columbia, clearly recognized the central importance of fisheries to First Nations by setting out the right to "carry on fisheries as formerly" in early treaties and later informing the House of Assembly that Aboriginal Peoples "were to be protected in their right

---

[5] Ann Garibaldi and Nancy Turner, "Cultural Keystone Species: Implications for Ecological Conservation and Restoration," *Ecology and Society* 9 (2004), 1.
[6] Garibaldi and Turner, "Cultural Keystone Species," p. 1.
[7] Garibaldi and Turner, "Cultural Keystone Species," p. 1.
[8] For a very detailed investigation see the proceedings of the Canadian Royal Commission on Aboriginal Peoples, Government of Canada, *Highlights from the Report of the Royal Commission on Aboriginal Peoples* (1996), archived online at http://www.aadnc-aandc.gc.ca/eng/1100100014597/1100100014637.
[9] Douglas C. Harris, *Landing Native Fisheries: Indian Reserves and Fishing Rights in British Columbia, 1849–1925* (Vancouver: UBC Press, 2008), p. 24. See, generally, Richard Mackie, *Trading beyond the Mountains: The British Fur Trade on the Pacific, 1763–1843* (Vancouver: UBC Press, 1997), pp. 221–30.

of fishing on the coast and in the bays of the Colony,"[10] thereby recognizing their rights. Until the 1870s, the fisheries were almost entirely Aboriginal, and the colonial government did not intervene.[11]

Once British Columbia joined Confederation in 1871, Aboriginal access to salmon increasingly was limited in parallel with the promotion of a nonindigenous commercial industrial fishery. In 1888, indigenous peoples in British Columbia were prohibited from selling fish, and their fishery was limited to what was termed an "Indian Food Fishery." The Dominion Fisheries Act of 1868 entered into force in British Columbia in 1877, and a clause that was added to the Salmon Fishery Regulations in 1888 stated that "Indians shall, at all times, have liberty to fish for the purpose of providing food for themselves but not for sale, barter or traffic, by any means other than drift nets, or spearing."[12]

Professor Harris explained the effect in his expert report, *The Recognition and Regulation of Aboriginal Fraser River Sockeye Salmon Fisheries to 1982*, to the Canadian federal Cohen Commission of Inquiry into the Decline of the Fraser River Sockeye Salmon:

> In addition to the commercial fishery, Aboriginal people also had access to a separately identified and regulated food fishery. The "Indian food fishery" was a category constructed in law that, while providing some limited protection for Aboriginal fishing, operated to marginalize whatever prior claim Aboriginal peoples had to the fisheries by virtue of their long history of fishing. In effect, the Indian food fishery performed the same role in the fisheries as the Indian reserve did on land; both were designed to contain the Aboriginal presence, opening a resource and territory to immigrants.[13]

Indigenous peoples have always seen and continue to see the distinction between the Indian food fishery and an economic fishery as a distortion because no such distinction existed in indigenous societies and economies. The Five Battlegrounds position paper drafted by indigenous peoples in British Columbia concludes that this distinction of the Indian food fishery by governmental regulation continues to constitute one of the main wedges in colonial rule that was established over

---

[10] "Douglas to House of Assembly, February 5, 1859," in *House of Assembly Correspondence Book, August 12, 1856 to July 6, 1859* (Victoria: William H. Cullen, Printer to the King's Most Excellent Majesty, 1918), pp. 46–47.

[11] *House of Assembly Correspondence Book*, p. 7.

[12] Douglas C. Harris, *Fish, Law, and Colonialism: The Legal Capture of Salmon in British Columbia* (Toronto: University of Toronto Press, 2001), p. 66 (quoting "Order-in-Council," *Canada Gazette* 22 (Nov. 26, 1888, 956)).

[13] Douglas C. Harris, *The Recognition and Regulation of Aboriginal Fraser River Sockeye Salmon Fisheries to 1982*, prepared for the Commission of Inquiry into the Decline of Sockeye Salmon in the Fraser River (Jan. 12, 2011).

indigenous peoples in British Columbia.[14] The direct effect of the government regulation was the economic marginalization of indigenous peoples to secure increased access to resources and land for nonindigenous actors. It persists to date.

3. INDIGENOUS RIGHTS RECOGNIZED IN THE CANADIAN CONSTITUTION

3.1. *Constitutional Protection for Aboriginal Title and Rights*

Indigenous peoples in Canada secured recognition of their Aboriginal and treaty rights in the Constitution Act of 1982.[15] The Canada Act[16] patriated the Canadian Constitution, which up until then consisted primarily of an enactment of the British Imperial Parliament, the British North America Act of 1867 (BNA Act), now referred to as the Constitution Act 1867, which contains among other things the division of powers between the federal government and the provinces.[17] Section 35 of the Constitution Act of 1982 provides constitutional status and protection to Aboriginal rights, stipulating that "The existing aboriginal and treaty rights of the aboriginal peoples of Canada are hereby recognized and affirmed."[18] In *Delgamuukw v. British Columbia*, the Supreme Court of Canada held that this constitutional protection extended to Aboriginal title, the collective land rights of indigenous peoples who have not signed treaties.[19]

Still, at the beginning of the sentence. The Canadian government failed to take active steps to implement this constitutional protection and recognize Aboriginal title and rights on the ground. As a result, Canadian courts have had to step in and give meaning to Aboriginal title and rights and their constitutional protection. The Supreme Court of Canada maintained, in cases such as *Calder et al. v. Attorney General of British Columbia*,[20] *Guerin v. the Queen*,[21] and *Delgamuukw*,[22] that Aboriginal title and rights are inherent rights, their essence is defined by indigenous laws, and hence they are sui generis.[23]

In *Delgamuukw*, the first indigenous land rights case after Section 35 entered into force, the court declared that sui generis Aboriginal title is based on the prior, continuous, and exclusive occupation of land and the legal effect given to occupation

---

[14] Reuben Ware, *Five Issues, Five Battlegrounds: An Introduction to the History of Indian Fisheries in British Columbia 1850–1930* (Coqualeetza Training Centre for the Stó:lō Nation, 1983), p. 8.
[15] Constitution Act, 1982, being Schedule B to the Canada Act 1982 (UK), c 11.
[16] Canada Act 1982 (UK), c 11.
[17] Constitution Act, 1867, 30 & 31 Vict, c 3 (UK), R.S.C. 1985, App. II, No. 5.
[18] Constitution Act, 1982, s. 35(1), (3).
[19] *Delgamuukw v. British Columbia*, [1997] 3 SCR 1010 at p. 1079–1081 and 1091–1095.
[20] *Calder et al. v. Attorney-General of British Columbia*, [1973] SCR 313.
[21] *Guerin v. The Queen*, [1984] 2 SCR 335.
[22] *Delgamuukw v. British Columbia*, [1997] 3 SCR 1010.
[23] *Delgamuukw*, p. 1066.

by the common law or by Aboriginal systems of land tenure law based on a territorial approach.[24]

The year 1846, the entry into force of the Oregon Boundary Treaty, has been established in the case law as the point in time when Aboriginal title crystallized in British Columbia. At that time indigenous peoples controlled all land and resources in what became the Province of British Columbia in 1857. Their economies flourished and indigenous trade networks were strong and started to interlink with those of nonindigenous traders. When the first trading posts were set up, indigenous peoples asserted their exclusive control over access to resources, such as the salmon fishery described in Section 2 of this chapter.[25]

British Columbia is the largest area in Canada and the United States where historically no treaties were signed with indigenous peoples, apart from the early Douglas treaties, mainly on Vancouver Island, and treaties that reached into the North of British Columbia. Indigenous peoples, especially in the Interior of British Columbia, have always maintained their inherent land rights. A number of tribes in the South Central Interior of British Columbia joined together in 1910 to assert their land rights and present their position to the then-federal Prime Minister Sir Wilfrid Laurier. In their declaration they rejected the position of the provincial government, which failed to recognize their land rights, and called for settling the land issue:

> When [the nonindigenous people] first came among us there were only Indians here. They found the people of each tribe supreme in their own territory.... We condemn the whole policy of the B[ritish] C[olumbia] government towards the Indian tribes of this country as utterly unjust, shameful and blundering in every way.... We demand that our land question be settled, and ask that treaties be made between the government and each of our tribes, in the same manner as accomplished with Indian tribes of the other provinces of Canada, and in the neighboring parts of the United States.[26]

The content of Aboriginal title is not restricted to those uses that generated Aboriginal rights, that is, "elements of a practice, custom or tradition integral to the distinctive culture of the Aboriginal group claiming the right."[27] The broad conceptualization of Aboriginal title involves the inherent land tenure systems that established various interests, responsibilities, and entitlements to use the territory that are distinct from other constitutionalized Aboriginal rights. In *Delgamuukw* the Supreme Court of Canada further recognized that Aboriginal title has an "inescapable economic

---

[24] *Delgamuukw*, p. 1082.
[25] Douglas C. Harris, *Landing Native Fisheries*, p. 18.
[26] From the Chiefs of the Shuswap, Okanagan and Couteau Tribes of British Colombia, *Memorial Sir Wilfrid Laurier, Premier of the Dominion of Canada*, Presented at Kamloops, B.C., Aug. 25, 1910, pp. 2, 6, http://www.secwepemc.org/files/memorial.pdf.
[27] Ibid., Memorial Sir Wilfrid Laurier, pp. 1087–88.

component"[28] along with a jurisdictional dimension, both of which are inherent to indigenous peoples' right to self-determination.

3.2. *Duty to Consult and Accommodate*

Following the judicial recognition of Aboriginal title in *Delgamuukw*, both federal and provincial governments persisted with their business-as-usual approach, authorizing development proposals and granting access to lands and resources without taking into account Aboriginal title and rights. This approach was challenged by the Haida Nation, which sought review of British Columbia's decision to transfer a large-scale, long-term tree farm license to Weyerhaeuser without taking into account and accommodating the potential impact on asserted Haida Aboriginal title and rights. The Supreme Court of Canada found that the Crown had violated the duty to consult the Haida Nation.[29] The duty to consult and accommodate is anchored in the constitutional principle of the honour of the Crown.[30] In the decision the Court considered how to reconcile preexisting Aboriginal sovereignty with assumed Crown sovereignty and pointed to the need to maintain the honour of the Crown that arises "from the Crown's assertion of sovereignty over an Aboriginal people and *de facto* control of land and resources that were formerly in the control of that people."[31] When situating the duties within these principles the Supreme Court has stated that "[t]he honour of the Crown is always at stake in its dealings with Aboriginal peoples."[32]

Under Canadian law, the duty to consult is triggered where: (1) the Crown has knowledge of an Aboriginal or treaty right; (2) the Crown has contemplated an action or a decision; and (3) the contemplated action may impact adversely the exercise of the Aboriginal or treaty right.[33]

These principles can serve as an example of how the issue of indigenous involvement in decision making plays out on the ground in a NAFTA member country. The duty to consult is forward-looking[34] and therefore applies to all future developments and decisions in indigenous territories: from major large-scale projects, such as pipelines and mining and overarching strategic decisions that could have widespread and long-term impacts, to smaller specific decisions, such as applications

---

[28] *Delgamuukw*, p. 1112.

[29] *Haida Nation v. British Columbia (Minister of Forests)*, [2004] 3 SCR 511.

[30] *Haida Nation*, paras. 16–18, 25–27. The honour of the Crown, has also been recently discussed by the Supreme Court of Canada in detail in *Manitoba Metis Federation, Inc. v. Canada (Attorney General)*, [2013] 1 S.C.R. 623.

[31] *Haida Nation*, at para. 32.

[32] *Haida Nation*, at para 16.

[33] First articulated in *Haida Nation*, at para. 35, and reiterated in *Rio Tinto Alcan Inc. v. Carrier Sekani Tribal Council*, [2010] 2 SCR 650.

[34] Rio Tinto Alcan Inc., at paras. 32–50; *Beckman v. Little Salmon/Carmacks First Nation*, [2010] 3 SCR 103 at 105–06.

for a specific permit. The Court has clearly warned the Crown that "[t]he multitude of smaller grievances created by the indifference of some government officials to aboriginal people's concerns, and the lack of respect inherent in that indifference has been as destructive of the process of reconciliation as some of the larger and more explosive controversies."[35]

To determine the content of the duty to consult and accommodate one has to assess the strength of the asserted rights and the seriousness of the potential adverse impacts that the proposed development would have on these rights.[36] As the Supreme Court of Canada stated in *Haida Nation*, "[t]he controlling question in all situations is what is required to maintain the honour of the Crown and to effect reconciliation between the Crown and the Aboriginal peoples with respect to the interests at stake."[37] In a situation where "the right and potential infringement is of high significance to the Aboriginal peoples, and the risk of non-compensable damage is high,"[38] the level of consultation required to maintain the honour of the Crown must be at its highest level. At this level, "[w]hen the consultation process suggests amendment of Crown policy, we arrive at the stage of accommodation."[39]

As the Canadian cases suggest, indigenous rights must be taken into account when decisions regarding land and resources are to be made. The seriousness of the economic, social, cultural, and environmental impacts has to be considered, since a proposed development or decision could negatively impact indigenous economies and cultures. By asserting their rights to address and avoid such potential impacts, indigenous peoples can contribute further to ensuring economically, socially, and environmentally sustainable development. At the highest end of the spectrum, the duty to consult and accommodate in an effort to obtain consent must be fulfilled if there could be severe impacts on proven rights of indigenous peoples.

3.3. *Tsilhqot'in Nation v. BC: A Game Changer*

The recent Supreme Court of Canada decision in *Tsilhqot'in Nation v. British Columbia*[40] resulted in the first declaration of Aboriginal title in Canadian history, which requires the implementation of Aboriginal title on the ground. That legislation, like the province's legal arguments in *Tsilhqot'in Nation*, has been based

---

[35] *Mikisew Cree First Nation v. Canada (Minister of Canadian Heritage)*, [2005] 3 SCR 388 at para 1.
[36] *Haida Nation*, at paras. 38–39.
[37] *Haida Nation*, at para. 45.
[38] *Haida Nation*, at para. 44.
[39] *Haida Nation*, at para. 47.
[40] *Tsilhqot'in Nation v. BC*, 2014 SCC 44. The author was one of the counsel in the Supreme Court for the Coalition of Union of British Columbia Indian Chiefs, the Okanagan Nation Alliance and the Shuswap Nation Tribal Council and their member communities, Okanagan, Adams Lake, Neskonlith, and Splatsin Indian Bands, interveners.

on what the Court referred to in its reasons as the government's "erroneous the-sis that only specific, intensively occupied areas can support Aboriginal title."[41] Instead, the Court maintained a broad territorial-use–based approach to Aborig-inal title, holding that a determination whether the respective indigenous peo-ples had the intention and capacity to control the land at the time of the asser-tion of sovereignty should take into account indigenous laws and factors such as the characteristics of the claimant group and the characteristics of the land in question.[42]

The Court's territorial approach to establishing title enables indigenous peoples to bring claims for larger parts of their territories. Once Aboriginal title is established the court made it clear that any developments would be subject to consent of the respective indigenous peoples or, absent consent, a stringent test where the Crown would have to justify the infringement of Aboriginal title. It is hard to imagine how substantive decisions regarding access and allocation could be justified by the Crown given that it does not retain any beneficial interest in the Aboriginal title lands and resources. The Court also warned that following a declaration of title the Crown might have to reassess prior conduct, which might require cancellation of a project that unjustifiably infringes Aboriginal title.[43]

Though noting that it was not necessary to its decision that on the facts the nation had established Aboriginal title, the Court went on to conclude that the legislation under which the Province had acted, namely the Forestry Act, did not apply to Aboriginal title lands, because the province had not contemplated that result. It noted that the legislation would have to be amended to apply to Aboriginal title lands.[44]

The Court also reiterated that indigenous peoples who assert Aboriginal title, but have not yet obtained a declaration of Title, have to be consulted by the Crown regarding any proposed developments that could negatively affect their asserted Aboriginal title and rights and if necessary accommodate them.[45] In conclusion, the Court went further, reminding both the Crown and proponents that the only way to obtain legal and economic certainty regarding proposed developments is to secure the consent of indigenous peoples:

> I add this. Governments and individuals proposing to use or exploit land, whether before or after a declaration of Aboriginal title, can avoid a charge of infringement or failure to adequately consult by obtaining the consent of the interested Aboriginal group.[46]

[41] *Tsilhqot'in Nation*, at para. 66.
[42] *Tsilhqot'in Nation*, at paras. 37, 41.
[43] *Tsilhqot'in Nation*, at paras 71–92.
[44] *Tsilhqot'in Nation*, at paras. 107–116.
[45] *Tsilhqot'in Nation*, paras. 78–88.
[46] *Tsilhqot'in Nation*, at para. 97.

Consent is the new recommended standard. Implied in it is indigenous jurisdiction and decision-making authority. Consent is not merely a procedural requirement, it has important substantive elements, requiring that indigenous peoples have to be provided with the necessary information regarding a proposed project, so they can make an informed decision. It also has a jurisdictional element, recognizing that indigenous peoples are decision makers regarding proposed developments in their territories.

3.4. *The Logging Cases and Indigenous Jurisdiction*

The issue of indigenous jurisdiction, especially vis-à-vis provincial jurisdiction, was not central to the *Tsilhqot'in Nation* case. It will be left to future cases to further delineate the interaction of those jurisdictions. The next cases in line are the Secwepemc Okanagan logging cases, which originated in 1999 when members of the respective nations went logging in their territories without a provincial permit in order to assert their Aboriginal title and jurisdiction over their land and resources. The province of British Columbia issued stop work orders pursuant to the provincial Forest Act, which prohibits the harvesting of timber without a provincial permit. In 2003, the Supreme Court found the resulting logging cases brought by the province against the Okanagan and Secwepemc to be cases of public importance, since they address issues regarding access to forestry resources and lands.[47] As a result, the logging cases received advance costs orders requiring that the province pay costs related to their litigation. This decision also set an important precedent and resulted in funding for the *Tsilhqot'in* case.[48]

The logging cases raised the issues of indigenous jurisdiction and control over access to forestry resources. Citing cost considerations, the province has long delayed the proceedings; the cases still have not been to trial fifteen years after they were initiated. In 2008, the British Columbia Court of Appeal found that "any definitive judgment on aboriginal title in [*Tsilhqot'in*] is bound to be influential in determining claims to aboriginal title here,"[49] leading to a further delay in the Logging Cases.

A limited Aboriginal right to harvest forestry resources was recognized by the Supreme Court of Canada in the New Brunswick case of *R. v. Sappier and R. v. Gray*;[50] as a result, the Province of British Columbia admitted Aboriginal rights to harvest trees for domestic purposes in the Browns Creek and Harper Lake

---

[47] *British Columbia (Ministry of Forests) v. Okanagan Indian Band*, [2003] 3 S.C.R. 371.
[48] *Tsilhqot'in Nation v. British Columbia*, [2007] BCSC 1700.
[49] *British Columbia (Minister of Forests) v. Okanagan Indian Band*, [2008] BCCA 107 at para. 29 (dismissing application for leave to appeal to the Supreme Court of Canada). The Secwepemc case has been stayed awaiting the outcome of the Okanagan case: *HMTQ v. Chief Ronnie Jules et al.*, [2005] BCSC 1312; *HMTQ v. Chief Ronnie Jules et al.*, Oral Reasons for Judgment (BCSC), Apr. 5, 2006.
[50] *R. v. Sappier; R. v. Gray*, [2006] 2 S.C.R. 686.

Watersheds, which had been subject to the logging litigation. Despite British Columbia's admissions and the ongoing litigation, the Province authorized logging of more than half the available timber in the Harper Lake Watershed, which has had a negative impact on water, fish, animals, and culturally important plants; affected traditional areas; disturbed spiritual areas; destroyed Secwepemc trail markers; and increased the possibility of flooding.[51] Since their cases were not moving at the domestic level, the Interior Nations of British Columbia went before international trade tribunals to assert their proprietary interests, as will be further discussed in Section 7 of this chapter.

4. INDIGENOUS PEOPLES AND THEIR RIGHTS AT INTERNATIONAL LAW AND REQUIREMENTS FOR NATIONAL IMPLEMENTATION

4.1. *International Principles and Obligations*

Under international law, indigenous peoples have the right to self-determination and "[b]y virtue of that right they freely determine their political status and freely pursue their economic, social and cultural development."[52] This right is set out in a number of binding treaties – specifically in Article 1 of the International Covenant on Civil and Political Rights (ICCPR) and the International Covenant on Economic Social and Cultural Rights (ICESCR), jointly known as the Decolonization Treaties – to which all NAFTA member states are parties.[53] Hence, they are required to implement the respective international obligations. The international community collectively has agreed that the right to self-determination applies to indigenous peoples, as set out in Article 3 of the UN Declaration on the Rights of Indigenous Peoples (UNDRIP),[54] which contains the same wording specific to indigenous peoples.

The right to self-determination of all peoples is a foundational right under international law and has the status of *jus cogens*.[55] Under the Vienna Convention on the Law of Treaties, *jus cogens* is "a peremptory norm of general international law [which] is a norm accepted and recognized by the international community of

---

[51] *British Columbia (Forests and Range) v. Okanagan Indian Band*, [2010] BCSC 1088 at paras. 16, 17, 40–45.

[52] International Covenant on Civil and Political Rights (ICCPR), G.A. Res. 2200A (XXI), U.N. Doc. A/6316 (Mar. 23, 1976); International Covenant on Economic, Social and Cultural Rights (ICESCR), G.A. Res. 2200A (XXI), U.N. Doc. A/6316 (Jan. 3, 1976). Arts. 1, paras. 1, of both covenants set out that: "All peoples have the right of self-determination. By virtue of that right they freely determine their political status and freely pursue their economic, social and cultural development."

[53] Ibid.

[54] United Nations Declaration on the Rights of Indigenous Peoples. G.A. Res. 61/295, U.N. Doc. A/61/L.67 (Sept. 13, 2007) [hereinafter UNDRIP].

[55] James Crawford, *Brownlie's Principles of Public International Law*, 8th ed. (Oxford, U.K.: Oxford University Press, 2012), p. lxxviii; Hugh M. Kindred et al., eds., *International Law Chiefly as Interpreted and Applied in Canada*, 7th ed. (Toronto: Emond Montgomery Publications, 2007), pp. 70–78; John H. Currie, *Public International Law*, 2nd ed. (Toronto: Irwin Law, Inc., 2008), pp. 56–66.

States as a whole as a norm from which no derogation is permitted and which can be modified only by a subsequent norm of general international law having the same character."[56] On the basis of this, NAFTA member states are obligated under their national constitutions and international obligations to properly implement the indigenous right to self-determination, including in the context of international trade and economic decision making.

In order to properly implement indigenous rights, NAFTA member states should look to UNDRIP, which by now has been endorsed by all NAFTA member states. It articulates the right to self-determination and other international human rights principles that have direct application or form part of customary international law. For example, UNDRIP, Article 8.2(b), imposes an obligation on the State to prevent any action that has the aim or effect of dispossessing indigenous peoples of their lands, territories, and resources.[57] Article 18 protects their right to participate in decision making through their own institutions,[58] and Article 19 imposes an obligation on the State to obtain their "free, prior and informed consent before adopting and implementing legislative or administrative measures that may affect them,"[59] such as regulation of resource development. Notably, Articles 25 through 29 articulate several of the rights of indigenous peoples, as well as state obligations in relation to their traditionally owned, occupied, and used lands, territories, waters, and other resources and to uphold state obligations as caretakers of these resources for the benefit of future generations.[60]

UNDRIP further has articulated free prior informed consent (PIC) as the minimum standard to be met when dealing with resource development. Specifically, Article 32 states:

1. Indigenous peoples have the right to determine and develop priorities and strategies for the development or use of their lands or territories and other resources.

2. States shall consult and cooperate in good faith with the indigenous peoples concerned through their own representative institutions in order to obtain their free and informed consent prior to the approval of any project affecting their

---

[56] Vienna Convention on the Law of Treaties, done at Vienna May 23, 1969, 1155 U.N.T.S. 331 (entered into force Jan. 27, 1980), arts. 53, 64.

[57] UNDRIP, G.A. Res. 61/295, U.N. Doc. A/61/L.67 (Sept. 13, 2007), art. 8.

[58] Ibid., art. 18. Article 18 states: "Indigenous peoples have the right to participate in decision-making in matters which would affect their rights, through representatives chosen by themselves in accordance with their own procedures, as well as to maintain and develop their own indigenous decision-making institutions."

[59] Ibid., art. 19. Article 19 states: "States shall consult and cooperate in good faith with the indigenous peoples concerned through their own representative institutions in order to obtain their free, prior and informed consent before adopting and implementing legislative or administrative measures that may affect them."

[60] Ibid., arts. 25–29.

lands or territories and other resources, particularly in connection with the development, utilization or exploitation of mineral, water or other resources.

3. States shall provide effective mechanisms for just and fair redress for any such activities, and appropriate measures shall be taken to mitigate adverse environmental, economic, social, cultural or spiritual impact.[61]

Where a proposed development stands to have very serious impacts on the economy, culture, and spirituality of the indigenous peoples, indigenous governance structures have to be engaged to ensure that indigenous laws are followed and impacts are mitigated.

PIC is being implemented increasingly at the international and local levels. In the *Saramaka* case, the Inter-American Court of Human Rights ruled that when "large-scale development or investments projects that would have a major impact within [the affected indigenous peoples'] territory, the State has a duty, not only to consult with the [affected indigenous peoples], but also to obtain their free, prior, and informed consent, according to their customs and traditions."[62]

As a matter of customary international law, PIC should be adopted in domestic decision-making processes. James Anaya, the UN Special Rapporteur on indigenous peoples, has commented that

> [w]here property rights are affected by natural resource extraction, the international norm is developing to also require actual consent by the indigenous people concerned . . . the state's consultations with indigenous peoples must at least have the objective of achieving consent. . . . If consent is not achieved, there is a strong presumption that the project should not go forward. If it proceeds, the state bears a heavy burden of justification to ensure the indigenous peoples share in the benefits of the project, and must take measures to mitigate its negative effects . . . and . . . the state must show that indigenous concerns were heard and accommodated.[63]

4.2. *National Application in Canadian Law*

In the *Quebec Secession Reference*, the Supreme Court of Canada found that the right to self-determination "is now so widely recognized in international conventions that the principle has acquired a status beyond 'convention' and is considered a general principle of international law"[64] and hence is a free-standing source of international

---

[61] Above note 54, art. 32.

[62] *Case of the Saramaka People v. Suriname, Preliminary Objections, Merits, Reparations, and Costs,* Inter-Am. Ct. H.R. (ser. C) No. 172 (Nov. 28, 2007), para 134.

[63] James Anaya, "Indigenous Peoples' Participatory Rights in Relation to Decisions About Natural Resource Extraction: The More Fundamental Issue of What Rights Indigenous Peoples Have in Lands and Resources," *Arizona Journal of International and Comparative Law* 22 (2005), 17, http://www.ajicl.org/AJICL2005/vol221/Anaya%20Formatted%20Galleyproofed.pdf.

[64] *Reference re Secession of Quebec,* [1998] 2 SCR 217 at para. 114.

law. Furthermore, a long line of Canadian jurisprudence has clearly established that "Canada's international obligations and relevant principles of international law are ... instructive in defining [constitutional rights]," and that they "should be presumed to provide at least as great a level of protection as is found in the international human rights documents that Canada has ratified."[65]

The Court has also offered an interpretation as to how the right to self-determination arises in Canada:

> In summary, the international law right to self-determination only generates, at best, *a right to external self-determination in situations of former colonies; where a people is oppressed,* as for example under foreign military occupation; *or where a definable group is denied meaningful access to government to pursue their political, economic, social and cultural development.* In all three situations, the people in question are entitled to a right to external self-determination *because they have been denied the ability to exert internally their right to self-determination.*[66]

Canadian courts[67] and Royal commissions[68] have repeatedly established that indigenous peoples in Canada have been subject to colonization and remain oppressed and marginalized as a direct result of government regulation and the failure to implement Aboriginal title and rights pursuant to Section 35 of the Constitution Act of 1982.[69]

5. NONRECOGNITION OF INDIGENOUS RIGHTS RESULTS IN LEGAL AND ECONOMIC UNCERTAINTY

As early as 1990, Indian and Northern Affairs Canada (INAC) commissioned a study by the international accounting firm, then called Price Waterhouse, on the economic value of uncertainty associated with indigenous land claims in British Columbia.[70] It set out the impact that legal uncertainty related to indigenous land

---

[65] *Divito v. Canada (Public Safety and Emergency Preparedness)*, [2013] 3 SCR 157at paras 22–23; *Health Services and Support-Facilities Subsector Bargaining Assn. v. British Columbia*, [2007] 2 SCR 391 at para 70.

[66] *Reference re Secession of Quebec*, 2 SCR 217 at para. 138 (emphasis added).

[67] *R. v. Ipeelee* [2012] 1 SCR 433 at para. 60; *Gladue v. The Queen* [1999] 1 SCR 688 at para. 61; *R. v. Williams* [1998] 1 SCR 1128 at para 58.

[68] Royal Commission on Aboriginal Peoples, *Report of the Royal Commission on Aboriginal Peoples, Volume 1: Looking Forward, Looking Back* (Ottawa: Supply and Services, 1996), pp. 165–173, http://www.collectionscanada.gc.ca/webarchives/20071115053257/www.ainc-inac.gc.ca/ch/rcap/sg/sgmm_e.html (last visited June 4, 2014); see generally Canadian Human Rights Commission, *Report on Equality Rights of Aboriginal People* (Ottawa: CHRC, 2013), http://www.chrc-ccdp.gc.ca/sites/default/files/equality_aboriginal_report.pdf.

[69] Constitution Act, 1982, being Schedule B to the Canada Act 1982 (U.K.), c. 11, at s. 35.

[70] Price Waterhouse, Economic Value of Uncertainty Associated with Native Claims in B. C. (March 1990) (unpublished).

rights had on the British Columbian economy. It found that all major commercial-industrial sectors in British Columbia consider land right issues as generating uncertainty for companies, including the right of access to lands and resources.

One option for the Canadian federal government would have been to revise its Comprehensive Claims Policy in line with the demands of indigenous peoples in British Columbia and base it on the recognition of Aboriginal title, so as to create clarity and legal certainty. This way, the policy could have been brought in line with the Supreme Court of Canada decisions recognizing Aboriginal title as the collective proprietary interests of indigenous peoples in their territories, despite arguments from the provincial and federal governments that it had been extinguished or are extremely limited, which was rejected in *Tsilhqot'in Nation*. In fact, since *Delgamuukw*, Canada and British Columbia have had to report contingent liabilities for outstanding Aboriginal title litigation and land claims in their financial statements.[71]

Instead of recognizing Aboriginal title in its Comprehensive Claims Policy, the federal and provincial governments have maintained the British Columbia Treaty Commission (BCTC) process for negotiation of land claims based on that now-outdated Policy.[72] Under this process, indigenous peoples can access and borrow funds to negotiate a comprehensive land claims agreement, where their inherent land rights are modified and limited to rights enshrined in an agreement that will cover only a small part of their territory as settlement lands. This policy and process have been described as a risk management strategy for the government. In effect, the establishment of the BCTC can be linked directly to the Price Waterhouse Report, as a means of mitigating the risk to their investors. In their financial statements, the governments point to the negotiations under the BCTC in return as their way of addressing those liabilities.[73] The BCTC has since commissioned further studies, from Price Waterhouse Coopers, that ironically nowadays report on how lack of progress in their negotiations causes uncertainty for investment.[74]

But there are indigenous peoples in British Columbia who refuse to negotiate under Canada's policies that violate international human and indigenous rights standards and aim at de facto extinguishment of Aboriginal title. In order to confront

[71] See, for example, Summary Financial Statements, Province of British Columbia for the Fiscal Year Ended March 31, 2010; Public Accounts of Canada, 2005, Summary Report and Financial Statements [hereinafter Financial Statements].

[72] For more information on the terms on the basis of which Canada negotiates Comprehensive Claims see Government of Canada, Aboriginal Affairs and Northern Development Canada, *Comprehensive Claims* (2012), http://www.aadnc-aandc.gc.ca/eng/1100100030577/1100100030578 (last visited June 4, 2014).

[73] For example: Summary Financial Statements, Province of British Columbia for the Fiscal Year Ended March 31, 2010; Public Accounts of Canada, 2005, Summary Report and Financial Statements.

[74] See generally Price Waterhouse Coopers, Financial and Economic Impacts of Treaty Settlements in B.C., Report to the BC Treaty Commission (2009).

these government policies that continue to marginalize indigenous economies, they have made their independent indigenous submissions to international trade tribunals, which will be further discussed in following sections.

Economic uncertainty for investors and project proponents in indigenous territories persists. As a result, more and more proponents have attempted to negotiate and sign agreements with indigenous peoples regarding developments in their territories, even absent government recognition of their indigenous rights. These agreements constitute implicit recognition of Aboriginal title and rights and their economic dimension.

Disregard of the powerful position of indigenous peoples has resulted in a great deal of economic uncertainty for provinces and resource developers alike. For example, when the Province of Ontario unilaterally granted the mining proponent Platinex, Inc., a permit to drill and explore for minerals, and then failed to adequately consult, the Kitchenuhmaykoosib Inninuwug (KI) defended their lands from destruction in accordance with their laws.[75] In the end, Ontario spent millions of dollars buying back mineral claims from proponents. A similar case occurred in Algonquin territory, where Ontario and the proponent Frontenac Ventures disregarded a moratorium under Algonquin law, which led to blockades, extensive litigation, and ultimately the suspension of exploration.[76]

As the UN Special Rapporteur on the Rights of Indigenous Peoples has stated, "the prevailing model of resource extraction is one in which an outside company, with backing by the State, controls and profits from the extractive operation, with the affected indigenous peoples at best being offered benefits in the form of jobs or community development projects that typically pale in economic value in comparison to profits gained by the corporation."[77] Indigenous peoples are opposing this model where others benefit from indigenous lands and resources and indigenous peoples are left with the negative effects. An alternative model based on recognition of indigenous rights and jurisdiction would take into account indigenous values and laws and internalize the costs of the proposed development to indigenous peoples and the environment. Substantial funds would have to be set aside for mitigation of impacts, environmental monitoring, and remediation. Finally, benefits would have to be shared with indigenous peoples, remunerating them in relation to the resources taken from their territory and compensation for any damage caused and loss to indigenous economies. Such a model would ensure much more economically, socially, and culturally sustainable development.

---

[75] *Platinex Inc. v. Kitchenuhmaykoosib Inninuwug First Nation*, [2008] ONCA 620.
[76] *Frontenac Ventures Corp. v. Ardoch Algonquin First Nation*, [2008] ONCA 534.
[77] Special Rapporteur on the Rights of Indigenous Peoples, *Extractive Industries and Indigenous Peoples*, Human Rights Council, U.N. Doc. A/HRC/24/41 (July 1, 2013) (by James Anaya), para. 4.

6. ENSURING SUSTAINABLE DEVELOPMENT AND PROTECTION OF BIODIVERSITY

6.1. *In General*

Today there continues to be a strong correlation and overlap between biodiversity and cultural and linguistic diversity, meaning that the highest concentrations of biodiversity can be found in areas of linguistic diversity, such as the remaining territories under the control of indigenous peoples worldwide. Research further has confirmed that indigenous peoples' interaction with the ecosystems and the different species continues to enhance biodiversity.[78]

Indigenous Peoples hold traditional knowledge, which along with "[p]ractices of aboriginal peoples to maintain and enhance their lands, waters, and living resources are derived from generations of experimentation and observation, leading to an understanding of complex ecological and physical principles. 'Indigenous peoples are uniquely positioned in their close and long-standing environmental relationships, yet the survival of many indigenous cultures is severely threatened by insensitive economic development, by coercive education systems, by assimilation into the modes of production and inexorable movement toward market economies of the dominant society, and by the escalating ecological destruction of peoples' homelands and resources. Indeed, worldwide, the knowledge base for traditional ecological knowledge and wisdom (TEKW) is threatened, and so are the possibilities for continued expression and reproduction of this knowledge and the mode of production that it engenders.'"[79]

The Convention on Biological Diversity (CBD) recognizes traditional knowledge as central to in situ conservation of biological diversity and stipulates in Article 8(j) that each contracting party shall

> [s]ubject to its national legislation, respect, preserve and maintain knowledge, innovations and practices of indigenous and local communities embodying traditional lifestyles relevant for the conservation and sustainable use of biological diversity and promote their wider application with the approval and involvement of the holders of such knowledge, innovations and practices and encourage the equitable sharing of the benefits arising from the utilization of such knowledge, innovations and practices.[80]

---

[78] For a summary of this research please refer to Luisa Maffi, "Linguistic, Cultural and Biological Diversity," *Annual Review of Anthropology* 34 (2005), 599–617.

[79] Nancy Turner et al., "Traditional Ecological Knowledge and Wisdom of Aboriginal Peoples in British Columbia," *Ecological Applications* 10 (2000), 1276.

[80] The CBD was negotiated under the auspices of the United Nations Environment Programme (UNEP) and opened for signature in June 1992 at the UN Conference on Environment and Development, also known as the Earth Summit, it entered into force on December 29, 1993 and in 2014 it counts 193 member countries, including Canada and Mexico, but not the United States of America.

The Convention language from 1992 makes it clear that any wider application of traditional knowledge of indigenous peoples requires their approval, which today is reflected in the internationally recognized principle of PIC of indigenous peoples when it comes to access to their knowledge and also increasingly to their resources and lands. This has a clear jurisdictional element. Just like states claim national sovereignty over biological diversity, making access subject to their PIC, indigenous peoples equally control access to their traditional knowledge. They are recognized as the holders of that knowledge, which is under their control and not the control of the state.

The CBD and the other Rio Conventions, including the UN Framework Convention on Climate Change (UNFCCC), were adopted at the Earth Summit in Rio in 1992, and the CBD entered into force on December 29, 1993, just three days before NAFTA and the North American Agreement on Environmental Cooperation (NAAEC). Indigenous peoples have been actively engaged in the development of the international framework regarding biodiversity. The first Conferences of the Parties (COP) discussed, and COP 4 (May 1998, Bratislava, Slovakia) established, the Ad Hoc Open-ended Inter-Sessional Working Group on Article 8(j) and Related Provisions (Article 8(j) working group), mandated to address, *inter alia,* application and development of legal and other forms of protection of traditional knowledge, innovations, and practices.[81] The working group since has met biannually in each intersessional period, and indigenous representatives have participated in its proceedings on equal footing with state representatives, setting an important precedent for indigenous involvement in international environmental negotiations. Indigenous peoples have been participating actively in all elements of CBD work, including its work on access and benefit sharing (ABS), which developed in parallel with the work under the Article 8(j) working group. The Convention's work on ABS was also initiated at COP 4 when a regionally balanced expert panel on ABS was established, followed by the formal creation of a working group on ABS to develop guidelines and other approaches on PIC and mutually agreed terms (MAT), participation of stakeholders, benefit-sharing mechanisms, and the preservation of traditional knowledge.[82] Since ABS relates to access to genetic resources, parties recognized that traditional knowledge of indigenous peoples plays an important role in locating and fully understanding the properties of genetic resources. At the early stages of the negotiations, PIC was mainly discussed in terms of state PIC to access genetic resources within indigenous peoples' territory, but indigenous peoples asserted that indigenous PIC regarding access to traditional knowledge and associated genetic

---

[81] International Institute for Sustainable Development, "First Meeting of the Ad Hoc Open-Ended Inter-Sessional Working Group on Article 8(j)," *Earth Negotiations Bulletin* 9 (March 27, 2000), http://www.iisd.ca/download/asc/enb09144e.txt.

[82] International Institute for Sustainable Development, "Summary of the Sixth Meeting of the Working Group on Article 8(j) of the Convention on Biological Diversity: November 2–6, 2009," *Earth Negotiations Bulletin* 9 (Nov. 9, 2009), 2, http://www.iisd.ca/download/pdf/enb09482e.pdf.

resources would also be required. It took another decade to finally have indigenous PIC recognized in the Nagoya Protocol on Access to Genetic Resources and the Fair and Equitable Sharing of Benefits Arising from their Utilization ("Nagoya Protocol"), which entered into force in October 2014.[83] This never would have been possible without the full participation of indigenous representatives in the CBD and the increased awareness that indigenous knowledge is the key to locating and unlocking many of the properties of genetic resources,[84] based on the long-term interaction of indigenous peoples with their land and resources.

The Nagoya Protocol sets out specific obligations in relation to benefit-sharing and access to genetic resources and traditional knowledge associated with such resources, when the general commitment to fair and equitable benefit-sharing was already set out in the CBD and established as one of its objectives.[85]

As noted in the commentary on the Nagoya Protocol, it is the first international agreement to set out legally binding benefit-sharing obligations arising from the use of the traditional knowledge of indigenous peoples in research and development.[86] Morgera and Tsiumani note that

> [i]n that regard, the Nagoya Protocol makes reference to qualitatively different concept of benefit-sharing – namely, *intra*-State benefit-sharing as opposed to *inter*-State benefit-sharing discussed above. In other words, in the case of traditional knowledge, benefit-sharing makes reference to an internal, State-to-community contribution to sustainable development and equity.[87]

The international obligation to ensure benefit-sharing with indigenous peoples is in itself a recognition of the proprietary interests of indigenous peoples in their lands and resources. Even more so the international obligation to secure indigenous prior informed consent to access, as set out in the Nagoya Protocol in relation to access to traditional knowledge and also associated genetic resources,[88] recognizes indigenous

---

[83] Nagoya Protocol on Access to Genetic Resources and the Fair and Equitable Sharing of Benefits Arising from Their Utilization to the Convention on Biological Diversity, Oct. 29, 2010, U.N. Doc. UNEP/CBD/COP/10/27 (Jan. 20, 2011) [hereinafter Nagoya Protocol].

[84] See generally Suneetha M. Subramanian and Balakrishna Pisupati, eds., *Traditional Knowledge in Policy and Practice: Approaches to Development and Human Well-Being* (Tokyo: United Nations University Press, 2010); Manuel Ruiz and Ronnie Vernooy, eds., *The Custodians of Biodiversity: Sharing Access to and Benefits to Genetic Resources* (London: Earthscan, 2012).

[85] See generally Morten W. Tvedt and Tomme Young, *Beyond Access: Exploring Implementation of the Fair and Equitable Sharing Commitment in the CBD* (Gland, Switzerland: IUCN, 2007); Natalie Stoianoff, ed., *Accessing Biological Resources: Complying with the Convention on Biological Diversity* (The Hague: Kluwer Law International, 2004).

[86] Nagoya Protocol, Oct. 29, 2010, U.N. Doc. UNEP/CBD/COP/10/27 (Jan. 20, 2011), arts. 5(5), 7; Elisa Morgera et al., *Unraveling The Nagoya Protocol: A Commentary on the Nagoya Protocol on Access and Benefit-Sharing to the Convention on Biological Diversity* (The Netherlands: Brill Publishers 2014).

[87] Elisa Morgera and Elsa Tsioumani, "The Evolution of Benefit-Sharing: Linking Biodiversity and Community Livelihoods," *Review of European Community and International Environmental Law* 19 (2010), 150–51.

[88] Nagoya Protocol, Oct. 29, 2010, U.N. Doc. UNEP/CBD/COP/10/27 (Jan. 20, 2011), arts. 6, 7.

jurisdiction and control over their knowledge and resources. It is important that these rights be taken into account in international trade and also when making decisions regarding access and proposed developments.

6.2. *Indigenous Peoples' Participation in Implementation of the NAAEC*

Some commentators have argued that where the CBD creates a framework for protecting global biodiversity, the NAAEC strives to do the same for North American biodiversity, which is especially significant in light of the fact that the United States is not a party to the CBD, but it is bound by the NAAEC.[89]

While the NAAEC mentions neither biodiversity nor indigenous peoples, they are covered under its broad objectives: to foster the protection and improvement of the environment in the territories of the parties for the well-being of present and future generations, and promote sustainable development based on cooperation and mutually supportive environmental and economic policies. Even more so, indigenous peoples can play a key role in meeting the objectives, since they hold important intergenerational knowledge that is key to establishing baselines and protecting the environment, and also developed practices of sustainable development.

Looking at the substantive work on conservation, biological diversity, sustainable use, and benefit sharing under the CBD, the implementation of the NAAEC would equally benefit from the full and equal participation of indigenous peoples. It is fair to say that to date no similar processes and substantive arrangements for indigenous participation have been put into place, and as a result indigenous involvement in the work of the NAAEC has fluctuated considerably and not been as prevalent. This is not to say that the NAAEC has not recognized the important role that indigenous peoples have to play in ensuring sustainable development in North America.

Securing involvement of indigenous peoples in CEC work has been brought up several times since 1998 by the Joint Public Advisory Committee (JPAC) in their Advice to Council letters.[90] A General Recommendation from 2002 (ADV/02–11) sums up the general tenor of these expressions:

> Repeatedly, the need for efforts to engage indigenous peoples in the programs and projects of the CEC was raised. This is an issue that has preoccupied JPAC for some years and despite specific recommendations to Council, which they adopted

---

[89] Robert L. Glicksman, "The CEC's Biodiversity Conservation Agenda," in David L. Markell and John H. Knox (eds.), *Greening NAFTA: The North American Commission for Environmental Cooperation* (Stanford, Calif.: Stanford University Press, 2003), p. 60.

[90] Commission for Environmental Cooperation, Joint Public Advisory Committee (JPAC), Advice to Council 99–05, J/99–05/ADV/Rev. 1, *Expanding the Involvement of the North American Public, Including Indigenous Peoples in the Work of the Commission for Environmental Cooperation*; JPAC, Advice to Council 99–10, J/99–10/ADV/Rev.3, *Promoting the Involvement of Indigenous Peoples in the Work of the Commission for Environmental Cooperation*.

in their own statement, we see few concrete improvements. JPAC strongly urges Council to direct the Secretariat to improve this situation.[91]

The Recommendation specifically noted the divergence in terms of integration of indigenous knowledge in comparison to the CBD and recommended its full integration in the CEC work program:

> Nowhere in the program area (on biodiversity conservation) is there mention of either the importance or the need to work with indigenous knowledge, despite its integration into many United Nations processes and the explicit reference to it in the Convention on Biological Diversity. All projects in this program area should be assessed for how and where they could benefit from working with indigenous knowledge and adjusted accordingly.[92]

In 2003 a report was commissioned entitled *Participation of Indigenous Peoples in the CEC*, which emphasized that

> [t]he amount of territory under different forms of aboriginal jurisdiction is growing significantly, particularly in Canada. There, between 30 and 40 percent of the territory will be under some form of aboriginal management in the future (amounting to between 14 and 19 percent of the total area of North America).[93]

In 2004 JPAC issued a comprehensive recommendation under ADV/04–01 that notably recommended a commitment from Council to "to consistently appoint Indigenous Persons to the JPAC National and Governmental Advisory Committees (NAC and GAC)" and the creation and funding of a permanent position at the Secretariat to be staffed by an indigenous person in order to ensure indigenous involvement.[94]

In 2006, a response from Council suggested that it would discuss this at the next Joint JPAC-Council session,[95] but there was never any substantive implementation of the recommendations, which might explain the continued limited or lack of involvement of indigenous peoples in CEC work and lack of integration of indigenous knowledge into the work program. In CBD work the creation of permanent staff positions related to traditional knowledge and indigenous peoples has been demonstrated to result in increased indigenous involvement. So the CEC might want to reconsider these recommendations and take active steps to secure increased indigenous involvement.

---

[91] JPAC, Advice to Council 02–11, J/02–03/ADV/02–11/Rev.1, Commission for Environmental Cooperation Proposed Program Plan and Budget for 2003–2005.
[92] Ibid.
[93] John Reid, *Participation of Indigenous Peoples in the CEC*, submitted to the Secretariat of the Commission for Environmental Cooperation (2003), p. 1.
[94] JPAC, Advice to Council 04–01, Securing the Long-term Involvement of Indigenous Peoples in the Activities of the Commission for Environmental Cooperation.
[95] Letter from Judith Ayres, Alternate U.S. Representative to JPAC, June 23, 2006.

In addition to benefiting from indigenous involvement in CEC work, the special standing that indigenous peoples have in international law can lend more power or credence to NAAEC processes. Arguably, the NAAEC has suffered from a power imbalance vis-à-vis its (bigger) sister agreement, NAFTA, which contains many strong substantive provisions and enforcement mechanisms. Alleged violations of international trade agreements can lead to imposition of remedies, such as countervailing duties.

Indigenous rights have to be taken into account in international trade because they do not have just social, cultural, and environmental elements; they also have an economic dimension. As already established, indigenous peoples maintained their own sustainable economies prior to contact, and they have rights to continue those economies, which puts them in a powerful position when dealing with environmental issues, as well as proposed developments and access to their lands and resources.

As previously stated, the internationally recognized right to self-determination and the indigenous right to prior informed consent have a jurisdictional dimension. When states claim the right to prior informed consent to access, that means that they control access to the respective resources, and usually access requires going through processes administered by the competent national authority.

Similarly, where indigenous peoples have the right to prior informed consent, they control access to the respective knowledge and resources and have to be decision makers regarding access to them. Indigenous processes and procedures for implementing indigenous PIC should be based on indigenous laws and sui generis processes, since they constitute the essence of indigenous rights.

7. THE ECONOMIC DIMENSION OF INDIGENOUS RIGHTS

The case of indigenous peoples from the Interior of British Columbia, who asserted their indigenous land rights and jurisdiction over forestry resources in their territory as described in Section 3.4 of this chapter, is particularly interesting. The delays in the domestic courts previously described constitute evidence of a lack of effective domestic remedies given that the case has still not been to trial fifteen years after its initiation. Accordingly, the Secwepemc and Okanagan Nations took the issues raised in the logging cases that began in 1999 to international fora, bringing the issue of nonrecognition of Aboriginal title before the World Trade Organization (WTO) and NAFTA tribunals, after the Supreme Court of Canada had already rejected the extinguishment arguments of Canada and the provinces and maintained Aboriginal title in the *Delgamuukw* decision.[96] In all cases the independent indigenous

---

[96] Delgamuukw v. British Columbia, [1997] 3 SCR 1010.

submissions were accepted.[97] This not only recognized that indigenous rights have an economic dimension, but it also showed how indigenous peoples, whose rights have cultural, economic and environmental dimensions, can help bridge the so-called trade and environment divide.

The indigenous peoples in the Interior of British Columbia, who were making the submissions, depend on larger territories to sustain their people, since they have mixed-use economies, including hunting, fishing, and food gathering, while the coastal indigenous economies could accumulate substantive wealth centered around fish and aquatic resources. Hence, some of the largest territories belong to indigenous peoples in the Interior of British Columbia who have refused to negotiate modern land claims agreements with the federal and provincial government, because the Comprehensive Claims Policy underlying those negotiations fails to recognize Aboriginal title and rights. This policy has been found to violate international human rights standards by a number of UN human rights bodies.[98]

Unfortunately international human rights agreements, similar to MEAs, lack enforcement mechanisms, so indigenous peoples from the Interior of British Columbia decided to bring the failure to recognize their Aboriginal rights before international trade tribunals.

Failure to provide effective national remedies opens the way for direct complaints to international tribunals and human rights bodies. For example, the Hul'qumi'num Treaty Group was successful in proving the lack of effective national remedies in dealing with Aboriginal title in their complaint to the Inter-American Commission on Human Rights, supported by amicus submissions of the logging litigants, outlining the failure of the courts to address issues related to Aboriginal title in a timely and effective manner.[99]

---

[97] World Trade Organization (WTO), United States – Preliminary Determinations with Respect to Certain Softwood Lumber from Canada, WT/DS/236 (Apr. 15, 2002); WTO United States – Final Countervailing Duty Determination with Respect to Certain Softwood Lumber from Canada, WT/DS257/4 (Jan. 21, 2003); WTO, Appeal of the Decision in United States – Final Countervailing Duty Determination with Respect to Certain Softwood Lumber from Canada, WT/DS257/4 (Oct. 20, 2003).

[98] For example the UN Committee on Economic Social and Cultural Rights (CESCR) described their concerns in their concluding observations on Canada in 2006:

"16. The Committee, while noting that the State party has withdrawn, since 1998, the requirement for an express reference to extinguishment of Aboriginal rights and titles either in a comprehensive claim agreement or in the settlement legislation ratifying the agreement, remains concerned that the new approaches, namely the "modified rights model" and the "non-assertion model", do not differ much from the extinguishment and surrender approach. It further regrets not having received detailed information on other approaches based on recognition and coexistence of rights, which are currently under study."

[99] Inter-Am. Comm'n H.R., Report No. 105/09, Petition 529–07, Admissibility, Hul'qumi'num Treaty Group, Oct. 30, 2009, paras. 31–43, http://www.cidh.oas.org/annualrep/2009eng/Canada592.07eng.htm (last visited June 4, 2014).

Most of the timber and lumber harvested from the territories of indigenous peoples in the Interior of British Columbia is exported,[100] with softwood lumber constituting one of the largest export items from Canada to the United States. So indigenous leaders from the Interior of British Columbia decided to inform purchasers of softwood lumber, including U.S. consumers, that indigenous peoples had not been remunerated for the lumber taken from their territories.

At the same time, the long-standing U.S.–Canada Softwood Lumber dispute was reigniting in the early 2000s, with the U.S. lumber industry alleging that Canada's stumpage program did not ensure a fair market price was paid for harvesting softwood lumber, constituting a subsidy in violation of international trade law.[101] Indigenous peoples added to that equation that they have also not been remunerated for the lumber extracted from their territories. They pointed to Canada's Comprehensive Claims Policy as the vehicle for providing this additional subsidy, since it does not recognize Aboriginal title as an indigenous proprietary interest in land and resources and thus companies do not have to remunerate indigenous peoples.[102]

Indigenous peoples from the Interior of British Columbia became the first indigenous peoples ever to have made an independent submission to an international trade tribunal. In early 2002, the WTO tribunal hearing Canada's complaint against the U.S. preliminary countervailing duty determination officially accepted this indigenous submission.[103] In an unprecedented move they openly notified parties about their acceptance and asked the parties to the dispute and third parties to comment on the indigenous submissions. It was clear that the WTO was taking the submission seriously, since it was the first time they had to conceptualize around the proprietary interests of indigenous peoples in international trade disputes.

Quickly realizing the power of the arguments recognizing the economic dimension of Aboriginal title and rights, indigenous peoples from other parts of Canada, whose territories were also subject to softwood lumber extraction, joined the Interior Nations in their submissions before the WTO and NAFTA. Panels set up under Chapter 19 of NAFTA have experts nominated by the two disputing member parties. Nevertheless, the panel hearing the Softwood Lumber dispute opted to accept the independent indigenous submissions now submitted jointly by indigenous peoples

[100] For more information about the Canadian Softwood Lumber industry, see Government of Canada, Statistics Canada, *Manufacturing at a Glance: The Canadian Lumber Industry, 2003 to 2012* (2013), http://www.statcan.gc.ca/daily-quotidien/131112/dq131112a-eng.htm (last visited June 4, 2014).
[101] Richard Herring, *Decision Memorandum on New Subsidy Allegations: Certain Softwood Lumber Products from Canada to Melissa Skinner* (Washington, D.C.: Office of AD/CVD Enforcement IV, 2001).
[102] Interior Alliance, Independent Indigenous Submission to WTO Tribunal considering Preliminary Determinations with Respect to Certain Softwood Lumber from Canada, WT/DS 236 (2002) (unpublished).
[103] WTO, United States – Preliminary Determinations with Respect to Certain Softwood Lumber from Canada, Report of the Panel, WT/DS 236/R (November 1, 2002), para 7.2.

from across Canada under the umbrella of the Indigenous Network on Economies and Trade (INET). This was despite the arduous opposition of Canada,[104] focusing mainly on their assertion of sovereignty and exclusive control over lands and resources. The acceptance[105] of the independent indigenous submissions, in light of these arguments, was a recognition that indigenous rights have to be taken into account when it comes to international trade, and indigenous peoples have to be part of decision making regarding access to their lands and resources. Failure to do so can result in economic uncertainty for investors and potentially even international trade remedies.

At the height of the U.S. countervailing duty investigation and the U.S.–Canada Softwood Lumber dispute, billions had been collected in countervailing duties against Canadian exports. While the U.S. industry wanted to ensure that these monies were not returned to the Canadian industry, which they argued had been subsidized, they indicated readiness to share some of these monies with indigenous peoples in Canada who had not been remunerated for the lumber extracted from their territories.[106] In the end this was precluded by the U.S.–Canada Softwood Lumber agreement,[107] but indigenous peoples still had succeeded in raising increased awareness about indigenous proprietary interests in the international market place.

8. CONCLUSION

Indigenous proprietary interests, combined with increased international recognition of indigenous rights to control access to their lands and resources, make indigenous peoples important subjects of international law, ranging from international human rights to environmental and international trade law. Indigenous peoples may indeed hold the key to securing sustainable development in North America. Indigenous knowledge contains the most long-term data about different ecosystems in North America, which can be built on to ensure more environmentally, socially, and economically sustainable development. At the same time, investments will only be secure in the long term if indigenous rights are properly taken into account. This was further underlined by the recent Supreme Court of Canada in *Tsilhqot'in v.*

---

[104] Weil, Gotshal, & Manges LLP, Washington, D.C., Joint Opposition of Canadian Parties to the Motions of the Indigenous Network on Economies and Trade and the Natural Resources Defense Council for Leave to Participate as Amicus Curiae, November 25, 2002.

[105] *In the matter of Certain Softwood Lumber Products from Canada: Final Affirmative Countervailing Duty Determination*, Order granting the motion of leave to participate as amicus curiae on behalf of INET, Secretariat File No. USA-CDA-2002–1904–03, NAFTA Article 19.04 Binational Panel Review (Mar. 5, 2003).

[106] Memorandum, Update on the Softwood Lumber Agreement to Indigenous Nations under INET (2004) (unpublished), p. 5.

[107] Softwood Lumber Agreement Between the Government of Canada and the Government of The United States Of America, U.S.-Can., Sept. 12, 2006, E105072, http://www.treaty-accord.gc.ca/text-texte.aspx?id=105072&lang=eng (last visited June 4, 2014).

British Columbia, discussed in Section 3.3, which recognized Aboriginal title based on a territorial approach and also reminded investors and governments that they should seek the consent of indigenous peoples prior to accessing their lands and resources as the only way to secure economic and legal certainty.[108] This requires recognition of Aboriginal title on the ground. Furthermore, the case of indigenous peoples from the Interior of British Columbia who asserted their indigenous land rights and jurisdiction over forestry resources in their territory is an important case that could set important precedent for international recognition of indigenous rights. By bringing the issue of the Canadian government's failure to recognize their land rights before WTO and NAFTA tribunals in the U.S.–Canada Softwood Lumber dispute, and having their independent indigenous submissions accepted in all cases, they have already established that indigenous rights have an economic dimension and have to be taken into account in international trade law.

Finally indigenous peoples are in the best position to bridge, and in many ways already are bridging, the so-called trade and environment divide by asserting and implementing their rights, which have cultural, economic, and environmental dimensions.

---

[108] *Tsilhqot'in v. British Columbia*, 2014 SCC 44.

Climate Change, Sustainable Development, and NAFTA

Regional Policy Harmonization as a Basis for Sustainable Development

Freedom-Kai Phillips

1. INTRODUCTION

Climate change has emerged as an increasingly prevalent threat globally. Although NAFTA Parties are employing individual policy measures domestically, the NAAEC has the additional potential to assist Parties in combating climate change together in a comprehensive and efficient manner. Capitalizing on the experience of the European Union, NAFTA Parties have an opportunity to integrate their individual climate change strategies. By leveraging lessons learned, Parties can collectively increase policy effectiveness and decrease costs of implementation.

While the formal integration of Canada, Mexico, and the United States through the North American Free Trade Agreement (NAFTA)[1] has brought many benefits, principally economic prosperity and political cooperation, it has not led to growth in regional environmental protection measures. With the effects of global warming becoming increasing apparent, the opportunity has become ripe for a reevaluation of the initial political compromises around environmental measures made at the onset of the NAFTA accord. This chapter puts forward policy recommendations to enhance harmonization of regional climate change mitigation measures through the legal framework established under NAFTA as an aspect of a broader sustainable development policy.

First, this chapter analyzes how environmental issues are incorporated into NAFTA and the North American Agreement on Environmental Cooperation (NAAEC) in order to develop policy recommendations, with a particular focus on how climate change is influencing decision makers. Second, it outlines the process Parties use to address the issue of climate change in relation to sustainable

---

[1] North American Free Trade Agreement between the Government of the United States of America, the Government of Canada and the Government of the United Mexican States, San Antonio, December 17, 1992, in force January 1, 1994, (1993) 32 ILM 296; Can TS 1994 No 2.

development, with attention to the shortcomings of the programs employed. Finally, it discusses strategies used successfully in the European Union (EU) and applies them to the NAFTA context to lay out pragmatic steps to address climate change as an aspect of sustainable development strategic planning. Ultimately, NAFTA Parties have a unique opportunity to systematically respond to climate change by capitalizing on institutional framework established through the NAAEC.

2. NAFTA, THE ENVIRONMENT, AND CLIMATE CHANGE IN NORTH AMERICA

Free trade initiatives have historically raised many fears for the environmentally minded, with many arguing that environmental concerns are allowed to play a subordinate role to market liberalization.[2] Although the early stages of NAFTA negotiations were criticized for this reason, the final accord and subsequent side agreement on environmental cooperation – the NAAEC – have proven to be a resilient compromise between the divergent interests of the Parties.

This section summarizes NAFTA's environmental potential by first outlining the NAFTA accord with a focus on sections of environmental significance. Second, it discusses the NAAEC and the role of the Commission for Environmental Cooperation (CEC). Finally, it reviews the current state of the environment in North America, aiming to illustrate the necessity of immediate action. On the whole, NAFTA has laid a flexible framework to empower Parties to collectively harmonize mitigation and adaptation measures to address climate change as part of broader sustainable development efforts.

2.1. *NAFTA's Environmental Obligations*

NAFTA is an example of parallel yet interdependent integration in relation to sustainable development, with the core trade agreement complementing parallel agreements on labor and the environment.[3] Proponents of free trade have dubbed NAFTA the "greenest trade agreement on record."[4] I do not disagree with such views, as I recognize the complex nature of negotiated agreements as a whole and the difficulties faced by the Parties in achieving more robust environmental standards. The few

---

[2] Ian Sheldon, "Trade and Environment Policy: A Race to the Bottom?" (2006) 57:3 *Journal of Agricultural Economics* 365–392, http://aede.osu.edu/sites/aede/files/publication_files/Trade%20and%20Environmental%20Policy.pdf.

[3] Marie-Claire Cordonier Segger and Ashfaq Khalfan, *Sustainable Development Law: Principles, Practices and Prospects* (Oxford: Oxford University Press, 2004) at 103–107, 195.

[4] Greg Block, "Trade and Environment in the Western Hemisphere: expanding the North American Agreement on Environmental Cooperation into the Americas" (2003) 33 *Environmental Law* 501–546 at 503.

references to the environment in the final accord are a testament to two major issues at play. First, the United States and Canada were highly influential in the overall negotiations. Were it not for their collective pressure, the trade and environment debate would not have occurred whatsoever. Second, and arguably more important, was the need for Mexican economic liberalization and the willingness of the Mexican government to accept environmental obligations as the price of concluding the trade agreement. The allure of a rapid injection of foreign capital into the Mexican market was the basis of the ultimate compromise, rather than a truly altruistic environmental agenda on the part of the Mexican Government.[5] Therefore, although NAFTA is principally a trade agreement, the final accord has numerous explicit and implicit environmental and sustainable development references.

2.1.1. Preamble

While the incorporation of environmental elements into NAFTA was a political compromise, they appear throughout the preamble. As an underlying influence, the goals of economic integration and trade liberalization are to be accomplished "in a manner consistent with environmental protection and conservation." Moreover, the NAFTA framework is aimed at promoting "sustainable development," preserving domestic flexibility to "safeguard the public welfare," and "strengthen[ing] the development and enforcement of environmental laws and regulations."[6] Environmental considerations became a fundamental element of the NAFTA regime despite the underlying motivations of the Parties.[7]

2.1.2. Empowering Parties to Protect Human Health, Safety, and the Environment

Chapters 7 and 9 of NAFTA give Parties the ability to address issues affecting human health, safety, and the environment. First, Parties can determine their own levels of protection for health, safety, and the environment.[8] This section acknowledges varying levels of development among Canada, Mexico, and the United States and emphasizes national sovereignty to account for the differences. Second, although NAFTA encourages Parties to use international standards as reference points, nothing in the agreement hinders a Party pursuing a legitimate objective from "adopting, maintaining or applying" a more rigorous standard if the result is greater

---

[5] Gustavo Alanis-Ortega and Ana Karina González-Lutzenkirchen, "No Room for the Environment: The NAFTA Negotiations and the Mexican Perspective on Trade and the Environment," in Carolyn L. Deere and Daniel C. Esty (eds.), *Greening the Americas: NAFTA's Lessons for Hemispheric Trade* (Cambridge Mass.: MIT Press, 2002) 41–60.

[6] NAFTA, Preamble.

[7] Cordonier Segger and Khalfan, *Sustainable Development Law*, p. 196.

[8] NAFTA, Article 713(1).

environmental protection.[9] This flexibility allows Parties to pursue increased levels of domestic environmental protection rather than being bound to a single standard.

Third, Parties are able to conduct a scientific and technical risk assessment prior to importation to ensure that social and environmental standards are not compromised. Moreover, if scientific data are insufficient to ensure compliance with domestic environmental standards, Parties may install temporary trade-restrictive protective measures until sufficient data are available.[10] Unique to NAFTA, this precautionary clause allows states to preemptively ensure that materials are safe prior to importation, in stark contrast to the General Agreement on Trade and Tariffs (GATT),[11] which requires states to provide scientific evidence to justify a restriction on trade. Lastly, Parties are able to impose particular environmental requirements on investor activity to ensure that a given project is pursued in an environmentally sensitive manner.[12] Furthermore, Parties are restricted from lowering their domestic environmental standards to encourage investment.[13] Cumulatively, NAFTA's provisions do not undermine the domestic environmental standards of Parties. In comparison to other trade regimes – notably the World Trade Organization (WTO) – NAFTA affords Parties a higher level of domestic deference, allowing for substantially less legal conflict over acceptable environmental protection standards.

2.1.3. Multilateral Environmental Agreements and GATT Exceptions

Beyond formal empowerment clauses, NAFTA has two further aspects of particular importance for the environment. First, NAFTA is granted precedence over other international trade agreements, including the GATT, with the particular exception of multilateral environmental agreements (MEAs).[14] MEAs are granted a special role in relation to NAFTA. Parties recognized the importance of allowing for the incorporation of trade-related measures into an MEA as a means of ensuring compliance, to ensure trade liberalization does not trump environmental protection.[15] Second, although NAFTA takes precedence over GATT obligations, the environmental exception clauses found in GATT Article XX are explicitly incorporated into the agreement.[16] This ensures that Parties are not prevented from pursuing legitimate environmental policies that violate international trade principles – namely

---

[9] NAFTA, Article 905(3).

[10] NAFTA, Article 907(3).

[11] *General Agreement on Tariffs and Trade*, October 30, 1947, 58 U.N.T.S. 187, Can. T.S. 1947 No. 27 (entered into force January 1, 1948), Article XX.

[12] NAFTA, Article 1114(1).

[13] NAFTA, Article 1114(2).

[14] NAFTA, Articles 103 and 104.

[15] Gary C. Hufbauer and Jeffrey J. Schott, *NAFTA Revisited: Achievements and Challenges* (Washington, DC: Institute for International Economics, 2005) at 155.

[16] NAFTA Article 2101.

most favored nation (MFN) status and national treatment – provided that they are drafted and applied in a manner consistent with principles of trade law.

2.2. NAAEC and the Role of the Commission for Environmental Cooperation (CEC)

Resulting primarily from American congressional pressure to ensure that NAFTA would not result in large-scale capital flight or a "race to the bottom,"[17] rather than from true concern for environmental integrity, the NAAEC was forged to stabilize environmental standards while ensuring continued environmental dialogue and harmonization of environmental governance.[18] Regardless of the original intentions or motivations underlying its drafting, the incorporation of a formal *agreement* on the environment into a trade pact was a noteworthy accomplishment. The NAAEC aims to accomplish three main goals: (1) expand and enhance environmental standards while supporting sustainable development through cooperative initiatives; (2) enhance environmental compliance, transparency, and public participation; and (3) avoid environmentally based barriers to trade and mediate disputes.[19] Furthermore, it creates a trilateral forum for collective environmental improvement and enforcement.[20] These goals are to be accomplished through the creation of an institutional framework and dispute settlement process under the CEC. The CEC is comprised of a Council of Ministers, a Secretariat, and a Joint Public Advisory Committee (JPAC),[21] each of which will be outlined in the following. Finally, a segment will also be devoted to the environmental dispute settlement process set in place by the NAAEC.

2.2.1. Council of Ministers

The Council of Ministers is made up of "cabinet-level or equivalent representatives" from each of the Member States, who meet annually or at specially convened sessions to conduct business.[22] Acting as the governing body of the CEC, the Council has broad oversight functions, including approving the annual budget,[23] promoting environmental cooperation between the Parties,[24] and addressing any interpretive or

[17] Hufbauer and Schott, *NAFTA Revisited*, p. 157.
[18] Marie-Claire Cordonier Segger et al., *Ecological Rules and Sustainability in the Americas* (Winnipeg, Canada: IISD, 2002), p. 38.
[19] North American Agreement on Environmental Cooperation, September 14, 1993, in force January 1, 1994, (1993) 32 ILM 1480; Can TS 1994 No 3, Article 1.
[20] Ignacia S. Moreno et al., "Free Trade and the Environment: The NAFTA, the NAAEC and the implications for the Future" (1999) 12 *Tulane Environmental Law Journal* 405–478 at 422.
[21] NAAEC, Article 8(2).
[22] NAAEC, Articles 9(1)–(3).
[23] NAAEC, Article 10(1)(e).
[24] NAAEC, Article 10(1)(f).

functional questions that may arise during the implementation of the agreement.[25] Furthermore, the Council may make recommendations on numerous other areas including data gathering and analysis, pollution prevention strategies, environmental reporting standards, the use of financial instruments to support environmental goals, scientific and technical research development, strategies for raising public awareness, transboundary environmental pollution, strategies for the protection of various species and their habitats, environmental preparedness, environmental training and development, ecolabeling, and any other matters it deems necessary to address.[26] On the whole, the Council acts as a forum for high-level discussions, strategic planning, and intergovernmental and institutional cooperation pertaining to environmental concerns.

2.2.2. The Secretariat

If the Council is the brain of the CEC, then its body is most assuredly the Secretariat. A permanent institution based in Montreal, Canada, the Secretariat's primary focus is to act in a "technical, operational and administrative" capacity that supports the actions of the Council,[27] and to publish an annual report on the Council's activities.[28] Beyond its support role, the Secretariat also has an independent reporting function. First, it has a modest investigative role that allows for the publication of an expert report on any aspect relating to the cooperative components of the agreement, excluding matters relating to the failure of a Party to enforce domestic environmental standards.[29] Second, the Secretariat reviews complaints by members of civil society such as nongovernmental organizations (NGOs) and individual citizens about a Party's failure to adequately enforce its domestic environmental obligations.[30] Finally, the Secretariat can create and maintain a factual record, when instructed by the Council, of environmental complaints against the Parties.[31] It must be noted that these functions, other than the annual report, require a two-thirds majority vote to allow the Secretariat to proceed.

2.2.3. Joint Public Advisory Committee

A novel element of the NAAEC is the JPAC, comprised of fifteen members appointed in equal numbers by each Party from its National Advisory Committees.[32] In practice,

---

[25] NAAEC, Article 10(1)(d).
[26] NAAEC, Articles 10(2)(a)–(s).
[27] NAAEC, Article 11(5).
[28] NAAEC, Article 12.
[29] NAAEC, Article 13.
[30] NAAEC, Article 14.
[31] NAAEC, Article 15.
[32] NAAEC, Article 16(1).

JPAC is made up entirely of civil society representatives[33] and may offer advice to the Council on any subject under the scope of the agreement.[34] Furthermore, JPAC supports the Secretariat by providing relevant technical or scientific information when considering the creation of a factual record.[35] Functionally, the role of JPAC is to ensure active, informed, and competent public participation in the decision-making process and to facilitate public access to information.

2.2.4. Environmental Dispute Settlement Procedure

The NAAEC also has an environmental dispute settlement procedure incorporated into the agreement that allows any Party to file a written request for a consultation with another Party regarding that Party's repeated failure to enforce domestic environmental laws.[36] If these consultations are fruitless, a special session of the Council may be convened to discuss the matter further.[37] Again, if this does not resolve the matter adequately, the Council may convene an arbitral panel[38] composed of five members[39] selected from a standing roster of forty-five experts in environmental law or international trade disputes.[40]

Following its formation, the panel reviews the arguments put forward by the Parties, along with any relevant expert material. It submits a written report to the Parties within 180 days, outlining findings of fact, the judgment, and, if necessary, recommendations to resolve the dispute.[41] Within sixty days of the judgment, the report must be submitted to the Council along with a mutually agreed-upon action plan from the Parties to implement the Panel's recommendations.[42] Lastly, within 180 days of the Panel's findings, a Party may request a Panel to be reconvened to determine if the previously agreed-upon action plan was implemented adequately.[43]

It must be noted that although superficially this dispute settlement process seems quite robust, its utility is in fact limited by its scope and strength. First, the dispute must be related to the enforcement of environmental law as it relates to production of goods or services for trade between the Parties.[44] A notable exclusion from the definition of "environmental law" employed in the NAAEC agreement relates to

---

[33] NAAEC, Article 17. See http://www.cec.org/Page.asp?PageID=1226&SiteNodeID=208&BL_Expand ID=567.
[34] NAAEC, Article 16(4).
[35] NAAEC, Article 16(5).
[36] NAAEC, Article 22(1).
[37] NAAEC, Article 23.
[38] NAAEC, Article 24.
[39] NAAEC, Article 27(1)(a).
[40] NAAEC, Article 25.
[41] NAAEC, Article 31(2).
[42] NAAEC, Articles 32–33.
[43] NAAEC, Article 35.
[44] NAAEC, Article 24(1)(a).

extraction of natural resources.[45] Thus, many of the extraction methods that may have the worst environmental effects are outside the scope of inquiry. Second, if the panel awards a monetary penalty for environmental breach, it is paid to the Commission and then dispersed at the Council's discretion to enhance environmental enforcement in the deviant state.[46] Ultimately, these two shortcomings fundamentally limit the ability of Parties to deter environmentally detrimental action in another jurisdiction.

2.3. *Current State of Climate Change and Sustainable Development in North America*

Climate change and its impacts are no longer a matter of mainstream debate among policy makers and scientists.[47] As average global air and ocean temperatures rise, global warming's many risks to health, agricultural yields, and economic stability are amplified. In particular, experts have found problematic trends demonstrating that climate change has begun to redistribute global flows of fresh water,[48] undermine ecosystem integrity,[49] and increase vulnerability to extreme weather patterns.[50] Most pressingly, North America's disproportionately high contribution of global greenhouse gas (GHG) emissions must be reduced.

North America has the highest emissions levels in the world, with only seven percent of the global population but a quarter of total global emissions.[51] In per capita terms, Canada (22.8 tCO_2) and the United States (22.22 tCO_2) emit substantially higher levels of GHGs in comparison to Mexico (5.42 tCO_2).[52] In terms of an equitable distribution of implementation costs of a climate change adaptation, Canada and the United States will need to shoulder a considerable portion of the strategic and economic burden.[53] With the estimated cost of climate change in Canada proposed to grow from roughly $5 billion annually in 2020 to between

---

[45] NAAEC, Article 45(2)(b).

[46] NAAEC, Annex 34(3).

[47] Intergovernmental Panel on Climate Change, *Synthesis Report: An Assessment of the Intergovernmental Panel on Climate Change* (Cambridge, UK: Cambridge University Press, 2007), p. 30.

[48] United Nations Development Program, *Human Development Report 2007/2008 – Fighting Climate Change: Human Solidarity in a Divided World* (New York: United Nations, 2008), p. 94.

[49] UNDP, Human Development Report, p. 101.

[50] UNDP, Human Development Report, p. 98.

[51] Commission for Environmental Cooperation, *The North American Mosaic: an Overview of Key Environmental Issues* (June 2008), p. 8, http://www.cec.org/files/PDF//Mosaic-2008_en.pdf.

[52] United Nations, "Environmental Indicators: GHGs" Department of Economic and Social Affairs, (July 2010), http://unstats.un.org/unsd/environment/excel_file_tables/2010/GHG.xls.

[53] Henry Shue, "Subsistence Emissions and Luxury Emissions," (1993) 15 *Law & Policy* 39–59; Henry Shue, "Global Environment and International Inequality," (1999) 75 *International Affairs* 531–45; and Henry Shue, "Deadly Delays, Saving Opportunities: Creating a More Dangerous World?" in Stephen M. Gardiner, Simon Caney, Dale Jamieson, and Henry Shue (eds.), *Climate Ethics* (Oxford: Oxford University Press, 2010).

$21 and 43 billion by the 2050s,[54] political apathy is no longer an acceptable course of action.

A majority of North America's GHG emissions stem from two major sources. First, the conversion of fossil fuels into electricity for commercial purposes is the single largest contributor of GHGs, amounting for over half of North America's total share.[55] Second, and closely related, is the dominant role played by the highly energy dependant transport sector.[56] Both of these sectors need transformation through the use of available technological alternatives, collaboration, and focused research to mitigate their respective impact. Increased periods of sustained heat and rain have amplified the likelihood of wildfires[57] and waterborne disease,[58] put increased pressure on water systems,[59] and heightened the risk of vector-borne infectious diseases such as the West Nile virus.[60] These risks are particularly acute in Mexico where geography and infrastructural limitations decrease the government's ability to combat these concerns.

Climate change and sustainable development intersect under the United Nations Framework on Climate Change (UNFCCC) and the Kyoto Protocol, via the Clean Development Mechanism (CDM) and various supporting funds.[61] Despite this intersection, access to key tools for adaptation and mitigation is limited. As a result, NAFTA Parties lack the tools necessary to address increased environmental threats.[62] Regardless of the current economic difficulties associated with large-scale adjustment of the energy and transport sectors, long-term social, economic, and political costs will prove to be far more substantial if little is done. Integration of decision-making powers and coordination of national climate change policies is a worthwhile starting point, following Mexico's experience with the Intersecretarial Climate Change Commission (ICCC).[63] More broadly, Canada and the U.S.

---

[54] National Round Table on the Environment and the Economy (Canada), *Paying the Price: The Economic Impact of Climate Change in Canada* (National Round Table on the Environment and the Economy, 2011), p. 15, http://collectionscanada.gc.ca/webarchives2/20130322143132/http://nrtee-trnee .ca/wp-content/uploads/2011/09/paying-the-price.pdf.

[55] CEC, "North American Mosaic," p. 9.

[56] CEC, Destination Sustainability Reducing: Greenhouse Gas Emissions from Freight Transportation in North America, (CEC:2011), p. 23, http://www3.cec.org/islandora/en/item/4237-destination-sustainability-reducing-greenhouse-gas-emissions-from-freight-en.pdf.

[57] CEC, "North American Mosaic," p. 10.

[58] UNDP, *Human Development Report*, p. 106.

[59] UNDP, *Human Development Report*, p. 95.

[60] UNDP, *Human Development Report*, p. 106.

[61] Nathan E. Hultman, et al. "How Can the Clean Development Mechanism Better Contribute to Sustainable Development?" (2009) 38:2 *Ambio* 120.

[62] Duncan A. French, "Climate Change Law: Narrowing the Focus, Broadening the Debate," in Marie-Claire Cordonier Segger and C.G. Weeramantry (eds.), *Sustainable Justice: Reconciling Economic, Social and Environmental Law* (Leiden, Netherlands: Martinus Nijhoff Publishers, 2005) 273–283, pp. 275–279.

[63] Note: UNDP refers to this as the Interministerial Commission on Climate Change as that is the English translation, but the Mexican Government refers to it as the Intersecretarial Commission on Climate Change. For ease and consistency I will use the Mexican Government form. Arnoldo

have also begun to harmonize policies on fuel quality and motor vehicle efficiency. However, more than mere integration at the national level and limited international harmonization is needed. A clear climate change policy must be outlined and implemented nationally and harmonized among all NAFTA Parties. Without such a framework, progress will be inefficient at best and counterproductive at worst.

3. NATIONAL POLICIES TO ADDRESS CLIMATE CHANGE ACROSS NAFTA

Climate change has been on the collective political radar of NAFTA Parties for over two decades. However, little has been done to combat the increased threat posed by the continued degradation of the earth's climate. In fact, efforts to combat climate change have lost ground: the U.S. decision not to ratify the Kyoto Protocol also spurred Canada's abandonment of the process. These decisions are unfortunate in view of both countries' roles in NAFTA.[64] Observers may be led to the conclusion that the two largest collective emitters in the hemisphere are actively working against comprehensive climate policy. Again, this would also be a misrepresentation of the facts. NAFTA Parties are each implementing their own domestic responses to climate change with only varying degrees of harmonization. This section will outline the current climate policies utilized by NAFTA Parties, beginning with Canada, followed by the United States, and concluding with Mexico, and will focus on the various shortcomings found in these strategies.

3.1. *Canada and the Climate Question*

The government of Canada, under increased domestic as well as international pressure to respond to the issue, released a climate change initiative aimed at drastically decreasing the country's contribution to global GHG emissions. Over 2007–08 the Canadian national plan was outlined in "Turning the Corner: An Action Plan to Reduce Greenhouse Gases and Air Pollution"[65] and "Turning the Corner: Regulatory Framework for Industrial Greenhouse Gas Emissions," which modified the earlier plan in relation to industrial emissions.[66] Following the change in leadership of the Ministry of the Environment in 2008, there have been no further refinements to this plan.

Matus Kramer, "Adaptation to Climate Change in Poverty Reduction Strategies" (UNDP Human Development Report Occasional Paper, New York: United Nations, 2007), p. 15.

[64] D. Ljunggren, "Canada faces U.N. grilling over Kyoto abandonment," *Reuters*, November 12, 2006, http://uk.reuters.com/article/2006/11/13/science-environment-canada-dc-idUKN10223 729 2006 1113.

[65] Government of Canada, "Turning the Corner: An Action Plan to Reduce Greenhouse Gases and Air Pollution" (April 2007), http://www.centreforenergy.com/documents/presentations/PCEForums/Day2/LuncheonAddress/KendallWoo.pdf.

[66] Government of Canada, "Turning the Corner: Regulatory Framework for Industrial Greenhouse Gas Emissions" (March 2008), Environment Canada http://www.propanefacts.ca/upload/reports/RegulatoryFramework_GGM_March08.pdf. [Turning the Corner 2008]

The National Plan committed Canada to a formal reduction of total GHG emissions, in relation to 2006 levels, of 20 percent by 2020 and between 60 and 70 percent by 2050.[67] Although it suggests the incorporation of a mandatory fuel efficiency standard by model year 2011,[68] the proposal is aimed almost exclusively at industrial emissions. This includes the following sectors: electricity generation, oil and gas, pulp and paper, iron and steel, iron ore pelletizing, smelting and refining, cement, lime, potash, and chemicals and fertilizer.[69] Within each sector, existing facilities are required to reduce emission intensity by 18 percent below the 2006 baseline by the beginning of 2010, with a subsequent 2 percent reduction in every year following.[70] New facilities – coming into operation in 2004 or later – will be granted a three-year grace period, after which they too must reduce emission levels by 2 percent annually.[71] This emission intensity mechanism is also used in Alberta, the only province with emissions reduction legislation that is binding on large emitters.[72]

While targets were not established for "fixed process" emissions or a cleaner fuel standard,[73] a broad array of compliance mechanisms has also been integrated into the system to ease conformity with the proposed targets. First, a domestic offset system has been established. This system is designed to issue credits for "verified domestic reductions or removals" of GHG and is intended to provide a level of flexibility to the participating sectors, allowing them to invest in an offset program if facility reductions fall short of annual targets.[74] Once a system for cross-border emissions trading with the U.S. has been established, these projects will also be granted consideration. Second, emission credits may also be gained by investing in a CDM as defined under the Kyoto Protocol.[75] However, the total credit allowance that can be gained from CDM investment is capped at 10 percent to ensure that the program is not abused and that GHG reductions are primarily occurring domestically.[76] Third, firms that have been proactively addressing the climate change question over the past decade may be eligible for a onetime 15Mt "early action" bonus, which may be either banked or traded on the free market;[77] in Canada that means trading them on the Montréal Climate Exchange (MCeX), the only operating voluntary emission

---

[67] Ibid., 1.
[68] Ibid.
[69] Ibid., 2.
[70] Ibid., 7.
[71] Ibid., 3.
[72] Gary E. Taylor and Michael R Barrett, "Canada's Experience in Emissions Trading and Related Legal Issues," in David Freestone and Charlotte Streck (eds.), *Legal Aspects of Carbon Trading: Kyoto, Copenhagen and Beyond* (Oxford: Oxford University Press, 2009) 469–487, p. 469.
[73] Taylor and Barrett, "Canada's Experience," p. 473.
[74] Government of Canada, "Turning the Corner 2008," 17.
[75] Ibid., 18; Kyoto Protocol to the United Nations Framework Convention on Climate Change, December 11, 1997, 2303 UNTS 148, 37 ILM 22 (entered into force February 16, 2005), Article 12.
[76] Government of Canada, "Turning the Corner 2008," 18.
[77] Ibid.

trading regime.[78] Eligibility requirements seem unexpectedly low for such a large bonus, with firms required to incrementally reduce any of the accepted GHGs in a continuous fashion starting any time from 1992 to 2006.[79] Last, the establishment of a national technology fund will allow participating firms to meet a portion of their annual regulatory obligations by contributing to the fund.[80] The capital in the fund will then be used to invest in eligible GHG reduction technologies, providing the dual benefit of reducing domestic GHG levels while disseminating new technologies across sectors. Each compliance mechanism has a role to play in transitioning otherwise high-emission sectors into competitive yet environmentally conscious industries in a cost-effective manner.

Three Canadian provinces have also implemented climate change response plans: Alberta, Ontario, and British Columbia. Alberta passed the Climate Change and Emissions Management Act (CCEMA), which sets in place emission intensity reduction targets of 50 percent below 1990 levels.[81] The first compliance period saw 5.7 million tonnes of CO_2 offset, using a mixture of fund credits, internal offset programs, and performance credits.[82] Ontario set out emissions reduction targets in "Go Green, Ontario's Action Plan on Climate Change" as: 6 percent below 1990 GHG levels by 2014, 15 percent below 1990 GHG levels by 2020, and 80 percent below 1990 GHG levels by 2050.[83] Further, in 2008 Ontario and Quebec signed a Memorandum of Understanding (MoU) to establish a territorial hard cap-and-trade program, which could grow to include Manitoba and British Columbia through the Western Climate Initiative (WCI) north of the border and a California-led seven-state collective south of the border.[84] Last, British Columbia through its work with the WCI-set emissions reduction targets in the Greenhouse Gas Reduction Targets Act as: 33 percent below 2007 GHG levels by 2020 and 80 percent below 2007 GHG levels by 2050.[85] In 2008 British Columbia created a carbon tax,[86] established a proposed framework for a market-based cap-and-trade platform,[87] and passed legislation introducing a low-carbon fuel standard.[88]

Although the aforementioned framework seems initially promising, it contains shortcomings. First, its scope is limited to industry, and nonindustrial sectors –

[78] See Montréal Climate Exchange, http://www.mcex.ca/aboutGhg_canCarbonMarket_en.
[79] Government of Canada, "Turning the Corner 2008," 19.
[80] Ibid., 14–16.
[81] Climate Change and Emissions Management Act, SA 2003, c C-16.7, s 3.
[82] Taylor and Barrett, "Canada's Experience," p. 478.
[83] Province of Ontario, "Go Green, Ontario's Action Plan on Climate Change" (August 2007), p. 6, http://www.ene.gov.on.ca/stdprodconsume/groups/lr/@ene/@resources/documents/resource/stdo1_079169.pdf.
[84] Taylor and Barrett, "Canada's Experience," p. 479.
[85] Greenhouse Gas Reduction Targets Act, SBC 2007, c 42, s 2.
[86] Carbon Tax Act, SBC 2008, c 40.
[87] Greenhouse Gas Reduction (Cap and Trade) Act, SBC 2008, c 32.
[88] Greenhouse Gas Reduction (Renewable Energy and Low Carbon Fuel Requirements) Act, SBC 2008, c 16.

particularly transport and household emissions – must be incorporated to maximize GHG reductions. Second, the use of a 2006 GHG baseline is particularly troubling, as the Kyoto Protocol uses 1990 GHG levels – although it must be noted that Ontario and Quebec both use 1990 baselines independent of federal legislation.[89] By setting a reduction target of 20 percent below 2006 levels (721 Mt)[90] rather than below 1990 levels (592 Mt),[91] this presents a distorted view of Canada's GHG reduction efforts with regard to quantity or timing.[92] Third, the use of "emission intensity" as both a federal and provincial (Alberta) standard of measurement for industry reductions, rather than "total emissions" (Ontario and BC) is problematic. "Total emissions" is a straightforward measure for the total amount of GHGs put into the atmosphere in any given year, while emission intensity is the measure of total GHG emissions produced per unit of economic activity.[93] This difference not only distorts industrial emissions progress, but also fails to accurately represent domestic energy consumption levels. Harmonization of standards must come at both the provincial and the federal level, as multiple reporting measures across jurisdictions are unsustainable. Lastly, the proposed framework does not require a diversification of the energy mix, and in fact allows firms to buy their way out of emission reductions for the first few years. On the whole, Canada is attempting to move in the right direction. However, the proposed policy framework has crucial flaws.

3.2. *The United States and the Climate Question*

The United States is a global leader in many respects, but climate change policy is not one of them. Although the American government under the Clinton administration attended the Kyoto Protocol's negotiations and even signed it, the treaty was never submitted to Congress for ratification and thus is not binding.[94] The George W. Bush administration also proved to be quite hostile to the notion of binding international emission reduction targets.[95] Under the Obama administration, significant progress

---

[89] J. Montpetit, "McGuinty, Charest sign plan to cut emissions," *The Star*, June 2, 2008, http://www.thestar.com/News/Canada/article/435539.

[90] Environment Canada, "Information on Greenhouse Gas Sources and Sinks: Canada's 2006 Greenhouse Gas Inventory – A summary of Trends" (2006), p. 2, http://publications.gc.ca/collections/collection_2008/ec/En81-4-2006-1E.pdf.

[91] Environment Canada, "Information on Greenhouse Gas."

[92] Canada pledged to reduce its GHG emissions by five percent below 1990 levels by 2012; Kyoto Protocol at Article 3.

[93] Taylor and Barrett, "Canada's Experience"; Greenpeace, "Targeting Climate Change in Canada" (February 12, 2007), p. 2, http://www.greenpeace.org/canada/Global/canada/report/2008/11/targeting-climate-change-in-ca.pdf; A. Denny Ellerman and Ian Sue Wing, "Absolute vs. Intensity-Based Emission Caps," MIT Joint Program on the Science and Policy of Global Change, Report 100 (July 2003), http://web.mit.edu/globalchange/www/MITJPSPGC_Rpt100.pdf.

[94] John W. Gulliver and Keith A. Wheeler, "Diversified Leadership for Moving beyond a Carbon Economy in the United States," in Donald N. Zillman et al. (eds.), *Beyond the Carbon Economy* (New York: Oxford, 2008) 517–539, pp. 517–518.

[95] Gulliver and Wheeler, "Diversified Leadership," p. 518.

has been hampered by congressional division and domestic self-interest, but some progress has been made. In 2009, President Obama signed Executive Order 13514, which set out waste and pollution reduction targets for federal agencies along with an annual sustainability reporting requirement.[96] All federal agencies set and report on individual greenhouse gas and waste pollution to drive reductions, based on detailed guidance developed through an interagency work group composed of members from the Departments of Energy, Defence, Commerce, and the Interior.[97]

The Boxer-Lieberman-Warner bill brought congressional consideration of the issue. The bill would require the EPA to develop a regulatory framework for issuing carbon credits and offsets.[98] However, it was doomed to fail due to economic concerns.[99] While reduction efforts have occurred, the U.S. energy mix remains focused on fossil fuels,[100] nuclear power, and subsidized ethanol production,[101] with modest inroads into renewable energy sources (RES).[102] However, important developments driven by the private sector, state legislatures, and the judiciary have all played a role in the evolution of American climate policy. Each of these influences requires a focused discussion.

American corporations are quickly becoming champions of progressive climate change initiatives. Commentators have suggested that this progression can be grounded in three key and interrelated motivations: mitigation of corporate risk, economic opportunism, and a need for international stability.[103] Senior management in American corporations has been feeling pressure from both investors and consumers alike to proactively address climate change. In this regard, the laissez-faire attitude employed by the federal government is working as the private sector has responded positively to this public pressure. Corporate executives are finding

[96] The White House, "Executive Order 13514: Federal Leadership in Environmental, Energy and Economic Performance" (October 5, 2009), http://www.whitehouse.gov/assets/documents/2009fedleader_eo_rel.pdf.

[97] White House Council on Environmental Quality, "Revised Federal Greenhouse Gas Accounting and Reporting Guidance" (June 2012), http://www.whitehouse.gov/sites/default/files/microsites/ceq/revised_federal_greenhouse_gas_accounting_and_reporting_guidance_060412.pdf.

[98] "The Lieberman-Warner Climate Security Act (S. 2191)," http://www.gpo.gov/fdsys/pkg/BILLS-110s2191rs/pdf/BILLS-110s2191rs.pdf.

[99] James M. Inhofe, "The Economics of America's Climate Security Act of 2007: (S.2191, Lieberman-Warner Climate Bill)," White Paper May 2008, p. 14, http://www.inhofe.senate.gov/download/?id=a38e431a-1bd7-4b99-be75-33a3c5e39536&download=1.

[100] National Energy Policy Development Group, *Reliable, Affordable and Environmentally Sound Energy for America's Future* (Washington, DC: U.S. Government Printing Office, 2001), chapter 5–9, http://www.netl.doe.gov/publications/press/2001/nep/national_energy_policy.pdf; The White House, "Policy memorandum: American Made Energy" (June 18, 2008), http://georgewbush-whitehouse.archives.gov/news/releases/2008/06/20080618-9.html.

[101] The White House National Economic Council, "Advanced Energy Initiative" (February 2006), http://georgewbush-whitehouse.archives.gov/stateoftheunion/2006/energy/.

[102] National Renewable Energy Laboratory, *Renewable Electricity Futures Study – Volume 2: Renewable Electricity Generation and Storage Technologies* (Golden, CO: National Renewable Energy Laboratory, 2012), http://www.nrel.gov/docs/fy12osti/52409-2.pdf.

[103] Gulliver and Wheeler, "Diversified Leadership," p. 520.

innovative ways to adapt to climate change, if for no other reason than to uphold their fiduciary obligations to investors. However, this shift in public sentiment also provides a prime opportunity for well-positioned firms to maximize profit. With the rise of ecofriendly brands such as General Electric's "Ecomagination," which in two years turned an annual profit of $12 billion, there is proof that green initiatives are profitable.[104] Last, climate change will undoubtedly have an effect on the stability of international markets, particularly the NAFTA zone. This in many regards translates into a threat to national security. The private sector views proactive action to address climate change as having a dual benefit: preserving a stable economic order while increasing investor confidence.

Although little is being accomplished at the national level, American states have been far more productive. California has demonstrated clear leadership in this field. In 2006, the state legislature passed the Global Warming Solutions Act,[105] to focus the state in a greener direction and preemptively prepare California businesses to compete in other green jurisdictions.[106] The Act has two main features. First is the establishment of an emission reduction strategy to reduce GHG emissions to 1990 levels by 2020.[107] This strategy was established in 2009,[108] refined in 2010,[109] with a proposed updated draft upcoming in 2014.[110] Second, it allows for Parties to participate in an emissions trading system, in conjunction with the European Union and the Regional Greenhouse Gas Initiative (RGGI). Now, under the Western Climate Initiative,[111] California is linking its cap-and-trade program to other states and Canadian provinces. However, California is not the only state working in this area. The aforementioned RGGI is a coalition of nine states,[112] cooperating under the auspices of a nonprofit organization with a regional CO_2 Budget Trading Program.[113]

---

[104] Gulliver and Wheeler, "Diversified Leadership," pp. 524–525.

[105] State of California, Assembly Bill No. 32: California Global Warming Solutions Act of 2006, http://www.arb.ca.gov/cc/docs/ab32text.pdf.

[106] California, Global Warming Solutions Act of 2006, Chapter 2.

[107] Gulliver and Wheeler, "Diversified Leadership," pp. 527–528; California Global Warming Solutions Act, 38562(a), 38550.

[108] State of California, 2009 Climate Change Adaptation Strategy: A Report to the Governor of the State of California in Response to Executive Order S-13–2008 (2009), http://resources.ca.gov/climate_adaptation/docs/Statewide_Adaptation_Strategy.pdf.

[109] State of California, 2009 Climate Change Adaptation Strategy: First Year Progress Report to the Governor of the State of California (2010), http://www.energy.ca.gov/2010publications/CNRA-1000–2010-010/CNRA-1000–2010-010.pdf.

[110] State of California, Safeguarding California: Reducing Climate Risks: An Update to the 2009 California Climate Adaptation Strategy (Dec. 2013 *Public Draft*), http://resources.ca.gov/climate_adaptation/docs/Safeguarding_California_Public_Draft_Dec-10.pdf.

[111] Western Climate Initiative, http://www.wci-inc.org/.

[112] Participating States are Connecticut, Delaware, Maine, Maryland, Massachusetts, New Hampshire, New York, Rhode Island, and Vermont; Regional Greenhouse Gas Initiative Inc., http://www.rggi.org/rggi.

[113] Regional Greenhouse Gas Initiative, Regional Investment of RGGI CO_2 Allowance Proceeds, 2011 (Nov. 2012), available at: http://www.rggi.org/docs/Documents/2011-Investment-Report.pdf.

Although only in their infancy, the California legislation and RGGI show promise and are yet another example of state initiative far surpassing national policy.

Not to be overlooked, the U.S. Supreme Court has also spoken on the issue of climate change. In *Massachusetts* v. *EPA*,[114] the court considered whether CO_2 emissions from automobiles could be considered an "air pollutant" under the Clean Air Act (CAA), thus forcing the EPA to regulate them. The EPA argued that Congress never intended the EPA to regulate those substances; however, the court disagreed.[115] Admittedly, the court applied a strict reading of the CAA. Nevertheless, it found that automobile emission regulation did indeed fall under the jurisdiction of the EPA, thus bringing GHG emissions under the scope of current U.S. legislation.[116] Although the ruling is quite limited in scope, it nonetheless demonstrates that American agencies should be addressing climate change more rigorously.

Although the analysis presented here takes an optimistic view of U.S. climate change responses, the U.S. approach retains some flaws. First, the approach lacks national coordination. Absent guidance from Congress, the private sector and state legislatures have implemented their own policies. Second, the United States needs to take the lead, both within NAFTA and globally, in requiring implementation of national emission reduction targets, ratifying Kyoto, installing a mandatory national emissions trading system, and harmonizing the considerable variance among current carbon reduction projects.

3.3. *Mexico and the Climate Question*

The climate change picture in Mexico is substantially different than that of the United States or Canada. This holds true in many other respects than obvious differences in economic development. First, fossil fuels play a dominant role in the Mexican economy, in terms of satisfying domestic consumption needs and procuring foreign capital.[117] Second, because the domestic economy is so dependent on oil exports, it is particularly vulnerable to global market fluctuations. Finally, the oil sector is nationalized and highly regulated.[118] These three factors greatly influence the role that alternative energies can play in the country. Furthermore, as the United States is the primary importer of Mexican oil, any change in U.S. energy policies may destabilize the Mexican economy.[119]

Mexico's Intersecretarial Commission on Climate Change (ICCC) put forward a National Strategy on Climate Change in 2000, which was further revised in 2007.

---

[114] *Massachusetts* v. *EPA*, 549 U.S. 497; 127 S. Ct. 1438 (April 2, 2007).
[115] *Massachusetts* v. *EPA*, at p. 26.
[116] Gulliver and Wheeler, "Diversified Leadership," p. 530.
[117] José Juan González, "The Future of an Economy Based on Oil Exploitation: the Mexican Case," in Donald N. Zillman et al. (eds.), *Beyond the Carbon Economy*, Donald (New York: Oxford, 2008) 441–458 at 442.
[118] González, "The Future," pp. 442–443.
[119] González, "The Future," p. 444.

The goals of this new program are three-fold: first, identify emission reduction opportunities and develop domestic mitigation programs;[120] second, recognize the susceptibility of various economic and social sectors, as well as particular geographic regions, to the effects of climate change and develop regional capacity building projects to enhance response and adaptation capabilities;[121] and third, put forward policy goals and realistic strategies for the Special Climate Change Program that is planned to be an integral part of the 2007–12 National Development Plan (NDP).[122] Although earlier development and energy legislation touched on renewable energy technology integration,[123] the updated NDP is a step forward. It not only identifies particular GHG mitigation measures in specific sectors, but also incorporates the important and often overlooked aspect of land use planning to maximize GHG reductions and minimize long-term environmental effects.[124]

The Mexican Carbon Fund (FOMECAR) was founded in 2006 as a coordinated effort between the Mexican Ministry of the Ministry of Environment and Natural Resources (SEMARNAT) and the Mexican Bank for Foreign Trade (BANCOMEXT).[125] Its purpose is to provide technical, financial, and practical support to developers of emission reduction projects, as well as to assist in registering them under the Kyoto Protocol CDM. In 2012 Mexico passed the Climate Change Act to ensure a healthy environment, coordinate mitigation and adaptation efforts, and stabilize GHG emissions in accordance with Article 2 of the UNFCCC.[126] The Act also outlines powers of states and municipalities in developing and implementing policy;[127] creates the National Institute of Ecology and Climate Change (INECC) as a centralized coordinating body;[128] establishes sustainability, state responsibility, the precautionary approach, and competitiveness as guiding principles in policy development;[129] creates a new Climate Change Fund;[130] and establishes binding emission reduction targets.[131] By 2020 and 2050, Mexico aims to reduce its GHG

---

[120] Mexico, Intersecretarial Commission on Climate Change, "National Strategy on Climate Change (ENACC): Executive Summary – English" (2007), p. 3, http://www.un.org/ga/president/61/follow-up/climatechange/Nal_Strategy_MEX_eng.pdf.

[121] Mexico, "National Strategy."

[122] Mexico, "National Strategy."

[123] González, "The Future," p. 446.

[124] Mexico, "National Strategy," pp. 6–8.

[125] José Ramón Ardavín Ituarte, "How can Mexico take advantage of the CDM: the Mexican Carbon Fund" (PowerPoint presentation by the Ministry of the Environment and Natural Resources, Government of Mexico, November 2006), https://web.archive.org/web/20070612091811/ http://regserver.unfccc.int/seors/file_storage/vhbddq8z2vqor7e.pdf; also see FOMECAR official English website: https://web.archive.org/web/20080513230521/http://www.bancomext.com/Bancomext/public asecciones/secciones/11348/Inicio.htm.

[126] Mexico, Climate Change Act (2012), Article 2, online: http://www.diputados.gob.mx/LeyesBiblio/pdf/LGCC.pdf.

[127] Mexico, Climate Change Act, Articles 8–9.

[128] Mexico, Climate Change Act, Articles 13–25.

[129] Mexico, Climate Change Act, Article 26.

[130] Mexico, Climate Change Act, 16.

[131] Mexico, Climate Change Act, Transitional Provisions, Article 2.

emissions by 30 percent and 50 percent, respectively, below 2000 levels.[132] The Act also requires that 35 percent of electricity come from renewable sources by 2024.[133]

In 2013 the National Climate Change Strategy 10–20–40 Vision was published,[134] outlining the implementation of the Climate Change Act. The Strategy establishes six pillars of national climate change policy: (1) have cross-cutting and coordinated climate policies; (2) develop climate specific fiscal policies and financial instruments; (3) implement a platform for research and development of climate technologies and strengthening of institutional capacities; (4) promote the development of a climate culture; (5) implement mechanisms for measurement, reporting, and monitoring; and (6) strengthen strategic cooperation and international leadership.[135] These six pillars inform a vision that outlines ten-year, twenty-year, and forty-year goals.[136] Mexico must be commended for its progress and dedication to combating the global climate crisis. However, that progress is not without problems. Shortcomings are grounded more in institutional barriers to adaptation than in the flaws of any particular proposal. The most glaring roadblock is also the most problematic. By virtue of the Federal Constitution, the government forbids private investment in the energy sector.[137] This is a major hindrance to the integration of alternative energy sources into the country. Although energy rules were modified in 1997 to allow the entry of independent producers into the Mexican market, with the caveat that all energy produced must be sold to the Federal Commission of Electricity, these institutional barriers greatly undermine the ability of Mexico to procure investment, technological innovation, or implementation of CDM programs.[138] Overall, however, Mexico has demonstrated a keen awareness of the risks of climate change and has been proactive in taking the policy measures needed to support adaptation.

4. POLICY PROPOSALS FOR NAFTA PARTIES AND LESSONS LEARNED THROUGH THE EU

To reduce North America's excessively high GHG levels, the CEC can play an important role in coordination and implementation of a harmonized climate change mitigation and adaptation strategy. As noted, each of the NAFTA Parties has implemented various initiatives to address climate change. This is understandably based in different policy priorities, resources, and options. However, by harmonizing

---

[132] Mexico, Climate Change Act, Transitional Provisions, Article 2.
[133] Mexico, Climate Change Act, Transitional Provisions, Article 3(e).
[134] Mexico, National Climate Change Strategy. 10–20–40 Vision, (Ministry of the Environment and Natural Resources, 2013), http://mitigationpartnership.net/sites/default/files/encc_englishversion.pdf.
[135] Mexico, 10–20–40 Vision, pp. 24–26.
[136] Mexico, 10–20–40 Vision, pp. 22–23.
[137] *Constitución Política de los Estados Unidos Mexicanos*, Trigésima Quinta Edición, 1967, Article 27, http://portal.te.gob.mx/sites/default/files/consultas/2012/04/cpeum_ingles_ref_26_feb_2013_pdf_81046.pdf.
[138] González, "The Future," p. 452.

these initiatives across the NAFTA zone, with adaptations to account for regional differences, Parties can maximize emission reductions through mutually support-ive initiatives while simultaneously giving domestic industries the tools to support stability. Deference should be paid to the approaches employed by the EU when considering what polices to pursue and what method of implementation to adopt. Not only is the EU a global leader in green legislation, but its supranational struc-ture forces it to confront many of same considerations as a customs or trade union. The following comparative policy recommendations draw on the EU experience to support reducing GHG emissions across North America while establishing a stable and predictable climate framework for commercial stakeholders.

4.1. *Development of a Comprehensive Renewable Energy and Biofuel Policy*

A key step to emission reductions is the establishment of a comprehensive renew-able energy strategy for NAFTA that draws best practices from the common but differentiated legal approaches employed by the Parties. Part of the problem with addressing GHG emissions in North America is that both the public and private sectors lack a clear domestic vision for the role of renewable energy. This is the single biggest lesson that can be taken from the European experience. RES must play an increased role in any North American GHG reduction strategy, and that role must be clarified.[139] Furthermore, what is to be considered a "renewable energy source" must be clearly defined, with binding RES national consumption targets outlined and broad reporting mechanisms incorporated into any legal framework.[140] The success of the EU's initial Renewables Directive[141] brought about an updated Directive in 2009,[142] emphasizing the ever-growing need to functionally integrate RES into the energy mix. Specific action must be taken to encourage the expanded use of biofuels, particularly cellulose-based biodiesel. The EU in this regard passed the Biofuels Directive,[143] which required a 5.75 percent biofuel substitution in the

[139] North American Leaders Summit, "North American Leaders' Declaration on Climate Change and Clean Energy" (August 10, 2009), http://www.iisd.org/pdf/2009/na_leaders_declaration_climate.pdf; Government of Canada, http://www.pm.gc.ca/eng/news/2009/08/10/north-american-leaders-declaration-climate-change-and-clean-energy.
[140] All are incorporated into the *Renewables Directive*; see Martha M. Roggenkampet et al. (eds.) *Energy Law in Europe*, 2nd ed. (New York: Oxford, 2007), p. 1340.
[141] European Communities, Directive 2001/77/EC of the European Parliament and of the Council September 27, 2001 on the promotion of electricity produced from renewable energy sources in the internal market, [2001] O.J. L 283/33 of October 27, 2001.
[142] European Communities, Directive 2009/28/EC of the European Parliament and of the Council of April 23, 2009 on the promotion of the use of energy from renewable sources and amending and subsequently repealing Directives 2001/77/EC and 2003/30/EC, [2009] O.J. L 140/16 of May 6, 2009, http://eur-lex.europa.eu/LexUriServ/LexUriServ.do?uri=Oj:L:2009:140:0016:0062:en:PDF.
[143] European Communities, Directive 2003/30/EC of the European Parliament and of the Council of May 8, 2003 on the promotion of the use of biofuels or other renewable fuels for transport, [2003] O.J. L 123/42 of May 17, 2003.

transport sector by 2010 to reduce GHG emissions.[144] Heavy automobile use in North America makes this imperative particularly acute there.

Functionally, the CEC is uniquely placed to provide an ideal forum for coordination, policy development, and record keeping. As a high-level ministerial body, the Council of Ministers could act as a vehicle for trilateral discourse and debate. Further, policy consensus could be reached in this more intimate forum and then taken back to the domestic legislatures for consultation. Last, environmental data could be submitted and archived to monitor each Party's domestic progress. For any renewable energy policy to be successful and sustainable, long-term efficacy is paramount. It would be unwise for Parties to continue to individually employ inefficient mechanisms domestically. If a comprehensive renewable energy strategy were incorporated through the CEC, Parties would have common emission standards and baselines for industries, a mechanism for region-specific RES to drive emission reductions, and a sound reporting system allowing for transparency and trilateral oversight. This harmonization would reduce capital and carbon flight. A trilaterally negotiated emissions reduction agreement would be greatly beneficial in streamlining standards, incentivizing research and development, and cutting the overall costs of climate change adaptation.

4.2. *Continental Emission Trading Program*

In contrast to the voluntary trading markets in place in Canada and the United States, a second recommendation is the establishment of a NAFTA-wide Emission Trading System (ETS). Binding emission reduction targets require a mechanism to functionally integrate environmental compliance with economic productivity and incentivize innovation. Early on, the EU foresaw a prominent role for market-based initiatives in its overall GHG reduction strategy. In 2003, the EU established the EU ETS[145] as a cost-effective mechanism to, in the short term, reduce GHG emissions where it was cheapest to do so[146] while in the long term driving down the excessive cost of green technologies.

For similar reasons, a NAFTA-zone ETS could be established. Although the voluntary markets have been successful at encouraging support,[147] it will be the linking of carbon markets and the use of common and exchangeable credits that will drive reductions in cost and increases in trade.[148] Moreover, due to the highly divergent

---

[144] EC, Directive 2003/30/EC, Article 3(1)(b)(ii); Roggenkampet, *Energy Law*, p. 1356.

[145] European Communities, Directive 2003/87/EC of the European Parliament and of the Council of October 13, 2003 establishing a scheme for greenhouse gas emission allowance trading within the Community and amending Council Directive 96/61/EC, [2003] O.J. L 275/32 of October 25, 2003.

[146] Roggenkampet, *Energy Law*, p. 317.

[147] Richard G. Newell, William A. Pizer, and Daniel Raimi, "Carbon Markets: Past, Present, and Future" Resources for the Future: Discussion Paper (2013), p. 2, http://www.rff.org/RFF/Documents/RFF-DP-12–51.pdf.

[148] "Carbon Markets: Past, Present, and Future," p. 30.

nature of the carbon programs currently operating across NAFTA jurisdictions, organizations are left with the potential for uncertainty to hamper innovation.[149] A NAFTA-wide ETS system could harmonize credit dispersal criteria and definitions, align functional terminology, create common sectoral obligations, and standardize baselines, providing system-wide predictability and transparency while preserving certainty for investors and businesses. Again, the CEC could provide institutional support and structure for this program. The Council of Ministers would be an ideal forum for the development of recommended sectoral baselines. The Secretariat could provide an institutional skeleton and JPAC could act as a conduit for continued consultations between industry and government. The CEC provides an ideal forum to establish an institutional framework for a common emissions market for the benefit of all Parties.

4.3. *Specific Expansion of the CDM*

The CDM can be used to increase capital flow into Mexico's renewable energy and biofuel sectors. One of the major stumbling blocks to the reduction of Mexico's GHG emissions will undoubtedly be its dependence on fossil fuels both as a domestic energy source and as an export commodity.[150] It would also be inappropriate to demand that Mexico increase RES consumption without providing some support for capacity building to assist in the development of domestic green industries. To this end the CDM holds a key to potential success.

If a specific program were designed to allow for Canadian and U.S. investment in the Mexican renewable energy or biofuel sector through a CDM, such as cellulose-based biofuel derived from sugarcane, there would be unquestionable benefits across the board.[151] Mexico would gain from the expansion of vital sectors to rival its fossil fuel industry, would not violate its constitutional monopoly on energy production, would be provided with urgently needed infrastructural investment, and would lose little in return. The proportion of biofuel exports to the United States and Canada could grow. In this, the United States and Canada could gain consistent and secure access to a clean fuel, while offsetting domestic GHG emissions through ongoing CDM investment.

[149] Felix Mormann, "Enhancing the investor appeal of renewable energy," (2012) 42:3 *Environmental Law Journal* 681–734.
[150] José Juan González, "Mexico's dependence on fossil fuels and Climate Change policy" IUCN Academy of Environmental Law 2011 Colloquium, http://www.iucnael.org/en/component/docman/doc_download/1025-jose-juan.html.
[151] Bloomberg, "Moving Towards a Next-Generation Ethanol Economy Final Study" (Jan. 2012), http://www.novozymes.com/en/sustainability/benefits-for-the-world/biobased-economy/white-papers-on-biofuels/Documents/Next-Generation%20Ethanol%20Economy_full_report.pdf; Novozymes, "The Race Towards Cellulosic Ethanol (2011–2030)," http://www.novozymes.com/en/sustainability/benefits-for-the-world/biobased-economy/white-papers-on-biofuels/Documents/Infographic_race_towards_ethanol.pdf.

Functionally, Canada and the United States would need to gain first right to the importation of Mexican biofuel produced through their CDM investment with a covenant in the initial funding agreement, while the surplus could be freely sold on the international market. It should be noted, however, that biofuels is just one example of a sector where such an initiative could be pursued. Parties should allow the use of specific CDM regimes in cases where Canada and the U.S. would both benefit from investing in Mexico, providing Mexico with the tools necessary to respond to climate change.

5. CONCLUSION

In the global effort to combat the enduring threat of climate change, NAFTA Parties confront both an immense pressure from the international community to drastically cut GHG emissions and a significant opportunity to capitalize on the CEC institutional framework. Although initially a trade pact, NAFTA has fostered an integrated decision-making process in the environmental realm through the CEC,[152] which provides great potential to increase the efficiency and capacity of successful GHG mitigation measures while decreasing operational and technological costs in the process.[153]

The institutional skeleton set in place under the CEC provides an ideal legal structure for discourse, production of trilateral policy-oriented and policy-relevant recommendations, and public consultation.[154] The CEC's JPAC echoed this need for a trilateral climate agenda, noting that harmonization of emission standards, sharing of best practices, promotion of programs that promote reduction of energy consumption and carbon leakage, and use of the institutions as a trilateral working group will positively support future environmental and trade policy.[155] By implementing a common but differentiated renewable energy and biofuel strategy, Parties can hedge against capital and carbon flight. Furthermore, industries will benefit greatly from predictable, incremental, and clear-sighted sectoral targets for RES

---

[152] John Kirton, "Ten Years After: An Assessment of the Environmental Effectiveness of the NAAEC," in John M. Curtis and Aaron Sydor (eds.), *NAFTA at 10* (Minister of Public Works and Government Services Canada, 2006) 125–164, p. 133.

[153] There are less optimistic views proposed on the concrete benefits of mechanisms like the CEC. While these authors offer valid critiques, the political will necessary to fully realize the potential of multilateral institutions has not been truly present. See, for example, in this volume, Giselle Davidian, "Should Citizens Expect Procedural Justice in Nonadversarial Processes? Spotlighting the Regression of the Citizen Submission Process from NAAEC to CAFTA–DR," Section 6.

[154] Commission for Environmental Cooperation, "Positioning the CEC's Work on the Assessment of Trade and Environment Linkages for the Next Decade: Outcomes of the Experts' Roundtable" (Montreal, Canada: Commission for Environmental Cooperation, 2008), p. 13, http://www.cec.org/Storage/34/2597_Experts_Roundtable_-_Linkages_for_the_Next_Decade.pdf.

[155] Joint Public Advisory Committee of the Commission for Environmental Cooperation, "Re: JPAC Workshop on Climate Policy Coherence in North America" (Advice to Council NO:09–01 J/09–01/ADV/Final, August 13, 2009), http://www.cec.org/Page.asp?PageID=122&ContentID=2745.

and biofuel consumption, emission reduction levels, and research and development (R&D) spending.

Second, establishing a NAFTA-zone ETS will allow energy-intensive sectors to operate on an even playing field with common standards, requirements, and credit allocations. This will provide further predictability and encourage innovation and compliance. Lastly, by enhancing the CDM program within the NAFTA framework to allow for specific investment in the Mexican renewable energy and biofuel sectors, a conduit for technology transfer will be created while addressing infrastructural inadequacies.

The primary hindrances to effective climate change mitigation are barriers to the dissemination of essential technologies, lack of capital for adaptation, fear of large-scale capital and carbon flight, and lack of competitiveness due to increased environmental costs. However, the CEC provides an excellent forum for NAFTA Parties to overcome many of these barriers by applying lessons learned through the EU's experience.

12

The Principle of Public Participation in NAFTA Chapter 11 Disputes

Avidan Kent

1. INTRODUCTION

The principle of public participation and the international documents by which this principle was established have hardly ever been directly mentioned in investment treaties or by investment tribunals.[1] But as will be demonstrated in this chapter, elements of this principle have found their way into the domain of investment treaty

---

[1] The term "sustainable development" does appear in a few investment treaties, most notably in the preamble to the North American Free Trade Agreement Between the Government of Canada, the Government of Mexico and the Government of the United States, San Antonio, December 17, 1992, in force January 1, 1994 (1993), 31 ILM 296, Can TS 1994 No 2; preambles to Canadian Foreign Investment and Protection Agreements (FIPAs) and Free Trade Agreements (FTAs) signed with Peru (Agreement Between Canada and the Republic of Peru for the Promotion and Protection of Investments, November 14, 2006, in force June 20, 2007, E105078, Colombia (Canada–Colombia Free Trade Agreement, November 21, 2008, in force August 15, 2011), Panama (Treaty Between the Government of Canada and the Government of the Republic of Panama for the Promotion and Protection of Investments, Guatemala, September 12, 1996, in force February 13, 1998, C.T.S. 1998 No. 35), and Jordan (Agreement Between Canada and the Hashemite Kingdom of Jordan for the Promotion and Protection of Investments, Amman, June 28, 2009, in force December 14, 2009, E105176). See also the preamble of the Australia-Chile Free Trade Agreement (in force March 6, 2009). Other treaties, while not using the term "sustainable development" specifically, refer to the goals of sustainable development. See for example the preamble to the United States–Uruguay Bilateral Investment Treaty (BIT) (Treaty Between the United States of America and the Oriental Republic of Uruguay Concerning the Encouragement and Reciprocal Protection of Investment, Mar del Plata, November 2005, in force November 1, 2006). It should also be noted that the negotiated EU–Canada CETA (Comprehensive Economic and Trade Agreement, October 18, 2013) includes references to the Rio Declaration on Environment and Development, Rio de Janeiro, June 14, 1992, UN GAOR, UN Doc A/CONF.151/26 (vol. I), 31 ILM 874 (1992); the Johannesburg Declaration on Sustainable Development, A/Conf.199/20, September 4, 2002; and the Agenda 21 Proclamation of the United Nations Conference on Environment & Development, Rio de Janeiro, June 3–14, 1992. At this moment, however, it is not clear whether the CETA will include an investor-state arbitration provision. Another example is the European Free Trade Association–Singapore Free Trade Agreement, Eglisstadir, Iceland, June 26, 2002, in force January 1, 2003, which makes explicit reference to the *Universal Declaration of Human Rights* (GA Res 217 (III), UN GAOR, 3d Sess, Supp No 13, UN Doc A/810, December 10, 1984).

arbitration, even if it has not been mentioned expressly by name, and the current trend is certainly toward the increasing application of this principle.

This chapter examines the principle of public participation as it has been demonstrated in North American Free Trade Agreement's (NAFTA's) Chapter 11 investment disputes and in the arbitration rules governing these disputes. Chapter 11 represents one of the most advanced legal systems when it comes to the integration of this principle into investment treaty arbitration.

The groundbreaking approach adopted by NAFTA tribunals in this respect has had a significant influence on the field of international investment law. Indeed, important legal instruments such as the 2006 International Center for Settlement of Investment Disputes (ICSID) Arbitration Rules have incorporated some of the elements first adopted and recognized under the NAFTA framework. As an increasing number of investment treaties are being concluded, and in light of the fact that the field of international investment law is criticized as being closed, secretive, and biased toward the interests of foreign investors, the lessons learned from the NAFTA in this respect are very important.

2. THE PRINCIPLE OF PUBLIC PARTICIPATION AND ACCESS TO INFORMATION AND JUSTICE

2.1. *The Principle of Public Participation: In Essence*

The principle of public participation is often described as including three parts. The first includes the public's right to participate in decision-making processes in which sustainable development issues are involved. This part is based on the public's right to be actively involved in decisions that affect their lives,[2] and the people's right to express their opinions. This part is also intended to ensure good governance that is also transparent and responsive.

The second part in this typology – access to information – is perceived as a necessary condition for ensuring effective public participation. Access to information contributes to qualitative and informed participation, and it can be viewed as supporting both elements of good governance (informed decisions are better decisions) and the public's right to participate in decision making by fully understanding subject matters under discussion.[3]

The third part of the principle of public participation – access to judicial and administrative procedures – is necessary in order to ensure that people, whether

---

[2] See preamble to the Convention on Access to Information, Public Participation in Decision Making and Access to Justice in Environmental Matters, Aarhus, Denmark, June 25, 1998, UN Doc ECE/CEP43, http://www.unece.org/env/pp/documents/cep43e.pdf ("Aarhus Convention"); Paragraph 23.2 of the UN Agenda 21, above.

[3] For example, Paragraph 5.2 of the New Delhi Declaration, above, states that public participation: "requires a right of access to appropriate, comprehensible and timely information held by governments."

locals or foreigners, can participate in judicial and administrative processes in which sustainable development–related measures are being discussed and can claim compensation where harm has been done. This third part is less relevant for the discussion on investor–state arbitration and therefore will not be reviewed.[4]

2.2. *The Principle of Public Participation in International Law*

The concept of public participation in sustainable development decision-making processes has been recognized in several international documents. The modern inception of this concept in the field of international law can be attributed to the 1948 UN *Universal Declaration of Human Rights*, which stated that "[e]veryone has the right to take part in the government of his country, directly or through freely chosen representatives."[5] The following twenty years saw an evolution of this concept from a basic human right into a fundamental principle that also includes a focus on good governance and development. This evolution was manifested in the 1969 *UN Declaration on Social Progress and Development*:[6]

> Social progress and development require the full utilization of human resources, including, in particular: . . .
> (c) The active participation of all elements of society, individually or through associations, in defining and in achieving the common goals of development with full respect for the fundamental freedoms embodied in the Universal Declaration of Human Rights.

The recognition of the concept of public participation has also been expressed in other international documents from this period,[7] but as Professor Schrijver points out, it was not until the conclusion of the Rio Declaration and the UN Agenda 21 in 1992 that this concept received its international recognition as an international "principle."[8] Principle 10 of the Rio Declaration on Environment and Development states:[9]

> Environmental issues are best handled with the participation of all concerned citizens, at the relevant level. At the national level, each individual shall have

---

[4] This part specifically refers to the people's right to challenge measures related to environmental damage (see Principle 10 of the Rio Declaration, above; Article 9(3) of the Aarhus Convention, above) or "transboundary harm" (Paragraph 5.3 of the New Delhi Declaration, above), and to demand compensation from the state. This is clearly not within the domain of investor-state arbitrations, and is not related to this system.
[5] Article 21 (1) of the Universal Declaration of Human Rights, above.
[6] *Declaration on Social Progress and Development*, GA Res 2542 (XXIV), UN GAOR, 24th Sess (1969) UN Doc. A/RES/24/2542, December 11, 1969, Article 5.
[7] Most notably the International Covenant on Civil and Political Rights, December 19, 1966, in force March 23, 1976, 999 UNTS 171; Can TS 1976 No 47; and the *Inter-American Convention on Human Rights*, November 22, 1969, in force July 18, 1978, 1144 UNTS 123; OAS TIAS No 36.
[8] Nico Schrijver, *The Evolution of Sustainable Development in International Law: Inception, Meaning and Status* (Leiden: Martinus Nijhoff, 2008), p. 198.
[9] Rio Declaration, above.

appropriate access to information concerning the environment that is held by public authorities, including information on hazardous materials and activities in their
communities, and the opportunity to participate in decision making processes.
States shall facilitate and encourage public awareness and participation by making information widely available. Effective access to judicial and administrative
proceedings, including redress and remedy, shall be provided.

Paragraph 23.2 of the UN Agenda 21 elaborates:[10]

One of the fundamental prerequisites for the achievement of sustainable development is broad public participation in decision making. Furthermore, in the
more specific context of environment and development, the need for new forms
of participation has emerged. This includes the need of individuals, groups and
organizations to participate in environmental impact assessment procedures and to
know about and participate in decisions, particularly those which potentially affect
the communities in which they live and work. Individuals, groups and organizations
should have access to information relevant to environment and development held
by national authorities, including information on products and activities that have
or are likely to have a significant impact on the environment, and information on
environmental protection measures.

Following the Rio Declaration and Agenda 21, other international documents such
as the Johannesburg Declaration,[11] the Aarhus Convention (which recalls Principle
10 of the Rio Declaration[12]), and others[13] continued to affirm the international
commitment to the principle of public participation.

In 2002, the International Law Association (ILA), under the lead of Dr. Kamal
Hossain and Professor Nico Schrijver, adopted the ILA New Delhi Declaration of
Principles of International Law Relating to Sustainable Development, where the
principle of public participation received full confirmation. The ILA's formulation
of this principle summarizes the aforementioned developments and emphasizes the
importance of the principle for good governance on the one hand, and for human
rights on the other:[14]

---

[10] See further references to this principle in Agenda 21, above, at paras 8.3, 8.4(f), and 8.7.
[11] See, for example, Article 26 of the Johannesburg Declaration, above.
[12] Aarhus Convention, above.
[13] See also the *United Nations Convention on Biological Diversity*, June 5, 1992, in force December 29,
      1992, 1760 UNTS 79; 31 ILM 818; *United Nations Framework Convention on Climate Change*, New
      York, May 9, 1992, in force March 21, 1994, 31 ILM 849; North American Agreement on Environmental
      Cooperation, September 14, 1993, in force January 1, 1994, 32 ILM 1480 [NAAEC]; *United Nations
      Convention to Combat Desertification in Countries Experiencing Serious Drought and/or Desertifica-
      tion, Particularly in Africa*, Paris, October 17, 1994, in force December 26, 1996, 33 ILM 1328; see review
      in Kathleen Bottriell and Marie-Claire Cordonier Segger, "The Principle of Public Participation and
      Access to Information and Justice" (2005) CISDL "Recent Developments in International Law Related
      to Sustainable Development" Legal Working Paper Series, pp. 4–6.
[14] New Delhi Declaration, above.

5. The Principle of Public Participation and Access to Information and Justice

5.1. Public participation is essential to sustainable development and good governance in that it is a condition for responsive, transparent and accountable governments as well a condition for the active engagement of equally responsive, transparent and accountable civil society organizations, including industrial concerns and trade unions. The vital role of women in sustainable development should be recognized.

5.2. Public participation in the context of sustainable development requires effective protection of the human right to hold and express opinions and to seek, receive and impart ideas. It also requires a right of access to appropriate, comprehensible and timely information held by governments and industrial concerns on economic and social policies regarding the sustainable use of natural resources and the protection of the environment, without imposing undue financial burdens upon the applicants and with due consideration for privacy and adequate protection of business confidentiality.

5.3. The empowerment of peoples in the context of sustainable development requires access to effective judicial or administrative procedures in the State where the measure has been taken to challenge such measure and to claim compensation. States should ensure that where transboundary harm has been, or is likely to be, caused, individuals and peoples affected have non-discriminatory access to the same judicial and administrative procedures as would individuals and peoples of the State in which the harm is caused.

2.3. *The Principle of Public Participation and the NAFTA/NAAEC*

The concept of public participation has existed within the NAFTA framework ever since its inception. In fact, the public's involvement in the negotiation process leading up to the NAFTA was defined by scholars at the time as "unprecedented in the history of trade agreements."[15] The discussions on the potential environmental impact of the NAFTA indeed included open hearings, public roundtable sessions, and public forums.[16]

Following the conclusion of the NAFTA, the principle of public participation was explicitly included in the NAFTA's environmental side agreement, the North American Agreement on Environmental Cooperation (NAAEC). The Preamble to the NAAEC emphasizes "the importance of public participation in conserving, protecting and enhancing the environment."[17] Among the objectives of the NAAEC, Article 1(h) mentions the promotion of transparency and public participation with respect to the development of environmental regulation and policies.[18] Public participation

---

[15] Michael Gregory, "Environment, Sustainable Development, Public Participation and the NAFTA: A Retrospective" (1992) 7 *Journal of Environmental Law & Litigation* 99–174 at 99.

[16] Gregory, "Environment," above, 100–01.

[17] Preamble of the NAAEC, above.

[18] Article 1(h) of the NAAEC, above.

is also mentioned in other NAAEC provisions such as Article 4 ("publication"), which requires the Parties to publish legislative proposals and ensure that interested persons will be provided with the opportunity to comment on them;[19] in Article 7, which requires the Parties to open certain judicial and administrative proceedings to the public; and in numerous other provisions with respect to the work of the Commission for Environmental Cooperation.[20]

However, despite the strong emphasis placed on the principle of public participation in the NAAEC, Chapter 11 of the NAFTA does not include any reference to this principle. To the contrary, relevant provisions of Chapter 11[21] specifically address only the traditional parties to investment disputes (that is, foreign investors and host states) or the Parties to the treaty. It could be argued, however, that in light of Article 31(2)(a) of the Vienna Convention on the Law of Treaties,[22] the words of the NAAEC should be interpreted as also being relevant for Chapter 11. According to this argument, nondisputing parties (NDPs) can base their demand to intervene in Chapter 11 disputes on the principle of public participation. But despite the fact that NDPs have indeed raised Article 31(2)(a) of the Vienna Convention in the past with respect to the relevance of the NAAEC in Chapter 11 disputes,[23] to the best of the author's knowledge, no such claim was ever made with regard to the application of the principle of public participation.

But even without the application of such an argument, a modified version of this principle eventually did find its way into the Chapter 11 framework. The process through which the principle of public participation crept into the NAFTA Chapter 11 investor–state dispute settlement system, as well as its current application by tribunals, are at the heart of this chapter.

3. THE PRINCIPLE OF PUBLIC PARTICIPATION AND CHAPTER 11 OF THE NAFTA

International investment law is regulated through a network of over 2,750 international investment agreements (IIAs) and investment chapters in free trade agreements. Chapter 11 of the NAFTA is one of the earliest modern investment chapters, and probably the most researched and discussed legal instrument in this field. Like

---

[19] Article 4(2) of the NAAEC, above.
[20] See, for example, Articles 9(4), 9(7), 10(2)(f), 10(5), and 13(2)(e) of the NAAEC, above.
[21] See, for example, Articles 1128 (participation by a Party) and 1129 (access to documents) of NAFTA, above.
[22] Article 32(2)(a) of the Vienna Convention on the Law of Treaties, Vienna, May 23, 1969, in force January 27, 1980, 1155 UNTS 331; (1969) 8 ILM 697, states: "The context for the purpose of the interpretation of a treaty shall comprise . . . [A]ny agreement relating to the treaty which was made between all the parties in connection with the conclusion of the treaty."
[23] *Methanex Corporation v. The United States of America* (August 03, 2005), (NAFTA Chapter 11, UNCITRAL) (amicus curiae submissions by the International Institute for Sustainable Development) at para 23.

that of most investment treaties, the objective of Chapter 11 is the protection of foreign investment, based on the assumption that by providing foreign investors with treaty-based guarantees and a nonpoliticized dispute settlement mechanism, the flow of foreign investments will increase and contribute to the host state's development. As with most IIAs, Chapter 11 includes substantive legal provisions such as the protection of foreign investors from expropriation, protection from nationality-based discrimination (found in "national treatment" and "most favored nation" provisions), and the obligation to provide fair and equitable treatment to foreign investors.[24]

Like the majority of IIAs, Chapter 11 also opts for a rather unique dispute settlement mechanism that allows foreign investors to litigate treaty-based claims against host states before independent international arbitral panels. As these disputes are often claimed to be of public relevance, in many instances members of the general public have asked to gain access to these disputes, participate either as a third party or as a direct party, and access documents that are relevant to the dispute. In other words, investment tribunals are being asked by members of the public to de facto exercise the principle of public participation.

3.1. *Investment Treaty Arbitration versus the Principle of Public Participation: Challenges in the Application*

The assimilation of the principle of public participation into the investment treaty arbitration process (investor–state dispute settlement, or ISDS) is not without difficulties. Most notably, two key challenges must be faced. The first is with respect to the relevance of the principle of public participation to a process such as ISDS. The second concerns the conflicts that may arise between the practical application of this principle and the rationales behind the ISDS process. Addressing these challenges requires certain adaptations and compromises.

3.1.1. The Relevance of the Principle of Public Participation to the ISDS Process

The duty to provide for public participation is designed to ensure public participation in decision-making processes[25] and is traditionally required of states[26] or other sovereign entities. The arbitration process in this respect can hardly be seen as a classic decision-making process in which policies are being determined. Similarly, it is also difficult to view arbitrators as equivalent to states. In fact, the aim underlying the choice of the commercial arbitration model and the appointment of independent

---

[24] See, respectively, Articles 1110, 1102, 1103, 1105 of the NAFTA.
[25] See Principle 10 of the Rio Declaration, above, and paragraph 23.2 of Agenda 21, above.
[26] Paragraph 5.1 of the New Delhi Declaration specifically mentions "governments."

arbitrators in investor–state arbitrations is to distance this process from states' courts and the influence of the sovereign – which is also a party in these disputes. Indeed, these quasiprivate proceedings were designed to provide foreign investors with a nonpoliticized, commercially oriented dispute settlement mechanism. Therefore it can be argued that it seems unfit to demand sovereign obligations from those who were appointed to ensure independence from the sovereign and from the matters a sovereign must consider.

On the other hand, it should be remembered that whatever the original objective of the investor–state arbitration process is, the public ramifications of this system cannot be ignored. Arbitrators in this context are the interpreters of states' administrative measures and de facto apply a judicial review of these measures.[27] The subject matter of these arbitrations can also be of great public importance, and compensation awarded to private investors comes from taxpayers' pockets. Moreover, in their decisions, arbitrators can affect states' regulatory measures, or even "chill" a state from regulating a certain area in the future.[28] It can therefore be argued, in light of the public aspect of investment treaty arbitration and its influence over states' governance activities, that the application of the principle of public participation is justified.

Indeed, given the conflicting tensions described here, it is relatively well accepted today that at least to a certain extent, and perhaps with some modifications, the principle of public participation should be formally included within the investment arbitration system. This reality is reflected in legal instruments such as the 2006 ICSID Rules as well as in numerous "new generation" IIAs.[29] Attempts to balance these conflicting tensions have been made in the past by several tribunals, by creating a distinction between investment arbitrations in which purely contractual matters are discussed and investment arbitrations that involve issues that are of public importance.[30] In the latter, it was accepted that arbitrators cannot ignore

---

[27] This view is advocated by scholars such as Van Harten; see, for example, Gus Van Harten and Martin Loughlin, "Investment Treaty Arbitration as a Species of Global Administrative Law," (2006) 17 *European Journal of International Law*, 121; part 4 of this article; Gus Van Harten, *Investment Treaty Arbitration and Public Law* (New York: Oxford University Press, 2007).

[28] Although the existence of the "regulatory chill" is disputed in this respect, at least in some cases it seems to have taken place. See, for example, the case of Philip Morris threat of investment arbitration over Uruguay's antismoking rules, in Rory Carroll, "Uruguay bows to pressure over anti-smoking law amendments," The Guardian, July 27, 2010, http://www.guardian.co.uk/world/2010/jul/27/uruguay-tobacco-smoking-philip-morris.

[29] See, for example, the relevant provisions of the Dominican Republic-Central America's investment chapter (Washington, D.C., May 28, 2004, in force January 1, 2009). See also the model investment agreements of the U.S. (U.S. Model BIT (2012), http://www.ustr.gov/sites/default/files/BIT%20text%20for%20ACIEP%20Meeting.pdf) and Canada (Canada Model FIPA (2004), ITA, http://italaw.com/documents/Canadian2004-FIPA-model-en.pdf). Other examples include Chapter 10 of the Australia-Chile FTA, the Canada-Peru FIPA, above, and the U.S.-Uruguay BIT, above.

[30] Such a distinction was indeed made by investment tribunals, see *Suez, Sociedad General de Aguas de Barcelona S.A. and Vivendi Universal S.A v. Argentine Republic* (July 30, 2010), ICSID Case No.

the possibility that their decisions may affect public matters or their accountability toward the affected public.

3.1.2. The Rationale of the Investor–State Arbitration Process versus the Principle of Public Participation

The second challenge to be met in the integration of the principle of public participation into the process of investment-treaty arbitration concerns the conflict between some of the rationales for this system and the practical application of the principle. International investment law was designed to encourage foreign investors to invest in foreign territories. This system was designed to overcome the inherent lack of trust that foreign investors often have toward foreign governments by, inter alia, ensuring them a nonpoliticized, efficient, and commercially oriented dispute settlement mechanism. Yet acknowledging the need to apply the principle of public participation in this context can be seen as conflicting with the core objective of the investor–state dispute settlement mechanism.

The adoption of the principle of public participation, for example, can jeopardize the nonpoliticized, commercial nature of the arbitral process. For example, members of the public may attempt to apply pressure on foreign investors or even on arbitrators. During the ICSID *Biwater* arbitration, the foreign investor complained that the NDPs' campaign (entitled "Dirty aid, dirty water. Hands off Tanzania: Stop UK company Biwater's attempt to sue") was solely aimed at putting a stop to the arbitral proceedings.[31] The Tribunal indeed recognized in this case that public participation might negatively affect the dispute:[32]

> Given the media campaign that has already been fought on both sides of this case (by many entities beyond the parties to this arbitration), and the general media interest that already exists, the Tribunal is satisfied that there exists a sufficient risk of harm or prejudice, as well as aggravation, in this case to warrant some form of control.

Several eminent investment arbitrators and scholars have expressed their concerns in this respect. L. Yves Fortier has said:[33]

ARB/03/19 (Order in Response to a Petition for Transparency and Participation as *Amicus Curiae*, May 19, 2005), at para 20; with respect to discloser of materials to the public, see *Biwater Gauff (Tanzania) Ltd.* v. *United Republic of Tanzania* (July 24, 2008), ICSID Case No. ARB/05/22 (Procedural Order No. 3) at para 147; *Methanex Corporation* v. *The United States of America* (August 03, 2005), (NAFTA Chapter 11, UNCITRAL) (Decision of the tribunal on petitions from third persons to intervene as "Amici Curiae") at para 49; *Apotex Inc* v. *The United States of America* (June 14, 2013), (NAFTA, UNCITRAL) at para 30 ("Apotex I").

[31] *Biwater Gauff* (Procedural Order No. 3), above at para 16.

[32] *Biwater Gauff* (Procedural Order No. 3), above at para 146.

[33] L. Yves Fortier, "Investment Protection and the Rule of Law: Change or Decline?", Lecture given at the British Institute of International and Comparative Law, March 17, 2009, www.arbitration-icca .org/media/0/12392785460140/0732_001.pdf, p. 15.

Returning to the point I made earlier in respect of the de-politicization of dispute through use of the arbitral model of dispute resolution, a concern with "pre-award transparency", that is the participation of *amici curiae*, the publication of pre-award decisions, and the open hearings, among other measures, is that both claimants and respondents can use this kind of access as a weapon, contrary to the very principle of neutral, non-political dispute resolution.

Professor Thomas Wälde has added:[34]

> The introduction of amicus briefs by NGOs, which as a rule oppose the Claimant, impose the cost of review and attempted rebuttal. Amicus briefs can also directly or indirectly impugn the investor or the social acceptability of the investor's conduct, without supplying evidence or being subjected to cross-examination. Even if tribunals do not refer to such depreciatory comment, this does not mean that they are ineffectual (*"semper aliquid haeret"*).

Moreover, it is also possible that by opening investment disputes to third parties' participation, parties may lose a "certain flexibility and informality" which closed proceedings facilitate.[35] As a result, the possibility of reaching a compromise and amicably resolving disputes could be diminished.[36] This is especially harmful in the context of investor–state relationships, which are often long term and depend on the maintenance of a proper working relationship.

Last, public participation in investment disputes increases arbitration costs and prolongs the process, a fact that stands in contrast to the efficiency goal of the ISDS.[37] Certain rules of arbitration were in fact modified to emphasize the element of efficient process in light of increasing public participation.[38]

---

[34] Thomas W. Wälde, "'Equality of Arms' in Investment Arbitration: Procedural Challenges," in Katia Yannaca-Small (ed.), *Arbitration Under International Investment Agreements: A Guide to the Key Issues* (New York: Oxford University Press, 2010) 161 at 178.

[35] Vaughan Lowe, "Changing Dimension of International Investment Law" (2007) Oxford Legal Studies Research Paper Series, Working Paper No. 4/2007, http://papers.ssrn.com/sol3/papers.cfm/abstract_id1/4970727, 122.

[36] See also Federico Ortino, "External Transparency of Investment Awards" (2008) Society of International Economic Law, Working Paper No. 49/08, http://papers.ssrn.com/sol3/papers.cfm?abstract_id1/41159899, 13.

[37] *Methanex Amici Curiae decision*, above at para 50; the *Suez* Tribunals indeed mention the "extra burden which the acceptance of amicus curiae briefs may place on the parties" as an important consideration when deciding whether to grant a nonparty leave to submit amicus curiae briefs in *Suez*, *Amicus Curiae* order 2005, above at para 27; See also in *Biwater Gauff Ltd v. United Republic of Tanzania* (July 24, 2008), ICSID Case No. ARB/05/22 (ICSID), (Procedural Order No. 5) at paras 56–59. This consideration is also present in the United Nations Commission on International Trade Law *Arbitration Rules* (Vienna: United Nations, 2011); the International Centre for Settlement of Investment Dispute, *ICSID Convention, Regulations and Rules* (Washington, D.C.: ICSID, 2006); and the relevant NAFTA Free Trade Commission, "Statement of the Free Trade Commission on Non-Disputing Party Participation" (2003), http://www.international.gc.ca/trade-agreements-accords-commerciaux/assets/pdfs/Nondisputing-en.pdf.

[38] See Article 17(1) of the UNCITRAL Rules, above.

To conclude, the application of the principle of public participation is not without consequences, and therefore the assimilation of the principle within the ISDS process requires a certain compromise. On the one hand, states are increasingly willing today to incorporate the principle of public participation into the ISDS. On the other, in order to ensure that the application of this principle will not undermine the very raison d'être of the ISDS, certain safeguards must be created. As described in more detail in the following, this need to balance these tensions was indeed recognized by the Member States of the NAFTA, United Nations Commission on International Trade Law (UNCITRAL), and ICSID.

3.2. *The Principle of Public Participation in NAFTA Chapter 11 Disputes: The Regulatory Framework*

The principle of public participation is not mentioned in Chapter 11 of the NAFTA. Nor could it originally be found within the sets of arbitration rules that are relevant to NAFTA disputes, such as the UNCITRAL Arbitration Rules, the ICSID Arbitration Rules, and the ICSID Additional Facility (AF) Rules. The first steps toward the acceptance and integration of this principle into investment disputes were in fact made by NAFTA arbitrators, whose decisions revolutionized the approach of international investment tribunals toward the notion of public participation. Following these decisions, some of the arbitration rules have been amended and now contain, either implicitly or explicitly, certain aspects of the principle of public participation.

The rules governing NAFTA Chapter 11 disputes can be found in three main sources: the ICSID/ICSID AF Rules, the UNCITRAL Rules, and a body of notes and statements that were issued by the North American Free Trade Commission (FTC), most notably a "Statement of the Free Trade Commission on Non-Disputing Party Participation" issued in 2003 (FTC Statement),[39] and the "Notes of Interpretation of Certain Chapter 11 Provisions" issued in 2001 (Notes of Interpretation).[40]

3.2.1. NAFTA Chapter 11

Until 2001, there was nothing in the NAFTA's legal framework to imply that the principle of public participation applies with respect to investment disputes. However, following the *Methanex* and *UPS* disputes (discussed in the following), in which it was decided that tribunals possess "inherent powers" to accept NDPs' participation, the FTC issued a series of documents in which elements relevant to the principle of public participation were addressed.

---

[39] FTC Statement, above.

[40] NAFTA Free Trade Commission, "Notes of Interpretation of Certain Chapter 11 Provisions," July 31, 2001, http://www.international.gc.ca/trade-agreements-accords-commerciaux/disp-diff/nafta-interpr.aspx?lang=en&view=d.

3.2.1.1. THE NOTES OF INTERPRETATION. The context in which these documents were accepted by the FTC is important to understand: As Dumberry describes, at the time, Chapter 11 (as well as the investment arbitration regime in general) was enduring repeated attacks by civil society organizations.[41] Most notably, the closed nature of this system and the power granted to multinational corporations vis-à-vis sovereign states stood (and still stands) at the heart of this critique. These arguments did not fall on deaf ears; both Canada and the United States had already made supportive statements on these issues,[42] and indeed supported the applications made by several NGOs to participate in the proceedings of the *Methanex* arbitration.[43]

In light of this reality, following the *Methanex* and the *UPS* cases, the FTC issued several new and important documents. First, in July 2001, the FTC issued the Notes of Interpretation, addressing the matter of access to documents. In this statement, a relatively generous set of rules was prescribed; most notably, it was declared that no general rule of confidentiality applies on Chapter 11 arbitration proceedings, and that "nothing in the NAFTA precludes the Parties from providing public access to documents submitted to, or issued by, a Chapter Eleven tribunal."[44] Furthermore, it was also stated that the Parties agree to make such documents available to the public in a timely fashion. Three exceptions were made to this rule:[45] the first concerns confidential business information, the second addresses information that is protected from disclosure by domestic law, and the third refers to the restrictions imposed by other "relevant arbitral rules, as applied."

3.2.1.2. STATEMENT OF THE FREE TRADE COMMISSION ON NON-DISPUTING PARTY PRESENTATION. In 2003 the FTC adopted a statement with respect to the participation of NDPs in Chapter 11 disputes (most notably the submission of amicus curiae briefs).[46] The FTC Statement approved the *Methanex* and *UPS* Tribunals' conclusion that nothing in the NAFTA prohibits them from accepting NDPs' submissions, and recommends a set of procedures for making such submissions. The FTC Statement has been referred to (and relied upon) by ICSID tribunals (most notably the *Suez* Tribunal), and has undoubtedly influenced the design of later relevant arbitration rules such as the reformed ICSID Rules.

---

[41] Patrick Dumberry, "The Admissibility of *Amicus Curiae* Briefs by NGOs in Investor-States Arbitration: The Precedent Set by the *Methanex* Case in the Context of NAFTA Chapter 11 Proceedings" (2001) 1 *Non-State Actors and International Law* 201, 213; Marcia Staff and Christine Lewis, "Arbitration under NAFTA Chapter 11: Past, present, and future" (2003) 25 *Houston Journal of International Law* 301 at 328–329.

[42] Dumberry, "Admissibility," above, p. 213; Staff and Lewis, "Arbitration," above, pp. 328–29.

[43] See for a review of the proceedings International Institute for Sustainable Development, "Methanex Background," http://www.iisd.org/investment/dispute/methanex_background.asp.

[44] Paragraph 1(a) of the "NAFTA Notes of Interpretation," above.

[45] Paragraph 1(b)(ii)(c) of the "NAFTA Notes of Interpretation," above.

[46] FTC Statement, above.

The conditions recommended by the FTC Statement include a limitation on the length of submissions from NDPs (no more than five pages for the application and twenty pages for the submission itself) and broad disclosure obligations (including disclosure, inter alia, of membership, parent organizations, affiliation with a disputing party, and sources of funding). These rules are meant to ensure matters such as the efficiency of the arbitral process, the quality of the submissions, and their impartiality.

The FTC Statement further provides guidance as to the discretion to be applied by the tribunal.[47] According to these rules, arbitrators are expected to consider in reaching their decision the following considerations:

(a) the non-disputing party submission would assist the Tribunal in the determination of a factual or legal issue related to the arbitration by bringing a perspective, particular knowledge or insight that is different from that of the disputing parties;

(b) the non-disputing party submission would address matters within the scope of the dispute;

(c) the non-disputing party has a significant interest in the arbitration; and

(d) there is a public interest in the subject-matter of the arbitration.

Thus, the FTC's recognition of the principle of public participation is reflected in its language. First, the Statement specifically welcomes any "perspective, particular knowledge or insight" that is unrepresented by the Parties. The Statement also acknowledges that public participation can assist the tribunal and enhance the quality of its decisions. Last, contrary to other legal systems' approach to public participation at the time, the FTC Statement specifically dismisses the need to achieve both parties' consent to the public's participation and grants the tribunal the discretion to permit the public's participation even without such consent.

3.2.1.3. FTC JOINT STATEMENT. In 2004 a joint statement titled *A Decade of Achievement* was issued by the FTC ("Joint Statement"). While this statement was not drafted in the form of a legal agreement, the representatives of the three NAFTA member states jointly and explicitly expressed their view with respect to the Chapter 11 arbitrations' hearings:[48]

We were pleased Mexico has now joined Canada and the United States in supporting open hearings for investor-state disputes. In addition, we have agreed that

---

[47] Paragraph 6 of the FTC Statement, above.

[48] NAFTA Free Trade Commission, "Joint Statement: A Decade of Achievement," July 16, 2004, http://www.international.gc.ca/trade-agreements-accords-commerciaux/agr-acc/nafta-alena/js-sanantonio.aspx?lang=en&view=d.

the same degree of openness should apply to proceedings under the Dispute Settlement provisions of Chapter 20 of the NAFTA, and asked officials to develop rules governing open hearings for such proceedings.

This development was also inspired by the landmark approach of the *Methanex* Tribunal and the parties to this dispute, in which for the first time in the history of investment jurisprudence, the hearings on the merits were open to the general public. One of the amici in this case (the International Institute for Sustainable Development, IISD) indeed mentioned the importance of the open hearing process to their contribution in this case.[49] However, it should be noted that despite this landmark turn, the opening of hearings is still subject to parties' consent,[50] and indeed on some instances investors have declined to open their proceedings to the public.[51]

3.2.2. The ICSID/ICSID AF Rules

The other sources of legal rules that are relevant for the application of the principle of public participation in Chapter 11 disputes are the ICSID Rules of Arbitration and the ICSID AF Rules. The ICSID Rules are perhaps the most widely used set of arbitration rules in investment disputes today. As Mexico is currently not a party to the ICSID Convention, the ICSID Rules cannot be directly applied to any investment dispute between this country and U.S./Canadian investors, as well as between Mexican investors and Canada or the United States. However, nonparties may administer their investment disputes through ICSID in accordance with the ICSID AF rules. As the rules prescribed by the ICSID AF with respect to the principle of public participation (Article 41) are identical to those prescribed by the ICSID Rules (Rule 37(2)), the two frameworks will be discussed jointly.

Like NAFTA's Chapter 11, the original ICSID Rules did not address the principle of public participation. Also like Chapter 11, this situation was amended in light of certain decisions rendered by ICSID Tribunals. Most notably, following the *Suez* decision,[52] the ICSID Convention was amended to include a partial version of the principle of public participation, reflecting a careful balance of the conflicting

---

[49] See "Methanex Background," above.
[50] NAFTA 2022 Advisory Committee on International Private Commercial Disputes, "Minutes for the 14th Meeting/Santa Fe, New Mexico, September 26–28, 2004," http://www.nafta-alena.gc.ca/NAFTA/CMFILES/Meeting%20Minutes/Minutes14thmeetingSantaFe.pdf.
[51] *Chemtura Corp. v. Government of Canada* (2010), (NAFTA Chapter 11) (Confidentiality Order, January 21, 2008), http://www.naftalaw.org/Disputes/Canada/CromptonCorp/Crompton-Chemtura-Confidentiality.pdf, at para 10 [*Chemtura*, Confidentiality Order]; *Vito G. Gallo v. Government of Canada* (September 15, 2011), PCA Case No. 55798 (NAFTA Chapter 11) (Procedural Order No. 1), http://www.naftalaw.org/Disputes/Canada/Gallo/Gallo-Canada-Order1.pdf, at para 31.
[52] *Suez, Amicus Curiae* Order 2005, above.

forces. The result of this balancing is Rule 37(2) of the ICSID Rules (and the identical Article 41 of the ICSID AF Rules), which authorizes arbitrators to accept submissions of amicus briefs from the public, provided that:

   a. [T]he non-disputing party submission would assist the Tribunal in the determination of a factual or legal issue related to the proceeding by bringing a perspective, particular knowledge or insight that is different from that of the disputing parties;
   b. [T]he non-disputing party submission would address a matter within the scope of the dispute;
   c. [T]he non-disputing party has a significant interest in the proceeding.[53]

In addition to these conditions, Rule 37(2) safeguards the parties' interest in ensuring an efficient process, by indicating that the amicus submissions should not "disrupt the proceedings or unduly burden or unfairly prejudice either party."[54]

The only difference between Rule 37(2) and the FTC Statement discussed here is the latter's final condition, according to which the submission of amicus briefs shall be authorized only where "there is a public interest in the subject-matter of the arbitration."[55] ICSID tribunals, however, have included the public nature of the dispute as a reason to allow the public's participation.[56] In practice, therefore, the two sets can be seen as almost identical with respect to NDP's amicus submissions.

Like the NAFTA's conditions, the conditions of Rule 37(2) are aimed at ensuring that amicus submissions will genuinely assist the tribunal's work and will not unnecessarily undermine the investor's interests and the efficiency of the proceedings. ICSID's Rule 37(2), however, represents a slightly different compromise than that found in the NAFTA Chapter 11 framework. For example, unlike the NAFTA framework, Rule 37(2) remains silent on the subsequent right implied by the principle of public participation – the right to effective access to information. With respect to arbitral awards, Regulation 22 of ICSID's Administrative and Financial Regulations dictates that these will be published only with the consent of the parties. Furthermore, due to the objections of several member states,[57] the ICSID Rules do not allow open access to hearings (at least not without the consent of both parties).

[53] Rule 37(2) of the ICSID Rules, above.
[54] Rule 37(2) of the ICSID Rules, above.
[55] Paragraph 6 of the FTC Statement, above.
[56] Before the entering into force of the 2006 ICSID Arbitration Rules, the *Suez* Tribunal mentioned the public nature of the dispute (i.e. where cases are more than "simply a contract dispute") as a relevant condition. *Suez, Amicus Curiae* Order 2005, above at para 20.
[57] Antonio R. Parra, Preface to Nathalie Bernasconi-Osterwalder, "Transparency and Amicus Curiae in ICSID Arbitrations," in Cordonier Segger, Gehring, and Newcombe (eds.), *Sustainable Development in World Investment Law* (The Hague: Kluwer, 2010), pp. 189–90.

3.2.3. UNCITRAL Arbitration Rules

The UNCITRAL Rules are widely used in investment disputes and are often adopted by IIAs. In fact, the first investment tribunal to accept public participation in investment treaty arbitration – the *Methanex* tribunal – was governed by the UNCITRAL Rules. The application of the UNCITRAL Rules in the *Methanex* and the *UPS* decisions laid the foundation for the *Suez* Tribunal's (the first ICSID Tribunal to accept public participation) decision under the ICSID Rules, which in turn led to the modification of these Rules.

Despite the fact that Article 17 of the UNCITRAL Rules served as the original legal basis for permitting public participation in investment disputes, the UNCITRAL Rules on their own do not include a clear expression of the principle of public participation. In fact, credit for the introduction of this principle in the landmark UNCITRAL-governed disputes should be attributed to judicial activism demonstrated by the arbitrators in these cases, rather than to the legal text of the UNCITRAL Rules: Article 17 only states that the arbitral tribunal "may conduct the arbitration in such manner as it considers appropriate," but on this basis several tribunals have concluded that they have authority to accept amicus curiae briefs.[58] In the author's view, however, the fact that the recently (2010) revised rules did not amend this situation implicitly confirms this interpretation.

With respect to open hearings, Article 28(3) of the UNCITRAL Rules states that "[h]earings shall be held in camera unless the parties agree otherwise." Furthermore, there is nothing in the UNCITRAL Rules to suggest that the public has a right to access documents, including investment awards, or even to be notified as to the existence of an investment dispute.

This current state of affairs, it should be noted, is about to change. The UNCITRAL Working Group (UNCITRAL WG) has finalized a draft "rules on transparency" document, which was authorized by the member states in July 2013 (and came into effect in April 2014).[59] In these rules, the UNCITRAL member states have taken a far-reaching approach with respect to the principle of public participation. For example, it was decided that with limited exceptions, all hearings shall be opened

---

[58] See, for example, *Methanex Amici Curiae* Decision, above; *United Parcel Service of America Inc v. Canada*, (NAFTA Chapter 11, UNCITRAL) (Decision of the Tribunal on Petitions for Intervention and Participation as *Amici Curiae*).

[59] See United Nations Commission on International Trade Law, *UNCITRAL Rules on Transparency in Treaty-based Investor-State Arbitration* (effective date: April 2014); United Nations Commission on International Trade Law, "Report of Working Group II (Arbitration and Conciliation) of the Work of its Fifty-Eighth Session," New York, February 4–8, 2013, UN Doc. A/CN.9/765, http://daccess-dds-ny .un.org/doc/UNDOC/GEN/V13/808/19/PDF/V1380819.pdf/OpenElement; United Nations Commission on International Trade Law, "Settlement of Commercial Disputes: Draft UNCITRAL Rules on Transparency in Treaty-Based Investor-State Arbitration," February 28, 2013, UN Doc. A/CN.9/783, online: http://daccess-dds-ny.un.org/doc/UNDOC/GEN/V13/812/34/PDF/V1381234 .pdf/OpenElement.

to the general public.[60] Moreover, tribunals are in fact instructed to actively facilitate public access to the hearings by making sufficient "logistical arrangements."[61]

The UNCITRAL Rules on Transparency also prescribe a broad rule on access to documents: It is stated that a list of documents – including notice of arbitration, statements of claim, transcripts of hearings, orders, decisions, and awards – shall be made available to the general public.[62] It is further proposed that tribunals shall have the authority to make other documents, such as exhibits, publicly available.[63]

Moreover, in light of the fact that nothing in the current UNCITRAL Rules requires the parties to disclose that a dispute in fact exists, the new UNCITRAL Rules on Transparency prescribes that a registry of published information be established under the UNCITRAL.[64] With respect to the submission of NDP amicus curiae briefs, it was agreed that tribunals should accept them, provided that "any submission does not disrupt or unduly burden the arbitral proceedings, or unfairly prejudice any disputing party."[65]

Lastly, it should be noted that interests related to the efficiency and the integrity of the arbitral process were not abandoned in the new UNCITRAL Rules on Transparency, and the aforementioned liberal approach is somewhat limited by the Article 1(4), according to which:[66]

> Where the Rules on Transparency provide for the arbitral tribunal to exercise discretion, the arbitral tribunal in exercising such discretion shall take into account:
>
> (a) the public interest in transparency in treaty-based investor-State arbitration and in the particular arbitral proceedings, and
> (b) the disputing parties' interest in a fair and efficient resolution of their dispute.

3.2.4. New Generation of IIAs

Another important development with respect to the creeping acceptance of the principle of public participation in investment arbitration is the introduction of what is often described as a new generation of IIAs. Unlike the old generation, these new-generation IIAs are characterized as being more supportive of sustainable development goals, of the states' right to regulate, and often also of the public's right to participate in investor–state arbitration proceedings. These IIAs were largely influenced by the developments of Chapter 11 legislation and jurisprudence.

---

[60] UNCITRAL Rules on Transparency, above at Article 6.
[61] UNCITRAL Rules on Transparency, above at Article 6(3).
[62] UNCITRAL Rules on Transparency, above at Article 3.
[63] UNCITRAL Rules on Transparency, above at Article 3.
[64] UNCITRAL Rules on Transparency, above at Article 2 and 8.
[65] UNCITRAL Rules on Transparency, above at Article 5(4).
[66] UNCITRAL Rules on Transparency, above at Article 1(4). See further provisions with respect to the integrity of the arbitral process in Articles 7(6) and 7(7).

In the context of the NAFTA states, some of the treaties concluded by Canada and the United States can certainly be regarded as representative examples of new-generation IIAs.[67] The model IIAs designed by both these states are especially relevant. For example, the U.S. and Canadian model IIAs permit, under certain limitations, the submission of amicus briefs.[68] These model IIAs also include obligations to make key documents available to the general public[69] and permit the public's access to hearings.[70] It would appear that the United States and Canada were directly influenced by their experience with Chapter 11 in this respect.

The influence of Chapter 11 seems not to have ended there and can be found in other agreements as well. For example, a unique example of the creeping acceptance of the principle of public participation can be found in Article 10.21 of the Dominican Republic–Central American FTA (CAFTA–DR), titled "Transparency of Arbitral Proceedings." This Article includes, among others, instructions to make documents such as pleadings, submissions, minutes, orders, and awards available to the public, and to open the arbitral hearings to the public. Article 10.20 of the CAFTA–DR also grants tribunals the authority to accept amicus curiae briefs from third parties. This novel agreement was the source of a further somewhat revolutionary development with respect to public participation when based on the CAFTA–DR provisions; the first publicly webcast ICSID arbitration proceedings took place in 2010.[71]

Last, a recent, highly significant development in investment treaty making involves the future investment policy of the EU, which is expected to replace approximately 1,200 existing IIAs. In an announcement made in February 2013, the EU Commission stated that the EU will support the UNCITRAL WG recommendations on greater transparency in ISDS.[72] It was further announced that the EU will aspire to include obligations in its future IIAs to make arbitration documents available to the public, to open hearings to the public, and to permit the submission of amicus briefs.

---

[67] See in more detail in Chester Brown, "Bringing Sustainable Development Issues before Investment Treaty Tribunals," in Segger, Gehring, and Newcombe, *Sustainable Development*, above; Nathalie Bernasconi-Osterwalder, "Transparency and Amicus Curiae in ICSID Arbitration," in Segger, Gehring, and Newcombe, *Sustainable Development*, above.

[68] Article 39 of the Canada Model FIPA, above, and Article 28(3) of the United States Model BIT.

[69] See Article 29 of the U.S. Model BIT, above, and its somewhat less liberal equivalent – Article 38 of the Canadian Model FIPA, above, according to which the parties are still in a position to prohibit the publication of certain documents.

[70] Article 38 of the Canada Model FIPA, above, and Article 29(2) of the U.S. Model BIT, above.

[71] *Pac Rim Cayman LLC v. Republic of El Salvador* (May 31, and June 1, 2010), ICSID Case No. ARB/09/12, Public Hearing, http://icsid.worldbank.org/ICSID/FrontServlet?requestType=CasesRH&actionVal=OpenPage&PageType=AnnouncementsFrame&FromPage=Announcements&pageName=Announcement60.

[72] EU Commission Directorate-General for Trade, "EU backs new transparency standards for investor-state dispute settlement," Press release, February 11, 2013, http://trade.eceuropa.eu/doclib/press/index.cfm/id=868.

4. THE EVOLUTION OF THE PRINCIPLE OF PUBLIC PARTICIPATION IN NAFTA CHAPTER 11 JURISPRUDENCE

The previous part of this chapter reviewed the legal frameworks through which a somewhat restricted but nevertheless substantial principle of public participation has emerged. These legal reforms did not arise out of a vacuum, but were preceded and influenced by investment tribunals that had to face questions concerning public participation in light of legal lacunae. Investment jurisprudence continues today to develop and redefine the delicate balance between the application of the principle of public participation and the goals of the ISDS.

The next part of this chapter is therefore dedicated to the evolution of the principle of public participation within investment treaty jurisprudence. It will focus mainly on the cases conducted under NAFTA Chapter 11. A comparative review of other relevant investment cases will nevertheless be provided. This review will be performed in two parts; the first part will review tribunals' approaches toward the public's participation in investment arbitrations, whether as a party to a dispute or as a NDP. The second part will scrutinize these tribunals' approaches toward the public's right to access information, covering such matters as access to arbitration documents, awards, and oral hearings.

4.1. *Public Participation in NAFTA Jurisprudence*

The need to address the principle of public participation in the context of international investment law emerged when several representatives of the public (mostly NGOs) requested to actively participate in several investment disputes. These included requests for permission to submit written amicus curiae briefs at all stages of arbitration, to make oral presentations, to respond to investors' arguments, to respond to tribunals' questions, and even to join an arbitration as a party to the dispute. This chapter will focus on two types of participation: the submission of amicus curiae briefs and attempts to join as a party to arbitration. The first is perhaps the most common form of public participation in investment disputes. The second represents the fullest form of public participation and emphasizes the limits of this principle in investment disputes.

4.1.1. Amicus Curiae Briefs

Prior to the landmark decisions made by the *Methanex* and the *UPS* Tribunals, no investment tribunal had ever accepted an amicus brief. This situation was mainly the result of two elements. First, prior to these cases almost no attempts to submit amicus briefs were made. This lack of attempts to intervene in investment disputes is understandable as before the late 1990s, the field of international investment law was relatively dormant and unknown to the wider public. Similarly, public and academic attention to the adverse effects that investment arbitration may have on public policies was only in its early stage.

Second, as noted by the UPS Tribunal, the general practice of NDPs' interventions in international law at the time was "either ignored or given very low priority."[73] More specifically, to the best of the author's knowledge, no investment treaty at the time addressed issues relating to NDPs' participation. This situation, together with the fact that investment disputes are modeled along the lines of commercial arbitration, led to the impression that investment tribunals had no authority to accept such submissions. This approach was reflected by a decision made by the ICSID *Aguas del Tunari* Tribunal, which rejected the participation of several individuals and NGOs in the arbitral proceedings, claiming that the governing laws did not provide the Tribunal with the power to accept such an intervention from a nonparty.[74] The Tribunal's decision was relatively short (less than two pages) and no in-depth discussion was provided.

4.1.1.1. THE METHANEX AND THE UPS DECISIONS. Two decisions accepted by NAFTA tribunals have changed this state of affairs and have generally revolutionized the approach toward amicus curiae (and public participation in general) in international investment law. The first decision was given in January 2001 in the case between the Canadian Methanex Corporation and the United States, concerning a ban imposed by the state of California on a gasoline additive called MTBE.[75] This ban was based on environmental and health considerations. Following the commencement of proceedings, two petitions were submitted to the Tribunal by two NGOs, the IISD and Earthjustice,[76] requesting (among other things) the Tribunal's permission to file amicus briefs.[77]

As reasons, the IISD relied on three important arguments. First, it claimed that the legal issues raised in this case were of public importance as they defined the state's police power and regulatory flexibility. Second, the IISD argued that it possessed specific expertise with respect to the litigated questions and thus was in a position to support the tribunal's work. Last, it claimed that in light of the "notorious reputation"

---

[73] *UPS, Amici Curiae* Decision, above at para 40.

[74] *Aguas del Tunari, SA v. Republic of Bolivia*, ICSID Case No. ARB/02/3 (Letter sent by Professor David Caron, President of the Tribunal), http://italaw.com/cases/57.

[75] Methanex produces methane, a key ingredient in MTBE.

[76] *Methanex Corporation v. The United States of America* (August 03, 2005), (NAFTA Chapter 11, UNCITRAL) (Petition to the Arbitral Tribunal by the International Institute for Sustainable Development), http://naftaclaims.com/Disputes/USA/Methanex/MethanexAmicusStandingIISD.pdf; *Methanex Corporation v. The United States of America* (August 09, 2005), (NAFTA Chapter 11, UNCITRAL) (Petition to the Arbitral Tribunal by Earthjustice), http://naftaclaims.com/Disputes/USA/Methanex/MethanexAmicusStandingEarth.pdf.

[77] *Methanex*, Earthjustice Petition, above; *Methanex*, IISD Petition, above at para 5.1.

of Chapter 11–based arbitration, opening investment proceedings to the public would enhance the system's legitimacy.[78]

While the IISD emphasized a utilitarian approach according to which public participation is intended to support a tribunal's work, the second NGO, Earthjustice, addressed the issue of public participation from a human rights angle. Earthjustice presented itself as a representative "of serious public environmental and human health concerns" whose participation was required in order to safeguard the "democratic process."[79] More specifically, Earthjustice compared the arbitral process to the judicial litigation of constitutional questions involving issues such as private property rights and the state's authority to regulate, in both of which the importance of public participation is accepted.[80] The importance of public participation in resolving such "constitutional" issues, it was claimed, "is at least as great in this proceeding as in the analogous domestic proceedings."[81]

Both NGOs based their petitions on Article 15 of the UNCITRAL Rules (now Article 17), under which "the arbitral tribunal may conduct the arbitration in such manner as it considers appropriate."[82] This provision, these groups argued, grants a tribunal broad discretionary powers in such questions and authorizes it to accept the public's participation.[83] The two organizations further relied on WTO jurisprudence and Canadian and American domestic law as supportive, in their view, of this conclusion.[84]

The NGOs' arguments were only partly accepted by the *Methanex* Tribunal.[85] Most notably, the Tribunal did permit the submission of amicus curiae briefs. Relying on decisions made by tribunals such as the Iran–United States Claims Tribunal and the WTO, the *Methanex* Tribunal agreed that in light of Article 15, it enjoyed a wide discretion with respect to procedural questions.[86] The Tribunal accepted that *amicus* submissions may, in essence, place a burden on the parties to the arbitration ("this factor has weighted heavily with the Tribunal"[87]), but dismissed this problem by stating that in practice this burden "cannot be regarded as inevitably excessive for either Disputing Party."[88] Furthermore, the Tribunal also agreed that any such burden can be mitigated by imposing suitable restrictions as to the form and the substance of the submission.[89]

[78] *Methanex*, IISD Petition, above at para 3.
[79] *Methanex*, Earthjustice Petition, above at paras 2, 9.
[80] *Methanex*, Earthjustice Petition, above at paras 2, 10.
[81] *Methanex*, Earthjustice Petition, above at paras 2 and 10.
[82] Article 17(1) of the UNCITRAL Arbitration Rules, above.
[83] *Methanex*, Earthjustice Petition, above at para 17; *Methanex*, IISD Petition, above at para 4.2.
[84] *Methanex*, Earthjustice Petition, above at paras 23–24; *Methanex*, IISD Petition, above at para 4.6.
[85] *Methanex Amici Curiae* Decision, above.
[86] *Methanex Amici Curiae* Decision, above at paras 26–27, 31.
[87] *Methanex Amici Curiae* Decision, above at para 50.
[88] *Methanex Amici Curiae* Decision, above at para 36.
[89] *Methanex Amici Curiae* Decision, above at para 36.

It seems that the utilitarian approach presented by the IISD played a dominant role in the Tribunal's decision. The Tribunal, for example, addressed the question of how helpful the petitioners' submissions could be, and while it was unable to give an accurate answer to this question at the preliminary stage of the arbitration, it decided that it must assume that the submissions could indeed be of value.[90] Other factors considered by the Tribunal in its decision were the public interest in this dispute and the reputation of Chapter 11 arbitral process. With respect to the latter, the Tribunal stated:[91]

> Chapter 11 arbitral process could benefit from being perceived as more open or transparent; or conversely be harmed if seen as unduly secretive. In this regard, the Tribunal's willingness to receive amicus submissions might support the process in general and this arbitration in particular; whereas a blanket refusal could do positive harm.

While the *Methanex* Tribunal rejected the possibility that its decision could set a precedent in investment litigation with respect to the participation of NDPs in investment disputes, ten months later another NAFTA tribunal – the *UPS* Tribunal – further validated the criteria set by the *Methanex* Tribunal, leading up to the codification of these criteria in the FTC Statement two years later.

The *UPS* arbitration involved a dispute between the Canadian government and the United Parcel Service of America (a provider of courier services) in which the latter claimed that Canada's regulation of its mail sector (more specifically its favorable treatment of Canada Post) restricted the activities of foreign providers of mailing services in Canada. Following the initiation of this arbitration, two organizations, the Council of Canadians and the Canadian Union of Postal Workers, petitioned the Tribunal requesting, among other things, permission to submit amicus briefs.[92]

As with the *Methanex* arbitration, it was claimed that the subject matter of the arbitration was of public importance. The petitioners in this case, however, placed greater emphasis on the claim that their *own* interests were directly affected by the proceedings, so denying them the right to defend their interests would be "unfair and inconsistent with the principles of fundamental justice."[93]

The *UPS* Tribunal accepted the petition to submit amicus briefs. Basing its decision on the *Methanex* decision, the Tribunal agreed that Article 15 of the UNCITRAL Rules does indeed grant a tribunal the required authority to accept such briefs.[94] Also like the *Methanex* Tribunal, the *UPS* Tribunal emphasized that amicus

---

[90] *Methanex Amici Curiae* Decision, above at para 48.
[91] *Methanex Amici Curiae* Decision, above at para 49.
[92] *United Parcel Service of America Inc v. Canada*, (NAFTA Chapter 11, UNCITRAL) (Amicus petitions by the Canadian Union of Postal Workers and the Council of Canadians), http://naftaclaims.com/Disputes/Canada/UPS/UPSAmicusPetitionCUPW.pdf.
[93] *UPS*, Petition, above at para 2(1).
[94] *UPS, Amici Curiae* Decision, above at para 61.

submissions would not be permitted where they were "unduly burdensome for the parties" or "unnecessarily complicate[d] the Tribunal process."[95] In order to protect the efficiency of the proceedings and the parties' interests, the Tribunal imposed certain limitations on the participation of the amicus (for example, limits on lengths of the submissions and on the amicus's rights to call witnesses).[96] With regard to the criteria according to which amicus submissions would be permitted, the Tribunal confirmed the *Methanex* tests concerning the public nature of the dispute and the ability of the submissions to support the Tribunal's work.[97]

4.1.1.2. THE IMPACT OF THE METHANEX/UPS DECISIONS. Following the *UPS* and the *Methanex* decisions, a number of FTC statements were adopted that changed the regulatory framework of the NAFTA Chapter 11. The significance of these decisions was also noticed well beyond the North American context, and it was not long before ICSID Tribunals followed suit. In 2005, the question of public participation was raised in the ICSID *Suez* arbitration following the submission of a "Petition for Transparency and Participation as Amicus Curiae" by five NGOs.[98] The NGOs relied on the human rights angle of the public participation principle and claimed that "the case involved matters of basic public interest and the fundamental rights of people living in the area affected by the dispute in the case."[99] The petitioners asked both for the right to participate by presenting legal arguments via the submission of amicus curiae briefs and for the right to have unrestricted access to information (both to the hearing itself and to arbitration documents).[100] A similar request was made by a sixth NGO in parallel ICSID proceedings before the same arbitrators.[101]

With respect to the amicus submissions, despite the lack of specific reference to these in the ICSID Rules and without any similar precedent of an ICSID tribunal accepting such briefs, the *Suez* Tribunal concluded that it did have the power to accept them.[102] Inspired by the NAFTA's *Methanex* and *UPS* arbitrations and the FTC Statement that followed these arbitrations, the Tribunal concluded that according to Article 44 of the ICSID Rules, it was authorized to decide on a matter of

---

[95] *UPS, Amici Curiae* Decision, above at para 69.

[96] *UPS, Amici Curiae* Decision, above at para 69.

[97] *UPS, Amici Curiae* Decision, above at para 69.

[98] *Suez, Amicus Curiae* Order 2005, above.

[99] Aguas Provinciales de Santa Fe S.A., Suez, *Sociedad General de Aguas de Barcelona S.A. and Interaguas Servicios Integrales del Agua S.A. v. Argentine Republic,* Order in Response to a Petition for Participation as *Amicus Curiae,* March 17, 2006 ICSID Case No. ARB/03/17, (International Centre for Settlement of Investment Disputes), in para 1.

[100] Centro de Estudios Legales y Sociales et al. Petition for transparency and participation as amicus curiae in case no. ARB/03/19 before the International Centre for Settlement of Investment Disputes, Between Aguas Argentinas et al. and The Republic of Argentina, January 27, 2005.

[101] *Suez, Amicus Curiae* Order 2005, above.

[102] *Suez, Amicus Curiae* Order 2005, above.

procedure where no reference was made to it in the arbitration's governing laws.[103] The Tribunal gave three criteria according to which a request for the submission of an amicus curiae brief would be decided:

> a) the appropriateness of the subject matter of the case; b) the suitability of a given non-party to act as amicus curiae in that case, and c) the procedure by which the amicus submission is made and considered.[104]

Like the NAFTA tribunals, this Tribunal emphasized the public nature of the dispute:

> Given the public interest in the subject matter of this case, it is possible that appropriate nonparties may be able to afford the Tribunal perspectives, arguments, and expertise that will help it arrive at a correct decision.[105]

Following the *Suez* decision, the ICSID Arbitration Rules were also amended[106] to de facto codify three of the four conditions already prescribed by the FTC Statement, namely the ability of the amicus to assist the tribunal's work, its interest in the proceedings, and ensuring that the submission is within the scope of the arbitration. Indeed, as has been mentioned elsewhere, the close resemblance between the two regulatory frameworks allows NAFTA tribunals to search within ICSID decisions for "guidance" on the application of the FTC Statement.[107]

4.1.1.3. SUBSEQUENT NAFTA JURISPRUDENCE. Following the *Methanex* and the *UPS* cases, most NAFTA tribunals have continued to apply the principle of public participation in accordance with the conditions set by the FTC Statement and relying on these decisions. However, some tribunals – most notably the tribunals in a dispute between the Canadian corporation Apotex and the United States – have made some substantive comments on these conditions. This dispute was litigated simultaneously before two investment tribunals ("*Apotex I*"[108] and "*Apotex II*"[109]), both of which issued decisions concerning the participation of NDPs.

The *Apotex I* Tribunal seems to have stretched even further the acceptance of the principle of public participation in Chapter 11 disputes for reasons such as the efficiency of the process and the interests of the parties. First, with respect to the burden placed on the parties as a result of the *amicus* interventions, the *Apotex I* Tribunal emphasized that this should be balanced against the degree of public

---

[103] *Suez, Amicus Curiae* Order 2005, above at para 10; *Suez, Amicus Curiae* Order 2006, above at para 11.

[104] *Suez, Amicus Curiae* Order 2005, above at para 17.

[105] *Suez, Amicus Curiae* Order 2005, above at para 21.

[106] See Art. 37 of the ICSID Arbitration Rules.

[107] *Apotex Inc v. The United States of America* (June 14, 2013), (NAFTA, UNCITRAL) (Procedural Order No. 2) at para 19.

[108] *Apotex I*, above.

[109] *Apotex Holdings Inc and Apotex Inc v. The United States of America*, ICSID Case No. ARB(AF)/12/1, http://www.italaw.com/cases/1687 ("*Apotex II*").

importance attributed to the proceedings.[110] Unlike the previous tribunals, which approved such submissions only if they would not overly burden the parties (or were subject to the existence of sufficient safeguards), the *Apotex I* Tribunal's decision implies that the imposition of such a burden will not necessarily play a decisive role in the tribunal's conclusion and may indeed be tolerated in light of an exceptionally strong public interest.

Second, the *Apotex I* Tribunal also expanded the ruling of the *UPS* Tribunal concerning the scope of amicus intervention. The *UPS* Tribunal asserted that the issue of jurisdiction should not be within the scope of such submissions, as "the parties are fully able to present the competing contentions" on such an issue.[111] The *Apotex I* Tribunal, on the other hand, accepted the possibility that questions on jurisdiction will be addressed by NDPs in amicus submissions. The Tribunal explained that matters of public interest could be raised as part of the discussion on jurisdiction and that NDPs may be in a position to assist the tribunal on such questions.[112]

Third, the *Apotex I* Tribunal also emphasized that in matters of public interest, the requirement that the amicus present a particular perspective, particular knowledge, or expertise that is different from that of the disputing parties[113] should be interpreted very broadly. According to the Tribunal, the representation of as many voices and angles as possible will ensure that the interests in any given dispute are "properly canvassed" and accordingly will strengthen the arbitral process.[114] The *Apotex I* Tribunal in this particular respect was preceded by former statements made by the *Glamis* Tribunal, which indicated that in matters of public interest, leave to file amicus briefs should be granted "liberally."[115]

In the *Apotex I* arbitration, the Tribunal eventually ruled that even in light of such a broad interpretation of this condition, the amicus petition should be rejected as the NDP did not possess any knowledge, special perspective, experience, or expertise on any of the topics in question (that is, the pharmaceutical sector, drag law, international law, and so forth).[116] It seems, therefore, that despite the importance attributed to elements such as the representation of as many voices as possible, at least a minimal level of expertise or the ability to provide a unique perspective or insight is nevertheless necessary.[117] The Tribunal further stated that the NDP did

---

[110] *Apotex I*, Procedural Order No. 2, above at para 34.

[111] *UPS*, *Amici Curiae* Decision, above at para 71.

[112] *Apotex I*, Procedural Order No. 2, above at para 33.

[113] Paragraph 6(a) of the FTC Statement, above.

[114] *Apotex I*, Procedural Order No. 2, above at para 22.

[115] *Glamis Gold Ltd v. The United States of America* (June 8, 2009), (NAFTA Chapter 11, UNCITRAL) at para 286.

[116] *Apotex I*, Procedural Order No. 2, above at para 23.

[117] The amici's contribution in this case was described as "no more than a legal analysis of the terms of the NAFTA, and previous arbitral decisions on the concept of '*investment*', undistinguished and

not possess any significant interest in the arbitration and failed to explain what kind of public interest it sought to address in its submission.[118]

Despite its rejection of the amici's request, the *Apotex I* Tribunal's remarks reflect the increased importance of the human rights angle of the public participation principle. In essence, the Tribunal agreed that where issues of public importance are discussed, public participation may be permitted even if this complicates the proceedings or if the petitioner's particular knowledge is not so unique.

While it is not yet clear whether the *Apotex I* Tribunal's approach will be adopted by future investment tribunals, this development will certainly be interesting to follow. At the time of writing, however, the only cases in which these issues were considered, the *von Pezold* arbitration and the *Apotex II* arbitration, did not follow the liberal line suggested by the *Apotex I* Tribunal.

In the ICSID *von Pezold* arbitration,[119] the Tribunal adopted a more restrictive line of reasoning, refusing an application by indigenous communities from Zimbabwe to intervene as amici. These communities based their arguments, among other things, on international human rights law. The Tribunal denied these applications, asserting that such arguments were not within the scope of the dispute[120] and that the petitioners did not have a significant interest in the dispute.[121] While the Tribunal probably had other good reasons to reject the petition (it seems that the petitioners were not neutral[122]), the human rights rhetoric of the *Apotex I* Tribunal was not repeated in this case.

In the *Apotex II* arbitration, two amici requested to submit amicus petitions. The first was BNM, the same amicus that attempted (and failed) to submit an amicus brief at the *Apotex I* case. The *Apotex II* Tribunal rejected BNM's petition for the same reasons mentioned by the *Apotex I* Tribunal two years earlier.[123] A more interesting petition, however, was made by Mr. Barry Appleton, a leading investment lawyer. Based on his own expertise and extensive experience in investment litigation, Mr. Appleton asserted that he was in a position to assist the Tribunal by providing legal knowledge and expertise concerning the meaning of investment

---

uncoloured by any particular background or experience." See *Apotex I*, Procedural Order No. 2, above at para 23.

[118] *Apotex I*, Procedural Order No. 2, above at paras 27–31.

[119] *Bernard von Pezold and others v. Republic of Zimbabwe*, ICSID Case No. ARB/10/15.

[120] The Tribunal describe in this respect the scope of the dispute as limited to the "allegedly unlawful measures taken by the Respondent against the Claimant and their investments pursuant to the LRP." *Bernard von Pezold and others v. Republic of Zimbabwe*, ICSID Case No. ARB/10/15 (Procedural Order No. 2) at para 60.

[121] *Von Pezold*, above at para 60.

[122] *Von Pezold*, above para 61.

[123] *Apotex Holdings Inc and Apotex Inc v. The United States of America*, ICSID Case No. ARB(AF)/12/1 (Procedural Order on the Participation of the Applicant, BNM, as a Non-Disputing Party) at para 24.

treaty obligations.[124] However, the Tribunal rejected the possibility that legal expertise in itself was sufficient for satisfying the criterion set forth in section B(6)(a) of the FTC Statement. The Tribunal explained that the Parties' counsel were sufficiently knowledgeable and experienced to provide the Tribunal with the necessary legal insights and perspectives.[125]

4.1.2. Participation as Parties

On several occasions, representatives of the public have requested to receive the full status of a direct party to the dispute, which is perhaps the fullest possible form of public participation in any form of litigation. The petitioners in the ICSID *Tunari* arbitration requested, for example, "all rights of participation accorded to other parties to the claim."[126]

A similar request was also made in the *UPS* dispute, in which the Canadian Union of Postal Workers and the Council of Canadians both asked to receive standing as parties.[127] The petitioners argued that they each held a direct interest in the arbitration and therefore requested to be granted the right to defend these interests. Furthermore, the petitioners claimed that as certain rights in the arbitral process are reserved to parties alone (for example, choice of venue, consent to open the proceedings, and the rights to have one's views considered and to make submissions), it would be appropriate in this case to grant them such a status.[128]

In another NAFTA dispute, the *Merrill Ring* arbitration, a letter sent by the counsel representing three NDPs was considered by the Tribunal to be a request to join as party to the dispute.[129] The letter claimed that the NDPs had a "direct and public interest" in the dispute.[130]

These requests, it seems, went too far, as all three Tribunals denied the public representatives the right to join as a party to investment arbitration proceedings. The *Tunari* Tribunal held that it had no power to approve any form of public participation without specific instructions from the governing laws.[131] The *UPS* Tribunal likewise

---

[124] *Apotex Holdings Inc and Apotex Inc v. The United States of America*, ICSID Case No. ARB(AF)/12/1 (Procedural Order on the Participation of the Applicant, Mr. Barry Appleton, as a Non-Disputing Party) at paras 11, 30–34.

[125] *Apotex II*, Procedural Order on the Participation of the Applicant Mr. Barry Appleton, above at para 32.

[126] *Aguas del Tunari, SA v. Republic of Bolivia*, ICSID Case No. ARB/02/3 (Petition of La Coordinadora para la defensa del agua y vida et al.), http://italaw.com/cases/57 at 3.

[127] *UPS, Amici Curiae* Decision, above at 2.

[128] *UPS, Petition*, above at paras 50–60.

[129] It is doubtful, however, whether the content of this letter actually reflects such a request. The letter is available online: http://www.appletonlaw.com/files/Merrill/2.%20%20%20Ltr%20Shrybman%20to%20ICSID-BWA%20re%20Intent%20to%20file%20joint%20sub_27Jun08.pdf.

[130] Letter from Steven Shrybmen, above.

[131] Aguas del Tunari, above.

denied that it had authority to accept another party to the arbitration, basing its decision on the scope of the consent granted by the parties to the arbitration and the obligation an arbitral tribunal has to follow the parties' instructions in this respect.[132] The *Merrill Ring* Tribunal repeated the reasoning of the *UPS* Tribunal, and added that the governing laws (the NAFTA and the UNCITRAL Rules) restrict such a participation to only a "Party and an Investor of Another Party."[133]

4.2. *Access to Information in NAFTA Jurisprudence*

Access to information, as explained earlier, is routinely considered an inherent part of the principle of public participation. It is intended to support public participation and ensure its effectiveness. The most basic aspect of the right to information in the context of investment treaty arbitration is the right to know of the very existence of an investment dispute. Indeed, Vaughan Lowe has commented:[134]

> It would be a curious paradox if governments could be held liable to pay hundreds of millions of dollars of taxpayers' money in compensation to foreign investors because the government had failed to behave transparently and fairly, by a tribunal whose existence, proceedings and eventual award were kept a secret from those taxpayers.

This issue has been successfully accommodated in frameworks such as the NAFTA and ICSID, under which disputes are registered and their existence is made publicly known. This issue has also been recently confronted by the UNCITRAL member states, as under the new UNCITRAL Rules on Transparency the establishment of a repository has been prescribed.[135]

The right to have access to information is to be found in international investment law on several other levels as well. Three elements will be discussed in this respect: the public's right to have access to arbitration documents, the availability of oral hearings to the public, and the right to review arbitration awards.

4.2.1. Access to Arbitration Documents

Access to arbitration documents in investment treaty arbitrations is often requested by NDPs who wish to make their contribution more effective. This element was indeed stressed in petitions filed by amici in recent years,[136] but only rarely have

---

[132] *UPS, Amici Curiae* Decision, above at paras 35–43.
[133] *Merrill & Ring Forestry L. P. v. Canada*, (UNCITRAL), (Letter from the Tribunal, July 31, 2008).
[134] Lowe, "Changing Dimensions," above, p. 120.
[135] Article 8 of the UNCITRAL Rules on Transparency, above.
[136] See, for example, *Methanex*, IISD Petition, above at para 5.1(a); *Chevron Corp and Texaco Petroleum Corp v. The Republic of Ecuador*, UNCITRAL PCA Case No. 2009–23 (UNCITRAL) (Petition for participation as non-disputing parties) at para 1.2(3); *Biwater Gauff Ltd v. United Republic of Tanzania* (July 24, 2008), ICSID Cas No. ARB/05/22 (ICSID) (Petition for amicus curiae status), pp. 11–13.

these requests been granted without the consent of the parties to the arbitration. The reluctance to grant access to documents is also reflected in early NAFTA jurisprudence. The *Methanex* Tribunal emphasized that there is nothing in Chapter 11 to suggest that an amicus may receive any such documents, and that amici must be treated as "any other members of the public."[137]

Six months after the *Methanex* decision, the Notes of Interpretation were issued by the FTC. Concerning the matter of access to documents, the Notes mention:[138]

> Nothing in the NAFTA imposes a general duty of confidentiality on the disputing parties to a Chapter Eleven arbitration... from providing public access to documents submitted to, or issued by, a Chapter Eleven tribunal.... Each Party agrees to make available to the public in a timely manner all documents submitted to, or issued by, a Chapter Eleven tribunal.

Since the issuing of the Notes of Interpretation, NAFTA tribunals have tended to approve the publication of most documents submitted to or issued by them.[139] Indeed, today such documents can be easily accessed through online databases.[140] Interests such as confidentiality, however, were not entirely abandoned. The *Chemtura* and the *Gallo* Tribunals, for instance, ruled that prior to the publication of documents the parties to the arbitration shall be informed, providing them with the opportunity to raise objections.[141]

Here, again, the liberal approach presented by the NAFTA can be compared to the more restrictive approach of ICSID tribunals. For example, the *Suez* Tribunal rejected NDPs' requests for access to documents, stating that "the Petitioners have sufficient information even without being granted access to the arbitration record."[142] The Tribunal also mentioned that its preliminary decisions, already published on ICSID's website, contained sufficient information regarding the nature of the investor's claims.[143] The Tribunal further doubted the need to have access to the

---

[137] *Methanex, Amici Curiae* Decision, above at para 46.

[138] Paragraphs 1(a) and 1(b)(ii) of the "NAFTA Notes of Interpretation," above.

[139] See comments made by representatives of Canada and the United States, United Nations Commission on International Trade Law, "Settlement of Commercial Disputes: Transparency in Treaty-Based Investor-State Arbitration," UNCITRAL Working Group II 54th Sess, February 7–11, 2011, UN Doc. A/CN.9/WG.II/WP.163, http://www.iiiglobal.org/component/jdownloads/finish/635/3970.html.

[140] See, for example, www.italaw.com and www.naftaclaims.com, as well as the NAFTA Parties' official websites.

[141] *Chemtura*, Confidentiality Order, above, paras 11–12; *Vito G. Gallo v. Government of Canada* (September 15, 2011), PCA Case No. 55798 (NAFTA Chapter 11) (Confidentiality Order, June 4, 2008), http://www.naftalaw.org/Disputes/Canada/Gallo/Gallo-Canada-Confidentiality-Order.pdf, paras 5–6.

[142] *Suez, Sociedad General de Aguas de Barcelona S.A. and Vivendi Universal S.A v. Argentine Republic* (July 30, 2010), ICSID Case No. ARB/03/19 (Order in response to a petition by five nongovernmental organizations for permission to make an amicus curiae submission) at para 24.

[143] *Suez*, Order in response to NGOs, above at para 24.

arbitration documents, as the petitioners asked to offer views on general issues, and that in any case their role "is not to challenge arguments or evidence put forward by the Parties. This [was] the Parties' role."[144]

The ICSID *Biwater* Tribunal addressed this issue from a different perspective. It claimed that since the NDPs at issue were not party to the dispute, they should concern themselves only with the broad policy issues in which they were qualified to contribute and in which they claimed to be experts. For this reason, it was explained, they did not need access to arbitration documents.[145]

Last, the *AES* Tribunal adopted a different justification for its refusal to allow access to documents, denying such access simply based on the lack of the Parties' consent.[146]

In 2009, the ICSID *Foresti* Tribunal did allow access to several of the documents submitted to the Tribunal in order to allow NDPs to focus their contributions on the relevant issues by learning the Parties' positions.[147] This decision is especially unique as it allows access to the arbitration documents despite the investor's objections. This case, however, was discontinued by the Parties, and no documents were ultimately disclosed. Moreover, the approach displayed by the *Foresti* Tribunal does not reflect the general attitude displayed in ICSID and UNCITRAL jurisprudence.[148]

4.2.2. Access to Arbitration Hearings

Prior to the 2004 Joint Statement,[149] the *Methanex* and *UPS* tribunals denied access to the actual hearings themselves. These tribunals asserted that according to the UNCITRAL Rules, hearings are to be held in camera unless the parties agree otherwise.[150] But as already mentioned, in 2004 the three NAFTA member states expressed their support for opening the hearings of Chapter 11 disputes to the public. As Kinnear stated, "[o]pen hearings are now the norm" in Chapter 11 cases,[151] and indeed, such has been the case on numerous occasions.[152] It should be mentioned, however, that NAFTA tribunals still require the parties' permission prior to making

---

[144] *Suez*, Order in response to NGOs, above at para 25.

[145] *Biwater Gauff*, Procedural Order No. 5, above at para 65.

[146] *AES Summit Generation Ltd and AES-Tisza Erömü Kft. v. Republic of Hungary* (September 23, 2010), ICSID Case No. ARB/07/22, (Award) at para 3.22.

[147] *Piero Foresti, Laura de Carli & Others v. Republic of South Africa* (August 4, 2010), ICSID Case No. ARB(AF)/07/01, (Letter from the Tribunal to the Parties, October 5, 2009) at para 2.2–3.

[148] See, for example, *Suez*, Order in response to NGOs, above at para 25; *Biwater Gauff*, Procedural Order No. 5, above at para 65; AES Award, above at para 3.22.

[149] *NAFTA* Free Trade Commission, "Joint Statement," above.

[150] *UPS*, Amici Curiae Decision, above at para 67; *Methanex*, above at para 42.

[151] Meg Kinnear and Robin Hansen, "The Influence of NAFTA Chapter 11 in the BIT Landscape," (2005) 12 *UC Davis Journal of International Law & Policy* 101, 111.

[152] Open hearings were held inter alia in *UPS*, above, *Glamis*, above, *Grand River*, above, and *Methanex*, above.

the hearing open to the public,[153] and that on several occasions such permission was indeed denied.[154]

This is another occasion on which the ICSID framework represents a far less liberal approach. Following the instructions of Article 32 of the ICSID Rules of Arbitration, both the *Suez* and the *Biwater* Tribunals held that without the parties' consent, tribunals cannot permit any third party's attendance at the arbitral hearings.[155] The *Biwater* Tribunal further added that "the privacy of the arbitral hearing [is] a central element of the arbitral process."[156] This approach was reiterated in the *Foresti* arbitration.[157]

It should be noted, however, that several tribunals have agreed that the parties to the arbitration are entitled to *discuss* the arbitral proceedings publicly.[158] This, to a certain extent, can assist public representatives who wish to obtain information about a certain dispute – especially as the position of these NDPs usually supports the position of the state.

This subsection would not be complete without mention of the new platforms made available by technological developments. Most notably, since 2010 several ICSID tribunals have followed the practice of other noninvestment international tribunals[159] and enabled the webcasting of arbitral proceedings to the general public.[160] Such online access to arbitration hearings has not yet been accepted by NAFTA tribunals, despite the requests made by NGOs.[161] The importance of this particular technological platform is quite obvious, especially in disputes that

---

[153] See clarifications made soon after the issuing of the joint statement in NAFTA Advisory Committee on International Private Commercial Disputes, "Minutes for the 14th meeting," above. See also the practice of tribunals: At the *Canfor* arbitration, the Tribunal stated: "Finally, as you know, the parties have agreed to make the hearing open to the public. The hearing is thus broadcast live in a separate room within the ICSID premises." *Canfor Corp. v. United States of America* (NAFTA Chapter 11) (Hearing Transcript, December 7, 2004), http://www.naftaclaims.com/Disputes/USA/Canfor/Canfor-Jurisdiction-Transcript-DayOne.pdf, pp. 11–12.

[154] See *Chemtura*, Confidentiality Order, above; *Gallo*, Procedural Order No. 1, above.

[155] *Suez, Amicus Curiae* Order 2005, above at para 6; *Suez, Amicus Curiae* Order 2006, above at para 7; *Biwater Gauff*, Procedural Order No. 5, above at paras 70–71.

[156] *Biwater*, Prodedural Order No. 3, above at para 124.

[157] *Foresti*, letter, above at para 4.

[158] *Biwater*, Procedural Order No. 3, above. The *Biwater* Tribunal cited at paras 121–29 in this respect other decisions made by the *Metalclad*, the *Amco* and *Loewen* Tribunals. The Tribunal has also mentioned that there are several limitations in this respect, such as the "Non-Aggravation/Non-Exacerbation" of the Dispute, at para 135.

[159] See, for example, the practice of the International Court of Justice. For example, the reading of the Court's Advisory Opinion in the *Legal Consequences of the Construction of a Wall in the Occupied Palestinian Territory* was broadcast live on the Court's web site online: http://www.icj-cij.org/docket/?pr=74&code=mwp&p1=3&p2=4&p3=6&case=131&k=5a&PHPSESSID=334ec2af0583186bc57cfa3546381679.

[160] See, for example, *Pac Rim Cayman LLC v. Republic of El Salvador*, ICSID Case No. ARB/09/12; *Railroad Development Corporation v. Republic of Guatemala*, ICSID Case No ARB/07/23.

[161] See CIEL, "Webcasting as a tool to increase transparency in dispute settlement proceedings," 2010, http://www.ciel.org/Publications/Webcasting_21Jun10.pdf.

are international in nature, as it permits public access to these hearings without the inconvenience and expense of travel. Furthermore, as these proceedings are uploaded to the Internet, this type of broadcast also allows access to hearings at later times, permitting those wishing to follow the proceedings to do so with more flexibility.[162]

4.2.3. Access to Arbitration Awards

Another fundamental aspect of access to information is the publication of investment awards. Without having ready access to awards, the public cannot scrutinize the arbitral process, nor can it understand the justifications for decisions accepted against states' measures. The position adopted by the NAFTA member states in this respect reflects the principle of public participation: Annex 1137.4 of Chapter 11 states that in disputes to which either Canada or the United States is party, awards will be made public.[163] Furthermore, according to paragraph 1(b)(ii) of the Notes of Interpretation, the Parties agree to make awards available to the public in a timely manner.[164] This approach is considered rather liberal within the field of international investment law: in comparison, according to the ICSID Rules, awards shall be published only with the consent of both parties.[165] A similar rule currently also applies with respect to UNCITRAL-governed investment awards.[166]

5. CONCLUSION: THE PRINCIPLE OF PUBLIC PARTICIPATION UNDER NAFTA CHAPTER 11

The principle of public participation has not only crept into the field of international investment law but has also evolved from within it. This principle was originally envisioned to ensure public participation in decision-making processes and was required of states. The acceptance of this principle (albeit a limited version) in the field of investment arbitration, both by investment treaties and tribunals, reflects the principle's evolution: it is now perceived as applying also to quasiprivate entities such as investment tribunals in order to ensure public participation in areas that only indirectly affect the public interest, such as investment disputes, rather than in classic decision-making mechanisms.

---

[162] See on this issue, Luke Eric Peterson, "The Expending Audience for Open Arbitration Hearings," (2012) Kluwer Arbitration Blog, http://kluwer.practicesource.com/blog/2012/the-expanding-audience-for-open-arbitration-hearings.

[163] Annex 1137.4 of NAFTA, Chapter 11, above.

[164] "NAFTA Notes of Interpretation," above.

[165] See Rule 48(4) of the ICSID Rules, above.

[166] See Rules 34(5) of the UNCITRAL Rules, above.

The process of integrating the principle of public participation within the ISDS has required certain adaptations both by the ISDS and of the principle itself. On the one hand, it is now relatively widely accepted that investment tribunals can no longer deny public participation where public interests could be affected. On the other, investment tribunals and rules still impose certain limitations on the application of the principle. Despite these limitations, the rules of the NAFTA currently reflect a higher degree of willingness to adopt the principle of public participation than is found in other competing institutions, such as the ICSID. The approach demonstrated in the NAFTA in this respect has served as an inspirational source for many important developments in the world of international investment law.

But should NAFTA member states be content with the current situation? In the author's view, the NAFTA's decision makers must pay attention to recent developments in the global arena in order to evaluate their own policies and examine new ideas. This is so especially in light of the fact that since the middle of the last decade, no noticeable developments concerning the principle of public participation have taken place under the NAFTA, while considerable progress has been made elsewhere.

And where should NAFTA decision makers search for inspiration? First, they should look across the Atlantic Ocean. The EU is currently in the process of changing its member states' IIAs for EU IIAs. These treaties are expected to include an ambitious approach with respect to the principle of public participation. As mentioned earlier in Section 3.2.4, the EU Commission has already announced that the EU will adopt the new UNCITRAL Rules on Transparency in ISDS[167] and will include elements that currently do not exist under the NAFTA framework, such as a clear rule on open access to hearings. Another suggestion raised as part of the debate on future EU investment policy concerns the possibility of granting NDPs the status of a party to investment disputes.[168] It therefore seems that the EU is trying to raise the bar with respect to public participation even further. While the ideas mentioned by EU decision makers may be accepted, modified, or even rejected, they should at least be considered in order to avoid ossification.

Second, much can be learned from the new UNCITRAL Rules on Transparency, most notably when it comes to access to hearings. Access to NAFTA Chapter 11 dispute hearings is still subject to investors' consent. While the reasons for such a restrictive approach are clear, the author believes that there are better ways to balance interests of privacy and confidentiality with the need to open Chapter 11's

---

[167] EU Commission, "EU backs new transparency standards," above.
[168] European Parliament, *Report on the Future European International Investment Policy*, March 22, 2011, (2010/2203/INI), http://www.europarl.europa.eu/sides/getDoc.do?type=REPORT&reference=A7-2011 -0070&language=EN, p 3.

ISDS. For example, as prescribed by Article 6(2) of the UNCITRAL Rules on Transparency, when specific sensitive confidential information is discussed, arbitrators may make appropriate arrangements to preserve this confidentiality, such as instructing NDPs to temporarily leave the hearing.[169] Furthermore, reflecting the FTC Statement rules on the submission of amicus briefs, it could be decided that tribunals will be authorized to open hearings only where there is a public element in the dispute.

On the same issue, NAFTA decision makers should examine the use of new technological platforms, most notably webcasting. The importance of the webcasting tool has been mentioned both by prominent investment law reporters and by amici.[170] While other institutions (see, for example, the ICSID, based on the provisions of the CAFTA-DR) are increasing the use of webcasting in order to enhance the transparency of public hearings, such technology has not yet been adopted in NAFTA disputes. In the only Chapter 11 case in which this issue was raised (the *Canadian Cattlemen* case),[171] despite approving a one-way transmission of the hearings to the claimants' distant location, the Tribunal refused applications made by NGOs to make such a transmission public.

Third, the current NAFTA Chapter 11 rules are set, among other things, as recommendations (the rules on amicus submissions) and as a nonbinding expression of intentions (the FTC Joint Statement on access to hearings). As the importance of public participation in investment disputes gains recognition, and as investment tribunals are increasingly asked to deal with requests to participate, the case for adopting a comprehensive and binding set of rules on this matter is becoming clear. One such possible set of rules that all three NAFTA member states have been involved in the making of is the new UNCITRAL Rules on Transparency. The progressive approach expressed in these rules seems to reflect the general attitude of the NAFTA member states, as seen in their declarations and practice.

Last, the possibility of permitting NDPs to join the dispute as a party should not be entirely ruled out. This possibility may be considered in those extreme and relatively rare cases in which significant interests of a certain party are being discussed, and the position of this party is not represented by the host state. Perhaps a more relaxed version of this rather extreme suggestion would be to permit the amicus, in similar cases, some of the rights that are usually reserved for the parties, such as effective legal representation and the rights to interrogate witnesses, to bring evidence, or to raise legal and factual arguments before the tribunal. Such rights can also be limited in scope in order to avoid imposing a disproportionate burden on the parties, and such interventions can even be subject to the payment of costs.

---

[169] Article 6(2) of the UNCITRAL Rules on Transparency, above.
[170] CIEL, "Webcasting," above; and Peterson, "Expanding Audience," above.
[171] *Cases regarding the Border Discloser due to BSE Concerns* (Procedural Order No. 3, August 3, 2007), UNCITRAL (NAFTA).

To conclude, the NAFTA framework has always been considered to be an advanced legal system with respect to the integration of the principle of public participation in international investment law. However, much is happening in international fora, and in order to keep pace with these developments, as well as with the rising global standards for transparency and participation, NAFTA decision makers should follow these developments and reevaluate the application of the principle of public participation in Chapter 11's investment disputes.

13

Preventing Environmental Deterioration from International Trade and Investment

How China Can Learn from NAFTA's Experience to Strengthen Domestic Environmental Governance and Ensure Sustainable Development

Danni Liang and Jingjing Liu

1. INTRODUCTION

The North American Free Trade Agreement (NAFTA),[1] ratified in 1994, is the first free trade agreement to openly incorporate environmental provisions. Its enforcement generated wide criticism on the impact of trade on environmental degradation, with the focus on its Chapter 11, which provides for investment protection.[2] The critical debate places itself in wider debates of the status and legitimacy of international investment treaties and treaty-based arbitration. NAFTA Chapter 11 has been compared to the "Magna Carta" of foreign investors, which means the Chapter is overly protective of investors and, as a result, inappropriately infringes on a state's ability to regulate investment within its borders.[3] While foreign investors cheered for the profound rights under Chapter 11, many observers worried about the negative effects on the host state's sovereignty under this treaty, especially in the sense that it allows foreign investors to bring their claims against host states directly.[4] In addition, some of the Chapter 11 arbitration cases touch upon sensitive public interest issues such

---

[1] North American Free Trade Agreement, U.S.-Can.-Mex., Dec. 17, 1992, 32 I.L.M. 289 (1993), 32 I.L.M. 605 (1993) [hereinafter NAFTA].

[2] See, e.g., Jeffery Atik, "*Repenser* NAFTA Chapter 11: A Catalogue of Legitimacy Critiques," *Asper Review of International Business & Trade Law* 3 (2003), 215; John Wickham, "Toward a Green Multilateral Investment Framework: NAFTA and the Search for Models," *Georgetown International Environmental Law Review* 12 (2000), 617; Michael Wiable et al., "The Backlash against Investment Arbitration. Perceptions and Reality," *Wolters Kluwer Law & Business* (2010).

[3] Elizabeth Whitsitt, "NAFTA Fifteen Years later: the Successes, Failures and Future Prospects of Chapter 11," *IISD Investment Treaty News* (Feb. 17, 2009), http://www.iisd.org/itn/2009/02/17/nafta-fifteen-years-later-the-successes-failures-and-future-prospects-of-chapter-11/ (last visited March 14, 2014).

[4] Joseph de Pencier, "Investment, Environment and Dispute Settlement: Arbitration Under NAFTA Chapter Eleven," *Hastings International & Comparative Law Review* 23 (2000), 411–12.

as protecting the environment and public health, an important component of a government's regulatory framework. In light of the startling sum of monetary damages arising from the awards, anxiety among government agencies and civil society groups increases.[5]

The bulk of the aforesaid debate is centered around the lack of transparency and public participation in the investor–state arbitration process, particularly in cases that involve public interest, as well as the call for multinational corporations to shoulder adequate social responsibilities when they pursue profit maximization.[6] Environmental protection should not be sacrificed in the tide of trade liberalization, just as the harmonization of sustainable development and global economic has been affirmed as one of the key objectives of free trade agreements (FTAs) and bilateral investment treaties (BITs).[7] It is also the objective of the Chinese government when negotiating FTAs and BITs with other countries.[8] On April 7, 2008, China concluded an FTA with New Zealand (China-NZ FTA), which entered into force on October 1, 2008. This is the first bilateral FTA China has signed with a developed country. The Chapter 11 under the China-NZ FTA, which specifies both the substantial provisions of investment protection and investor–state arbitration clause, is similar to the Chapter 11 under NAFTA. In addition, China and New Zealand signed an Environment Cooperation Agreement[9] to reaffirm the international commitments,

---

[5] See Charles H. Brower, II, "Investor-State Disputes Under NAFTA: A Tale of Fear and Equilibrium," *Pepperdine Law Review* 29 (2001), 44; Howard Mann and Konrad von Moltke, *NAFTA's Chapter 11 and the Environment: Addressing the Impacts of the Investor-State Process on the Environment* (Winnipeg, Canada: International Institute for Sustainable Development, 1999), 5, http://www.iisd.org/pdf/nafta.pdf; Kevin Banks, "NAFTA's Article 1110 – Can Regulation Be Expropriation?," NAFTA: Law & Business Review of the Americas 5 (1999) 501–03.

[6] See Brower, above note 5, p. 44; Mann and von Moltke, above note 5, p. 5; Banks, above note 5, pp. 500–01.

[7] "A perusal of the content of the 17 IIAs concluded in 2012 for which texts are available shows that they increasingly include sustainable-development oriented features. Of these IIAs, 12 (including 8 BITs) refer to the protection of health and safety, labour rights, environment or sustainable development in their preamble; 10 (including 6 BITs) have general exceptions – e.g. for the protection of human, animal or plant life or health, or the conservation of exhaustible natural resources; and 7 (including 4 BITs) contain clauses that explicitly recognize that parties should not relax health, safety or environmental standards to attract investment." See United Nations Conference on Trade and Development, World Investment Report 2013: Global Value Chains: Investment and Trade for Development (Geneva: United Nations Publications, 2013), pp. 102–03, http://unctad.org/en/PublicationsLibrary/wir2013_en.pdf.

[8] See, e.g., Agreement for the Promotion, Facilitation and Protection of Investment, China-Japan-Korea, May 13, 2012, http://www.mofa.go.jp/announce/announce/2012/5/pdfs/0513_01_01.pdf. The signatories "[r]ecogniz[e] that these objectives can be achieved without relaxing health, safety and environmental measures of general application." Ibid., Preamble. "Each Contracting Party recognizes that it is inappropriate to encourage investment by investors of another Contracting Party by relaxing its environmental measures. To this effect each Contracting Party should not waive or otherwise derogate from such environmental measures as an encouragement for the establishment, acquisition or expansion of investments in its territory." Ibid., Art. 23.

[9] Environment Cooperation Agreement, China-N.Z. (2008), http://chinafta.govt.nz/1-The-agreement/1-Key-outcomes/0-downloads/ECA-NZ.pdf.

including those agreed to by the Parties in multilateral environmental agreements and the commitment of the Parties to develop the content of their bilateral agenda and to share the knowledge and experience gained in the fields related to economic development and environmental protection.[10]

Nowadays China has concluded more than 10 FTAs and 130 BITs. Most of them include comprehensive investment protection rules and investor–state dispute settlement provisions, but not all of these FTAs and BITs address the harmonization of economic development and environmental protection as does the China-NZ FTA.[11] Although China has not yet faced assaults by foreign investors arising from domestic regulatory measures that protect the environment or other aspects of public interest undertakings, given the increasing outbound and inbound investment, China should prepare for such challenges from foreign investors by carefully balancing economic growth and sustainable development, and regulatory sovereignty and commitments under the FTAs and BITs.

This chapter will discuss the lessons China should learn from the NAFTA experience of addressing impacts of free trade on the environment, in particular the concerns over the potential for a "race to the bottom" in light of lax environmental regulations and weak enforcement in China.

2. LESSONS FROM NAFTA CHAPTER 11 AND THE DANGER OF INVESTOR–STATE ARBITRATION CASES TO A NATION'S ENVIRONMENTAL REGULATORY SYSTEM

2.1. *Case Studies under NAFTA Chapter 11*

2.1.1. The *Methanex* Case

Methanex is a Canadian-based manufacturer of methanol, a component of the gasoline additive MTBE (methyl tertiary-butyl ether). Methanex does not manufacture the MTBE itself, but a significant percentage of the methanol it produces was used in the making of MTBE. Methanex was the largest supplier in California of MTBE. The challenged regulatory measures were based on a University of California study on MTBE's impact on the environment. The study revealed that MTBE poses a significant risk to public health and the environment, mainly through polluting surface water and groundwater in the state. On December 3, 1999, Methanex claimed compensation from the United States in the amount of approximately U.S. $970 million for losses caused by the State of California's ban on the sale and use of

---

[10] Ibid., pp. 2–3.
[11] The BITs concluded by China and other countries are available at http://tfs.mofcom.gov.cn/article/Nocategory/201111/20111107819474.shtml; the FTAs concluded by China and other countries are available at http://fta.mofcom.gov.cn/index.shtml.

MTBE by alleging a violation by the United States of Articles 1105(1) and 1110(1) of NAFTA Chapter 11.[12] This was rejected by the Tribunal,[13] which nonetheless allowed a second amended claim, submitted by Methanex in November 2002, in which Methanex alleged a violation of Article 1102. The main allegation was that the California government imposed the ban due to a political deal with a rival company that makes ethanol, a substitute for methanol and MTBE as a gasoline additive, and the ethanol producer, Archer Daniels Midland (ADM), had used political donations to improperly influence the decision of California Governor Davis in a manner that breached the protection of foreign investors according to NAFTA Chapter 11 in favor of domestic producers of ethanol.[14]

In rejecting Methanex's claim, the Tribunal appealed to the "effect and purpose" approach, and it found no unfair treatment of Methanex's alleged violation of international law norms under NAFTA Article 1105 and no expropriation or measures tantamount to expropriation under Article 1110. For the second point, the tribunal announced a defining indirect expropriation in the following analysis that should please the environmental community:[15]

> In the Tribunal's view, Methanex is correct that an intentionally discriminatory regulation against a foreign investor fulfils a key requirement for establishing expropriation. But as a matter of general international law, a non-discriminatory regulation for a public purpose, which is enacted in accordance with due process and, which affects, inter alios, a foreign investor or investment is not deemed expropriatory and compensable unless specific commitments had been given by the regulating government to the then putative foreign investor contemplating investment that the government would refrain from such regulation.[16]

The Methanex Case has attracted attentions worldwide related to the contradiction between the environmental regulatory measures of host states and protection of foreign investors under the international investment agreement (IIA). This case is also a landmark case in the history of investor–state arbitration under NAFTA Chapter 11 in several aspects.

First, it was the first Tribunal to allow public hearings and participation by nondisputing parties, including submission of amici curiae briefs by environmental

[12] Methanex Corporation v. United States of America, ICSID, Final Award of the Tribunal on Jurisdiction and Merits, Pt. I, Preface, paras. 1, 2 (Aug. 3, 2005), http://naftaclaims.com/Disputes/USA/Methanex/Methanex_Final_Award.pdf [hereinafter Methanex Final Award].

[13] Ibid. Pt. IV, Ch. F, para. 6. The procedural history of this case is complex and disputed; all relevant documentation is available at http://www.naftaclaims.com/disputes_us_methanex.htm.

[14] Ibid. Pt. I, Preface, para. 5.

[15] See Howard Mann, *The Final Decision in Methanex v. United States: Some New Wine in Some New Bottles* (Winnipeg, Canada: International Institute for Sustainable Development, 2005), p. 6, http://www.iisd.org/pdf/2005/commentary_methanex.pdf; see also Todd Weiler, "Methanex Corp. v. U.S.A.: Turning the Page on NAFTA Chapter Eleven?," *Journal of World Investment & Trade* 6 (2005), 918.

[16] Methanex Final Award, above note 12, Pt. IV, Ch. D, para. 7.

nongovernmental organizations (NGOs),[17] which made a significant contribution to promoting transparency in the investor–state arbitration process. By virtue of a NAFTA Free Trade Commission decision in October 2003,[18] a process for amicus submissions in Chapter 11 cases has been established. In addition, the International Center for Settlement of Investment Disputes (ICSID) Arbitration Rules 2006 incorporates transparency requirements, including public hearings, open access to documents, and amicus submissions.[19] On July 11, 2013, after nearly three years of negotiations in the UNCITRAL Working Group on Arbitration, UNCITRAL adopted the UNCITRAL Rules on Transparency in Treaty-based Investor–State Arbitration.[20] Furthermore, recent IIAs incorporate the transparency requirements, mostly those with the United States as a Party,[21] since such provisions have been included in both the 2004 and 2012 U.S. Model BITs. It has been widely acknowledged that the Methanex case represents a milestone in the transition of the investor–state arbitration from a process behind the doors to a more transparent, accessible, and accountable process, especially when public interest and sustainable development are concerned.[22]

Second, the Tribunal's jurisprudence relieves the concerns of the civil society community, since a transnational corporation will be required to prove a direct causal link between the environmental protection measures and the corporation's

---

[17] On August 25, 2000, the International Institute for Sustainable Development (IISD) submitted the first recorded petition for access to the investor–state proceedings as an amicus curiae. An IISD petition was followed shortly by a second petition from other American-based NGOs. See *Methanex Corporation v. United States of America*, ICSID, Petitioner's Final Submissions Regarding the Petition of the International Institute for Sustainable Development to the Arbitral Tribunal for Amicus Curiae Status, para. 40 (Oct. 16, 2000), http://www.naftaclaims.com/Disputes/USA/Methanex/MethanexAmicusStandingIISDFinal.pdf.

[18] NAFTA Free Trade Commission, *Statement of the Free Trade Commission on Non-disputing Party Participation* (Oct. 7, 2003), http://www.sice.oas.org/TPD/NAFTA/Commission/Nondispute_e.pdf.

[19] ICSID Rules of Procedure for Arbitration Proceedings, Rules 32(2), 37(2) (2006), https://icsid.worldbank.org/ICSID/StaticFiles/basicdoc/CRR_English-final.pdf; ICSID Additional Facility Rules, Arts. 39(2), 41(3) (2006), https://icsid.worldbank.org/ICSID/StaticFiles/facility/AFR_English-final.pdf.

[20] United Nations Information Service "UNCITRAL Adopts Transparency Rules for Treaty-based Investor-State Arbitration and Amends the UNCITRAL Arbitration Rules" (July 12, 2013), http://www.unis.unvienna.org/unis/pressrels/2013/unis186.html (last visited March 14, 2014).

[21] See, e.g., Treaty Concerning the Encouragement and Reciprocal Protection of Investment, U.S.-Rwanda, Art. 29, Feb. 19, 2008; U.S.-Uruguay, Art. 29, Nov. 4, 2005. The U.S.-Rwanda BIT and U.S.-Uruguay BIT are both available at http://www.ustr.gov/trade-agreements/bilateral-investment-treaties/bit-documents (last visited March 14, 2014). See also U.S.-CAFTA-DR FTA Art. 10.21; U.S.-Chile FTA, Art. 10.20; U.S.-Columbia FTA, Art. 10.21, U.S.-Peru FTA, Art. 10.21; U.S.-Korea FTA, Art. 10.21; U.S.-Morocco FTA, Art. 10.20; U.S.-Singapore FTA, Art. 15.21; U.S.-Oman FTA, Art. 10.20; U.S.-Panama FTA, Art. 10.21. The FTAs are available at http://www.ustr.gov/trade-agreements/free-trade-agreements (last visited March 14, 2014).

[22] Howard Mann, Review of the Decision on Jurisdiction of the Methanex Tribunal, August 5, 2002, (2002), p. 7, http://www.iisd.org/pdf/2002/trade_methanex_analysis.pdf; see also Amokura Kawharu, "Public Participation & Transparency in Investment Arbitration: Recent Developments and Future Challenges," (2007), pp. 3–4, http://150.203.86.5/Cipl/Conferences_SawerLecture/2007/ANZSIL%202007/Publications/Amicus%20Notes%2006.07_Amokura.pdf.

business, not just alleged loss or a negative effect suffered by the foreign investor.[23] Before rejecting all the claims made by Methanex, the Tribunal undertook an extensive review of the regulatory measures of the California government in three stages: enactment of legislation, scientific study and assessment of risks, and executive action based on the results of the study.[24] Above all, the Tribunal examined the merits of the legislation, the California Senate bill, and concluded that there was no sufficient evidence to show the discriminatory intent to harm the foreign investor and to benefit the native competitor.[25] The Tribunal pointed out that Methanex's technical criticism against the study by the University of California (UC) was without merit.[26] At least, the objectivity of the UC study on the MTBE was reaffirmed by the Tribunal.[27] As to the ban itself, the Tribunal found that the governor's discretion was limited by the legislation and by the UC study.[28] "The tribunal's award clearly shows its displeasure with the implausibility of Methanex's claim of discriminatory intent and the willingness of Methanex to pursue such a claim with little or no evidence to support its speculative inferences."[29]

Finally, with respect to the minimum standard of fair and equitable treatment, the Tribunal explained "in applying this standard it is relevant that the treatment is in breach of *representations made by the host State which were reasonably relied upon by the claimant.*"[30] No such commitments were given to Methanex, which means Methanex did not enter the U.S. market because of special representations made to it.

On the issue of legitimate expectation of a foreign investor, which can successfully sustain a claim of regulatory expropriation when certain conditions are met, the Tribunal concluded that the distinct investment-backed expectations of regulatory stability will change according to the regulatory environment:

> Methanex entered a political economy in which it was widely known, if not notorious, that governmental environmental and health protection institutions at the federal and state level, operating under the vigilant eyes of the media, interested corporations, non-governmental organizations and a politically active electorate, continuously monitored the use and impact of chemical compounds and commonly prohibited or restricted the use of some of those compounds for environmental

---

[23] Methanex Final Award, above note 12, Pt. IV, Ch. E, para. 18.
[24] Sanford E. Gaines, *Environmental Policy Implications of Investor-State Arbitration under NAFTA Chapter 11* (Montreal: Commission for Environmental Cooperation, 2005), p. 35, http://www.cec.org/Storage/58/5068_Final-Gaines-T-E-Symposium05-Paper_en.pdf.
[25] Methanex Final Award, above note 12, Pt. IV, Ch. E, paras. 18–22.
[26] Methanex Final Award, above note 12, Pt. IV, Ch. E, para. 19.
[27] Methanex Final Award, above note 12, Pt. IV, Ch. E, paras. 21–22.
[28] Gaines, above note 24, p. 35.
[29] Gaines, above note 24, p. 35.
[30] Methanex Final Award, above note 12, Pt. IV, Ch. D, para. 8. (quoting *Waste Management, Inc., v. United Mexican States*, ICSID Case No. ARB(AF)/00/3, para. 98 (Apr. 30, 2004), 43 I.L.M. 967 (2004)).

and/or health reasons. Indeed, the very market for MTBE in the United States was the result of precisely this regulatory process.[31]

2.1.2. The *Metalclad* Case[32]

Metalclad is an American enterprise that initiated the first investor-state case under NAFTA Chapter 11. Metalclad alleged that Mexico, through its local governments of San Luis Potosi (SLP) and Guadalcazar, interfered with its development and operation of a hazardous waste landfill. Metalclad claimed that this interference was a violation of NAFTA Articles 1102 (National Treatment), 1103 (Most-Favored-National Treatment), 1105 (International Minimum Standard Treatment), 1106 (Performance Requirements), and 1110 (Expropriation).[33] In 1993, Metalclad exercised its option to buy COTERIN, a locally incorporated company, through its own locally incorporated subsidiary ECONSA, while COTERIN was in possession of the federal and state permits for the facility, after the federal environmental authorities granted the construction and operating permits to COTERIN and after the new governor of SLP supposedly gave assurances of his support for the project.[34] However, local opposition to reopening the facility surfaced and the governor began to speak out against the facility. While consulting with federal environmental officials and receiving extensions of time on its federal permits, Metalclad continued to construct the landfill facility and completed the construction in early 1995. However, local protestors prevented the site from operating.[35] Finally the city of Guadalazar refused to grant the permit, which was the key issue of the Metalclad's argument. On September 23, 1997, the state governor issued an ecological decree, which established a natural area for the protection of a local rare species of cactus, encompassing the Metalclad's proposed landfill site.[36]

The Tribunal found that Mexico had denied Metalclad fair and equitable treatment[37] and the actions of Mexico were tantamount to an uncompensated expropriation of Metalclad's investment,[38] and awarded Metalclad recovery of its expenses in constructing the landfill facility.[39] Mexico appealed the award to the British Columbia Supreme Court, since the seat of arbitration was in Vancouver, British Columbia. In 2001, the Court uphold the Tribunal's conclusion that Mexico's

[31] Ibid., Pt. IV, Ch. D, para. 9.
[32] *Metalclad Corporation v. The United Mexican States*, ICSID Case No. ARB(AF)/97/1, Award (Aug. 30, 2000), http://naftaclaims.com/Disputes/Mexico/Metalclad/MetalcladFinalAward.pdf [hereinafter Metalclad Award].
[33] Ibid., para. 1.
[34] Ibid., paras. 28–31.
[35] Ibid., paras. 37–44.
[36] Ibid., paras. 59–61.
[37] Ibid., para. 101.
[38] Ibid., para. 112.
[39] Ibid., para. 131.

domestic measures in relation to the Ecological Decree had in effect constituted indirect expropriation, while annulling other parts of the award concerning the events leading up to the denial of the municipal permit. Judge Tysoe in his Judgment and Reasons for Decision set aside the part of the award issued by the Tribunal on the Metalclad case based on the violation of Article 1105 because the Tribunal's incorporation of the obligation of transparency into the standard was beyond its jurisdictional powers.[40] In the end Mexico paid Metalclad the amount of the final award, a sum of U.S. $16.7 million.[41]

Another two cases against Mexico concerned breaches of contract of waste disposal services, submitted by Robert Azinian[42] and by Waste Management, Inc.,[43] and both cases were dismissed on jurisdictional grounds without addressing the merits of the respective claims. However, the environmental regulatory measures related to waste management policies in Mexico have been frequently challenged by foreign investors, which triggered the debate on the effects of NAFTA Chapter 11 on environmental regulatory powers of host state Parties.[44]

The Metalclad case reveals the importance of transparency of host states' environmental regulations, since the Tribunal placed great reliance in its reasoning on the lack of transparency of the permit approval process. In the counter-memorial in the Metalclad case, Mexico argued that Article 1105 had to be interpreted in the context of other provisions of NAFTA, including Article 1114 and the Preamble, and also the ancillary NAAEC,[45] which means that NAFTA itself allowed environmental considerations to be taken into account in interpreting the State's obligations toward foreign investors.

The criticism pointed out that the Tribunal intentionally evaded other objectives stated in the Preamble of NAFTA, such as to strengthen the development and enforcement of environmental laws and regulations.[46] It seems transparency of the local legal regime is given priority over environmental concerns of the host state

---

[40] Metalclad, Judgment and Reasons for Decision, paras. 68–76 (May 2, 2001), http://naftaclaims.com/ Disputes/Mexico/Metalclad/MetalcladJudgement.pdf.

[41] Metalclad Award, above note 32, para. 131.

[42] *Robert Azinian et al., v. The United Mexican States*, ICSID Case No. ARB (AF)/97/2, Award (Nov. 1, 1999), http://naftaclaims.com/Disputes/Mexico/Azinian/AzinianFinalAward.pdf.

[43] *Waste Management, Inc. v. United Mexican States*, ICSID Case No. ARB(AF)/00/3, Award (Apr. 30, 2004), 43 I.L.M. 967 (2004), http://naftaclaims.com/Disputes/Mexico/Waste/WasteFinalAwardMerits .pdf.

[44] E.g., Mary Bottari, "NAFTA's Investor 'Rights', A Corporate Dream, A Citizen Nightmare," *Multinational Monitor* 22 (Apr. 2001), http://lege.net/blog.lege.net/ratical.org/co-globalize/mmNAFTA2001 .pdf; Gabriel Cavazos Villanueva and Luis F. Martinez Serna, "Private Parties in the NAFTA Dispute Settlement Mechanisms: The Mexican Experience," *Tulane Law Review* 77 (2003), 1017.

[45] Metalclad, Mexico's Counter-Memorial, para. 838 (Feb. 17, 1998), http://naftaclaims.com/Disputes/ Mexico/Metalclad/MetalCladMexicoCounterMemorial.pdf.

[46] Joel C. Beauvais, Note, "Regulatory Expropriations under NAFTA: Emerging Principles & Lingering Doubts," *New York University Environmental Law Journal* 10 (2002), 246–47.

government. The Metalclad award also revealed the tension between the Mexican federal government's eagerness to attract foreign investment and local citizens' concerns about environmental issues. After the Metalclad case, new legislation to regulate the sector of hazardous waste disposal more effectively was introduced in Mexico.[47] The publicity surrounding the Metalclad arbitration and the final award of compensation led also to unprecedented initiatives toward greater regulatory transparency in Mexico.[48] The Mexican Senate expressly cited NAFTA's espousal of clear and transparent regulations as beneficial to both domestic and foreign investors.

2.1.3. The *Chemtura* Case[49]

The U.S.-based Chemtura's corporate predecessor, the Crompton Corporation, first signaled that it would sue Canada on the grounds of the phase-out of the toxic agrochemical Lindane in 2001. The corporation awaited the final outcome of the regulatory processes in Canada before submitting its claim. In 2005, Chemtura sought more than $80 million in compensation for the alleged expropriation of its investment, and the failure by Canada to provide fair and equitable treatment according to NAFTA Chapter 11.[50] While used for a long time as a pesticide in various agricultural contexts, Lindane has been banned in a growing number of countries. Chemtura alleged that the decision by Canada's Pest Management Regulatory Agency to ban Lindane on health and environmental grounds lack a rigorous scientific risk assessment.[51]

In its counter-memorial, Canada contended that Chemtura was seeking to hold the Canadian Government "responsible for the fact that it can no longer profit from the sale of a toxic chemical that has been internationally banned based on demonstrated health and environmental concerns."[52] Canada also maintained that the measures to ban Lindane were "a valid exercise of Canada's police powers to protect public health and the environment."[53] In the Methanex case, the Tribunal stressed that legitimate nondiscriminatory regulation of a chemical substance fell within the police powers rule. In addition, Canada emphasized that the regulatory process exhibited ample due process and that Chemtura had had no assurances from regulators that pesticide regulations would remain unchanged over time.[54]

47 See Gaines, above note 24, pp. 14–15.
48 Gaines, above note 24, pp. 14–15.
49 *Chemtura Corporation v. Government of Canada* (formerly *Crompton Corporation v. Government of Canada*), UNCITRAL, Award (August 2, 2010), http://www.italaw.com/sites/default/files/case-documents/ita0149_0.pdf [hereinafter Chemtura Award].
50 Ibid., paras. 92–96.
51 Ibid., paras. 126, 148.
52 Chemtura, Canada's Counter-Memorial, para. 16 (Oct. 20, 2008), http://www.naftaclaims.com/Disputes/Canada/CromptonCorp/Crompton-Chemtura-CounterMemorial.pdf.
53 Ibid., para. 500.
54 Ibid., para. 16.

In August 2010, the Tribunal rejected all claims advanced by Chemtura, and the claimant was ordered to bear the costs of the arbitration and reimburse Canada for certain costs associated with the proceeding.[55] The Tribunal decided no "substantial deprivation" of Chemtura's assets which might be an expropriation under NAFTA Chapter 11.[56] The most important aspect was that the Tribunal signaled that Canada's actions fell within that country's police powers under international law.[57] However, the argument over the police powers exception and whether it may exempt a host country from paying compensation for some regulatory measures, which otherwise amounts to indirect expropriation of a foreign investor's assets, has never disappeared.[58]

Although Canada won an important victory in the Chemtura case, it is unclear what kind of impacts the Chemtura award may have on similar cases in the future. On August 25, 2008, the U.S. giant Dow AgriSciences served a Notice of Intent to Submit a Claim to Arbitration under NAFTA Chapter 11, for losses allegedly caused by a Quebec's 2006 law banning the use of cosmetic lawn pesticides containing the active ingredient 2,4-D.[59] This case was settled in May 2011,[60] though it has been sharply criticized by environmental groups and some Canadian politicians.[61] In August 2010, Canada agreed to compensate forestry giant AbitibiBowater Inc. $130 million to settle a claim under Chapter 11 that the company assets in Newfoundland and Labrador were illegally seized by the province.[62] Despite uncertainties surrounding the cases after the Chemtura award, the Chemtura case shows that a balance between the needs to implement appropriate environmental measures and to protect foreign investment is possible.

The challenges made to Canada's chemicals regulations generated anxieties among the civil society community. In an interview, Kathleen Cooper, a senior researcher with the Canadian Environmental Law Association, a nonprofit, public

---

[55] Chemtura Award, above note 49, p. 80.

[56] Chemtura Award, above note 49, para. 265.

[57] Chemtura Award, above note 49, para. 266.

[58] See L. Yves Fortier, CC, QC, and Stephen L. Drymer, "Indirect Expropriation in the Law of International Investment: I Know It When I See It, or Caveat Investor," *Asia Pacific Law Review* 13 (2005), 79; see also Christopher Gibson, "A Look at the Compulsory License in Investment Arbitration: the Case of Indirect Expropriation," *American University International Law Review* 25 (2010), 357.

[59] *Dow AgroSciences, LLC v. Government of Canada*, Notice of Intent to Submit a Claim to Arbitration under Article 1119 of NAFTA, paras. 3–8 (Aug. 25, 2008), http://www.international.gc.ca/trade-agreements-accords-commerciaux/assets/pdfs/disp-diff/dow-01.pdf.

[60] Ibid., Settlement Agreement (May 25, 2011), http://www.international.gc.ca/trade-agreements-accords-commerciaux/assets/pdfs/disp-diff/dow-03.pdf.

[61] Kathleen Cooper et al., "Seeking a Regulatory Chill in Canada: the Dow Agrosciences NAFTA Chapter 11 Challenge to the Quebec Pesticides Management Code," *Golden Gate University Environmental Law Journal* 7 (2014), 48–49, http://digitalcommons.law.ggu.edu/gguelj/vol7/iss1/4.

[62] Bertrand Marotte, "Ottawa Wins NAFTA Challenge Brought by U.S. Chemical Maker," *Globe and Mail* (Aug. 23, 2012), http://m.theglobeandmail.com/report-on-business/ottawa-wins-nafta-challenge-brought-by-us-chemical-maker/article1690616/?service=mobile (last visited March 14, 2014).

interest group, expressed concerns that chemical producers can invoke NAFTA to "undermine the decisions of democratically-elected governments."[63]

2.2. NAFTA *Chapter 11's Crisis of Legitimacy*

Two decades ago, investor–state arbitration was almost unknown beyond the academic circle and Parties involved in the negotiations of international investment treaties. It started to attract public attention in the mid-1990s after claims were advanced by investors under NAFTA Chapter 11 and numerous BITs. In 2012, fifty-eight new cases were initiated, which constituted the highest number of known treaty-based disputes ever filed in a single year, and the total number of known treaty-based cases rose to 514 by the end of 2012.[64] Since most arbitration forums do not maintain a public registry of claims, the total number of cases is likely to be higher. It "confirms that foreign investors are increasingly resorting to investor-state arbitration."[65] While claimants "have challenged a broad range of government measures," including those related to revocations of licenses, breaches of investment contracts, irregularities in public tenders, changes to domestic regulatory frameworks, withdrawal of previously granted subsidies, direct expropriations of investments, and tax measures,[66] the challenges to environmental measures have continued to be the most remarkable. In 2012, Canada was put on notice with respect to two potential claims under NAFTA Chapter 11 – one of them arose out of the moratorium on offshore wind farms introduced by the Government of Ontario (pending further research into such farms' environmental and health effects), which allegedly destroyed the claimant's contractual rights.[67] The other is on the ground of banning oil and gas activities in certain areas.[68]

Judge Brower[69] has suggested that there is an emerging crisis of legitimacy for international arbitration, and such crisis may be deeper than the surface of the

---

[63] Luke Eric Peterson, "Analysis: Stricter Chemicals Regulations by Canada Attract NAFTA Lawsuits," *Investment Arbitration Reporter* 1 (Oct. 22, 2008), http://www.iareporter.com/downloads/20100107_15/download.

[64] United Nations Conference on Trade and Development, IIA Issues Note (No.1), *Recent Developments in Investor-State Dispute Settlement* (May 2013) p. 1, http://unctad.org/en/PublicationsLibrary/webdiaepcb2013d3_en.pdf.

[65] Ibid.

[66] Ibid., p. 3.

[67] *Windstream Energy, LLC v. Government of Canada*, Notice of Intent to Submit a Claim to Arbitration under Chapter 11 of NAFTA, paras. 36–37 (Oct. 17, 2012), http://italaw.com/sites/default/files/case-documents/italaw1141.pdf.

[68] *Lone Pine Resources, Inc. v. Government of Canada*, Notice of Intent to Submit a Claim to Arbitration under Chapter 11 of NAFTA, para. 2 (Nov. 8, 2012), http://italaw.com/sites/default/files/case-documents/italaw1156.pdf.

[69] Charles N. Brower is a judge of the Iran–United States Claims Tribunal in the Hague, Netherlands, and special counsel in the Washington, D.C., office of New York's White & Case.

investor–state arbitration itself.[70] It goes to the basic objective and scope of IIAs, and to the substantive and procedural aspects of the investor–state arbitration regime those IIAs contain. Over the past twenty years, IIAs are moving beyond postinvestment protection to provide a right to establishment and even preestablishment rights for foreign investors.[71] This development is based on economic liberalization theory: the fewer the constraints on capital, the more mobile it will be and more efficiently it will be allocated from an economic perspective.[72] The improvement of foreign investors' rights under IIAs means the erosion of host states' sovereignty,[73] such as the governments' regulatory powers to control their own resources for economic growth and sustainable development, given that foreign investors have plenty of rights and no responsibilities while the rights of host states are not mentioned in most IIAs. NAFTA is different from most of the other IIAs, since its substantive rules for investor protection go beyond traditional protection from direct expropriation.[74] Due to the broad discretion of arbitrators, the national treatment, the most-favored-nation treatment, and the fair and equitable treatment provided under NAFTA have worked increasingly against the three Parties.

Moreover, the ad hoc tribunals that enforce the obligation of host states to protect foreign investors under IIAs have issued divergent decisions, since the arbitrators are not constrained by stare decisis. The decisions are made behind the scenes even though some of the cases involve significant public interest. The critics of NAFTA Chapter 11 argue that secretive and unaccountable NAFTA tribunals elevate investor interests over important state legislative and administrative policy interests.[75]

The reformation of NAFTA Chapter 11 started in 2001. For example, its lack of transparency has decreased as amicus curiae and nondisputing parties were allowed to intervene in the arbitral proceeding, public hearing, and arbitral documents in the Methanex case[76] and in most of the following NAFTA Chapter 11 cases, particularly

[70] Charles N. Brower, "A Crisis of Legitimacy," *National Law Journal* (Oct. 7, 2002), http://www.lancaster.ac.uk/fass/law/intlaw/ibuslaw/docs/brower2002.pdf.

[71] Howard Mann, "International Investment Agreements: Building the New Colonialism?," *American Society of International Law Proceedings* 97 (2003), 248.

[72] Ibid. pp. 248–49.

[73] Peter Muchlinski, "Corporations and the Uses of Law: International Investment Arbitration as a 'Multilateral Legal Order,'" *Oñati Socio-Legal Series* 1 (2011), 5, http://opo.iisj.net/index.php/osls/article/viewFile/61/211.

[74] Howard Mann and Konrad von Moltke, *Protecting Investor Rights and the Public Good: Assessing NAFTA's Chapter 11* (Winnipeg, Canada: International Institute for Sustainable Development, 2002), p. 1, http://www.iisd.org/trade/ilsdworkshop/pdf/background_en.pdf.

[75] Luke Eric Peterson, "Investor Rights and Wrongs: Suffering from 'Calligroeconomania,'" *IISD Commentary* (Dec. 2002) (originally published in the *Toronto Star*, June 14, 2002, at A22), http://www.iisd.org/pdf/2002/commentary_trade_3.pdf.

[76] *Methanex Corporation v. United States*, Decision of the Tribunal on Petitions from Third Persons to Intervene as "Amici Curiae," Pt. I, paras. 1–4 (Jan. 15, 2001), http://naftaclaims.com/Disputes/USA/Methanex/MethanexDecisionReAuthorityAmicus.pdf.

when the tribunals are dealing with cases of significant environmental protection, public health, and other public interest implications.[77] More transparency of the investor–state arbitration procedures helps reduce some of the concerns of civil society groups that IIAs such as NAFTA Chapter 11 pose a threat to the public interest of host countries.

NAFTA Chapter 11 has certainly proven itself to be a "dynamic laboratory,"[78] and most contracting parties are seriously considering reforming the current direction of IIAs, including substantive rules and investor–state dispute settlement provisions in their negotiations. Anxious about their legitimate environmental measures being challenged and also concerned about the relationship between sustainable development and economic globalization, the contracting parties are trying to include environmental provisions when negotiating IIAs. The NAFTA preamble states that the Parties shall: "Undertake each of the preceding [investment and trade objectives] in a manner consistent with environmental protection and conservation; Preserve their flexibility to safeguard the public welfare; Promote sustainable development; Strengthen the development and enforcement of environmental laws and regulations."[79] The Energy Charter Treaty's (ECT's) preamble makes note of international environmental agreements with energy-related aspects and "[r]ecogniz[es] the increasingly urgent need for measures to protect the environment."[80] The 2004 U.S. Model BIT's preamble establishes that the Parties "[d]esir[e] to achieve these objectives in a manner consistent with the protection of health, safety, and the environment, and the promotion of internationally recognized labor rights."[81] This preamble has been copied into the 2012 U.S. Model BIT.[82]

Besides the preamble, a new environmental provision headed by "Investment and Environment" has been included in some recent IIAs, such as Article 1114 of NAFTA and Article 12 of the 2004 U.S. Model BIT. Such articles express the parties' recognition that it is "inappropriate to encourage investment by weakening or reducing the protections afforded in domestic environmental laws."[83] And such articles provide

---

[77] See Mary Bottari et al., *NAFTA Chapter 11 Investor-to-State Cases: Bankrupting Democracy* (Washington, D.C.: Public Citizen's Global Trade Watch, 2001), http://www.citizen.org/documents/ACF186 .PDF.

[78] Charles N. Brower, "NAFTA's Investment Chapter: Dynamic Laboratory, Failed Experiment, and Lessons for the FTAA," *American Society of International Law Proceedings* 97 (2003), 251, 257.

[79] NAFTA, above note 1, Preamble, 32 I.L.ML at 297.

[80] See Energy Charter Treaty, Preamble, Dec. 17, 1994, in Energy Charter Secretariat (ed.), *The Energy Charter and Related Documents* (Brussels: Energy Charter Secretariat, 2004), http://www.encharter .org/fileadmin/user_upload/document/EN.pdf.

[81] 2004 U.S. Model Bilateral Investment Treaty, http://www.state.gov/documents/organization/117601 .pdf.

[82] 2012 U.S. Model Bilateral Investment Treaty, http://www.state.gov/documents/organization/188371 .pdf.

[83] 2004 U.S. Model BIT, above note 81, Art. 12; see also NAFTA, above note 1, Art. 1114, 32 I.L.M. at 642. ("The Parties recognize that it is inappropriate to encourage investment by relaxing domestic health, safety or environmental measures.")

that each party "shall strive to ensure that it does not waive or otherwise derogate from, or offer to waive or otherwise derogate from" domestic environmental laws "in a manner that weakens or reduces the protections afforded in those laws as an encouragement for the establishment, acquisition, expansion, or retention of an investment in its territory."[84] If a party considers that the other party has offered such an encouragement, it may request consultations, and the two parties "shall consult with a view to avoiding any such encouragement."[85] Furthermore, such articles also make it clear that nothing in the BIT shall be construed to prevent a party from adopting, maintaining, or enforcing any measure otherwise consistent with the BIT that it considers appropriate to ensure that investment activity in its territory is undertaken in a manner sensitive to environmental concerns.[86] The point is that the environmental article in the U.S. Model BIT applies to measures adopted or maintained by a party with respect to all investments in its territory, not only covered investments. The environmental provision is intended to promote environmental protection and prevent host state actions from undermining the effectiveness of environment laws, regardless of the nationality of ownership of the investment such actions seek to attract.[87] Ultimately, these environmental provisions strive to deter the host country from racing to the bottom in order to attract foreign investment. For instance, the U.S.-Uruguay BIT;[88] the United States, Central-America and the Dominican Republic FTA; and the FTAs signed by the U.S. with Singapore, Chile, Morocco, Oman, Australia, Peru, and Colombia, respectively, contain such identical environmental articles.

Although the labor and environmental provisions in the 2012 U.S. Model BIT[89] are not subject to compulsory arbitration, they include a requirement that countries enforce their own labor and environmental laws, subject to consultations. This means there is no formal mechanism to directly enforce these provisions. Despite the concern of racing to the bottom to attract foreign investment, it has been generally recognized that international investment flow and economic growth have a positive impact on labor and environmental protection in less-developed states.[90] Labor and environmental groups called for the Obama administration to make labor and

---

[84] 2004 U.S. Model BIT, above note 81, Art. 12; see also NAFTA, above note 1, Art. 1114, 32 I.L.M. at 642. ("[A] Party should not waive or otherwise derogate from, or offer to waive or otherwise derogate from, such measures as an encouragement for the establishment, acquisition, expansion or retention in its territory of an investment of an investor.")

[85] 2004 U.S. Model BIT, above note 81, Art. 12.

[86] E.g. United States, Central-America and the Dominican Republic FTA, Art. 10.11, http://www.ustr .gov/sites/default/files/uploads/agreements/cafta/asset_upload_file328_4718.pdf.

[87] Kenneth J. Vandevelde, U.S. *International Investment Agreements* (New York: Oxford University Press, 2009), p. 744.

[88] U.S.-Uruguay BIT, above note 21, Art.12.

[89] 2012 U.S. Model BIT, above note 82, Arts. 12, 13.

[90] Kathryn McConnell, "Trade Deals Can Boost Labor, Environment Protections, USTR Says," *United States Embassy, IIP Digital* (Feb. 19, 2014), http://iipdigital.usembassy.gov/st/english/article/2014/02/ 20140219293644.html#axzz2ubaLg2MX (last visited March 14, 2014).

environmental protection obligations more enforceable, at least through state–state dispute resolution mechanisms, in recent U.S. FTAs with Panama, Colombia, and Peru.[91] However, the final text of the 2012 U.S. Model BIT came as a disappointment to labor and environmental groups because the modifications of these labor and environmental provisions were too mild. Critics pointed out that these provisions set a bad example and may undermine the ability of the U.S. to conclude BITs with developing countries and promote the labor and environmental protection purposes that international investment should bring about.[92] In other words, the new Model BIT may hinder negotiations of new BITs with certain countries,[93] such as China, India, and Vietnam.

As mentioned previously, violating such environmental provisions does not constitute a cause of action under either the investor–state or the state–state dispute resolution system. Therefore, these provisions have traditionally been considered as soft law under IIAs, as compared to provisions such as the national treatment, the most-favored-nation treatment, and the fair and equitable treatment. However, as a whole, the investor–state arbitration tribunals should consider the objectives of an international investment treaty as well as its context. When the treaty in question expressly addresses matters related to the environment and public health, it is crucial to interpret the substantive protections in the treaty within the context of relevant environmental and health provisions.[94]

3. IIAS SIGNED BY CHINA AND THEIR ENVIRONMENTAL PROVISIONS

As China becomes increasingly integrated into the world economy, its inbound and outbound investment has been growing robustly despite the worldwide financial crisis and economic depression in recent years. China continues to be the most favored destination for foreign investment.[95] In addition, the Twelfth Five-Year Plan, the country's core national economic policy for the period of 2011–2015, encourages Chinese enterprises to invest abroad.[96] It is estimated that China's cumulative outbound investments in nonfinancial sectors were around $366 billion and inbound

---

[91] Paolo Di Rosa, "The New 2012 U.S. Model BIT: Staying the Course," *Kluwer Arbitration Blog* (June 1, 2012), http://kluwerarbitrationblog.com/blog/2012/06/01/the-new-2012-u-s-model-bit-staying-the-course/ (last visited March 14, 2014).

[92] Arthur Stamoulis, "Labor, Environmental Provisions in Model BIT Spark Divergent Reactions," *Citizens Trade* (April 25, 2012), http://lists.citizenstrade.org/pipermail/ctcfield-citizenstrade.org/2012-April/002020.html (last visited March 14, 2014).

[93] Di Rosa, above note 91.

[94] Rahim Moloo and Justin Jacinto, "Environmental and Health Regulation: Assessing Liability Under Investment Treaties," *Berkeley Journal of International Law* 29 (2011), 10.

[95] United Nations Conference on Trade and Development, *World Investment Report 2012: Towards a New Generation of Investment Policies* (Geneva: United Nations Publications, 2012), p. xvi, http://www.unctad-docs.org/files/UNCTAD-WIR2012-Full-en.pdf [hereinafter UNCTAD World Investment Report 2012].

[96] China's Twelfth Five Year Plan (2011–2015), Ch. 52, § 2, http://cbi.typepad.com/china_direct/2011/05/chinas-twelfth-five-new-plan-the-full-english-version.html.

investments were around $712 billion in total at the end of 2011.[97] Much of the outbound investment has been directed at mergers and acquisitions abroad.[98] By the end of 2012, the overall number of IIAs worldwide reached 3,196, including 2857 BITs and 339 other IIAs.[99] China has concluded more than 140 BITs and 12 FTAs so far,[100] most of which include investor–state arbitration provisions.[101] In 2012, China, Japan, and South Korea concluded the trilateral investment agreement and the three Contracting Parties have also agreed to start the negotiation of an FTA, which will account for one-fifth of both world population and the global GDP.[102] This trilateral investment treaty includes an environmental provision, which states that the Contracting Party recognizes that it is inappropriate to encourage foreign investments "by relaxing its environmental measures" and "should not waive or otherwise derogate from such environmental measures as an encouragement for the establishment, acquisition or expansion of investments in its territory."[103]

China and Canada also signed a BIT in 2012, which is not ratified by the Canadian government yet.[104] The China-Canada FIPA provides that "[t]he Contracting Parties recognize that it is inappropriate to encourage investment by waiving, relaxing, or otherwise derogating from domestic health, safety or environmental measures."[105] The treaty also includes a general exception provision that provides that "nothing in this Agreement shall be construed to prevent a Contraction Party from adopting or maintaining measures, including environmental measures."[106] As to the expropriation provision, the Contracting Parties agree that measures designed and applied to

---

[97] UNCTAD World Investment Report, above note 96, p. 174.
[98] Ibid., p. 71.
[99] United Nations Conference on Trade and Development, *World Investment Report 2013: Global Value Chains: Investment and Trade for Development* (Geneva: United Nations Publications, 2013), p. 101, http://unctad.org/en/PublicationsLibrary/wir2013_en.pdf.
[100] A list of China's BITs is available at http://www.unctad.org/sections/dite_pcbb/docs/bits_china.pdf. The text of each BIT is available at http://www.unctadxi.org/templates/docsearch____779.aspx (last visited March 14, 2014).
[101] E.g., China-Canada BIT, Art. 20 (2012); China-Belgium-Luxemburg BIT, Art. 8 (2005); China-Uzbekistan BIT, Art. 12 (2011); China-Nigeria BIT, Art. 9 (2001); Modification of the China-Cuba BIT, Art. 10 (2007).
[102] Yu Lintao, "Three's Company: China, South Korea and Japan Consider Free Trade Agreement," *Beijing Review* (May 24, 2012), http://www.bjreview.com.cn/world/txt/2012–05/21/content_454898.htm (last visited March 14, 2014).
[103] Agreement for the Promotion, Facilitation and Protection of Investment, China-Japan-Korea, above note 10, Art. 23.
[104] Opponents of the China-Canada BIT state that it favors China's interests, while leaving Canada's natural resources vulnerable to control by foreign companies. In addition, the treaty would permit Chinese investors to bring claim against the host government if implementing environmental regulations have an negative impact on projects of foreign investors. The proposed Enbridge Northern Gateway pipeline is an example. E.g., Lauren Krugel, "Tom Mulcair: China-Canada FIPA Threat to Alberta's Natural Resources Control," *Huffington Post* (Nov. 13, 2012), http://www.huffingtonpost.ca/2012/11/13/tom-mulcair-alberta-natural-resources-china-canada-fipa_n_2126606.html (last visited March 14, 2014).
[105] China-Canada BIT, above note 101, Art. 18.
[106] China-Canada BIT, above note 101, Art. 33.

protect the legitimate public objectives for the well-being of citizens, such as health, safety, and the environment, do not constitute indirect expropriation.[107]

Believing that international investment is a significant driver for national economic growth, job creation, and exports, China will continue to push its IIAs policy to promote greater access for Chinese companies to enter other countries' markets and more openness of its own domestic market for access by foreign investors as well. On May 24, 2011, the first investor–state arbitration case against China was filed before the ICSID, which was submitted by a Malaysian company called Ekran Berhad.[108] The dispute concerned Ekran's right to a leasehold over a piece of land in the Chinese province of Hainan. The value of this piece of land was estimated to be over U.S. $5.7 million, and the lease had been revoked by the local government.[109] While little is known about the details of the case, the case was based on the China-Malaysia BIT that entered into force on March 31, 1990.[110] As China has signed more than 140 IIAs with other countries since 1982, the international society has been expecting the first investor–state arbitration case against China for a long time.[111] On May 16, 2013, the parties filed a request for the discontinuance of the proceeding pursuant to ICSID Arbitration Rule 43(1) and the Secretary-General of ICSID issued a procedural order taking note of the discontinuance of the proceeding.[112] It is obviously too early to predict whether Ekran's claim will mark the beginning of a new era for arbitration cases brought by foreign investors against China, but this case sent a strong message that domestic regulatory measures could trigger investor–state arbitrations against the Chinese government.

4. CHINA'S SIGNIFICANT ENVIRONMENTAL CHALLENGES AND THE DEVELOPMENT OF ITS ENVIRONMENTAL LEGAL AND GOVERNANCE FRAMEWORK

After three decades of rapid economic development, China, as the second largest economy in the world, is facing a wide range of challenges on the environmental, energy, and climate change front. Both its people and the international community have called upon the Chinese government to enhance its efforts to reduce pollution, protect natural resources, and tackle the tricky issue of global warming. In 2013 alone, a series of air pollution episodes in several Chinese cities made international headlines. Experts from the Chinese Academy of Social Science attributed the growing air

---

[107] China-Canada BIT, above note 101, Annex B.10.
[108] *Ekran Berhad v. People's Republic of China*, ICSID Case No. ARB/11/15 (May 24, 2011), https://icsid .worldbank.org/ICSID/FrontServlet?requestType=GenCaseDtlsRH&actionVal=ListConcluded (last visited March 14, 2014).
[109] "First ICSID Case Against China," *WunschARB* (May, 30, 2011), http://www.wunscharb.com/news/ first-icsid-case-against-china (last visited March 14, 2014).
[110] Ibid.
[111] Ibid.
[112] Ekran Berhad, above note 108.

pollution largely to China's rapid development and a significant increase in primary energy consumption as a result.[113] In addition to causing economic damages, such serious air pollution could trigger cancer and affect fertility.[114] A recently released report by the same government think tank showed that China has the second worst air pollution in the world, after India.[115] After an evaluation of different countries' ecological status, environmental management capacity, and the balance between economic development and conservation, the report drew a conclusion that China ranked merely 87th out of 133 countries in overall environmental competitiveness.[116]

Thirty-eight percent of the 456 cities in China had acid rain in the first six months of 2013.[117] Government data from 2013 also showed nearly 30 percent of the groundwater and 60 percent of the surface water in China was classified as of either "poor" or "very poor" quality.[118] Already the largest greenhouse gases emitter in the world, China's per capita emissions continue to grow and are now higher than the global average and equal to or even higher than those of some countries in Europe.[119] Growing pollution has a direct impact on Chinese citizens' daily lives and shapes their perception of the country's environmental future. According to a survey of over 3,000 Chinese respondents by the Pew Research Center in 2013, the public's concern about China's air and water quality is increasing.[120] According to the survey report, 47 percent of the respondents rated air pollution a very big problem, an increase of 11 percent from 2012, while 40 percent said water pollution is a very big problem, compared with 33 percent in 2012.[121]

In addition, pollution has already surpassed land disputes to become the main cause of social unrest in China.[122] When planned projects may have an impact on

[113] "Gov. Think Tank Warns over Worsening Haze in Chinese Cities that Could Affect Fertility," *Caijing* (Nov. 5, 2013), http://english.caijing.com.cn/2013-11-05/113524242.html?utm_source=The+Sinocism+China+Newsletter&utm_campaign=62e90439c8-Sinocism11_06_13&utm_medium=email&utm_term=0_171f237867-62e90439c8-29577665 (last visited March 14, 2014).

[114] Ibid.

[115] Li Jing, "Study Shows How China's Air Quality Affects its Global Competitiveness," *South China Morning Post* (Jan. 11, 2014), http://www.scmp.com/news/china/article/1402682/study-shows-how-chinas-air-quality-affects-its-global-competitiveness (last visited March 14, 2014).

[116] Ibid.

[117] Ashley Kindergan, "China Will Soon Embark On A Decade-Long 'Green Cycle,'" *Business Insider* (Jan. 11, 2014), http://www.businessinsider.com/credit-suisse-china-green-cycle-2014-1 (last visited March 14, 2014).

[118] Ibid.

[119] William Schulte et al., "China Regulates CO2 Emissions," *Vermont Law Top 10 Environmental Watch List 2014*, http://watchlist.vermontlaw.edu/china-regulates-co2-emissions/ (last visited March 14, 2014).

[120] Pew Research Global Attitudes Project, *Environmental Concerns on the Rise in China* (Washington, D.C.: Pew Research Center, 2013), p. 1, http://www.pewglobal.org/files/2013/09/Pew-Global-Attitudes-Project-China-Report-FINAL-9-19-132.pdf.

[121] Ibid.

[122] "Chinese Anger Over Pollution Becomes Main Cause of Social Unrest," *Bloomberg News* (March 6, 2013), http://www.bloomberg.com/news/2013-03-06/pollution-passes-land-grievances-as-main-spark-of-china-protests.html (last visited March 14, 2014).

local environment and public health, Chinese citizens have become increasingly active in participating in the government's environmental decision-making process, and this requires the government to rethink its traditional approach of focusing on GDP growth only, according to a leading Chinese environmental activist.[123]

Considering the daunting environmental challenges facing China, one may think it lacks environmental laws and regulations to address pollution and natural resources degradation. Quite to the contrary, China's environmental legislative framework began to take shape in 1979 when the Environmental Protection Law (for Trial Implementation)[124] was enacted by the national legislature. The following three decades witnessed the promulgation of an impressive set of statutes and regulations to reduce pollution, protect natural resources, and conserve energy use. China is also in the process of drafting a comprehensive law on climate change. As pointed out by Peking University Professor Wang Jin, statutes related to environmental protection, natural resources, energy, circular economy, and clean production accounted for over 10 percent of all the statutes enacted by the National People's Congress and its Standing Committee. Even though there are some areas that lack relevant legislations, China's environmental legal framework in general is complete.[125]

Accompanying the overall rapid development of China's environmental legal framework is the country's increasing attention to the foreign investment aspects of its environmental regulatory regime. While pollution control was rarely addressed in China's foreign-investment laws in the early 1980s, the subsequent three decades witnessed an increasingly stringent and detailed set of rules, mostly through the foreign-investment approval process and technology or production process guidelines, to make foreign-investment projects more likely to take environmental protection into consideration. This is laudable since the Chinese government has been granting numerous legal incentives and protections that favor foreign investors over domestic businesses, but it has not given privileges in the arena of environmental rules or standards to foreign investors for the purpose of attracting their investment.[126] Unlike the practices in some other countries, China did not create a weaker set of requirements for the environmental impact assessments of foreign-invested projects, exempt foreign companies from pollution monitoring, or set more lax pollution discharge standards for foreign firms.[127]

[123] Ibid.
[124] Environmental Protection Law of the People Republic of China (for Trial Implementation), enacted on Sept. 13, 1979 by the Standing Committee of the National People's Congress.
[125] Wang Jin, "Remarks at the Special Third Forum on Legal Mechanism To Ensure Achievement of Environmental Protection Targets Under the 12th Five-Year Plan" (Sept. 21, 2011). The notes of this event can be found at http://www.acef.com.cn/news/lhhdt/2011/0921/9040.html (last visited March 14, 2014).
[126] Phillip Stalley, *Foreign Firms, Investment, and Environmental Regulation in the People's Republic of China* (Stanford, CA: Stanford University Press, 2010), p. 56.
[127] Ibid., p. 75.

However, the increasingly comprehensive set of environmental regulations has not translated into better environmental quality in China because the country has encountered enormous difficulties in effectively enforcing its existing environmental laws. The statutes' lack of enforceability is an important contributing factor. In China, it is not uncommon for government agencies to pass environmental laws that look good on paper but are unenforceable in reality because the language of these laws lacks clarity and practicality.[128] Local government's obsession with economic growth, weak regulatory infrastructure, lack of financial and human resources, and a fledging judiciary with limited authority to check government power have created significant barriers to improved environmental management.[129] Weak enforcement of environmental law is exacerbated in poorer regions that lack comparative advantage to attract foreign capital and, as a result, are more willing to ignore or completely disregard established environmental standards.[130]

Back in the 1980s and 1990s, government officials, businesses, and the majority of Chinese people acknowledged the priority afforded to economic development and viewed environmental deterioration as a price they had to pay. However, starting in the 2000s, environmental consciousness was rising, as was the political will to fight against pollution.[131] More recently, a series of high-profile air and water pollution incidents made visible the devastating economic and health impacts of environmental degradation on people's daily lives, and have gradually changed the public's environmental awareness and made it increasingly clear to the government that providing a clean and healthy environment is no less important than GDP growth. It is not uncommon to see the public, who worry about the environmental consequences of industrial projects, pressure local governments to cancel or relocate planned projects. In 2012, the city of Ningbo halted plans to produce the chemical paraxylene at a China Petroleum & Chemical Corp. plant, and the city of Qidong scrapped plans for a waste discharge pipeline project after local residents protested.[132] In 2013, authorities in the southern city of Shenzhen asked Shenzhen Energy Group to stop preparatory work for constructing a new coal-fired power plant, as a result of strong public opposition over air pollution concerns, even though this coal power plant project had received approval earlier from China's National Energy Administration to begin preliminary work.[133]

---

[128] Ibid., p. 140.

[129] Jingjing Liu and Adam Moser, "Environmental Law – China," in Klaus Bosselmann et al. (eds.), *The Encyclopedia of Sustainability Vol. 3: the Law and Politics of Sustainability* (Great Barrington, MA: Berkshire Publishing Group, 2011), p. 222.

[130] Stalley, above note 126, p. 15.

[131] Rachel E. Stern, *Environmental Litigation in China: A Study of Political Ambivalence* (Cambridge: Cambridge University Press, 2013), p. 32.

[132] "Chinese Anger Over Pollution Becomes Main Cause of Social Unrest," above note 122.

[133] "China Cancels Planned Coal-fired Plant," *Electric Light & Power* (Aug. 9, 2013), http://www.elp.com/articles/2013/8/china-cancels-planned-coal-fired-plant.html (last visited March 14, 2014).

Meanwhile, civil society has become increasingly active in shaping China's environmental governance landscape through a diverse array of activities ranging from environmental education, protecting biodiversity, and promoting a low-carbon lifestyle to providing comments on national environmental legislations, demanding disclosure of environmental information held by the government, and initiating public interest lawsuits across the country. By hearing a growing number of environmental cases, including disputes of a public interest nature, Chinese judges, in particular those serving in many of the recently created specialized environmental courts, have gradually accrued experience in adjudicating more complex and technical environmental lawsuits, and exhibited increasing sophistication in fashioning innovative and feasible solutions.[134] Such a dynamic environmental governance background presents new, uncertain, and complex challenges to the Chinese government and foreign investors when navigating the intricate relationship between environmental protection and foreign investment.

5. LESSONS FOR CHINA FROM NAFTA TO ENSURE SUSTAINABLE DEVELOPMENT AND BETTER ENVIRONMENTAL GOVERNANCE

Early on in the reform era and more recently in the period around China's entrance into WTO in 2002, Chinese government leaders believed in the benefits of foreign trade and investment on protecting China's environment – for example, helping generate income necessary to strengthen environmental protection efforts, facilitating Chinese firms' access to advanced clean production technology, and compelling China to adopt more stringent environmental standards and best international practices – and such a view is also shared by the international business community.[135] The reality, as testified by the coexistence of the miraculous economic growth and abysmal environmental record in China in the past three decades, is more complicated. On one hand, multinational companies comply with China's environmental laws, many going beyond compliance, and they also influence and work with their Chinese partners to strengthen the latter's environmental compliance as part of their Environment, Health, and Safety (EHS) practices. On the other hand, a significant portion of the foreign investment in China, particularly that invested by firms from developing countries in a domestic Chinese jurisdiction not necessarily attractive to foreign investors, is of low quality both in terms of the environmental strategy of foreign investors and more broadly in terms of the negative environmental impacts generated.[136]

---

[134] Jingjing Liu, "Environmental Justice with Chinese Characteristics: Recent Developments in Using Environmental Public Interest Litigation to Strengthen Access to Environmental Justice," *Florida Agricultural & Mechanical University Law Review* 7 (2012), 259.

[135] Stalley, above note 126, pp. 4–5.

[136] Stalley, above note 126, pp. 110, 201.

The growing concern of the Chinese people about pollution, food safety, and public health has provided impetus for and will continue to push the government to enhance its governance capacity and devote more resources to protecting the environment. The public's desire for better environmental quality and the government's response will continue to shape the investment environment for foreign capital. Although China has not yet been challenged by investor–state arbitration claims that are based on domestic environmental regulatory measures, given the trend of pollution issues constantly occupying the front page of media reports and the increasingly tough environmental protection measures, it will not be a surprise to see China facing arbitration claims brought by foreign investors on environmental grounds. Just like Mexico's experience with foreign investors' frequent challenges of its own waste management measures, it is not too difficult to imagine similar claims against China where increasingly stringent environmental standards and regulatory measures are challenged by foreign investors who took advantage of a particular region's eagerness for foreign capital, lax environmental standards, and/or weak environmental enforcement.

As mentioned earlier, the Metalclad case prompted more effective legislation to regulate hazardous waste disposal in Mexico. In China, public pressure prioritizes the need to fill in any legislative gaps, pass better environmental laws, and impose tougher measures to control pollution. The Environmental Protection Law was recently amended. Another major environmental statute, the Air Pollution Prevention and Control Law, is currently under revision.[137] China is also in the process of drafting a soil pollution law to tackle soil contamination and the associated food safety concerns. In September 2013, the Chinese government issued a five-year air pollution action plan that imposed some of the most stringent emission standards the world has ever seen that will apply to utilities, cement, and steel producers over the next two years: China's sulfur oxide limit for steelmakers will be between one-third and one-half of what is available in Europe, and coal-fired power plants will be permitted to emit only half the air pollutants permitted to their Japanese and European counterparts.[138] In addition to stricter rules on paper, enforcement of environmental laws is expected to be strengthened at different levels of local government.[139] A circular recently released by the Organization Department of the Communist Party of China Central Committee called for a more balanced work evaluation system of

---

[137] Another major environmental statute, the Water Pollution Prevention and Control Law, was passed by the Standing Committee of China's National People's Congress on May 11, 1984, and went through substantial revisions in 1996 and 2008.

[138] Kindergan, above note 117.

[139] In his excellent study on the impacts of foreign investment on China's environmental governance, Phillip Stalley conducted extensive interviews with industry representatives of domestic and foreign firms in China and these interviews revealed that most representatives believed environmental enforcement against both domestic and foreign firms is increased in recent years, with foreign firms subjected to a higher level of scrutiny. See Stalley, above note 126, pp. 89–90.

local Party and government officials by downplaying the obsession with economic growth and focusing more on the environment.[140] According to the circular, gross regional product (GRP) and its growth rates should not be the only main indicator when evaluating local officials' work achievements, and greater emphasis should be placed on indicators related to the waste of resources, environmental protection, elimination of excess capacity, and production safety.[141]

In addition to improved regulatory framework and enforcement, another aspect of China's environmental governance practice that may expose the government to foreign investor claims is related to transparency in its environmental decision-making process. The Metalclad case highlighted the importance of transparency in Mexico's permit approval process and the country's environmental regulations in general, and this is a good lesson for China, which needs to think seriously about its governance skills and practices when it comes to foreign investment. Although significant efforts have been made to improve transparency in environmental law-making and decision-making processes in China, transparency is still a goal to strive for rather than a reality. For example, environmental authorities typically do not disclose the EIA reports to the public. In addition, the more significant and controversial the environmental impact for a project (and therefore the stronger the public's interest would be in knowing the environmental impact), the less likely the EIA is made available.[142] Even if the public can access such EIA reports, the validity and quality of these reports may be questionable. In November 2013, the Ministry of Environmental Protection penalized thirty-four EIA institutions for falsifying document or providing assessment reports of poor quality.[143] Given the problematic practices related to EIAs, local governments could potentially face challenges to their environment-related decisions from foreign investors on grounds of lacking transparency.

As mentioned previously, among the broad range of government measures challenged by the claimants in investor–state arbitrations, environmental measures constitute a very significant portion. Although the Chinese government has not faced any such challenges yet to its environmental regulatory measures, given the depth and breadth of its environmental problems and the central government's desire to strengthen environmental protection efforts, China could potentially be in a vulnerable position to investor–state arbitration claims on environmental grounds; for example, the local government could cancel a planned industrial project by a foreign investor because of residents' opposition, even though this project may have gone through the relevant regulatory approval process. The fact that China

[140] Xinhua, "Local Officials to Obsess Less over Growth," *Global Times* (Dec. 10, 2013), http://www .globaltimes.cn/content/831125.shtml#.Uq8RWRaD5lK (last visited March 14, 2014).

[141] Ibid.

[142] Stalley, above note 126, p. 51.

[143] Xinhua, "China's Environmental Watchdog Punishes Agencies," *China.org.cn* (Nov. 6, 2013), http://china.org.cn/environment/2013–11/06/content_30515692.htm (last visited March 14, 2014).

lacks experience with this type of arbitration claim is notable and should remind the Chinese government of the urgency to minimize exposure to such claims by improving its governance capacity to strike the delicate balance between foreign investment and sustainable development. It should also prepare itself for this type of claims by developing relevant strategies and plans. This situation is further complicated by the fact that China has a centralized system, and the central government is held responsible when local governments make mistakes related to foreign investment that lead to investor-state arbitration claims. Given that local government officials are very likely to know little about investor-state arbitration and its legal implications, it is important for the central government to develop programs that help raise local officials' awareness of this issue for the purpose of minimizing its legal risks.

6. CONCLUSION

In the midst of citizens' growing demand for better environmental quality and the paramount weight the government places on maintaining social stability, the delicate balance between foreign investment and sustainable development is constantly tested in China, a country that has little experience with investor–state arbitration claims on environmental grounds or investor–state arbitration claims in general. Although China has started to realize the importance of harmonizing economic growth with environmental protection in international trade and investment by incorporating environmental provisions in some of its FTAs and BITs, it has not yet developed a solid understanding of the potential foreign investment-related legal challenges presented by its increasingly stringent environmental regulatory framework and the lack of transparency in environmental decision-making process, in particular how the central government may be held liable when local governments make unwarranted commitments related to environmental measures for the purpose of attracting foreign investment or scrap foreign-invested projects over public concern of significant environmental impact.

Going forward, China should consider incorporating provisions related to environmental protection and sustainable development into all of the FTAs and BITs it plans to sign. More importantly, the central government should stay alert to and be prepared for potential investor–state arbitration claims arising out of the country's increasingly comprehensive and sophisticated environmental legal system and local residents' desire to keep pollution away from their communities. It should also ensure that such awareness of potential exposure to arbitration claims by foreign investors flows down to the local level of governments who are seeking foreign investment and are tasked with protecting local environment at the same time.

PART III

Proposals for Reform and Lessons Going Forward

14

Pathways of Influence in the NAFTA Regime and Their Implications for Domestic Environmental Policy Making in North America

Sébastien Jodoin

1. INTRODUCTION

Over the last twenty years, scholars in law, economics, and political science have examined the impacts of the North American Free Trade Agreement (NAFTA) and its two side agreements – the North American Agreement on Environmental Cooperation (NAAEC) and the North American Agreement on Labor Cooperation (NAALC) – on various elements and indicators of sustainable development[1] such as economic growth;[2] jobs, wages, and income inequality;[3] corporate performance;[4] pollution levels;[5] and labor standards.[6]

While this body of scholarship has taken on the difficult task of disentangling NAFTA's effects from those of other significant economic, social, and political phenomena, the narrower question of whether and how NAFTA and its side agreements have influenced domestic policy-making processes and outcomes has received

---

[1] For an overview of the first decade of this scholarship, see Gary Clyde Hufbauer and Jeffrey J. Schott, *NAFTA Revisited: Achievements and Challenges* (Washington, DC: Institute for International Economics, 2005).

[2] See, e.g., Lorenzo Caliendo and Fernando Parro, "Estimates of the Trade and Welfare Effects of NAFTA" (National Bureau of Economic Research Working Paper No. 18508, 2012); David Karemera and Kalu Ojah, "An industrial analysis of trade creation and diversion effects of NAFTA" (1998) 13:3 *Journal of Economic Integration* 400–425.

[3] See, e.g., Victoria Hottenrott and Stephen Blank, "Assessing NAFTA – Part II: The Impact of NAFTA on Jobs, Wages, and Income Inequality" (Lubin School of Business Working Paper 12–1–1998, 1998).

[4] See, e.g., Priscilla S. Wisner and Marc J. Epstein, "'Push' and 'Pull' Impacts of NAFTA on Environmental Responsiveness and Performance in Mexican Industry" (2005) 45:3 *MIR: Management International Review* 327–347.

[5] See, e.g., Tun-Hsiang Yu, Man-Keun Kim and Seong-Hoon Cho, "Does Trade Liberalization Induce More Greenhouse Gas Emissions? The Case of Mexico and the United States under NAFTA" (2010) 93:2 *American Journal of Agricultural Economics* 545–552.

[6] See, e.g., Alfredo Hualde and Miguel Angel Ramírez, "The Impact of the NAFTA Treaty on Wage Competition, Immigration, Labor Standards and Cross-border Co-operation" (2001) 7:3 *Transfer: European Review of Labour and Research* 494–514.

relatively little attention. When scholars have turned to this latter issue, their work has tended to be compartmentalized around particular sources of policy influence: NAFTA and its dispute settlement processes (especially Chapter 11),[7] the implementation of its side agreements and the activities of their associated institutions,[8] or the market-driven processes of policy change fostered by trade liberalization.[9] Moreover, this analysis is more often than not anchored in largely binary analytical frameworks that aim to establish whether NAFTA has led to downward or upward pressures on environmental and social regulation.[10] As a result, much of the existing scholarship fails to effectively grapple with the complexity and contradictions of how a fragmented regime such as NAFTA exerts policy influence at the domestic level[11] and thus leaves unresolved the question of whether and to what extent NAFTA has altered the ability of policy-makers to regulate economic, environmental, and social matters in a manner consistent with the objective and principles of sustainable development.[12]

In this chapter, I seek to develop a theoretical account of how various elements of the NAFTA regime may affect domestic policy processes and outcomes in Canada, Mexico, and the United States, with a particular focus on the environment as an illustrative issue area. To this end, I draw inspiration from Bernstein and Cashore, who recognize the role of, and intersections between, four main "pathways" of policy influence: international rules, international norms, markets, and direct access to policy-making.[13] While some of these pathways have already been addressed in the existing literature on NAFTA, they have rarely been analyzed from the perspective of their policy influence and have seldom been studied together. I aim in this chapter to examine how the various pathways of influence in the NAFTA regime may affect the development and implementation of environmental policy in complex and intersecting ways that are not reducible to the "race-to-the-bottom" and "race-to-the-top" hypotheses that dominate existing scholarship in this area.

[7] See sources cited in Section 2 of this chapter.
[8] See sources cited in Section 3 of this chapter.
[9] See sources cited in Section 4 of this chapter.
[10] Contrast David Vogel, *Trading Up: Consumer and Environmental Regulation in a Global Economy* (Cambridge, MA: Harvard University Press, 1995), with Per G. Fredriksson and Daniel L. Millimet, "Is There a Race to the Bottom in Environmental Policies? The NAFTA" (First North American Symposium on Assessing the Linkages between Trade and Environment, CEC, 2000).
[11] For similar criticisms of the broader literature on globalization and public policy, see Steven Bernstein and Benjamin Cashore, "Globalization, Four Paths of Internationalization and Domestic Policy Change: The Case of EcoForestry in British Columbia, Canada" (2000) 33:1 *Canadian Journal of Political Science* 67–99.
[12] Compare Donald S. Macdonald, "Chapter 11 of NAFTA: What Are the Implications for Sovereignty?" (1998) 24 *Canada-United States Law Journal* 281–288 and George Hoberg, "Trade, Harmonization, and Domestic Autonomy" (2001) 3 *Journal of Comparative Policy Analysis* 191–217.
[13] Steven Bernstein and Benjamin Cashore, "Complex Global Governance and Domestic Policies: Four Pathways of Influence" (2012) 88:3 *International Affairs* 585–604. It is worth noting that while I draw on the typology developed by Bernstein and Cashore, the way that I define these different pathways differs from their work in a number of ways.

I proceed as follows. I successively analyze the policy influence exerted by NAFTA's international rules (Section 2), its direct access mechanisms (Section 3), its market force (Section 4), and its international norms (Section 5). I begin each section by providing a brief overview of the literature that has developed around these four pathways of influence, with a particular focus on their relevance for studying the domestic policy influence of regional trade agreements (RTAs). Drawing on existing findings, I then review how the NAFTA regime's pathways of policy influence have affected domestic environmental policy-making. It must be stressed that much of my analysis of the NAFTA regime is meant to be illustrative of how these different pathways operate and is far from comprehensive or conclusive. I close the chapter by discussing the tensions and synergies that may exist across these pathways for promoting environmental sustainability within North America and by laying out an agenda for further empirical research on NAFTA's complex relationship with domestic policy-making in the field of sustainable development.

2. THE POLICY INFLUENCE OF NAFTA'S INTERNATIONAL RULES

RTAs can affect domestic policy-making through the influence of their international rules and their related compliance mechanisms. Rationalism has emerged as one of the leading accounts for explaining the ability of international rules, especially in the context of regional and international economic law, to affect the policies of the governments that sign on to them.[14] Rationalist explanations conceive of the commitment to international rules as resulting from the rational, self-interested, and utility-maximizing behavior of governments.[15] A government's decision to ratify an RTA thus depends on whether the benefits of ratification (particularly the expectation that other governments will abide by the agreement, thereby generating economic gains from the liberalization of trade and investment) outweigh its costs (most notably the abandonment of protectionist policies and the domestic repercussions that may result therefrom).[16] In some cases, while governments may prefer the status quo to joining a new trade agreement, they may nonetheless decide

---

[14] An alternate take on the domestic influence of international law is provided by constructivist research that argues that when rules adhere to certain norms concerning the legitimacy and fairness of rule-making, they may inspire a sense of fidelity from those actors to whom they are addressed (Jutta Brunnée and Stephen Toope, *Legitimacy and Legality in International Law. An Interactional Account* (Cambridge, UK: Cambridge University Press, 2010). (The potential for NAFTA to adhere to this constructivist account of international law is discussed in Hoi Kong's Chapter 15 of this book.) For my part, I provide a constructivist analysis of the influence of NAFTA's international norms in Section 5.

[15] Andrew T. Guzman, "A Compliance-Based Theory of International Law" (2002) 90 *California Law Review* 1823–1888; Kenneth W. Abbott and Duncan Snidal, "Hard and Soft Law in International Governance" (2000) 54:3 *International Organization* 421–436.

[16] Judith Goldstein and Lisa Martin, "Legalization, Trade Liberalization, and Domestic Politics," (2000) 54:3 *International Organization* 603–632 at 630–632.

to join in order to avoid being the only country left outside of the agreement in question.[17]

Similar cost-benefit calculations are also seen to underlie the decisions of a government to comply with an RTA on an ongoing basis. First, governments may comply with an RTA (or a decision issued by one of its dispute settlement mechanisms) to reap the rewards associated with trade liberalization, on the expectation that the other parties will also continue to abide by the terms of the RTA.[18] Second, governments may also respect an RTA to avoid the costs associated with noncompliance, whether sanctions imposed by a third party dispute settlement mechanism or the adoption of retaliatory trade measures by another party.[19] Finally, and most importantly, rationalists argue that governments usually decide to comply with an RTA in order to obtain or preserve the reputational benefits that accrue from compliance vis-à-vis their trading partners and key domestic audiences. For all of these reasons, rationalists hold that the establishment of mechanisms that can provide transparent and credible information about the behavior of other governments, so as to monitor and sanction shirking and free-riding, will be key to ensuring high levels of compliance with RTAs.[20]

Conceiving of NAFTA as a body of international rules is familiar to legal scholars, and there is an extensive literature discussing the legal implications of NAFTA and the NAAEC for environmental law and policy.[21] As far as NAFTA is concerned, most scholars agree that the real import of its trade and investment rules lies not in their substantive implications for environmental policies, but rather in the procedural standards that they require for their adoption and implementation.[22] While NAFTA enshrines the right of governments to adopt regulatory standards that serve a legitimate purpose – including public safety; the protection of human, animal, or plant life or health; and environmental or consumer protection[23] – it also sets

---

[17] Lloyd Gruber, "Power Politics and the Free Trade Bandwagon" (2001) 34:7 *Comparative Political Studies* 703–741 (arguing that Mexico and Canada supported the adoption of NAFTA to avoid being the only country left out of a trade agreement with the United States).

[18] Beth A. Simmons, "Compliance with International Agreements" (1998) 1:1 *Annual Review of Political Science* 75–93 at 80–81.

[19] James McCall Smith, "The Politics of Dispute Settlement Design: Explaining Legalism in Regional Trade Pacts" (2000) 54:1 *International Organization* 137–180 at 145–147.

[20] Abbott and Snidal, "Hard and Soft Law," 426–427.

[21] See, e.g., Pierre Marc Johnson and André Beaulieu, *The Environment and NAFTA: Understanding and Implementing the New Continental Law* (Washington, DC: Island Press, 1996).

[22] Stephen Zamora, "NAFTA and the Harmonization of Domestic Legal Systems: The Side Effects of Free Trade" (1995) 12 *Arizona Journal of International and Comparative Law* 401 at 410–411. See also Howard Mann, *Assessing the Impact of NAFTA on Environmental Law and Management Processes* (Winnipeg, Manitoba: IISD, 2000) at 7–25.

[23] See, e.g., North American Free Trade Agreement between the Government of the United States of America, the Government of Canada and the Government of the United Mexican States, San Antonio, December 17, 1992, in force January 1, 1994, (1993) 32 ILM 296; Can TS 1994 No 2, Articles 712(1), 904(1), and 1114(1). See also NAFTA, Article 1114(2) (recognizing that "it is inappropriate to encourage investment by relaxing domestic health, safety or environmental measures").

out a number of restrictive conditions for the adoption of such standards.[24] While these types of conditions do not inherently prevent governments from adopting laws and policies to protect the environment,[25] many scholars speculate that they place too great an evidentiary and procedural burden on regulatory authorities and thus increase the costs and complexities of environmental policy-making.[26]

For its part, the NAAEC reiterates that the Parties have the right to develop, modify, and implement their own environmental policies and adds that "each Party shall ensure that its laws and regulations provide for high levels of environmental protection and shall strive to continue to improve those laws and regulations."[27] Most significantly, the NAAEC commits each Party to "enforce its environmental laws and regulations through appropriate governmental action";[28] to "ensure that judicial, quasi-judicial or administrative enforcement proceedings are available under its law to sanction or remedy violations of its environmental laws and regulations";[29] and to ensure that private parties have "appropriate access to administrative, quasi-judicial or judicial proceedings for the enforcement of the Party's environmental laws and regulations."[30] Finally, the NAAEC also sets out a number of procedural and transparency requirements for environmental policy-making.[31] Upon NAFTA's passage, commentators cited these provisions, and their associated dispute settlement mechanisms discussed in the following pages to argue that NAFTA could serve as a model agreement for reconciling environmental and trade concerns.[32]

Existing scholarship suggests, however, that these two sets of international rules have had modest effects, if any, on environmental policy-making in Canada, Mexico, and the United States. As far as environmental policy-making *processes*

[24] Among other things, the trade and investment disciplines in NAFTA require that these must be "necessary" to achieve the legitimate objective for which they were established (Articles 712(1) and 904(4)); they must be based on scientific principles and evidence, including a risk assessment, when appropriate (Articles 712(3) and 907(1)); they must not "arbitrarily or unjustifiably discriminate" against the goods or services of another party (Articles 712(4) and 907(2)); they must follow a number of procedural requirements regarding prior notice, points for inquiry or disclosure of information to third parties (Articles 718, 910, and 912).

[25] See Daniel C. Esty and Damien Geradin, "Market Access, Competitiveness, and Harmonization: Environmental Protection in Regional Trade Agreements" (1997) 21 *Harvard Environmental Law Review* 265–336 at 310–316.

[26] Paulette L. Stenzel, "Can NAFTA's Environmental Provisions Promote Sustainable Development?" (1995) 59 *Albany Law Review* 423–480 at 436–439.

[27] North American Agreement on Environmental Cooperation, September 14, 1993, in force January 1, 1994, (1993) 32 ILM 1480; Can TS 1994 No 3, Article 3.

[28] NAEEC, Article 5(1).

[29] NAEEC, Article 5(2).

[30] NAEEC, Article 6(2).

[31] NAEEC, Articles 4 and 7.

[32] See, e.g., Stefan R. Miller, "Comment: NAFTA: A Model for Reconciling the Conflict between Free Trade and International Environmental Protection" (1994) 56 *University of Pittsburgh Law Review* 483–533. For a more pessimistic view, see James E. Bailey, "Free Trade and the Environment – Can NAFTA Reconcile the Irreconcilable?" (1993) 8 *American University Journal of International Law and Policy* 839–901.

are concerned, there is some evidence that Mexico's decision to reform its administrative procedures was triggered, in part, by NAFTA's due process and transparency provisions.[33] On the other hand, while there has been some convergence in the processes for developing and implementing environmental policies in Canada and the United States, this is generally not attributed to NAFTA, but to the diffusion of international ideas concerning "new" approaches to environmental policy-making.[34] With respect to the *enforcement* of environmental regulations, scholarly assessments of the impact of the NAAEC have been uniformly negative.[35] While Mexico did improve its record of enforcing environmental law and regulations in the immediate aftermath of NAFTA's passage, this is generally attributed to the influence of NAFTA's market forces, not its international rules.[36] Indeed, the provision of sanctions and remedies for violations of environmental law has been cited in a survey of key policy actors in the NAFTA regime as the NAAEC's least successful area of implementation.[37]

In rationalist terms, the limited influence of these international rules on environmental policy-making can be explained by two factors. First, while NAFTA is generally lauded for the high level of precision of its international rules,[38] the rules that apply to the development and application of environmental policies are framed in more general language that requires interpretation and application in particular cases.[39] This lack of precision provides a wider margin of discretion to policy-makers and may undermine one Party's confidence that another Party will comply with these rules. Moreover, imprecision reduces the visibility of violations and the potential that they will be detected by other Parties, thus limiting the reputational consequences associated with breaching these rules.[40]

---

[33] Zamora, "NAFTA and Harmonization," 411; Mark Aspinwall, "NAFTA-ization: Regionalization and Domestic Political Adjustment in the North American Economic Area" (2009) 47:1 *Journal of Common Market Studies* 1–24 at 7–10.

[34] George Hoberg, Keith Banting, and Richard Simeon, "North American Integration and the Scope for Domestic Choice: Canada and Policy Sovereignty in a Globalized World," Prepared for the Annual Meeting of the Canadian Political Science Association, June 6–8, 1999, Sherbrooke, Quebec, at 6; Michael Howlett, "Beyond Legalism? Policy Ideas, Implementation Styles and Emulation-Based Convergence in Canadian and U.S. Environmental Policy" (2000) 20:3 *Journal of Public Policy* 305–329.

[35] See, e.g., Chris Wold, "Evaluating NAFTA and the Commission for Environmental Cooperation: Lessons for Integrating Trade and Environment in Free Trade Agreements" (2008) 28 *Saint Louis University Public Law Review* 201–252 at 227–232.

[36] See Section 4 of this chapter.

[37] Joseph F. DiMento and Pamela M. Doughman, "Soft Teeth in the Back of the Mouth: The NAFTA Environmental Side Agreement Implemented" (1997) 10 *Georgetown International Environmental Law Review* 651–742 at 695.

[38] Frederick W. Abbott, "NAFTA and the Legalization of World Politics: A Case Study" (2000) 54:3 *International Organization* 519–547 at 529–530.

[39] Esty and Geradin, "Market Access," 310–315.

[40] Kenneth W. Abbott et al., "The Concept of Legalization" (2000) 54:3 *International Organization* 401–419 at 412–415.

Second, the dispute resolution mechanisms established to monitor and sanction violations of these international rules have also proven to be largely ineffective due to the relatively low level of authority that they have been delegated.[41] For one thing, the general mechanisms established to resolve disputes relating to the trade and investment disciplines in NAFTA (Chapter 20) and the environmental provisions of the NAAEC (Articles 22–36) must be initiated by a NAFTA Party. A dispute has yet to be initiated under either of these mechanisms since their creation. Many scholars thus argue that they are likely to remain inert due to the Parties' reluctance to trigger an escalating spiral of retribution on environmental matters.[42]

In addition to these general interstate dispute resolution mechanisms, NAFTA and the NAAEC also provide for two mechanisms that may be triggered by non-governmental claimants. Under Chapter 11, private investors of one of the Parties have the right to bring an arbitral claim against another Party to challenge the compatibility of environmental regulations with the investment disciplines.[43] As several claims have been brought to challenge the introduction of new environmental regulations and have resulted in fines and penalties or out-of-court settlements, many scholars have argued that NAFTA's Chapter 11 has created a "regulatory chill" that may induce policy-makers to refrain from adopting new environmental regulations, out of concern that they will be subject to a suit from private investors.[44] While these Chapter 11 cases provide concrete examples of influence over policy decisions in particular cases,[45] the claim of a more pervasive regulatory chill seems rather speculative. Further empirical research is needed to assess whether knowledge of Chapter 11 challenges to environmental regulations has in fact spread throughout policy networks at various levels in North America and has accordingly modified the incentives of policy-makers in environmental matters.

The NAAEC similarly creates a complaints mechanism that is directly accessible to nongovernmental organizations and citizens. Upon receipt of an eligible

---

[41] Abbott, "NAFTA and Legalization," 535–543.
[42] In relation to the NAAEC interstate mechanisms, see John Kirton, "Ten Years After: An Assessment of the Environmental Effectiveness of the NAAEC," in John M. Curtis and Aaron Sydor (eds.), *NAFTA@10* (Ottawa: Minister of Public Works and Government Services Canada, 2006) 125–164 at 150.
[43] Although investment arbitral awards under NAFTA may not invalidate legislation, they may result in significant fines and can be enforced by national courts. See Howard Mann and Howard von Moltke, *NAFTA's Chapter 11 and the Environment: Addressing the Impacts of the Investor-State Process on the Environment* (Winnipeg, Manitoba: International Institute for Sustainable Development, 1999); Julie Soloway, "NAFTA's Chapter 11 – The Challenge of Private Party Participation" (1999) 16:2 *Journal of International Arbitration* 1–14.
[44] See Geneviève Dufour, "Le chapitre 11 de l'ALÉNA: son impact sur la capacité de l'État d'agir pour le bien public et de gérer le risque" (2012) 17:1 *Lex Electronica* 1–32 at 8–10 (and sources cited therein).
[45] The Ethyl case is an oft-cited example. See Kyla Tienhaara, "What You Don't Know Can Hurt You: Investor-State Disputes and the Protection of the Environment in Developing Countries" (2006) 6:4 *Global Environmental Politics* 73–100 at 94–96.

submission alleging the failure of a Party to effectively enforce its environmental law, the Secretariat of the Commission for Environmental Cooperation (CEC) may request information from the Party in question, and upon a two-thirds vote of the CEC, it may prepare a factual record on the matter.[46] There is some evidence that the submissions process, in combination with media and political pressure, has played a role in triggering improvements in policy implementation and decision making in particular cases.[47] However, many scholars have been critical of the perceived efforts of the Parties to undermine the submissions process and have noted moreover that the release of a factual record in most cases has not produced any changes in environmental decision making, law, and policy.[48] On the whole, the submissions process cannot be said to have played a significant role in improving overall levels of enforcement of environmental law in North America, due, in part, to the lack of support that it has received from the Parties and the actions that they have taken to narrow its scope and hamper its effectiveness.[49]

NAFTA is generally seen as benefiting from a relatively high compliance rate due to the precision of its rules and the self-interest and reciprocity that make continued compliance advantageous for all three Parties.[50] On the other hand, the international rules with the greatest potential to affect environmental policy-making are largely imprecise and are not, moreover, subject to the types of dispute resolution mechanisms that might interpret provisions and clarify obligations; monitor, detect, and publicize violations; or effectively and reliably sanction violations, thereby increasingly restricting the autonomy of policy-makers in environmental matters.[51] In this context, and without denying the impacts of NAFTA's Chapter 11 mechanism and the NAAEC's citizen submissions process on environmental decision making in a handful of cases, it cannot be said that NAFTA's international rules have had

---

[46] NAAEC, Articles 14–15.

[47] John Kirton, "International Institutions, Sustainability Knowledge and Policy Change: The North American Experience," in Frank Biermann, Sabine Campe and Klaus Jacob (eds.), *Proceedings of the 2002 Berlin Conference on the Human Dimensions of Global Environmental Change: Knowledge for the Sustainability Transition: The Challenge for Social Science* (Amsterdam, Netherlands: Global Governance Project, 2004) 127–137 at 130–133; Jonathan Graubart, "Giving Meaning to New Trade-Linked 'Soft Law' Agreements on Social Values: A Law-In-Action Analysis of NAFTA's Environmental Side Agreement" (2002) 6 *UCLA Journal of International Law & Foreign Affairs* 425–462 at 442–443.

[48] Wold, "Evaluating NAFTA," 231–232; Linda J. Allen, "The North American Agreement on Environmental Cooperation: Has It Fulfilled Its Promises and Potential? An Empirical Study of Policy" (2012) 23:1 *Colorado Journal of International Environmental Law and Policy* 121–199 at 146–159.

[49] Chris Wold et al., "The Inadequacy of the Citizen Submission Process of Articles 14 & 15 of the North American Agreement on Environmental Cooperation" (2004) 26 *Loyola of Los Angeles International and Comparative Law Review* 415–444; David J. Blair, "The CEC's Citizen Submission Process: Still a Model for Reconciling Trade and the Environment?" (2003) 12:3 *The Journal of Environment and Development* 295–324.

[50] See Abbott, "NAFTA and Legalization."

[51] See Robert Keohane, Andrew Moravcsik, and Anne-Marie Slaughter, "Legalized Dispute Resolution: Interstate and Transnational" (2000) 54:3 *International Organization* 457–488 at 488.

a pervasive effect – positive or negative – on environmental policy processes and outcomes in North America.

3. THE POLICY INFLUENCE OF NAFTA'S DIRECT ACCESS MECHANISMS

RTAs can influence domestic policy-making through the activities of their direct access mechanisms, including "through direct funding, education, training, assistance and capacity-building, and possibly even through attempts at cogovernance via partnerships between domestic and international public and private actors and authorities."[52] Given the relatively meager resources at the disposal of NAFTA's institutions and their low level of autonomy vis-à-vis state Parties,[53] there has been little scope for direct access interventions that seek to coerce or induce domestic policy change through the provision of funding (such as conditional aid).[54] As such, the potency of NAFTA's direct access mechanisms lies in their ability to trigger processes of policy learning, through which policy-makers may develop new understandings of the appropriateness and viability of policy objectives, interventions, and implementation designs.[55]

RTAs can support processes of policy learning in one of two ways. First, their associated institutions may generate and communicate their own policy knowledge to domestic policy-makers through the production and dissemination of policy briefs and reports; the organization of conferences, meetings, and training sessions; and the delivery of technical assistance projects and consultancies.[56] Depending on its credibility and format, such knowledge can directly alter the policy preferences of targeted audiences of policy-makers or serve as a political resource that can be leveraged by receptive policy-makers to persuade other policy-makers to change their preferences.[57] Second, RTAs may provide opportunities for policy-makers to exchange knowledge about the strengths and weaknesses of policy experiences elsewhere and identify new solutions to policy problems.[58] In this second regard, the

---

[52] Bernstein and Cashore, "Complex global governance," 593.

[53] See generally Stephen Zamora, "Rethinking North America: Why NAFTA's Laissez Faire Approach to Integration is Flawed, and What to do About It" (2011) 56 *Villanova Law Review* 631–670.

[54] Frank Dobbin, Beth Simmons, and Geoffrey Garrett, "The Global Diffusion of Public Policies: Social Construction, Coercion, Competition, or Learning?" (2007) 33 *Annual Review of Sociology* 449–472 at 455; Thomas J. Biersteker, "Reducing the Role of the State in the Economy: A Conceptual Exploration of IMF and World Bank Prescriptions" (1990) 34:4 *International Studies Quarterly* 477–492.

[55] Peter May, "Policy Learning and Failure" (1992) 12:4 *Journal of Public Policy* 331–354.

[56] Mitchell A. Orenstein, *Privatizing Pensions. The Transnational Campaign for Social Security Reform* (Princeton, NJ: Princeton University Press, 2008) at 63–66; Dobbin, Simmons, and Garrett, "Global Diffusion," 461–462.

[57] Orenstein, *Privatizing Pensions*, 89; Paul F. Steinberg, *Environmental Leadership in Developing Countries: Transnational Relations and Biodiversity Policy in Costa Rica and Bolivia* (Cambridge, MA: MIT Press, 2001) at 12–13.

[58] Claire Dunlop, "Policy Transfer as Learning: Capturing Variation in what Decision-makers Learn from Epistemic Communities" (2009) 30:3 *Policy Studies* 289–311.

role of the RTA's institutions is facilitative, rather than pedagogical, and consists in supporting transnational policy networking, dialogue, and coordination among policy-makers themselves.[59]

Although NAFTA is often presented as a test case for inducing economic and political integration without institutions,[60] it has given rise to countless trilateral intergovernmental bodies, committees, and working groups.[61] I will briefly discuss how the policy learning activities of two such bodies – the Free Trade Commission (FTC) and the aforementioned CEC – may have affected environmental policy-making at the domestic level. The FTC is a trilateral body comprised of cabinet-level representatives (or their alternates) of each Party and supported by a Secretariat. It serves to oversee NAFTA's implementation, appoint arbitrators for various dispute settlement bodies, and supervise the activities of the two dozen committees and working groups established to facilitate regulatory harmonization.[62] The FTC itself and its Secretariat do not exert much policy influence – the former is "neither seen nor heard, aside from a semiannual meeting and joint statement"[63] and the latter has been described as a fiction: "far from a supranational organ, it is a loose collection of coordinating offices in the three countries."[64] Perhaps the FTC's most known contribution lies in the interpretative statement that it issued in July 2001 regarding Chapter 11.[65]

Instead, the real policy influence in the FTC lies with the committees and working groups that bring together officials and bureaucrats from departments across the three Parties to discuss coordination and harmonization in various areas such as agriculture, land transportation, automobiles, pesticides, and sanitary and phytosanitary standards. These bodies have significantly increased contact and interactions between low-ranking officials and technical officials in all three governments, thereby generating mutual understanding, building trust, supporting transgovernmental networking, and creating momentum for uniformization,[66] which have resulted in the adoption of harmonized standards in a number of fields.[67] In their

---

[59] Dobbin, Simmons, and Garrett, "Global Diffusion," 461–462; Richard Rose, "What is Lesson-drawing?" (1991) 11:1 *Journal of Public Policy* 3–30; Diane Stone, "Global Public Policy, Transnational Policy Communities, and Their Networks" (2008) 36:1 *Policy Studies Journal* 19–38.

[60] Frederick M. Abbott, "Integration Without Institutions: The NAFTA Mutation of the EC Model and the Future of the GATT Regime" (1992) 40:4 *The American Journal of Comparative Law* 917–948.

[61] CEC, "NAFTA's Institutions – The Environmental Potential and Performance of the NAFTA Free Trade Commission and Related Bodies" (Montreal: CEC, 1997).

[62] NAFTA, Articles 2001–2002.

[63] Hufbauer and Schott, *NAFTA Revisited*, 61.

[64] Zamora, "Rethinking North America," 638.

[65] Gabrielle Kaufmann-Kohler, "Interpretive Powers of the Free Trade Commission and the Rule of Law," in Emmanuel Gaillard and Frédéric Bachand (eds.), *Fifteen Years of NAFTA Chapter 11 Arbitration* (Huntington, NY: Juris, 2011), 175–194.

[66] Aspinwall, "NAFTA-ization," 10–12.

[67] Stephen Clarkson, "Reform from Without versus Reform from Within: NAFTA and the WTO's Role in Transforming Mexico's Economic System," in Joseph Tulchin and Andrew Selee (eds.), *Mexico's Politics and Society in Transition* (Boulder, CO: Lynne Rienner, 2002) 215–254.

first three years, these committees grappled with numerous issues at the intersections of trade and the environment, with some committees setting common standards that increased levels of protection for the environment (as in the case of the transportation of dangerous goods) and other committees unwilling to act to set standards (such as automotive standards).[68] Given the important role that these committees are playing in standard-setting in areas of direct relevance to the environment, further research is needed to assess their aggregate implications for environmental policy-making. One aspect that is well documented, however, is that there has been little coordination between the FTC and the CEC and thus little progress has been made within the FTC on the general objective of reconciling trade and environmental objectives.[69]

The CEC was created to support the implementation of the NAAEC. It includes a trilateral Council of cabinet-level officials to oversee its activities, a Secretariat that develops and administers its programs, and a Joint Public Advisory Committee (JPAC) bringing together multiple stakeholders from each country.[70] Apart from its previously discussed role in resolving disputes and receiving citizen submissions, the CEC performs two important functions. First, the CEC undertakes voluntary environmental cooperative initiatives within its four programmatic areas: biodiversity conservation; law and policy; environment, economy, and trade; and pollutants and health.[71] The voluntary cooperative initiatives supported by the CEC have resulted in the establishment of networks and initiatives to improve and facilitate cooperation between officials on issues such as marine protected areas and bird conservation;[72] projects to build and strengthen the capacity of policy-makers and officials in environmental matters, especially in Mexico;[73] and regional actions and registries on such matters as pollution releases and transfers as well as chemicals that have resulted in domestic policy changes throughout North America.[74] In addition, the JPAC has emerged as a key institution for facilitating informal exchanges among multiple stakeholders and making recommendations on sensitive issues such as the enforcement of environmental policy.[75] While the CEC's role in promoting and facilitating cooperation in environmental issues is frequently seen by practitioners and scholars as its most successful area of intervention,[76] Kirton nonetheless points

---

[68] CEC, *NAFTA's Institutions*, 26–48.
[69] Allen, "The NAAEC," 134–135, 161–165; Kirton, "Ten Years After," 147.
[70] NAAEC, Articles 8–11.
[71] Allen, "The NAAEC," 133.
[72] Greg Block, "The CEC Cooperative Program of Work," in David L. Markell and John H. Knox (eds.), *Greening NAFTA: The North American Commission for Environmental Cooperation* (Palo Alto, CA: Stanford University Press, 2002) 25–37.
[73] Kirton, "Ten Years After," 132.
[74] Wold, "Evaluating NAFTA," 226–227; Allen, "The NAAEC," 175–190; Mark S. Winfield, "North American Pollutant Release and Transfer Registries: A Case Study in Environmental Policy Convergence," in Markell and Knox, *Greening NAFTA*, 38–56.
[75] Kirton, "Ten Years After," 138.
[76] DiMento and Doughman, "Soft Teeth," 693–694.

out that "the CEC has found it difficult to attract regular senior level participation from the corporate and economic community, which has limited its ability to influence the powerful national departments for trade, finance, agriculture and energy, and the international organizations and institutions they control."[77]

Second, the CEC also plays a key role in generating and diffusing policy-salient knowledge and data on a variety of environmental issues, including problems that are specific to a particular location and those that concern the continent as a whole, stock-taking scientific assessments in particular sectors, and the environmental effects of NAFTA.[78] By marshaling scientific data, building on the expertise of the CEC Secretariat, and collaborating with scientists and experts in each NAFTA Party, these policy knowledge products have come to be seen as credible by many policy actors and stakeholders in the NAFTA regime.[79] Scholars disagree about the actual impact that these knowledge products have had on policy-making. Some scholars argue that they have spurred intergovernmental negotiation, galvanized public support for greater environmental action, and contributed to legal and policy reforms, especially in Mexico.[80] Allen's process-tracing analysis shows, however, that the CEC's independent reporting on environmental issues has done little more than raise the prominence of environmental issues in particular situations and that its work on integrating trade and the environment has not managed to convince policy-makers to take action to address the environmental impacts of trade.[81]

NAFTA's direct access mechanisms thus appear to have exerted some measure of influence over environmental policy-making processes and outcomes by facilitating policy learning among policy-makers interacting with one another, sharing information, and developing common standards and initiatives within the FTC's working groups and the CEC's voluntary cooperative initiatives.[82] These activities have created two epistemic communities[83] – one dedicated to trade liberalization and regulatory harmonization, and the other committed to addressing environmental problems of regional significance.[84] While existing research suggests that the latter community has contributed to positive outcomes for environmental policy-making in a few particular cases and issues, further research is required to assess the environmental implications of the FTC's standard-setting activities. Most importantly, the lack of overlap and coordination between these two communities has undoubtedly limited the ability of the NAFTA regime's learning mechanisms to

[77] Kirton, "Ten Years After," 135.
[78] Kirton, "International Institutions"; Allen, "The NAAEC," 169–175.
[79] Kirton, "International Institutions," 146.
[80] Wold, "Evaluating NAFTA," 232–233; Kirton, "International Institutions."
[81] Allen, "The NAAEC," 169–175.
[82] Zamora, "NAFTA and Harmonization," 417–418; Aspinwall, "NAFTA-ization," 19.
[83] Emanuel Adler and Peter M. Haas, "Conclusion: Epistemic Communities, World Order, and the Creation of a Reflective Research Program" (1992) 46:1 *International Organization* 367–390.
[84] Allen, "The NAAEC," 164.

make positive and transformative contributions to environmental policy-making in North America.

4. THE POLICY INFLUENCE OF NAFTA'S MARKET FORCES

RTAs can exert influence on domestic policy-making through economic competition, which leads policy-makers to respond to the policies of competing jurisdictions as a means of increasing or maintaining economic resources.[85] An earlier wave of scholarship suggested that such competition would result in a generalized "race to the bottom" in social and environmental regulation, as policy-makers sought to lower the costs of doing business in their jurisdictions in order to attract foreign investment.[86] While economic competition has clearly resulted in policy convergence in terms of less restrictive investment rules and capital controls and lower rates of corporate taxation, most scholars argue that it has not led to a generalized rollback of social and environmental policies.[87]

In fact, many scholars argue that trade liberalization may instead trigger an upward process of convergence that may induce policy-makers to increase the stringency of their domestic regulations. Vogel has labeled this phenomenon "the California effect," referring to situations where policy-makers seek to improve their regulatory performance in line with the higher requirements set by an important foreign export market to which they seek to gain or maintain access.[88] Trade agreements between high- and low-regulating jurisdictions generally include provisions that aim to create a level regulatory playing field and thus provide opportunities for the former to pressure the latter into adopting more stringent regulatory standards.[89] As well, the adoption of higher regulatory standards or improved social or environmental performance may itself be explicitly set as a precondition for joining an RTA or otherwise gaining enhanced or preferential access to a foreign export market.[90] On the other hand, Bechtel and Tosun point out that low-regulating jurisdictions may

---

[85] Dobbin, Simmons, and Garrett, "Global Diffusion," 461–462.

[86] David C. Korten, *When Corporations Rule the World* (London: Earthscan, 1995); Gareth Porter, "Trade Competition and Pollution Standards: 'Race to the Bottom' or 'Stuck at the Bottom'" (1999) 8:2 *The Journal of Environment and Development* 133–151.

[87] See, e.g., Fabrizio Gilardi, "Transnational Diffusion: Norms, Ideas, and Policies," in Walter Carlsnaes, Thomas Risse, and Beth Simmons (eds.) *Handbook of International Relations* (London, UK: Sage Publications, 2013) 453–477 at 462–463; Daniel W. Drezner, "Globalization and Policy Convergence" (2001) 3:1 *International Studies Review* 53 at 57–60.

[88] Vogel, *Trading Up*, 259–260. See also Brian Greenhill, Layna Mosley, and Aseem Prakash, "Trade-based Diffusion of Labor Rights: A Panel Study, 1986–2002" (2009) 103:4 *American Political Science Review* 669–690.

[89] Vogel, *Trading Up*, 263–265.

[90] Emilie Hafner-Burton, "Trading Human Rights: How Preferential Trade Agreements Influence Government Repression" (2005) 59 *International Organization* 593–629; Frank Schimmelfennig and Ulrich Sedelmeier, "Governance by Conditionality: EU Rule Transfer to the Candidate Countries of Central and Eastern Europe" (2004) 11:4 *Journal of European Public Policy* 661–679.

"fake" an interest in policy convergence by adopting policy changes that they have no intention of enforcing in order to reap the rewards of increased or preferential access to foreign markets.[91] The effectiveness of economic competition as a mechanism of domestic policy influence thus depends not only on the degree to which a jurisdiction is dependent on access to foreign markets or investments, but also on the ability of high-regulating jurisdictions and regional trade institutions to monitor and sanction the failure of a low-regulating jurisdiction to implement conditional domestic policy changes.[92]

Despite the fears expressed twenty years ago, there is no evidence that the regional economic integration fostered by NAFTA has resulted in a race to the bottom in environmental regulation.[93] One potential explanation is that the compliance costs associated with environmental regulations are relatively unimportant for corporations when compared to other types of costs and do not therefore play a significant role in their decisions to locate or relocate their operations.[94] This reduces the incentives that policy-makers may have to reduce the stringency of their environmental regulations as a means of improving their economic competitiveness. Moreover, it should also be mentioned that NAFTA's main contribution in market terms has been to strengthen existing economic ties between the United States and Canada (which were already bound by a preexisting bilateral trade agreement) as well as significantly increase levels of bilateral trade and investment between the United States and Mexico. Although there are some economic sectors that subsist within a true North American dynamic, regional economic integration in North America remains partial and incomplete.[95]

While there is no evidence that NAFTA's market dynamics have negatively affected the stringency of environmental policy in North America, the possibility

[91] Michael M. Bechtel and Jale Tosun, "Changing Economic Openness for Environmental Policy Convergence: When Can Bilateral Trade Agreements Induce Convergence of Environmental Regulation?" (2009) 53 *International Studies Quarterly* 931–953 at 948–949. See also Christoph Knill, Jale Tosun, and Stephan Heichel, "Balancing Competitiveness and Conditionality: Environmental Policy-Making in Low-Regulating Countries" (2008) 15:7 *Journal of European Public Policy* 1019–1040.
[92] Vogel, *Trading Up*, 7; Bechtel and Tosun, "Changing Economic Openness," 945.
[93] See, e.g., Shanti Gamper-Rabindran, "NAFTA and the Environment: What Can the Data Tell Us?" (2006) 54:3 *Economic Development and Cultural Change* 605–633.
[94] See, in the context of NAFTA, Elizabeth T. Cole, and Prescott C. Ensign, "An Examination of US FDI Into Mexico And Its Relation To Nafta: Understanding the Effects of Environmental Regulation and the Factor Endowments that Affect the Location Decision" (2005) 19:1 *International Trade Journal* 1–30. See generally Arik Levinson, "The Missing Pollution Haven Effect: Examining Some Common Explanations" (2000) 15:4 *Environmental and Resource Economics* 343–364.
[95] M. Angeles Villarreal and Ian F. Fergusson, *NAFTA at 20: Overview and Trade Effects* (Washington, DC: Congressional Research Service, 2013); Isidro Morales, *Post-NAFTA North America. Reshaping the Economic and Political Governance of a Changing Region* (Basingstoke, NH: Palgrave MacMillan, 2008) at 77–121. Isidro Morales, *Post-NAFTA North America. Reshaping the Economic and Political Governance of a Changing Region* (Basingstoke, NH: Palgrave MacMillan, 2008), pp. 77–121. Although trade and investment between Canada and Mexico has also increased, its relative importance for both countries is modest: Morales, *Post-NAFTA*, 91–92.

of gaining increased access to the American market did create important economic incentives for Mexican policy-makers to improve the stringency of their environmental laws and regulations, especially in the lead-up to and immediate aftermath of NAFTA's passage.[96] While the dynamics of economic competition generated by the NAFTA regime led to positive changes in the development and implementation of environmental policies in Mexico in the early 1990s, assessments of Mexico's record over the succeeding decade and a half are mixed. While some scholars argue that there have been continual improvements in the adoption of higher environmental regulations,[97] others emphasize that the enforcement of environmental regulations remains insufficient and has even declined after a NAFTA-induced spike.[98] This leads Bechtel and Tosun to conclude that initial commitments made by Mexico in order to secure NAFTA accession are an example of what they call "deceptive environmental policy convergence."[99]

Bechtel and Tosun's conclusion appears rather harsh in two respects. First, it fails to acknowledge that Mexico's failure to enforce more stringent environmental regulations may result from its limited capabilities and resources and its enduring economic challenges,[100] rather than its policy intentions.[101] Moreover, there is no reason to expect that Mexico would achieve improvements in all aspects of its environmental policies; rather, it is more reasonable to assume that its performance might improve in some areas, and not others. For instance, one might have expected that Mexico's performance would improve in relation to issue areas that would be most visible to American policy-makers and stakeholders, such as industrial production aimed at the U.S. export market.[102] As such, it is reasonable to conclude

---

[96] Vogel, *Trading Up*, 237–246; Bryan W. Husted and Jeanne M. Logsdon, "The Impact of NAFTA on Mexico's Environmental Policy" (1997) 28 *Growth and Change* 24–48; Michael D. Madnick, "NAFTA: A Catalyst for Environmental Change in Mexico" (1993) 11:1 *Pace Environmental Law Review* 9; Laura Carlsen and Hilda Salazar, "Limits to Cooperation: A Mexican Perspective on the NAFTA's Environmental Side Agreement and Institutions," in Carolyn L. Deere and Daniel C. Esty (eds.), *Greening the Americas: NAFTA's Lessons for Hemispheric Trade* (Cambridge, MA; MIT Press, 2002) 221–246; Wisner and Epstein, "'Push' and 'Pull,'" 329–330.

[97] Husted and Logsdon, "The Impact of NAFTA."

[98] Stephen P. Mumme, "Environmental Policy and Politics in Mexico," in Uday Desai (ed.), *Ecological Policy and Politics in Developing Countries* (Albany, NY: State University of New York Press, 1998) 183–203; Stephen P. Mumme and Donna Lybecker, "Environmental Capacity in Mexico: An Assessment," in Hartmut Weidner and Martin Jänicke (eds.), *Capacity Building in National Environmental Policy* (Berlin, Germany: Springer, 2002) 311–328; Claudia Schatan, "Lessons from the Mexican Environmental Experience: First Results from NAFTA," in Diana Tussie (ed.), *The Environment and International Trade Negotiations: Developing Country Stakes* (London, UK: MacMillan, 2000) 167–187.

[99] Bechtel and Tosun, "Changing Economic Openness," 943.

[100] Mumme, "Environmental Policy," 192.

[101] See David Vogel, "Trading up and Governing across: Transnational Governance and Environmental Protection" (1997) 4:4 *Journal of European Public Policy* 556–571; Abram Chayes and Antonia Chayes, "On Compliance" (1993) 47:2 *International Organization* 175–205.

[102] See Arik Levinson, "Offshoring Pollution: Is the United States Increasingly Importing Polluting Goods?" (2010) 4:1 *Review of Environmental Economics and Policy* 63–83 at 66–67.

that NAFTA inserted environmental issues onto the domestic policy agenda in Mexico, as has been recorded with respect to other treaty ratification processes.[103] However, in the absence of regional trade institutions to monitor and sanction compliance with the NAAEC or American institutions to do so in relation to the informal promises made by the Mexican government upon accession, there is no reason to believe that NAFTA's market pathway would lead to lasting or ever-increasing improvements in environmental policy. While NAFTA did result in a modest California Effect in its early stages, this was doomed to be short-lived in the absence of causal mechanisms that could maintain or increase economic incentives for stringent environmental policies.[104]

5. THE POLICY INFLUENCE OF NAFTA'S INTERNATIONAL NORMS

RTAs can affect domestic policy-making by generating and diffusing international norms that provide intersubjective understandings that redefine the identities of actors and give meaning to their behavior.[105] Domestic policy-makers may be social-ized into adopting policy beliefs that conform with international norms[106] through interactions with domestic and international interlocutors in the context of political debates,[107] a transnational network,[108] an epistemic community,[109] the activities of an international organization,[110] and a variety of transnational legal and regulatory processes.[111] In its deepest form, socialization leads to internalization whereby an

---

[103] Beth A. Simmons, *Mobilizing for Human Rights: International Law in Domestic Politics* (Cambridge: Cambridge University Press, 2010) at 127–129 (discussing the agenda-setting effects of treaty ratification debates in the field of human rights).

[104] See, on the other hand, the potential for "racheting up" identified in legality verification systems: Benjamin Cashore and Michael W. Stone, "Can Legality Verification Rescue Global Forest Governance? Analyzing the Potential of Public and Private Policy Intersection to Ameliorate Forest Challenges in Southeast Asia" (2012) 18 *Forest Policy and Economics* 13–22.

[105] Andrew T.F. Lang, "Reconstructing Embedded Liberalism: John Gerard Ruggie and Constructivist Approaches to the Study of the International Trade Regime" (2006) 9:1 *Journal of International Economic Law* 81–116 at 113–114.

[106] Jeffrey T. Checkel, "International Institutions and Socialization in Europe: Introduction and Framework" (2005) 59:4 *International Organization* 801–826.

[107] Thomas Risse and Kathryn Sikkink, "The Socialization of International Human Rights Norms into Domestic Politics: Introduction," in Thomas Risse, Stephen C. Ropp, and Kathryn Sikkink (eds.), *The Power of Human Rights. International Norms and Domestic Change* (Cambridge, UK: Cambridge University Press, 1999) 1–38, p. 1.

[108] Jacqui True and Michael Mintrom, "Transnational Networks and Policy Diffusion: The Case of Gender Mainstreaming" (2001) 45:1 *International Studies Quarterly* 27–57.

[109] Emanuel Adler and Peter M. Haas, "Conclusion: Epistemic Communities, World Order, and the Creation of a Reflective Research Program" (1992) 46:1 *International Organization* 367–390.

[110] Martha Finnemore, "International Organizations as Teachers of Norms: The United Nations Education, Scientific, and Cultural Organization and Science Policy" (1993) 47:4 *International Organization* 565–597.

[111] Harold Hongju Koh, "Why Do Nations Obey International Law?" (1996) 106 *Yale Law Journal* 2599–2659.

international norm achieves a "taken-for-granted quality" that makes "conformance with the norm almost automatic."[112] When policy-makers internalize an international norm, this affects their conception of the appropriateness of alternative policy beliefs and options.[113]

Scholars considering the influence of international norms in international trade and investment law have emphasized the role that economic agreements can play in reconstituting the intersubjective context and web of meaning in which policy-making takes place.[114] As Lang argues:

> While we spend a great deal of time analysing which kinds of measures are prohibited by trade law and which are not, we spend little time analysing the separate question of which kinds of measures trade law helps to constitute as an intervention (or as a "barrier", or as "protectionism", or whatever) and the processes by which it does so. I am not referring here to the kinds of definitional discussions common in legal commentary, but rather to the categories into which trade law encourages us to divide the world. If constructivists are right, this constitutive function of trade law, by which we learn to attribute particular meanings to behaviour, may represent a far more important way in which trade law affects outcomes in the international trading system.[115]

Another insight that emerges from constructivist research on international trade law is that the construction of regional markets both requires and triggers the development of international norms.[116] As demonstrated by Fligstein and Stone Sweet in the context of the EC/EU, the creation of a new market may generate a series of feedback loops that drive the simultaneous development of related institutions. The loop begins with the establishment of rules that create new opportunities for market actors. The resulting economic activity then leads market actors to lobby for additional rule-setting to resolve any ensuing problems and expand markets further. To the extent that new institutional arrangements are responsive to these demands, this will generate market activity and foster additional need for institutional development and regulatory harmonization from market actors.[117]

---

[112] Martha Finnemore and Kathryn Sikkink, "International Norm Dynamics and Political Change" (1998) 52:4 *International Organization* 887–917 at 904–905.

[113] A shallower form of socialization is acculturation: Ryan Goodman and Derek Jinks, "How to Influence States: Socialization and International Human Rights Law" (2004) 54:3 *Duke Law Journal* 621–704 at 626.

[114] Moshe Hirsch, "The Sociology of International Economic Law: Sociological Analysis of the Regulation of Regional Agreements in the World Trading System" (2008) 19:2 *European Journal of International Law* 277–299 at 281.

[115] Lang, "Reconstructing Embedded Liberalism," 113.

[116] Francesco Duina, "Regional Market Building as a Social Process: An Analysis of Cognitive Strategies in NAFTA, the European Union and Mercosur" (2004) 33:3 *Economy and Society* 359–389.

[117] Neil Fligstein and Alec Stone Sweet, "Constructing Polities and Markets: An Institutionalist Account of European Integration" (2002) 107:5 *American Journal of Sociology* 1206–1243.

Unlike the other pathways discussed in this chapter, there has been very little research on the role and influence of international norms within the NAFTA regime[118] or more broadly within the process of North American integration.[119] On the other hand, many scholars have made norm-related claims that the CEC has supported the development of "an international common law of the environment,"[120] given greater prominence to environmental matters and promoted messages concerning the compatibility of economic and environmental objectives,[121] and helped create a sense of a "North American environmental identity and constituency."[122] For the most part, the evidence does not suggest that the NAAEC or its institutions have engendered particularly important or influential international norms for environmental policy-making, even on basic issues such as what retrogression in environmental law might mean or what levels of participation might be appropriate in environmental decision-making.[123] Indeed, the NAAEC's institutions have only provided partial opportunities for generating new international norms on environmental policy issues and for socializing policy-makers into following them. This can be explained by a number of issues discussed in Sections 2 and 3 of this chapter, such as the lack of independence and limited authority of the CEC's citizens submissions process; the inertia of the dispute settlement process as concerns the implementation of the NAAEC; the limited resources, mandate, and standing of the CEC and its Secretariat; and the dearth of interactions between policy-making networks operating in the economic and environmental spheres.

On the other hand, further research is needed to assess whether and how NAFTA's international norms on trade and economic matters have affected environmental policy-making. Hirsh argues that the norms spread by trade agreements may extend beyond the limited context of trade liberalization and may serve to transmit a broader set of liberal values and contribute to the formation of regional political communities.[124] The ability of norms to reconstitute the identity of policy-makers may lead them to "understand their primary role in international economic life as facilitators of transnational commerce, rather than some other role."[125] As Lang emphasizes, this has clear implications for understanding the implications of a trade agreement on policy-making: "the clear message is that we should not only be interested in the way the trade regime prohibits certain kinds of regulation, we

[118] Duina, "Regional Market Building," 361.
[119] Laura Spitz, "The Evolving Architecture of North American Integration" (2009) 80 *University of Colorado Law Review* 101–157.
[120] DiMento and Doughman, "Soft Teeth," 741.
[121] Kirton, "Ten Years After," 139–140, 144.
[122] Aspinwall, "NAFTA-ization," 15.
[123] DiMento and Doughman, "Soft Teeth," 705–716.
[124] Hirsch, "Sociology of International Economic Law," 289.
[125] Lang, "Reconstructing Embedded Liberalism," 114.

should also pay attention to the ways in which, by the operation of intersubjective understandings, states come to see certain kinds of regulation as not in their own interest."[126] Given the prevalence of discourses that oppose economic and environmental objectives among politicians and commentators in North America, the hypothesis that NAFTA's international norms may have contributed to the development of new understandings of the very nature of policy-making in environmental matters deserves further investigation.

6. CONCLUSION

The NAFTA regime is many things – a body of international rules and associated compliance mechanisms, a set of institutions for fostering transnational learning and collaboration, a market for regional trade and investment, and a vehicle for generating and disseminating international norms. As the Table 14.1 evinces, the pathways of influence framework used in this chapter makes it possible to study the full range of formal and informal processes through which NAFTA may affect environmental policy-making processes and outcomes at the domestic level. Yet, in spite of the many different opportunities offered by the NAFTA regime to change the incentives and ideas of policy-makers on environmental matters, one important lesson from my analysis is that NAFTA does not appear to have actually exerted pervasive, sustained, or significant influence on environmental policy-making in North America over the last twenty years.

While the existing literature has uncovered numerous instances of NAFTA's policy influence, these tend to be limited in their effects to a particular location or case (NAFTA's Chapter 11 process, the CEC's citizen's submission process, and the CEC's voluntary environmental cooperative initiatives) or a time period (Mexico's actions to improve its environmental policy performance in the lead-up to and after accession). On balance, while it cannot be said that NAFTA has made much of a contribution to improving environmental policy-making in North America, the opposite claim of negative influence is not substantiated either. These findings suggest that North American jurisdictions have retained a greater measure of policy resilience than many activists and scholars have been willing to recognize. Indeed, research in comparative law and public policy in North America emphasizes instead that in many issue areas, policy-makers have retained their regulatory autonomy as a result of the path dependence of policy-making processes and institutions and the restraining influence of federal structures.[127]

Ultimately, an analysis across the pathways discussed here demonstrates that the NAFTA regime has not been given, nor has it developed, the institutional capacities

---

[126] Lang, "Reconstructing Embedded Liberalism," 114.
[127] H. Patrick Glenn, "Conflicting Laws in a Common Market? The NAFTA Experiment" (2000) 76 *Chicago-Kent Law Review* 1789–1819; Hoberg, "Trade."

TABLE 14.1. *NAFTA's Pathways of Influence and their Implications for Environmental Policy-Making*

	Rules	Learning	Markets	Norms
Primary Causal Mechanism	Compliance driven by the calculations of policy-makers, responding to incentives and disincentives provided by the behavior of others and dispute settlement mechanisms.	Learning by policy-makers driven and facilitated by international institutions.	Competition among policy-makers to attract capital or gain access to foreign markets.	Socialization of policy-makers that develop and internalize international norms.
Application to the NAFTA Regime	Rules in NAFTA and the NAAEC and their dispute settlement bodies may constrain policy-makers in the development of environmental policy-making or induce them to enforce their environmental laws.	The FTC and the CEC may facilitate policy learning among policy-makers interacting with one another, sharing information, and developing common standards and initiatives within standard-setting working groups and voluntary environmental cooperative initiatives.	Like other RTAs between low- and high-regulating countries, NAFTA may provide leverage for the United States to pressure Mexico into improving its environmental policy performance.	NAFTA and its associated institutions may have facilitated interactions between policy actors and provided opportunities for the development and diffusion of international norms.
Implications for Environmental Policy-Making	The NAFTA Chapter 11 investor/state process has negatively affected the environmental policy-making efforts of domestic authorities in a few cases. Further research is needed to assess the validity of the regulatory chill hypothesis on a broader scale. The NAAEC citizen submission process has led to positive changes in the development and enforcement of environmental laws in a few cases.	The FTC's standard setting committees have influenced environmental policy-making, though further research is needed to assess the extent and implications of this influence. The CEC has influenced environmental policy-making in a number of limited cases and has strengthened the capacity of Mexican officials to address environmental issues. It has failed, however, to exert greater influence on trade/economic policy-making.	NAFTA has led to improvements in environmental policy-making and implementation in Mexico in the lead-up to and during accession, but this has not been sustained in the long term.	The NAAEC has not generated international norms that have strengthened environmental policy-making in North America. Further research is required to assess the extent to which international norms generated and diffused through NAFTA may have reshaped the identity of policy-makers to emphasize the importance of economic trade and development over environmental issues and considerations.

to exert significant influence on domestic policy-making in the environmental field. For one thing, the limited independence, authority, and resources of the institutions created by NAFTA, especially with respect to the reconciliation of trade and environmental issues, has hindered the effectiveness of the direct access pathway along with every other pathway. The lack of stronger dispute settlement mechanisms to monitor and sanction failures to effectively enforce environmental laws has reduced the incentives to compliance on its own terms as well as failed to reinforce processes of policy learning, competition, and socialization along the other pathways. Likewise, the weaknesses associated with the CEC's institutional architecture have hindered its ability to generate new policy-salient knowledge and facilitate interactions between economic and environmental policy-makers, thus encumbering the effectiveness of the learning and norms pathways. On this basis, NAFTA appears to provide a case study of a regime in which the potential synergies across pathways of influence have not been activated. Of course, the very same institutional factors that may explain why NAFTA has failed to significantly improve the prospects for environmental sustainability in North America also explain why its negative implications have been limited. Those who want to strengthen the regulatory powers and capacities of NAFTA should be cognizant of the potential advantages and disadvantages of this option for domestic policy-making in environmental matters.

That being said, it is also possible that existing scholarship has simply not uncovered the most durable and significant ways in which the NAFTA regime has affected environmental policy-making in North America. As highlighted earlier, there are a number of gaps in our understanding of the policy influence of NAFTA, most notably the purported claim of Chapter 11's "regulatory chill," the implications of the standard-setting activities of the FTC, and the diffusion and effect of international norms that may have redefined the appropriate scope of policy-making in environmental matters. While the rules, markets, and direct access pathways have garnered significant attention from scholars, the norms pathway has been understudied and the broader relationship between the first three pathways and processes of policy change has not received much attention either.

A related series of important research questions relate to the *indirect* pathways through which NAFTA may have affected policy-making. To begin with, it is quite possible that NAFTA has most effectively influenced policy-making through its influence on the development of new free trade agreements, especially between the United States and other countries.[128] Moreover, the NAFTA regime, whether through the activities of its institutions, its market changes, or simply by providing opportunities for policy advocacy and change, may have led to the emergence

---

[128] Wold et al., "Inadequacy," 235–244.

of networks of civil society advocates,[129] lawyers,[130] and business people.[131] Further research is needed to understand how the pathways of influence within the NAFTA regime intersect with policy actors, with processes, and, at the domestic level, with civil society organizations[132] and government officials,[133] and thus provide indirect opportunities for shaping domestic environmental policy-making processes and outcomes.

The questions identified here await further refinement and call for additional empirical research focusing on the pathways through which the NAFTA regime has influenced environmental policy-making in North America. While there have been countless articles examining provisions and institutions in the NAFTA regime (including many provisions that exist on paper only), the broad variety of ways in which NAFTA's pathways of policy influence have interacted with domestic policy actors and processes has attracted little attention. Absent an empirically grounded understanding of how the NAFTA regime has actually affected policy-making in economic, social, and environmental matters, scholars are unlikely to make much headway in understanding its implications for sustainable development and identifying opportunities for enhancing its positive contributions to sustainability.

[129] Zamora, "Rethinking North America," 652–653; Raul Pacheco-Vega, "Democracy by Proxy: Environmental NGOs and Policy Change in Mexico," in Aldemaro Romero and Sarah E. West (eds.), *Environmental Issues in Latin America and the Caribbean* (London, UK: Springer, 2005) 231–249; Jonathan Graubart, *Legalizing Transnational Activism: The Struggle to Gain Social Change From NAFTA's Citizen Petitions* (University Park, PA: Penn State University Press, 2008).
[130] Glenn, "Conflicting Laws," 125.
[131] Maurice Schiff and Yanling Wang, "Regional Integration and Technology Diffusion: The Case of NAFTA" (Policy Research Working Paper 3132, Washington DC: The World Bank, 2003).
[132] Allen, "The NAEEC," 192; Kirton, "Ten Years After," p. 135; Zamora, "Rethinking North America," 660–661; Aspinwall, "NAFTA-ization," 19.
[133] Aspinwall, "NAFTA-ization," 15–16.

15

The Citizen Submissions Process in the NAAEC

Theory and Practice in Deliberative Democratic Institutional Design for Transnational Institutions

Hoi L. Kong*

1. INTRODUCTION

Deliberative democratic theory is well established at the level of national and subnational orders and has influenced institutional design debates in a range of areas. Substantial literatures incorporating deliberative democratic insights have developed in the fields of constitutional and administrative law,[1] and institutional designs have been proposed at national and subnational government scales.[2] There has been comparatively less work done at the transnational level, and perhaps for good reason.[3] In the absence of representative, global democratic institutions, it is

* I express my gratitude to the participants in a workshop at the Commission on Environmental Cooperation, sponsored by the Commission, the North American Consortium on Legal Education, Vermont Law School, and the Faculty of Law of McGill University for excellent comments. I am also grateful to the participants in a seminar at the Lauterpracht Centre of Cambridge University for insights on an early draft of this paper. I am particularly grateful to Catherine MacKenzie and Marcus Gehring for the extent and generosity of their comments. I would like to acknowledge the excellent feedback from the participants in a seminar at the World Trade Institute in Geneva, including Shaheeza Lalani, who generously hosted me. I thank my colleague Sébastien Jodoin for his read of the text and his written suggestions. For excellent research assistance, I thank Andra Syvanen, and for outstanding editorial work, I thank William Stephenson. Finally, I would like to thank the Social Sciences and Humanities Research Council of Canada for its support of my research on deliberative democracy of which this chapter and book are a part.

[1] For a recent constitutional contribution, see Conrado Hubner Mendes, *Constitutional Courts and Deliberative Democracy* (Oxford: Oxford University Press, 2013). For a significant contribution in the administrative law literature, see Glen Staszewski, "Political Reasons, Deliberative Democracy, Administrative Law" (2012) 97 *Iowa Law Review* 849.

[2] For an example of a deliberative democratic proposal that aims to have national effects, see Bruce Ackerman and James S. Fishkin, *Deliberation Day* (New Haven, CT: Yale University Press, 2004). For a prominent analysis of deliberative democracy at the subnational level, see Iris Marion Young, *Inclusion and Democracy* (Oxford: Oxford University Press, 2000).

[3] For present purposes, I use the expression "transnational law" in a broad sense that includes a narrower one. These two senses have been captured by Gregory Shaffer, who writes: "the concept of transnational

difficult to conceive of how many of the rich debates that arise in the national and subnational context can be transposed to the transnational order.[4] In particular, if one were to attempt to locate deliberative innovations in formal processes of law-making and regulation, one would immediately be confronted with the problem of how to ground them in legitimating democratic institutions, given the challenges involved in creating representative, global governmental forms.[5]

By focusing on transnational discourses, John Dryzek has offered a prominent attempt to side-step this problem. He defines a discourse as "a shared set of assumptions and capabilities embedded in language that enables its adherents to assemble bits of sensory information that come their way into coherent wholes. Because discourses are social as well as personal, they act as sources of order by co-ordinating the behaviour of the individuals who subscribe to them."[6] Dryzek goes further to claim that "the contestation of discourses should be central to a model of deliberative democracy, provided that the contest can be engaged by a broad variety of competent actors under unconstrained conditions."[7] Transnational discourses, argues Dryzek, are created and propagated in networks that are comprised of civil society actors who bring their local interpretations of issues to bear on deliberation and debates. He writes: "Networks emerge when individuals or groups that are similarly situated in one important respect, but different in most other respects, decide that their common interest would benefit from joint action."[8] Transnational deliberative democracy, for Dryzek, seems to be constituted of contests among and within networks over the contents and influence of various discourses, at least when these contests are conducted in accordance with "norms of openness, respect, reciprocity, and equality."[9]

---

law can be narrower or broader, depending on the concept's user, but it generally comprises legal norms that apply across borders to parties located in more than one jurisdiction.... From a broader conception, transnational legal orders can subsume international law but also encompass legal rules and norms that have effects across borders without any binding agreement among states, whether they are created by international organizations, intergovernmental networks, or private actors, and whether they are of a hard or soft law nature" ("Transnational Legal Process and State Change" (2012) 37 *Law & Social Inquiry* 229 at 232–3).

I focus in this paper on the practices of transnational organizations, but I do not intend thereby to imply that the term "transnational law" should exclude forms of regulation that can be created by networks of nonstate actors, including nongovernmental organizations and market participants. For an articulation of transnational law that expressly includes these other modes of regulation, see Schaffer, "Transnational Legal Process," pp. 235–6.

[4] See generally Nico Krisch, *Beyond Constitutionalism: The Pluralist Structure of Postnational Law* (Oxford: Oxford University Press, 2010), p. 266.

[5] Ibid., p. 267.

[6] John S. Dryzek, *Deliberative Democracy and Beyond: Liberals, Critics, Contestations* (Oxford: Oxford University Press, 2000), p. 121.

[7] Ibid., p. 122.

[8] Ibid., p. 134. The anti-biopiracy network is among the examples he gives of transnational discourses and the networks that constitute them (p. 134).

[9] Ibid., p. 135.

Following the example of Dennis Thompson,[10] Dryzek goes further and asks how intergovernmental organizations (IGOs) can include the civil society members of these kinds of networks, in their decision-making processes. One form of inclusion involves welcoming the members of these civil society networks in international negotiations, and he gives as examples of international governmental organizations that incorporate these perspectives "UNESCO, UNICEF, the UN Environment Programme, and the Human Rights Commission."[11] Yet Dryzek, writing in 2000, notes that forms of inclusion are limited: "Actively inclusive representation, in which an IGO would sponsor a civil society group and foster its power within the organization, is possible to imagine, but I can think of no examples in practice, and no discussions of its desirability in theory."[12]

In this paper, I will examine the citizen submission process of the North American Agreement on Environmental Cooperation (NAAEC) which, even at the time of Dryzek's writing, was celebrated as an institution that approaches the kind of inclusion for which he advocated. I will endeavor to demonstrate how deliberative democracy offers a theoretical framework that (1) justifies this form of inclusion, (2) explains why and how the NAAEC falls short of fully realizing its deliberative democratic potential, and (3) proposes reforms to the process that reflect a principled and pragmatic understanding of the NAAEC's limits. This chapter will proceed in three parts. Section 2 offers an account of deliberative democracy that attempts to demonstrate why and how it can be extended to the transnational context. Section 3 examines in detail the structure and processes of the NAAEC and shows how the citizen submissions process inspired hopes that resonate with the aspirations of deliberative democratic theory, yet has been widely understood to have been a disappointment. Section 4 proposes reforms that acknowledge the limits of the NAAEC, while seeking to vindicate deliberative democratic aspirations.

2. FULLER, DELIBERATIVE DEMOCRACY, AND TRANSNATIONAL LAW

The ambitions of this section are modest. I do not aim to offer a general theoretical justification for transnational institutions that would demonstrate how and under what conditions they can be considered to be democratically legitimate. Instead, I aim to achieve the more limited goal of showing how *some* forms of transnational law can be justified in deliberative democratic terms. I have narrowed the inquiry in two main ways. First, I examine a discrete subset of forms of *transnational law*. I will be examining an instrument that would typically be characterized as soft law, and I will endeavor to show how it should be understood and justified in normative terms *as law*. Second, I am not attempting to offer a *general democratic* justification

---

[10] Dennis F. Thompson, "Democratic Theory and Global Society" (1999) 7 *Journal of Political Philosophy* 111, cited in Dryzek, *Deliberative Democracy and Beyond*, pp. 132–3.

[11] Ibid., p. 137.

[12] Ibid., p. 136.

for this form of law, but a specific, deliberative democratic justification, and I will show how this justification overlaps with the characterization of soft law, as law.

2.1. *Fuller and Transnational Law*

I begin by situating my discussion in general debates about transnational law and articulating a justification for this form of law that draws on the jurisprudence of Lon Fuller. I am not alone in finding in Fuller inspiration for a conception of international law. Jutta Brunée and Stephen Toope, with their "interactional theory," have provided the most extended articulation of a Fullerian international law. They draw the link between relationships of reciprocity and legal norms when they write that

> within *all* systems of legal normativity, even state systems of law, social norms are constructed through rhetorical activity and social practice, producing increasingly influential mutual expectations or shared understandings of actors. In turn, if these shared understandings are reinforced through action based upon Fuller's criteria of legality, it becomes possible to generate obligation, or fidelity to law.[13]

The authors extend these ideas of legality and reciprocity, which are central to Fuller's jurisprudence, to the international sphere when they stress that "law is only possible within specific times and places where actors have developed certain basic understandings about what they hope to achieve together."[14] It is when these basic understandings are present and when specific legal forms exist through which parties can reason together and reinforce their mutual obligations that, according to Brunée and Toope, legal relations in the international sphere can be said to exist.

The authors stress that the participants in this law-making exercise are diverse and include actors other than states, such as "[i]nternational organizations, [nongovernmental organizations, or] NGOs, corporations, informal intergovernmental expert networks, and a variety of other groups [which] are actively engaged in the creation of shared understandings and the promotion of learning amongst states and other international actors."[15] Moreover, they note that one advantage of this conception of law is that it can more easily account for some forms of international law, including custom and soft law, than alternative, positivist theories. Unlike positivist theories, the interactional account does not need to make recourse to hypothetical consent in order to explain why custom should be considered law.[16] And unlike those theories, the interactional account can justify considering "soft law" as law, even if it is not incorporated into the decisions of formal adjudicative bodies.[17] Custom and soft law

[13] Ibid., p. 34.
[14] Ibid., p. 42.
[15] Ibid., p. 45.
[16] Ibid., p. 47.
[17] Ibid., p. 51.

can be considered to be law because when "they are rooted in shared understandings and adhere to the conditions of legality, they generate fidelity."[18]

Another theorist who draws on Fuller to derive an account of transnational regulation is Benedict Kingsbury. He claims that "global administrative law" consists of "shared sets of norms and norm-guided practices that are in some cases regarded as obligatory, and in many cases are given some weight, even where they are not obviously part of national (state) law or standard inter-state law."[19] Kingsbury's claim rests on a distinctive conception of law, which does not understand the norms and practices that "are not obviously part of national (state) law or standard inter-state law" to be supplements or nonlegal alternatives to international law. Kingsbury rather argues that these norms and practices can themselves be a form of law. In order to arrive at this conclusion he draws on Fuller.

According to Fuller, laws that conform to the rule of law address themselves to citizens in ways that create a relationship of reciprocity between lawgiver and citizen. It is this relationship of reciprocity that constitutes the basis of legitimacy of a legal order, and if a lawgiver undermines this relationship, through, for instance, acting like a tyrant, the resulting governance order is no longer one of law and the citizen has no obligation of fidelity toward it.[20] Kingsbury similarly argues that rule of law principles in the transnational context have the effect of "channelling, managing, shaping and constraining political power."[21] Whereas a positivist conception of international law focuses on the binding effects of law, the Fullerian conception directs attention instead to law's capacity to facilitate the pursuit of the public good by those publics who are affected by global administrative law.[22] The relevant publics include (1) global administrative public entities, apart from states;[23] (2) states and agencies of a particular state;[24] and (3) individuals and other private actors.[25] Moreover, according to Kingsbury, a norm or practice in the global administrative law context does not necessarily become law because it emanates from an authoritative

---

[18] Ibid., p. 51.

[19] Benedict Kingsbury, "The Concept of 'Law' in Global Administrative Law" (2009) 20 *European Journal of International Law* 23 at 26.

[20] See Kristen Rundle, *Forms Liberate: Reclaiming the Jurisprudence of Lon L. Fuller* (Portland, OR: Hart, 2012), chapter 1. Macdonald has argued, in a Fullerian framework, that laws offer hypotheses of interaction that citizens can construct and interpret. See, e.g., Roderick A. Macdonald, "The Fridge Door Statute" (2001) 47 *McGill Law Journal* 11 at 33. Jeremy Waldron calls this aspect of Fuller's conception of the rule of law "self-application" (*Dignity, Rank, and Rights* (New York: Oxford University Press, 2012), p. 53).

[21] Kingsbury, "The Concept of 'Law,'" p. 32.

[22] On this difference in emphasis, see Benedict Kingsbury, "Legal Positivism as Normative Politics: International Society, Balance of Power and Lassa Oppenheim's Positive International Law" (2002) 13 *European Journal of International Law* 401 at 424–5.

[23] Kingsbury, "The Concept of 'Law,'" p. 36. Kingsbury gives as an example of such an entity the World Trade Organization.

[24] Ibid., 37.

[25] Ibid., 37–8. For an analysis of Fuller that understands the facilitative function to be central to his conception of law, see Rundle, *Forms Liberate*.

source, such as the sovereign wills of states. Instead, Kingsbury argues that a norm or practice becomes law by virtue of the fact that it satisfies the normative requirements of "publicness" and Kingsbury, like Brunée and Toope, finds inspiration in Fuller's conception of the rule of law to make this argument.[26] According to Kingsbury, the norms and practices of global administrative law satisfy the requirements of "publicness" even if they have not been authorized or delegated by states,[27] and he sets out an indicative list of principles that gives specific content to this general idea of publicness, in much the same way that Fuller sets out a set of indicia that give specific content to his idea of the rule of law.[28]

We will see in the following how the citizen submissions process of the NAAEC, in both its aspirations and content, can be understood to fit within the ambit of these Fullerian-inspired theories of transnational regulation, but for now I want to make clear my reasons for invoking them. I should emphasize that I do not intend to engage broad debates about the nature and content of international law, as they are beyond the scope of this chapter and my competence. Moreover, I do not primarily intend to undertake an argument about whether the citizens submissions process should be characterized as international law. Instead, I intend to show how a Fullerian conception of transnational law provides a normative standard against which to evaluate the citizen submission process of the NAAEC. Yet before I articulate that argument, I will endeavor to examine the overlap between this Fullerian understanding of law and theories of deliberative democracy that have been developed in the transnational context. The analysis will demonstrate that the Fullerian account of transnational law can be placed on firm normative ground that justifies a particular set of transnational legal phenomena.

2.2. *Deliberative Democracy and Transnational Regulation*

The theory of deliberative democracy has diverse elements and strands, and any attempt to offer a complete picture of it in a space as short as this section will necessarily fail. My aim in this section is therefore limited: I will offer a stylized version of deliberative democratic theory that, I hope, neither unduly simplifies nor exaggerates the significance of central aspects of that theory. I begin by identifying the core concern of deliberative democratic theory, as well as some articulations of its constitutive principles. The core claim has been articulated by Gutmann: "Personal freedom and political equality are valuable to the extent that they express or support individual autonomy – the willingness and ability of persons to shape their lives through rational deliberation."[29] Gutmann continues that "persuasion is

[26] Kingsbury, "The Concept of 'Law,'" p. 31. Kingsbury directly links his conception of global administrative law to Fuller's ideas about the "inner morality of law" (ibid., 38–9).

[27] Ibid., 40.

[28] Ibid., 32. The list includes the principles of legality, rationality, proportionality, the rule of law and human rights (ibid., 32–3).

[29] Amy Gutmann, "Democracy." in Robert E. Godin, Philip Pettit, and Thomas Pogge (eds.), *A Companion to Contemporary Political Philosophy*, 2nd ed. (Oxford: Wiley-Blackwell, 2007), p. 527. This

the most justifiable form of political power because it is the most consistent with respect for the autonomy of persons and their capacity for self-government."[30] The central challenge for deliberative democrats who address issues of governance and institutional design lies in identifying means of safe-guarding the autonomy interests of citizens, and ensuring that when political power is exercised against citizens it is guided by norms of persuasion. Joshua Cohen developed this point when he argued that state action is legitimate when it *manifestly* results from the deliberation of citizens.[31]

Authors have proposed a variety of principles as candidates for evaluating whether a given set of institutions or outcomes safeguards the value of autonomy. Gutmann and Thompson for instance, identify the principles of reciprocity, publicity, and accountability.[32] According to the authors, "[t]he basic premise of reciprocity is that citizens owe one another justifications for the institutions, laws, and public policies that collectively bind them."[33] Further, "[t]he principle of publicity requires that reason-giving be public in order that it be mutually justifiable. The principle of accountability specifies that officials who make decisions on behalf of other people, whether or not they are electoral constituents, should be accountable to those people."[34]

With these general arguments about the nature of deliberative democracy in view, we can see how they can be applied in the transnational context and how they fit within the Fullerian view of transnational law that we surveyed earlier. Consider first a prominent treatment of deliberative democratic theory in the transnational context. Dennis Thompson has argued that the theory offers the conceptual resources necessary to deal with the challenges to democratic theory *in general* that are posed by transnational regulation. The challenge that is most pertinent to the present discussion is what he calls "'the problem of many majorities,' the fact that decision-making authority is dispersed, and that no majority has an exclusive and overriding claim to democratic legitimacy."[35] These challenges are endemic to areas of transnational regulation, such as international environmental law, in which the costs of polluting

---

paragraph draws on material previously published in Hoi L. Kong, "Election Law and Deliberative Democracy: Against Deflation" (2015) 5 Journal of Parliamentary and Political Law 35 at 36.

[30] Gutman, "Democracy".

[31] Cohen writes: "Because the members of a democratic association regard deliberative procedures as the source of *legitimacy*, it is important to them that the terms of their association not merely *be* the results of their deliberation but also be *manifest* to them as such." Joshua Cohen, "Deliberation and Democratic Legitimacy," in *Philosophy, Politics, Democracy: Selected Essays* (Cambridge, MA: Harvard University Press, 2009), p. 22.

[32] Amy Gutmann and Dennis Thompson, *Democracy and Disagreement Democracy and Disagreement* (Cambridge, MA: Belknap Press, 1996), p. 12.

[33] Amy Gutmann and Dennis Thompson, *Why Deliberative Democracy?* (Princeton, NJ: Princeton University Press, 2004), p. 133.

[34] Ibid., p. 135.

[35] Thompson, "Democratic Theory," p. 112.

in one jurisdiction are imposed on the inhabitants of multiple states, each of which may belong to a transnational entity that itself constitutes, however weakly, a polity whose inhabitants are comprised of all its member states. In this example, there are according to Thompson at least three majorities affected: those of the polluter state, those of the affected state, and those of the transnational entity.[36] A second challenge, which he calls the problem of disagreement about rights, lies in the fact that "[t]he scope of liberal rights is expanding, bringing more disagreement about what their content should be and about who should enforce them."[37] These kinds of disagreements arise in the domestic context, as is evident in disagreements about what kinds of rights should be protected in a given polity and how they should be protected.[38] In the transnational context, these and similar kinds of moral dis-agreements are heightened, as the numbers of cultural differences and potential regulatory institutions multiply.[39]

Thompson has argued that deliberative democracy provides normative and insti-tutional design resources for responding to these challenges. According to him, the problem of many majorities can be solved by making public officials accountable to all those who are affected by their decisions, and not only those who are found within a specific political jurisdiction, governed by its particular majority. Thomp-son argues that if this extension of the concept is broadly accepted, overlapping lines of accountability will develop, and so individuals will not be placed in a position of being subject to official action whose authors they cannot hold to account.[40] The institutional design proposal that he offers in support of this notion of accountability is a forum "in which representatives could speak for the ordinary citizens of foreign states, presenting their claims and responding to counter-claims of representatives of the host state."[41] The response to the problem of reasonable disagreement lies similarly in a normative prescription and an institutional design proposal. Thomp-son argues that deliberative democratic theory calls on parties to disagreements to "search for significant points of convergence between their own moral understand-ings and those of the citizens whose positions, taken in their more comprehensive forms, they reject."[42] The institutional solution lies in creating processes in which

---

[36] In the example Thompson gives of transborder environmental pollution, he discusses the polluting state, the state that receives the pollution, and a hypothetical forum in which disputes about this kind of pollution can be addressed (ibid., pp. 120–2). Thompson also discusses the three majorities identified in the main text when he addresses the question of whether children of migrant laborers should be eligible for education grants in a member country of the European Union. In that case, the three majorities involved were Germany, Italy, and the European Union (ibid. pp. 111–2).

[37] Ibid., at p. 113.

[38] Thompson gives the example of conflicts between East and West Germany over the right to an abortion (ibid., 115).

[39] Ibid.

[40] Ibid., 121.

[41] Ibid., 121.

[42] Ibid., 124.

rights claims can be "proposed, established, challenged and revised in an ongoing process."[43]

2.3. *Overlaps between Fullerian and Deliberative Democratic Conceptions of Transnational Regulation*

The overlaps between these general deliberative democratic insights into transnational regulation and the scholarship offering a Fullerian interpretation of transnational law arise at three points. Consider first the general issue of accountability. In much the same way that Kingsbury conceives of global administrative law as controlling exercises of power and requiring that those who wield power account to those who are subject to it, one of the deliberative democratic theorist's core concerns in the transnational context is how to hold transnational actors accountable through obligations of reason-giving. The second point of overlap lies in the restrictions that are placed on the content of those reasons. We have seen that deliberative democrats require in general and in the transnational context in particular that the reasons offered be public, in the sense that those who are addressed by the reasons could reasonably be expected to accept them. Brunnée and Toope's arguments about the importance of shared understandings in transnational law can be seen, in a deliberative democratic light, as providing the content of these reasons, or, at the very least, the framework in which public reasons can be articulated. The third point of contact between the transnational deliberative democrats and the Fullerian transnational legal theorists lies in their shared institutional focus. As we have seen, the Fullerians define law in terms of its coherence with principles such as reciprocity and publicity, which resonate with the terminology of deliberative democratic theory. The Fullerians tell us why we should consider particular regimes to *be* transnational law, while the deliberative democrats make clear why it *should matter from the perspective of political theory* that particular institutional forms correspond to the Fullerian conception of transnational law. In what follows, I will endeavor to show how the particular legal regime of the citizen submissions process can be understood to evince and fall short of the Fullerian and deliberative democratic accounts of transnational law that have been surveyed here. This argument will aim to test the plausibility of those accounts and to determine how both they and the institutions that I examine can be refined.

3. THE CITIZEN SUBMISSIONS PROCESS: PROMISE, CRITIQUES, AND REFORM

Before discussing the details of the submissions regime, I will very briefly lay out some of the background history of the agreement, as well as its institutional structure. In

---

[43] Ibid., 123.

order to gain support for the passing of NAFTA from environmental groups, the Clinton administration proposed a trilateral side agreement that would aim to respond to their concerns, including three that are particularly pertinent for our discussion: (1) the creation of "pollution havens" in Mexico, as foreign investment would be directed there, and "environmental degradation and loss of natural resources there" would result;[44] (2) the compromising of domestic environmental standards, as a result of trade-related challenges;[45] and (3) the exclusion of the public from participating in trade disputes.[46] Environmental groups pressed for the creation of a North American Commission on the Environment that would include "a permanent Secretariat with independent power to conduct investigations and prepare reports and [that would be] advised by a nongovernmental board of citizens" and "increased public participation in dispute settlement."[47] The North American Agreement on Environmental Cooperation (NAAEC) reflects some of these demands, but, argue John Knox and David Markell, it should be primarily understood as an attempt to prevent pollution havens.[48] The authors note that the agreement neither protects domestic environmental legislation from trade challenges under NAFTA, nor does it provide for public participation in dispute resolution.[49] Nonetheless, it does target domestic regulation when it obliges member Parties to effectively enforce their environmental laws and regulations and it provides, through Sections 14 and 15, a procedure for direct citizen involvement in overseeing this obligation.[50] In this respect and others, the NAAEC should be seen as a compromise that attempts to give effect to some of the aspirations of environmental groups, while yielding to political exigencies. With this historical grounding established, I will now turn to providing a brief overview of the institutional structure that the NAAEC creates, before discussing in detail Sections 14 and 15.

3.1. Structure and Process

The NAAEC creates the Commission for Environmental Cooperation (CEC), which is comprised of (1) the Council, on which sit the cabinet-level representatives of the Parties or their representatives, and which is the governing body of the Commission[51]; (2) the Secretariat, which provides "technical, administrative and

---

[44] John H. Knox and David L. Markell, "The Innovative North American Commission for Environmental Cooperation," in David L. Markell and John H. Knox (eds.), *Greening NAFTA: The North American Commission for Environmental Cooperation* (Stanford, CA: Stanford University Press, 2003), p. 4.

[45] Ibid., p. 6.

[46] Ibid., p. 7.

[47] Ibid., pp. 7–8.

[48] Ibid., p. 9.

[49] Ibid.

[50] Ibid.

[51] North American Agreement on Environmental Cooperation, Mexico City, September 8, 1993, in force January 1, 1994, 32 ILM 1480, art. 9(1) [NAAEC].

operational support to the Council"[52] and is headed by an Executive Director, who is chosen by the Council for one three year term that may be renewed for an additional three years,[53] and staffed by appointees of the Executive Director, who makes his selections taking into consideration candidates proposed by the Parties and the Joint Public Advisory Committee, as well as questions of national representation.[54] Finally, the Joint Public Advisory Council includes fifteen members, with equal numbers of members from each Party country, and it "may provide advice to the Council on any matter within the scope of this Agreement"[55] and "may provide relevant technical, scientific or other information to the Secretariat."[56]

This interlocking structure of political actors, independent experts, and ordinary citizens creates the potential for tensions, as will become evident in the following discussion of critiques of the citizen submissions process. That process is governed by Articles 14 and 15 of the NAAEC. According to Article 14, "[t]he Secretariat may consider a submission from any non-governmental organization or person asserting that a Party is failing to effectively enforce its environmental law" and sets out the conditions of admissibility for a claim.[57] Once the Secretariat has found that these are met, it "shall determine whether the submission merits requesting a response from the Party" and that inquiry is guided by a set of factors.[58] If the Secretariat determines that a response is merited, "it shall forward to the Party a copy of the submission and any supporting information provided with the submission."[59] The Party must then, within a time limit, advise the Secretariat "whether the matter is the subject of a pending judicial or administrative proceeding, in which case the Secretariat shall proceed no further,"[60] as well as "any other information that the Party wishes to submit."[61]

---

[52] Ibid., Art. 11(5).
[53] Ibid., Art. 11(1).
[54] Ibid., Art. 16(1).
[55] Ibid., Art. 16(4).
[56] Ibid., Art. 16(5).
[57] Ibid., Art. 14. According to Article 14(1) of the NAAEC the conditions include that the submission "(a) is in writing in a language designated by that Party in a notification to the Secretariat; (b) clearly identifies the person or organization making the submission; (c) provides sufficient information to allow the Secretariat to review the submission, including any documentary evidence on which the submission may be based; (d) appears to be aimed at promoting enforcement rather than at harassing industry; (e) indicates that the matter has been communicated in writing to the relevant authorities of the Party and indicates the Party's response, if any; and (f) is filed by a person or organization residing or established in the territory of a Party."
[58] Ibid., Art. 14(2): "In deciding whether to request a response, the Secretariat shall be guided by whether: (a) the submission alleges harm to the person or organization making the submission; (b) the submission, alone or in combination with other submissions, raises matters whose further study in the process would advance the goals of this Agreement; (c) private remedies available under the Party's law have been pursued; and (d) the submission is drawn exclusively from mass media reports."
[59] Ibid., Art. 14(2).
[60] Ibid., Art. 14(3)(a).
[61] Ibid., Art. 14(3)(a)(1). Included is information, such as "(i) whether the matter was previously the subject of a judicial or administrative proceeding, and (ii) whether private remedies in connection

If the Secretariat considers that a submission is warranted, it must "inform the Council and provide its reasons."[62] If the Council, "by a two-thirds vote, instructs it to do so," it must prepare a factual record.[63] According to Article 15(4), the Secretariat then must prepare the record, considering relevant information that "(a) is publicly available; (b) submitted by interested non-governmental organizations or persons; (c) submitted by the Joint Public Advisory Council; or (d) developed by the Secretariat or by independent experts." Once the record is completed, the Secretariat must provide a draft copy to the Council that any Party may provide comments on.[64] The Secretariat must then incorporate any comments that it finds appropriate and submit it to the Council,[65] which by a two-thirds vote may be decide whether to make the report public.[66]

3.2. *Deliberative Democratic and Fullerian Rationales for the CEC*

Now that we have seen the salient aspects of the NAAEC's history, structure, and process, we can identify the ways in which the CEC and the submissions process satisfy the requirements of a Fullerian and deliberative democratic conception of transnational law. Let us begin with Toope and Brunée's conception of reciprocity. Recall that according to this Fullerian ideal, law arises from the shared understandings of those who are subject to its authority and provides a framework through which those understandings can be constructed and legitimated. Moreover, we saw earlier that one advantage of this Fullerian conception is that it can explain why "soft law" should be considered law, even in the absence of enforcement mechanisms, which more positivist conceptions of transnational law would understand to be a defining feature of law. We saw further that these elements of a Fullerian conception of transnational law resonate with deliberative democratic principles such as reciprocity and publicity, and provide the conditions under which those subject to law can understand themselves to be the addressees of public reasons, or reasons that they could reasonably be expected to accept. The CEC and the citizen submission process satisfy these elements of the Fullerian and deliberative conception of transnational law, and, moreover, respond to what Thompson has called the problem of many majorities, by creating institutions through which governments can be incentivized to consider the interests of multiple polities. To understand how the institutions of the CEC achieve this end, I turn now briefly to network theory.

with the matter are available to the person or organization making the submission and whether they have been pursued."
[62] Ibid., Art. 15(1).
[63] Ibid., Art. 15(2).
[64] Ibid., Art. 15(5).
[65] Ibid., Art. 15(6).
[66] Ibid., Art. 15(7).

Network theorists have long argued that the unitary, sovereign state actor is not the only or even the primary actor in transnational law. Instead, they argue, transnational law often gains its efficacy through the shared understandings and interactions of actors in the legislative, administrative, and judicial branches of multiple states, who then influence their respective states to give effect to transnational obligations.[67] The structure of the CEC can be considered to be an instance of network regulation, as it facilitates interactions among the environmental ministries of the member states and, in addition, creates opportunities for NGOs to coordinate activities across borders. This is in part a function of the ambitions of the institution and the regime. As Knox and Markell note, the CEC was designed to be the first organization that could address any environmental issue, arising anywhere on the continent.[68] In addition, the mandate of the Council is broad, as under Article 10, it may make recommendations on a long and open-ended list of topics.[69] Similarly, the Secretariat is authorized under Article 13 to prepare a report on any matter within the scope of the annual program, without council authorization, and on any other environmental matter related to the cooperative functions of the NAAEC, unless the council objects by a two-thirds vote.[70] Moreover, and more specifically and concretely with respect to the citizen submissions process, environmental activists from the member countries have in the past filed submissions together and have worked together on initiatives related to the procedure, including writing letters advocating change.[71] With each of these activities, the CEC and the citizen submission process create basic conditions through which diverse actors in the international sphere can forge common understandings and a shared discourse that provide the basis for broad acceptance of the legal regime of the NAAEC. Finally, the participation

[67] See, e.g., see Anne-Marie Slaughter, *A New World Order* (Princeton, NJ: Princeton University Press, 2004)

[68] Knox and Markell, "The Innovative North American Commission," p. 10.

[69] Mark S. Winfield, "North American Pollutant Release and Transfer Registries: A Case Study for Environmental Policy Convergence," in David L. Markell and John H. Knox (eds.), *Greening NAFTA: The North American Commission for Environmental Cooperation* (Stanford, CA: Stanford University Press, 2003), pp. 48–9. The Council has issued an annual report on North American pollutant releases and transfers, which analyzes data from jurisdictions in the U.S. and Canada and compared the performance of facilities. These reports provoked media attention, have incentivized actors to respond, and have enabled NGO monitoring of facilities. Moreover, Council put public pressure on the Mexican government to implement a mandatory pollutant release and transfer registries (PRTR) system and provided technical and financial support (ibid., p. 47).

[70] Examples of such reports include the Silva Reservoir report, which was undertaken at the request of environmental groups. The Secretariat constituted a panel of experts to examine the causes of a migratory bird die-offs in a reservoir located in Mexico and to propose recommendations. Jorge Soberón et al., *The Death of Migratory Birds at the Silva Reservoir (1994–95)* (Montreal: Secretariat of the Commission for Environmental Cooperation, 1995), http://www3.cec.org/islandora/en/item/1618-death-migratory-birds-silva-reservoir-1994-95-en.pdf.

[71] John H. Knox and David L. Markell, "Evaluating Citizen Petition Procedures: Lessons from an Analysis of the NAFTA Environmental Commission" (2012) 47 *Texas International Law Journal* 505 at 528.

of coalitions of environmental groups from different member parties, challenging member states to enforce their environmental laws, resembles Thompson's proposal for enabling members of polities to contest the actions of governments not their own.[72] The deliberative democrat's problem of multiple majorities, therefore, is in part solved by the institutional structure of the citizen submissions process under the NAAEC.

We saw earlier that Kingsbury's Fullerian conception of transnational law involves an element in addition to Toope and Brunée's notion of reciprocity, and that the deliberative democratic view of transnational law addresses itself to a set of concerns beyond the many majorities problem. The transnational theory derived from Kingsbury focuses on the concept of "publicness," while the challenge Thompson identifies is about the fact of widespread and reasonable disagreement in transnational relations. I will close this section by examining how the citizen submissions process embodies a key element of publicness; the next section of this chapter, which focuses on criticisms of the process, will examine the pertinence of the challenge of reasonable disagreement.

Although Kingsbury's concept is open-ended in its incorporation of multiple principles, its core concern is one shared by deliberative democrats and Fuller himself, namely that those who wield authority should be answerable to those who are subject to that authority. This underlying concern is expressed in Kingsbury's principle of rationality, which is one of the sub-elements of his concept of publicness; it is present in Thompson and Gutmann's principle of accountability, and it underwrites Fuller's claim that law does not involve a one-way projection of authority, but rather involves the subject of law in the construction and interpretation of law's meaning and application.[73] The citizen submissions process embodies this notion of accountability by enabling citizens and civil society groups to directly contest the authority of states and by giving them and any state subject to the process a role in mutually constructing, with the mediating role of the Secretariat, factual records that implicitly call upon states to justify themselves.

It is worth mentioning a feature that distinguishes the citizen submissions process from Kingsbury's global administrative law. Whereas the latter focuses on processes that render *transnational actors* accountable, the NAAEC regime uses a transnational forum to hold *states* accountable.[74] This international spotlight and the means of

---

[72] For an excellent overview of the means by which coalitions of activist groups have made use of the citizen submissions process, see Jonathan Graubart, *Legalizing Transnational Activism: the Struggle to Gain Social Change from NAFTA's Citizen's Petitions* (University Park, PA: Pennsylvania State University Press, 2008).

[73] For the argument against law as a one-way projection of authority, see Lon Fuller, *The Morality of Law* (New Haven, CT: Yale University Press, 1969), p. 192.

[74] On this point, see Kal Raustiala, "Citizen Submissions and Treaty Review in the NAAEC," in David L. Markell and John H. Knox (eds.), *Greening NAFTA: The North American Commission for Environmental Cooperation* (Stanford, CA: Stanford University Press, 2003), p. 260.

triggering it have been identified as sources of the process's strength. For instance, the spotlight aims to draw media attention to the state, as its actions are the target of a factual record, and thereby opens the state up to domestic repercussions, such as the threat of electoral defeat,[75] and international repercussions, including diplomatic pressure and the potential that international partners will withdraw from cooperative ventures.[76] Moreover (and to change metaphors) scholars have claimed that a "fire-alarm" procedure such as the citizen submissions process has advantages relative to an investigative system that is under centralized control.[77] Fire alarms, in the domestic and transnational context, enable private actors to identify problems that governments either may miss or may choose not to act upon.[78] The citizen submissions process is one such fire alarm.

Finally, the specifically transnational nature of the citizen submissions process provides an opportunity to hold states to account for environmental failures that may be barred by domestic law.[79] These benefits of the citizen submissions process, which are consistent with, but go beyond Kingsbury's theory of global administrative law, have a deliberative democratic pedigree. In its spotlight and fire-alarm functions, the citizen submissions process evinces the deliberative democratic ideal of public accountability, by making public actors answerable, at the initiative of citizens. Of course, the process has not been without controversy and it is to criticisms of it that I now turn. We shall see that the responses to these criticisms can also be framed in deliberative democratic terms.

3.3. *Critiques of the Process*

A range of criticisms has been directed against the process. Two are especially pertinent to our current discussion. First, authors have argued that the Council is put in an apparent conflict of interest. It has the authority to determine whether a

---

[75] Raymond MacCallum, "Evaluating the Citizen Submission Procedure Under the North American Agreement on Environmental Cooperation" (1997) 8 *Colorado Journal of International Environmental Law and Policy* 395 at 422.

[76] David G. Schiller, "Great Expectations: the North American Commission on Environmental Cooperation Review of the Cozumel Pier Submission" (1997) 28 *University of Miami Inter-American Law Review* 437 at 474.

[77] Raustiala, "Citizen Submissions," p. 257.

[78] Ibid., p. 264.

[79] On this point, in the U.S. context, see Marirose J. Pratt, "The Citizen Submission Process of the NAAEC: Filling the Gap in Judicial Review of Federal Agency Failures to Enforce Environmental Laws" (2006) 20 *Emory International Law Review* 741. Scholars have also noted that the more frequent recourse to the process by Mexican and Canadian groups is due to the relatively fewer opportunities to hold governments to account for failure to enforce their environmental laws. On this point, see Tseming Yang, "The Effectiveness of the NAFTA Environmental Side Agreement's Citizen Submission Process: A Case Study of Metales y Derivados" (2006) 76 *University of Colorado Law Review* 443.

factual record will be prepared, but since the Council is comprised of the member states, the target of any potential record will play a role in the deliberations about whether a record should go forward.[80] Second, authors have noted that the procedure is toothless, either because it includes no possibility of enforcement or because there is no continuing monitoring.[81] I will turn to the second criticism when I address measures for reform, but I will address the first criticism in this section, and in particular a specific controversy over Council's actions in narrowing the scope of the factual record.

Observers have noted that in several prominent instances, the Council, in instructing the Secretariat to prepare a factual record, has in addition narrowed the scope of the inquiry that was proposed in the submission and recommended by the Secretariat.[82] This narrowing of the factual record has transformed claims about systemic failures to enforce state law into inquiries over a few specific instances of nonenforcement, thus trivializing the exercise. In one instance, such an authorization resulted in the submitter withdrawing a submission.[83] Narrowing of records is a problem because it undermines the faith that civil society has in the CEC and the citizen submission process and therefore potentially cancels out the deliberative democratic and Fullerian benefits that I identified earlier. The impact is potentially particularly grave insofar as it is unauthorized by the plain meaning of Article 15, which only gives the Council the power to approve the record that the Secretariat has recommended. It is difficult to see how narrowing the record, in the face of clear meaning of the text, would incentivize civil society to participate in the process and to create thereby the shared understandings and network effects that are important to establishing the conditions for legitimacy for the NAAEC. Rather, such actions by the Council would seem likely to cause actors to doubt the impartiality and good faith of the institutions of the CEC.[84] The doubt created by narrowing the records also puts into question the citizen submissions process as a site of contestation and accountability. It is difficult to see how the process can be understood to hold to account a state whose representatives can change, without justification, the terms under which it is being challenged.

---

[80] For a statement of the conflict, see David J. Blair, "The CEC Citizen Submission Process: Still a Model for Reconciling Trade and the Environment?" (2003) 12 *The Journal of Environment Development* 295 at 318.

[81] See, e.g., Yang, "Effectiveness of the Citizen Submission Process," p. 478; David Markell, "The Role of Spotlighting Procedures in Promoting Citizen Participation, Transparency, and Accountability" (2010) 45 *Wake Forest Law Review* 425 at 451.

[82] See Chris Wold et al., "The Inadequacy of the Citizen Submission Process Articles 14 & 15 of the North American Agreement on Environmental Cooperation" (2004) 26 *Loyola of Los Angeles International and Comparative Law Review* 415 at 434.

[83] Knox and Markell, "Evaluating Citizen Petition Procedures."

[84] David L. Markell, "Governance of International Institutions: A Review of the North American Commission for Environmental Cooperation's Citizen Submissions Process" (2005) 30 *North Carolina Journal of International Law and Commercial Regulation* 759 at 790.

This is indeed a serious challenge to the process and its deliberative democratic legitimacy. Yet the solution to the challenge lies in the deliberative democratic potential of the institution itself. In order to see why this is the case, it is perhaps helpful to characterize the controversy in the deliberative democratic terms that we have already been using. Recall that according to Thompson, one of the great challenges of transnational regulation is that it multiplies the extent of reasonable disagreement beyond that which exists at the national level. We might say that what we are faced with in the controversy over the scope of factual records is reasonable disagreement over the proper role of political actors in the NAAEC regime. That tension is built right into the agreement itself, as it gives the Council a right to comment that civil society actors, who are the primary beneficiaries of the act, do not enjoy. It also provides the Council with the power to determine whether a factual record is to be prepared at all, and, if so, whether it is to be made public.[85] These privileges reflect the fact that the NAAEC is at the same time a document of political compromise among political actors, who sought to protect their self-interest, and a treaty that creates a forum for democratic deliberation and contestation.

The institutional response to this challenge can be found in Thompson's institutional proposal for responding to reasonable disagreement, namely the creation of forums in which parties can deliberate about their disagreements.[86] The actions of the Council have been subject to pointed criticism by the JPAC, including by means of an "advice letter," and in response to the attention drawn to the practice, the Council refrained from continuing to engage in them.[87] Moreover, as a result of a recently concluded consultation process, interpretive guidelines were developed that expressly rejected a proposal to codify the practice of narrowing factual records.[88] This result, as well as the processes that generated it, suggest that although the threats posed by the Council's actions potentially seriously undermined the deliberative potential of the citizen submissions process, the response to that threat was to be found in deliberative practices themselves. To the extent that the actions reflected reasonable disagreement about the appropriate role of political actors in the process, the deliberative forums provided by the NAAEC itself offered a path to resolution.

3.4. *Reforms*

Let me conclude this chapter by responding to the claim that the process is toothless, because it neither provides enforcement mechanisms nor offers continuing oversight after the production of a factual record. The responses to this claim will allow us to

---

[85] Yang, "Effectiveness of the Citizen Submission Process," p. 473.
[86] Thompson, "Democratic Theory," p. 122.
[87] John H. Knox, "Fixing the CEC Submissions Procedure: Are the 2012 Revisions Up to the Task" (2014) 7 *Golden Gate University Environmental Law Journal* 81, p. 88.
[88] Knox, "Fixing the CEC Submissions Procedure," p. 81.

address a lingering doubt about the citizen submission process, namely that because it is soft law, it should not be considered to be law at all. The first thing to note is that what scholarship we have on the effectiveness of the process suggests that the spotlight function works in some instances. Scholars have described discrete policy changes that were responses to factual records, such as in the very first *Cozumel* case, which reduced the size of the proposed project, reduced the impacts of commercial shrimp farming in Nayarit, led to the cleanup of a lead smelter in Tijuana, and led to greater efforts to reduce illegal logging in Sierra Tarahumara.[89] This evidence might offer a modest response to the criticism of soft law as nonlaw, namely that the conditions for *Fullerian* law have been met, because the actors on the ground understand the citizen submission process to be a significant normative force. The conditions for reciprocity, filtered through the regulatory form of law, have provided meaningful direction for state action, and, in Kingsbury's terms, have channeled and controlled the exercise of political power. A stronger response might say that the positivist misunderstands the nature of law, and in particular international law. We do not overcome the problem of multiple majorities and reasonable disagreement by fiat and command but by mutual agreement and understanding. The fact that in a given instance of transnational regulation there is an absence of effective means of implementation is suggestive of this lack of shared understanding. Law is absent for this reason, and not because there is an absence of coercive enforcement measures.

Yet even if one accepts this interpretation of international law and soft law, in general, and the citizen submissions process, in particular, one might object to the current configuration of the process on Fullerian and deliberative democratic grounds. If the overarching goal of the process is to ensure accountability, then the process as currently configured would seem to be overly dependent on contingent factors for its success. To understand this claim, it is perhaps helpful to briefly examine Jonathan Graubart's assessment of the process. Consistent with the tenor of this chapter's argument, Graubart claims that the "lack of binding authority does not render a transnational quasijudicial mechanism ineffective."[90] Rather, he argues that by giving a legal form to what would otherwise be a simple political dispute, activists can give "greater status" to their claims, and if activists can mobilize broad support for their cause, they can increase "pressure on the target government to comply with the soft-law process."[91] The contingent nature of such a process's prospect for success is highlighted when he writes that "[a]ctivists enjoy the best prospects for using the mechanisms effectively when the governments support the general process and/or the underlying values at issue."[92] In some ways, this qualification fits with the argument advanced by the Fullerian view of transnational law advanced in this

---

[89] Knox and Markell, "Evaluating Citizen Petition Procedures," p. 527.
[90] Graubart, *Legalizing Transnational Activism*, p. 140.
[91] Ibid.
[92] Ibid.

paper. According to that view, as articulated by Toope and Brunée, transnational regulation only has the quality of law when it rests on shared understandings of law and legal forms facilitate interactions that are tied to these shared understandings.

Even with this qualification in place, it would seem that the citizen submissions process could be altered in order to increase the likelihood that governments will be answerable to citizens. As it stands, if a government, in the face of a factual record, makes the political calculation that it will not suffer political repercussions from ignoring the record, it will do so. Markell has argued that this was what happened in the *Migratory Bird Treaty Act* case, where the relevant U.S. agency did not change its actions after the publication of the factual record.[93] A solution to this problem, which respects the parties' choice to adopt a soft law instrument, would aim to increase the accountability of states, without subjecting them to formal compliance mechanisms. Along these lines, Knox and Markell have advocated for ongoing monitoring of the problems identified in the factual records[94] and Wold et al. argue that a model can be found in article 17.8(8) of the Dominican Republic–Central American–United States Free Trade Agreement (DR-CAFTA), which empowers a transnational body to issue recommendations for how a government that fails to enforce its environmental laws can monitor its enforcement activities.[95]

To close this chapter, I will suggest a second, specifically Canadian response to the problem of accountability posed by the citizen submissions process. Canada's involvement in the CEC was the subject of extended analysis by Environment Canada in a 2007 report.[96] The elements of the report most relevant to the present analysis are its claim that the CEC has had limited influence on the Canadian government's activities[97] and that it is perceived as such by Canadian stakeholders.[98] One way of addressing this perceived lack of effectiveness might be to incorporate the results of the citizen submissions process into domestic Canadian law. The Auditor General Act allows a Canadian resident to petition the Auditor General "about an environmental matter in the context of sustainable development that is the responsibility of [departments specified in the legislation]."[99] The Auditor General is required to forward the petition "within fifteen days after the day on which it is received to the appropriate Minister for the department."[100] Within specified

---

[93] Markell, "The Role of Spotlighting," p. 451.

[94] John H. Knox, "A New Approach to Compliance with International Environmental Law: The Submissions Procedure of the NAFTA Environmental Commission" (2001) 28 *Ecology Law Quarterly* 1 at 122; Markell, "The Role of Spotlighting," 458; Knox and Markell, "Evaluating Citizen Petition Procedures," 537.

[95] Wold et al., "Inadequacy of the Citizen Submission Process," 443.

[96] Environment Canada, "Evaluation of Canada's Participation in the Commission for Environmental Cooperation (CEC)" (Ottawa: Environment Canada, 2007).

[97] Ibid., pp. 20–1.

[98] Ibid.

[99] *Auditor General Act*, RSC 1985, c. A-17, s. 22(1).

[100] Ibid.

time periods, the Minister is required to send an acknowledgement of the petition, reply to the person who made it, and copy the Auditor General.[101] In addition, the Commissioner is under a duty to monitor, which includes the power to undertake any "examinations and inquiries that the Commissioner considers necessary in order to monitor... the extent to which [relevant departments] have met the objectives, and implemented the plans set out in their own sustainable development strategies."[102] Finally, the Commissioner is obliged to report annually on "anything that the Commissioner considers should be brought to the attention of Parliament in relation to environmental and other aspects of sustainable development."[103] Within this structure, it seems possible that a petitioner could refer to a factual record compiled pursuant to the citizen submissions process in a petition to the Auditor General. Once this is done, the Commissioner would be under a duty to monitor and report on a failure of any federal department to effectively enforce its own sustainable development legislation, either because such a failure falls within the scope of a department's own sustainable development strategy or because it falls within the discretion of the Commissioner to include in his or her annual report. In this instance, dual recourse to the transnational and national mechanisms would render the former more effective by increasing the burden of accountability on the Canadian federal government.

4. CONCLUSION

This chapter has sought to achieve two broad goals. First, it has aimed to provide a deliberative democratic justification for transnational institutions, and in particular for soft law instruments that rely on citizen participation for their effectiveness. Second, it has analyzed a specific regime, the citizen submissions process of the CEC, in light of that theoretical framework. In the course of its analysis, the chapter has touched on debates about the nature of international law, but has not entered deeply into them. In closing, I would like to place those debates in the context of a more general discussion about the normative significance of legal forms.[104]

This chapter has addressed a topic in what has been described as "international environmental law": a subset of public international law, which is itself "a body of law created by States for States to govern problems that arise between States."[105]

---

[101] Ibid., ss. 22(2) and 22(3).

[102] Ibid., s. 23(1)(a).

[103] Ibid., s. 23(2).

[104] The following paragraph draws on material previously published in Hoi L. Kong, "The Disaggregated State in Transnational Environmental Regulation" (2013) 78 *Missouri Law Review* 443.

[105] Lakshman D. Guruswamy, *International Environmental Law in a Nutshell*, 4th ed. (St. Paul, MN: West, 2012), p. 1. Authors note that public international law governs international organizations and nonstate actors, as well as states. See, e.g., Philippe Sands, *Principles of International Environmental Law*, 2nd ed. (Cambridge: Cambridge University Press, 2003).

International environmental law is further typically defined in terms of its author-itative and binding sources[106] and the subject matter it regulates, namely the environment.[107] As we have seen here, various theorists of international law have argued against the positivist conception of international law that underlies this understanding of international environmental law, and it is perhaps worthwhile to articulate the outlines of this positivist conception. Positivists generally understand binding effects to be a necessary feature of international law. Perhaps the strongest version of this positivist vision can be found in command theories of international law.[108] Additional versions of international law positivism that emphasize other, typ-ically Hartian, aspects of the positivist tradition also typically define[109] international law, generally, and international environmental law, in particular, in terms of their binding effects.[110]

The Fullerian conceptions of international law that I have described react to this version of international law, and it is worth asking whether this reaction has normative significance. One might reject such significance and simply claim that the positivist view of international law is descriptively inadequate, because it does not capture important features of international law, including customary and soft law. As we have seen, this is one aspect of the position of Toope and Brunée. To close this chapter, I would like to point to another aspect of their argument, which has broad implications for legal theory. According to Toope and Brunée's reading of Fuller, law can never be simply a one-way projection of authority from law giver to law receiver. Quoting Fuller, they write: "law depends for its existence 'on effective interaction and cooperation between citizens and lawmaking and law-applying officials.'"[111] This

---

[106] The standard enumeration of the sources of international law is found in Article 38(1) of the Statute of the International Court of Justice, June 26, 1945, in force October 24, 1954, TS 993, 59 Stat. 1031: treaties, international custom, general principles of law, and the subsidiary sources. In addition to these binding sources of authority, international environmental law is governed by soft law or nonbinding agreements that are lower on the hierarchy of sources (see Ulrich Beyerlin and Thilo Marauhn, *International Environmental Law* (Oxford: Hart, 2011), pp. 291–4).

[107] For various definitions of the "environment" in international law, see Sands, *Principles of International Environmental Law*, pp. 15–8.

[108] I am aware that such an essentially "command theory" of international law is not accepted by all international law positivists. For a description of the command theory, see Mehrdad Payandeh, "The Concept of International Law in the Jurisprudence of H.L.A. Hart" (2010) 21 *European Journal of International Law* 967 at 969–70. Whether one views international law as conforming to the command theory or the more sophisticated versions of international law positivism, it remains the case that authors typically define international law, generally, and international environmental law, in particular, in terms of their binding effects.

[109] For normative accounts of positivism that do not rest on such a command theory, see ibid. and Kingsbury, "The Concept of 'Law.'"

[110] See, e.g., Sands, *Principles of International Environmental Law*, p. 12. In this standard view, interna-tional law, in its legislative function creates "laws and principles which impose binding obligations requiring states and other members of the international community to conform to certain norms of behaviour." The administrative function of international law involves the application of these principles and norms.

[111] Toope and Brunée, *Legitimacy and Legality*, p. 23.

function of law rests on a particular view of human autonomy, which, according to the authors' interpretation of Fuller, "is best understood in relational terms – as human interaction in social institutions."[112] Law, in this view, enables citizens to reason with norms and to stand in a particular relationship with respect to officials who make and apply laws. That relationship is one in which citizens can, as Toope and Brunée argue, interpret and apply the law in specific contexts.[113]

The analysis of the relationship between deliberative democracy and transnational law sketched out here suggests a complementary feature of the Fullerian view of law, namely that in order for laws to be legitimate, lawmakers have to be accountable to those who are subject to those laws. Accountability can take many forms, and the process described in this chapter provides only one example. Moreover, we have seen in this chapter that legal regimes can have varying degrees of effective accountability. For the Fullerian, this might imply that "law can exist by degrees, so it is possible to talk about law that is being constructed; law is not an all-or-nothing proposition."[114] Nonetheless, there is a minimum threshold of accountability, below which a regime of rules cannot plausibly purport to be law. The debates surrounding the citizen submissions process can be understood in this light. Those who criticize the process might be interpreted to be arguing that the regime lacks even a minimum degree of accountability, while those who are more optimistic claim that it has crossed a threshold of accountability and that it can be altered to be rendered more effective in this respect. Note that this way of framing the debate focuses on the effects of law on citizens, rather than on definitions or categories. Such a view of law and international law places the citizen at the very center of theoretical concern and is for this reason, according to the Fullerian and deliberative democratic view articulated here, normatively valuable.

[112] Ibid., p. 21.
[113] Ibid., p. 23.
[114] Ibid., pp. 22–3.

16

Assessing ENGO Influence in North American Environmental Politics

The Double Grid Framework

Raul Pacheco-Vega[1]

1. INTRODUCTION

There has been much debate regarding the effects of trade on environmental quality. Although the inextricable linkages between free trade and environment are not under discussion, the causal mechanisms and exact effects that increased transnational commercial activity has on specific ecosystems are, and the evidence has been inconclusive. However, there are significant collateral or indirect environmental consequences of the North American Free Trade Agreement (NAFTA). Innovative citizen participation mechanisms and strong cross-border mobilization of environmental activists are but two examples. In this chapter, I summarize the results of empirical investigations I have conducted on the coalition-building mechanisms deployed by environmental nongovernmental organizations (ENGOs) involved in the development and use of information dissemination policy instruments such as the pollutant release and transfer registries (PRTRs) over the last fifteen years. These instruments are designed to change the behavior of the polluter through indirect (civil society) pressure. Communities that are affected by contaminants released by a specific plant can use the information provided by the pollutant release inventory to apply pressure to company management to reduce these emissions. Derived from

[1] My intellectual debts are all too many to cite here. Collaborative research with Kathryn Harrison and Mark Winfield has sharpened my thinking on the politics of PRTR design and implementation. Thanks are due to Paul Ruesch for editorial help, Manolo Velazquez for superb research assistance, and Jonathan Fox, Inger Weibust, Kathryn Hochstetler, Steve Mumme, Michele Betsill, Elisabeth Corell, for their insightful comments on research leading to this paper. I gratefully acknowledge the North American Commission on Environmental Cooperation (NACEC) for financial support to attend the PRTR project meetings. I am extremely thankful to each and every one of the people I have interviewed for my research on PRTRs. All errors, of course, remain mine. The views presented in this chapter are of the author alone and should not be deemed as representing the position or view of the NACEC or any other organization or individual mentioned in the chapter. None of the people or organizations mentioned in this work is, in any way, responsible for the way I have interpreted their ideas and suggestions.

an increased emphasis on nonregulatory measures, PRTRs have steadily gained popularity, enhanced by the signing of the Aarhus Convention on Access to Information and Environmental Justice.

The North American Commission for Environmental Cooperation (NACEC),[2] a trinational intergovernmental body created as a result of the North American Agreement on Environmental Cooperation (NAAEC), the environmental aspect of NAFTA, has spent considerable resources (human, material, and financial) fostering the exchange of information, capacity-building, and the formation of transnational communities of ENGOs interested in several issue areas across North America. By providing these ENGOs with financial support to attend meetings, facilitating cross-border collaboration and information sharing, and widely disseminating research output generated, the CEC facilitated the formation of ENGO transnational coalitions. Furthermore, the CEC has helped these ENGOs further their agendas by empowering and encouraging them to participate in trinational meetings, which the ENGOs would probably not have been able to attend otherwise.

My research provides empirical evidence that significant coalition-building occurred as a result of NACEC's efforts, and that this trinational coalition did effect policy change in the design of Mexico's PRTR.[3] The aforementioned studies are based on in-depth interviews conducted both in Spanish and in English during several field seasons from 2001 to 2004, as well as official document analyses, reviews of journalistic accounts, and the like. I have previously outlined the many methodological challenges in the study of transnational coalition influence on domestic policy change.[4] In "The Politics of Information Dissemination," we used the policy transfer framework to try and explain whether the Mexican PRTR would have reached the point of maturity it has now if the CEC had not existed.[5] We found that the Mexican Registro de Emisiones y Transferencia de Contaminantes (RETC) has reached the point where it is right now largely as a result of CEC's efforts to push for convergence of North American PRTRs. My research has focused on unpacking the degree of influence that international institutions (such as NACEC) have on domestic policymaking as well as the long-term effects and

---

[2] NACEC is also referred to as CEC (Commission for Environmental Cooperation). In this paper, I use both acronyms interchangeably.

[3] See Raul Pacheco and Peter N. Nemetz, "Business-not-as-usual: Alternative policy instruments for environmental management," in *Proceedings of the 5th IRE Annual Workshop: Addressing the Knowledge Crisis in Water and Energy: Linking Local and Global Communities* (Vancouver: Institute for Resources and Environment, 2001); Kathryn Harrison et al., "The politics of information dissemination: The role of policy transfer in the development of Mexico's pollutant release inventory," in *Proceedings of the Annual Meeting of the American Association for Public Policy Analysis and Management* (Washington, D.C.: APPAM, 2003); Raul Pacheco-Vega, "Democracy by proxy: Environmental NGOs and policy change in Mexico," in Aldemaro Romero and Sarah Elizabeth West (eds.), *Environmental Issues in Latin America and the Caribbean* (Dordrecht: Springer, 2005), p. 231.

[4] Pacheco and Nemetz, "Business-not-as-usual."

[5] Harrison et al., "The politics of information dissemination."

stability of policy change over time.[6] This chapter builds on previous research and outlines a proposed methodology that can be used to assess the degree of influence of ENGO coalitions on domestic policy-making.

The chapter is organized as follows. In Section 2, I provide a bit of background on how civil society organizations have traditionally been involved in issues surrounding the NAAEC. In this section I also briefly summarize empirical findings and theoretical propositions I have tested in my research. Section 3 provides a brief review of the literature on how academics have examined the influence of ENGOs in domestic and international policy design and implementation. I briefly describe two proposed methodologies to assess influence.[7] This section also describes some of the theoretical and methodological challenges facing researchers interested in assessing influence. Since my research attempts to evaluate ENGO influence on domestic policy-making, in Section 4 I depart from these two methodologies and propose a framework that attempts to capture the subtleties of assessing transnational ENGO coalition influence on domestic policy-making, the double-grid framework. Finally, in Section 5, I provide some discussion and closing remarks.

2. CIVIL SOCIETY INVOLVEMENT IN THE DESIGN AND IMPLEMENTATION OF THE NORTH AMERICAN AGREEMENT ON ENVIRONMENTAL COOPERATION

When Mexico was entering NAFTA, discussions on the environmental effects of increased international trade got increasingly heated.[8] U.S.-based ENGOs claimed that plants located within U.S. territory would be relocating south of the border in an attempt to escape stringent environmental regulations. The argument of a Mexican pollution haven was too loaded to escape. Through heavy lobbying and vocal outcries, a group of U.S. ENGOs was able to influence the way in which

---

[6] Partial results from this paper have been presented in Raúl Pacheco-Vega, Inger Weibust, and Jonathan Fox, "Lessons from the Citizen Submissions on Enforcement Matters (CSEM) to the North American Commission for Environmental Cooperation (NACEC)," in Ismael Aguilar Barajas et al. (eds.), *Senderos de integración silenciosa en América del Norte* (Mexico City: El Colegio de Mexico, 2010), and Raúl Pacheco-Vega, "Las denuncias ciudadanas sobre cumplimientoambiental en América del Norte (1996–2012): perspectivas sobre la sociedad civilambientalista norteamericana" (2013) 8 *Norteamérica* 77. I worked with Inger Weibust and Jonathan Fox on a comparative project assessing the effectiveness of NACEC's citizen submission on enforcement matters mechanism (CSEM). This project was funded by the Programa de Investigacion y Estudios sobre la Region de America del Norte (PIERAN) based at the Colegio de Mexico. I gratefully acknowledge PIERAN's funding to undertake this component of the project.

[7] These methodologies are found in the following two articles: Bas Arts and Piet Verschuren, "Assessing political influence in complex decision-making: An instrument based on triangulation" (1999) 20 *International Political Science Review* 411; Michele M. Betsill and Elisabeth Corell, "NGO influence in international environmental negotiations: A framework for analysis" (2001) 1 *Global Environmental Politics* 65.

[8] See Pierre M. Johnson and André Beaulieu (eds.), *The environment and NAFTA: Understanding and implementing the new continental law* (Washington, D.C.: Island Press, 1996).

NAFTA and its side agreement (NAAEC) were worded.[9] Another popular argument was also wielded by civil society: the "race to the bottom" hypothesis. ENGOs claimed that the agreement would bring American (and Canadian) environmental standards down to the lowest common denominator.

Ten years after NAFTA and NAAEC were first implemented, evidence of a Mexican pollution haven and a North American "race to the bottom" is still inconclusive. Kevin Gallagher is one of the researchers who have undertaken thorough research around these two arguments. His 2004 book provides evidence that Mexican factories comply with environmental regulations just as much as their U.S. counterparts, lending very little support to the pollution haven hypothesis.[10] Furthermore, evidence on whether there is a "race to the bottom" in North America is scant and inconclusive. However, we do find evidence of indirect environmental effects in the form of increased participation of nonstate actors.

Citizen participation in North American environmental policy-making has steadily increased, greatly as a result of the CEC's strategies and programs.[11] Two mechanisms were specifically designed to allow for citizen participation within the CEC: the Citizen Submission on Enforcement Matters (CSEM) and the Joint Public Advisory Committee (JPAC).

The first, the CSEM mechanism, is based on Articles 14 and 15 of NAAEC. This mechanism provides civil society organizations with the opportunity to play a "whistleblower" role. Any concerned citizen from any of the three countries can prepare and present a submission to the CEC Secretariat denouncing a country for failing to comply with its own environmental laws.[12] The CEC Secretariat's Office of Submissions on Enforcement Matters reviews the submission and assesses whether the submission actually warrants a response from the concerned country.

An interesting feature of the CSEM mechanism is that citizens from any country can present a submission against any country. A Mexican citizen can denounce lack of compliance with environmental regulation in Mexico, Canada, or the United States, with the same opportunity afforded to American and Canadian citizens. Some submissions against Mexico have actually come from Canadian and/or American ENGOs. This sounds reasonable, as the perception seems to be that Mexican environmental standards are the weakest of all three countries. But a closer examination of the historical patterns of citizen submissions shows interesting patterns.

 9 See Barbara Hogenboom, "Cooperation and polarisation beyond borders: The transnationalisation of Mexican environmental issues during the NAFTA negotiations" (1996) 17 *Third World Quarterly* 989. A detailed account on the history of how the NAAEC came about is outside the scope of this paper. For such accounts, see Johnson and Beaulieu, *The environment and NAFTA.*
10 Kevin P. Gallagher, *Free trade and the environment: Mexico, NAFTA and beyond* (Palo Alto, Calif.: Stanford University Press, 2004).
11 Raul Pacheco and Obdulia Vega, "Cooperación internacional para la protección ambiental: la formación de coaliciones en perspectiva" (2003) 43 *Foro Internacional* 403.
12 NACEC, "Bringing the facts to light: A guide to Articles 14 and 15 of the North American Agreement on Environmental Cooperation" (Montréal: North American Commission for Environmental Cooperation, 2001).

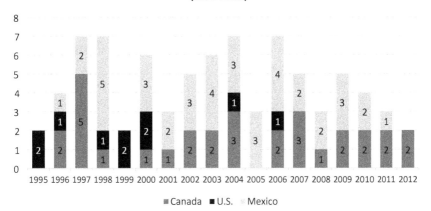

FIGURE 16.1. Number of submissions per year against each of the three North American countries. (*Source*: Author's own calculations based on NACEC's reported submissions. N = 81. Data as of Nov. 16, 2013.)

For example, in a five-year span (1999–2004), U.S. ENGOs have only sent in three submissions (see Figure 16.1). Why is it that U.S. ENGOs are not presenting more submissions? Given that U.S. ENGOs were so vocal about the need to strengthen environmental standards in Mexico and Canada, it would seem natural that U.S. ENGOs would make more frequent use of a mechanism that was put in place precisely as a response to their concerns.

As innovative as the CSEM mechanism is, it has been strongly criticized, primarily by concerned government officials who debate the validity of the ENGO's claims of regulatory noncompliance. Some Mexican officials have argued that, because the petitioners had not exhausted all other potential avenues (such as domestic lobbying), their submission should have been dismissed.

The process itself has been criticized as having procedural and structural design flaws. In 2000, the CEC Council called for comments on Articles 14 and 15 and commissioned the JPAC to produce a report on lessons learned from the CSEM process. A number of responses were collected and analyzed by JPAC and the CEC Secretariat. Criticisms included the fact that some ENGO groups use the mechanism before exhausting domestic remedies. Council Resolution 01–06 provided a response to JPAC's report on lessons learned regarding the Article 14 and 15 process that amended the procedures for citizen submissions. Despite challenges facing the CSEM mechanism, mounting evidence indicates that indeed this mechanism has helped ENGOs raise their profile and advance their agendas.[13]

---

[13] For example, see, generally, in this collection, Giselle Davian, "Should Citizens Expect Procedural Justice in Nonadversarial Processes? Spotlighting the Regression of the Citizen Submission Process

Issues of legitimacy of ENGO claims are still the subject of heated debates. Particularly, discussions are centered on whether or not ENGOs who present a citizen submission to the CEC Secretariat have exhausted all other possible avenues. It would be very hard for the Secretariat to verify whether ENGOs did indeed explore each and every other option to pressure the target domestic government.

It should be noted, though, that while this concern may be legitimate, the mechanism itself is designed to provide additional avenues for citizen participation, regardless of whether they participate within the domestic or international arenas. The choice of a second-order pressure mechanism (lobbying and raising awareness by asking an intergovernmental body to intervene) over a first-order pressure mechanism (direct lobbying with domestic government officials) is still part of a broad array of ENGO strategies that could be considered as valid as any other strategy.[14] So when we attempt to evaluate the CSEM mechanism, we should also consider that the mere fact that ENGOs are now comfortable and knowledgeable submitting their concerns for review to the CEC is already a sign of increased citizen participation in environmental policy-making in North America. Therefore, the mechanism is fulfilling at the very least one of its most important objectives.

In addition to the CSEM mechanism, two other very relevant avenues for citizen participation in North American environmental policy are the JPAC and the participation of civil society representatives in public meetings and advisory committees to NACEC's programs. The JPAC is a trinational, multistakeholder advisory committee that provides input and advice to the CEC council on matters related to the CEC programs and projects. Each government nominates an individual who represents industry, government, academia, civil society, and so on. The JPAC is composed of fifteen individuals (five nationals of each country).[15] While the composition of the JPAC may or may not reflect a wide variety of interests and viewpoints, the idea in and of itself is a good one. However, the JPAC does not provide steering direction nor does it have any binding powers. It provides advice, and it is up to the Council to determine whether or not it adopts any recommendations.

In this chapter, I have chosen not to discuss the JPAC at length since it is not a mechanism that provides for ample citizen participation in and of itself. Only one civil society representative per country sits on the JPAC and generally speaking he or she comes from a highly recognized ENGO or is highly recognized as an individual. For example, long-time Mexican toxic reduction activist Laura Silvan de Durazo was

---

from NAAEC to CAFTA-DR" (Chapter 2); Freedom-Kai Phillips, "Climate Change, Sustainable Development, and NAFTA: Regional Policy Harmonization as a Basis for Sustainable Development" (Chapter 11).

[14] The terminology of first-order and second-order mechanisms is described in detail in Pacheco and Nemetz, "Business-not-as-usual"; Pacheco-Vega, "Democracy by proxy."

[15] The actual wording is "15 citizens" but it is clear that these citizens aren't randomly chosen, hence why I use the term "individual."

a member of the JPAC for a long time. Regina Barba-Pirez, the former head of the coalition of environmental groups Union de Grupos Ambientalistas, previously an activist and now with the Mexican Secretariat of Environment and Natural Resources (SEMARNAT), was two-time Chair of the JPAC during her tenure. Gustavo Alanis, a renowned environmental lawyer from the Mexican Center for Environmental Law (CEMDA), was chair of JPAC a few times.

Participation in NACEC's consultative groups and public meetings is a far better and more open mechanism for citizen participation.[16] Academics and civil society organizations are frequently funded to travel to participate in NACEC's meetings. This financial support is provided on a demonstrated-need basis. At a Consultative Group meeting for the North American PRTR Project held in Alexandria, Virginia, in October 2003, several ENGO representatives publicly indicated that their participation would have not been possible had it not been for the CEC's financial support.[17]

I have previously described the active role that the CEC took in fostering transnational coalition building and ENGO collaboration around the Mexican PRTR.[18] I will briefly summarize here what I saw as the main effects that these transnational coalitions had on Mexican toxics policy throughout the period of 1999 to 2014. While the Canadian and U.S. toxic release inventories (National Pollutant Release Inventory, NPRI, and Toxic Release Inventory, TRI, respectively) mandated that all firms that complied with certain criteria should report to TRI and NPRI in terms of pollutants emitted and transferred, the Mexican RETC was entirely voluntary from design. On December 6, 2001 the RETC became mandatory, and once the definite regulation that governs RETC has been fully implemented, it will be very similar to NPRI and TRI. My research indicates that Mexican ENGOs were able to influence the Mexican government to accept a change in policy on the reporting mode to the RETC around 2001.

I argue that Mexican ENGOs used coalition-formation strategies to pressure the Mexican government to effectively change the voluntary format of reporting to RETC. These coalitions used first-order and second-order pressure transmission mechanisms that allowed them to have a long-lasting impact on the design and implementation of RETC. Many of the Mexican ENGO representatives who fought for mandatory reporting now sit on the Mexican consultative group for RETC and have regular meetings with the RETC team at SEMARNAT. Many observers view this as a resounding success story of ENGO-government collaboration.

---

[16] I currently sit on the Consultative Group for the North American Pollutant Release and Transfer Registry Project.

[17] Cf. CEC, *Taking Stock. 2002 North American Pollutant Releases and Trabnsfers*, p. 33 (Montreal, 2005).

[18] See Pacheco and Nemetz, "Business-not-as-usual"; Harrison et al., "The politics of information dissemination"; Pacheco-Vega, "Democracy by proxy"; Pacheco-Vega, "Las denuncias ciudadanas."

3. LITERATURE REVIEW: HOW DO NGOS INFLUENCE POLICY AND TO WHAT EXTENT?

The debate on whether NGOs are indeed able to effect policy change is still strong. Discussions have yielded many different (and frequently opposing) views on NGO influence. Neil Harrison makes an important point. He says that we should focus not on whether NGOs influence policy, but on *how* and *under what circumstances* NGOs are able to exert such influence. This type of analysis is not an easy task. In the concluding remarks of this paper, I give several examples of how and under what circumstances Mexican ENGOs have been able to influence domestic policy change, based on my own findings and some revelations from other scholars. In this section, I briefly review recent scholarship that focuses on nonstate actor influence on policy-making, particularly international environmental negotiations.

One example that does not focus on transnational coalition influence on international negotiations is Kathryn Hochstetler's study of environmental movements within the La Plata river basin in Argentina. She analyzes coalition mobilization to block construction of a transnational water superhighway along the La Plata river system and finds that long-term NGO influence is largely determined by domestic capacity and acceptance of international norms.[19]

Michele Betsill and Elisabeth Corell proposed a methodological framework to analyze NGO influence based on the notion of influence defined by David Knoke. Their methodological piece does a wonderful job of reviewing the state of the art on NGO influence,[20] and their empirical piece applies their framework to a case study of the United Nations Convention on Climate Change and the United Nations Convention on Desertification.[21] However, their analyses are focused primarily on NGO influence on international environmental negotiations.[22] I won't go in detail into their framework,[23] but I will summarize the basic points of their findings.

Betsill and Corell argue that there are two important dimensions to the notion of influence, one related to what NGOs do to make information available and the other related to whether and how other actors change their behavior accordingly.

---

[19] See Kathryn Hochstetler, "After the boomerang: Environmental movements and politics in the La Plata river basin" (2002) 2 *Global Environmental Politics* 35.

[20] Betsill and Corell, "NGO influence in international environmental negotiations."

[21] Elisabeth Corell and Michele M. Betsill, "A comparative look at NGO influence in international environmental negotiations: Desertification and climate change" (2001) 1 *Global Environmental Politics* 86.

[22] Corell and Betsill edited a volume on NGO influence that also includes Humphreys's and Skodvin's and Andresen's recent articles in the journal *Global Environmental Politics*. See David Humphreys, "Redefining the issues: NGO influence on international forests negotiations" (2004) 4 *Global Environmental Politics* 51 and Tora Skodvin and Steinar Andresen, "Nonstate influence in the International Whaling Commission, 1970–1990" (2003) 3 *Global Environmental Politics* 61.

[23] I would not do justice to their very thorough piece of research, as the reader can check their findings on GEP.

Furthermore, they note that NGO influence may be observed both in the outcome of the negotiations as well as in the negotiating process.[24]

In a recent study on international forests negotiations, David Humphreys applies the Betsill and Corell framework to evaluate the degree to which NGOs have influenced textual outputs on international forest policy since the mid-1980s.[25] Humphreys examines NGO influence in forest-related issues at the United Nations Commission for Environment and Development (UNCED), the World Commission on Forests and Sustainable Development, the Intergovernmental Panel on Forests, and the Intergovernmental Forum on Forests. He finds, among other things, that NGOs can be more influential when there is some degree of agreement on textual outputs that are favorable already to NGO agendas, and when they frame recommendations in language that is nonthreatening to powerful political and economic interests.

Tora Skodvin and Steinar Andresen used a multilevel approach to examine NGO influence around the International Whaling Commission from 1970 to 1990. They found that domestic channels of influence may be equally or even more important than international channels of influence linked to the international decision-making level. Their study attempts to include nonstate influence on international policy-making that takes place via domestic channels.[26] This paper departs from Skodvin and Andresen's analysis in that its focus is on transnational nonstate actor influence on domestic policy-making.

Bas Arts and his collaborators have studied nonstate actor involvement on international environmental negotiations such as the Biodiversity Convention and the Climate Change Convention.[27] They found several strategies used by NGOs to exert political influence. Notions of power and perception are the main determinants of influence according to Arts' understanding of political influence.

Arts and Verschuren's framework is predicated on the premise that political influence is dependent on power, resources, and ideologies. Their methodological paper describes the EAR instrument, which is intended to assess political influence.[28] "E" refers to the perception of a key player of his/her own influence or lack thereof. "A" refers to the perception of the target agent on whether the agent exerting the influence has or does not have any meaningful influence. And "R" refers to an assessment

---

[24] Betsill and Corell, "NGO influence in international environmental negotiations," p. 81.

[25] See Humphreys, "Redefining the issues."

[26] Skodvin and Andresen, "Nonstate influence in the International Whaling Commission," p. 65.

[27] See Bas Arts, *The political influence of global NGOS: Case studies on the Climate and Biodiversity Conventions* (Utrecht: International, 1998); Arts and Verschuren, "Assessing political influence"; Bas Arts and Sandra Mack, "Environmental NGOs and the Biosafety Protocol: A case study in political influence" (2003) 19 European Environment 19.

[28] Arts and Verschuren, "Assessing political influence." EAR refers to the acronym ego-perception (E), alter-perception (A), researcher's analysis (R).

by the researcher of whether E and A are actually true, through an evaluation of "goal-achievement," "intervention," and "participation."

Bas Arts and Sandra Mack describe three methods to assess political influence: the reputation method, the position method, and the decision-making method.[29] For Arts and Mack, ENGOs are influential if they are perceived as such. When the target agent perceives the actor as being capable of exerting influence, and acts upon that perception, Arts and Mack say that influence has occurred. This framework does pose the challenge of identifying actual perceptions of the involved actors. However, it also provides an interesting starting point. The methodology I propose in the following can be used in addition to Betsill and Corell's or any of Arts's suggested methods.

Finally, Lars Gulbrandsen and Steinar Andresen build a framework that analyzes NGO influence in terms of access to international negotiations, goal-attainment, and *ego* and *alter* perceptions of NGO influence.[30] Their approach resonates with that of Arts and Verschuren.[31] In Gulbrandsen and Andresen's study of the design and implementation of rules for compliance, sinks, and the flexibility mechanisms under the United Nations Framework Convention on Climate Change (UNFCCC), they found that different NGOs use different strategies, target different actors, and seek to achieve different goals. They also found that NGOs, generally speaking, believed they had a larger degree of influence in the negotiations than other respondents did.

This brief survey of recent literature highlights the need to consider NGO influence in terms of (among other factors) access to target actors, goal-attainment, domestic and international sources of influence, power, and perceptions of both target agent and influential agent. The following section presents a framework that attempts to add to the dimensions already considered by the aforementioned scholars.

4. A PROPOSED METHODOLOGY TO ASSESS TRANSNATIONAL ENGO INFLUENCE ON DOMESTIC POLICYMAKING: THE DOUBLE-GRID FRAMEWORK

In a published report by the Swedish Institute of International Affairs, Corell and Betsill summarize the results of an academic workshop on NGO influence. Beatriz Torres, one of the participants in the workshop, indicated that if there was high political contention, NGO influence decreases. In the empirical cases I have examined, I have found that while the process of changing the reporting mode of RETC was highly contentious, NGOs were able to be influential because they used both

[29] See Arts and Mack, "Environmental NGOs and the Biosafety Protocol."
[30] Lars H. Gulbrandsen and Steinar Andresen, "NGO influence in the implementation of the Kyoto Protocol: Compliance, flexibility mechanisms and sinks" (2004) 4 *Global Environmental Politics* 54.
[31] Arts and Verschuren, "Assessing political influence."

TABLE 16.1. *Structural Dimensions of NGO Influence on Domestic Policy-making*

Influential Agent (NGO)	Target Agent (Country)
Relative networking capabilities (highly networked/isolated)	Relative strength to international/ intergovernmental pressures (strong/weak)
Relative lobbying strength (weak/strong)	Domestic political climate (amenable to citizen participation/closed to citizen participation)

first-order and second-order pressure mechanisms. If they had only used first-order pressure mechanisms (direct lobbying), their influence would have probably been much less.

I suggest that there are other dimensions that need to be studied in order to adjust any methodology analyzing NGO influence in the domestic policy arena. I propose that to assess NGO influence on domestic policymaking we look at the structural dimensions presented in Table 16.1.

This framework is compatible with Corell and Betsill's methodology as well as with Arts and Verschuren's research instrument. What my framework emphasizes is the need to evaluate domestic factors of the target country and intrinsic factors of the influential NGO. The framework presented in Table 16.1 allows us to create two grids to assess degree of influence. Both grids connect intrinsic factors of NGOs and domestic factors of the target country.

Grid 1 (transnational influence grid; Figure 16.2) compares NGO networking capabilities with target country's receptiveness to international pressures (particularly

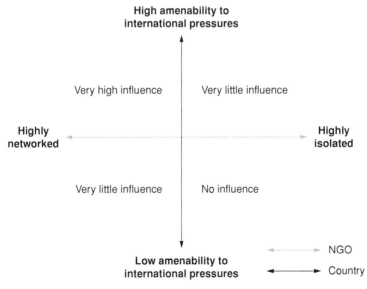

FIGURE 16.2. Grid 1: Transnational influence grid.

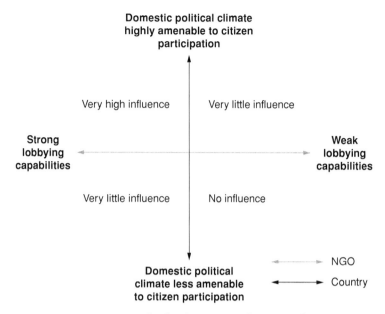

FIGURE 16.3. Grid 2: Domestic influence grid.

those of an intergovernmental body). Grid 1 allows us to determine whether a country would be highly influenced by NGOs given the country's responsiveness to external (transnational or intergovernmental) pressures. The level of NGO influence would be dependent not only on the responsiveness of the country but also on the strength of the coalition.[32]

Grid 2 (Figure 16.3) compares lobbying strength with domestic political climate. Grid 2 (domestic influence grid) allows us to determine whether the target country would be influenced through domestic NGO lobbying depending on receptivity to citizen participation of the target country. If the results of Grid 2 indicate that the target country would not be amenable to citizen participation under conditions of strong lobbying by ENGOs, we could infer that ENGOs would use second-order mechanisms. Furthermore, second-order mechanisms would be effective depending on the results of Grid 1. If the target country is highly responsive to international pressure and faces lobbying from strong ENGOs, we can infer that ENGOs would be more influential.

The double-grid framework is still very much in its developmental stages and therefore requires further refinement. It does emphasize, though, the need to assess domestic factors when studying NGO influence in domestic policy-making.

[32] See Jonathan Fox's increasing density of relations table in Jonathan Fox, "Lessons from Mexico-US civil society coalitions" in David Brooks and Jonathan Fox (eds.), *Cross-border dialogues: U.S.-Mexico social movement networking* (La Jolla, Calif.: UC San Diego Center for U.S.-Mexican Studies, 2002), p. 341.

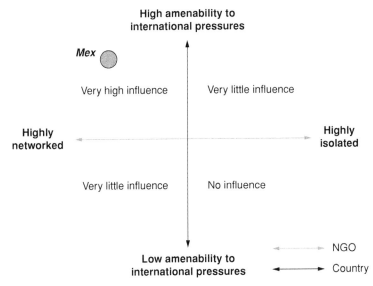

FIGURE 16.4. Grid 1: Transnational influence grid, applied to RETC.

Applying the double-grid framework to the RETC case is rather straightforward (see Figures 16.4 and 16.5).

The transnational influence grid (Grid 1) shows that Mexican ENGOs were highly networked thanks in great part to the CEC providing funding for an Internet-based listserve that led to the surge of a trinational coalition that strongly pressured the Mexican government to change the mode of voluntary reporting to mandatory. Grid 1 also shows that the Mexican government was susceptible of being "blamed and shamed"[33] into changing the reporting method. Therefore, we conclude that transnational ENGOs were in fact able to exert a high degree of influence.

Grid 2 shows that Mexican ENGOs were able to successfully lobby the Mexican legislature to pass the motion of mandatory RETC reporting as they had learned from their American and Canadian counterparts how to assemble successful campaigns. Their participation in CEC consultative groups also gave them insight into alternate lobbying strategies. Furthermore, the domestic political climate was one of increasing openness. With discussions of a new bill proposing a new Federal Law of Access to Public Government Information,[34] Mexican government officials were increasingly pressured to disclose previously guarded information and make it public. Therefore, the political climate was one that allowed for ENGOs to have a higher degree of influence on the Mexican government.

[33] See Pacheco and Nemetz, "Business-not-as-usual"; Harrison et al., "The politics of information dissemination"; Pacheco-Vega, "Democracy by proxy."
[34] *Ley Federal de Acceso a la Informacion Publica Gubernamental*, Official Gazette of the Federation (June 11, 2002, as amended July 7, 2014).

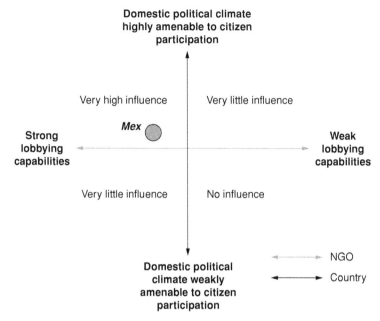

FIGURE 16.5. Grid 2: Domestic influence grid, applied to RETC.

Two caveats are in order, though. First, in order to test the double grid framework, we need to search for comparable cases where transnational civil society was involved and no policy change took effect (in order to find counterfactuals). While process tracing can be a useful tool,[35] finding cases where the influence of a variable is not present in order to compare relative effects of the same variable is very difficult. Also, we needed to find ways to position a particular case within a specific axis. For example, on Grid 2, how can we quantitatively assess the relative openness of a nation-state to citizen participation? At the time of writing, I am only using one particular case and I am also assessing where to place it within the two axes. Forthcoming work will explore ways in which we can make these assessments more straightforward and reproducible.

Second, in any study of nonstate actors' influence on international environmental negotiations or domestic politics, we need to recognize that there is an inherent interplay among international environmental institutions, states, and nonstate actors.[36] Unpacking the exact degree of influence of each variable is still very hard to do.

---

[35] Paul Steinberg, "New Approaches to Causal Analysis in Policy Research" (Paper presented at the Annual Meeting of the American Political Science Association, Chicago, September 2, 2004).

[36] See Kal Raustiala, "States, NGOs, and international environmental institutions" (1997) 41 *International Studies Quarterly* 710.

5. DISCUSSION AND CONCLUSION REMARKS

This paper set out to show that while it is very difficult to assign causation to NGO activities and find causal connections between NGO coalition formation, influence mechanisms, and environmental quality, we can argue that the formation of transnational coalitions is, indeed, an indirect environmental effect of NAFTA. Determining the extent to which these ENGOs ultimately improve environmental quality is a methodological challenge that requires a serious investment of research time and effort. However, it could be argued that, by lobbying for more stringent environmental regulation and better compliance of national environmental laws, ENGOs could effectively be improving environmental quality. A lengthy discussion on this topic goes beyond the scope of this paper.

Despite heated debates on the topic, it is clear that NGOs do influence domestic politics. The circumstances under which they are able to exert such influence are very context-specific. For example, I find that Mexican ENGOs were able to effect change on RETC-related policy thanks to a number of factors. Among these I consider as key CEC involvement and funding, transnational collaboration and exchange of information among North American ENGOs, a receptive federal environmental agency (SEMARNAT), and the lobbying efforts of Mexican ENGO coalitions that targeted the Mexican Chamber of Deputies and the Senate. Generally speaking, we can argue that ENGOs can influence domestic policy if most of the listed factors are present. This proposition still needs rigorous testing, although it provides a basis on which to develop further research projects.

Assessing ENGO influence on domestic policy-making presents us with many challenges. One of the top challenges is to actually find causal mechanisms that demonstrate that NGOs actually changed the way an actor would have behaved had they not influenced such actor. In a very recent (confidential) interview, a former SEMARNAT official mentioned that he firmly believed that the success story of RETC becoming mandatory had indeed been the result of lobbying efforts of Mexican ENGOs on the Chamber of Deputies and the Senate. If these ENGOs had not targeted the Legislature, the motion to pass a mandatory mode of reporting for RETC would not have been possible. Thus we are able to find a direct connection between something that the influential actor had done and the actual way in which the target actor would have behaved had it not been for these ENGOs' lobbying efforts.

Given the nature of social-science research, we will always struggle with assigning causation, particularly when it comes down to NGO-related research. However, one can be hopeful that empirical evidence gathered through several methods (triangulation, semistructured interviews, etc.) will enhance our understanding of the complex processes surrounding nonstate actors' involvement in environmental policy-making, both at the domestic and international levels. The double-grid

framework I propose in this paper is just a small step toward enhancing our understanding of how NGOs influence domestic policy-making.

LIST OF REFERENCES

Arts, B. (1998). *The political influence of global NGOS: Case studies on the Climate and Biodiversity Conventions.* Utrecht, The Netherlands, International.

Arts, B. and S. Mack (2003). "Environmental NGOs and the Biosafety Protocol: A case study in political influence." *European Environment* 19: 19–33.

Arts, B. and M. Noortmann, et al., eds. (2001). *Non-state actors in international relations.* London, Ashgate.

Arts, B. and P. Verschuren (1999). "Assessing political influence in complex decision-making: An instrument based on triangulation." *International Political Science Review* 20(4): 411–424.

Betsill, M. M. and E. Corell (2001). "NGO influence in international environmental negoti-ations: A framework for analysis." *Global Environmental Politics* 1(4): 65–85.

Corell, E. and M. M. Betsill (2001). "A comparative look at NGO influence in international environmental negotiations: Desertification and climate change." *Global Environmental Politics* 1(4): 86–107.

Fox, J. (2002). "Lessons from Mexico-US civil society coalitions." In *Cross-border dialogues. U.S.-Mexico social movement networking.* D. Brooks and J. Fox, eds. La Jolla, CA, Center for U.S.-Mexican Studies, University 8: 341–418.

Gallagher, K. B. (2004). *Free trade and the environment. Mexico, NAFTA and beyond.* Palo Alto, CA, Stanford University Press.

Gulbrandsen, L. H. and S. Andresen (2004). "NGO influence in the implementation of the Kyoto Protocol: Compliance, flexibility mechanisms and sinks." *Global Environmental Politics* 4(4): 54–75.

Harrison, K., R. Pacheco Vega, et al. (2003). *The politics of information dissemination: The role of policy transfer in the development of Mexico's pollutant release inventory.* Annual Meeting of the American Association for Public Policy Analysis and Management, Washington, DC, APPAM.

Hochstetler, K. (2002). "After the boomerang: Environmental movements and politics in the La Plata river basin." *Global Environmental Politics* 2(2): 35–57.

Hogenboom, B. (1996). "Cooperation and polarisation beyond borders: The transnational-isation of Mexican environmental issues during the NAFTA negotiations." *Third World Quarterly* 17(5): 989–1005.

Humphreys, D. (2004). "Redefining the issues: NGO influence on international forests nego-tiations." *Global Environmental Politics* 4(2): 51–74.

Johnson, P. M. and A. Beaulieu, eds. (1996). *The environment and NAFTA: Understanding and implementing the new continental law.* Washington, DC, Island Press.

NACEC (2001). *Bringing the facts to light: A guide to Articles 14 and 15 of the North American Agreement on Environmental Cooperation.* Montreal, QC, North American Commission for Environmental Cooperation.

Pacheco, R. and P. N. Nemetz (2001). *Business-not-as-usual: Alternative policy instruments for environmental management.* 5th IRE Annual Workshop: Addressing the Knowledge Crisis in Water and Energy: Linking Local and Global Communities, Vancouver, BC, Institute for Resources and Environment, UBC.

Pacheco, R. and O. Vega (2003). "Cooperación internacional para la protección ambiental: La formación de coaliciones en perspectiva." *Foro Internacional* 43(2): 403–428.

Pacheco-Vega, R. (2005). "Democracy by proxy: Environmental NGOs and policy change in Mexico." In *Environmental Issues in Latin America and the Caribbean*. A. Romero and S. West, eds. Dordrecht, The Netherlands, Springer Publishers.

Pacheco-Vega, R. (2013). Las denuncias ciudadanas sobre cumplimiento ambiental en América del Norte (1996–2012): Perspectivas sobre la sociedad civil ambientalista norteamericana. *Norteamérica*, 8(1), 77–108.

Pacheco-Vega, R., Weibust, I., & Fox, J. (2010). Lessons from the Citizen Submissions on Enforcement Matters (CSEM) to the North American Commission on Environmental Cooperation (NACEC). In I. Aguilar Barajas, N. A. Fuentes Flores, R. López Villicaña, J. Schiavon Uriegas, B. Torres Ramírez, & J. L. Valdés Ugalde (Eds.), Senderos de Integración Silenciosa en América del Norte (pp. 173–205). Ciudad de México: Programa Interinstitucional de Estudios sobre la Región de América del Norte (El Colegio de México) & Centro de Investigaciones sobre América del Norte (Universidad Nacional Autónoma de México).

Raustiala, K. (1997). "States, NGOs, and international environmental institutions." *International Studies Quarterly* 41: 710–740.

Skodvin, T. and S. Andresen (2003). "Nonstate influence in the International Whaling Commission, 1970–1990." *Global Environmental Politics* 3(4): 61–86.

Steinberg, P. (2004). *New approaches to causal analysis in policy research*. American Political Science Association, Chicago, IL.

Index

Kirton, John, 39, 339–340
Kitchenuhmaykoosib Inninuwug (KI), 233
knowledge products, CEC, 340
Knox, John, 82, 158, 360, 363, 369
Kong, Hoi L., xii, 11
Kyoto Protocol, 23

labeling requirements, genetically engineered
  materials, 186–187
labor provisions, U.S. Model BIT, 315–316
Laguna del Tigre Fonpetrol Guatemala, 66
Lake Chapala II submission, 90–91, 157–158,
  160–162, 167
Lake Chapala submission, 214
Lake Roosevelt, sediment contamination in,
  211
land rights. *See* Aboriginal title and rights
landfill, *Metalclad* case regarding, 308–310
Lang, Andrew T.F., 345, 346–347
law. *See also* environmental law under SEM
    process; international law; investment treaty
    arbitration
  CEC Secretariat consideration of, 81–85
  global administrative, 355–356
  in Secretariat's interpretation of Article 45(3),
    103
legal uncertainty due to non-recognition of
    indigenous rights, 231–233
legality, in Fullerian conception of international
    law, 354
Ley de Aguas Nacionales (LAN), Mexico, 90–91
LGEEPA (General Law of Ecological Balance
    and Environmental Protection), Mexico, 163
Liang, Danni, xii, 10–11
liberalized trade. *See specific trade agreements;*
    trade liberalization
Lindane agro-chemical, 310–312
Liu, Jingjing, xii, 10–11
livestock. *See* ILOs in Mexico
living modified organisms (LMOs), 182. *See also*
    agricultural biotechnology
Logging Cases, Canada
  submission to international tribunals, 239–242
  before Supreme Court of Canada, 227–228
LOS (UN Convention on the Law of the Sea), 191
Los Remedios National Park II submission, 110–111
Los Remedios National Park submission, 93
Lowe, Vaughan, 294

MA (Millennium Ecosystem Assessment), 194
Mack, Sandra, 382
maize, genetically engineered, 170–171, 187–188.
    See also agricultural biotechnology
majorities, problem of many

deliberative democracy in transnational context,
    357–358
  and SEM process, 362–364
manure, problems related to in ILOs, 157–158
Marine Ecoregions of North America (CEC), 198
marine environment. *See also specific assessment
    platforms*
  assessment platforms, 193–195
  Baja to Bering project, 200, 214
  CEC tools for, 192, 195–201
  connecting CEC tools to assessment platforms,
    201–203
  overview, 9, 191–193
Marine Protected Areas (MPAs), ecological
    scorecards for, 199–201
Markell, David, 158, 360, 363, 369
market forces, influence on domestic policy,
    341–344, 348
markets, regional, and international norms, 345
Massachusetts v. EPA, 259
MCeX (Montréal Climate Exchange), 254–255
McGill University Faculty of Law, 6
McRae, Donald M., 95
MEAs (multilateral environmental agreements),
    247–248
Mendel, Gregor, 172
mercury in waterways, SEM submissions related
    to, 215
Merrill & Ring Forestry L. P. v. Canada, 293, 294
*Metalclad Corporation v. The United Mexican
    States*, 308–310
Metales y Derivados submission, 59, 60, 88–89, 92
*Methanex Corporation v. The United States of
    America*
  amicus curiae briefs, 295
  decision on, 286–288
  impact of, 289–290
  lessons for China's environmental regulatory
    system, 304–308
  open hearing process, 280, 296
Methanex SEM submission, 103–104
methanol, 304–305
Methyl Tertiary-Butyl Ether (MTBE), 304–305
Mexican Carbon Fund (FOMECAR), 260
Mexico. *See also* ILOs in Mexico; *specific
    investment arbitration cases; specific SEM
    submissions*
  approach to agricultural biotechnology
    regulation, 182–185
  Article 14(3)(a), inferred opinions toward, 110–111
  Article 415 of Federal Criminal Code, 88–89
  authority to enforce law, 85
  biodiversity laws, SEM submissions based on,
    91

CPSIA information can be obtained
at www.ICGtesting.com
Printed in the USA
LVHW052225070119
603029LV00021B/253